Marketing

CANADIAN EDITION

PHILIP KOTLER
Northwestern University

GORDON H.G. McDOUGALL
Wilfrid Laurier University

GARY ARMSTRONG
University of North Carolina

Prentice-Hall Canada Inc.
Scarborough, Ontario

Canadian Cataloguing in Publication Data

Kotler, Philip.
    Marketing

Canadian ed.
Includes bibliographical references and index.
ISBN 0-13-558495-7

1. Marketing.   2. Marketing—Management.
I. McDougall, Gordon H. G., 1942–   .   II. Armstrong,
Gary.   III. Title.

HF5415.K67 1988   658.8   C87-094963-2

© 1988 by Prentice-Hall Canada Inc., Scarborough, Ontario

Original U.S. edition published by
Prentice-Hall, Inc., Englewood Cliffs, New Jersey, U.S.A.
© 1987 by Prentice-Hall, Inc.

This edition is authorized for sale in Canada only.

Prentice-Hall, Inc., Englewood Cliffs, New Jersey
Prentice-Hall International, Inc., London
Prentice-Hall of Australia, Pty., Ltd., Sydney
Prentice-Hall of India Pvt., Ltd., New Delhi
Prentice-Hall of Japan, Inc., Tokyo
Prentice-Hall of Southeast Asia (Pte.) Ltd., Singapore
Editora Prentice-Hall do Brasil Ltda., Rio de Janeiro
Prentice-Hall Hispanoamericana, S.A., Mexico

ISBN 0-13-558495-7

Production Editor: Kateri Lanthier
Designer: Bruce Bond
Production Coordinator: Matt Lumsdon
Cover design: David Peden
Cover photograph: J. Panjer, Hot Shots Stock Shots Inc.
Chapter opening photographs: Chapter 1   Peter Redman, *Financial Post*
                             Chapter 9   Human Computing Resources
                                         Corporation
                             Chapter 13 George Hunter, Manitoba
                                         Department of Industry and Commerce

Typographer: Compeer Typographic Services Limited
Printed and bound in Canada by John Deyell Company

    2 3 4 5   92 91 90 89 88

Contents

9 Designing Products: Products, Brands, Packaging, and Services ————— 207

Cases

Vignettes

Each chapter presents a marketing vignette or story that leads into the chapter material.

Preface

Marketing is designed to help students learn about the basic concepts and practices of modern marketing in an enjoyable and practical way. As marketing is all around us, we all need to know something about it. Most students are surprised to find out how widely marketing is used. Marketing is used not only by manufacturing companies, wholesalers, and retailers, but by all kinds of individuals and organizations. Lawyers, accountants, and doctors use marketing to manage demand for their services, as do hospitals, museums, and performing arts groups. No politician can get the needed votes, and no resort can attract the needed tourists, without developing and carrying out marketing plans.

People throughout organizations need to know how to define and segment a market and develop need-satisfying products and services for chosen target markets. They must know how to price their offerings to make them attractive and affordable, and how to choose middlemen to make their products available to customers. They also need to know how to advertise and promote products so that customers will know about and want them. Clearly, marketers need a broad range of skills in order to sense, serve, and satisfy consumer needs.

Students also need to know about marketing in their roles as consumers and citizens. Someone is always trying to sell us something, so we need to recognize the methods they use. When students enter the job market, they must conduct a form of marketing research to find the best opportunities and the best ways to market themselves to prospective employers. Many will start their careers with marketing jobs in sales forces, in retailing, in advertising, in research, or in one of numerous other marketing areas.

Approach and Objectives

Several factors guided the development of *Marketing*. Most marketing students want a broad picture of the basics, but they do not want to drown in a sea of details. They want to know not only about important marketing principles and concepts, but also how these concepts are applied in actual marketing management practice. Furthermore, they want a text that presents the complex and fascinating world of marketing in an easy-to-grasp, lively, and enjoyable way.

Marketing covers important marketing principles and concepts that are supported by research and evidence from economics, the behavioral sciences, and modern management theory. Yet the text takes a practical marketing management approach. Concepts are applied through examples in which well-known and little-known companies assess and solve their marketing problems. Illustrations, boxed exhibits, and cases present further applications.

Finally, *Marketing* makes marketing easy and enjoyable to learn. The book includes stories that reveal the drama of modern marketing: the retail success of Dylex, the battle of the Canadian breweries, the pricing decision of Crown Royal, the strategy of Bombardier, world product mandating, and Pennington's segmentation strategy. Dozens of other examples and illustrations throughout each chapter also reinforce key concepts and bring marketing to life for the student.

Thus *Marketing* gives the student a complete, manageable, managerial introduction to the basics of marketing. Its style, level, and extensive use of examples and illustrations make the book comprehensive and enjoyable to read.

Learning Aids

Many aids are provided within this book to help students learn about marketing. The main aids are:

- **Chapter objectives** Each chapter begins with objectives that prepare the student for the chapter material and identify learning goals.
- **Opening vignettes** Each chapter starts with a dramatic marketing story that introduces the chapter material and arouses student interest.
- **Figures, photographs, and illustrations** Throughout each chapter, key concepts and applications are illustrated.
- **Exhibits** Additional examples and important information are highlighted in exhibits throughout the text.
- **Summaries** Each chapter ends with a summary that wraps up the main points and concepts.
- **Review questions** Each chapter has a set of review questions covering the main chapter points.
- **Key terms** Key terms are highlighted within each chapter, and a list of key term definitions is provided at the end of each chapter.
- **Case studies and exercises** Cases and exercises for class or written discussion are provided at the end of the book. They challenge students to apply marketing principles to companies in various situations.
- **Appendix** The appendix ''Marketing Arithmetic'' provides additional, practical information for students.

- **Glossary** At the end of the book, an extensive glossary provides quick reference to the key terms found in the book.
- **Indexes** A name index and a subject index help students quickly find information and examples in the book.

Supplements

A successful marketing course requires more than a well-written book. It requires a dedicated teacher and a complete set of supplemental learning and teaching aids. The following aids support *Marketing*:

- **Instructor's Manual** The comprehensive Instructor's Manual contains chapter overviews, lecture outlines, reviews of objectives and key terms, answers to chapter discussion questions, and analyses of all cases.
- **Test Item File** The Test Item File contains about 1900 multiple choice and true-false questions. The file is also computerized for the instructor's convenience.
- **Study Guide** For each chapter, the Study Guide contains a chapter review, sample questions with answers to help students test their knowledge, and two sets of exercises that help students learn and apply chapter terms and concepts.
- **Transparencies** The Transparencies package includes almost 100 transparency masters, as well as a set of colour transparencies for the instructor's use.

Acknowledgments

In preparing the Canadian edition of *Marketing*, I would like to acknowledge a number of people who assisted in the preparation of this book. First, my marketing colleagues at Wilfrid Laurier who offered various ideas and comments. Second, Arlene Bennett, who wrote a number of the cases, reviewed many others, and prepared various teaching notes. Third, Janet Campbell, Jennifer Dilella, Shirley Gates, Elsie Grogan, Susan Kirkey, and Maureen Nordin, who cheerfully and professionally provided secretarial assistance. A special thanks to Elsie, as this is the fourth time we have worked together on a book. I would also like to thank the reviewers: Douglas W. Snetsinger of the University of Toronto, David Sutherland of Fanshawe College, Auleen Carson of the University of New Brunswick, and William E. Avery of Durham College. Finally, the individuals at Prentice-Hall Canada — Yolanda de Rooy, who strives for quality, and Kateri Lanthier, who strives for accuracy — made the project worthwhile.

I am dedicating the book to Betty, Michael, and Sandy.

GORDON H.G. McDOUGALL

Marketing

CANADIAN EDITION

Social Foundations of Marketing: Meeting Human Needs

Chapter Objectives

After reading this chapter, you should be able to:
1. Define marketing and discuss its role in the economy.
2. Compare the four marketing management philosophies.
3. Explain how marketing is used by organizations.

Marketing touches all Canadians every day of our lives. We wake up to a Viking radio alarm clock (produced in Hong Kong), which is playing a Bryan Adams song followed by a Wardair commercial advertising a vacation flight to Florida. We brush our teeth with Crest, gargle with Listermint, shower with Zest (all products made by Canadian subsidiaries of U.S. parents). We put on our Pierre Cardin shirts (made in Canada but licenced from France), GWG jeans (made in Canada), and Greb shoes (made in Canada). We pour some Maple Leaf milk and prepare a bowl of Cheerios (again, made by a Canadian subsidiary of a U.S. firm). We sweeten a cup of Nescafé (produced by the Canadian subsidiary of a European firm) with two teaspoons of Lantic sugar. We drive to work in a Mazda (made in Japan) and at lunchtime we purchase a T-shirt (made in Hong Kong). During work, we phone business firms in Vancouver, Montreal, and Halifax via a telecommunication system developed by Northern Telecom (a Canadian company). Arriving home we get our mail and find a Canadian Tire catalog, a letter from the Toronto-Dominion Bank offering various financial services, and coupons saving us money on our favorite brands. Later that night we watch Bill Cosby on cable television. Our day ends with CBC's The National. As Canadians, we benefit from products from all over the world. Our marketing system has made these products available to us with little effort on our part. We support this standard of living, in part, by marketing our resources to other countries. Marketing is important to Canadians because of the global nature of our community.

What Is Marketing?

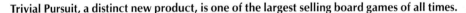

What does the term marketing mean? Most people mistakenly think of marketing only as selling and promotion. And no wonder! Canadians are bombarded with television commercials, newspaper ads, direct mail, and sales calls. Someone is always trying to sell something. It seems that we cannot escape death, taxes, or selling.

Therefore many students are surprised to learn that the most important part of marketing is not selling: Selling is only the tip of the marketing iceberg. Selling is only one of several marketing functions, and often not the most important one. If the marketer does a good job of identifying consumer needs, developing good products, and pricing, distributing, and promoting them effectively, these goods will sell very easily.

Everyone knows about "hot" products that attract consumers in droves. When Trivial Pursuit was first offered for sale, when compact disc players were introduced to the Canadian market, and when McCain's introduced frozen pizza, the manufacturers of these products were swamped with orders. They had designed the "right" products — not "me-too" products that simply followed a trend, but products that offered new benefits.

Peter Drucker, a leading management thinker, put it this way:[1]

> The aim of marketing is to make selling superfluous. The aim is to know and understand customers so well that the product or service fits them and sells itself.

Trivial Pursuit, a distinct new product, is one of the largest selling board games of all times.

James Hertel

This does not mean that selling and promotion are unimportant, but rather that they are part of a larger "marketing mix," a set of marketing tools that work together to affect the marketplace.

Here is our definition of marketing:

Marketing is human activity directed at satisfying needs and wants through exchange processes.[2]

To explain this definition, we will look at the following terms: **needs**, **wants**, **demands**, **products**, **exchange**, **transactions**, and **markets**.

Needs

The most basic concept underlying marketing is that of human needs, which we define as follows:

A human need is a state of felt deprivation in a person.

Humans have many complex needs. They include basic physical needs for food, clothing, warmth, and safety; social needs for belonging and affection; and individual needs for knowledge and self-expression. These needs are not created by marketing, but are a basic part of human makeup.

When a need is not satisfied, the person is unhappy. An unsatisfied person will either look for an object that will satisfy the need or try to reduce the need. People in industrial societies try to find or develop objects that will satisfy their desires. In developing societies people may have to focus on meeting basic needs, or reducing their desires to what is available.

Wants

A second basic concept in marketing is that of human wants.

Human wants are the form human needs take as shaped by culture and individual personality.

A hungry person in Bali may want mangoes, suckling pig, and beans. A hungry person in Canada may want a hamburger, French fries, and a Coke. Wants can be described in terms of objects that will satisfy needs. As a society evolves, the wants of its members expand. The people are exposed to more objects that arouse their interest and desire. Producers try to make a connection between what they produce and people's needs.

Sellers often confuse wants and needs. A manufacturer of drill bits may think that the customer needs a drill bit, but what the customer really needs is a hole. These sellers suffer from "marketing myopia."[3] They are so taken with their products that they focus only on existing wants and lose sight of underlying customer needs. They forget that a physical product is only a tool to solve a consumer problem. These sellers have trouble if a new product comes along that serves the need better or more cheaply. The customer will have the same need but will want the new product.

Demands

People may have almost unlimited wants but have limited resources. They choose products that produce the most satisfaction for their money.

Wants become demands when backed by buying power.

It is easy to list the demands in a society at a given time. In a single year, 26 million Canadians might purchase 5 billion eggs, 2.2 billion kilograms of chicken, 338 million liters of ice cream, 175 million kilograms of fish, 1 million cars, and 12 billion cups of tea. These and other consumer goods and services lead in turn to a demand for more than 15 million tons of steel, 10 million tons of cement, and many other industrial goods. These are a few of the demands in a $450 billion economy.

Consumers view products as bundles of benefits and choose products that give them the best bundle for their money. Thus a Toyota means basic transportation, a low price, and fuel economy. A Cadillac means comfort, luxury, and status. People choose the product whose benefits add up to the most satisfaction, given their wants and resources.

Products

Human needs, wants, and demands suggest that there are products to satisfy them. We define product as follows:

A product is anything that can be offered to a market for attention, acquisition, use, or consumption that might satisfy a want or need.

Suppose a person feels the need to be more attractive. We will call all the products that can satisfy this need the **product choice set**. The set may include such products as new clothes, hair styling services, a Caribbean suntan, and exercise classes. These products are not all equally desirable. The more available and less expensive products, such as clothing and a new haircut, are likely to be purchased first.

We can represent a specific product and a specific want as circles, and represent the product's want-satisfying ability by the degree to which it covers the want circle. Figure 1-1 shows that product A does not satisfy want X, that product B partially satisfies want X, and that product C completely satisfies want X. Product C would be called an **ideal product**. The closer the product

FIGURE 1-1
Three Degrees of Want Satisfaction

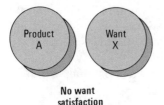

No want
satisfaction

Partial want
satisfaction

Complete want
satisfaction

Our seals will steal your heart!

Now . . . a fine new home for our appealing seals . . . the Gordon & Mary Russell Seal Pool where you can indulge in closeup admiration of the Aquarium's collection of playful harbour seals. Feeding times — daily — 11:45 a.m., 2:45 p.m., 6 p.m.

Vancouver Aquarium

Stanley Park . . . Open daily
Call 682-1118 for information

Products do not have to be physical objects. A visit to the aquarium can satisfy a need for adventure, an educational experience, or entertainment.

matches the consumer's want, the more successful the producer will be. Thus producers should find out what consumers want and provide products that come as close as possible to satisfying these wants.

The concept of product is not limited to physical objects. Anything capable of satisfying a need can be called a product. In addition to goods and services, this includes **persons**, **places**, **organizations**, **activities**, and **ideas**. A consumer decides which entertainers to watch on television, places to go on a vacation, organizations to contribute to, and ideas to support. To the consumer, these are all products. If the term product does not seem to fit at times, we can use the term satisfier, resource, or offer. All describe something of value to someone.

Exchange

Marketing occurs when people decide to satisfy needs and wants through exchange.

Exchange is the act of obtaining a desired object from someone by offering something in return.

Exchange allows people to concentrate on producing things they are good at producing and trading them for needed items made by others. The society ends up producing much more than under any alternative plan.

Exchange is the core concept of marketing.[4] For an exchange to take place, several conditions must be satisfied. There must be at least two parties, and each must have something of value to the other. Each party must want to deal with the other party and each must be free to accept or reject the other's offer.

Finally, the parties must be able to communicate their decisions and deliver the product or service.

These conditions make exchange possible. Whether exchange actually takes place depends on whether the parties come to an agreement. If they agree, we conclude that the act of exchange leaves each party better off (or at least not worse off) because each was free to reject or accept the offer.

Transactions

As exchange is the core concept of marketing, a transaction is its unit of measurement.

A transaction consists of a trade of values between two parties.

We must be able to say that A gives X to B and gets Y in return. Jones gives $400 to Smith and obtains a television set. This is a classic **monetary transaction**, but not all transactions involve money. In a **barter transaction**, Jones might give a refrigerator to Smith in return for the television set. A transaction involves at least two things of value, conditions that are agreed to, a time of agreement, and a place of agreement.

In the broadest sense, the marketer tries to bring about a response to some offer. The response may be more than "buying" or "trading" goods and services in the narrow sense. A political candidate wants a response called "votes," a church wants "joining," a social action group wants "adoption of the idea." Marketing consists of actions taken to obtain a desired response from a target audience to some product, service, idea, or other object.

Markets

The concept of transactions leads to the concept of a market.

A market is the set of actual and potential buyers of a product.

To understand the nature of a market, imagine a primitive economy with only four persons: a fisherman, a hunter, a potter, and a farmer. Figure 1-2 shows three different ways in which these traders could meet their needs. In the first case, **self-sufficiency**, they gather the needed goods for themselves. Thus the hunter spends most of the time hunting, but also takes time to fish, make pottery, and farm to obtain the other goods. The hunter is therefore less efficient at hunting, and the same is true of the other three people.

In the second case, **decentralized exchange**, each person sees the other three as potential "buyers" who make up a market. Thus the hunter may make separate trips to trade goods with the fisherman, the potter, and the farmer to exchange meat for their goods. In the third case, **centralized exchange**, a new person called a merchant appears and locates in a central area called a market-place. Each trader brings goods to the merchant and trades for other needed goods. Thus the hunter transacts with one "market" to obtain all the needed

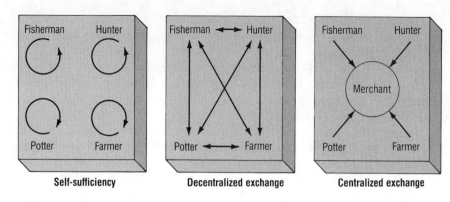

Fisherman	Hunter		Fisherman ⟷ Hunter		Fisherman	Hunter
Potter	Farmer		Potter ⟷ Farmer		Potter	Farmer
Self-sufficiency			**Decentralized exchange**		**Centralized exchange**	

FIGURE 1-2
Evolution toward Centralized Exchange

goods, rather than with three other persons. Merchants and central marketplaces greatly reduce the total number of transactions needed to accomplish a given volume of exchange.[5]

Markets, such as the Kitchener Farmers' Market, bring buyers and sellers together to make transactions.

James Hertel

As the number of persons and transactions increases in a society, the number of merchants and marketplaces also increases. In advanced societies, markets need not be physical places where buyers and sellers interact. With modern communications and transportation, a merchant can advertise a product on late evening television, take orders from hundreds of customers over the phone, and mail the goods to the buyers on the following day without having had any physical contact with the buyers.

A market can grow up around a product, a service, or anything else of value. For example, a labor market consists of people who are willing to offer their work in return for wages or products. Various institutions such as employment agencies and job-counseling firms will grow up around a labor market to help it function better. The money market is another important market that emerges to meet the needs of people so that they can borrow, lend, save, and protect money. The donor market emerges to meet the financial needs of non-profit organizations.

Marketing

The concept of markets finally brings us full circle to the concept of marketing. Marketing means working with markets to bring about exchanges for the purpose of satisfying human needs and wants. Thus we return to our definition of marketing as human activity directed at satisfying needs and wants through exchange processes.

Exchange processes involve work. Sellers have to search for buyers, identify their needs, design good products, promote them, store and deliver them, and set prices. Such activities as product development, research, communication, distribution, pricing, and service are core marketing activities.

Although we normally think of marketing as being carried on by sellers, buyers also carry on marketing activities. Consumers are "marketing" when they search for the goods they need at prices they can afford. Company purchasing agents are "marketing" when they track down sellers and bargain for good terms. A **seller's market** is one in which sellers have more power and buyers have to be the more active "marketers." In a **buyer's market**, buyers have more power and sellers have to be more active "marketers."

In the early 1950s the supply of goods began to grow faster than the demand. Marketing became identified with sellers trying to find buyers. This book will take this point of view and examine the marketing problems of sellers in a buyer's market.

Marketing Management ━━━━━━━━━━

Those who engage in exchange activities learn over time how to market more effectively. We define marketing management as follows:

Marketing management is the analysis, planning, implementation, and control of programs designed to create, build, and maintain beneficial exchanges with target buyers for the purpose of achieving organizational objectives.

Most people think of a marketing manager as someone who finds enough customers for the company's current output. However, this view is too limited. The organization has a desired level of demand for its products. At various times, there may be no demand, adequate demand, irregular demand, or too much demand. Marketing managers are concerned not only with finding and increasing demand, but also with changing or even reducing it. Marketing management seeks to affect the level, timing, and nature of demand in a way that will help the organization achieve its objectives. Simply put, marketing management is **demand management**.

By marketing managers, we mean company people who are involved in marketing analysis, planning, implementation, and control activities. They include sales managers and salespeople, advertising executives, sales promotion people, marketing researchers, product managers, and pricing specialists. We will say more about these marketing jobs in Chapters 2 and 3.

Marketing Management Philosophies

We have described marketing management as carrying out tasks to achieve desired exchanges with target markets. What philosophy should guide these marketing efforts? What weight should be given to the interests of the organization, customers, and society? Very often the interests of these groups conflict. Clearly, marketing activities should be carried out under some philosophy.

There are four competing concepts under which organizations conduct their marketing activity: the production, selling, marketing, and societal marketing concepts.

The Production Concept

The production concept is one of the oldest philosophies guiding sellers.

The production concept holds that consumers will favor products that are available and highly affordable, and therefore management should focus on improving production and distribution efficiency.

The production concept is a reasonable philosophy in two types of situations. The first is where the demand for a product is greater than the supply. Here management should look for ways to increase production. The second situation is where the product's cost is high, and improved productivity is needed to bring it down. Henry Ford's whole philosophy was to perfect the production of the Model T so that its cost could be brought down and more people could afford it. He joked about offering people any color car as long as it was black. Today Texas Instruments (TI) follows this philosophy of increased production and lower costs in order to bring down prices. It won a major share of the hand-calculator market with this philosophy. Lower prices and greater availability are not a guarantee of success, however. When TI used the same strategy in the digital watch market, it failed. Although the watches were priced low, customers did not find TI's watches attractive. TI again tried the same strategy in the home computer market and lost over $300 million before it abandoned the field.[6]

Some service organizations also follow the production concept. Many medical and dental practices use assembly-line principles, as do some government agencies such as unemployment offices and license bureaus. Although this procedure results in many cases being handled per hour, this type of management is open to charges of being unfriendly and impersonal.

The Selling Concept

Many organizations follow the selling concept.

> *The selling concept holds that consumers will not buy enough of the organization's products unless the organization undertakes a large selling and promotion effort.*

The selling concept is practiced hardest with "unsought goods," those that buyers normally do not think of buying, such as insurance, encyclopedias, and funeral plots. These industries are good at tracking down prospective buyers and taking a hard sell approach to convince them of product benefits. Hard selling also occurs with sought goods, such as automobiles.

> From the moment the customer walks into the showroom, the auto salesman "psychs him out." If the customer likes the floor model, he may be told that there is another customer about to buy it and that he should decide on the spot. If the customer balks at the price, the salesman offers to talk to the manager to get a special concession. The customer waits ten minutes and the salesman returns with "the boss doesn't like it but I got him to agree." The aim is to "work up the customer" to buy on the spot.[7]

The Marketing Concept

The marketing concept is a more recent business philosophy.[8]

> *The marketing concept holds that achieving organizational goals depends on determining the needs and wants of target markets and delivering the desired satisfactions more effectively and efficiently than competitors.*

The marketing concept has been stated in colorful ways, such as "Find a need and fill it"; "Make what you can sell instead of trying to sell what you can make"; and "We make the hamburger a beautiful thing" (Harvey's).

The selling concept and the marketing concept are frequently confused. Figure 1-3 compares the two concepts. The selling concept starts with the company's existing products and calls for heavy selling and promoting to achieve profitable sales. The marketing concept starts with the needs and wants

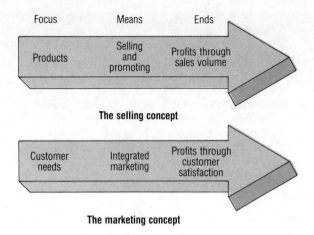

FIGURE 1-3
The Selling and Marketing Concepts Contrasted

of the company's target customers. The company integrates all the activities that will affect customer satisfaction and makes its profit by creating and maintaining customer satisfaction. Under the marketing concept companies produce what consumers want, and in this way satisfy consumers and make profits.

Many companies have adopted the marketing concept. We know that Procter & Gamble, IBM, Dylex, and McDonald's follow this concept faithfully (see Exhibit 1-1). We also know that the marketing concept is practiced more in consumer goods companies than in industrial goods companies, and more in large companies than in small companies. Also, many companies claim they practice the concept but do not. They have the forms of marketing — such as a marketing vice-president, product managers, marketing plans, marketing research — but not the substance.[9] Several years of hard work are needed to turn a sales-oriented company into a market-oriented company.

Recently, critics have contended that the marketing concept with its strong adherence to identifying and satisfying the needs and wants of buyers may stifle product innovation. Two McGill researchers argue that:

> Inventors, scientists, engineers, and academics, in the normal pursuit of scientific knowledge, gave the world the telephone, the phonograph, the electric light, and in more recent times, the laser, xerography, instant photography, and the transistor. In contrast, worshippers of the marketing concept have bestowed upon mankind such products as newfangled potato chips, feminine hygiene deodorant, and the pet rock.[10]

Market-driven behavior, which focuses entirely on the consumer, may be a factor in the economic decline of North America. Consider the following:

> Deferring to a market-driven strategy without paying attention to its limitations is, quite possibly, opting for customer satisfaction and lower risk in the short run

EXHIBIT 1-1
McDonald's Applies the Marketing Concept

McDonald's Corporation, the fast-food hamburger retailer, is a master marketer. In only three decades, McDonald's has served over 50 billion hamburgers to people in Canada and 42 other countries. With over 10 000 outlets, it commands $11 billion in annual sales and a 19% share of the fast-food market, far ahead of Burger King (6.5%) and Wendy's (4.0%). Credit for this leading position belongs to a strong marketing orientation. McDonald's knows how to serve people and adapt to changing consumer wants.

Before McDonald's, consumers could get hamburgers in restaurants or diners, but they often encountered poor hamburgers, slow and unfriendly service, unattractive decor, unclean conditions, and a noisy atmosphere. In 1955 Ray Kroc, a 52-year-old salesman of milkshake-mixing machines, became excited about a string of seven restaurants owned by Richard and Maurice McDonald. Kroc liked their fast-food restaurant concept and bought the chain for $2.7 million. Kroc decided to expand the chain by selling franchises to others.

In Canada, McDonald's opened in June 1967, with a single store in Richmond, British Columbia. George A. Cohon, President of McDonald's Restaurants of Canada Limited, opened a store in London, Ontario, in November 1968, to mark entry into the Eastern Canadian market. Surprisingly, in the early years McDonald's lost money in Canada. Then in 1971, George Cohon made a dramatic move. He cut prices at McDonald's by 20% across the board. Sales jumped by 25% and have grown ever since.

McDonald's marketing philosophy is captured in the motto of "Q.S.C. & V.," which stands for quality, service, cleanliness, and value. Customers enter a spotlessly clean restaurant, walk up to a friendly hostess, receive a good-tasting hamburger within five minutes, and eat it there or take it out. There are no jukeboxes or telephones to create a teenage hangout. There are also no cigarette machines or newspaper racks. McDonald's became a family affair, appealing strongly to children.

As times changed, so did McDonald's. It expanded its sitdown sections, improved decor, launched a breakfast menu, added new food items, and opened new outlets in high-traffic areas. For example, McDonald's was ready for Expo 86 in Vancouver. It had five restaurants on the Expo 86 site, including McBarge — a floating restaurant — and served between 60 000 and 70 000 customers every day. In Canada , McDonald's is a great marketing success story. More than one million Canadians a day visit one of the nearly 500 McDonald's restaurants. The company has 50 000 employees and makes annual purchases of more than 23 million kilograms of beef, 32 million kilograms of potatoes, 26 million dozen buns, and 10 million kilograms of chicken products.

McDonald's has mastered the art of serving consumers. It monitors product and

at the expense of superior products in the future. Satisfied customers are crucially important, of course, but not if the strategy for creating them is responsible as well as for unnecessary product proliferation, inflated costs, unfocused diversification, and a lagging commitment to new technology and new capital equipment.[11]

Any business that is solely marketing oriented may be omitting some impor-

McDonald's floating restaurant at Expo 86 in Vancouver.

service quality through continuous customer surveys, and puts great energy into improving hamburger production methods to simplify operations, bring down costs, and speed up service. McDonald's' focus on consumers has made it the world's largest food service organization.

Sources: John F. Love and McDonald's Corporation, *McDonald's: Behind the Arches*, Toronto: Bantam Books, 1986; and Wynne Thomas, "Compelling Story of Common Sense Marketing," *Marketing*, November 24 1986, p. 11-12.

tant dimensions in determining its future directions. For some firms the key to success may depend on technology or production. For example, technology is critical in the computer field. In pulp and paper and in steel, two important Canadian industries, lower production costs have more impact than any marketing techniques that could be used. While the marketing concept is an extremely valuable approach, in some situations other orientations may be more suitable.[12]

The Societal Marketing Concept

The societal marketing concept is the newest concept.

The societal marketing concept holds that the organization should determine the needs, wants, and interests of target markets and deliver the desired satisfactions more effectively and efficiently than competitors in a way that maintains or improves the consumer's and the society's well-being.

The societal marketing concept questions whether the pure marketing concept is appropriate in an age of environmental problems, resource shortages, rapid population growth, worldwide inflation, and neglected social services.[13] Is the firm that senses, serves, and satisfies individual wants always doing what is best for consumers and society in the long run? The pure marketing concept overlooks possible conflicts between short-run consumer wants and long-run consumer welfare.

Consider the Coca-Cola Company. People see it as being a highly responsible corporation producing fine soft drinks that satisfy consumer tastes. Yet consumer and environmental groups have voiced concerns that Coke has little nutritional value, can harm teeth, contains caffeine, and adds to the litter problem with one-way disposable bottles.

These kinds of concerns led to the societal marketing concept. The concept calls upon marketers to balance three considerations in setting their marketing policies. Originally, companies based their marketing decisions largely on short-run company profit. Over time, companies began to recognize the long-run importance of satisfying consumer wants, and introduced the marketing concept. Now they are beginning to think of society's interests when making decisions. The societal marketing concept calls for balancing all three considerations—company profits, consumer wants, and society's interests.

The Goals of the Marketing System

Marketing affects so many people in so many ways that it inevitably stirs controversy. Some people intensely dislike modern marketing activity, charging it with such sins as ruining the environment, bombarding the public with senseless ads, creating unnecessary wants, and teaching greed to youngsters. Consider the following comments on advertising:

The squandering of resources only begins the problem. The consumption binge which television has done so much to push has been fouling air, water, roads, streets, fields, and forests—a trend we failed or declined to recognize until almost irreversible. It has given us garbage statistics as staggering as our consumption statistics, and closely related to them.[14]

Others vigorously defend marketing:

> Aggressive marketing policies and practices have been largely responsible for the high material standard of living in North America. Today through mass, low-cost marketing we enjoy products which once were considered luxuries, and which still are so classified in many foreign countries.[15]

It is clear that various social commentators have vastly different views on the meaning and contribution of marketing. The major breakthrough in the last 30 years has been the recognition that sellers not only must take buyers' wants into account but must start with them.

What is now happening is that business is going through another learning phase and is discovering that it must also take the interests of citizens into account. Marketing, at its highest level of practice, is a balanced serving of the combined interests of sellers, buyers, and citizens. This approach helps to ensure the long-run profitability and survival of businesses in an increasingly competitive and turbulent marketplace.

The Rapid Adoption of Marketing

Most people think that marketing is carried on only in large companies operating in capitalistic countries. The truth is that marketing is carried on within and outside the business sector in all kinds of countries.

In the Business Sector

In the business sector, different companies became interested in marketing at different times. A few U.S. companies, such as General Electric, General Motors, Sears, Procter & Gamble, and Coca-Cola, saw marketing's potential almost immediately. Marketing spread most rapidly in consumer packaged goods companies, consumer durables companies, and industrial equipment companies—in that order. The importance of marketing was quickly appreciated by many Canadian firms in these industries because of their close ties with U.S. companies and the similarity of the marketing systems. For example, in a recent survey of the chief executives of large Canadian companies, marketing experience was considered essential for the top position.[16] Producers of such commodities as steel, chemicals, and paper adopted marketing later, and many still have a long way to go.

Within the past decade consumer service firms, especially airlines and banks, have moved toward modern marketing. Marketing is also beginning to attract the interest of insurance and stock brokerage companies, such as Dominion Securities Pitfield, and they are learning to apply marketing effectively.

The latest business groups to take an interest in marketing are professionals such as lawyers, accountants, physicians, and architects. Until recently, professional associations have not allowed their members to engage in price competition, client solicitation, and advertising. Today accounting firms such as

Fee.

No fee.

$12 annually or a transaction charge of 15¢.

$12 annually or 15¢ (min. monthly 50¢)
per transaction.

$12 annually or $6 plus 10¢ per transaction.

15¢ per transaction, up to $1.00 monthly.

$12 annually.

User fees as of August 25th, 1983.

No fee, no transaction charges.

The intelligent choice.

Most bank credit cards charge you a fee just to use them. The Bank of Montreal MasterCard does not.

In fact, Bank of Montreal MasterCard is the only credit card of Canada's five largest banks, that you can use as much as you want without charging you a fee.

All transactions (excluding cash advances) are free as long as you pay your balance in full by the due date.

And payments of your MasterCard statement can be mailed or made at any Instabank or branch of Bank of Montreal.

We've never charged our credit card customers a user fee at the Bank of Montreal. And we don't intend to start now.

If you don't want to pay to have a credit card, why should you?

Find out more.

Bank of Montreal

Consumer service firms, such as banks, have enthusiastically adopted marketing.

Clarkson Gordon are advertising to small businesses, and firms such as Price Waterhouse are advertising to the energy sector. Lawyers in some provinces are now advertising and competing on price. Predictions are that other provinces will soon follow. Dentists are devising new marketing techniques to increase their business, including advertising. In Manitoba and British Columbia, dentists are accepting payment by credit cards. In Ontario, dentists and doctors are setting up offices in department stores and malls and offering extended hours.[17]

In the International Sector

Marketing is practiced not only in North America, but in the rest of the world. In fact, several European and Japanese multinationals—companies like Nestlé, Siemens, Toyota, and Sony — have often outperformed their North American competitors. Multinationals have introduced and spread modern marketing practices throughout the world. As a result, management in smaller countries is beginning to ask: What is marketing? How does it differ from plain selling? How can we introduce marketing into the firm? Will it make a difference?

In socialist countries, marketing has traditionally had a bad name. However, such marketing functions as marketing research, branding, advertising, and sales promotion are now spreading rapidly. The U.S.S.R. now has over 100 state-operated advertising agencies and marketing research firms.[18] Several companies in Poland and Hungary have marketing departments, several socialist universities teach marketing, and Romania is adopting a modified form of the marketing concept.[19]

In the Nonprofit Sector

Marketing is currently attracting the interest of nonprofit organizations such as colleges, hospitals, police departments, museums, and symphony orchestras.[20] Consider the following developments:

- Many universities in Canada are operating at a deficit because of declining enrollments and increasing costs. In Ontario, the possibility of closing smaller universities has been discussed for over a decade.

- Many cultural performance groups cannot attract large enough audiences. Even those that have seasonal ticket sellouts, such as the Winnipeg Symphony Orchestra, face huge operating deficits at the end of the year.

- Many nonprofit organizations that flourished in earlier years — the YMCA, Salvation Army, Girl Guides, and Women's Christian Temperance Union — are re-examining their mission in an effort to reverse a decline in membership.

These organizations have marketplace problems. Their administrators are struggling to keep them alive in the face of changing consumer attitudes and reduced financial resources. Many such institutions have turned to marketing as a possible answer to their problems.

Governments are also showing an increasing interest in marketing. Canada Post has developed a number of marketing plans for its operations, and the federal government is the largest advertiser in Canada. Both federal and provincial government agencies are involved in marketing energy conservation, anti-smoking, and other public causes. Other organizations, such as Crown corporations and marketing boards, are using marketing to solve some of their problems.

Plan of the Book

The following chapters will expand on the marketing topics introduced in this chapter. Chapter 2 discusses strategic planning and the marketing management process. Chapter 3 looks at how marketing strategies and programs are planned, implemented, and controlled by people in the organization's marketing department.

Chapters 4 and 5 look at the ways marketers seek attractive opportunities in the marketing environment. In Chapter 4 we discuss the importance of marketing research and information in preparing company and marketing plans, and in analyzing the marketing environment. Chapter 5 describes the actors and forces in the rapidly changing marketing environment.

Chapters 6, 7, and 8 examine the key characteristics of the company's markets. Chapter 6 examines consumer markets; Chapter 7 looks at organizational markets. Chapter 8 describes the art of selecting appropriate markets. The marketer first segments the market, then selects target segments and positions the company's products in chosen segments.

Chapters 9 through 17 look at the major marketing activities of the firm — designing, pricing, placing, and promoting products and services. In these chapters we will look at the various concepts that guide marketing managers and at the techniques they use to develop attractive offers and market them successfully.

The final three chapters look at topics of current interest. Chapter 18 discusses international marketing; Chapter 19 discusses services and nonprofit marketing. The last chapter, "Marketing and Society," returns us to the basic question of marketing's role and purpose in society, its contributions, and its shortcomings.

The book ends with an appendix that presents the marketing arithmetic used by marketing managers when making many decisions.

Summary

Marketing touches everyone's life. It is the means by which a standard of living is developed and made available to people. Many people confuse marketing with selling, but marketing occurs long before and after the selling event. Marketing actually combines many activities, such as marketing research, product development, distribution, pricing, advertising, and personal selling. These activities are designed to sense, serve, and satisfy consumer needs while meeting the organization's goals.

Marketing is directed at satisfying needs and wants through exchange processes. The key concepts of marketing are needs, wants, demands, products, exchange, transactions, and markets. Marketing management is the analysis, planning, implementation, and control of programs designed to create, build, and maintain beneficial exchanges with target markets for the purpose of achieving organizational objectives. Marketers must be good at managing the level of demand, since actual demand can be different from what the organization wants.

Marketing management can be conducted under four different marketing philosophies. The production concept holds that consumers will favor products that are available at low cost, and therefore management's task is to improve production efficiency and bring down prices. The selling concept holds that consumers will not buy enough of the company's products unless they are stimulated through heavy selling and promotion. The marketing concept holds that a company should research the needs and wants of a well-defined target market and deliver the desired satisfactions. The societal marketing concept holds that the company should generate customer satisfaction and long-run societal well-being as the key to achieving organizational goals.

Interest in marketing is growing as more organizations in the business sector, in the international sector, and in the nonprofit sector recognize how marketing can improve performance.

Questions for Discussion

1. Identify and discuss the main functions of marketing.
2. The historian Arnold Toynbee has criticized marketing practice in North America, saying that consumers are being manipulated into purchasing products that aren't required to satisfy the "minimum material requirements of life" or "genuine wants." What is your position? Defend it.
3. Define marketing in your own words.
4. Peter Drucker, a leading management authority and consultant, has stated that "The aim of marketing is to make selling superfluous." Explain Drucker's comment.
5. Although McDonald's Corporation has been praised for applying the marketing concept, it has also been criticized for practicing a selling orientation. What might have caused this criticism?
6. Contrast the marketing management philosophies of the production concept and the marketing concept with respect to the firm's attitude toward the

customer and product offering, the role of marketing research, the importance of profit, and the role of the sales force.

7. Procter & Gamble's success is often credited to the company being a good "listener." How does this relate to the marketing concept?

8. Why has marketing been used by many nonprofit organizations in recent years? Elaborate on a specific example.

Chapter 1 Key Terms

Demands   Human wants that are backed by buying power.

Exchange   The act of obtaining a desired object from someone by offering something in return.

Human need   A state of felt deprivation in a person.

Human want   The form that a human need takes as shaped by culture and individual personality.

Market   The set of actual and potential buyers of a product.

Marketing   Human activity directed at satisfying needs and wants through exchange processes.

Marketing concept   The marketing management philosophy that holds that achieving organizational goals depends on determining the needs and wants of target markets and delivering the desired satisfactions more effectively and efficiently than competitors.

Marketing management   The analysis, planning, implementation, and control of programs designed to create, build, and maintain beneficial exchanges with target buyers for the purpose of achieving organizational objectives.

Marketing manager   A person who is involved in marketing analysis, planning, implementation, and control activities.

Product   Anything that can be offered to a market for attention, acquisition, use, or consumption that might satisfy a need or want.

Production concept   The philosophy that consumers will favor products that are available and highly affordable, and therefore management should focus on improving production and distribution efficiency.

Selling concept   The idea that consumers will not buy enough of the organization's products unless the organization undertakes a large selling and promotion effort.

Societal marketing concept   The idea that the organization should determine the needs, wants, and interests of target markets and deliver the desired satisfactions more effectively and efficiently than competitors in a way that maintains or improves the consumer's and society's well-being.

Transaction   A trade between two parties that involves at least two things of value, agreed upon conditions, a time of agreement, and a place of agreement.

Cases for Chapter 1 ▬▬▬▬▬▬▬▬▬▬▬▬▬▬▬▬▬▬▬▬

Strategic Planning and the Marketing Management Process

Chapter Objectives

After reading this chapter, you should be able to:
1. Discuss company wide strategic planning and its four steps.
2. Describe how companies develop mission statements and objectives.
3. Explain how companies evaluate and develop their "business portfolios."
4. Discuss marketing's role in strategic planning.
5. Describe the marketing management process and the forces that influence it.

In 1973, Dylex Limited had sales of $132 million and net earnings of $4.5 million. By the end of 1985 sales were over $2 billion and net earnings were $47 million. This phenomenal growth has made Dylex Canada's largest specialty fashion retailer, capturing over 10% of the total Canadian apparel sales. Factors responsible for the company's success include innovative merchandising and the ability to adapt to changing markets. Dylex has over 1100 retail stores in most major shopping malls in Canada and controls over 1500 stores in the United States. The stores are designed to appeal to specific segments of the market. For the female shopper, Dylex has six different chains:

Fairweather/Daniel Hechter
Latest in fashionable moderately priced women's clothing and accessories for the 15-30 age group.

B.H. Emporium
Value priced fashionable merchandise for the younger shopper.

Braemar
Selected lines of fashionable sportswear, dresses, and coats.

Suzy Shier/L.A. Express
Medium-priced fashionable merchandise for the younger market.

Town and Country/Petites
Medium-priced contemporary coats, dresses, and sportswear.

Harry Rosen Women
Beautiful and tasteful clothing for the professional woman.

Rubys/Feathers/Fantasia/Diva
Fashionable and moderately priced footwear.

For the male shopper, three chains offer distinct product lines:

Tip Top
Suits and accessories for the broad middle group of consumers.

Big Steel Man
Latest in fashionable moderately priced clothing for the younger man.

Harry Rosen
Quality and fashion for the professional and executive.

For the family shopper there are three chains:

Thrifty's
Casual wear and accessories for active lifestyles.

Bi-Way
Low cost clothing and housewares for budget-conscious consumers.

Drug World
Wide range of discount products.

Dylex pays close attention to their consumers. They constantly fine-tune their knowledge by extensive market analysis and surveys. As a Fairweather executive explains, "We track our markets in a very sophisticated way and learn as much about them as possible. We went into junior sizes because this is the mass market, and we went after the biggest segment of that market in a special way that would appeal to them. Our research enables us to identify our customers, and our market share." An executive with Suzy Shier states, "We strive to pres-

ent a unique fashion statement specifically geared to our smaller store and endeavor to offer original styling from world markets to give customers a different look than is generally available and at competitive prices." Big Steel Man has a well defined marketing plan consisting of upbeat advertising, store-by-store profiling, and extensive market research. The focus on quality and value, the targeting of very fashionable clothing at young men, and the careful selection and training of personnel all contribute to the dramatic sales growth of Big Steel Man.

Dylex's top management uses formal planning to see that all of these retail stores work together to achieve the company's overall growth and profit goals. They begin by defining Dylex's corporate mission. Next, they translate the company mission into specific objectives for the various stores. Then strategies are planned for achieving the objectives.

Finally, guided by the company's overall strategic plan, managers throughout Dylex prepare marketing, financial, production, personnel, and other plans for the stores and various manufacturing operations. A large company such as Dylex cannot survive in its fast-changing environment by making last-minute decisions and trusting to luck. Managers must use formal planning to position the company for long-run success.[1]

All companies must look ahead and develop long-term strategies to meet the changing conditions in their industries. No one strategy is best for all companies. Each company must find the game plan that makes the most sense given its situation, opportunities, objectives, and resources. The hard task of selecting an overall company strategy for long-run survival and growth is called strategic planning.

Marketing plays an important role in strategic planning. It provides information to help prepare the strategic plan. In turn, strategic planning defines marketing's role in the organization. Guided by the strategic plan, marketing works with other departments in the organization to help achieve overall strategic objectives.

In this chapter, we will look first at the organization's overall strategic planning. Next we will discuss marketing's role in the organization as defined by the overall strategic plan. Then we will look at the marketing management process — the process that marketers undertake to carry out their role in the organization.

Thrifty's targets the active lifestyle.

Overview of Planning

Benefits of Planning

Many companies operate without formal plans. In new companies, managers are so busy that they have no time for planning. In mature companies, many managers argue that they have done well without formal planning and therefore planning cannot be too important. They resist taking the time to prepare a written plan. They argue that the marketplace changes too fast for a plan to be useful—it would end up collecting dust.

Yet formal planning can yield a number of benefits. Melville Branch lists these benefits as follows: (1) Planning encourages management to think ahead systematically; (2) leads to better coordination of company efforts; (3) leads to clearer performance standards for control; (4) causes the company to sharpen its objectives and policies; (5) better prepares the company for sudden developments; (6) improves interactions between company executives.[2]

Kinds of Plans

Companies usually prepare annual plans, long-range plans, and strategic plans. The **annual plan** describes the current marketing situation, company objectives, marketing strategy for the year, action program, budgets, and controls. Top management approves this plan and uses it to coordinate marketing activities with production, finance, and other areas of the company.

The **long-range plan** describes the major factors and forces affecting the organization over the next several years. It includes long-term objectives, the major marketing strategies that will be used to attain them, and the resources required. This long-range plan is reviewed and updated each year so that the company always has a current long-range plan.

The company's annual and long-range plans deal with current businesses and how to keep them going. Management must also plan which businesses the company should stay in and which new ones it should pursue. The environment is full of surprises, and management must design the company to withstand shocks. Strategic planning enables the firm to take advantage of opportunities by adapting to its constantly changing environment.

Strategic Planning

Strategic planning sets the stage for the rest of the planning in the firm. We define it as follows:

> Strategic planning is the process of developing and maintaining a strategic fit between the organization's goals and capabilities and its changing marketing opportunities. It relies on developing a clear company mission, supporting objectives, a sound business portfolio, and coordinated functional strategies.

The steps in the strategic planning process are shown in Figure 2-1. At the corporate level the company first defines its overall purpose and mission. This

FIGURE 2-1
Steps in Strategic Planning

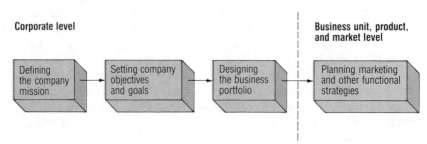

mission is then broken down into detailed supporting objectives that guide the whole company. Next, headquarters decides what portfolio of businesses and products is best for the company, and how much support to give each one. Each business and product unit must in turn develop detailed marketing and other functional plans that support the company-wide plan. Thus marketing planning occurs at the business unit, product, and market levels. It supports company strategic planning with more detailed planning for specific marketing opportunities. We discuss each of the strategic planning steps in more detail below.

Defining the Company Mission

An organization exists to accomplish something. At first it has a clear purpose or mission, but over time its mission may become unclear as the organization grows and adds new products and markets. Alternatively, the mission may remain clear, but some managers may no longer be interested in it. Or the mission may remain clear, but may no longer be best given new conditions in the environment.

When management senses that the organization is drifting, it must renew its search for purpose. It is time to ask: What is our business? Who is the customer? What is value to the customer? What will our business be? What should our business be?[3] These simple-sounding questions are among the most difficult the company will ever have to answer. Successful companies continually raise these questions and answer them carefully and fully.

Many organizations develop formal mission statements that answer these questions.

A mission statement is a statement of the organization's purpose, what it wants to accomplish in the larger environment.

A clear mission statement acts as an "invisible hand" that guides people in the organization so that they can work independently and yet collectively toward overall organizational goals.

Companies traditionally defined their business in product terms, such as "We manufacture video games," or in technological terms, such as "We are a chemical-processing firm." But some years ago, Theodore Levitt proposed that market definitions of a business are better than product or technological definitions.[4] Products and technologies eventually become out of date, but basic market needs may last forever. A market-oriented mission statement defines the business in terms of serving particular customer groups or needs.

Management should avoid making its mission too narrow or too broad. A lead pencil manufacturer that says it is in the communication equipment business is stating its mission too broadly. Mission statements should be specific and realistic. Many mission statements are written for public relations purposes and lack specific, workable guidelines. The statement "We want to be the leading company in this industry producing the highest-quality products with the best service at the lowest prices" sounds good, but it will not help the company make tough decisions.

Setting Company Objectives and Goals

The company's mission needs to be turned into detailed supporting objectives for each level of management. Each manager should have objectives and be responsible for reaching them. This system is known as **management by objectives**.

For example, a major objective may be to "improve profits." Profits can be improved by increasing sales or reducing costs. Sales can be increased by increasing the company's share of the Canadian market and entering new foreign markets. These become the company's current marketing objectives.

Marketing strategies must be developed to support these marketing objectives. To increase its Canadian market share, the company could increase the availability and promotion of its product. To enter new foreign markets, the company could cut prices. These are the broad marketing strategies.

Each marketing strategy should be spelled out in greater detail. For example, increasing the product's promotion will call for more salespeople and advertising, both of which will have to be carefully planned. In this way the firm's mission is translated into a set of objectives for the current period. The objectives should be as specific as possible. The objective to "increase our market share" is not as useful as to "increase our market share to 15% by the end of the second year."

Designing the Business Portfolio

Guided by the company's mission statement and objectives, management must now plan its business portfolio.

> A company's business portfolio is the collection of businesses and products that make up the company.

The best business portfolio carefully matches the company's strengths and weaknesses with opportunities in the environment. The company must (1) analyze the current business portfolio and decide which businesses should receive more or less investment, and (2) develop growth strategies for adding new products or businesses to the portfolio.

Analyzing the Current Business Portfolio

The major tool in strategic planning is **business portfolio analysis**, whereby management evaluates the businesses that make up the company. The company will want to put strong resources into its more profitable businesses and phase down or drop its weaker business. It can keep its portfolio of businesses up to date by strengthening or adding growing businesses and withdrawing from declining businesses.

Management's first step is to identify the key businesses that make up the company. These can be called the strategic business units.

> A strategic business unit (SBU) is a unit of the company that has a separate mission and objectives, and that can be planned independently from other

company businesses. An SBU can be a company division, a product line within a division, or sometimes a single product or brand.

Identifying SBUs can be very difficult. In a large corporation, should SBUs be defined at the level of companies, divisions, product lines, or brands? Thus, defining basic business units for portfolio analysis is often a complex task.

The next step in business portfolio analysis calls for management to assess the attractiveness of its various SBUs and decide how much support each deserves. In some companies, this is done informally. Management looks at the company's collection of businesses or products and uses judgment to decide how much each SBU should contribute and receive. Other companies use formal portfolio planning methods.

The purpose of strategic planning is to find ways in which the company can best use its strengths to take advantage of attractive opportunities in the environment. Most standard portfolio analysis methods evaluate SBUs on two important dimensions—the attractiveness of the SBU's market or industry, and the strength of the SBU's position in that market or industry. The best-known of these portfolio planning methods was developed by the Boston Consulting Group, a leading management consulting firm.[5]

Using the Boston Consulting Group (BCG) approach, a company classifies all its SBUs in the **growth-share matrix** shown in Figure 2-2. On the vertical axis, **market growth rate** provides a measure of market attractiveness. On the horizontal axis, **market share** serves as a measure of company strength in the market. By dividing the growth-share matrix in the way indicated, four types of SBUs can be distinguished.

FIGURE 2-2
The BCG Growth Share Matrix

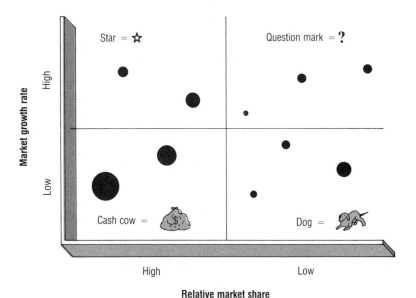

Relative market share

Stars   Stars are high-growth, high-share businesses or products. They often need heavy investment to finance their rapid growth. Eventually their growth will slow down, and they will turn into cash cows.

Cash cows   Cash cows are low-growth, high-share businesses or products. These established and successful SBUs need less investment to hold their market share. Thus they produce a lot of cash that the company uses to pay its bills and support other SBUs that need investment.

Question marks   Question marks are low-share business units in high-growth markets. They require a lot of cash to hold their share, let alone increase it. Management has to think hard about which question marks it should try to build into stars and which should be phased out.

Dogs   Dogs are low-growth, low-share businesses and products. They may generate enough cash to maintain themselves, but do not promise to be a large source of cash.

Once it has classified its SBUs, the company must determine what role each will play in the future. One of four strategies can be pursued for each SBU. The company could invest more in the business unit in order to **build** its share. Second, it could invest just enough to **hold** the SBU's share at the current level. Third, it could **harvest** the SBU, increasing its short-term cash flow regardless of the long-term effect. Finally, the company could **divest** the SBU by selling it or phasing it out and using the resources elsewhere.

As time passes, SBUs change their position in the growth-share matrix. Each SBU has a life. Many SBUs start out as question marks, and move into the star category if they succeed. They later become cash cows as market growth falls, then finally turn into dogs toward the end of their life cycle. The company needs to add new products and units continually so that some of them will become stars and eventually cash cows to help finance the other SBUs.

The BCG and other formal methods that were developed in the 1970s revolutionized strategic planning. However, such approaches have limitations. They can be difficult, time-consuming, and costly to implement. Management may find it difficult to define SBUs and measure market share and growth. In addition, these approaches focus on classifying current businesses, but provide little advice for future planning. Management must still use judgment to set the business objectives for each SBU, to decide what resources each will be given, and to figure out which new businesses should be added.

These formal approaches have some additional drawbacks:

These overly quantitative techniques caused companies to place a great deal of emphasis on market-share growth. As a result, companies were devoting too much time to corporate portfolio planning and too little to hammering out strategies to turn sick operations into healthy ones or to ensure that a strong business remained strong. In too many instances, strategic planning degenerated into acquiring growth businesses that the buyers did not know how to manage and selling or milking to death mature ones.[6]

Many companies have dropped these formal methods to use more custom-ized strategic planning approaches better suited to situations of their compa-nies. Most large Canadian companies use some form of strategic planning analysis.[7] Such analysis is no solution for finding the best strategy. But it can help management to better understand the company's overall situation, to see how each business or product contributes, to better assign resources to its businesses, and to better orient the company for future success.

Developing Growth Strategies

Beyond evaluating current businesses, designing the business portfolio involves finding future businesses and products the company should consider. One useful device for identifying growth opportunities is the **product/market expansion grid**.[8] This grid is shown in Figure 2-3. We will apply it to a well-known company, Warner-Lambert Canada:

> Warner-Lambert Canada, the largest subsidiary of the U.S. firm Warner-Lambert, manufactures health care and consumer products. The company has annual sales in Canada of over $225 million. Warner-Lambert Canada operates four divisions, each manufacturing several products: Personal Products Division (health and beauty aids including Listerine mouthwash, Schick blades, and Bromo Seltzer); Adams Brand Division (confectionery products including Chiclets, Dentyne, and Trident); Parke-Davis Division (ethical health care products including Sinutab and Benylin); and Deseret Division (medical and surgical products).

Market Penetration

First, Warner-Lambert Canada (WLC) management considers whether the com-pany's major brands can achieve deeper market penetration by increasing sales to present customers without changing the products in any way. For example, to increase Listerine sales, the company might cut prices, increase advertising, get Listerine into more stores, or obtain better shelf positions for Listerine. Basically, management would like to increase usage by current customers and attract customers of other brands to Listerine.

FIGURE 2-3
Market Opportunity Identification through the Product/Market Expansion Grid

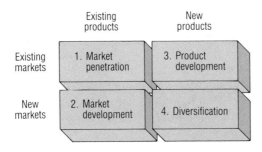

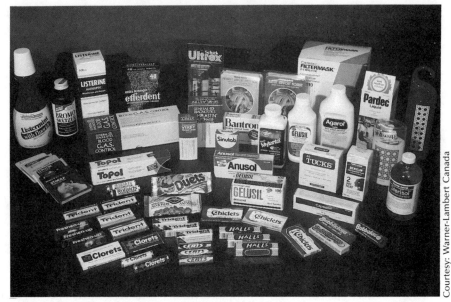

Warner-Lambert Canada operates in all sections of the product/market expansion grid.

Market Development

Second, WLC management considers possibilities for market development — identifying and developing new markets for current products. For example, managers at WLC review **demographic markets** — infants, preschoolers, teenagers, young adults, senior citizens—to see if any of these groups can be encouraged to buy or buy more of its mouthwash. The managers look at **institutional markets** — hotels, airlines, hospitals — to see if sales to these buyers can be increased. The managers also review **geographical markets** to see if these markets can be developed. All these are market development strategies.

Product Development

Third, the management considers product development—offering modified or new products to current markets. Listerine mouthwash could be offered in new sizes, or with new ingredients, or in new packaging, all representing possible product modifications. WLC could also launch new brands to appeal to different users, or it could launch other health care products that its current customers might buy. In fact, WLC launched a new brand of mouthwash, Listermint, and then modified the branch and relaunched it as Listermint with Fluoride. These are product development strategies.

Diversification

Fourth, WLC could consider diversification. It could start up or buy businesses that are entirely outside of its current products and markets. For example, the company could enter such "hot" industries as fitness equipment and health foods. Some companies try to identify the most attractive emerging industries. They feel that half the secret of success is to enter attractive industries instead of trying to be efficient in an unattractive industry.

Planning Functional Strategies

The company's strategic plan establishes what kinds of businesses the company will be in, and the company's objectives for each. Then within each business unit, more detailed planning must take place. Each functional department — marketing, finance, accounting, purchasing, manufacturing, personnel, and others—must plan what role it will play in reaching overall strategic objectives.

Each functional department deals with different publics to obtain inputs the business needs, such as cash, labor, raw materials, research ideas, manufacturing processes, and others. For example, marketing brings in revenues by negotiating exchanges with consumers. Finance arranges exchanges with lenders and stockholders to obtain cash. Therefore, the marketing and finance departments must work together to obtain needed funds for the business. Similarly, the personnel department supplies labor, and purchasing obtains materials needed for operations and manufacturing.

Marketing's Role in Strategic Planning

There is considerable overlap between overall company strategy and marketing strategy. Marketing looks at consumer needs and the company's ability to satisfy them; these same factors guide the company mission and objectives. As most company strategy planning deals with marketing variables such as market share, market development, and growth, it is sometimes hard to separate strategic planning from marketing planning. In fact, in some companies, strategic planning is called "strategic marketing planning."

Marketing plays a key role in the company's strategic planning in several ways. First, marketing provides a guiding philosophy: company strategy should revolve around serving the needs of important consumer groups. Second, marketing provides inputs to strategic planners by helping to identify attractive market opportunities and to assess the firm's potential for taking advantage of them. Finally, marketing designs strategies within individual business units for reaching the unit's objectives.[9]

Marketing and the Other Business Functions

There is much confusion about marketing's importance in the firm. In some firms it is just another function; all functions count in the company and none

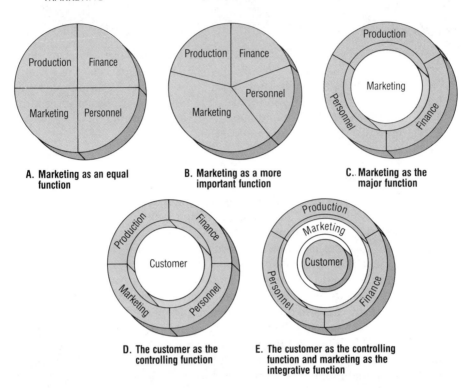

FIGURE 2-4
Alternative Views of Marketing's Role in the Company

takes leadership. This view is illustrated in Figure 2-4A. If the company faces slow growth or a sales decline, marketing may become more important for a period of time (Figure 2-4B).

Some marketers claim that marketing is the major function of the firm. They quote Drucker's statement: "The aim of the business is to create customers." They say it is marketing's job to define the company's mission, products, and markets and to direct the other functions in the task of serving customers (Figure 2-4C). Enlightened marketers, however, prefer to put the customer at the center of the company. They argue that all functions should work together to sense, serve, and satisfy the customer (Figure 2-4D).

Finally, some marketers say that marketing still needs to be in a central position to be certain that customers' needs are understood and satisfied (Figure 2-4E). These marketers argue that the firm cannot succeed without customers, so the key task is to attract and hold customers. Customers are attracted by promises and held through satisfaction, and marketing defines the promise and ensures its delivery. But the actual consumer satisfaction is affected by the performance of other departments, so marketing needs influence over these other departments if consumers are to be satisfied.

The Marketing Management Process

The strategic plan defines the company's overall mission and objectives. Within each business unit, marketing plays a role in helping to accomplish the overall strategic objectives. Marketing's role and activities in the organization are shown in Figure 2-5, which summarizes the entire **marketing management process** and the forces influencing company marketing strategy.

Target consumers are in the center. The company identifies the total market, divides it into smaller segments, selects the most promising segments, and focuses on serving and satisfying these segments. It designs a marketing mix made up of factors under its control—product, price, place, and promotion. To find the best marketing mix and put it into action, the company engages in

FIGURE 2-5
Factors Influencing Company Marketing Strategy

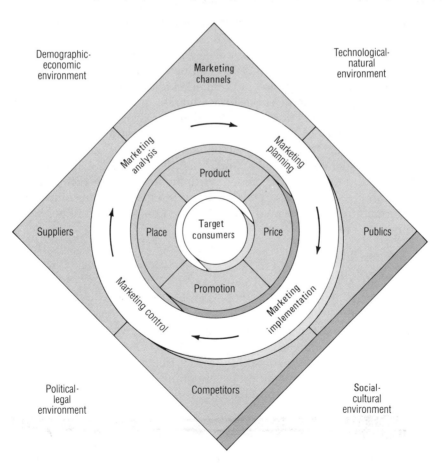

marketing analysis, planning, implementation, and control. Through these activities, the company watches and adapts to the marketing environment.

We will now look briefly at each factor in the marketing management process. In later chapters, we will discuss each factor in more depth.

Target Consumers

Companies know that they cannot satisfy all consumers in a given market, at least not all consumers in the same way. There are too many different kinds of consumers with too many different kinds of needs. Some companies are in a better position to serve certain segments of the market. Therefore, each company must study the total market, and choose the segments it can profitably serve better than competitors. This involves four steps: demand measurement and forecasting, market segmentation, market targeting, and market positioning.

Demand Measurement and Forecasting

Suppose a company is looking at possible markets for a potential new product. The company first needs to make a careful estimate of the current and future size of the market and its various segments. To estimate current market size, the company would identify all competing products, estimate their current sales, and determine whether the market is large enough.

Equally important is the future market growth. Companies want to enter markets that show strong growth prospects. Growth potential may depend on the growth rate of certain age, income, and nationality groups that use the product more. Growth may also be related to larger developments in the environment, such as economic conditions, the crime rate, and life style changes. Forecasting the effects of these environmental forces is difficult, but it must be done in order to make a decision about the market. The company's marketing information specialists will probably use complex techniques to measure and forecast demand.

Market Segmentation

Suppose the demand forecast looks good. The company now has to decide how to enter the market. The market consists of many types of customers, products, and needs, and the marketer has to determine which segments offer the best opportunity to achieve company objectives. Consumers can be grouped in various ways based on geographic factors (regions, cities), demographic factors (sex, age, income, education), psychographic factors (social classes, life-styles), and behavioral factors (purchase occasions, benefits sought, usage rates).

The process of classifying customers into groups with different needs, characteristics, or behavior is called market segmentation.

Every market is made up of market segments, but not all ways of segmenting the market are equally useful. For example, Bromo Seltzer would gain little by distinguishing between male and female users of the product category if both respond the same way to marketing stimuli.

A market segment consists of consumers who respond in a similar way to a given set of marketing stimuli.

In the car market, consumers who choose the biggest, most comfortable car no matter what its price make up one market segment. Another market segment would be customers who care mainly about price and operating economy. It would be very difficult to make one model of car the first choice of every consumer. Companies are wise to focus their efforts on meeting the distinct needs of one or more market segments. They should study the geographic, demographic, behavioral, and other characteristics of each market segment to evaluate its attractiveness as a marketing opportunity.

Market Targeting

A company can enter one or many segments of a given market. A company with limited skills or resources can decide to serve only one segment. Alternatively,

Segmentation and targeting: Procter & Gamble Canada identifies segments and serves a number of the segments through targeting.

Courtesy: Procter & Gamble Canada

a company might choose to serve several related segments, perhaps those that have different kinds of customers who have the same basic wants. A large company might decide to offer a complete range of products to serve all the market segments.

Most companies enter a new market by serving a single segment, and if this proves successful, they add segments. Large companies eventually seek full market coverage. They want to be the "General Motors" of their industry. GM says that it makes a car for every "person, purse, and personality." The leading company normally has different products designed to meet the special needs of each segment.

Market Positioning

Once a company has decided which market segments to enter, it must decide what "positions" it wants to occupy in those segments. A product's **position** is the place the product occupies in consumers' minds relative to competitors. If a product is perceived to be exactly like another product on the market, consumers would have no reason to buy it. Thus marketers plan positions that distinguish their products from competing products, and that give them the greatest strategic advantage in their target markets.

> Market positioning is arranging for a product to occupy a clear, distinctive, and desirable place, relative to competing products, in the minds of target consumers.

For example, the Hyundai automobile is positioned on low price; Jaguar is positioned as "a blending of art and machine"; Saab is "the smartest car ever built." Procter & Gamble positions its Crest brand as the "Family Dental Plan" toothpaste, and its Pearl Drops brand as the toothpaste that "cleans tobacco stains."

To plan a product's position, the company first identifies the existing positions of all the products and brands currently serving its market segments. Next, the company determines what consumers want with respect to major product attributes. The company then selects a position based on its product's ability to satisfy consumer wants better than the products of competitors. Finally, it develops a marketing program that communicates and delivers the product's position to target consumers.

Developing the Marketing Mix

Once the company has decided upon its positioning strategy, it is ready to begin planning the details of the marketing mix. The marketing mix is one of the major concepts in modern marketing. We define it as follows:

> The marketing mix is the set of controllable marketing variables that the firm blends to produce the response it wants in the target market.

The marketing mix consists of everything the firm can do to influence the

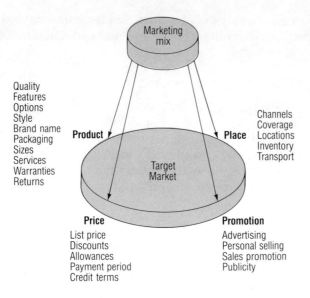

Quality
Features
Options
Style
Brand name
Packaging
Sizes
Services
Warranties
Returns

Product

Channels
Coverage
Locations
Inventory
Transport

Place

Target
Market

Price

List price
Discounts
Allowances
Payment period
Credit terms

Promotion

Advertising
Personal selling
Sales promotion
Publicity

FIGURE 2-6
The Four Ps of the Marketing Mix

demand for its product. The many possibilities can be collected into four groups of variables known as the "four Ps:" **product**, **price**, **place**, and **promotion**.[10] The particular marketing variables under each P are shown in Figure 2-6.

Product stands for the "goods-and-service" combination the company offers to the target market. Thus WLC's Listermint "product" consists of 500 millilitres of green liquid in a plastic package with a list of ingredients in both French and English.

Price stands for the amount of money customers have to pay to obtain the product. For Listermint, WLC suggests retail and wholesale prices, discounts, allowance, and credit terms. Its "price" has to be in line with the perceived value of the product, or buyers will purchase competing products.

Place stands for company activities that make the product available to target consumers. Thus WLC chooses wholesalers and retailers, urges them to display and advertise the product, checks on shelf stock, and arranges product shipping and storage.

Promotion stands for activities that communicate the merits of the product and persuade target customers to buy it. Thus WLC buys advertising, hires salespeople, sets up sales promotions, and arranges publicity for Listermint.

Managing the Marketing Effort

The company wants to design and put into action the marketing mix that will best achieve its objectives in its target markets. This involves four marketing management functions — **analysis**, **planning**, **implementation**, and **control**. These functions are discussed briefly below and more fully in Chapter 3.

Marketing Analysis

Management of the marketing function begins with a complete analysis of the company's situation. The company must analyze its markets and marketing environment to find attractive opportunities and avoid environmental threats. It must analyze company strengths and weaknesses, and current and possible marketing actions, to determine which opportunities it can best pursue. Marketing analysis feeds information and other inputs to each of the other marketing management functions.

Marketing Planning

Through strategic planning, the company decides what it wants to do with each business unit. Marketing planning involves deciding on marketing strategies that will help the company attain its overall strategic objectives. A detailed marketing plan is needed for each business, product, or brand. For example, suppose WLC decides that its Chiclets chewing gum should be built further because of its strong growth potential. The brand manager of Chiclets will then develop a marketing plan to carry out Chiclets' growth objective.

Marketers must continually plan their analysis, implementation, and control activities.

Courtesy: Procter & Gamble Canada

Marketing Implementation

Good marketing analysis and planning are only a start toward successful company performance—the marketing plans must be implemented well. It is often easier to design good marketing strategies than to put them into action.

People at all levels of the marketing system must work together to implement marketing strategy and plans. People in marketing must work closely with people in finance, purchasing, manufacturing, and other company departments. Many outside people and organizations must help with implementation —suppliers, resellers, advertising agencies, research firms, and the advertising media. All must work together effectively to implement the marketing program.

The implementation process consists of five elements—action programs, the company's organizational structure, decision and reward systems, human resources, and company climate and culture. To successfully implement its marketing plans and strategies, the company must blend these elements into a cohesive program.

Marketing Control

Many surprises are likely to occur as marketing plans are implemented. The company needs control procedures to make sure that its objectives will be achieved. Companies want to make sure that they are achieving the sales, profits, and other goals set in their annual plans. This involves stating well-defined goals, measuring ongoing market performance, determining the causes of any serious gaps in performance, and deciding on the best corrective action to close the gaps. This may call for improving the ways in which the plan is being implemented, or even changing the goals.

Companies should also stand back from time to time and look at their overall approach to the marketplace. The purpose is to make certain that the company's objectives, policies, strategies, and programs remain appropriate in the face of rapid environmental changes. Giant companies such as Massey-Ferguson fell on hard times because they did not watch the changing marketplace and make the proper adaptations. A major tool used for such strategic control is the **marketing audit**, which is described in Chapter 3.

The Marketing Environment

Managing the marketing function would be hard enough if the marketer had to deal only with the controllable marketing mix variables. However, the company operates in a complex marketing environment that consists of uncontrollable forces to which the company must adapt. The environment produces both threats and opportunities. The company must carefully analyze its environment so that it can avoid the threats and take advantage of the opportunities.

Companies may think that they have few opportunities, but they may simply be failing to think strategically about what business they are in and what strengths they have. Every company faces many opportunities. Companies can search for new opportunities casually or systematically. Many companies find new ideas by simply keeping their eyes and ears open to the changing marketplace. Other organizations use formal methods for analyzing the marketing environment.

Not all opportunities are right for every company. A marketing opportunity must fit the company's objectives and resources. Thus personal computers are an attractive industry, but not for every company. For example, we sense that personal computers would not be right for McDonald's. McDonald's seeks a high level of sales, growth, and profits from the fast-food business. And even though McDonald's has very large resources, it lacks the technical knowhow, industrial marketing experience, and special distribution channels needed to successfully sell personal computers.

The company's marketing environment includes forces close to the company that affect its ability to serve its consumers, such as other company departments, channel members, suppliers, competitors, and publics. It also includes broader demographic/economic forces, political/legal forces, technological/ecological forces, and social/cultural forces. The company must consider all of these actors and forces when developing and positioning its offer to the target market.

Summary

Strategic planning involves developing a strategy for long-run survival and growth. Marketing helps in strategic planning, and the overall strategic plan defines marketing's role in the company. Marketers undertake the marketing management process to carry out their role in the organization.

Not all companies use formal planning or use it well. Yet formal planning offers several benefits, including systematic thinking, better coordination of company efforts, sharper objectives, and improved performance measurement, all of which can lead to improved sales and profits. Companies develop three kinds of plans—annual plans, long-range plans, and strategic plans.

Strategic planning sets the stage for the rest of company planning. The strategic planning process consists of developing the company's mission, objectives and goals, business portfolio, and functional plans.

Developing a sound mission statement is a challenging undertaking. The mission statement should be market-oriented, feasible, motivating, and specific if it is to direct the firm to its best opportunities. The mission statement then leads to supporting objectives and goals, in a system known as management by objectives.

From here, strategic planning calls for analyzing the company's business portfolio and deciding which businesses should receive more or less resources. The company might use a formal portfolio planning method such as the BCG growth-share matrix. But most companies are now designing more customized portfolio planning approaches that better suit their unique situations.

Beyond evaluating current strategic business units, management must plan for growth into new businesses and products. The product-market expansion grid shows four avenues for growth. Market penetration involves more sales of current products to current customers. Market development involves identifying new markets for current products. Product development involves offering new or modified products to current markets. Finally, diversification involves starting businesses entirely outside of current products and markets.

Each of the company's functional departments provides inputs for strategic planning. Once strategic objectives have been defined, management within each business must prepare a set of functional plans that coordinates the activities of the marketing, finance, manufacturing, and other departments. Each department has a different idea about which objectives and activities are most important. The marketing department stresses the consumer's point of view. Marketing managers must understand the points of view of the other functions and work with other functional managers to develop a system of plans that will best accomplish the firm's overall strategic objectives.

To fulfill their role in the organization, marketers engage in the marketing management process. Consumers are at the center of the marketing management process. The company divides the total market into smaller segments and selects the segments it can best serve. It then designs its marketing mix to attract and satisfy these target segments. To find the best mix and put it into action, the company engages in marketing analysis, marketing planning, marketing implementation, and marketing control. Through these activities, the company watches and adapts to the marketing environment.

Questions for Discussion

1. Planning is critical to the success of an organization. Identify, in your own words, the benefits of planning.

2. Why is strategic planning such an important process for organizations moving into the 1990s?

3. Briefly describe the four types of strategic business units (SBUs) developed by the Boston Consulting Group. Classify Ford's current automobile models in each of the four categories. Defend your choices.

4. Explain how McDonald's Corporation could use the product/market expansion grid to identify growth opportunities.

5. If a company has adopted the marketing concept, it will want to blend the different business functions (departments) to produce customer satisfaction. Comment.

6. Summarize the marketing management process.

7. Identify the four Ps of the marketing mix and list some typical decisions companies make for each element of the mix.

8. It is argued that the success of L'eggs panty hose is due to the company's

understanding of the marketing-mix factors. Discuss the important marketing-mix variables as they relate to L'eggs.

9. Marketers do not operate in a vacuum; that is, they must take into account those factors and forces beyond their control that may have an effect on their ability to serve the target customers. Identify those uncontrollable elements that must be considered during market strategy planning.

Chapter 2 Key Terms

Business portfolio   The collection of businesses and products that make up the company.

Cash cows   Low-growth, high-share businesses or products — established and successful units that generate cash that the company uses to pay its bills and support other business units that need investment.

Diversification   A strategy for company growth by starting up or acquiring businesses outside the company's current products and markets.

Dogs   Low-growth, low-share businesses and products that may generate enough cash to maintain themselves, but do not promise to be a large source of cash.

Market development   A strategy for company growth by identifying and developing new market segments for current company products.

Market penetration   A strategy for company growth by increasing sales of current products to current market segments without changing the product in any way.

Market positioning   Arranging for a product to occupy a clear, distinctive, and desirable place, relative to competing products, in the minds of target consumers.

Market segment   A group of consumers who respond in a similar way to a given set of marketing stimuli.

Market segmentation   The process of classifying customers into groups with different needs, characteristics, or behavior.

Marketing mix   The set of controllable marketing variables that the firm blends to produce the response it wants in the target market.

Mission statement   A statement of the organization's purpose, or what it wants to accomplish in the larger environment.

Product development   A strategy for company growth by offering modified or new products to current market segments.

Question marks   Low-share business units, in high-growth market, that require a lot of cash to hold their share or build into stars.

Stars   High-growth, high-share businesses or products. They often require heavy investment to finance their rapid growth.

Strategic business unit (SBU)   A unit of the company that has a separate mission and objective, and which can be planned independently from other company businesses. An SBU can be a company division, a product line within a division, or sometimes a single product or brand.

Strategic planning   The process of developing and maintaining a strategic fit between the organization's goals and capabilities and its changing marketing opportunities. It relies on developing a clear company mission, supporting objectives, a sound business portfolio, and coordinated functional strategies.

Cases for Chapter 2

Planning, Implementing, and Controlling Marketing Programs

Chapter Objectives

After reading this chapter, you should be able to:
1. Identify the sections of a marketing plan and what each section contains.
2. Describe the elements of the marketing implementation process.
3. Compare different ways of organizing the marketing department.
4. Explain the three ways in which companies control their marketing activities.

In the late 1950s and early 1960s, independent hardware stores in Canada were under attack. Besieged by the mass merchandisers — the discount and chain stores — on one side and the aggressive tactics of hardware-automotive outlets like Canadian Tire on another, many independents fell by the wayside. A major problem for these independents was trying to keep stock on hand to satisfy their customers. A typical hardware store in Canada may carry up to 24 000 items — an inventory that many independents found difficult to control by means of "looking at the shelf and seeing how many we have."

One man was concerned about the future of the independent hardware dealer. In 1963, Walter Hachborn, a partner in a wholesale hardware firm in St. Jacob's, Ontario, began organizing small hardware dealers. They formed a wholesale cooperative, Home Hardware, by purchasing Hachborn's former business. Hachborn then organized other wholesalers so that,

today, United Hardware supplies over 900 independent dealers across Canada under the Home Hardware umbrella. Total dealer sales now exceed $1 billion annually.

What Hachborn recognized was that the hardware business requires planning, implementation, and control. A Home Hardware dealer (an independent business person) can now access a system that can provide store designs and layouts, prepare advertising, suggest retail prices based on market research, and, most important, automatically control inventory. The dealer goes over his stock weekly with a portable, battery-operated "order entry unit." By means of a keyboard and the telephone, his current stock is automatically transmitted to St. Jacob's. For the independent hardware dealer, planning and control of a 24 000-item product line is now possible — thanks to computers, some sophisticated programming, and Walter Hachborn.[1]

In this chapter, we will look more closely at each marketing management function — analysis, planning, implementation, and control. Figure 3-1 shows the
relationship between these marketing activities. The company first develops
overall strategic plans. These companywide strategic plans are then translated
into marketing and other plans for each division, product, and brand.

Through implementation, the company turns the strategic and marketing
plans into measures to achieve the company's strategic objectives. Marketing
plans are implemented by people in the marketing organization, who work with
others inside and outside the company. Control consists of measuring and evaluating the results of marketing plans and activities, and taking corrective action
to make sure objectives are being reached. Marketing analysis provides the
information and evaluations needed for all of the other marketing management
activities.

We will discuss planning first to review all the factors that marketers must
consider when designing marketing programs. However, this does not mean
that planning always comes first, or that planning ends before marketers move
on to the other activities. Figure 3-1 shows that planning and the other activities
are closely related. Marketers must plan their analysis, implementation, and
control activities; analysis provides inputs for planning, implementation, and
control; control provides feedback for future planning and implementation.

In the remainder of this chapter, we will discuss marketing planning, and
how plans are implemented and controlled by people in the marketing department. In Chapter 4 we will examine many of the tools used in marketing
analysis.

FIGURE 3-1

The Relationship between Analysis, Planning, Implementation, and Control

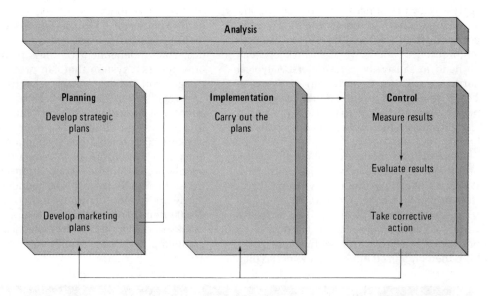

Marketing Planning

The strategic plan defines the company's overall mission and objectives. Within each business unit, functional plans must be prepared — including marketing plans. If the business unit consists of many product lines, brands, and markets, plans must be written for each. Marketing plans might include product plans, brand plans, or market plans.

What does a marketing plan look like? Our discussion will focus on product or brand plans. A product or brand plan should contain the following sections: executive summary, current marketing situation, threats and opportunities, objectives and issues, marketing strategies, action programs, budgets, and controls (see Figure 3-2).

Executive Summary

The marketing plan should open with a short summary of the main goals and recommendations to be presented in the plan. Here is a short example:

> The 1988 Marketing Plan seeks a significant increase over the preceding year in company sales and profits. The sales target is $80 million, a planned 20% sales gain. This increase is attainable because of the improved economic, competitive, and distribution picture. The target operating margin is $8 million, a 25% increase over last year. To achieve these goals, the sales promotion budget will be $1.6 million, or 2% of projected sales. The advertising budget will be $2.4 million, or 3% of projected sales. . . [More detail follows.]

The executive summary helps top management to quickly find the major points of the plan. A table of contents should follow the executive summary.

Current Marketing Situation

The first major section of the plan describes the target market and the company's position in it. The marketing planner provides the following information:

FIGURE 3-2
Components of the Marketing Plan

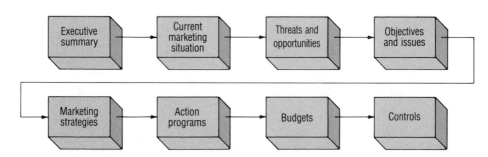

Market description Here the market is defined, including the major market segments. The planner shows the size of the market (in units or dollars) in total and by segment for the past several years. The plan reviews customer needs and factors in the marketing environment that may affect customer purchasing.

Product review Here the plan shows sales, prices, contribution margins, and net profits for each of the major products in the product line for the past several years.

Table 3-1 shows an example of how data might be presented for a product line. Row 1 shows the total industry sales in units growing at 5% annually until 1987, when demand declined slightly. Row 2 shows the company's market share hovering around 3%, although it reached 4% in 1986. Row 3 shows the average price for the product rising about 10% a year except the last year, when it rose 4%. Row 4 shows variable costs — materials, labor — rising each year. Row 5 shows that the gross contribution margin per unit — the difference between price (row 3) and unit variable cost (row 4) — rose in the first few years and remained at $100 in the latest year. Rows 6 and 7 show sales volume in units and dollars, and row 8 shows the total gross contribution margin, which rose until the latest year, when it fell. Row 9 shows that overheads remained constant during 1984 and 1985 and increased to a higher level during 1986 and 1987 due to an increase in manufacturing capacity. Row 10 shows net contribution mar-

TABLE 3-1
Historical Product Data

Variable	Columns	1984	1985	1986	1987
1. Industry sales — in units		200 000	210 000	220 500	220 000
2. Company market share		0.03	0.03	0.04	0.03
3. Average price per unit $		200	220	240	250
4. Variable cost per unit $		120	125	140	150
5. Gross contribution margin per unit $	$(3-4)$	80	95	100	100
6. Sales volume in units	(1×2)	6 000	6 300	8 820	6 600
7. Sales revenue $	(3×6)	1 200 000	1 386 000	2 116 800	1 650 000
8. Gross contribution margin $	(5×6)	480 000	598 500	882 000	660 000
9. Overhead $		200 000	200 000	350 000	350 000
10. Net contribution margin $	$(8-9)$	280 000	398 500	532 000	310 000
11. Advertising and promotion $		80 000	100 000	100 000	90 000
12. Sales force and distribution $		70 000	100 000	110 000	100 000
13. Marketing research $		10 000	12 000	15 000	10 000
14. Net operating profit $	$(10-11-12-13)$	120 000	186 500	307 000	110 000

gin, that is, gross contribution margin less overhead. Rows 11, 12, and 13 show marketing expenditures on advertising and promotion, sales force and distribution, and marketing research. Finally, row 14 shows net operating profit after marketing expenses. The picture is one of increasing profits until 1987, when profits fell to about one-third of the 1986 level. Clearly the product manager needs to find a strategy for 1988 that will once again restore healthy growth in sales and profits to the product line.

Competition   *Here the plan identifies major competitors and each of their strategies with respect to product quality, pricing, distribution, and promotion. The section also shows the market shares held by the company and each competitor.*

Distribution   *Here the plan describes recent sales trends and developments in the major distribution channels.*

Threats and Opportunities

This section requires the manager to look ahead for major threats and opportunities that the product might face. The purpose is to help the manager anticipate important developments that can have an impact on the firm. Managers should list as many threats and opportunities as they can imagine. Suppose the manager at Imperial Tobacco Limited/Limitée came up with the following list:

1. The Canadian Medical Association, in a landmark brief to the House of Commons, states that health hazards created by cigarette smoking represent ''an unrivalled tale of illness, disability, and death.''

2. The federal government has banned smoking in all federal buildings, and many municipalities have prohibited smoking in public places. The federal government has also banned all cigarette advertising.

3. Air Canada has banned smoking on many flights.

4. Imperial's research lab is close to finding a way to turn lettuce into an enjoyable but harmless tobacco.

5. In the past six years, the light, ''low-tar'' segment of the cigarette market has tripled.

   The first three items are **threats**. Not all threats call for the same attention or concern — the manager should assess how likely it is that each threat will occur, and how much harm it would cause. The manager should then focus on the most probable and harmful threats, and prepare plans in advance to meet them.
   The last two items in the list are marketing opportunities:

A company marketing opportunity is an attractive arena for marketing action in which the company would enjoy a competitive advantage.

   The manager should assess each opportunity according to its potential attractiveness and the company's probability of success. Figure 3-3 shows that the company should pursue only the opportunities that fit its objectives and resources. Every company has objectives based on its business mission. In addition, each opportunity requires that the company have certain amounts of capital and know-how. Companies can rarely find ideal opportunities that exactly fit their objectives and resources. Developing opportunities involves risks. When evaluating opportunities, the manager must decide whether the expected returns justify this risk.

FIGURE 3-3
Evaluating a Company Marketing Opportunity in Terms of Company Objectives and Resources

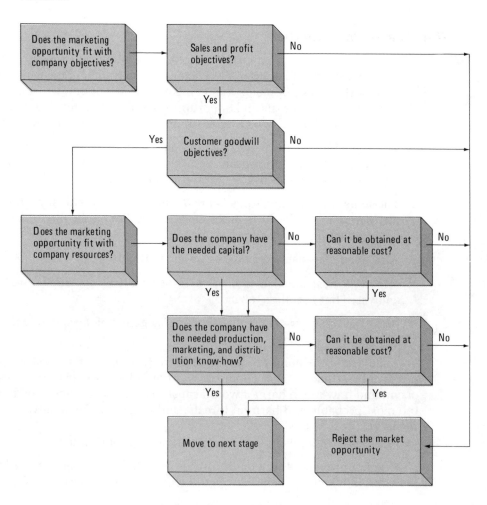

Objectives and Issues

Having studied the product's threats and opportunities, the manager can now set objectives and consider issues that will affect them. The objectives should be stated as goals that the company would like to reach during the plan's term. For example, the manager might want to achieve a 15% market share, a 20% pretax profit on sales, and a 25% pretax profit on investment. Suppose the current market share is only 10%. This poses a key issue: How can market share be increased? The manager will want to consider the major issues involved in trying to increase market share.

Marketing Strategies

In this section, the manager outlines the broad marketing strategy or "game plan" for attaining the objectives. We define marketing strategy as follows:

Marketing strategy is the marketing logic by which the business unit hopes to achieve its marketing objective. It consists of specific strategies for target markets, marketing mix, and marketing expenditure level.

Marketing strategy should spell out the market segments on which the company will focus. These segments differ in their needs and wants, responses to marketing, and profitability. The company would be smart to put its effort and energy into those market segments it can best serve from a competitive point of view. It should develop a marketing strategy for each targeted segment.

The manager should outline specific strategies for such marketing mix elements as new products, field sales, advertising, sales promotion, prices, and distribution. The manager should explain how each strategy responds to the threats, opportunities, and key issues spelled out earlier in the plan.

The manager should also map out the marketing budget that will be needed to carry out its strategies. The manager knows that higher budgets will produce more sales, but is looking for the marketing budget that will produce the best profit picture.

Action Programs

The marketing strategies should be turned into specific action programs that answer the following questions: *What* will be done? *When* will it be done? *Who* is responsible for doing it? *How much* will it cost? For example, the manager may want to step up sales promotion as a key strategy for winning market share. A sales promotion action plan should be drawn up that outlines special offers and their dates, trade shows entered, new point-of-purchase displays, and other promotions. The action plan shows when activities will be started, reviewed, and completed.

Budgets

The action plans allow the manager to make a supporting budget that is essentially a projected profit and loss statement. On the revenue side, it shows the forecasted number of units that could be sold and the average net price. On the expense side, it shows the cost of production, physical distribution, and marketing. The difference is the projected profit. Higher management will review the budget and approve or modify it. Once approved, the budget is the basis for materials buying, production scheduling, manpower planning, and marketing operations.

Controls

The last section of the plan outlines the controls that will be used to monitor progress. Typically, goals and budgets are spelled out for each month or quarter. This means that higher management can review the results each period and spot businesses or products that are not meeting their goals. The managers of these businesses and products have to explain the problems and the corrective actions they will take.

Implementation

Planning good strategies is only a start toward successful marketing. A brilliant marketing strategy will count for little if the company fails to implement it properly.

> Marketing implementation is the process that turns marketing strategies and plans into marketing actions in order to accomplish strategic marketing objectives.

Implementation involves day-to-day, month-to-month activities that effectively put the marketing plan to work. Whereas marketing planning addresses the *what* and *why* of marketing activities, implementation addresses the *who, where, when,* and *how*.

Implementation is difficult — it is often easier to think up good marketing strategies than to carry them out. In addition, managers often have trouble diagnosing implementation problems. It is usually hard to tell whether poor performance was caused by poor strategy, poor implementation, or both.[2]

The Implementation Process

People at all levels of the marketing system must work together to implement marketing plans and strategies. People in the marketing department, in other company departments, and in outside organizations can either help or hinder marketing implementation. The company must find ways to coordinate all these actors and their activities.

The implementation process is shown in Figure 3.4.[3] The figure shows that marketing strategy and marketing performance are linked by an implementation system consisting of five related elements: action programs, an organization structure, decision and reward systems, human resources, and managerial climate and company culture.

FIGURE 3-4
The Marketing Implementation Process

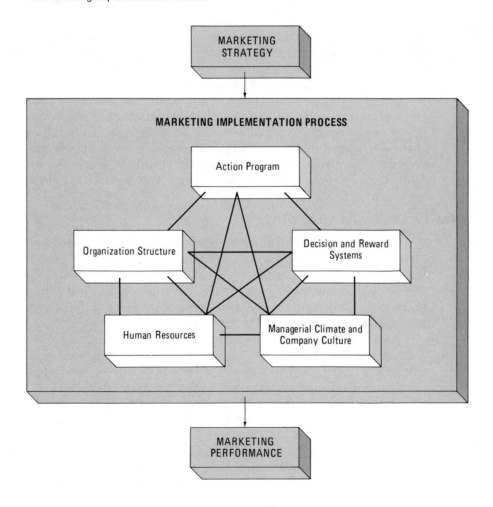

The Action Program

To implement marketing plans, people at all company levels make decisions and perform tasks. At Procter & Gamble, implementation of a plan to introduce a stream of high-quality new products requires day-to-day decisions and actions by many people inside and outside the organization. In the marketing organization, marketing researchers test new product concepts and scan the marketplace for new product ideas. For each new product, marketing managers make decisions about target segments, branding, packaging, pricing, promoting, and distributing. Salespeople are hired, trained and retrained, directed, and motivated.

Marketing managers work with other company managers to get support for promising new products. They talk with engineering about product design. They talk with manufacturing about production and inventory levels. They talk with finance about funding and cash flows, with the legal staff about patents and product safety issues, and with personnel about staffing and training needs. Marketing managers also work with outside people. They meet with advertising agency people to plan ad campaigns, and with the media to obtain publicity support. The sales-force urges retailers to advertise the new products, give them lots of shelf space, and use company displays.

The action program pulls all of these people and activities together. It identifies the decisions and actions needed to implement the marketing program. It also gives responsibility for these decisions and actions to specific people in the company. Finally, the action program provides a timetable that states when decisions must be made and when actions must be taken. The action program shows what must be done, who will do it, and how decisions and actions will be coordinated to reach the company's marketing objectives.

The Organization Structure

The company's formal organization structure plays an important role in implementing marketing strategy. The structure breaks up the company's work into well-defined jobs, assigns these jobs to people and departments, and improves efficiency through specialization. The structure then coordinates these specialized jobs by defining formal ties between people and departments, and by setting lines of authority and communication.

Companies with different strategies need different organization structures. A small firm developing new products in a fast-changing industry might need a flexible structure that encourages individual action — a decentralized structure with lots of informal communication. A more established company in a more stable market might need a structure that provides more integration — a more centralized structure with well-defined roles and communication "through proper channels."

In their study of successful companies, Peters and Waterman found the companies had many common structural characteristics that lead to successful implementation.[4] For example, their structures tended to be informal, decentralized, simple, and lean.

Some of the conclusions in the Peters and Waterman study have been questioned because the study focused on high-technology and consumer goods companies operating in rapidly changing environments.[5] The structures used by these companies may not be right for other types of firms in different situations. Many of the study's excellent companies will need to change their structures as their strategies and situations change.

Decision and Reward Systems

Decision and reward systems include formal and informal operating procedures that guide such activities as planning, information gathering, budgeting, recruiting and training, control, and personnel evaluation and rewards. Consider a company's compensation system. If it compensates managers for short-run results, they will have little incentive to work toward long-run objectives. Many companies are designing compensation systems that will overcome this problem. Here is an example:[6]

> One company was concerned that its annual bonus system encouraged managers to ignore long-run objectives and focus on annual performance goals. To correct this, the company changed its bonus system to include rewards for both annual performance and for reaching "strategic milestones." Under the new plan, each manager works with planners to set two or three strategic objectives. At the end of the year, the manager's bonus is based on both operating performance and on reaching the strategic objectives. Thus the bonus system encourages managers to achieve more balance of the company's long-run and short-run needs.

Human Resources

Marketing strategies are implemented by people, so successful implementation requires careful human resources planning. At all levels, the company must fill its structure and systems with people who have the necessary skills, motivation, and personal characteristics. Company personnel must be recruited, assigned, trained, and maintained.

The selection and development of executives and other managers are especially important for implementation. Different strategies call for managers with different personalities and skills. New venture strategies need managers with entrepreneurial skills; holding strategies require managers with organizational and administrative skills; and retrenchment strategies call for managers with cost-cutting skills. The company must carefully match its managers to the needs of the strategies to be implemented.

Managerial Climate and Company Culture

The company's managerial climate and company culture can make or break marketing implementation. Managerial climate involves the way company managers work with others in the company. Some managers take command, delegate little authority, and keep tight controls. Others delegate many responsibilities, encourage their people to take initiative, and communicate informally. No one managerial style is best for all situations. Different strategies may require different leadership styles. The style that is best varies with the company's structure, tasks, people, and environment.

Company culture is a system of values and beliefs shared by people in an organization. It is the company's collective identity and meaning. The culture informally guides the behavior of people at all company levels. Peters and Waterman found that excellent companies have strong and clearly defined cultures.

> Without exception, the dominance and coherence of culture proved to be an essential quality of the excellent companies. Moreover, the stronger the culture and the more it was directed toward the marketplace, the less need there was for policy

TABLE 3-2

Questions About the Marketing Implementation System

Organization structure
What is the organization's structure?
What are the lines of authority and communication?
What is the role of task forces, committees, or similar mechanisms?

Systems
What are the important systems?
What are the key control variables?
How do product and information flow?

Action program
What are the tasks to be performed and which are critical?
How are they accomplished, with what technology?
What strengths does the organization have?

Human resources
What are their skills, knowledge, and experience?
What are their expectations?
What are their attitudes toward the firm and their jobs?

Climate and culture
Are there shared values that are visible and accepted?
What are the shared values and how are they communicated?
What are the dominant management styles?
How is conflict resolved?

Fit
Does each component above support marketing strategy?
Do the various components fit together well to form a cohesive framework for implementing strategy?

Source: Adapted from David L. Aaker, *Strategic Market Management* (New York: Wiley, 1984), p. 151. © 1984, John Wiley & Sons, Inc.

manuals, organization charts, or detailed procedures and rules. In these companies, people way down the line know what they are supposed to do in most situations because the handful of guiding values is crystal clear.[7]

Table 3-2 shows a list of questions companies should ask about each element of the implementation system. Successful implementation depends on how well the company blends the five activities into a cohesive program that supports its strategies.

Marketing Department Organization

The company must design a marketing department that can carry out marketing analysis, planning, implementation and control. In this section, we will focus on how marketing departments within companies are organized. If the company is very small, one person might end up doing all the marketing activities such as research, selling, advertising, and customer service. As the company expands, a marketing department organization emerges to plan and carry out marketing activities. In large companies, this department contains many marketing specialists. Thus General Mills has product managers, salespeople and sales managers, market researchers, advertising experts, and other specialists.

Modern marketing departments can be arranged in several ways. A company will set up its marketing department in the way that best helps it meet its marketing objectives.

Functional Organization

The functional organization is the most common form of marketing organization. Marketing specialists are in charge of different marketing activities, or functions. Figure 3-5 shows five specialists: marketing administration manager, advertising and sales promotion manager, sales manager, marketing research

FIGURE 3-5
Functional Organization

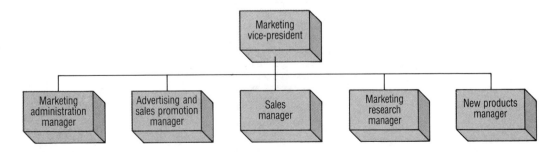

manager, and new products manager. Other specialists might include a customer service manager, a marketing planning manager, and a distribution manager.

The main advantage of a functional marketing organization is that it is simple to administer. On the other hand, this form by itself is less and less effective as the company's products and markets grow. First, it becomes difficult to make plans for each different product or market, and products that are not favorites of the functional specialists get neglected. Second, as the functional groups compete with each other to gain more budget and status, top management has trouble coordinating all the marketing activities.

Geographic Organization

A company selling all across the country often uses a geographic organization for its salesforce. Figure 3-6 shows one national sales manager, four regional sales managers, 24 zone sales managers, 192 district sales managers, and 1 920 salespersons. Geographic organization allows salespeople to settle into a territory, get to know their customers, and work with a minimum of travel time and cost.

FIGURE 3-6
Geographic Organization

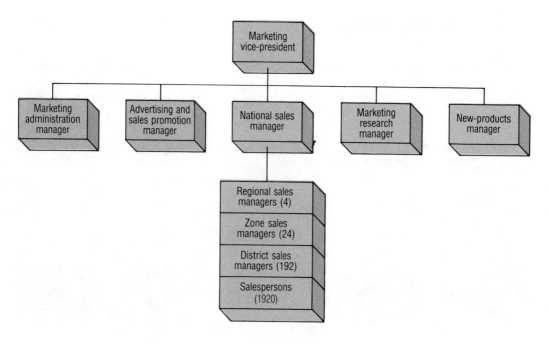

Product Management Organization

Companies with many products or brands often create a product management organization. The product or brand management organization is headed by a product manager. This manager supervises several product group managers, who in turn supervise product managers in charge of specific products (see Figure 3-7). The product manager's job is to develop and implement a complete strategy and marketing program for a specific product or brand. A product management organization makes sense if the company has many very different products.

Product management first appeared in the Procter & Gamble Company in 1927. A new company soap, Camay, was not doing well, and a young P&G executive was assigned to give his exclusive attention to developing and promoting this product. He was successful, and the company soon added other product managers.

Since then, many firms, especially in the food, soap, toiletries, and chemical industries, have set up product management organizations. Because many of these firms operate in both Canada and the United States — Colgate-Palmolive, Procter & Gamble, General Foods, Bristol-Myers — the product management concept is common to both countries.[8] The Canadian subsidiary of General

FIGURE 3-7
Product Management Organization

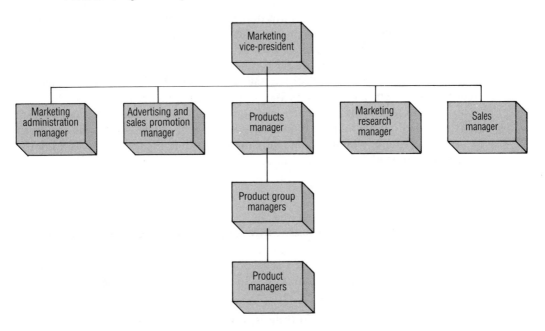

Foods, for example, uses a product management organization within each of its two major divisions, food services and groceries. Each product area within the grocery division has a product manager. A group product manager might be in charge of cereals, pet foods, or beverages. Within the cereal product group, there are separate product managers for nutritional cereals, children's pre-sweetened cereals, family cereals, and miscellaneous cereals. This organizational structure also extends to General Foods' subsidiaries, including Hostess Food Products, White Spot Limited, and Canterbury Foods.

The product management organization has many advantages. First, the product manager coordinates the whole marketing mix for the product. Second, the product manager can sense and react quickly to product problems. Third, smaller brands get more attention because they have their own product manager. Fourth, product management is an excellent training ground for young executives as it involves them in almost every area of company operations. For example, the presidents of 16 Canadian companies obtained some of their training at Procter & Gamble.[9]

However, a price is paid for these advantages. First, product management creates some conflict and frustration. Product managers are often not given enough authority to carry out their responsibilities effectively. Second, product managers become experts in their product but rarely become experts in any functions. Third, the product management system often costs more than expected due to higher payroll costs.

Market Management Organization

Many companies sell one product line to many different types of markets. For example, IBM sells electric typewriters to consumer, business, and government markets. Stelco sells steel to the railroad, construction, and public utility industries. When different markets have different needs and preferences, a market management organization might be best for the company.

A market management organization is similar to the product management organization shown in Figure 3-7. Market managers are responsible for developing long-range and annual plans for the sales and profits in their markets. They have to coax help from marketing research, advertising, sales, and other functions. This system's main advantage is that the company is organized around the needs of specific customer segments.

Marketing Control

Because many surprises will occur during the implementation of marketing plans, the marketing department has to engage in constant marketing control.

> *Marketing control is the process of measuring and evaluating the results of marketing strategies and plans, and taking corrective action to ensure that marketing objectives are attained.*

TABLE 3-3
Types of Marketing Control

Type of Control	Prime Responsibility	Purpose of Control	Approaches
I. Annual plan control	Top management Middle management	To examine whether the planned results are being achieved	Sales analysis Market-share analysis Marketing expense-to-sales ratios Customer attitude tracking
II. Profitability control	Marketing controller	To examine where the company is making and losing money	Profitability by: Product Territory Market segment Trade channel Order size
III. Strategic control	Top management Marketing auditor	To examine whether the company is pursuing its best marketing opportunities and doing this efficiently	Marketing audit

There are three types of marketing control (see Table 3-3). *Annual plan control* involves checking ongoing performance against the annual plan, and taking corrective action when necessary. *Profitability control* involves determining the actual profitability of different products, territories, markets, and channels. *Strategic control* involves looking at whether the company's basic strategies are well matched to its opportunities.

Annual Plan Control

The purpose of annual plan control is to ensure that the company achieves the sales, profits, and other goals set out in its annual plan. It involves the four steps shown in Figure 3-8. First, management must set monthly or quarterly goals in the annual plan. Second, management must measure its performance in the marketplace. Third, management must evaluate the causes of any differences between expected and actual performance. Fourth, management must

FIGURE 3-8
The Control Process

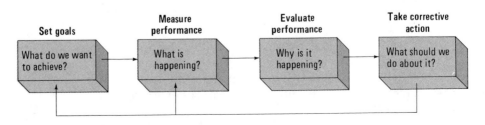

take corrective action to close the gaps between its goals and its performance. This may require changing the action programs, or even changing the goals.

What specific control tools are used by management to check on performance? The four main tools are sales analysis, market-share analysis, marketing expense-to-sales analysis, and customer attitude tracking.

Sales analysis consists of measuring and evaluating actual sales in relation to sales goals. This might involve finding out whether specific products and territories are producing their expected share of sales. Suppose the company sells in three territories, and expected sales were 1500 units, 500 units, and 2000 units, respectively, adding up to 4000 units. The actual sales volume was 1400 units, 525 units, and 1075 units. Thus territory one fell short by 7 percent; territory two had a 5 percent surplus; and territory three fell short by 46 percent! Territory three is causing most of the trouble. The sales vice-president can check into territory three to see why performance is poor.

Company sales do not reveal how well the company is doing relative to competitors. A sales increase could be due to better economic conditions in which all companies gained, rather than to improved company performance in relation to competitors. Management needs to use **market share analysis** to track the company's market share. If the company's market share goes up, it is gaining on competitors; if its market share goes down, it is losing to competitors.

Annual plan control requires making sure that the company is not overspending to achieve its sales goals. Thus, marketing control also includes **expense-to-sales analysis**. Watching the ratio of marketing expenses to sales will help keep marketing expenses in line.

Alert companies use **customer attitude tracking** to check the attitudes of customers, dealers, and other marketing system participants. By becoming aware of changes in customer attitudes before they affect sales, management can take earlier action. The main customer attitude tracking systems are complaint and suggestion systems, customer panels, and customer surveys.

Profitability Control

Besides annual plan control, companies also need profitability control to measure the profitability of their various products, territories, customer groups, channels, and order sizes. This information will help management determine whether any products or marketing activities should be expanded, reduced, or eliminated.

For example, suppose a lawnmower company wants to determine the profitability of selling its lawnmowers through three types of retail channels: hardware stores, garden supply shops, and department stores. Using profitability analysis, management would first identify all the expenses involved in selling, advertising, and delivering the product. Next, it would assign these expenses to each type of channel according to the effort and dollars spent on each channel. Finally, a profit and loss statement is prepared for each channel to see how much each is contributing to overall company profits.

If the analysis shows that one of the channels is unprofitable, the company can take one of many corrective actions. Suppose the company finds that it is actually losing money selling through garden supply shops. It might eliminate only the weakest garden supply shops. It might offer a program to train people in these shops to sell lawnmowers more effectively. The company could cut channel costs by reducing the sales calls and promotional aid going to garden supply shops. As a last resort, the company could drop the channel altogether.

Strategic Control

From time to time, companies need strategic control to critically review their overall marketing effectiveness. Marketing strategies and programs can quickly become out of date. Each company should now and then reassess its overall approach to the marketplace, using a tool known as the marketing audit.[10] We define marketing audit as follows:

> *A marketing audit is a comprehensive, systematic, independent, and periodic examination of a company's environment, objectives, strategies, and activities to determine problem areas and opportunities, and to recommend a plan of action to improve the company's marketing performance.*

The marketing audit covers all major marketing areas of a business, not just a few trouble spots. It is normally conducted by an objective and experienced outside party who is independent of the marketing department. The marketing audit should be carried out periodically, not only when there is a crisis. It promises benefits for the successful company as well as for the company in trouble.

The marketing auditor should be given freedom to interview managers, customers, dealers, salespeople, and others who might throw light on marketing performance. Table 3-4 is a guide to the kinds of questions the marketing auditor will ask. Not all these questions are important in every situation. The auditor will develop a set of findings and recommendations based on this information. The findings may come as a surprise or even a shock to management. Management decides which recommendations make sense, and how and when to implement them.

TABLE 3-4
Parts of the Marketing Audit

Part I — Marketing environment audit
The Macroenvironment
A. Demographic
   1. What major demographic developments and trends pose opportunities or threats to this company?
   2. What actions has the company taken in response to these developments and trends?

B. Economic
   1. What major developments in income, prices, savings, and credit will impact the company?
   2. What actions has the company been taking in response to these developments and trends?

CONTINUED

TABLE 3-4   CONTINUED
Parts of the Marketing Audit

C. Natural
1. What is the outlook for the cost and availability of natural resources and energy needed by the company?
2. What concerns have been expressed about the company's role in pollution and conservation, and what steps has the company taken?

D. Technological
1. What major changes are occurring in technology? What is the company's position in technology?
2. What major generic substitutes might replace this product?

E. Political
1. What laws now being proposed could affect marketing strategy and tactics?
2. What federal, provincial, and local actions should be watched? What is happening in pollution control, equal employment opportunity, product safety, advertising, price control, and other areas that affect marketing strategy?

F. Cultural
1. What is the public's attitude toward business and toward the products produced by the company?
2. What changes in consumer and business life styles and values might affect the company?

The Task Environment
A. Markets
1. What is happening to market size, growth, geographic distribution, and profits?
2. What are the major market segments?

B. Customers
1. How do customers rate the company and its competitors on reputation, product quality, service, salesforce, and price?
2. How do different customer segments make their buying decisions?

C. Competitors
1. Who are the major competitors? What are their objectives and strategies, their strength and weaknesses, their sizes and market shares?
2. What trends will affect future competition for this product?

D. Distribution and dealers
1. What are the main channels for bringing products to customers?
2. What are the efficiency levels and growth potentials of the different channels?

E. Suppliers
1. What is the outlook for the availability of key resources used in production?
2. What trends are occurring among suppliers in their pattern of selling?

F. Marketing service firms
1. What is the cost and availability outlook for transportation services, warehousing facilities, and financial resources?
2. How effectively is the advertising agency performing?

G. Publics
1. What publics provide particular opportunities or problems for the company?
2. What steps has the company taken to deal effectively with each public?

Part II — Marketing strategy audit

A. Business mission
1. Is the business mission clearly stated in market-oriented terms? Is it feasible?

B. Marketing objectives and goals
1. Are the corporate and marketing objectives stated in the form of clear goals to guide marketing planning and performance measurement?
2. Are the marketing objectives appropriate, given the company's competitive position, resources, and opportunities?

TABLE 3-4   CONTINUED
Parts of the Marketing Audit

C. Strategy

1. What is the core marketing strategy for achieving the objectives? Is it sound?
2. Are enough resources (or too many) budgeted to accomplish the marketing objectives?
3. Are the marketing resources allocated optimally to market segments, territories, and products?
4. Are the marketing resources allocated optimally to the major elements of the marketing mix — such as product quality, service, salesforce, advertising, promotion, and distribution?

Part III — Marketing organization audit

A. Formal structure

1. Does the marketing officer have adequate authority and responsibility over company activities that affect the customer's satisfaction?
2. Are the marketing activities optimally structured along functional, product, end user, and territorial lines?

B. Functional efficiency

1. Are there good communication and working relations between marketing and sales?
2. Is the product management system working effectively? Are product managers able to plan profits or only sales volume?
3. Are there any groups in marketing that need more training, motivation, supervision, or evaluation?

C. Interface efficiency

1. Are there any problems between marketing and manufacturing, R&D, purchasing, or financial management that need attention?

Part IV — Marketing systems audit

A. Marketing information system

1. Is the marketing intelligence system producing accurate, sufficient, and timely information about marketplace developments?
2. Is marketing research being adequately used by company decision makers?

B. Marketing planning system

1. Is the marketing planning system effective?
2. Are sales forecasting and market potential measurement soundly carried out?
3. Are sales quotas set on a proper basis?

C. Marketing control system

1. Are control procedures adequate to ensure that the annual plan objectives are being achieved?
2. Does management periodically analyze the profitability of products, markets, territories, and channels of distribution?
3. Are marketing costs being examined periodically?

D. New-product development system

1. Is the company well organized to gather, generate, and screen new-product ideas?
2. Does the company do adequate concept research and business analysis before investing in new ideas?
3. Does the company carry out adequate product and market testing before launching new products?

Part V — Marketing productivity audit

A. Profitability analysis

1. What is the profitability of the company's different products, markets, territories, and channels of distribution?
2. Should the company enter, expand, contract, or withdraw from any business segments, and what should be the short- and long-run profit consequences?

B. Cost-effectiveness analysis

1. Do any marketing activities seem to have excessive costs? Can cost-reducing steps be taken?

CONTINUED

TABLE 3-4 CONTINUED
Parts of the Marketing Audit

Part VI — Marketing function audits

A. Products
1. What are the product line objectives? Are these objectives sound? Is the current product line meeting the objectives?
2. Are there products that should be phased out?
3. Are there new products that are worth adding?
4. Would any products benefit from quality, feature, or style modifications?

B. Price
1. What are the pricing objectives, policies, strategies, and procedures? To what extent are prices set on cost, demand, and competitive criteria?
2. Do the customers see the company's prices as being in line with the value of its offer?
3. Does the company use price promotions effectively?

C. Distribution
1. What are the distribution objectives and strategies?
2. Is there adequate market coverage and service?
3. Should the company consider changing its degree of reliance on distributors, sales representatives, and direct selling?

D. Advertising, sales promotion, and publicity
1. What are the organization's advertising objectives? Are they sound?
2. Is the right amount being spent on advertising? How is the budget determined?
3. Are the ad themes and copy effective? What do customers and the public think about the advertising?
4. Are the advertising media well chosen?
5. Is sales promotion used effectively?
6. Is there a well-conceived publicity program?

E. Sales force
1. What are the organization's sales-force objectives?
2. Is the sales force large enough to accomplish the company's objectives?
3. Is the sales force organized along the proper principles of specialization (territory, market, product)?
4. Does the sales force show high morale, ability, and effort?
5. Are the procedures adequate for setting quotas and evaluating performances?
6. How is the company's sales force rated in relation to competitors' sales forces?

Summary

This chapter has examined how marketing strategies are planned, implemented, and controlled.

Each business has to prepare marketing plans for its products, brands, and markets. The main components of a marketing plan are: executive summary, current marketing situation, threats and opportunities, objectives and issues, marketing strategies, action programs, budgets, and controls.

It is often easier to plan good strategies than to carry them out. To be successful, companies must implement the strategies effectively. Implementation is the process that turns marketing strategies into marketing actions. The implementation process links marketing strategy and plans with marketing performance. The process consists of five related elements. The action program identifies crucial tasks and decisions needed to implement the marketing plan, assigns them to specific people, and sets up a timetable. The organization structure defines tasks and assignments, and coordinates the efforts of the company's people and units. The company's decision and reward systems guide activities such as planning, information, budgeting, training, control, and personnel evaluation and rewards. Well-designed action programs, organization structures, and systems can encourage good implementation.

Successful implementation also requires careful human resources planning. The company must recruit, allocate, develop, and maintain good people. It must carefully match its managers to the requirements of the marketing programs being implemented. The company's managerial climate and company culture can make or break implementation. Company climate and culture guide people in the company — good implementation relies on strong and clearly defined cultures that fit the chosen strategy.

Each element of the implementation system must fit company marketing strategy. Moreover, successful implementation depends on how well the company blends the five elements into a cohesive program that supports its strategies.

Most of the responsibility for implementation goes to the company's marketing department. Modern marketing departments are organized in a number of ways. The most common form is the functional marketing organization, in which marketing functions are headed by separate managers reporting to the marketing vice-president. Another form is the product management organization, in which products are assigned to product managers who work with functional specialists to develop and achieve their plans. Another form is the market management organization, in which major markets are assigned to market managers who work with functional specialists.

Marketing organizations carry out three types of marketing control. Annual plan control involves monitoring current marketing results to make sure that the annual sales and profit goals will be achieved. The main tools are sales analysis, market-share analysis, marketing expense-to-sales analysis, and customer attitude tracking. If underperformance is detected, the company can implement several corrective measures.

Profitability control calls for determining the actual profitability of the firm's products, territories, market segments, and channels. Strategic control makes sure that the company's marketing objectives, strategies, and systems fit with the current and forecasted marketing environment. It uses the marketing audit to determine marketing opportunities and problems and to recommend short-run and long-run actions to improve overall marketing performance.

Questions for Discussion

1. If the marketing management process is simplified to include the planning, implementation, and control of marketing programs, identify the most important element in the process and defend your choice.

2. Explain the importance of a company's formal organization in implementing a marketing strategy.
3. What are the major advantages and disadvantages of organizing by function, geography, product, or market?
4. Identify the three types of marketing control and discuss the purpose of each.
5. A friend of yours is planning to open a restaurant. He realizes that marketing "control" is essential for success. How would you advise him on the ways he might exercise marketing control in his new venture?
6. What are the relative advantages and disadvantages of customer attitude tracking when compared with the other annual plan control approaches?
7. The heart of the strategic control process is the marketing audit. Briefly discuss the characteristics and purpose of this concept.

Chapter 3 Key Terms

Action program   A detailed program that shows what must be done, who will do it, and how decisions and actions will be coordinated to implement marketing plans and strategy.

Annual plan control   Evaluation and corrective action to ensure that the company achieves the sales, profits, and other goals set out in its annual plan.

Company culture   A system of values and beliefs shared by people in an organization, the company's collective identity and meaning.

Company marketing opportunity   An attractive arena for marketing action in which the company would enjoy a competitive advantage.

Functional organization   An organization structure in which marketing specialists are in charge of different marketing activities or functions such as advertising, marketing research, sales management, and others.

Geographic organization   An organization structure in which a company's national sales force (and perhaps other functions) specializes by geographic area.

Managerial climate   The company climate resulting from the way managers work with others in the company.

Market management organization   An organization structure in which market managers are responsible for developing plans for sales and profits in their specific markets.

Marketing audit   A comprehensive, systematic, independent, and periodic examination of a company's environment, objectives, strategies, and activities to determine problem areas and opportunities, and to recommend a plan of action to improve the company's marketing performance.

Marketing control   The process of measuring and evaluating the results of marketing strategies and plans, and taking corrective action to ensure that marketing objectives are attained.

Marketing implementation   The process that turns marketing strategies and plans into marketing actions in order to accomplish strategic marketing objectives.

Marketing strategy   The marketing logic by which the business unit hopes to achieve its marketing objectives. Marketing strategy consists of specific strategies for target markets, marketing mix, and marketing expenditure level.

Product management organization   An organization structure in which product managers are responsible for developing and implementing marketing strategies and plans for a specific product or brand.

Profitability control   Evaluation and corrective action to ensure the profitability of a company's various products, territories, customer groups, trade channels, and order sizes.

Strategic control   A critical review of the company's overall marketing effectiveness.

Cases for Chapter 3

Marketing Research and Information Systems

Chapter Objectives

After reading this chapter, you should be able to:
1. Discuss the importance of information to the company.
2. Define the marketing information system and discuss its parts.
3. Describe the four steps in the marketing research process.
4. Identify the different kinds of information a company might use.
5. Compare the advantages and disadvantages of various methods of collecting information.

In May of 1985, the Coca-Cola Company made what now appears to have been a spectacular marketing blunder. After 99 successful years, it set aside its long-standing rule — "don't mess with Mother Coke" — and dropped its original formula Coke! In its place came New Coke, which had a sweeter, smoother taste. The company boldly announced the exciting new taste with a flurry of advertising and publicity in both Canada and the United States.

At first, amid the introductory fanfare, New Coke sold well in both countries. But sales soon went flat in the U.S., and the stunned public reacted. Coke began receiving more than 1500 phone calls and many sacks of mail each day from angry consumers. A group called Old Cola Drinkers staged protests, handed out tee-shirts, and threatened to start a class-action suit unless Coca-Cola brought back the old formula or made it public. Business analysis and the media debated the decision, and some marketing experts predicted that New Coke would be the "Edsel of the Eighties."

After just two months, the Coca-Cola Company brought old Coke back. Called Coke Classic, it sold side-by-side with New Coke on supermarket shelves. The company said that New Coke would remain its "flagship" brand,

but consumers had a different idea. By the end of 1985, Classic was outselling New Coke in supermarkets by two to one. By the end of 1986, Coke Classic was the company's main brand and New Coke was the also-ran.

The situation was similar in Canada, but there was less of an emotional outburst from consumers. One reason was that Canadians had been drinking a sweeter blend of Coke, much like the new product, for over 45 years. In fact, when new Coke was introduced in Canada, the sweetness level was not changed and only a slight change was made in the ratio of syrup to carbonated water. The Canadian president of Coca-Cola said that Canadians had raised little outcry against old Coke's disappearance. However, a Canadian hot-line was established to let consumers tell Coca-Cola what they thought of the change. In three weeks 575 000 Canadian callers said they wanted old Coke back and the company re-introduced it as Coke Classic. As in the U.S., by the end of 1986 Coke Classic was outselling New Coke.

Why was New Coke introduced in the first place? What went wrong? Many analysts blame the blunder on poor marketing research.

In the early 1980s, although Coke was still

the leading soft drink, it was slowly losing market share to Pepsi in both Canada and the U.S. For years, Pepsi had successfully mounted the "Pepsi Challenge," a series of televised taste tests showing that consumers preferred the sweeter taste of Pepsi. In Canada, Coke's share of the $2.2 billion soft drink market fell from 28% in 1982 to 22% in 1984. The story was much the same in the U.S. market, which is ten times the size of the Canadian market. Coca-Cola had to do something to stop the erosion of its market share — the solution appeared to be a change in Coke's taste.

Coca-Cola began the largest new product research project in the company's history. It spent over two years and $4 million on research before settling on a new formula. It conducted some 200 000 taste tests in Canada and the U.S. —30 000 on the final formula alone. In the blind tests, 60% of consumers chose the new Coke over the old, and 52% chose it over Pepsi. Research showed that New Coke would be a winner and the company introduced it with confidence. So what happened?

Looking back, Coke's marketing research appears to have been too narrowly focused. The research looked only at taste; it did not explore how consumers felt about dropping the old Coke and replacing it with a new version. As one expert noted, the research consisted mostly of "blind comparisons, which took no account of the total product . . . name, history, packaging, cultural heritage, image—a rich mix of tangible and intangible." Brand loyalty—that certain something that makes a consumer keep buying over and over again—is an elusive quality. It begins with the customer's preference for a product on the basis of objective reasons: the

drink is sweeter, the paper towel is more absorbent. But when a branded product like Coke has been around for a long time it can become part of a person's self-image. The company failed to measure these deep emotional ties. Coke's symbolic meaning turned out to be more important to many consumers than its taste. More complete marketing research would have detected these strong emotions, and explored how consumers *feel* about the product.

Coke's managers may also have used poor judgment in interpreting the research findings and planning strategies around them. For example, they took the finding that 60% of consumers preferred New Coke's taste to mean that the new product would win in the marketplace—as when a political candidate wins with 60% of the vote. But it also meant that 40% still wanted the old Coke. By dropping the old Coke, the company trampled the taste buds of its large core of local Coke drinkers who didn't want a change. The company might have been wiser to leave the old Coke alone and introduce New Coke as a brand extension, as it later did successfully with Cherry Coke.

The Coca-Cola Company has one of the largest, best managed, and most advanced marketing research operations in North America. Good marketing research has kept the company on top of the rough-and-tumble soft-drink market for decades. Nevertheless marketing research is far from an exact science. Consumers are full of surprises, and anticipating them can be awfully difficult. If the Coca-Cola Company can make a large marketing research mistake, any company can.[1]

In carrying out marketing analysis, planning, implementation, and control, marketing managers need information at almost every turn. They need information about customers, competitors, dealers, and other forces in the marketplace. Marion Harper put it this way: "To manage a business well is to manage its future; and to manage the future is to manage information."[2] This chapter looks at how information is gathered and how it is organized in a useful way.

Understanding consumers, the environment, competitive activities, and government intentions is a difficult task. Marketers often require substantial amounts of information to anticipate consumer and environmental changes. Although sellers always need more marketing information, the supply never seems sufficient. Marketers complain that they cannot gather enough of the accurate and useful information they need.

Marketing managers continually need more and better information. With advances in research and computer techniques, companies have a greater capacity to provide managers with information, but often have not made good use of it. Many companies are now studying the information needs of their managers, and designing information systems to meet these needs.

The Marketing Information System

We define the marketing information system as follows:[3]

> *A marketing information system (MIS) is a structure of people, equipment, and procedures to gather, sort, analyze, evaluate, and distribute needed, timely, and accurate information to marketing decision makers.*

The marketing information system concept is illustrated in Figure 4-1. The MIS begins and ends with the marketing managers. First, the MIS interacts with

FIGURE 4-1
The Marketing Information System

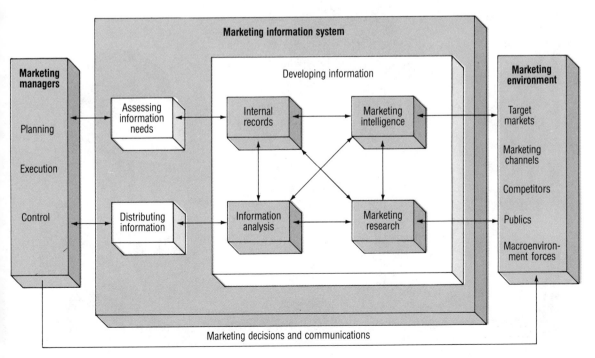

these managers to assess their information needs. Next, it develops the needed information from internal company records, marketing intelligence activities, and the marketing research process. Information analysis processes the information to make it more useful. Finally, the MIS distributes information to managers in the right form and at the right time to help them in marketing planning, implementation, and control.

We will now take a closer look at the functions of the company's marketing information system.

Assessing Information Needs

A good marketing information system balances the information that managers would *like* to have against what they really *need* and what is *feasible* to offer. The company begins by interviewing managers to find out what information they would like. But managers do not always need all the information they ask for, and they may not think carefully and ask for what they really need. Moreover, sometimes the MIS cannot supply all the information that managers request. However, with today's information technology, most companies can

Information abounds—the problem is to give managers the right information at the right time.

provide much more information than managers can actually use. Too much information can be as harmful as too little.

Busy managers may ignore vital information, or may not know to ask for some types of information. For example, managers might need to know that a competitor plans to introduce a new product during the coming year. Because they do not know about the new product, they do not think to ask about it. The MIS must watch the marketing environment and provide decision makers with information they should have in order to make key marketing decisions.

Sometimes the company cannot provide the needed information because it is not available or because of MIS limitations. For example, a brand manager might want to know how much competitors will change their advertising budgets next year and how these changes will affect industry market shares. The information on planned budgets is probably not available. Even if it is, the company's MIS may not be advanced enough to forecast resulting changes in market shares.

Finally, the company must decide whether the benefits of having an item of information are worth the costs of providing it. Both value and cost are often hard to assess. By itself, information has no worth — its value lies in how it is used. Although methods have been developed for calculating the value of information,[4] executives often must rely on subjective judgment. Similarly, while the company can add up the costs of the people and equipment that make up a marketing information system, or the costs of a marketing research project, the cost of a specific information item may be difficult to calculate.

The costs of obtaining, processing, storing, and delivering information can add up quickly. In many cases, additional information will do little to change or improve a manager's decision, or the costs of the information will exceed the returns from the better decision that results. For example, suppose a company estimates that launching a new product without any further information will yield a profit of $500 000. The manager believes that additional information will improve the marketing mix and allow the company to make $525 000. It would be foolish to pay $30 000 to obtain the extra information.

Developing Information

The information needed by marketing managers can be obtained from internal company records, marketing intelligence, and marketing research. The information analysis system then processes this information to make it more useful for managers.

Internal Records

Most marketing managers use internal records and reports regularly, especially for day-to-day planning, implementation, and control decisions. The company's accounting department provides financial statements and keeps detailed records of sales and orders, costs, and cash flows. Manufacturing reports on production schedules, shipments, and inventories. The salesforce reports information on reseller reactions and competitor activities. Research studies conducted for one department may provide useful information for several others. Managers can use information gathered from these and other sources within the company to evaluate performance and to detect problems and opportunities.

Here are examples of how companies use internal records information in marketing decisions:

- Canadian Tire store managers, through the use of point-of-sale computer terminals, have instant access to sales patterns. The computers can trigger re-orders when needed to avoid stockouts and also reduce or stop orders for slow-moving stock.

- Many Loblaw's and A&P stores have installed computer scanners at the checkouts. The scanners supply the store managers with daily sales information on all products. The effect of the weekly advertisements is monitored through the total sales volume by store each day.

- Toronto's Pizza Pizza has developed a computer system called BOSS (Best Operating Systems Solution). BOSS allows the home delivery pizza company to improve its service (30 minutes from order to delivery) and also to analyze who is buying, who isn't, and why.[5]

Information from internal records can usually be obtained more quickly and cheaply than information from other sources, but it also presents some problems. Because it was collected for other purposes, the information may be incomplete or in the wrong form for making marketing decisions. For example, accounting department sales and cost data used for preparing financial statements must be adapted for use in evaluating product, salesforce, or channel performance. In addition, the many different areas of a large company produce great amounts of information; keeping track of it all is difficult. The marketing information system must gather, organize, process, and index this mountain of information so that managers can find and use it easily and quickly.

Marketing Intelligence

Marketing intelligence is happenings data.

> Marketing intelligence is everyday information about developments in the marketing environment that helps managers prepare and adjust marketing plans.

The marketing intelligence system determines what intelligence is needed, collects it by searching the environment, and delivers it to the appropriate marketing managers.

Marketing intelligence can be gathered from many sources. Much intelligence can be collected from the company's own personnel — executives, engineers, scientists, purchasing agents, and the salesforce. Yet company people are often busy and fail to pass on important information. The company must convince its people of their importance as intelligence gatherers, train them to spot new developments, and urge them to report intelligence back to the company.

The company must also encourage suppliers, resellers, and customers to pass along important intelligence. Information on competitors can be obtained from what they say about themselves in annual reports, speeches and press releases, and advertisements. The company can also learn about competitors from what others say about them in business publications and at trade shows. Companies can also use the Access to Information Act to determine which competitors have received contracts with the Canadian federal government. The company can also watch what competitors do — it can buy and analyze their products, monitor their sales, and check for new patents.

Companies also buy intelligence information from outside suppliers. The A.C. Nielsen Company sells bimonthly data (based on a sample of 465 stores) on brand shares, retail prices, percentage of stores stocking the item, and percentage of stockout stores. The ISL Consumer Panel, on a quarterly basis, measures purchasing behavior of over 3000 Canadian households. The Daniel Starch Company regularly measures the readership of advertisements appearing in Canadian periodicals. Compusearch provides information on the consumer spending potential for a wide variety of product categories including household furnishings, transportation, and recreation. Clipping services are hired to report on competitors' ads, advertising expenditures, and media mixes.

Some companies set up an office to collect and circulate marketing intelligence. The staff scans major publications, summarizes important news, and sends news bulletins to marketing managers. It develops a file of intelligence information and helps managers to evaluate new information. These services greatly improve the quality of information available to marketing managers.

Marketing Research

Managers cannot always wait for information to arrive in bits and pieces from the marketing intelligence system. They often require formal studies of specific situations. For example, *Maclean's* magazine wants to know current readers' attitudes toward format changes in the magazine. The Toronto-Dominion Bank wants to know the effect of opening some of their branches on Saturday. In such situations, the marketing intelligence system will not provide the necessary detailed information. Furthermore, managers normally do not have the skill or time to obtain the information on their own. They need formal marketing research.

We define marketing research as follows:

Marketing research is the systematic design, collection, analysis, and reporting of data and findings relevant to a specific marketing situation facing the company.

Marketing researchers have steadily expanded their activities in Canada and the United States (see Table 4-1). The ten most common activities are measurement of market potentials, market share analysis, the determination of market characteristics, sales analysis, studies of business trends, short-range

TABLE 4-1

Types of Marketing Research Performed by Companies in Canada and the United States

Type of research	Percent performing research Canada	U.S.
Advertising research		
A. Motivation research	25%	47%
B. Copy research	33	61
C. Media research	36	68
D. Studies of ad effectiveness	42	76
E. Studies of competitive advertising	38	67
Business economics and corporate research		
A. Short-range forecasting (up to 1 year)	51	89
B. Long-range forecasting (over 1 year)	50	87
C. Studies of business trends	49	91
D. Pricing studies	50	83
E. Plant and warehouse location studies	35	68
F. Acquisition studies	41	73
G. Export and international studies	33	49
H. MIS (Management Information System)	41	80
I. Operations Research	34	65
J. Internal company employees	39	76
Corporate responsibility research		
A. Consumer "right to know" studies	16	18
B. Ecological impact studies	16	23
C. Studies of legal constraints on advertising and promotion	29	46
D. Social values and policies studies	18	39
Product research		
A. New product acceptance and potential	48	76
B. Competitive product studies	54	87
C. Testing of existing products	52	80
D. Packaging research: design or physical characteristics	41	65
Sales and market research		
A. Measurement of market potentials	59	97
B. Market share analysis	61	97
C. Determination of market characteristics	60	97
D. Sales analysis	58	92
E. Establishment of sales quotas, territories	54	78
F. Distribution channel studies	49	71
G. Test markets, store audits	35	59
H. Consumer panel operations	33	63
I. Sales compensation studies	37	60
J. Promotional studies of premiums, coupons, sampling, deals, etc.	28	58

Source: Dik Warren Twedt, ed., *1983 Survey of Marketing Research* (Chicago: American Marketing Association, 1983), p. 41, and Joyce Cheng, David Conway, and George Haines Jr., "Marketing Research in Canada: A 1985 Update," in *ASAC Marketing Proceedings*, Thomas G. Muller (ed.), Whistler, 1986, p. 297.

forecasting, competitive product studies, long-range forecasting, marketing information systems studies, and testing of existing products. Firms in the United States generally spend more on marketing research and conduct more research than Canadian firms. The reason, in part, is the smaller size of both the Canadian economy and Canadian firms.

Every marketer needs research. A company can do marketing research in its own research department or have some or all of it done outside. Whether a company uses outside firms depends on the skills and resources within the company. Fifty percent of Canadian large companies have their own marketing research departments. A company with no research department will have to buy the services of research firms. But even companies with their own departments often use outside firms to do special research tasks or special studies. In total, Canadian firms spend over $200 million annually on marketing research.[6]

The Marketing Research Process

This section describes the four steps in the marketing research process (Figure 4-2): defining the problem and research objectives, developing the research plan, implementing the research plan, and interpreting and presenting the findings. We will illustrate these steps with the following situation:

> Some years ago, Pacific Western Airlines was primarily a commuter airline serving British Columbia and Alberta. The company also operated an extensive network of scheduled routes to the Northwest Territories. In the late 1970s and the early 1980s, however, Pacific Western was able to expand its routes; a merger with another airline and a relaxation of the government regulation of the industry enabled Pacific Western to fly to over 45 destinations, from Toronto in the East to Victoria in the West, and from Seattle in the South to Resolute in the Northwest Territories. The airline served more destinations in its geographic region than Air Canada and CP Air combined. While the commuter role remained important to Pacific Western, the relaxation of regulations permitted the airline to fly nonstop between many of its destinations in direct competition with Air Canada and CP Air. In these markets, Pacific Western had historically operated commuter or multi-stop flights in contrast to the nonstop flights offered by its competitors. Pacific Western needed a new advertising campaign to let people know about its expansion. To design the most effective campaign, however, the marketing department had to do extensive research to learn more about the airline market.

FIGURE 4-2
The Marketing Research Process

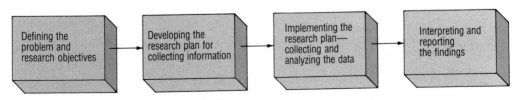

Defining the Problem and Research Objectives

The first step in research calls for the marketing manager and marketing researcher to define the problem carefully and agree on the research objectives. If the marketing manager tells the marketing researcher, "Gather data on the airline market," he or she is likely to be disappointed with the results. Hundreds of aspects of the market can be researched. If the research findings are to be useful, they must bear on a decision problem facing the company. Information is too costly to collect, and allowing the problem to be defined vaguely or incorrectly is wasteful. Consider old saying: A problem well defined is half solved.

The marketing manager and the marketing researcher in the Pacific Western case agreed that the problem was that Pacific Western did not attract as many passengers as desired. This led to two further problems: (1) How do passengers choose their airline? and (2) How might more passengers be induced to fly Pacific Western?

At this point, the managers need to set the research objectives. The objectives may be *exploratory*—to gather some preliminary data to throw more light on the problem and possibly suggest some hypotheses. They may be *descriptive*—to describe certain phenomena, such as how many people fly, or how many people have heard of Pacific Western. Finally, they may be *causal*—to test a hypothesis about some cause-and-effect relationship, such as a fare cut of $15 that would increase passenger traffic by at least 10%. Managers often start with exploratory research and later follow with descriptive or causal research.

The statement of the problem and research objectives will guide the entire research process. The manager and researcher should put the statement in writing to be certain that they agree on the purpose and expected results of the research.

Developing the Research Plan

The second step of the marketing research process calls for determining the information needed and developing a plan for gathering it efficiently.

Determining Specific Information Needs

Research objectives must be translated into specific information needs. For example, suppose Pacific Western decides to do research to find out how consumers will react to a new proposal that stand-by passengers would be allowed a 50% discount on ticket prices. This research might call for the following specific information:

- The demographic and economic characteristics of current users.

- Consumer purchase patterns for tickets: for example, the number of business users who buy their tickets at the airport.

- The number of business versus tourist travelers on Pacific Western Airlines.

Pacific Western's managers will need this information, and many other types of information to decide whether or not to introduce the new fare.

Researchers often find secondary data in a variety of external sources.

Surveys of Secondary Information

To meet the manager's information needs, the researcher can gather secondary data, primary data, or both.

Secondary data consist of information that already exists somewhere, having been collected for another purpose.

Primary data consist of information collected for the specific purpose at hand.

Researchers usually start by gathering secondary data. Table 4-2 shows many secondary data sources, including **internal** and **external** sources. Secondary data can usually be obtained more quickly and at a lower cost than primary data. In the case of the Pacific Western project, the researchers could find a great deal of secondary data on the air travel market. For example, Statistics Canada publications provide data on the size, growth, and market shares of the various carriers. The Canadian Transport Commission has published numerous studies on the characteristics, attitudes, and behavior of air travelers. Similarly, various travel agencies have data that may reveal how air travelers choose their carriers.

TABLE 4-2
Sources of Secondary Data

A variety of secondary data sources are available to obtain information on markets, consumer expenditures, corporate and financial performance, and import and export activity.

I. **Market information** — including market size, growth trends, product technology, marketing developments, trade practices, and economic and political trends.

    A. Newspapers and business periodicals — for information on commerce, industry, specific companies, and investment in Canada. Most newspapers contain a business section. Newspapers and magazines that focus specifically on business include: *The Globe and Mail's Report on Business, The Financial Post, The Financial Times, Canadian Business, The Canadian Business Review, The Business Quarterly,* and *Business Week.*

    B. Marketing journals — for information on marketing activities and topics. The major journals are *Marketing, ASAC Marketing Proceedings, Advertising Age,* and *The Journal of Marketing.*

    C. Government sources — for information on virtually all aspects of the economy from price changes to production of automobiles, Statistics Canada is the major source. The Statistics Canada catalog provides details of both regular and special studies. In addition, all three levels of government (federal, provincial, and municipal) collect and provide data on a wide range of business topics. At the federal and provincial level, the department / ministry involved with industry, trade, and commerce is the most common source for business information.

    D. Industry trade magazines and associations — for information on a specific industry (e.g. automobiles, appliances). The two main sources are trade associations and trade journals. The *Canadian Advertising Rates and Data* book identifies the trade journals by industry.

    E. Handbooks and surveys — for information on consumer incomes and expenditures by product category, economics activity by industrial category, and a series of extremely useful statistics on the Canadian economy. Three important sources are: (1) *Handbook of Consumer Markets*, published by the Conference Board of Canada, (2) *The Financial Post Survey of Markets*, and (3) *Market Research Handbook*, published by Statistics Canada.

II. **Consumer expenditures** — including income and expenditure data. The sources listed above frequently contain information in this area. Government sources and handbooks and surveys would be the most relevant sources.

III. **Corporate and financial performance** — including company history, size, ownership, and subsidiaries. Again, in addition to the above sources, *The Financial Post* provides annual surveys of industrial, oil, mining, and investment companies that offer details about the company, past sales and earnings, and subsidiaries. Dun and Bradstreet business reports include financial information on companies as well as credit ratings. A number of trade indexes are available that provide a classification of companies by product and / or industry. These include the *Canadian Trade Index, National List of Advertisers*, and *Fraser's Canadian Trade Directory*. Finally, the annual reports of publicly-held companies will provide specific details on the financial performance of a particular firm.

IV. **Import and export activity** — including trade activities between Canada and other nations. The major source of trade data is Statistics Canada and the relevant publications include the *Summary of External Trade, Exports by Commodities* and *Imports by Commodities*.

Secondary data also present problems. The needed information may not exist as researchers can rarely obtain all the data they need from secondary sources. Even where the data can be found, they might not be very usable. The researcher must evaluate secondary information carefully to make certain it is **relevant**, **accurate**, **current**, and **impartial**.

Secondary data provide a good starting point for research and often help to define the problem and research objectives. In most cases, however, secondary sources cannot provide all the needed information, and the company must collect primary data.

TABLE 4-3
Planning Primary Data Collection

Research Approaches	Contact Methods	Sampling Plan	Research Instruments
Observation	Mail	Sampling unit	Questionnaire
Survey	Telephone	Sample size	Mechanical instruments
Experiment	Personal	Sampling procedure	

Planning Primary Data Collection

Some managers collect primary data by dreaming up a few questions and finding some people to interview. Data collected in this way might be useless or, even worse, misleading. Table 4-3 shows that designing a plan for primary data collection calls for decisions on research approaches, contact methods, sampling plan, and research instruments.

Research Approaches

Observational research is the gathering of primary data by observing relevant people, actions, and situations. For example:

- A food products manufacturer sends researchers into supermarkets to find out the prices of competing brands or how much shelf space and display support retailers give its brands.

- A bank evaluates possible new branch locations by checking the locations of competing branches, traffic patterns, and neighborhood conditions.

- A maker of personal care products pretests its ads by showing them to people and measuring eye movements, pulse rates, and other physical reactions.

- A department store chain sends observers posing as customers to its stores to check on store conditions and customer service.

- A museum checks the popularity of various exhibits by noting the amount of floor wear around them.

   Observational research can be used to obtain information that people are unwilling or unable to provide. In some cases, observation may be the only way to obtain the needed information. On the other hand, some responses simply cannot be observed: feelings, attitudes, motives, and personal behavior. Long-run or infrequent behavior is also difficult to observe. Because of these limitations, researchers often use observation in combination with other data collection methods.

   Survey research is the approach best suited for gathering descriptive information. A company that wants to know about people's knowledge, attitudes, preferences, or buying behavior can often find out by asking them directly.

Survey research can be structured or unstructured. Structured surveys use formal lists of questions asked of all respondents in the same way. Unstructured surveys let the interviewer probe respondents and guide the interview, according to their answers.

Survey research may be direct or indirect. In the direct approach, the researcher asks direct questions about behavior or thoughts — for example, "Why don't you buy clothes at Eaton's?" Using the indirect approach, the researcher might ask, "What kinds of people buy clothes at Eaton's?" From the response to this indirect question, the researcher may be able to discover why the consumer avoids Eaton's clothing — in fact, it may suggest reasons the consumer is not consciously aware of.

Survey research is the most widely used method for primary data collection, and it is often the only method used in a research study. The biggest advantage of survey research is its flexibility. It can be used to obtain many different kinds of information in many different marketing situations. Depending on the survey design, it may also provide information more quickly and at lower cost than the observational or experimental research.

Survey research also has some problems. Sometimes people are unable to answer survey questions because they cannot remember or never thought about what they do and why. Alternatively, people may be unwilling to answer questions asked by unknown interviewers or about things they consider private. Busy people may not take the time. Respondents may answer survey questions even when they do not know the answer, in order to appear smarter or more informed, or they may try to help the interviewer by giving pleasing answers. Careful survey design can help to minimize these problems.

Whereas observation is best suited for exploratory research and surveys for descriptive research, *experimental research* is best suited for gathering causal information. Experiments involve selecting matched groups of subjects, giving them different treatments, controlling unrelated factors, and checking for differences in group responses. Thus experimental research tries to explain cause-and-effect relationships. Observation and surveys may be used to collect information in experimental research.

Before adding a new sandwich to the menu, researchers at McDonald's might use experiments to answer such questions as the following:

- How much will the new sandwich increase McDonald's sales?

- How will the new sandwich affect the sales of other menu items?

- Which advertising approach would have the greater effect on sales of the sandwich?

- How would different prices affect the sales of the product?

- Should the new item be targeted toward adults, children, or both?

For example, to test the effects of two different prices, McDonald's could set up the following simple experiment. It could introduce the new sandwich at one price in its restaurants in one city, and at another price in restaurants in another similar city. If the cities are very similar, and if all other marketing efforts for the sandwich are the same, then differences in sales in the two cities could be related to the price charged. More complex experiments could be designed to include other variables and other locations.

Contact Methods

Information can be collected by mail, telephone, or personal interview. Table 4-4 shows the strengths and weaknesses of each of these contact methods.

Mail questionnaires have many advantages. They can be used to collect large amounts of information at a low cost per respondent. Respondents may give more honest answers to more personal questions on a mail questionnaire than to an unknown interviewer in person or over the phone. No interviewer is involved to bias the respondent's answers.

Mail questionnaires also have some disadvantages. They are not very flexible: they require simple and clearly worded questions; all respondents answer the same questions in a fixed order; and the researcher cannot adapt the questionnaire based on earlier answers. Mail surveys usually take longer to complete, and the response rate — the number of people returning completed questionnaires — is often very low. The researcher often has little control over the mail questionnaire sample. Even with a good mailing list, it is often hard to control *who* at the mailing address fills out the questionnaire.

Telephone interviewing is the best method for gathering information quickly, and it provides greater flexibility than mail questionnaires. Interviewers can explain questions that are not understood. They can skip some questions or probe more on others, depending on the respondent's answers. Telephone interviewing allows greater sample control. Interviewers can ask to speak to respondents with the desired characteristics or even by name, and response rates tend to be higher than with mail questionnaires.

Telephone interviewing also has drawbacks. The cost per respondent is higher than with mail questionnaires, and people may not want to discuss

TABLE 4-4
Strengths and Weaknesses of the Three Contact Methods

	Mail	Telephone	Personal
1. Flexibility	Poor	Good	Excellent
2. Quantity of data that can be collected	Good	Fair	Excellent
3. Control of interviewer effects	Excellent	Fair	Poor
4. Control of sample	Fair	Excellent	Fair
5. Speed of data collection	Poor	Excellent	Good
6. Response rate	Poor	Good	Good
7. Cost	Good	Fair	Poor

Source: Adapted with permission of Macmillan Publishing Company from *Marketing Research: Measurement and Method*, 3rd ed., by Donald S. Tull and Del I. Hawkins. Copyright © 1984 by Macmillan Publishing Company.

Courtesy: Consumer Contact Ltd.

A marketing research team is conducting telephone interviewing.

personal questions with an interviewer. Using an interviewer increases flexibility, but also introduces interviewer bias. The way interviewers talk, small differences in how they ask questions, and other differences may affect respondents' answers. Different interviewers may interpret and record responses differently, or under time pressures some interviewers might cheat by recording answers without asking questions.

Personal interviewing takes two forms, individual and group interviewing. **Individual interviewing** involves talking with people in their homes or offices, on the street, or in shopping malls. The interviewer must gain their cooperation, and the time involved can range from a few minutes to several hours. Sometimes a small payment is given to people in return for their time.

Group interviewing consists of inviting six to ten people to gather for a few hours with a trained interviewer to talk about a product, service, or organization. The interviewer needs objectivity, knowledge of the subject and industry, and some understanding of group and consumer behavior. The participants are normally paid a small sum for attending. The meeting is held in a pleasant place and refreshments are served to create an informal atmosphere. The interviewer starts with broad questions before moving to more specific issues, and encourages free and easy discussion, hoping that the group dynamics will bring out actual feelings and thoughts. At the same time, the interviewer "focuses" the discussion — hence the name *focus group interviewing*. The comments are recorded through note taking or on videotapes that are later studied to understand the consumers' buying process. Focus group interviewing is becoming one of the major marketing research tools for gaining insight into consumer thoughts and feelings.[7]

Personal interviewing is very flexible and can be used to collect large amounts of information. Trained interviewers can hold the respondent's attention for a long time and can explain difficult questions. They can guide interviews, explore issues, and probe as the situation requires. Personal interviews can be used with any type of questionnaire. Interviewers can show subjects actual products, advertisements, and packages, and observe reactions and behavior. In most cases, personal interviews can be conducted fairly quickly.

The main drawbacks of personal interviewing are costs and sampling problems. Personal interviews may cost three to four times as much as telephone interviews. Group interview studies usually use small sample sizes to keep time and costs down, and it may be difficult to generalize from the results. Because interviewers have more freedom in personal interviews, there is a greater problem of interviewer bias.

Which contact method is best depends on what information the researcher wants, and on the number and types of respondents to be contacted. Advances in computers and communications have had an impact on methods of obtaining information. For example, some research firms now do Computer Assisted Telephone Interviewing (CATI) using a combination of WATS lines and data-entry terminals. The interviewer reads a set of questions from a video screen and types the respondent's answers right into the computer. This process eliminates data editing and coding, reduces errors, and saves time. Other research firms have set up terminals in shopping centers—respondents sit down at a terminal, read questions from a screen, and type their own answers into the computer.

Sampling Plan

Marketing researchers usually draw conclusions about large groups of consumers by studying a small sample of the total consumer population. A sample is a segment of the population elected to represent the population as a whole. Ideally, the sample should be representative so that the researcher can make accurate estimates of the thoughts and behaviors of the larger population.

Designing the sample calls for three decisions. First, who is to be surveyed? This is not always obvious. For example, to study the decision-making process for a family automobile purchase, should the researcher interview the husband, wife, other family members, dealership salespeople, or all these people? The researcher must determine what information is needed and who is most likely to have it.

Second, how many people should be surveyed? Large samples give more reliable results than small samples. However, it is not necessary to sample the entire target market or even a large portion to get reliable results. If well chosen, samples of less than 1% of a population can often provide good reliability.

Third, how should the the people in the sample be chosen? They might be chosen at random from the entire population (a **probability sample**), or the researcher might select people who are easiest to obtain information from (a **convenience sample**). Alternatively, the researcher might interview a specified number of people in each of several demographic groups (a **quota sample**). These and other ways of drawing samples have different costs and time limitations, and different accuracy and statistical properties. Which method is best depends on the needs of the research project.

Research Instruments

In collecting primary data, marketing researchers have a choice of two main research instruments—the questionnaire and mechanical devices.

The **questionnaire** is by far the most common instrument. Broadly defined, a questionnaire consists of a set of questions presented to a respondent for his or her answers. The questionnaire is very flexible as there are many ways to ask questions. Questionnaires need to be carefully developed and tested before they can be used on a large scale. We can usually spot several errors in a carelessly prepared questionnaire (see Exhibit 4-1 on p. 94).

In preparing a questionnaire, the marketing researcher must decide what questions to ask, the form of the questions, the wording of the questions, and the ordering of the questions. Questionnaires too often leave out questions that should be answered, and include questions that cannot be answered, or will not be answered, or need not be answered. Each question should be checked to see that it contributes to the research objectives.

FIGURE 4-3
Types of Questions

	Closed-End Questions				
Name	**Description**	**Example**			
Dichotomous	A question offering two answer choices.	"In arranging this trip, did you personally phone Pacific Western?" Yes ☐ No ☐			
Multiple choice	A question offering three or more answer choices.	"With whom are you traveling on this flight?" No one ☐ Spouse ☐ Spouse and children ☐ Children only ☐ Business associates/friends/relatives ☐ An organized tour group ☐			
Likert scale	A statement where respondent shows the amount of agreement/ disagreement.	"Small airlines generally give better service than large ones." Strongly disagree 1 ☐	Disagree 2 ☐	Neither agree nor disagree 3 ☐	Agree 4 ☐	Strongly agree 5 ☐
Semantic differential	A scale is inscribed between two bipolar words, and the respondent selects the point that represents the direction and intensity of his or her feelings.	Pacific Western Airlines Large [X] — Small Experienced — [X] Inexperienced Modern — [X] — Old-fashioned			
Importance scale	A scale that rates the importance of some attribute from "not at all important" to "extremely important."	"Airline food service to me is:" Extremely important 1	Very important 2	Somewhat important 2	Not very important 4	Not at all important 5
Rating scale	A scale that rates some attribute from "poor" to "excellent."	"Pacific Western's food service is:" Excellent 1	Very good 2	Good 3	Fair 4	Poor 5

The *form* of the question can influence the response. Marketing researchers distinguish between closed-end and open-end questions. Closed-end questions include all the possible answers, and subjects make choices among them. Figure 4-3 shows the most common forms of closed-end questions. Open-end questions allow respondents to answer in their own words. The questions take various forms; the main ones are shown in Figure 4-3. Open-end questions often reveal more because respondents are not limited in their answers, and, as a result, are especially useful in exploratory research where the researcher is trying to find out how people think, rather than measuring how many people think in a certain way. Closed-end questions, on the other hand, provide answers that are easier to interpret and tabulate.

Care should be used in the *wording* of questions. The researcher should use simple, direct, and unbiased wording. The questions should be pretested before they are widely used. Care should also be taken in the *ordering* of questions. If possible, the first question should create interest. Difficult or personal questions should be asked last so that respondents do not become defensive. The questions should come up in a logical order.

Open-End Questions		
Name	**Description**	**Example**
Completely structured	A question that respondents can answer in an almost unlimited number of ways.	"What is you opinion on Pacific Western Airlines?"
Word association	Words are presented, one at a time, and respondents mention the first word that comes to mind.	"What is the first word that comes to your mind when you hear the following?" Airline _____ Travel _____ Pacific Western _____
Sentence completion	Incomplete sentences are presented, one at a time, and respondents complete the sentence.	"When I choose an airline, the most important consideration in my decision is _____
Story completion	An incomplete story is presented, and respondents are asked to complete it.	"I flew Pacific Western a few days ago. They gave me a cold sandwich to eat. This aroused in me the following thoughts and feelings." Now complete the story.
Picture completion	A picture of two characters is presented, with one making a statement. Respondents are asked to identify with the other and fill in the empty balloon.	Fill in the empty balloon.
Thematic Apperception Tests (TAT)	A picture is presented, and respondents are asked to make up a story about what they think is happening or may happen in the picture.	Make up a story about what you see.

EXHIBIT 4-1
A "Questionable" Questionnaire

Suppose the following questionnaire had been prepared by a summer camp director to be used in interviewing parents of prospective campers. How do you feel about each question?

1. What is your income to the nearest hundred dollars?
   People do not necessarily know their income to the nearest hundred dollars nor do they want to reveal their income that closely. Furthermore, a questionnaire should never open with such a personal question.

2. Are you a strong or a weak supporter of overnight summer camping for your children?
   What do "strong" and "weak" mean?

3. Do your children behave themselves well in a summer camp?
   Yes(   ) No (   )
   "Behave" is a relative term. Besides, will people want to answer this? Furthermore, is "yes" or "no" the best way to allow a response to the question? Why is the question being asked in the first place?

4. How many camps mailed literature to you last April? This April?
   Who can remember this?

5. What are the most salient and determinant attributes in your evaluation of summer camps?
   What are "salient and determinant attributes"? Don't use big words on me.

6. Do you think it is right to deprive your child of the opportunity to grow into a mature person through the experience of summer camping?
   Loaded question. How can one answer "yes," given the bias?

Although questionnaires are the most common research instrument, **mechanical instruments** are also used. For example, a galvanometer measures the strength of a subject's interest or emotions aroused by an exposure to an ad or picture. The galvanometer picks up the minute degree of perspiration that accompanies emotional arousal. The tachistoscope flashes an ad to a subject at exposures ranging from less than one-hundredth of a second to several seconds. After each exposure, the respondents describe everything they recall. Eye cameras are used to study respondents' eye movements to determine at what points their eyes land first, and how long they linger on a given item. The audiometer is an electronic device attached to television sets in homes to record when the set is on and to which channel it is tuned.[8]

Presenting the Research Plan

The marketing researcher should summarize the research plan in a written proposal. A written proposal is especially important when the research project will be large and complex, or when an outside firm carries out the research. The proposal should cover the management problems to be addressed, the research objectives, the information to be obtained, the sources of secondary information or methods for collecting primary data, and how the results will help management decision making. The proposal should also include research costs. A written research plan or proposal ensures that the marketing manager and researchers have considered all important aspects of the research, and that they agree on why and how the research will be done.

Implementing the Research Plan

The researcher next puts the marketing research plan into action. This involves collecting, processing, and analyzing the information. Data collection can be done by the company's marketing research staff or by outside firms. The company keeps more control over the collection process and data quality by using its own staff. However, outside firms that specialize in data collection can often do the job more quickly and at lower cost.

The data collection phase of the marketing research process is generally the most expensive and the most subject to error. The researcher should watch the fieldwork closely to make sure that the plan is correctly implemented and to guard against problems with contacting respondents, with respondents who refuse to cooperate or who give biased or dishonest answers, and and interviewers who make mistakes or take shortcuts.

The collected data must be processed and analyzed to pull out important information and findings. Data from questionnaires is checked for accuracy and completeness, and coded for computer analysis. The researcher applies standard computer programs to prepare tabulations of results and to compute averages and other measures for the major variables.

Interpreting and Reporting the Findings

The researcher must now interpret the findings, draw conclusions, and report them to management. The researcher should not try to overwhelm managers with numbers and fancy statistical techniques—the data will overwhelm them. The researcher should present major findings that are relevant to the major decisions faced by management. The study is useful when it reduces the amount of uncertainty facing marketing executives.

The Pacific Western case illustrates the potential benefits of market research. Pacific Western's marketing researchers found that most people still thought of Pacific Western as the smallest and least aggressive carrier in its region even though it flew to more destinations in the West than Air Canada and CP Air combined, and carried more passengers than CP Air. Air travelers preferred large carriers and carriers with which they were familiar.

Canadian Airlines International Limited, the new airline formed in the merger of CP Air and Pacific Western.

In response to these findings, Pacific Western launched an advertising campaign positioning itself as "The Competition." The objective of the campaign was to familiarize travelers and potential travelers with Pacific Western, its routes, and its equipment. The campaign was designed to present Pacific Western as a major competitor to Air Canada and CP Air and, by so doing, raise the awareness and improve the perception of the airline.

Television, newspaper and magazine ads carried such messages as:

• Know the Competition

• The Competition Is Everywhere

• The Competition Sizes Up

Pacific Western's business continued to grow. After the advertising campaign, a larger number of passengers began to use the airline. The marketing research and resulting advertising campaign were successful in making the airline better known and more widely used.[9] In late 1986, Pacific Western purchased CP Air and became the second largest airline in Canada.

Marketing Research in Smaller Organizations

In this section we have looked at the marketing research process—from defining research objectives to interpreting and reporting results—as a lengthy, formal process carried out by large marketing companies. However, many small businesses and nonprofit organizations also use marketing research. Almost any organization can find informal, low-cost alternatives to the formal and complex marketing research techniques used by research experts in large firms (see Exhibit 4-2).

EXHIBIT 4-2
Marketing Research in Small Businesses and Nonprofit Organizations

Managers of small businesses and nonprofit organizations often think that marketing research can be done only by experts in large companies with big research budgets. However, many of the marketing research techniques discussed in this chapter can also be used less formally by smaller organizations at little or no expense.

Managers of small businesses and nonprofit organizations can obtain good marketing information simply by **observing** things around them. For example, retailers can evaluate new locations by observing vehicle and pedestrian traffic. They can visit competing stores to check on facilities and prices. They can evaluate their customer mix by recording how many and what kinds of customers shop in the store at different times. Competitor advertising can be monitored by collecting advertisements from local media.

Managers can conduct informal **surveys** using small convenience samples. The director of an art museum can learn what patrons think about new exhibits by conducting informal "focus groups"—inviting small groups to lunch and having discussions on topics of interest. Retail salespeople can talk with customers visiting the store; hospital officials can interview patients. Restaurant managers might make random phone calls during slack hours to interview consumers about where they eat out and what they think of various restaurants in the area.

Managers can also conduct their own simple **experiments**. For example, by changing the themes in regular fundraising mailings and watching results, a nonprofit manager can find out much about which marketing strategies work best. By varying newspaper advertisements, a store manager can learn the effects of ad size and position, price coupons, and media used.

Small organizations can obtain most of the secondary data available to large businesses. In addition, many associations, local media, chambers of commerce, and government agencies provide special help to small organizations. Local newspapers often provide information on local shoppers and their buying patterns.

Sometimes volunteers and colleges are willing to help carry out research. Nonprofit organizations can often use volunteers from local service clubs and other sources. Many colleges are seeking small businesses and nonprofit organizations to serve as cases for projects in marketing research classes.

As we have seen, secondary data collection, observation, surveys, and experiments can be used effectively by small organizations with small budgets. Although such informal research is less complex and costly, it must still be done carefully. Managers must carefully think through the objectives of the research, formulate questions in advance, recognize the biases introduced by smaller samples and less skilled researchers, and conduct the research systematically. If carefully planned and implemented, such low-cost research can provide reliable information for improving marketing decision making.

Source: Based on information found in Alan R. Andreasen, "Cost-Conscious Marketing Research," *Harvard Business Review*, July-August, 1983, pp. 74-79, and other sources.

Information Analysis

Information gathered by the company's marketing intelligence and marketing research systems often requires further analysis. Managers may need help to apply the research to marketing problems and decisions. Assistance might include more advanced statistical analysis to learn more about the relationships within a set of data and their statistical reliability. Such analysis allows management to go beyond means and standard deviations in the data, and allows managers to answer such questions as:

- What are the major variables affecting my sales and how important is each one?

- If I raised my price 10% and increased my advertising expenditures 20%, what would happen to sales?

- What are the best predictors of consumers who are likely to buy my brand versus my competitor's brand?

- What are the best variables for segmenting my market, and how many segments exist?

Information analysis might also involve a collection of mathematical models that will help marketers make better decisions. Each model represents some real system, process, or outcome. These models can help answer the questions of **what if** and **which is best**. In the past 20 years, marketing scientists have developed a great number of models to help marketing managers make better marketing mix decisions, design sales territories and sales call plans, select sites for retail outlets, develop optimal advertising mixes, and forecast new product sales.[10]

Distributing Information

Marketing information has no value until managers use it to make better marketing decisions. The information gathered through marketing intelligence and marketing research must be distributed to the right marketing managers at the right time. Most companies have centralized marketing information systems that provide managers with regular performance reports, intelligence updates, and reports on the results of studies. Managers need these routine reports for making regular planning, implementation, and control decisions. However, marketing managers may also need particular information for special situations and on-the-spot decisions. For example, a sales manager having trouble with a large customer wants a summary of the account's sales and profitability over the past year. As another example, a retail store manager whose store has run out of a best-selling product wants to know the current inventory levels in the chain's other stores. In companies with centralized information systems, these managers must request the information from the MIS staff and wait; often the information arrives too late to be useful.

Recent developments in information handling have caused a revolution in information distribution. With advances in microcomputers, software, and

communications, many companies are decentralizing their marketing information systems. They are giving managers direct access to information stored
in the system.[11] In some companies, marketing managers can use a desk terminal
to tie into the company's information network. Without leaving the desk, they
can obtain information from internal records or outside information services,
analyze the information using statistical packages and models, prepare reports
on a word processor, and communicate with others in the network through
telecommunications.

Such systems offer exciting prospects. They allow the managers to get the
information they need directly and quickly, and to tailor it to their own needs.
As more managers develop the skills needed to use such systems, and as
improvements in the technology make them more economical, more and more
marketing companies will use decentralized marketing information systems.

Summary

In carrying out their marketing responsibilities, marketing managers need a
great deal of information. Despite the growing supply of information, managers
often lack enough information of the right kind or have too much of the wrong
kind. To overcome these problems, many companies are taking steps to improve
their marketing information systems.

A well-designed marketing information system begins and ends with the
user. It first assesses information needs by interviewing marketing managers
and surveying their decision environment to determine what information is
desired, needed, and feasible to offer.

The MIS next develops information and helps managers to use it more
effectively. Internal records provide information on sales, costs, inventories,
cash flows, and accounts receivable and payable. Such data can be obtained
quickly and cheaply, but must often be adapted for marketing decisions. The
marketing intelligence system supplies marketing executives with everyday
information about developments in the external marketing environment. Intelligence can be collected from company employees, customers, suppliers, and
resellers, or by monitoring published reports, conferences, advertisements,
competitor actions, and other activities in the environment.

Marketing research involves collecting information relevant to a specific
marketing problem facing the company. Every marketer needs marketing
research, and many companies have their own marketing research departments.
Marketing research involves a four-step process. The first step consists of the
manager and researcher carefully defining the problem and setting the research
objectives. The objectives may be exploratory, descriptive, or causal. The second step consists of developing the research plan for collecting data from primary and secondary sources. Primary data collection calls for choosing a
research approach (observation, survey, experiment), choosing a contact
method (mail, telephone, personal), designing a sampling plan (whom to survey, how many to survey, and how to choose them) and developing research
instruments (questionnaire, mechanical). The third step consists of imple-

menting the marketing research plan by collecting, processing, and analyzing the information. The fourth step consists of interpreting and reporting the findings. Further information analysis helps marketing managers to apply the information and provides advanced statistical procedures and models to develop more rigorous findings from information.

Finally, the marketing information system distributes information gathered from internal sources, marketing intelligence, and marketing research to the right managers at the right times. More and more companies are decentralizing their information systems through distributed processing networks that allow managers to have direct access to information.

Questions for Discussion

1. What role should marketing research play in helping a firm to implement the marketing concept?
2. How does a marketing information system differ from a marketing intelligence system?
3. Identify and discuss the major steps in the marketing research process.
4. List some research tasks for the following areas: distribution decisions, product decisions, advertising decisions, personal selling decisions, pricing decisions.
5. Explain why defining the problem and research objective is often the hardest step in the research process.
6. Researchers usually start the data gathering process by examining secondary data. Define secondary data and explain its advantages and disadvantages.
7. Which type of research would be the most appropriate in the following situations, and why?
   a. Post Cereals wants to investigate the effect children have on the actual purchase of its products.
   b. Your college bookstore wants to gather some preliminary information on how students feel about the merchandise and service provided by the bookstore.
   c. McDonald's is considering locating a new outlet in a fast-growing suburb.
   d. Gillette wants to test the effect of two new advertising themes for its Right Guard lime stick deodorant sales in two cities.

Chapter 4 Key Terms

Causal research   Marketing research to test hypotheses about cause-and-effect relationships.

Descriptive research   Marketing research to better describe marketing problems, situations, or markets—such as the market potential for a product, or the demographics and attitudes of consumers.

Experimental research The gathering of primary data by selecting matched groups of subjects, giving them different treatments, controlling related factors, and checking for differences in group responses.

Exploratory research Marketing research to gather preliminary information that will help to better define problems and suggest hypotheses.

Focus group interviewing Personal interviewing which consists of inviting six to ten people to gather for a few hours with a trained interviewer to talk about a product, service, or organization. The interviewer "focuses" the group discussion on important issues.

Marketing information system (MIS) A structure of people, equipment, and procedures to gather, sort, analyze, evaluate, and distribute needed, timely, and accurate information to marketing decision makers.

Marketing intelligence Everyday information about developments in the marketing environment that helps managers prepare and adjust marketing plans.

Marketing research The systematic design, collection, analysis, and reporting of data and findings relevant to a specific marketing situation facing the company.

Observational research The gathering of primary data by observing relevant people, actions, and situations.

Primary data Information collected for the specific purpose at hand.

Sample A segment of the population selected for marketing research to represent the population as a whole.

Secondary data Information that already exists somewhere, having been collected for another purpose.

Survey research The gathering of primary data by asking people questions about their knowledge, attitudes, preferences, and buying behavior.

Cases for Chapter 4

The Marketing Environment

Chapter Objectives

After reading this chapter, you should be able to:
1. Describe the environmental forces that affect the company's ability to serve its customers.
2. Explain how changes in the demographic and economic environments affect marketing decisions.
3. Identify the major trends in the firm's natural and technological environments.
4. Discuss the key changes occurring in the political and cultural environments.

Understanding the changing Canadian environment is a difficult task for many marketers. Shifting demographics are creating new opportunities and threats in the marketplace. For example, between 1986 and 1996, the number of Canadians under 35 years of age will decline by 7% and the number over 35 will increase by 25%. The biggest increase will occur as the Baby Boomers enter middle age — there will be 1.6 million more adults in the 35 to 49 age group, an increase of 32% from 1986.

Not only is the median age of the population shifting, but Canadians are getting married later in life, the average family size is declining, the number of working mothers is increasing, and the divorce rate is increasing. Ignoring these changes can lead to dire consequences in the marketplace — as the Campbell Soup Company learned in the early 1980s.

By 1982, Campbell Soup had become a stodgy, conservative company with declining sales in the highly competitive packaged foods industry. As the market changed, consumers did not want just a can of soup, they also wanted increased convenience, sophistication, and variety. Per capita consumption of soup had decreased and Campbell was losing share in a declining market. The story was the same for TV dinners and tomato juice, as market share for Campbell was flat or declining in these product categories.

In 1983, Campbell hired a new president who was given the task of turning the company around. The president, David Clark, defined the company's mission as operating in the "well-being" business and focused on meeting and responding to the ever-changing needs of Canadian consumers. Campbell's objective was to be in the top 5% of all Canadian packaged goods companies. To accomplish this goal, it dramatically increased research and development and marketing expenditures to support the launching of new products and repositioning of existing products. Many of these products were targeted at the growing, health-conscious, convenience food market, which is prepared to pay more for value-added, higher quality products. As well, products were designed to satisfy the needs of those Canadians who were eating four meals a day, with the last two meals consisting of lighter convenience foods.

The new and rejuvenated products in Campbell's line include:

- Chunky Soups, "The Soup That Eats Like a Meal."

- Calorie-Reduced Soups, with half the calories of regular soup.

- Prego Spaghetti Sauce, a premium sauce.

- Le Menu, a premium-quality frozen food dinner.

- V-8 Juice, repackaged and positioned as a drink that is nutritious and delicious.

By more closely monitoring the changing Canadian consumer environment, Campbell has been able to identify and capture new opportunities in the marketplace. Since 1983, sales, market share, and profits have steadily increased; these increases strongly indicate that Campbell is on the right track in adapting to developments in the marketing environment.[1]

The marketing environment consists of uncontrollable forces that surround the company. To be successful, the company must adapt its marketing mix to trends and developments in this marketing environment.

We define a company's marketing environment as follows:

A company's marketing environment consists of the actors and forces outside the firm that affect marketing management's ability to develop and maintain successful transactions with its target customers.

The changing and uncertain marketing environment deeply affects the company. Instead of changing slowly and predictably, the environment can produce major surprises and shocks. Which oil companies in 1971 would have predicted the end of cheap energy in the years that followed, or the changes in the government's position on Canadian ownership of the oil industry, or the decline in world oil prices in 1985? How many managers at Gerber Foods foresaw the end of the baby boom? Which auto companies foresaw the huge impact Ralph Nader and consumers would have on their business decisions? The marketing environment offers both opportunities and threats, and the company must use its marketing research and marketing intelligence systems to monitor the changing environment.

The marketing environment is made up of a microenvironment and a macroenvironment. The microenvironment consists of the forces close to the company that affect its ability to serve its customers—the company, marketing channel firms, customer markets, competitors, and publics. The macroenvironment consists of the larger societal forces that affect the whole microenvironment—demographic, economic, natural, technological, political, and cultural forces. We will first look at the company's microenvironment and then at its macroenvironment.

The Company's Microenvironment

The job of marketing management is to create attractive products for its target markets. However, marketing management's success will be affected by the rest of the company, middlemen, competitors, and various publics. These actors in

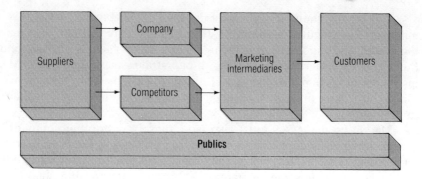

FIGURE 5-1
Major Actors in the Company's Microenvironment

the company's *microenvironment* are shown in Figure 5-1. Marketing managers cannot simply focus on the target market's needs. They must also watch all actors in the company's microenvironment. This chapter will examine the company, suppliers, middlemen, customers, competitors, and publics — in that order. We will illustrate the role and impact of these actors by referring to Pro Cycle of Quebec, a large Canadian bicycle producer. Pro Cycle markets four major brands of bicycles: Velo Sport, Peugeot, Lovell, and C.C.M.

The Company

In making marketing plans, marketing management at Pro Cycle must take into account other company groups such as top management, finance, research and development (R&D), purchasing, manufacturing, and accounting. All these groups form the company microenvironment (see Figure 5-2).

FIGURE 5-2
Company Microenvironment

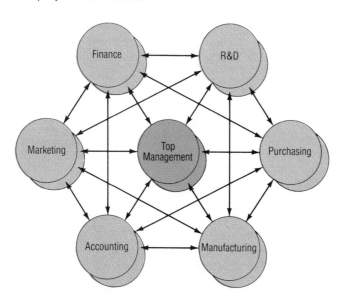

Top management at Pro Cycle consists of the bicycle division's general manager, the executive committee, the chief executive officer, the chairman of the board, and the board of directors. These higher levels of management set the company's mission, objectives, broad strategies, and policies. Marketing managers must make decisions within the plans made by top management. Marketing plans must be approved by top management before they can be implemented.

Marketing managers must also work closely with other company departments. Finance is concerned with finding and using funds to carry out the marketing plan. R&D focuses on the problems of designing safe, attractive bicycles or new products such as mountain bicycles. Purchasing obtains supplies and materials, while manufacturing is responsible for producing the desired number of bicycles. Accounting measures revenues and costs to help marketing judge how well it is achieving its objectives. All these departments have an impact on the marketing department's plans and actions.

Suppliers

Suppliers are firms and individuals that provide the resources needed by the company to produce goods and services. For example, Pro Cycle must obtain steel, aluminum, rubber tires, gears, seats, and other materials to produce bicycles. It also must obtain labor, equipment, fuel, electricity, computers, and other factors of production.

Developments with suppliers can seriously affect marketing. Marketing managers need to watch price trends of their key inputs. Rising supply costs may force price increases that can harm the company's sales volume. Marketing managers must also watch supply availability. Supply shortages, labor strikes, and other events can lose sales in the short run and damage customer goodwill in the long run.

Marketing Intermediaries

Marketing intermediaries are firms that help the company to promote, sell, and distribute its goods to final buyers. They include middlemen, physical distribution firms, marketing service agencies, and financial intermediaries.

Middlemen

Middlemen are business firms that help the company find customers or make sales to them. These include wholesalers and retailers who buy and resell merchandise (they are often called **resellers**). Pro Cycle's primary method of marketing bicycles is to sell them to dealers, who resell them at a profit.

Why does Pro Cycle use middlemen? The answer is that middlemen perform important functions more cheaply than Pro Cycle can by itself. They stock bicycles in locations convenient to customers. They show and deliver bicycles when consumers want them. They advertise the bikes, and negotiate terms of sale. Pro Cycle finds it better to work through middlemen than to try to own and operate its own massive system of outlets.

Courtesy: Pro Cycle

The forces in Pro Cycle's micoenvironment affect the marketing of its bicycles.

Selecting and working with middlemen is not easy. No longer do manufacturers have many small, independent middlemen from which to choose. They now face large and growing middlemen organizations. More and more bicycles are being sold through large corporate chains (such as Eaton's and Canadian Tire), and large wholesalers, retailers, and franchise chains. These groups have great power to dictate terms or shut the manufacturer out of large markets. Manufacturers must work hard to get "shelf space."

Physical Distribution Firms

Physical distribution firms help the company to stock and move goods from their origin to their destination. Warehouses are firms that store and protect goods before they move to the next destination. Transportation firms include railroads, trucking companies, airlines, ships, and other companies that specialize in moving goods from one location to another. A company has to decide on the best ways to store and ship goods, balancing such considerations as cost, delivery, speed, and safety.

Marketing Services Agencies

Marketing services agencies—marketing research firms, advertising agencies, media firms, and marketing consulting firms—help the company to target and promote its products to the right markets. When the company decides to use one of these agencies, it must choose carefully, since these firms vary in creativity, quality, service, and price. The company has to review the performance of these firms regularly and consider replacing those that no longer perform well.

Financial Intermediaries

Financial intermediaries include banks, credit companies, insurance companies, and other companies that help finance transactions or insure risk associated with the buying and selling of goods. Most firms and customers depend on financial intermediaries to finance their transactions. The company's marketing performance can be seriously affected by rising credit costs or limited credit or both. For this reason, the company has to develop strong relationships with important financial institutions.

Customers

The company needs to study its customer markets closely. The company can operate in five types of customer markets. These are shown in Figure 5-3 and defined below:

Consumer markets   *Individuals and households that buy goods and services for personal consumption*

Industrial markets   *Organizations that buy goods and services for further processing or for use in their production process*

Reseller markets   *Organizations that buy goods and services in order to resell them at a profit*

Government markets   *Government agencies that buy goods and services in order to produce public services or transfer these goods and services to others who need them*

International markets   *Foreign buyers, including consumers, producers, resellers, and governments*

FIGURE 5-3
Basic Types of Customer Markets

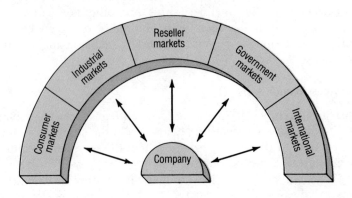

Pro Cycle may sell bicycles in all these markets. It might sell some bicycles directly to consumers through factory outlets. Producers might purchase the bicycles to deliver goods or ride around the plant. It might sell bicycles to bicycle wholesalers and retailers, who resell them to consumer and producer markets. It could sell bicycles to government agencies. Pro Cycle might also sell bicycles to foreign consumers, producers, resellers, and governments. Each market type has special characteristics that call for careful study by the seller.

Competitors

Every company faces a wide range of competitors. The marketing concept states that, to be successful, the company must satisfy the needs and wants of consumers better than the competition. Therefore, marketers must do more than simply adapt to the needs of target consumers. They must also adapt to the strategies of competitors who are serving the same target consumers. Companies must gain strategic advantage by strongly positioning their offerings against competitors' offerings in the minds of consumers.

No single competitive marketing strategy is best for all companies. Each firm must consider its size and industry position compared to competitors. Large firms with dominant positions in an industry can use certain strategies that smaller firms cannot afford, but being large is not enough. There are both winning and losing strategies for large firms; and small firms can find strategies that give them better rates of return than large firms. Both large and small firms must find marketing strategies that best position them against competitors in their markets.

In deciding on a marketing strategy Pro Cycle must consider competition from large Canadian firms like TI Raleigh Industries and Gervin Company, as well as from smaller specialty builders such as Cycles Marinoni and Bicylesport. Competition also comes from foreign manufacturers who export to Canada in spite of high tariffs. Pro Cycle must consider a variety of both foreign and domestic competitors in considering its strategy.

Publics

The company's marketing environment also includes various publics. We define public as follows:

A public is any group that has an actual or potential interest in or impact on an organization's ability to achieve its objectives.

A company can prepare marketing plans for its major publics as well as its customer markets. Suppose the company wants some response from a particular public, such as its goodwill, favorable word of mouth, or donations of time or money. The company would have to design an offer to this public that is attractive enough to produce the desired response.

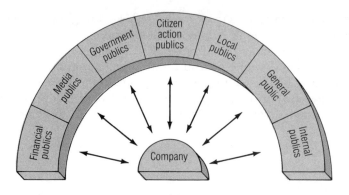

FIGURE 5-4
Types of Publics

Every company is surrounded by seven types of publics (see Figure 5-4):

Financial publics   *Financial publics influence the company's ability to obtain funds. Banks, investment houses, and stockholders are the major financial publics. Pro Cycle seeks the goodwill of these groups by issuing annual reports and showing the financial community that its house is in order.*

Media publics   *Media publics are those that carry news, features, and editorial opinion. They include newspapers, magazines, and radio and television stations. Pro Cycle is interested in getting more and better media coverage.*

Government publics   *Management must take government developments into account. Pro Cycle's marketers must respond to issues of product safety, truth-in-advertising, dealers' rights, and others. Pro Cycle must consider joining with other bicycle manufacturers to lobby for better laws.*

Citizen action publics   *A company's marketing decisions may be questioned by consumer organizations, environmental groups, minority groups, and others. For example, parent groups are lobbying for greater safety in bicycles. Pro Cycle has the opportunity to be a leader in product safety design. Pro Cycle's public relations department can help it to stay in touch with consumer groups.*

Local publics   *Every company has local publics such as neighborhood residents and community organizations. Large companies usually appoint a community relations officer to deal with the community, attend meetings, answer questions, and contribute to worthwhile causes.*

General public   *A company needs to be concerned about the general public's attitude toward its products and activities. The public's image of the company affects its buying. To build a strong "corporate citizen"* image, Pro Cycle will lend its officers to community fund drives, make large contributions to charity, and set up systems for consumer complaint handling.

Internal publics   A company's internal publics include blue-collar workers, white-collar workers, volunteers, managers, and the board of directors. Large companies develop newsletters and other ways to inform and motivate their internal publics. When employees feel good about their company, this positive attitude spills over to external publics.

The Company's Macroenvironment

The company and its suppliers, marketing intermediaries, customers, competitors, and publics all operate in a larger *macroenvironment* of forces that shape opportunities and pose threats to the company. The company must watch and respond to these forces, which are "uncontrollables." The macroenvironment consists of the six major forces shown in Figure 5-5. The remaining sections of this chapter will examine these forces and show how they affect marketing plans.

Demographic Environment

Demography is the study of human populations in terms of size, density, location, age, sex, race, occupation, and other statistics. The demographic environment is of major interest to marketers because people make up markets. The most important demographic trends are described here.[2]

FIGURE 5-5
Major Forces in the Company's Macroenvironment

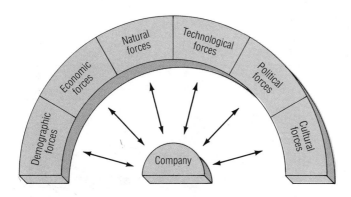

Changing Age Structure of the Canadian Population

The single most important demographic trend in Canada is the changing age structure of the population. The Canadian population is getting older for two reasons. First, there is a slowdown in the **birthrate**, so there are fewer young people to pull the population's average age down. Second, **life expectancy** is increasing, so there are more older people to pull the average age up.

The Canadian population stood at 26 million in 1987 and may increase to 27 million by the year 1996. During the baby boom that followed World War II and lasted until the early 1960s, the annual birthrate reached an all-time high. The baby boom was followed by a "birth dearth," and by the mid-1970s the birthrate had fallen sharply. The annual number of births forecast for the late 1980s is about 375 000, compared to a peak of 479 000 in 1959. This decrease was caused by smaller family sizes resulting from the desire to improve personal living standards, the increasing desire of women to work outside the home, and improved birth control.

The second factor in the general aging of the population is increased life expectancy. Current average life expectancy is 75 years; 73 for males and 80 for females. This increasing life expectancy and the declining birthrate are producing an aging population. The Canadian median age is now 30 and is expected to reach 33 by the year 2000.

The changing age structure of the population will result in different growth rates for various age groups over the decade (see Figure 5-6), and these differences will strongly affect the targeting strategies of marketers. Growth trends for six age groups are summarized below.

FIGURE 5-6
Projected Age-Group Shifts, 1986-1996

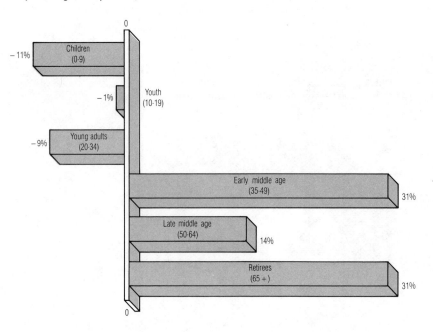

Children   The number of infants to nine year olds will decline by 11% in the next ten years. This will mean that markets for baby toys, clothes, furniture, and food will decline in the next few years.

Youths   The number of ten to 19 year olds will drop slightly during the decade. This means slower sales growth for jeans manufacturers, movie and record companies, colleges, and others who target the teen market.

Young Adults   This group will decline during the 1980s and in the next decade as the ''birth dearth'' generation moves in. Marketers who sell to the 20 to 34 age group—furniture makers, life insurance companies, sports equipment manufacturers—can no longer rely on increasing market size for increases in sales. They will have to work for bigger shares of smaller markets.

Early middle age   The baby boom generation will be moving into the 35 to 49 age group, creating huge increases. This group is a major market for larger homes, new automobiles, clothing, entertainment, and investments.

Late middle age   The 50 to 64 age group will increase over the next decade. This group is a major market for eating out, travel, clothing, and recreation.

Retirees   The over-65 group will increase by 31% over the decade, and will continue to grow. This group has a demand for retirement communities, quieter forms of recreation, single-portion food packaging, and medical goods and services.

Thus the changing age structure of the Canadian population will strongly affect future marketing decisions.

The Changing Canadian Family

The Canadian ideal of the two-children, two-car suburban family has been losing some of its luster. There are many forces at work. People are marrying later and having fewer children. The average age of couples marrying for the first time has been rising over the years and now stands at 25 years for males and 23 for females. Couples with no children under 18 now make up about 38% of all families. Of those families that have children, the average number of children is 2.2, down from 3.5 in 1955.

There has also been an increase in the number of working mothers. More than half of the mothers with children at home hold a job. Their incomes contribute 40% of the household's income, and influence the purchase of higher-quality goods and services. Marketers of tires, automobiles, insurance, and travel service are increasingly directing their advertising to working women. All these changes are accompanied by a shift in the traditional roles and values of husbands and wives, with the husband assuming more domestic functions such as shopping and childcare. As a result, husbands are becoming more of a target market for food and household appliance marketers.

James Hertel

As more married women enter the labor force, more husbands take on domestic responsibilities, including shopping for food and household goods.

Finally, the number of non-family households is increasing. Many young adults leave home and move into apartments. Other adults choose to remain single. Still others are divorced or widowed people living alone. Today, over 32% of all households are non-family households or single-parent households. In Canada, over 1.8 million people live alone (20% of all households). This group needs smaller apartments, inexpensive and smaller appliances, furniture, and furnishings, and food that is packaged in smaller sizes. Their car preferences are different. Ford Motor Company of Canada has designed a "two seater" car to capture a special niche in this growing "singles" market, which has doubled in the past two decades and continues to grow.[3] Singles are also a market for various services that enable them to meet each other, such as singles bars, tours, and cruises.

Geographic Shifts in Population

Canadians are a mobile people. About one out of ten, or 2.6 million Canadians, move each year. Among the major trends are the following:

Movement West, then East   In the past decade many Canadians moved west; between 1976 and 1986 when Canada's population increased by 11%, Alberta's population increased by 27% and British Columbia's by 19%. However, between 1986 and 1996 when Canada's population is projected to increase by 7%, Ontario's population is projected to increase by 9% and the population of the Maritimes is projected to increase by 9%. These shifts in population are caused, in part, by the economic climates in the various regions of Canada. The population shifts offer opportunities for home builders and retailers in the faster growth areas and threats for the same marketers in the lower growth regions.

Movement from rural to urban areas   People have been moving from rural to urban areas for over a century. Cities show a faster pace of living, more commuting, higher incomes, and greater variety of goods and services than can be found in the small towns and rural areas across Canada. The largest cities, such as Toronto, Montreal, and Vancouver, account for most of the sales of expensive furs, perfumes, luggage, and works of art. These cities also support the opera, ballet, and other forms of "high culture" (see Exhibit 5-1). Recently, however, there has been a slight shift of population back to small towns and rural areas.

Movement from the city to the suburbs   Cities have become surrounded by suburbs. Statistics Canada calls concentrated urban areas Census Metropolitan Areas (CMAs). About 56% of the nation's population live in the 23 CMAs. The CMAs constitute the primary market focus of many firms. The 23 CMA markets with future projections are listed in Table 5-1. Companies use the CMAs in researching the best geographical segments for their products and in deciding where to buy advertising time.

A large number of Canadians live in the suburbs. Suburbs are characterized

TABLE 5-1
The Top 23 CMA Markets in Canada, 1986 and 1996 Estimate

Rank 1986	Rank 1996 E	CMA	Population 1986	Population 1996 E
1	1	Toronto	3 074 000	3 310 000
2	2	Montreal	2 910 000	2 959 000
3	3	Vancouver	1 339 000	1 512 000
4	4	Ottawa-Hull	781 000	860 000
5	5	Calgary	696 000	904 000
6	6	Edmonton	673 000	790 000
7	7	Quebec	622 000	699 000
8	8	Winnipeg	622 000	664 000
9	9	Hamilton	597 000	626 000
10	10	St. Catharines-Niagara	324 000	342 000
11	11	Kitchener	310 000	337 000
12	12	Halifax	299 000	333 000
13	14	London	299 000	320 000
14	13	Victoria	266 000	323 000
15	15	Windsor	238 000	227 000
16	16	St. John's	177 000	218 000
17	17	Oshawa	165 000	196 000
18	18	Regina	165 000	179 000
19	19	Sudbury	151 000	144 000
20	20	Saskatoon	148 000	160 000
21	21	St. John	133 000	141 000
22	23	Chicoutimi-Jonquière	130 000	130 000
23	22	Thunder Bay	127 000	135 000

Source: *Marketing Research Handbook 1985-86*, Statistics Canada, Catalog #63-224.

EXHIBIT 5-1
Toronto: The Affluent City

In the Toronto Census Metropolitan Areas, approximately 5000 people earn more than $150 000 per year. Toronto has more people earning over $150 000 per year than Montreal, Vancouver, and Ottawa-Hull combined. One of the reasons is that over 25% of all managers and professionals in Canada live in Toronto. As well, 491 of the largest Canadian companies have head offices in Toronto.

Because of this affluence, Toronto is the best Canadian market for luxury cars (over 2300 new BMW's and Mercedes-Benz's are sold each year), upper-class stores and boutiques (such as Holt Renfrew and Creeds), and upscale restaurants. Toronto is also the major market for the American Express Platinum card. To qualify for the card you need to have an annual income of over $150 000 and spend at least $10 000 per year on the card.

Source: Stanley Oziewics, "Toronto the Wealthy," *The Globe and Mail*, November 8 1986, pp. 1, 15.

by more casual, outdoor living, greater neighbor interaction, higher incomes, and younger families. Suburbanites buy station wagons, home workshop equipment, garden furniture, lawn and gardening tools, and outdoor cooking equipment. Retailers have acknowledged the suburbs by building branch department stores and suburban shopping centers.

A Better-Educated and More White-Collar Population

In 1981, 36% of Canadian adults had completed some post-secondary education. By 1990, the number will increase to 40% or over 8 million adults. The rising number of educated people will increase the demand for quality products, books, magazines, and travel. It suggests a decline in television viewing, because college-educated consumers watch less TV than the population at large.

The workforce is becoming more white-collar. Forty percent of Canadian workers are employed in white collar jobs (sales, clerical) and 25% of the workforce are in professional, managerial, and administrative occupations. One-third of the workforce are in blue-collar occupations. The category with the greatest annual increase in employment in the past decade was professionals, followed by white-collar, and then blue-collar workers.

Demographic trends are highly reliable for the short and intermediate run. There is little excuse for a company to be suddenly surprised by a demographic development. Companies can list the major demographic trends, then spell out what the trends mean for them. This is done in Table 5-2 for three industries. In the case of airlines, for example, each trend is expected to have a positive sales and profit impact.

TABLE 5-2
The Impact of the Changing Population Mix on Three Industries

Trends	Airlines	Apparel	Consumer Electronics
Baby boom generation matures	Many will have more money for travel as they get older. √√√	Will spend more on clothes as they age; shift from casual to higher quality. √√√	Rising incomes provide means to buy better-quality stereos, TVs, etc. √√
More elderly persons	They have the time to travel but inflation may rob them of the means. √	Older people spend less on clothing.	Little demand from this group; often forced to make do with older products.
More working women	Second income allows more females to take trips; more single women have money. √√√	Career women need more clothing and have the money to buy it. √√√	Can buy more and higher-priced merchandise. √√
Smaller family units	More disposable income per member; more economical to fly than drive. √√	A shift toward higher-quality, higher-margin merchandise. √√	More income per capita; electronic entertainment replaces family activities. √√

√√√ Very positive   √√ Positive   √ Mildly positive

Source: *Chicago Tribune*, April 8, 1979, Sec. 5, p. 1. Copyright © 1979 by Standard & Poor's Corp., 345 Hudson St., New York, N.Y. 10014. Reproduction by permission.

The children born between 1945 and the early 1960s in Canada, about 6 500 000, are referred to as the *baby boom* generation, or "Boomies."[4] Not only do the Boomies have a disproportionate influence on Canadian society, but they bring new attitudes and values with them to the marketplace. In contrast to their older brothers and sisters (the pre-Boomies) they act and behave in different ways:

	Pre-Boomies	**Boomies**
Status Symbols	Cars	Stereo sets
Children	4	1.8
Shelter	Houses	Apartments
Breadwinners	Husband	Husband and wife
Child rearing	Mother	Day care
University courses	Arts	Business administration
Finance	Savings	Credit cards

Economic Environment

The *economic environment* consists of factors that affect consumer purchasing power and spending patterns. Markets require buying power as well as people. Total purchasing power depends on current income, prices, savings, and credit. Marketers should be aware of major trends in income and of changing consumer spending patterns.

Changes in Income

In response to past economic conditions, many Canadians have turned to more cautious buying. To save money, they are buying more store brands and fewer national brands. Many companies have introduced economy versions of their products and turned to price appeals in their advertising. Some consumers have postponed purchases of durable goods, while others purchased them out of fear that prices would be higher the next year. Many families began to feel that a large home, two cars, foreign travel, and private higher education were beyond their reach.

In recent years, however, economic conditions have improved. Current projections suggest that real income will rise modestly through the mid-1990s. The baby boom generation will be moving into its prime wage-earning years, and the number of small families headed by dual-career couples will increase greatly. It is forecast that by 1995, over 75% of the women in the 25 to 44 age group will be working, and 50% of the 45-64 age group will be employed. These more affluent groups will demand higher quality and better service, and they will be willing to pay for it. These consumers will spend more on time-saving products and services, travel and entertainment, physical fitness products, cultural activities, and continuing education.

Marketers should pay attention to income distribution as well as average income. Income distribution in Canada is still very skewed. At the top are upper-class consumers, whose spending patterns are not affected by current economic events. These consumers are a major market for luxury goods. There is a comfortable middle class that is somewhat careful about its spending but is able to afford expensive clothes, minor antiques, and a small boat or cottage. The working class must stick close to the basics of food, clothing, and shelter and must try hard to save. Finally, the underclass (persons on welfare and many retirees) have to count their pennies when making even the most basic purchases.

In 1986, about 5% of working Canadians made over $50 000 annually, 15% made between $30 000 and $50 000, 21% made between $20 000 and $30 000, 29% made between $10 000 and $20 000, and 30% made less than $10 000. Income differences also exist between the various regions of Canada because of local economic activity and employment levels. The median income in the Maritime provinces is about 20% below the average for all of Canada, and Ontario, Alberta, and British Columbia exceed the average. Marketers need to take these geographic differences into account when planning their programs.

Changing Consumer Spending Patterns

Table 5-3 shows the consumer spending patterns for major goods and services categories between 1960 and 1990. Food, housing, household operations, and transportation use up most household income. Over time, however, the food, clothing, and personal care bills of households have been falling, while the housing, transportation, and recreational bills have been increasing. Some of these changes were noted over a century ago by Ernest Engel, who studied how people shifted their spending as their income rose. He found that as family

TABLE 5-3
Percentage Distribution of Consumption Expenditures, 1960, 1970, 1980, and 1990 Estimate

Expenditure	1960	1970	1980	1990 E
Food, beverages, tobacco	25.3	22.3	20.3	20.0
Housing	17.7	19.6	18.4	19.8
Household operations	10.2	9.5	9.2	8.5
Transportation	13.1	13.8	14.7	14.5
Medical-care expenses	6.4	3.5	3.3	3.5
Clothing and footwear	8.6	8.1	6.9	6.8
Recreation and education	5.9	8.9	10.2	12.5
Personal business	4.8	6.1	9.1	8.5
Personal care	7.4	8.0	7.3	7.4
Other	.6	.2	.5	.5

Sources: Lawrence R. Small, ed., *Handbook of Canadian Markets*, 1979, The Conference Board of Canada, Ottawa, October 1979, and *Market Research Handbook*, 1985-86 Statistics Canada, Catalog 63-224, Ottawa, February, 1986.

income rises, the percentage spent on food declines, the percentage spent on housing and household operations remains constant, and the percentage spent on other categories and savings increases. Engel's "laws" have generally been supported by later studies.

Changes in such major economic variables as income, cost of living, interest rates, and savings and borrowing patterns have a large impact on the marketplace. Companies monitor these variables with economic forecasting. Businesses do not have to be wiped out by a downturn in economic activity. With adequate warning, they can take steps to reduce their costs and ride out the economic storm.

Natural Environment

The *natural environment* contains natural resources that are needed as inputs by marketers, or that are affected by marketing activities. During the 1960s, public concern grew over whether the natural environment was being damaged by the industrial activities of modern nations. Popular books raised concerns about shortages of natural resources, and about the damage to water, earth, and air caused by industrial activities. Watchdog groups such as Pollution Probe sprang up, and legislators proposed measures to protect the environment. Marketers should be aware of the following trends in the natural environment.

Shortages of Raw Materials

Air and water may seem to be infinite resources, but some groups see long-run dangers. Environmental groups have lobbied for a ban on certain propellants used in aerosol cans because of their potential damage to the ozone layer. Water is already a problem in some parts of the world.

Renewable resources, such as forests and food, have to be used wisely.

Companies in the forestry business are required to reforest timberlands in order to protect the soil and to ensure enough wood supplies to meet future demand. Food supply can be a major problem because the amount of farmable land is limited, and more and more of it is being developed for urban areas.

Nonrenewable resources, such as oil, coal, and various minerals, pose a serious problem:

> . . . it would appear at present that the quantities of platinum, gold, zinc, and lead are not sufficient to meet demands ... silver, tin, and uranium may be in short supply even at higher prices by the turn of the century. By the year 2050, several more minerals may be exhausted if the current rate of consumption continues.[5]

The marketing implications of these shortages are many. Firms using scarce minerals face large cost increases, even if the materials remain available. They may not find it easy to pass these costs on to the consumer. Firms engaged in research and development and exploration can help by developing new sources and materials.

Increased Cost of Energy

One nonrenewable resource, oil, has created the most serious problem for future economic growth as the major industrial economies of the world depend heavily on it. Until economical energy substitutes can be developed, oil will continue to dominate the global political and economic picture. Large increases in the price of oil during the 1970s (from $2.23 per barrel in 1970 to $34.00 per barrel in 1982) created a frantic search for alternative forms of energy. Companies are searching for practical ways to harness solar, nuclear, wind, and other forms of energy.

Increased Levels of Pollution

Industry will almost always damage the quality of the natural environment. Consider the disposal of chemical and nuclear wastes, the dangerous mercury levels in the ocean, the problem of acid rain in Canada's lakes, the quantity of DDT and other chemical pollutants in the soil and food supply, and the littering of the environment with nonbiodegradable bottles, plastics, and other packaging materials.

The public's concern creates a marketing opportunity for alert companies. It creates a large market for pollution control solutions such as scrubbers and recycling centers.

Government Intervention in Natural Resource Management

Marketing management needs to pay attention to the natural environment. Business can expect strong controls from government and pressure groups. Canadian companies face an array of federal, provincial, and municipal regulations that prohibit or restrict their activities in these areas. Instead of opposing regulation, business should help develop solutions to the material and energy problems facing the nation.

Technological Environment

The most dramatic force shaping people's destiny is technology. The *techno-logical environment* consists of forces that affect new technology, creating new product and market opportunities. Technology has released such wonders as penicillin, open-heart surgery, and the birth control pill. In contrast, it has produced such horrors as the hydrogen bomb, nerve gas, and the submachine gun. Technology has also produced such mixed blessings as the automobile, television, and white bread. Our attitude toward technology depends on whether we are more impressed with its wonders or with its blunders.

Every new technology replaces an older technology. Transistors hurt the vacuum-tube industry, photocopiers hurt the carbon-paper business, the auto hurt the railroads, and television hurt the movies. Instead of adopting the new technologies, older industries fought or ignored them, and their businesses declined.

New technologies create new markets and opportunities. The marketer should watch the following trends in technology.

Faster Pace of Technological Change

Many of today's common products were not available even a hundred years ago. Sir John A. Macdonald did not know of automobiles, airplanes, phono-graphs, radios, or the electric light. Sir Robert Laird Borden did not know of television, aerosol cans, home freezers, automatic dishwashers, room air con-ditioners, antibiotics, or electronic computers. William Lyon MacKenzie King did not know of photocopies, synthetic detergents, tape-recorders, birth control pills, or earth satellites. John Diefenbaker did not know of personal computers, digital watches, video-recorders, or word processors. Companies that do not keep up with technological change will soon find their products out of date, and will miss new product and market opportunities.

Unlimited Opportunities

Scientists today are working on a wide range of new technologies that will revolutionize our products and production processes. The most exciting work is being done in biotechnology, solid-state electronics, robotics, and materials science.[6] Scientists today are working on the following promising new products and services:

Practical solar energy	Commercial space shuttle	Happiness pills
Cancer cures	Lung and liver cures	Electric cars
Chemical control of mental health	Household robots that cook and clean	Electronic anesthetic for pain killing
Desalinization of seawater	Nonfattening, tasty, nutritious foods	Totally safe and effective contraceptives

Scientists also speculate on fantasy products such as small flying cars, single-person rocket belts, three-dimensional television, space colonies, and human clones. The challenge in each case is not only technical but commercial — to make practical, affordable versions of these products.

R&D Budgets

In order to capture the potential offered by innovation, companies and governments must invest in research and development (R&D). In contrast to the United States, where R&D expenditures are about 2.3% of the gross national product, Canada spends around 1% of its gross national product on R&D. While this amounted to over $6 billion in 1986, most industrialized nations spend over 2% of gross national product on R&D.[7] As one example, the level of R&D as a percentage of industrial output is about five times lower in Canada than in the U.S.[8] In addition, a study of innovation in the U.S. reported a much higher ratio of engineering and design to R&D than was observed in Canada.[9]

The result of this low R&D activity in Canada is a deficiency in the innovative capability of many Canadian firms. Frequently these firms, particularly the subsidiaries of multinationals, rely on parent companies to transfer technology to Canada. This leads to Canadian firms following technology rather than being in the forefront. It may also lead to lower profits and lower sales in foreign markets.[10] The industries spending the most on R&D in Canada are in the "high-tech" sector; notably communications, computer hardware and software, and aerospace. They typically invest 5% to 10% of sales on R&D versus less than 2% for resource industries.

Marketers need to understand the changing technological environment and how new technologies can serve human needs. They need to work closely with R&D people to encourage more market-oriented research. With new ideas, they must be alert to possible negative aspects that might harm the users and bring about distrust and opposition.

Political Environment

Marketing decisions are strongly affected by developments in the *political environment*. The political environment is made up of laws, government agencies, and pressure groups that influence and limit various organizations and individuals in society. We will look at the main political trends and what they mean to marketing management.

Legislation Regulating Business

Legislation affecting business has increased steadily over the years. This legislation has been enacted for a number of reasons. The first is to **protect companies** from each other. Business executives all praise competition but try to neutralize it when it touches them. For example, the old Combines Investigation Act contained a section that made it an indictable offence to form a merger by which competition in an industry is lessened against the interests of the public (i.e., consumers, producers, or others). The enforcement of this section of the act was not successful.[11] When proposals for a new competition policy for Canada were put forth, business firms, in general, opposed them.[12] The history of mergers in Canada suggests that many firms prefer to **buy** market share (through merging with competitors) rather than **compete** for it. The Bay-Simpson's merger is an example of this strategy. This type of merger activity, and that of newspaper chains such as Thompson's, have led to new laws to define and prevent unfair competition. The Competition Act, enacted in 1986, contains new provisions for mergers and anti-competitive conduct.

The second purpose of government regulation is to **protect consumers** from unfair business practices. Some firms, if left alone, would make poor products, tell lies in their advertising, and deceive through their packaging and pricing. Unfair consumer practices have been defined and are enforced by various agencies such as the Department of Consumer and Corporate Affairs at the federal level. In addition, various provincial consumer departments have been established to protect consumers. Many managers become incensed with each new consumer law, and yet a few have said that "consumerism may be the best thing that has happened . . . in the past 20 years."[13]

The third purpose of government regulation is to **protect the interests of society** against unrestrained business behavior. Profitable business activity does not always create a better quality of life. Regulation arises to make certain that firms take responsibility for the social costs of their production or products.

New laws and their enforcement will continue or increase. Business executives must watch these developments when planning their products and marketing programs. Marketers need to know about the major laws protecting competition, consumers, and society. The main federal laws are listed in Table 5-4. In addition, each province has its own set of laws for marketing activities.

TABLE 5-4
Major Federal Legislation Affecting Marketing

The Competition Act
The Competition Act is the major legislative act affecting the marketing of companies in Canada. Specific sections and the relevant areas are:

Section 33: Mergers — Forbids mergers by which competition is, or is likely to be, lessened to the detriment of, or against, the interests of the public.

Section 34: Pricing — Forbids a supplier to charge different prices to competitors purchasing like quantities of goods (price discrimination). Forbids price-cutting that lessens competition (predatory pricing).

Section 36: Pricing and Advertising — Forbids advertising prices that misrepresent the "usual" selling price (misleading price advertising).

Section 38: Pricing — Forbids suppliers to require subsequent resellers to offer products at a stipulated price (resale price maintenance).

Other selected Acts that have an impact on marketing activities:

National Trade Mark and True Labelling Act — established the term "Canada-Standard" or "C.S." as a national trade mark; requires certain commodities to be properly labelled or described in advertising for the purpose of indicating material content or quality.

Consumer Packaging and Labelling Act — provides a set of rules to ensure that full information is disclosed by the manufacturer, packer, or distributor. Requires that all prepackaged products bear the quantity in French and English in metric as well as traditional Canadian standard units of weight, volume, or measure.

Motor Vehicle Safety Act — established mandatory safety standards for motor vehicles.

Food and Drug Act — prohibits the advertisement and sale of adulterated or misbranded foods, cosmetics, and drugs.

In Quebec, for example, Bill 101 requires that all labels have the same information in French as in English.

Government Agency Enforcement

When the Department of Consumer and Corporate Affairs was set up in 1967, it was assumed that it would be a dominating force in protecting consumer rights in Canada. While the department has been active in the investigation of misleading price advertising, critics have argued that the department and the federal government have responded more to powerful special interest groups than to consumer interests.[14]

Growth of Public Interest Groups

The number and power of public interest groups have increased during the past two decades. The most successful is Ralph Nader's Public Citizen group, which "watchdogs" consumer interests. Nader built consumerism into a major social force, first with his successful attack on unsafe automobiles, and then through investigations of meat processing, truth-in-lending, auto repairs, insurance, and X-ray equipment. In Canada, the Consumers Association of Canada has led the fight to improve packages and labelling, standards for hockey helmets, children's car seats, inspection of meat plants and many other consumer areas.[15] Other Canadian consumer interest groups that have had an impact on marketing activities include Phil Edmunston's "Rusty Ford" group, Greenpeace, Pollution Probe, and Energy Probe.

Cultural Environment

The cultural environment is made up of institutions and other forces that affect society's basic values, perceptions, preferences, and behavior. People grow up in a particular society that shapes their basic beliefs and values. They absorb a world view that defines their relationship to themselves and others. The following cultural characteristics can affect marketing decision making.

Persistence of Cultural Values

People in every society hold many beliefs and values. Their core beliefs and values usually persist over time. For example, most Canadians believe in work, the institution of marriage, charity, and honesty. These beliefs shape more specific attitudes and behaviors found in everyday life. Core beliefs and values are passed on from parents to children and are reinforced by schools, churches, business, and government.

Secondary beliefs and values are more open to change. Believing in marriage is a core belief, while believing that people should get married early is a secondary belief. Family planning marketers could argue more effectively that people should get married later rather than that they should not get married at all. Marketers have some chance of changing secondary values, but little chance of changing core values.

Subcultures

In Canada there are at least two major societies, English and French. While these two share some core beliefs and values, major differences also exist. For example, French consumers in Quebec have a predisposition to rely more on their senses—touch, taste, smell, hearing—when making a purchase decision. The French consumer also tends to be "conservative" in purchasing, an expression of low risk-taking behavior. Finally, these two values combine to produce a third, called "non-price rationale," which means that consumers who are satisfied with a brand will not switch because of price considerations.[16] Other major differences between these two cultures will be discussed in the next chapter.

Along with the two major cultures, a large number of **subcultures** exist in Canada. These are groups of individuals who hold different beliefs and values from the cultural mainstream. For example, immigrants form subcultures because they have had different experiences and may have different beliefs and values. Sizeable communities of Italian, Ukrainian, German, and Chinese consumers exist in Canada. These communities are often served by their own newspapers and radio stations. Marketing to these groups requires special efforts because of the different patterns of consumer wants and behaviors.

Shifts in Secondary Cultural Values

Although core values are fairly consistent, cultural swings do take place. Consider the impact of the hippies, the Beatles, Elvis Presley, Michael Jackson, Bruce Springsteen, and other culture heroes on young people's hairstyles, clothing, and sexual norms. Marketers have a keen interest in anticipating cultural shifts in order to spot new marketing opportunities or threats. For example, the percentage of people who value physical fitness and well-being has been going up steadily over the years, especially in the under-30 group and the upscale group. Marketers will want to cater to this trend with appropriate products and communication appeals.

Summary

The company must start with the marketing environment when searching for opportunities and monitoring threats. The marketing environment consists of all the actors and forces that affect the company's ability to transact effectively with the target market. The company's marketing environment can be divided into the microenvironment and the macroenvironment.

The microenvironment consists of five components. The first is the company's internal environment—its several departments and management levels—as it affects marketing management's decision making. The second component includes the marketing channel firms that cooperate to improve the value of the product: the suppliers and marketing intermediaries (middlemen, physical distribution firms, marketing service agencies, financial intermediaries). The third component consists of the five types of markets in which the company can sell: the consumer, producer, reseller, government, and international markets. The fourth component consists of the competitors facing the company. The fifth component consists of all the publics that have an actual or potential interest in or impact on the organization's ability to achieve its objectives: financial, media, government, citizen action, and local, general, and internal publics.

The company's macroenvironment consists of major forces that shape opportunities and pose threats to the company: demographic, economic, natural, technological, political, and cultural.

The demographic environment shows a changing age structure in the Canadian population, a changing Canadian family, geographic population shifts, and a better-educated and more white-collar population. The economic environment shows changes in real income and consumer spending patterns. The natural environment shows coming shortages of certain raw materials, increased pollution levels, and increasing government intervention in natural resource management. The technological environment shows rapid technological change, unlimited opportunities for innovation, concentration on minor improvements rather than major discoveries, and increased regulation of technological change. The political environment shows increasing business regulation and the growth of public interest groups. The cultural environment shows the endurance of core values.

Questions for Discussion

1. Compare and contrast a company's microenvironments and macroenvironments.
2. How do publics differ from consumers? Explain by using a specific example.
3. Identify and briefly describe the six major components of a firm's macroenvironment.
4. It has been estimated that by 1990 approximately one-quarter of all Canadian families may be headed by only one adult. Discuss the impact this may have on marketers.
5. The average age in Canada is continuing to increase. Identify the reasons why the average age is increasing and the challenge it represents for marketers.
6. Identify and discuss several examples of new products that have been introduced to the market as a result of technological innovation.
7. Life style studies show a positive trend in the attitude that "meal preparation should take as little time as possible." How would this affect the sales of frozen vegetables?
8. The political environment has become increasingly active. How have the Consumers Association of Canada and the actions of the Department of Consumer and Corporate Affairs affected marketing decision making in recent years?

Chapter 5 Key Terms

Baby boom   The major increase in the annual birthrate following World War II and lasting until the early 1960s. The "baby boomers," now moving into middle age, are a prime target for marketers.

Company marketing environment   The actors and forces outside the firm that affect marketing management's ability to develop and maintain successful transactions with its target customers.

Cultural environment   Institutions and other forces that affect society's basic values, perceptions, preferences, and behaviors.

Demography   The study of human populations in terms of size, density, location, age, sex, race, occupation, and other statistics.

Economic environment   Factors that affect consumer purchasing power and spending patterns.

Macroenvironment   The larger societal forces that affect the whole microenvironment — demographic, economic, natural, technological, political, and cultural forces.

Marketing-intermediaries   Firms that help the company to promote, sell, and distribute its goods to final buyers; they include middlemen, physical distribution firms, marketing service agencies, and financial intermediaries.

Microenvironment   The forces close to the company that affect its ability to serve its customers — the company, market channel firms, customer markets, competitors, and publics.

Natural environment   Natural resources that are needed as inputs by marketers or that are affected by marketing activities.

Political environment   Laws, government agencies, and pressure groups that influence and limit various organizations and individuals in society.

Public   Any group that has an actual or potential interest in or impact on an organization's ability to achieve its objectives.

Suppliers   Firms and individuals that provide the resources needed by the company and its competitors to produce goods and services.

Technological environment   Forces that create new technologies, creating new product and market opportunities.

Cases for Chapter 5

Consumer Markets and Consumer Buying Behavior

Chapter Objectives

After reading this chapter, you should be able to:
1. Define the consumer market, and construct a simple model of consumer buying behavior.
2. Name the four major factors that influence consumer buying behavior.
3. List the stages in the buyer decision process.

A well-known slogan "You are what you eat" is causing concern among many marketers in the Canadian food industry. Due to shifts in demographics — in particular the aging of the Canadian population, changes in lifestyles, and new family structures — consumers are modifying their eating habits. Consider the following:

- Canada is a greying society — the average age of Canadians is increasing and by 1996 almost 7.6 million Canadians (28% of the population) will be over 50 years old. As well, there will be a 7% decline in the number of Canadians under 35. Older people need fewer calories than younger people, so total consumption of food is likely to decline in the future.

- The "well-being" syndrome is important for many Canadians and this translates to desire for physical fitness, good nutrition, and a healthy lifestyle. Consumers are concerned about what and how much they eat.

These demographic changes and other factors are causing a revolution in Canada's $46 billion food business. Those companies that respond quickly to changing consumer trends

are gaining sales and profits. Campbell Soup is one of them. Faced with a decline of 2% each year in sales of canned foods, and flat sales in the overall frozen food market, Campbell introduced Le Menu, a new high-priced line of frozen dinners. Le Menu was positioned as a gourmet-quality food that can be cooked in a microwave oven and served without any hassle. Sales of "gourmet" frozen dinners increased by 277% in one year, and Le Menu was one of the leaders.

Some companies have ignored or been slow to catch on to these trends. The meat industry, particularly beef producers, did not realize how much consumers were changing their eating habits. In 1976, consumption of red meats (beef, pork, and lamb) peaked at an annual per capita amount of 51.4 kilograms. Ten years later it had declined to 38.3 kilograms, which translates into lost revenues of about $2.6 billion for the red meat industry. Pork producers are finally responding to the trends. They have developed the "light" pork steak, a boneless chop made from lean, grain-fed pigs and trimmed of fat, that contains only half the calories of the "old" pork chop. This is the first major change made in pork in 20 years, and it seems to have worked. After six years of declining consumption, pork showed a 5% increase in 1986.

The marketers of fish, a product that has less fat and fewer calories than meat have also been winners. Moreover, the fat in fish is polyunsaturated, as opposed to the saturated fats in meat. Red Lobster, a chain of seafood restaurants, has set up shop in many sites formerly occupied by Ponderosa, a chain of steak houses. Red Lobster now has over 40 restaurants in Canada and expects yearly sales in each restaurant of over $2 million.

Marketers who fail to understand consumers and how their behaviors change over time will face a troubled future. Consumers need food, but what they buy is determined by their wants. Today, many want foods that fit an active, healthy lifestyle. Marketers who match these wants are more likely to survive and prosper than those who don't.[1]

Marketers have to be extremely careful in analyzing consumer behavior. Buying behavior is never simple, yet understanding it is the essential task of marketing management.

This chapter will explore the dynamics of consumer behavior and the consumer market:

The consumer market consists of all the individuals and households who buy or acquire goods and services for personal consumption.

The discussion will focus on the Canadian consumer market. In a later chapter, international markets will be considered. However, it is important to note that approximately one-third of all the goods and services that Canadians produce are sold in other countries. The Canadian consumer market is only one-tenth the size of the American consumer market, and Canada has less than 1% of the world's population. While it makes sense to start with the Canadian consumer market, many firms consider Canada just one of many markets in which they could operate.

In 1986, the Canadian consumer market consisted of about 26 million persons who consumed over $317 billion worth of goods and services — over $12 000 worth for every man, woman, and child. Each year this market grows by over 250 000 persons and another $15 billion.[2]

Consumers vary tremendously in age, income, education level, and tastes. Marketers have found it worthwhile to develop products and services tailored to the needs of specific consumer groups. If a market segment is large enough, some companies may set up special marketing programs to serve this market. Here are two examples of special consumer groups:

French consumers Constituting the second largest ethnic group in Canada (26% of the population) are over 6 000 000 French-speaking consumers, most of whom live in Quebec, Ontario, and New Brunswick. These consumers differ from other Canadians in a number of ways, some of which are discussed in Exhibit 6-1. Appealing to the French consumer requires knowledge of language, culture, and socio-economic characteristics of this target market. Some firms have taken English ad campaigns and had a literal translation done. For example, "car wash" literally translated meant "car enema" in French (lavement d'auto); "chicken to take out" has ended up as "chicken to go out with" (poulet pour sortir).[3]

University students as consumers   This group of over 400 000 consumers represents a total market of $2.4 billion. On average they spend $140 a month on discretionary items such as records, entertainment and stereo equipment. They spend disproportionately on sports equipment as the majority participate in some form of physical exercise including swimming, jogging, skiing and tennis. The one problem for marketers is that they cannot easily be reached by media as they are classified as light television viewers and radio listeners. Most read the campus and daily newspapers but few read national magazines (only 16% on average read *Maclean's*).[4]

Other consumer submarkets, for example, women, the elderly, or a cultural community like the Italians, also provide good opportunities for tailored marketing programs.

The 26 million consumers in Canada buy an incredible variety of goods and services. We will now look at how consumers make their choices among these products.

EXHIBIT 6-1
Are There Really Major Cultural Differences Between English and French Consumers?

Various studies that have looked at the differences between French and English consumers (or Quebec consumers and the rest of Canada) have reached conclusions such as:

- French-Canadian families serve more home-made soup than English-Canadian families.
- French-Canadian homemakers buy more packaged soups and cake mixes than canned soups and ready-made cakes.
- Quebec consumers drink more soft drinks per capita than the rest of Canada.
- French Canadians drink less Canadian whiskey than does the rest of Canada.
- The French Canadian, compared to other Canadians, shops less in chain stores.

These differences exist for three possible reasons: (1) true cultural differences, (2) socio-economic differences, or (3) differences in marketing strategies—particularly distribution—in Quebec. Few researchers have examined differences in culture or consumer behavior in the French market beyond socio-economic and marketing differences. For example, many of the studies ignored the fact that the population in Quebec had less formal education than other Canadians. In 1976, 31% of the Quebec population had less than nine years of formal schooling, while in the rest of Canada, only 23% of the population had as little schooling. Education, a determinant of social class, has been shown to influence some types of product choice and usage levels. However, were the differences in buying behavior due to cultural or educational differences? Similarly, many of the early studies did not control for income when there were substantial differences between Quebec (lower average income) and the rest of Canada. For example, in 1955, personal income per capita in Quebec was 85% of the national average, in 1965 it was

Exhibit 6-1 continued

CLIENT: PROCTER & GAMBLE INC.
PRODUIT: Secret
TITRE: "MOMENTS TENDRES"
DURÉE: 30 Sec. T.V.

(MUSIQUE D'AMBIANCE
DOUCE)
SAMANTHA: Chut...

BRETT: (S'APPROCHANT DU
BÉBÉ POUR LE SENTIR):
Hmmm! la poudre pour bébé...

SAMANTHA: C'est moi
que sens ça!

BRETT: Toi?
(SOURIRE MOQUEUR)

VHC: Oui, le nouveau Secret
en bâton ovale, parfumé à la
poudre pour bébé, nous aide
à rester bien au sec et bien
fraîche, toute la journée.

BRETT: Hmmm!

SAMANTHA: ...Et Secret est
spécialement conçu pour nous,
les femmes!

BRETT: Et moi?
SAMANTHA: Jean, ne fais
pas le bébé!

VHC: Le nouveau Secret en
bâton ovale, parfumé à la
poudre pour bébé... chut...

Procter & Gamble targets the French Canadian market.

88%, and in 1973 it was 90%. Again, the level of income has an effect on consumer behavior.

Four studies did consider cultural differences while controlling for income or education level. Their conclusions were that consumption patterns are different between Quebec and Ontario households (Palda, Thomas) and that both French males and females held different activities, interests, opinions, and behaviors than their English counterparts (Tigert). For example, the French-Canadian female is more oriented toward home, family, and kitchen, more interested in baking, and more fashion and appearance conscious. As a result, French-speaking families, compared to English-speaking families, use more staples, less frozen vegetables, consume more soft drinks, beer, and wine, and consume less hard liquor (Schaninger, et al.).

Some differences may also be due to marketing strategies. In Quebec, wine and beer are sold in "mom and pop" corner grocery stores. These products are significant "traffic generators" for these stores, with consumers buying many other food products in addition to their beverages. As a result, the major supermarket chains hold a lower market share of total foods sales than in other provinces. This and other external factors account for some differences in preferences and purchasing behavior.

It is dangerous to assume that an identical marketing strategy can have the same results with both English and French consumers. By 1981, the average income of consumers in Quebec was virtually the same as the rest of Canada and retail sales per capita in 1986 were only 4% below the national average. However, Quebec consumers spent more than the rest of Canadian consumers in food stores (15% more), hardware stores (15% more), furniture, appliance, television and radio stores (25% more), and in service stations (15% more). The Quebec consumers spent less on motor vehicles (9% less), and in book and stationery stores (31% less). Some of these differences in spending patterns are due to culture. The marketer must also consider the media habits of Quebeckers; they watch more television than do other Canadians and listen to more radio. The marketer can get an understanding of these differences and the implications for strategy through specific research studies on the French market.

Sources: Bruce Mallen, "French Canadian Consumer Behavior," Advertising and Sales Executive Club of Montreal, 1977; Maurice Brisebois, "Industrial Advertising and Marketing in Quebec," *The Marketer,* Spring-Summer 1966, pp. 10, 13; Bruce Mallen, "How Different is the French-Canadian Market?" *The Business Quarterly,* Fall 1967, pp. 59-66; E. Clifford, "Tippers Reflect Diverse Tastes of National Mosaic," *The Globe and Mail,* June 30 1979; *The Financial Post, Canadian Markets,* 1981, and *Canadian Markets,* 1982; Morris B. Holbrook and John A. Howard, "Frequently Purchased Non-durable Goods and Services," in *Selected Aspects of Consumer Behavior* (Washington: National Science Foundation, 1977), pp. 189-222; William L. Marr and Donald G. Paterson, *Canada: An Economic History* (Toronto: Macmillan of Canada, 1980), p. 426; Kristian S. Palda, "A Comparison of Consumer Expenditures in Quebec and Ontario," *Canadian Journal of Economics and Political Science,* February 1967, p. 26; Dwight R. Thomas, "Culture and Consumer Consumption: Behavior in English and French Canada," *Proceedings,* Marketing Division, CAAS Conference, Edmonton, 1975; Douglas J. Tigert, "Can a Separate Marketing Strategy for French Canada be Justified: Profiling English-French Markets Through Life Style Analysis," in Donald N. Thompson and David S.R. Leighton, eds., *Canadian Marketing: Problems and Prospects* (Toronto: Wiley of Canada, 1973), pp. 113-142; William Johnson, "Francophones Have Closed Income Gap," *The Globe and Mail,* January 20 1984, p. 11; *Market Research Handbook,* 1983, Statistics Canada, Catalog 63-224, Ottawa, November 1983. For further information on differences between English and French markets see Gail Chiasson, "The Quebec Market," *Marketing,* October 21 1981, pp. 21-52, "The Quebec Report," *Marketing,* June 13 1983, pp. 11-31; Charles M. Schaninger, Jacques C. Bourgeois, and W. Christian Buss, "French-English Canadian Subcultural Consumption Differences," *Journal of Marketing,* Spring 1985, pp. 82-92, and "Quebec Report," *Marketing,* May 27 1985, pp. 33, 36.

A Model of Consumer Behavior

In earlier times, marketers could learn about consumers through the daily experience of selling to them. As firms and markets have grown in size, however, many marketing decision makers have lost direct contact with their customers. Most managers have had to turn to consumer research. They are spending more money than ever to study consumers in an attempt to learn: Who buys? How do they buy? When do they buy? Where do they buy? Why do they buy?

The central question is: How do consumers respond to various marketing stimuli the company might use? The company that really understands how consumers will respond to different product features, prices, and advertising appeals has a great advantage over its competitors. Therefore companies and academics have heavily researched the relationship between marketing stimuli and consumer response. Their starting point is the simple stimulus-response model shown in Figure 6-1. This figure shows that marketing and other stimuli enter the consumer's "black box" and produce certain responses. Marketers must figure out what is in the buyer's "black box."

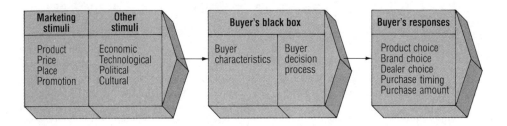

FIGURE 6-1
Detailed Model of Buyer Behavior

On the left in Figure 6-1, marketing stimuli consist of the four Ps—product, price, place, and promotion. Other stimuli include major forces and events in the buyer's environment—economic, technological, political, and cultural. All these stimuli enter the buyer's black box, where they are turned into a set of observable buyer responses shown on the right—product choice, brand choice, dealer choice, purchase timing, and purchase amount.

The marketer must understand how the stimuli are changed into responses inside the consumer's black box. The black box has two parts. First, the buyer's characteristics influence how he or she perceives and reacts to the stimuli. Second, the buyer's decision process itself affects outcomes. This chapter looks first at buyer characteristics as they affect buying behavior. It then examines the buyer decision process.

Personal Characteristics Affecting Consumer Behavior

Consumer purchases are strongly influenced by cultural, social, personal, and psychological characteristics. These factors are shown in Figure 6-2. For the most part they cannot be controlled by the marketer, but they must be taken into account. We want to examine the influence of each factor on a buyer's behavior. We will illustrate these characteristics for the case of a hypothetical consumer named Betty Smith:

> Betty Smith is a married college graduate who works as a brand manager in a leading consumer packaged-goods company. She currently wants to find a new leisure time activity that will offer some contrast to her working day. This need has led her to consider buying a camera and taking up photography. Many characteristics in her background will affect the way she goes about looking at cameras and choosing a brand.

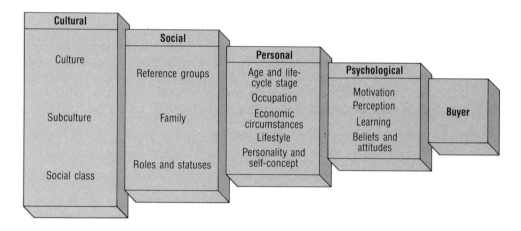

FIGURE 6-2
Detailed Model of Factors Influencing Behavior

Cultural Factors

Cultural factors exert the broadest and deepest influence on consumer behavior. We will look at the role played by the buyer's culture, subculture, and social class.

Culture

Culture is at the root of a person's wants and behavior. Human behavior is largely learned. The child growing up in a society learns basic values, perceptions, wants, and behaviors from the family and other key institutions.

Betty Smith's desire for a camera is a result of being raised in a modern society where camera technology and a whole set of consumer learnings and values have developed. Betty knows what cameras are. She knows how to read instructions on how to operate cameras, and her society has accepted the idea of women photographers. In another culture, for example, an aboriginal tribe in central Australia, a camera may mean nothing. It may simply be a curiosity.

Subculture

Each culture contains smaller subcultures, or groups of people with shared value systems based on common life experiences and situations. Nationality groups such as the Italians, Portuguese, and Germans are found within large communities and have distinct ethnic tastes and interests. Religious groups such as Catholics, Protestants, Lutherans, and Jews are subcultures with their own preferences and taboos. Racial groups such as the Chinese have distinct culture styles and attitudes. Geographical areas such as parts of the Maritimes have distinct subcultures with characteristic life styles.

Betty Smith's interest in various goods will be influenced by her nationality, religion, race, and geographical background. These factors will affect her food preferences, clothing choices, recreation, and career goals. Subcultures attach different meanings to picture taking, which could affect Betty's interest in cameras and the brand she buys.

Social Class

Almost every society has some form of social class structure.

> *Social classes are relatively permanent and ordered divisions in a society whose members share similar values, interests, and behaviors.*

Social scientists have identified the six social classes shown in Table 6-1.[5]

Social class is not indicated by a single factor such as income, but is measured as a combination of occupation, income, education, wealth, and other variables. Marketers are interested in social class because people within a given social class tend to have similar behavior, including buying behavior.

Social classes show distinct product and brand preferences in such areas as clothing, home furnishings, leisure activity, and automobiles. Betty Smith's social class may affect her camera decision. She may have come from a higher social class background. In this case, her family probably owned an expensive camera and may have dabbled in photography. The fact that she thinks about "going professional" is also in line with a higher social class background.

TABLE 6-1
Characteristics of Six Major Social Classes

---

1. Upper uppers (less than 1 percent)

The social elite with inherited wealth and a well-known family background. They give large sums to charity, maintain more than one home, and send their children to the finest schools. They are a market for jewelry, antiques, homes, and vacations. They often buy and dress conservatively. While small as a group, their consumption decisions trickle down and are imitated by the other social classes.

2. Lower uppers (about 2 percent)

Persons who have earned high income or wealth from the professions or business. They usually come from the middle class. They tend to be active in social and civic affairs and buy the symbols of status for themselves and their children, such as expensive homes, schools, yachts, swimming pools, and automobiles. They want acceptance in the upper-upper stratum, which is more likely to be achieved by their children than themselves.

3. Upper middles (12 percent)

Persons who possess neither family status nor unusual wealth. They are primarily concerned with "career." They have attained positions as professionals, independent businesspersons, and corporate managers. They believe in education and want their children to develop professional or administrative skills so that they will not drop into a lower stratum. They are joiners and highly civic-minded. They are the quality market for good homes, clothes, furniture, and appliances.

4. Lower middles (30 percent)

Primarily "white collars" (office workers, small-business owners), "gray collars" (mailmen, firemen), and "aristocrat blue collars" (plumbers, factory foremen). They want "respectability." They have conscientious work habits and adhere to culturally defined norms and standards, including going to church and obeying the law. The home is important, and lower middles like to keep it neat and "pretty." They buy conventional home furnishings and do a lot of their own work around the home. They prefer clothes that are neat and clean rather than high-styled.

5. Upper lowers (35 percent)

The largest social class segment, including blue-collar working class of skilled and semiskilled factory workers. While they seek respectability, their main drive is security, "protecting what they have." The working-class husband has a strong "all-male" self-image, being a sports enthusiast, outdoorsman, and heavy smoker and beer drinker. Working-class wives often hold full- or part-time jobs to bring in extra income. Those not working spend most of their time in the house cooking, cleaning, and caring for their children.

6. Lower lowers (20 percent)

The bottom of society consisting of poorly educated, unskilled laborers. They are often out of work and on some form of public assistance. Their housing is typically substandard and located in slum areas. They often reject middle-class standards of morality and behavior. They buy more impulsively. They often do not evaluate quality, and they pay too much for products and buy on credit.

Source: Adapted from James F. Engel, Roger D. Blackwell, and David T. Kollat, *Consumer Behavior*, Third ed. (New York: Holt, Rinehart & Winston, 1978), pp. 127-28.

Social Factors

A consumer's behavior is also influenced by social factors, such as the consumer's reference groups, family, and social roles and status.

Reference Groups

A person's behavior is influenced by many reference groups.

Reference groups are groups that have a direct (face-to-face) or indirect influence on the person's attitudes or behavior.

Reference groups have a significant influence on a person's norms, life style, and buying behavior.

Reference groups that have a direct influence and to which a person belongs are called membership groups. Some are primary groups with whom there is regular informal interaction, such as family, friends, neighbors, and co-workers. Some are secondary groups, which are more formal and have less regular interaction. They include organizations such as religious groups, professional associations, and trade unions.

People are also influenced by groups to which they do not belong. An aspirational group is one to which the individual wishes to belong. For example, a teenage hockey player may aspire to play someday for the Edmonton Oilers. He identifies with this group although there is no face-to-face contact.

Marketers try to identify the reference groups of their target markets. Reference groups influence a person in at least three ways. They expose the person to new behaviors and life styles. They influence the person's attitudes and self-concept because he or she wants to "fit in." They also create pressures to conform that may affect the person's product and brand choices (see Exhibit 6-2).

The importance of group influence varies across products and brands.[6] It tends to be strongest when the product is visible to others whom the buyer respects. Purchases of products that are bought and used privately are not much affected by group influences because neither the product nor the brand will be noticed by others. If Betty Smith buys a camera, both the product and the brand will be visible to others she respects. Her decision to buy the camera and her

EXHIBIT 6-2
Home-Party Selling—Using Reference Groups to Sell

An increasingly popular form of nonstore selling involves throwing sales parties in homes and inviting friends and acquaintances to see merchandise demonstrated. Each year, more than one million Canadians, mostly women, hold home parties to sell personal care or home items. The women at these parties spend over $300 million annually, mainly on cosmetics and kitchen products. Home parties in Canada now account for 30% of the direct sales market. Companies such as Mary Kay Cosmetics and Tupperware Home Parties are masters at this form of selling and have enjoyed good sales and profits. Here is how home-party selling works.

A Mary Kay "beauty consultant" (there are 12 000 in Canada) will ask different neighbors to hold small beauty shows in their homes. The neighbor will invite her friends for a few hours of informal socializing and refreshment. Within this congenial atmosphere, the Mary Kay consultant will give a two-hour beauty plan and free makeup lessons to the guests, hoping that the majority of the guests will buy some of the cosmetics just demonstrated. The hostess receives a commission of approximately 15% on sales plus a discount on personal purchases. About 60% of the guests are likely to purchase something, partly because they want to look good in the other women's eyes.

There are at least 35 different home-party companies in Canada selling cosmetics, cookware, household products, dresses, shoes, and lingerie. Mary Kay Cosmetics, now 25 years old, uses a highly motivational approach, rewarding its saleswomen for recruiting new consultants—called "offspring"—and honoring the top saleswomen at the annual convention by naming them Queens of Personal Sales and giving them a pink Cadillac to drive for an entire year. Mary Kay's enterprise depends on her sharp understanding of women and how they can influence each other in the buying process.

Sources: David D. Seltz, "The Party-Plan Concept," in *Handbook of Innovative Marketing Techniques* (Reading, Mass.: Addison-Wesley, 1981), pp. 3-11; Helen Kohl, "Enterprise Begins at Home," *The Financial Post Magazine*, October 15 1982, pp. 20-28; and David Olive, "All the Way with Mary Kay," *Canadian Business*, November 1984, pp. 77-81.

brand choice may be strongly influenced by some of her groups. Friends who belong to a photography club may influence her to buy a good camera.

Family

Family members can have a strong influence on the buyer's behavior. The family is the most important consumer-buying organization in society and it has been researched extensively. Marketers are interested in the roles and influence of the husband, wife, and children in the purchase of different products and services.

Five different roles and influences can be identified:

1. ***Initiator***   The initiator is the person who first suggests or thinks of buying the particular product or service.

2. **Influencer**   *An influencer is a person whose views or advice carry some weight in making the final decision.*

3. **Decider**   *The decider is a person who ultimately determines any part of or the entire buying decision: whether to buy, what to buy, how to buy, when to buy, or where to buy.*

4. **Buyer**   *The buyer is the person who makes the actual purchase.*

5. **User**   *The user is the person(s) who consumes or uses the product or service.*

Husband-wife involvement varies widely by product category. The wife has traditionally been the main buyer for the family, especially for food and clothing. This situation is changing with the increased number of working wives and the willingness of husbands to do more of the family purchasing. Marketers of basic products would therefore be making a mistake to continue to think of women as the main or only purchasers of their product.

In the case of expensive products and services, husbands and wives more often make joint decisions. In the case of Betty Smith buying a camera, her husband will play an influencer role. He may have an opinion about her purchase of a camera and the kind of camera to buy. At the same time, she will be the primary decider, purchaser, and user.

The ways in which families make decisions also depend on whether or not the household has children. In a study of where and when to take a vacation, Filiatrault and Ritchie found that although Canadian husbands tended to dominate the "vacation" decision in families with children, joint decision making was more prevalent in couples with no children.[7] As a result, marketers might consider different approaches to "couples" versus "families" in promoting vacation travel.

Roles and Status

A person may belong to many groups — family, clubs, organizations. The person's position in each group can be defined in terms of *role* and *status*. With her parents, Betty Smith plays the role of daughter; in her family, she plays the role of wife; in her company, she plays the role of brand manager. A role consists of the activities a person is expected to perform according to the persons around him or her. Each of Betty's roles will influence some of her buying behavior.

Each role carries a status reflecting the general esteem accorded it by society. The role of brand manager has more status in this society than the role of daughter. As a brand manager, Betty will buy the kind of clothing that reflects her role and status.

Personal Factors

A buyer's decisions are also influenced by personal characteristics such as the buyer's age and life-cycle stage, occupation, economic situation, life style, and personality and self-concept.

Age and Life-Cycle Stage

People change the goods and services they consume over their lifetimes. They eat baby food in the early years, a wide variety of foods in the growing and mature years, and special diets in the later years. People's taste in clothes, furniture, and recreation is also age-related.

Buying is also shaped by the stage of the **family life cycle**. Nine stages of the family life cycle are listed in Table 6-2, along with the financial situation and typical product interests of each group. Marketers often define their target markets in terms of life-cycle stages, and develop appropriate products and marketing plans.[8]

TABLE 6-2
An Overview of the Family Life Cycle and Buying Behavior

Stage in family life cycle	Buying or behavioral pattern
1. Bachelor stage: Young single people not living at home	Few financial burdens. Fashion opinion leaders. Recreation-oriented. Buy: basic kitchen equipment, basic furniture, cars, equipment for the mating game, vacations.
2. Newly married couples: Young, no children	Better off financially than they will be in near future. Highest purchase rate and highest average purchase of durables. Buy: cars, refrigerators, stoves, sensible and durable furniture, vacations.
3. Full nest I: Youngest child under six	Home purchasing at peak. Liquid assets low. Dissatisfied with financial position and amount of money saved. Interested in new products. Like advertised products. Buy: washers, dryers, TV, baby food, chest rubs and cough medicines, vitamins, dolls, wagons, sleds, skates.
4. Full nest II: Youngest child six or over	Financial position better. Some wives work. Less influenced by advertising. Like larger-sized packages, multiple-unit deals. Buy: many foods, cleaning materials, bicycles, music lessons, pianos.
5. Full nest III: Older married couples with dependent children	Financial position still better. More wives work. Some children get jobs. Hard to influence with advertising. High average purchase of durables. Buy: new, more tasteful furniture, auto travel, nonnecessary appliances, boats, dental services, magazines.
6. Empty nest I: Older married couples, no children living with them, head in labor force	Home ownership at peak. Most satisfied with financial position and money saved. Interested in travel, recreation, self-education. Make gifts and contributions. Not interested in new products. Buy: vacations, luxuries, home improvements.
7. Empty nest II: Older married, no children living at home, head retired	Drastic cut in income. Keep home. Buy: medical appliances, medical care products that aid health, sleep, and digestion.
8. Solitary survivor, in labor force	Income still good but likely to sell home.
9. Solitary survivor, retired	Same medical and product needs as other retired group; drastic cut in income. Special need for attention, affection, and security.

Sources: William D. Wells and George Gubar, "Life Cycle Concepts in Marketing Research," *Journal of Marketing Research*, November 1966, pp. 355-63, here p. 362. Also see Patrick E. Murphy and William A. Staples, "A Modernized Family Life Cycle," *Journal of Consumer Research*, June 1979, pp. 12-22; and Janet Wagner and Sherman Hanna, "The Effectiveness of Family Life Cycle Variables in Consumer Expenditure Research," *Journal of Consumer Research*, December 1983, pp. 281-91.

Some changes in this family life-cycle concept have been suggested because a number of demographic shifts have altered the composition of the "typical" Canadian family.[9] Three major shifts have occurred. First, the overall decline in family size will mean that the "full nest" stages may no longer be the predominant portion of the family life cycle. Second, the tendency to delay the time of first marriage will increase the amount of time women and men spend in the bachelor stage. Third, the increased rate of divorces in Canada, from about 3000 in 1960 to over 70 000 in 1986, suggests that a new category of "divorced" should be incorporated into the stages. To illustrate, the number of single-parent families in Canada, because of divorce or other reasons, exceeds 11% of all households or more than 720 000 families.[10] With the changing sizes of these stages and the development of new stages, new opportunities are appearing for marketers, including a dramatic increase in the demand for day care facilities.

Occupation

A person's occupation affects the purchase of goods and services. A blue-collar worker may buy work clothes, work shoes, lunch boxes, and bowling recreation. A company president may buy expensive clothes, air travel, country club membership, and a large sailboat. Marketers try to identify the occupational groups that have an above-average interest in their products and services. A company can even specialize in making products needed by a given occupational group. As an example, Mark's Work Wearhouse has targeted part of its retail offering to meet the needs of workers in physical occupations, such as construction workers.

Economic Situation

A person's economic situation will greatly affect product choice. A person's economic situation consists of spendable income, savings, assets, borrowing power, and attitude toward spending versus saving. For example, a study of Canadian buyers of furniture and appliances found that financial constraints lead consumers to search longer and delay major purchases.[11] Thus, Betty Smith can consider buying an expensive Nikon if she has enough spendable income, savings, or borrowing power. Marketers of income-sensitive goods closely watch trends in personal income, savings, and interest rates. If economic indicators point to a recession, marketers can take steps to redesign, reposition, and reprice their product.

Life Style

People coming from the same subculture, social class, and even occupation may have quite different life styles.

> Life style is a person's pattern of living as expressed in his or her activities, interests, and opinions.

Life style captures something more than the person's social class or personality. It profiles a person's whole pattern of acting and interacting in the world. The technique of measuring life styles is known as **psychographics**.[12] It involves measuring dimensions related to activities, interests, and opinions. Using these measures, 14 Canadian life style types have been identified, such as ''Sue, the social single'' and ''Steve, the hard hat.''[13]

 People's life styles affect their buying behavior. Betty Smith, for example, can choose to live like a capable homemaker, a career woman, or a free spirit. She plays several roles, and her way of reconciling them expresses her life style. If she becomes a professional photographer, this would change her life style, in turn changing what and how she buys. When preparing strategies, marketers must search for relationships between the product or brand and life style groups.[14]

Personality and Self-Concept

Each person's distinct personality will influence his or her buying behavior.

> *Personality is a person's distinguishing psychological characteristics that lead to relatively consistent and lasting responses to his or her environment.*

Personality is usually described in terms of such traits as self-confidence, sociability, affiliation, and achievement.[15] Personality can be useful in analyzing consumer behavior for some product or brand choices. For example, a beer company may discover that heavy beer drinkers tend to be very sociable and aggressive. This suggests a possible brand image for the beer, and the type of people to show in the advertising. Many marketers use a concept related to personality — a person's **self-concept** (also called self-image). All of us have a complex mental picture of ourselves. For example, Betty Smith may see herself as outgoing, creative, and active. Therefore, she will favor a camera that projects the same qualities. If the Nikon is promoted as a camera for outgoing, creative, and active people, then its brand image will match her self-image. Marketers should try to develop brand images that match the self-image of the target market.[16]

Psychological Factors

A person's buying choices are also influenced by four major psychological factors — motivation, perception, learning, and beliefs and attitudes.

Motivation

We saw that Betty Smith became interested in buying a camera. Why? What is she really seeking? What needs is she trying to satisfy?

 A person has many needs at any given time. Some needs are **biological**, arising from states of tension such as hunger, thirst, or discomfort. Other needs are **psychological**, arising from states of tension such as the need for recognition, esteem, or belonging. Most of these needs will not be strong enough to motivate the person to act at a given point in time. A need becomes a motive when it is aroused to a sufficient level of intensity.

A motive (or drive) is a need that is sufficiently pressing to direct the person to seek satisfaction of the need.

Psychologists have developed theories of human motivation. Two of the most popular — the theories of Sigmund Freud and Abraham Maslow — have quite different meanings for consumer analysis and marketing.

Freud's Theory of Motivation

Freud assumes that people are largely unconscious about the real psychological forces shaping their behavior. He suggests that people repress many urges as they grow up. These urges are never eliminated or under perfect control; they emerge in dreams, in slips of the tongue, in neurotic and obsessive behavior, or ultimately in psychoses.

According to Freud's theory, a person does not fully understand his or her motivation. If Betty Smith wants to purchase an expensive camera, she may describe her motive as wanting a hobby or career. At a deeper level, she may be purchasing the camera to impress others with her creative talent. At a still deeper level, she may be buying the camera to feel young and independent again.

Motivational researchers collect in-depth information from small samples of consumers to uncover the deeper motives for their product choices. They use various "projective techniques" to throw the ego off guard — techniques such as word association, sentence completion, picture interpretation, and role playing. Motivation researchers have reached some interesting and sometimes odd conclusions about what may be in the buyer's mind regarding certain purchases. They have suggested that:

- Consumers resist prunes because they are wrinkled-looking and remind people of sickness and old age.

- Men smoke cigars as an adult version of thumbsucking.

- Women prefer vegetable shortening to animal fats because the latter arouse a sense of guilt over killing animals.

- A woman is very serious when baking a cake because unconsciously she is going through the symbolic act of giving birth.

Maslow's Theory of Motivation

Abraham Maslow sought to explain why people are driven by particular needs at particular times.[17] Why does one person spend lots of time and energy on personal safety and another on acquiring the esteem of others? His answer is that human needs are arranged in a hierarchy, from the most pressing to the least pressing. Maslow's hierarchy of needs is shown in Figure 6-3.

The hierarchy, in order of importance, consists of **physiological** needs, **safety** needs, **social** needs, **esteem** needs, and **self-actualization** needs. A person will try to satisfy the most important needs first. When the most important need is satisfied, it will stop being a motivator for the present time, and the person will be motivated to satisfy the next most important need.

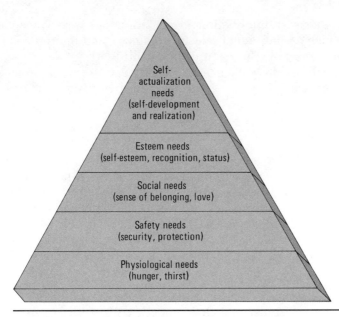

Adapted from *Motivation and Personality*, Second edition, Abraham H. Maslow, Copyright © 1970 by Abraham H. Maslow. Reprinted by permission of Harper & Row, Publishers, Inc.

FIGURE 6-3
Maslow's Hierarchy of Needs

For example, a starving man (need 1) will not take an interest in the latest happenings in the art world (need 5), nor in how he is seen or esteemed by others (needs 3 or 4), nor even in whether he is breathing clean air (need 2). But as each important need is satisfied, the next most important need will come into play.

What light does Maslow's theory throw on Betty Smith's interest in buying a camera? We can guess that Betty has satisfied her physiological, safety, and social needs; they do not motivate her interest in cameras. Her camera interest might come from a strong need for more esteem from others, or it might come from a need for self-actualization. She wants to be a creative person and express herself through photography.

Perception

A motivated person is ready to act. How the motivated person acts is influenced by his or her *perception* of the situation. Two people with the same motivation and in the same situation may act quite differently because they perceive the situation differently. Betty Smith might consider a fast-talking camera salesperson loud and phony. Another camera buyer might consider the same salesperson intelligent and helpful.

Why do people have different perceptions of the same situation? All of us learn about a stimulus by the flow of information through our five senses: sight, hearing, smell, touch, and taste. However, each of us receives, organizes, and interprets this sensory information in an individual way. Perception is the process by which an individual selects, organizes, and interprets information inputs to create a meaningful picture of the world.[18]

People can form different perceptions of the same stimulus because of three perceptual processes: selective exposure, selective distortion, and selective retention.

Selective Exposure

People are exposed to a great amount of stimuli every day. For example, the average person may be exposed to over 1500 ads a day. It is impossible for a person to pay attention to all these stimuli. Most will be screened out. Selective exposure means that marketers have to work especially hard to attract the consumer's attention. Their message will be lost on most people who are not in the market for the product. Even people who are in the market may not notice the message unless it stands out from the surrounding sea of other ads.

Selective Distortion

Even stimuli that consumers notice do not always come across in the intended way. Each person tries to fit incoming information into his or her existing mind set. Selective distortion describes the tendency of people to twist information into personal meanings. Betty Smith may hear the salesperson mention some good and bad points about a competing camera brand. Since she already has a strong leaning toward Nikon, she is likely to distort the points in order to conclude that Nikon is the better camera. People tend to interpret information in a way that will support what they already believe.

Selective Retention

People forget much that they learn. They tend to retain information that supports their attitudes and beliefs. Because of selective retention, Betty is likely to remember good points mentioned about the Nikon and forget good points mentioned about competing cameras. She remembers Nikon's good points because she "rehearses" them whenever she thinks about choosing a camera.

These three perceptual factors — selective exposure, distortion, and retention — mean that marketers have to work hard to get their messages through. This explains why marketers use so much drama and repetition in sending messages to their market.

Learning

When people act, they learn.

> *Learning describes changes in an individual's behavior arising from experience.*

Most human behavior is learned. Learning theorists say that learning occurs through the interplay of drives, stimuli, cues, responses, and reinforcement.

We saw that Betty Smith has a drive for self-actualization. A **drive** is a strong internal stimulus that calls for action. Her drive becomes a **motive** when it is directed toward a particular **stimulus object**, in this case a camera. Betty's response to the idea of buying a camera is conditioned by the surrounding cues. **Cues** are minor stimuli that determine when, where, and how the person responds. Seeing cameras in a shop window, hearing of a special sales price, and being encouraged by her husband are all cues that can influence Betty's **response** to the impulse to buy a camera.

Suppose Betty buys the camera. If the experience is **rewarding**, the probability is that she will use the camera more and more. Her response to cameras will be **reinforced**. Then the next time she buys a camera, or binoculars, or similar product, the probability is greater that she will buy a Nikon.

The practical significance of learning theory for marketers is that they can build up demand for a product by associating it with strong drives, using motivating cues, and providing positive reinforcement.

Beliefs and Attitudes

Through acting and learning, people acquire beliefs and attitudes. These in turn influence their buying behavior.

A belief is a descriptive thought that a person holds about something.

Betty Smith may believe that a Nikon takes great pictures, stands up well under hard use, and costs $550. These beliefs may be based on real knowledge, opinion, or faith. They may or may not carry an emotional charge. For example, Betty Smith's belief that a Nikon camera is heavy may or may not matter to her decision.

Marketers are very interested in the beliefs that people carry in their heads about specific products and services. These beliefs make up product and brand images, and people act on their beliefs. If some of the beliefs are wrong and prevent purchase, the marketer would want to launch a campaign to correct these beliefs.

People have attitudes regarding almost everything: religion, politics, clothes, music, food, and so on.

An attitude describes a person's enduring favorable or unfavorable cognitive evaluations, emotional feelings, and action tendencies toward some object or idea.[19]

Attitudes put people into a frame of mind to like or dislike things, moving toward or away from them. Betty Smith may hold such attitudes as "Buy the best," "The Japanese make the best products in the world," and "Creativity and self-expression are among the most important things in life." The Nikon camera therefore fits well into Betty's existing attitudes. A company would benefit greatly from researching the various attitudes people have that might bear on its product.

Attitudes are very difficult to change. A person's various attitudes fit into a pattern, and to change one attitude may require difficult adjustments in many others. A company would be well advised to fit its products into existing attitudes, rather than to try to change people's attitudes. There are exceptions, of course, where the great cost of trying to change attitudes may pay off.

We can now appreciate the many individual characteristics and forces acting on consumer behavior. The person's choice is the result of the complex interplay of cultural, social, personal, and psychological factors. Many of these factors cannot be influenced by the marketer. However, they are useful in identifying the buyers who may be more interested in the product.

The Buyer Decision Process

Now that we have looked at all the influences that affect buyers, we are ready to look at how consumers make buying decisions. Figure 6-4 shows the buyer decision process consisting of five stages: **problem recognition**, **information search**, **evaluation of alternatives**, **purchase decision**, and **postpurchase behavior**. This model emphasizes that the buying process starts long before the actual purchase and continues long after the purchase. It encourages the marketer to focus on the entire buying process, rather than just the purchase decision.[20]

FIGURE 6-4
Buyer Decision Process

This decision process model seems to imply that consumers pass through all five stages with every purchase they make. Whether or not a consumer passes through all five stages or skips or reverses some of these stages depends on the complexity of the product for the consumer. There are great differences between buying toothpaste, a tennis racket, an expensive camera, and a new car. Howard and Sheth have suggested that consumer buying can be viewed as problem-solving activity, and have distinguished three types of buying situations.[21]

Routinized Response Behavior

The simplest type of buying behavior occurs in the purchase of low-cost, frequently purchased items. Buyers have very few decisions to make as they are well acquainted with the product class, know the major brands, and have fairly clear preferences among the brands. They do not always buy the same brand because choice can be in fluenced by stockouts, special deals, and a wish for variety. In general, however, buyers' operations are routinized, and they are not likely to give much thought, search, or time to the purchase. The goods in this class are often called **low involvement** goods. Buyers often have a low interest in this class of goods and frequently purchase a particular brand through habit.

The marketer's task in this situation is twofold. With respect to current customers, the marketer should provide positive reinforcement. The brand's quality, stock level, and value must be maintained. With respect to potential customers, the marketer must break their normal buying habits by cues that call attention to the brand and its value in relation to the buyers' preferred brands. These cues include new features or benefits, point-of-purchase displays, price specials, and premiums.

Limited Problem Solving

Buying is more complex when buyers confront an unfamiliar brand in a familiar product class that requires information before making a purchase choice. For example, persons thinking about buying a new tennis racket may hear about a new oversized brand called the Prince. They may ask questions and look at ads to learn more about the new brand concept before choosing. This approach is described as limited problem solving because buyers are fully aware of the product class and the qualities they want, but are not familiar with all the brands and their features.

The marketer recognizes that consumers try to reduce risk through information gathering. The marketer must design a communication program that will increase the buyer's brand comprehension and confidence.

Extensive Problem Solving

Buying reaches its greatest complexity when buyers face an unfamiliar product class and do not know what criteria to use. For example, a man may become interested in buying a citizen-band receiver for the first time. He had heard brand names such as Cobra, Panasonic, and Lloyd's, but lacks clear brand concepts. He does not even know what product-class-attributes to consider in choosing a good citizen-band receiver. He is in a state of extensive problem solving.

The marketer of products in this class, often called **high-involvement goods**, must understand the information-gathering and evaluation activities of prospective buyers. The marketer's task is to facilitate the buyer's learning of the attributes of the product class, their relative importance, and the high standing of the brand on the more important attributes.

The model in Figure 6-4 shows all considerations that arise when a consumer faces a new and complex purchase situation. We will use this model to follow Betty Smith, in order to understand how she became interested in buying an expensive camera and the stages she went through to make the final choice.

Problem Recognition

The buying process starts when the buyer recognizes a problem or need. The buyer senses a difference between his or her actual state and a desired state. The need can be triggered by internal stimuli. One of the person's normal needs —hunger, thirst, sex—rises to a high enough level and becomes a drive. From previous experience, the person has learned how to cope with this drive and is motivated toward objects that he or she knows will satisfy this drive.

A need can also be triggered by external stimuli. Betty Smith passes a bakery and the sight of freshly baked bread stimulates her hunger; she admires a neighbor's new car; or she watches a television commercial for a Jamaican vacation. All of these can lead her to recognize a problem or need.

The marketer at this stage needs to determine the factors and situations that usually trigger consumer problem recognition. The marketer should research consumers to find out what kinds of needs or problems arose, what brought them about, and how they led to this particular product.

Betty Smith might answer that she felt the need for a new hobby when her busy season at work slowed down. She thought of cameras after talking to a friend about photography. By gathering such information, the marketer can identify the stimuli that most often trigger interest in the product and develop marketing programs that involve these stimuli.

Information Search

An aroused consumer may or may not search for more information. If the consumer's drive is strong and a satisfying product is near at hand, the consumer is likely to buy it then. If not, the consumer may simply store the need in memory and search for information bearing on the need.

At one level, the buyer may simply have "heightened attention." Here Betty Smith simply becomes more receptive to information about cameras. She pays attention to camera ads, cameras used by friends, and conversations about cameras.

Alternatively, Betty may actively search for information by looking for reading material, phoning friends, and gathering product information in other ways. How much searching she does will depend upon the strength of her drive, the amount of information she starts with, the ease of obtaining more information, the value she places on additional information, and the satisfaction she gets from searching.

How much search is undertaken can also be explained in part by perceived risk.[22] In many situations consumers are concerned that they make the right product and brand choice. They cannot be certain about the performance and psychosocial consequences of their purchase decision. This uncertainty produces anxiety or perceived risk. The three most common types of perceived risk are: **financial** — "Can I afford to purchase this product?"; **performance** — "Will this product work and continue to work to my satisfaction when I get it home?"; and **social** — "Will my family or friends, or reference groups approve of my purchase decision?"

Consumers develop strategies for reducing perceived risk. For example, consumers may search for more information in an attempt to make the "right" purchase decision. Consumers may look for a lower-priced brand to reduce financial risk, they may read *Canadian Consumer* or *Consumer Reports* to determine product reliability and reduce performance risk, or they may take along a friend or a "purchase pal" to obtain social approval and reduce social risk. Consumers may also use other strategies to reduce perceived risk, including delaying the purchase, purchasing national brands from well-known retailers, and buying brands that have warranties. Marketers need to understand the factors that provoke perceived risk in the consumer and attempt to provide information and support that will help reduce that risk.

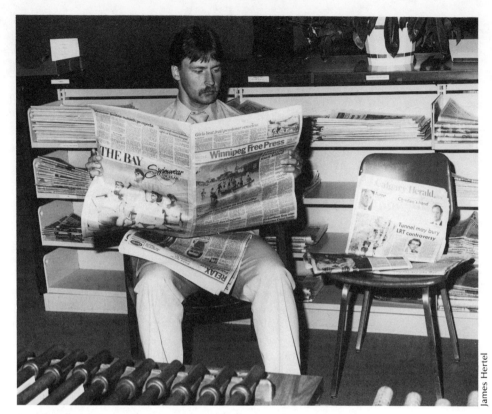

An advertisement can lead a consumer to recognize a need.

The consumer can obtain information from any of several sources. These include:

Personal sources: *family, friends, neighbors, acquaintances*

Commercial sources: *advertising, salespersons, dealers, packaging, displays*

Public sources: *mass media, consumer-rating organizations*

Experiential sources: *handling, examining, using the product*

The relative influence of these information sources varies with the product and the buyer. Generally the consumer receives the most information about a product from commercial sources, which are dominated by the marketer. The most effective sources, however, tend to be personal sources. Commercial sources normally inform the buyer, but personal sources legitimize or evaluate products for the buyer. For example, doctors normally learn of new drugs from commercial sources, but turn to other doctors for evaluation information.

As a result of gathering information, the consumer increases his or her awareness and knowledge of the available brands and their features. In looking for information, Betty Smith found out about the many camera brands available.

The information also helped her drop certain brands from consideration. A company must design its marketing mix to make prospects aware of and knowledgeable about its brand. If it fails to do this, the company must also learn which other brands customers consider, so that it knows its competition and can plan its appeals.

The marketer should carefully identify consumers' sources of information and the importance of each source. Consumers should be asked how they first heard about the brand, what information they received, and the importance they place on different information sources. This information is critical in preparing effective communication to target markets.

Evaluation of Alternatives

We have seen how the consumer uses information to arrive at a set of final brand choices. Now the question is: How does the consumer choose among the alternative brands? The marketer needs to know how the consumer processes information to arrive at brand choices. Unfortunately, there is no simple and single evaluation process used by all consumers, or even by one consumer in all buying situations. There are several evaluation processes.

Certain basic concepts will help explain consumer evaluation processes. First, we assume that each consumer sees a product as a bundle of **product attributes**. For cameras, these attributes include picture quality, ease of use, camera size, price, and others. Consumers will vary as to which of these attributes they consider relevant, and will pay the most attention to those attributes connected with their needs.

Second, the consumer will attach different **importance weights** to the attributes. That is, each consumer attaches importance to each attribute according to his or her unique needs and wants.

Third, the consumer is likely to develop a set of **brand** beliefs about where each brand stands on each attribute. The set of beliefs held about a particular brand is known as the **brand** image. The consumer's beliefs may vary from the true attributes because of his or her experience and the effect of selective perception, selective distortion, and selective retention.

Fourth, the consumer is assumed to have a **utility function** for each attribute. The utility function shows how the consumer expects total product satisfaction to vary with different levels of different attributes. For example, Betty Smith may expect her satisfaction from a camera to increase with better picture quality; to peak with a medium-weight camera as opposed to a very light or very heavy one; and to be higher for a 35-mm camera than for a 135-mm camera. If we combine the attribute levels where the utilities are highest, they make up Betty's ideal camera. The camera would also be her preferred camera if it were available and affordable.

Fifth, the consumer arrives at attitudes toward the different brands through an **evaluation procedure**. Consumers have been found to use one or more of several evaluation procedures, depending on the consumer and the buying decision.

We will illustrate these concepts with Betty Smith's camera buying situation. Suppose Betty has narrowed her choices to four cameras, and that she is primarily interested in four attributes—picture quality, ease of use, camera size, and price. Betty has formed beliefs about how each brand rates on each attribute. The marketer would like to be able to predict which camera Betty will buy.

Clearly, if one camera rated best on all the attributes, we could predict that Betty would choose it. However, the brands vary in appeal. Some buyers will choose using only one attribute, and their choices are easy to predict. If Betty wants picture quality above everything, she would buy the camera that she thinks has the best picture quality. Most buyers, however, consider several attributes, each with different importance. If we knew the importance weights that Betty assigns to the four attributes, we could predict her camera choice more reliably.

Marketers should study buyers to find out how they actually evaluate brand alternatives. With this knowledge, the marketer could take steps to influence the buyer's decision. Suppose Betty is inclined to buy a Nikon camera because she rates it highly on picture quality and ease of use. What strategies might another camera maker, say Minolta, use to influence people like Betty? There are several. Minolta could modify its camera so that it delivers better pictures or other features that consumers like Betty want. It could try to change buyer's beliefs about how its camera rates on key attributes, especially if consumers currently underestimate the camera's qualities. It could try to change buyers' beliefs about Nikon and other competitors. Finally, it could try to change the list of attributes that buyers consider, or the importance attached to these attributes. For example, it might advertise that all good cameras have about equal picture quality, and that its lighter weight, lower-priced camera is a better buy for people like Betty.

Purchase Decision

In the evaluation stage, the consumer ranks brands in the choice set and forms purchase intentions. Generally the consumer will buy the most preferred brand, but two factors can come between the purchase intention and the purchase decision. These factors are shown in Figure 6-5.[23]

The first is the **attitudes of others**. If Betty Smith's husband feels strongly that Betty should buy the lowest-priced camera to keep down expenses, the chances of Betty buying more expensive cameras may be reduced. How much another person's attitudes will affect Betty's choices depends on the strength

FIGURE 6-5

Steps between Evaluation of Alternatives and a Purchase Decision

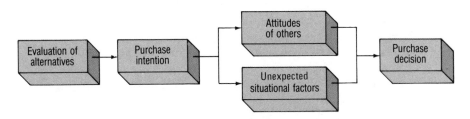

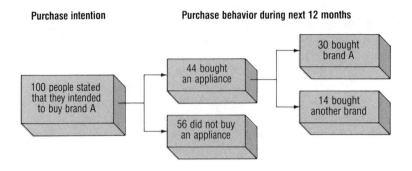

Purchase intention   **Purchase behavior during next 12 months**

FIGURE 6-6

Consequences of Purchase Intentions and Purchase Decisions

of the other person's attitudes toward her buying decision, and Betty's motivation to comply with the other person's wishes. The more intense the other person's attitudes and the closer the other person is to Betty, the more effect the other person will have.

Purchase intention is also influenced by **unexpected situational factors**. The consumer forms a purchase intention based on such factors as expected family income, expected price, and expected benefits from the product. When the consumer is about to act, unexpected situational factors may arise to change the purchase intention. Betty Smith may lose her job, some other purchase may become more urgent, or a friend may report being disappointed in that camera.

Thus preferences and even purchase intentions do not always result in actual purchase choice. They direct purchase behavior, but may not fully determine the outcome. Figure 6-6 shows a fairly typical outcome. In a study of 100 people who stated an intention to buy brand A of an appliance within the next 12 months, only 44 ended up buying the particular appliance, and only 30 purchased brand A.

Postpurchase Behavior

The marketer's job does not end when the product is bought. After purchasing the product, the consumer will be satisfied or dissatisfied, and will engage in postpurchase actions of interest to the marketer. What determines whether the buyer is satisfied or dissatisfied with a purchase? The answer lies in the relationship between the consumer's expectations and the product's perceived performance.[24] If the product matches expectations, the consumer is satisfied; if it falls short, the consumer is dissatisfied.

Consumers base their expectations on messages they receive from sellers, friends, and other information sources. If the seller exaggerates the product's performance, the consumer's expectations will not be met, which leads to dissatisfaction. The larger the gap between expectations and performance, the greater the consumer's dissatisfaction. This suggests that the seller should make product claims that faithfully represent the product's performance so that buyers are satisfied.

Satisfaction with the product will affect later behavior. A satisfied consumer is more likely to buy the product the next time and will speak well of the product to others. According to marketers, "A satisfied customer is our best advertisement."

Dissatisfied consumers may take any of several actions. They may return the product, or complain to the company and ask for a refund or exchange. They may go to a lawyer, or complain to other groups that might help them get satisfaction. Alternatively, buyers may simply stop buying the product or bad-mouth it to friends and others. In all these cases, the seller loses something.

Marketers can take steps to reduce consumer postpurchase dissatisfaction and to help customers feel good about their purchase. Automobile companies can send a letter to new car owners congratulating them on having selected a fine car. They can place ads showing satisfied owners driving their new cars. The companies can obtain customer suggestions for improvements and list the location of available services. They can write instruction booklets that reduce dissatisfaction, and send owners a magazine full of articles describing the pleasures of owning the new car.

Postpurchase communications to buyers have been shown to result in fewer product returns and order cancellations. Paying careful attention to customer dissatisfactions can help the company to spot and correct problems, resulting in increased postpurchase satisfaction for future buyers.

Understanding the consumer's needs and buying power is the foundation of successful marketing. By understanding how buyers go through problem recognition, information search, evaluation of alternatives, the purchase decision, and postpurchase behavior, the marketer can pick up many clues about how to meet the buyer's needs. By understanding the various participants in the buying process and the major influences on their buying behavior, the marketer can develop an effective marketing program to support an attractive offer to the target market.

Summary

Markets have to be understood before marketing strategies can be developed. The consumer market buys goods and services for personal consumption. It consists of many submarkets, such as the French-speaking population and university students, that may require special marketing programs.

Consumer behavior is influenced by the buyer's characteristics and by the buyer's decision process. Buyer characteristics include four major factors: cultural, social, personal, and psychological.

Culture is the most basic determinant of a person's wants and behavior. Marketers try to track cultural shifts that might suggest new ways to serve consumers. Subcultures are "cultures within cultures" that have distinct values and life styles. Social classes are subcultures whose members have similar social prestige based on occupation, income, education, wealth, and other variables. People with different cultural, subcultural, and social class characteristics have different product and brand preferences. Marketers may want to focus their marketing programs on the special needs of certain groups.

Social factors also influence a buyer's behavior. A person's reference groups — family, friends, social organizations, professional associations — strongly affect product and brand choices. The person's position within each group can be defined in terms of role and status. A buyer chooses products and brands that reflect his or her role and status.

The buyer's age, life-cycle stage, occupation, economic circumstances, life style, personality, and other personal characteristics influence his or her buying decisions. Young consumers have needs and wants different from those of older consumers; the needs of young married couples differ from those of retirees; consumers with higher incomes make different buying decisions from those who have less to spend. Consumer life styles — the whole pattern of acting and interacting in the world — are also an important influence on buyers' choices.

Finally, consumer buying behavior is influenced by four major psychological factors — motivation, perception, learning, and attitudes. Each of these factors provides a different perspective for understanding the workings of the buyer's "black box."

In buying something, the buyer goes through a decision process consisting of problem recognition, information search, evaluation of alternatives, purchase decision, and postpurchase behavior. The marketer must understand the buyer's behavior at each stage and what influences are operating. This helps the marketer to develop effective marketing programs for the target market.

Questions for Discussion

1. Identify and discuss the behavioral sciences that marketers use to study and understand consumers.
2. Discuss the importance of the "black box" component in the model of buyer behavior.
3. Explain the importance of reference groups and how they might influence a person.
4. Discuss how the family can be a strong influence on buying behavior.
5. Discuss the level of Maslow's hierarchy of needs that marketers of the following products are primarily attempting to satisfy: (a) smoke detectors, (b) telephone long-distance dialing, (c) Seagram's VO, (d) life insurance, (e) restaurant dining, and (f) transcendental meditation.
6. Apply the five stages in the decision process to your decision regarding which college to attend.
7. Why is the postpurchase behavior stage included in the model of the buying process?

Chapter 6 Key Terms

Attitude   A person's enduring favorable or unfavorable cognitive evaluations, emotional feelings, and action tendencies toward some object or idea.

Belief   A descriptive thought that a person holds about something.

Consumer market   All the individuals and households who buy or acquire goods and services for personal consumption.

Culture   The set of basic values, perceptions, wants, and behaviors learned by a member of society from family and other important institutions.

Learning   Changes in an individual's behavior arising from experience.

Life style   A person's pattern of living as expressed in his or her activities, interests, and opinions.

Motive (or drive)   A need that is sufficiently pressing to direct the person to seek satisfaction of the need.

Perception   The process by which an individual selects, organizes, and interprets information inputs to create a meaningful picture of the world.

Personal influence   The effect of statements made by one person on another's attitude or probability of purchase.

Personality   A person's distinguishing psychological characteristics that lead to relatively consistent and lasting responses to his or her own environment.

Reference groups   Groups that have a direct (face-to-face) or indirect influence on the person's attitudes or behavior.

Role   The activities a person is expected to perform according to the persons around him or her.

Social classes   Relatively permanent and ordered divisions in a society whose members share similar values, interests, and behaviors.

Status   The general esteem given to a role by society.

Subculture   A group of people with shared value systems based on common life experiences and situations.

Cases for Chapter 6

Organizational Markets and Organizational Buyer Behavior

Chapter Objectives

After reading this chapter, you should be able to:
1. Discuss how organizational markets differ from consumer markets.
2. Identify the major factors that influence organizational buyer behavior.
3. List and define the steps in the industrial buying decision process.
4. Explain how resellers and government buyers make their buying decisions.

There is a good chance that when a Canadian buys a soft drink or coffee from a vending machine, it is from VS Services. There is also a good chance that when a high-school student has a meal in the school cafeteria, when a patient or resident in a hospital, nursing, or retirement home has a meal, when a visitor has a hot dog at Toronto's Exhibition Stadium, or when a traveler has a bite to eat at Montreal International Airport, it is from VS Services.

VS Services concentrates on organizational markets — satisfying the needs of industry and government by offering such "products" as food services, catering services, linen and laundry services, and office catering services. Their major markets are hospitals and nursing homes, public and private schools, colleges and large universities, correctional facilities, and various industrial and business clients. These organizational markets offer tremendous potential for growth: VS Services has sales of over $300 million, and sales are increasing by over 15% each year.

Successful strategies in the industrial market often are similar to those taken in the consumer market, but there are some differences. Take VS Services' approach to the education market. If most high-school students had their way, the cafeterias would serve the McDonald's type of menu. If most school boards had their way, the cafeterias would serve only "wholesome" food. Both groups want a good price. To be selected for a school, a food service firm has to please both types of consumers — recognizing that they are dealing with organizations and individuals. VS Services introduced the Rainbow Program, which color-codes foods into four groups, each color representing a specific food group providing different basic nutritional requirements. By selecting one of the variety of dishes offered under each of the rainbow colors, students can choose foods they like while making sure they are receiving a nutritious meal. VS Services have also designed the "Itza Pizza" program and the "Gretel's Bake Shop" program for the educational market. The Campus Food Service division prepares and serves over 100 000 meals daily for the educational market.

The four major markets in which VS Services operates — health care, work, education, and leisure and recreation — require the company to consider a wide range of needs of both consumers and organizations. Thus VS Services faces the same challenges as consumer marketers, and some additional challenges.[1]

In one way or another most large companies sell to other organizations. Many industrial companies sell most of their products to organizations—companies such as Bombardier, Dofasco, and countless other large and small firms. Even large consumer products companies do organizational marketing. For example, Canada Packers makes many familiar products for final consumers, such as Tenderflake lard and Maple Leaf bacon. To sell these products to final consumers, Canada Packers must first sell them to the wholesale and retail organizations that serve the consumer market. Canada Packers also makes products, such as specialty chemicals, that are sold only to other companies.

Organizations make up a vast market. In fact, industrial markets involve many more dollars and items than consumer markets. Figure 7-1 shows the large number of transactions needed to produce and sell a simple pair of shoes. Hide dealers sell to tanners, who sell leather to shoe manufacturers, who sell shoes to wholesalers, who in turn sell shoes to retailers, who finally sell them to consumers. Each party in the chain buys many other goods and services as well. It is easy to see why there is more organizational buying than consumer buying—many sets of organizational purchases are made for only one set of consumer purchases.

Companies that sell to other organizations must do their best to understand organizational buyer behavior.

FIGURE 7-1
Organizational Transactions Involved in Producing and Distributing a Pair of Shoes

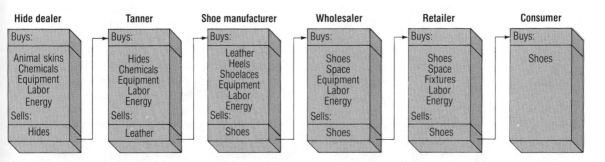

Organizational Markets

Types of Organizational Markets

We will examine three types of organizational markets: the industrial market, the reseller market, and the government market.

The Industrial Market

The *industrial market* consists of all the individuals and organizations that acquire goods and services that enter into the production of other products and services, which are then sold, rented, or supplied to others. The industrial market is huge: it consists of over 1 million organizations that generate an annual value added of over $120 billion and constitute a buying market for the goods of most firms.

The Reseller Market

The *reseller market* consists of all the individuals and organizations that acquire goods for the purpose of reselling or renting them to others at a profit. The reseller market includes over 44 000 wholesaling firms and 158 000 retailing firms that combine to purchase over $328 billion worth of goods and services a year.[2] Resellers purchase goods for resale and goods and services for conducting their operations. In their role as purchasing agents for their own customers, resellers purchase a vast variety of goods for resale — indeed, they purchase everything produced except for the few classes of goods that producers sell directly to customers.

The Government Market

The *government market* consists of governmental units — federal, provincial, and municipal — that purchase or rent goods and services for carrying out the main functions of government. In 1986, governments purchased about $100 billion worth of products and services, or 22% of the gross national expenditure.[3] Federal, provincial, and municipal government agencies buy an amazing range of products and services. They buy airplanes, sculpture, chalkboards, furniture, toiletries, clothing, fire engines, vehicles, and fuel. Governments represent a tremendous market for any producer or reseller.

Characteristics of Organizational Markets

In some ways, organizational markets are similar to consumer markets as both involve people who assume buying roles and make purchase decisions to satisfy needs. In many ways, however, organizational markets differ from consumer markets.[4] The main differences are in market structure and demand, the nature of the buying unit, and the types of decisions and the decision process.

Market Structure and Demand

The organizational marketer normally deals with far fewer, larger buyers than the consumer marketer. The Michelin Tire Company's fate in the industrial market depends on getting orders from one of the big three auto-makers. In contrast, when Michelin sells replacement tires to consumers, its potential market includes the owners of 10 million cars currently in use. Even in large organizational markets, a few buyers normally account for most of the purchasing.

Organizational markets are also more **geographically concentrated**. Seventy-one percent of the manufacturing establishments in Canada are concentrated in Ontario (41%) and Quebec (30%). These plants produce 79% of the output of Canadian manufacturers.[5] In fact, an even more narrow geographic area within these two provinces, referred to as the Windsor-Quebec corridor, contains most of the manufacturing plants.

Organizational demand is **derived demand** — it ultimately comes from the demand for consumer goods. General Motors buys steel because consumers buy cars. If consumer demand for cars drops, so will the demand for steel and all the other products used to make cars.

Many organizational markets have **inelastic demand**. Total demand for many industrial products is not much affected by price changes, especially in the short run. A drop in the price of leather will not cause shoe manufacturers to buy much more unless it results in lower shoe prices that increase consumer demand.

Finally, organizational markets have more **fluctuating demand**. The demand for many industrial goods and services tends to change more often and more quickly than the demand for consumer goods and services. A small percentage increase in consumer demand can cause large increases in industrial demand. Sometimes a rise of only 10% in consumer demand can cause as much as a 200% rise in industrial demand in the next period.

The Nature of the Buying Unit

As compared with consumer purchases, organizational purchases usually involve more buyers and more professional purchasing. Organizational buying is often done by trained purchasing agents who spend their work lives learning how to buy better. The more complex the purchase, the more likely that several persons will participate in the decision-making process. Buying committees made up of technical experts and top management are common in the buying of major goods.[6] This means that organizational marketers must have well-trained salespeople to deal with well-trained buyers.

Types of Decisions and the Decision Process

Organizational buyers usually face more complex buying decisions than consumer buyers. Purchases often involve large sums of money, complex technical and economic considerations, and interactions among many people at many levels of the buyer's organization. Because the purchases are more complex, organizational buyers may take longer to make their decisions. A company buying a large computer system may take many months or more than a year to select a supplier.

The organizational buying process tends to be more formalized than the consumer buying process. Large organizational purchases usually call for detailed product specifications, written purchase orders, careful supplier searches, and formal approval. The purchase process may be spelled out in detail in policy manuals.

Finally, in the organizational buying process, buyer and seller are often much more dependent on each other. Consumer marketers usually stay at a distance from their customers. But organizational marketers may roll up their sleeves and work closely with their customers during all stages of the buying process—from helping customers to define the problem, to finding solutions, to after-sale operation.

A Model of Organizational Buyer Behavior

Webster and Wind define *organizational buying* as "the decision-making process by which formal organizations establish the need for purchased products and services, and identify, evaluate, and choose among alternative brands and suppliers."[7] In trying to understand organizational buyer behavior, marketers must answer some hard questions. What kinds of buying decisions do organizational buyers make? How do they choose among suppliers? Who makes the decisions? What is the organizational buying decision process? What factors affect organizational buying decisions?

At the most basic level, marketers want to know how organizational buyers will respond to various marketing stimuli. A simple model of organizational buyer behavior is shown in Figure 7-2.[8] The figure shows that marketing and other stimuli affect the organization and produce certain buyer responses. The marketing stimuli consist of the four Ps: product, price, place, and promotion. The other stimuli consist of major forces in the environment: economic, technological, political, and cultural. All these stimuli enter the organization and are turned into buyer responses: product or service choice, supplier choice, order quantities, delivery times and terms, service terms, and payment terms. To design good marketing mix strategies, the marketer must understand what happens within the organization to turn the stimuli into purchase responses.

FIGURE 7-2
A Model of Organizational Buyer Behavior

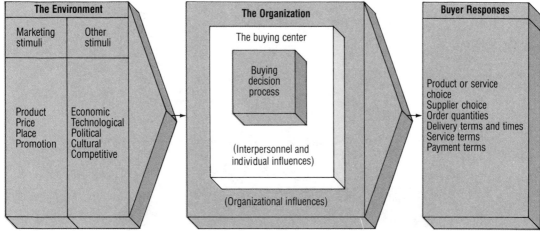

Within the organization, the buying activity consists of two major parts—the *buying center* (made up of all the people involved in the buying decision) and the buying decision process. The figure shows that the buying center and the buying decision process are influenced by internal organizational, interpersonal, and individual factors as well as by external environmental factors.

We will look at the various elements in this organizational buyer behavior model. For now we will focus on the largest and most important organizational market—the industrial market. Later in the chapter we will consider the special characteristics of reseller and government buyer behavior.

Industrial Buyer Behavior

We will examine four questions about industrial buyer behavior:

- What buying decisions do industrial buyers make?

- Who participates in the buying process?

- What are the major influences on buyers?

- How do industrial buyers make their buying decisions?

Industrial buyers purchase the raw materials, such as the coal for this steel plant, that companies use to make other products.

Courtesy: Dofasco

What Buying Decisions Do Industrial Buyers Make?

The industrial buyer faces a whole set of decisions in making a purchase. The number of decisions depends on the type of buying situation.

Major Types of Buying Situations

There are three major types of buying situations.[9] At one extreme is the straight rebuy, which is a fairly routine decision. At the other extreme is the new task, which may call for thorough research. In the middle is the modified rebuy, which requires some research. (For examples, see Figure 7-3.)

Straight Rebuy

In a straight rebuy, the buyer reorders something without any modifications. The order is usually handled on a routine basis by the purchasing department. The buyer chooses from suppliers on its "list," based on its past buying satisfaction with the various suppliers. The "in" suppliers try to maintain product and service quality. They often propose automatic reordering systems so that the purchasing agent will save reordering time. The "out" suppliers try to offer something new or exploit dissatisfaction so that the buyer will consider them. Outsuppliers try to get their foot in the door with a small order and then enlarge their "purchase share" over time.

Modified Rebuy

In a modified rebuy, the buyer wants to modify product specifications, prices, terms, or suppliers. The modified rebuy usually involves more decision participants. The "in" suppliers become nervous and have to put their best foot

FIGURE 7-3
Three Types of Industrial Buying Situations

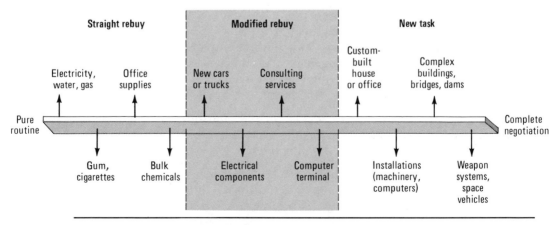

From *Marketing Principles*, Third edition, Ben M. Enis. Copyright © 1980, Scott, Foresman and Company. Reprinted by permission.

forward to protect the account. The "out" suppliers see it as an opportunity to make a "better offer" to gain some new business.

New Task

A company faces a new task when it buys a product or service for the first time. The greater the cost or risk, the larger the number of decision participants and the greater their information seeking. The new task situation is the marketer's greatest opportunity and challenge. The marketer not only tries to reach as many key buying influences as possible, but also provides help and information.

The Role of Systems Buying and Selling

Many buyers prefer to buy a whole solution to their problem and not make all the separate decisions involved. This solution, called *systems buying*, began with government buying of major systems. Instead of buying and putting all the components together, the government would ask for bids from suppliers who would assemble the package or system. The winning supplier would be responsible for buying and assembling the subcomponents.

Sellers have increasingly recognized that buyers like to purchase in this way and have adopted the practice of systems selling as a marketing tool. Systems selling has two parts. First, the supplier sells a group of interlocking products. For example, the supplier sells not only glue, but applicators and dryers as well. Second, the supplier sells a system of production, inventory control, distribution, and other services to meet the buyer's need for a smooth-running operation. Systems selling is a key industrial marketing strategy for winning and holding accounts.

Who Participates in the Industrial Buying Process?

Who does the buying of the billions of dollars worth of goods and services needed by the industrial market? Webster and Wind call the decision-making unit of a buying organization the buying center, defined as "all those individuals and groups who participate in the purchasing decision-making process, who share some common goals and the risks arising from the decisions."[10]

The buying center includes all members of the organization who play a role in the purchase decision process:

Users   Users are the members of the organization who will use the product or service. In many cases the users initiate the buying process and play an important role in defining the purchase specifications.

Influencers   Influencers are those members inside and outside of the organization who directly or indirectly influence the buying decision. They often help define specifications and also provide information for evaluating alternatives. Technical personnel are particularly important as influencers.

Buyers Buyers are organizational members with formal authority for selecting the supplier and arranging the terms of purchase. Buyers may help shape product specifications, but they play their major role in selecting vendors and negotiating within the purchase constraints. In more complex purchases, the buyers might include high-level officers of the company participating in the negotiations.

Deciders Deciders are organizational members who have either formal or informal power to select or approve the final suppliers. In the routine buying of standard items, the buyers are often the deciders. In more complex buying, the officers of the company are often the deciders.

Gatekeepers Gatekeepers are members of the organization who control the flow of information to others. For example, purchasing agents often have authority to prevent salespersons from seeing users or deciders. Other gatekeepers include technical personnel and even switchboard operators. The main impact of gatekeepers is to influence the inflow of information on buying alternatives.

The buying center is not a fixed and formally identified unit within the buying organization. It is a set of buying roles assumed by different persons for different purchases. Within the organization, the size and makeup of the buying center will vary for different products and for different buying situations. The buying center concept presents a major marketing challenge. The industrial marketer has to figure out: Who is involved in the decision? What decisions do they affect? What is their relative degree of influence? What evaluation criteria does each decision participant use? Consider the following example:

> McGaw sells disposable surgical gowns to hospitals. It tries to identify the hospital personnel involved in this buying decision. The decision participants turn out to be (1) the vice-president of purchasing, (2) the operating room administrator, and (3) the surgeons. Each party plays a different role. The vice-president of purchasing analyzes whether the hospital should buy disposable gowns or reusable gowns. If analysis favors disposable gowns, then the operating room administrator compares competing products and prices and makes a choice. This administrator considers the gown's absorbency, antiseptic quality, design, and cost, and normally buys the brand that meets requirements at the lowest cost. Finally, surgeons affect the decision later by reporting their satisfaction or dissatisfaction with the brand.

What Are the Major Influences on Industrial Buyers?

Industrial buyers are subject to many influences when they make their buying decisions. Some marketers assume that the major influences are economic. They think that buyers will favor the supplier who offers the lowest price, or the best product, or the most service. They concentrate on offering strong economic benefits to buyers.

Other marketers see the buyers as responding to personal motives. The buyers may seek favors, attention, or risk reduction. This view suggests that industrial marketers should look mostly at the human and social factors in the buying situation.

Industrial buyers actually respond to both economic and personal factors. When offers from suppliers are very similar, industrial buyers have little basis for rational choice. Since they can meet organizational goals with any supplier, buyers can consider personal factors. Where competing products differ greatly, industrial buyers are more accountable for their choice and pay more attention to economic factors.

The various groups of influences on industrial buyers — environmental, organizational, interpersonal, and individual — are listed in Figure 7-4 and described below.[11]

Environmental Factors

Industrial buyers are heavily influenced by factors in the current and expected economic environment, such as the level of primary demand, the economic outlook, and the cost of money. As the level of economic uncertainty rises, industrial buyers stop making new investments and attempt to reduce their inventories.

An increasingly important environmental factor is shortages in key materials. Many companies are now more willing to buy and hold larger inventories of scarce materials. Industrial buyers are also affected by technological, political, and competitive developments in the environment. The industrial marketer

FIGURE 7-4
Major Influences on Industrial Buying Behavior

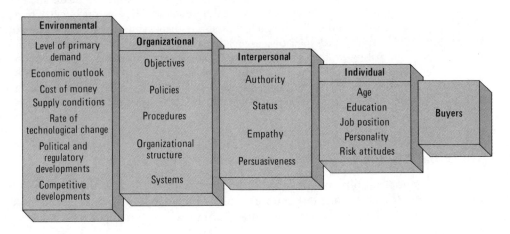

has to watch these factors, determine how they will affect the buyer, and try to turn these problems into opportunities.

Organizational Factors

Each buying organization has its own objectives, policies, procedures, structure, and systems. The industrial marketer has to know these as well as possible. Questions such as these arise: How many people are involved in the buying decision? Who are they? What are their evaluative criteria? What are the company's policies and limits on the buyers?

Interpersonal Factors

The buying center usually includes many participants; each affects and is affected by the others. In many cases, the industrial marketer will not know what kinds of group dynamics take place during the buying process. As Bonoma points out:

> Managers do not wear tags that say "decision maker" or "unimportant person." The powerful are often invisible, at least to vendor representatives.[12]

The buying center participant with the highest rank does not always have the most influence. Participants may have influence in the buying decision because they control rewards and punishments, because they are well liked, because they have special expertise, or because they are related by marriage to the company's president. Interpersonal factors are often very subtle. Where possible, industrial marketers try to understand these factors and design strategies that take them into account.

Individual Factors

Each participant in the buying decision process brings in personal motives, perceptions, and preferences. These are affected by age, income, education, professional identification, personality, and attitudes toward risk. Buyers have different buying styles. Some of the younger, higher-educated buyers are "computer freaks" and make in-depth analyses of competitive proposals before choosing a supplier. Other buyers are "tough guys" from the "old school" and play the sellers off against each other.

Industrial marketers must know their customers and adapt their tactics to environmental, organizational, interpersonal, and individual influences on the buying situation.

How Do Industrial Buyers Make Their Buying Decisions?

We now come to the issue of how industrial buyers move through the purchasing process. Robinson and others have identified eight stages of the industrial buying process.[13] They are listed in Table 7-1. The table shows that buyers facing the new task buying situation will go through all the stages of the buying process. Buyers making modified or straight rebuys will skip some of the stages. We will examine these steps for the typical new task buying situation.

Problem Recognition

The buying process begins when someone in the company recognizes a problem or need that can be met by acquiring a good or a service. Problem recognition can result from internal or external stimuli. Internally, the most common events leading to problem recognition are the following:

- The company decides to launch a new product and needs new equipment and materials to produce this product.

- A machine breaks down and needs new parts.

- Some purchased material turns out to be unsatisfactory, and the company searches for another supplier.

- A purchasing manager sees a chance to get better prices or quality.

Externally, the buyer may get some new ideas at a trade show, or see an ad, or receive a call from a salesperson who offers a better product or a lower price.

General Need Description

Having recognized a need the buyer next determines the general characteristics and quantity of the needed item. For standard items, this is not much of a problem. For complex items, the buyer will work with others — engineers,

TABLE 7-1
Major Stages of the Industrial Buying Process in Relation to Major Buying Situations

Stages of the Buying Process	Buying situations		
	New task	Modified rebuy	Straight rebuy
1. Problem recognition	Yes	Maybe	No
2. General need description	Yes	Maybe	No
3. Product specification	Yes	Yes	Yes
4. Supplier search	Yes	Maybe	No
5. Proposal solicitation	Yes	Maybe	No
6. Supplier selection	Yes	Maybe	No
7. Order routine specification	Yes	Maybe	No
8. Performance review	Yes	Yes	Yes

Source: Adapted from Patrick J. Robinson, Charles W. Faris, and Yoram Wind, *Industrial Buying and Creative Marketing* (Boston: Allyn & Bacon, 1967), p. 14.

When companies advertise to other companies, they point out how they can solve problems for that company.

users, consultants—to define the item. They will want to rank the importance of reliability, durability, price, and other attributes desired in the item.

The industrial marketer can help the buying company in this phase. Often the buyer is not aware of the value of different product characteristics. An alert marketer can help the buyer define the company's needs.

Product Specification

The buying organization next develops the item's technical specifications. A value analysis engineering team will be put to work on the problem. *Value analysis* is an approach to cost reduction in which components are carefully studied to determine if they can be redesigned or standardized or made by cheaper methods of production. The team will decide on the best product characteristics and specify them accordingly. Sellers too can use value analysis as a tool for breaking into an account. By showing a better way to make an object, outside sellers can turn straight rebuy situations into new task situations in which their company has a chance for business.

Supplier Search

The buyer now tries to find the best vendors. The buyer can look at trade directories, do a computer search, or phone other companies for recommendations. Some of the vendors will not be considered because they are not large enough to supply the needed quantity or because they have a poor reputation for delivery and service. The buyer will end up with a small list of qualified suppliers.

The newer the buying task, and the more complex and costly the item, the greater the amount of time spent in searching for suppliers. The supplier must make sure it is listed in major directories, and must build a good reputation in the marketplace. Salespeople should watch for companies in the process of searching for suppliers and make certain that their firm is considered.

Proposal Solicitation

The buyer will now invite qualified suppliers to submit proposals. Some suppliers will send only a catalog or a sales representative. If the item is complex or expensive, the buyer will need detailed written proposals from each potential supplier. The buyer will review the suppliers when they make their formal presentations.

Industrial marketers must therefore be skilled in researching, writing, and presenting proposals. Their proposals should be marketing documents, not just technical documents. Their presentations should inspire confidence, and help their companies stand out from the competition.

Supplier Selection

The members of the buying center now review the proposals and select a supplier(s). They will consider not only the technical competence of the various suppliers, but also their ability to deliver the item on time and provide necessary services. The buying center will often draw up a list of the desired supplier attributes and their relative importance. In selecting a chemical supplier, a buying center listed the following attributes in order of importance:

1. Technical support services
2. Prompt delivery
3. Quick response to customer needs
4. Product quality
5. Supplier reputation
6. Product price
7. Complete product line
8. Caliber of sales representatives
9. Extension of credit
10. Personal relationships
11. Literature and manuals

The members of the buying center will rate the suppliers against these attributes and identify the most attractive suppliers.

Buyers may attempt to negotiate with preferred suppliers for better prices and terms before making the final selections. In the end, they may select a single supplier or a few suppliers. Many buyers prefer multiple sources of supply as they will not be totally dependent on one supplier in case something goes wrong, and they will be able to compare the prices and performance of several suppliers.

Order Routine Specification

The buyer now writes the final order with the chosen supplier(s), listing the technical specifications, quantity needed, expected time of delivery, return policies, warranties, and so on. In the case of MRO items (maintenance, repair, and operating items), buyers are increasingly using blanket contracts rather than periodic purchase orders. Writing a new purchase order each time stock is needed is expensive. In addition, if buyers wrote fewer and larger purchase orders they would have to carry more inventory.

A blanket contract creates a long-term relationship in which the supplier promises to resupply the buyer as needed at agreed prices for a set time period. The stock is held by the seller; hence the name "stockless purchase plan." The buyer's computer automatically prints out an order to the seller when stock is needed. Blanket contracting leads to more single-source buying and the buying of more items from that single source. This locks the supplier in tighter with the buyer and makes it difficult for other suppliers to break in unless the buyer becomes dissatisfied with prices or service.

Performance Review

In this stage the buyer reviews supplier performance. The buyer may contact users and ask them to rate their satisfaction. The performance review may lead the buyer to continue, modify, or drop the seller. The seller's job is to monitor the same factor used by the buyer to make sure that the seller is giving the expected satisfaction.

We have described the buying stages that would operate in a new task buying situation. In the modified rebuy or straight rebuy situation, some of these stages would be compressed or bypassed. The eight-stage model provides a simple view of the industrial buying decision process. The actual process is usually much more complex.[14] Each organization buys in its own way, and each buying situation has unique requirements. Different buying center participants may be involved at different stages of the process. Although certain buying process steps usually occur, buyers do not always follow them in the same order, and they may add other steps. Often, buyers repeat certain stages more than once.

Reseller Buyer Behavior ▬▬▬▬▬▬▬▬▬▬▬▬▬▬▬▬

In most ways, reseller buyer behavior is like industrial buyer behavior. Reseller organizations have buying centers whose participants interact to make a variety of buying decisions. Their buying decision process starts with problem recognition and ends with decisions about which products to buy from which suppliers and under what terms. The buyers are affected by a wide range of environmental, organizational, interpersonal, and individual factors.

However, there are some important differences between industrial and reseller buying behavior. Resellers differ in the types of buying decisions they make, who participates in the buying decision, and how they make their buying decisions.

What Buying Decisions Do Resellers Make?

Resellers serve as purchasing agents for their customers, so they buy products and brands they think will appeal to their customers. They have to decide what product assortment to carry, what vendors to buy from, and what prices and terms to negotiate. The assortment decision is primary, and it positions the reseller in the marketplace. The reseller's assortment strategy will strongly affect its choice of which products to buy and which suppliers to buy from.

Resellers can carry products from only one supplier, or several related products or lines from a few suppliers, or a scrambled assortment of unrelated products from many suppliers. Therefore, a camera store might carry only Kodak cameras; many brands of cameras; cameras, radios, tape recorders, and stereo equipment; or all these plus stoves and refrigerators. The reseller's assortment will affect its customer mix, marketing mix, and supplier mix.

Who Participates in the Reseller Buying Process?

Who does the buying for wholesale and retail organizations? The reseller's buying center may include one or many participants assuming different roles. Some will have formal buying responsibility, and some will be behind-the-scenes influencers. In small "mom and pop" firms, the owner usually takes care of buying decisions. In large reseller firms, buying is a specialized function and a full-time job. The buying center and buying process vary for different types of resellers.

Consider supermarkets. In the headquarters of a supermarket chain, specialist buyers have the responsibility for developing brand assortments and listening to new brand presentations made by salespersons. In some chains these buyers have the authority to accept or reject new items. In many chains, however, they are limited to screening "obvious rejects" and "obvious accepts"; otherwise they must bring new items to the chain's buying committee for approval. Even when an item is accepted by a buying committee, chain-store managers may not carry it.

How Do Resellers Make Their Buying Decisions?

For new items, resellers use roughly the same buying process described for industrial buyers. For standard items, resellers simply reorder goods when the inventory gets low. The orders are placed with the same suppliers as long as their terms, goods, and services are satisfactory. Buyers will try to renegotiate prices if their margins drop due to rising operating costs. In many retail lines, the profit margin is so low (1 to 2% on sales in supermarkets, for example) that a sudden drop in demand or rise in operating costs will drive profits into the red.

Resellers consider many factors besides costs when choosing products and suppliers. Other criteria include expected consumer acceptance of the product, the amount of promotion the supplier will provide, merchandising help given by the supplier, purchase discounts, and others. Sellers stand the best chance when they can report strong evidence of consumer acceptance, present a well-designed advertising and sales promotion plan, and provide strong financial incentives to the retailer.

Several studies have attempted to rank the major criteria used by buyers, buying committees, and store managers. In one study of Canadian non-food retail chain buyers such as Shoppers' Drug Mart, Sears, Canadian Tire, and Eaton's, the major criteria used in their decision to accept a new product were:

- Expected profit contribution
- Supplier's ability to fill repeat orders quickly
- Product quality
- Retailer or dealer markup
- Product's meeting government regulations
- Competitive price
- Supplier's known track record
- Potential market volume
- Manufacturer's initial supply capabilities
- Product's fitting new trends in market[15]

Sellers are facing increasingly advanced buying on the part of resellers. They need to understand the changing needs of resellers and to develop attractive offers that help resellers serve their customers better. Table 7-2 lists several marketing tools used by sellers to make their offer to resellers more attractive.

TABLE 7-2
Vendor Marketing Tools Used with Resellers

Cooperative advertising, where the vendor agrees to pay a portion of the reseller's advertising costs for the vendor's product.

Preticketing, where the vendor places a tag on each product listing its price, manufacturer, size, identification number, and color; these tags help the reseller reorder merchandise as it is being sold.

Stockless purchasing, where the vendor carries the inventory and delivers goods to the reseller on short notice.

Automatic reordering systems, where the vendor supplies forms and computer links for automatic reordering of merchandise by the reseller.

Advertising aids, such as glossy photos, broadcast scripts.

Special prices for storewide promotion.

Return and exchange privileges for the reseller.

Allowances for merchandise markdowns by the reseller.

Sponsorship of in-store demonstrations.

Government Buyer Behavior

Government buying and industrial buying are similar in many ways, but they do have differences that must be understood by companies wishing to sell products and services to governments.[16] To succeed in the government market, sellers must locate key decision makers, identify the factors that affect buyer behavior, and understand the buying decision process.

Who Participates in the Government Buying Process?

Who does the buying of the billions of dollars of goods and services? Government buying organizations are found at the federal, provincial, and local levels. At the federal level, all government departments instigate the purchase of goods and supplies, although some of the purchasing for these departments is handled by Supply and Services Canada.[17] Its major function is to obtain goods and services of the best quality for the best price. At the provincial and municipal level, departments also have their own buying organizations that determine what is to be purchased and from whom.

What Are the Major Influences on Government Buyers?

Government buyers are affected by environmental, organizational, interpersonal, and individual factors. A unique aspect of government buying is that it is carefully watched by outside publics. At the federal level, members of parliament in the Opposition frequently query government expenditures. Probably the most visible watchdog is the Auditor General who provides an annual review of government buying and makes suggestions as to improvement in the efficiency of public spending. Many private groups also watch government agencies to see how they spend the public's money.

One of the markets for the de Havilland Dash 7 is the Canadian Armed Forces.

Courtesy: de Havilland Aircraft of Canada

Because spending decisions are subject to public review, government organizations get involved in much paperwork. Elaborate forms must be filled out and signed before purchases are approved. The level of bureaucracy is high, and marketers have to find a way to cut through the red tape. Noneconomic criteria are playing a growing role in government buying. The new criteria come out of government reform programs and call for favoring firms that are Canadian-owned or located in particular regions of the country.

How Do Government Buyers Make Their Buying Decisions?

Government buying practices often seem complex and frustrating to suppliers. However, the ins and outs of selling to government can be mastered in a short time. The government is generally helpful in spreading information about its buying needs and procedures. Government is often as anxious to attract new suppliers as the suppliers are to find customers. The Department of Supply and Services provides a *Weekly Bulletin of Business Opportunities* that lists contracts awarded to Canadian firms by federal departments and agencies.[18]

Government buying procedures fall into two types: the open bid and the negotiated contract. Open bid buying means that the government office invites bids from qualified suppliers for carefully described items, generally awarding a contract to the lowest bidder. The supplier must consider whether it can meet the specifications and accept the terms. For standard items, such as fuel or school supplies, the specifications are not a hurdle, but they may be a hurdle for nonstandard items. The government office is usually required to award the contract to the lowest bidder on a winner-take-all basis. In some cases, allowance is made for the supplier's better product or reputation for completing contracts.

In negotiated contract buying, the agency works with one or more companies and negotiates a contract with one of them covering the project and terms. This occurs primarily with complex projects — those involving major research and development cost and risk, or those for which there is little competition. The contract can be reviewed and renegotiated if the supplier's profits seem too high.

For a number of reasons, many companies that sell to the government have not been marketing-oriented. Total government spending is determined by elected officials, rather than by the efforts of marketing. The government buying has emphasized price, making suppliers invest their effort in technology to bring costs down. Where the product's characteristics are carefully specified, product differentiation is not a marketing factor. Furthermore, advertising and personal selling are of little importance in winning bids on an open bid basis.

Summary

Organizations make up a vast market. There are three major types of organizational markets—the industrial market, the reseller market, and the government market.

In many ways, organizational markets are like consumer markets, but in other ways they are much different. Organizational markets usually have fewer and larger buyers who are more geographically concentrated. Organizational demand is derived, largely inelastic, and more fluctuating. More buyers are usually involved in the organizational buying decision, and organizational buyers are better trained and more professional than consumer buyers. Organizational purchasing decisions are more complex and the buying process is more formal.

The industrial market includes firms and individuals that buy goods and services in order to produce other goods and services for sale or rental to others. Industrial buyers make decisions that vary with the three types of buying situations—straight rebuys, modified rebuys, and new tasks. The decision-making unit of a buying organization, called the buying center, may consist of many persons playing many roles. The industrial marketer needs to know: Who are the major participants? In what decisions do they exercise influence? What is their relative degree of influence? What evaluation criteria does each decision participant use? The industrial marketer also needs to understand the major environmental, organizational, interpersonal, and individual influences on the buying process. The buying process itself consists of eight stages: problem recognition, general need description, product specification, supplier search, proposal solicitation, supplier selection, order routine specification, and performance review. As industrial buyers become more sophisticated, industrial sellers must upgrade their marketing efforts.

The reseller market consists of individuals and organizations that acquire and resell goods produced by others. Resellers have to decide on their assortment, suppliers, prices, and terms. In small wholesale and retail organizations, buying may be carried on by one or a few individuals; in large organizations, by an entire purchasing department. With new items, the buyers go through a buying process similar to the one shown for industrial buyers; with standard items, the buying process consists of routines for reordering and renegotiating contracts.

The government market is a vast one that annually purchases billions of dollars of products and services for defense, education, public welfare, and other public needs. Government buying practices are highly specialized and specified, with open bidding or negotiated contracts characterizing most of the buying. Government buyers operate under the watchful eye of the Auditor General and many private watchdog groups. Hence they tend to fill out more forms, require more signatures, and respond more slowly in placing orders.

Questions for Discussion

1. Explain the concept of derived demand as it applies to organizational demand.
2. From your employment background, explain how your employer engaged in straight rebuy, modified rebuy, and new task buying.
3. What abilities should a purchasing agent have?

4. How would the participants in the industrial buying process differ between a small machine tool shop and Dofasco?

5. Discuss the major environmental factors that would influence Canadian Coachway's purchase of buses.

6. Identify the components of the government market and the types of products each buys that make it a significant marketing opportunity.

7. How do the buying influences on the government buyer differ from those on the industrial or reseller buyer?

Chapter 7 Key Terms

Buying center   All the individuals and groups who participate in the buying decision process, who share some common goals and the risks arising from the decisions.

Government market   Governmental units—federal, provincial, and municipal —that purchase or rent goods and services for carrying out the main functions of government.

Industrial market   All the individuals and organizations that acquire goods and services that enter into the production of other products and services, that are in turn sold, rented, or supplied to others.

Organizational buying   The decision-making process by which formal organizations establish the need for purchased products and services, and identify, evaluate, and choose among alternative brands and suppliers.

Reseller market   All the individuals and organizations that acquire goods for the purpose of reselling or renting them to others at a profit.

Systems buying   Buying a whole solution to a problem and not making all the separate decisions involved.

Value analysis   An approach to cost reduction in which components are carefully studied to determine if they can be redesigned or standardized or made by cheaper methods of production.

Cases for Chapter 7

CHAPTER *8*

Market Segmentation, Targeting, and Positioning

Chapter Objectives

After reading this chapter, you should be able to:
1. Define market segmentation, market targeting, and market positioning.
2. List and discuss the major bases for segmenting consumer and industrial markets.
3. Explain how companies identify attractive market segments and choose a market-coverage strategy.
4. Describe how companies can position their products for maximum advantage in the marketplace.

Pennington's Stores Limited, with over 160 retail outlets in nine provinces and the United States, sells over $85 million worth of merchandise each year. Chances are, however, that most Canadians have never heard of the store. Pennington's concentrates on just one particular market segment—overweight women and their clothing needs. By doing this, the company has grown rapidly with sales increasing about 15% each year, and holds a virtual monopoly in this market. The store motto says it all: "Where fashion has no size limit."

"Slim is in" and many women do not fit the mold. Statistics Canada data indicate that the percentage of overweight women is increasing because the percentage of overweight women increases with age and the average age of Canadian women is increasing. In one study, it was found that 42% of the women in the 20-29 age group were overweight, 65% between the ages of 40 and 64, and 80% of the 65 and over group. Surprisingly, most firms are not interested in this target market, preferring instead to focus on the *Vogue* or *Chatelaine* woman with her model figure. Eaton's and other retailers have made brief forays into this market but, for the most part, Pennington's is the leader and with good reason. The company's longtime partners first saw the possibilities of retailing large-size clothing back in 1947.

Pennington's strategy has these key elements: rapid expansion, widespread use of business-school graduates in middle management, and in-house control over merchandising, design, and advertising.

Pennington's has opened up about eight new stores a year since 1972. While most of the stores cater to the middle-class consumer through suburban shopping malls, in 1978 the company introduced Liz Porter stores — "an exciting new chain of boutiques geared towards a young, sophisticated clientele." These stores are targeted to the 25-to-40, career-oriented woman, and offer a medium-to-high price range. The merchandising mix emphasizes sports wear and ready-to-wear. In addition, for the lower-income consumer there are no-frills, self-service outlets called Pennington's Wearhouse.

In the early days, Pennington's had problems getting merchandise from manufacturers who cut most of their clothes in regular sizes.

As the company grew, they acquired more clout and now manufacturers pay some attention. However, the company still needs longer lead times because manufacturers do the biggest volume in regular sizes first. Clothing design work is done in-house, and most garments sold by Pennington's are designed by people at head office on the basis of experience, buying trips, and current styles. Over 70% of Pennington's merchandise is now developed in-house.

Advertising to this market could be a delicate problem. Pennington's tries to advertise on the basis of style and dignity. The newspaper and television ads are designed to "let the clothes do the talking" and the "glossy words" are kept to a minimum. The personal selling side is consistent with the store image as well. They hire overweight people as store clerks — in part because they can identify with the customer.

Pennington's has consistently increased its sales revenues each year. In addition, the company has a profit-to-sales ratio that is the envy of most retailers in Canada. It has done this by finding a target market and tailoring its offering to the needs of that segment.[1]

Organizations that sell to consumer and industrial markets recognize that they cannot appeal to all buyers in those markets, or at least not to all buyers in the same way. The buyers are too numerous, widely scattered, and varied in needs and buying practices. Different companies will be in better positions to serve certain segments of the market. Each company has to identify the parts of the market that it can serve best.

Sellers have not always practiced this philosophy. Their thinking passed through three stages:

Mass marketing   In mass marketing, the seller mass-produces, mass-distributes, and mass-promotes one product to all buyers. At one time Coca-Cola produced only one drink for the whole market, hoping it would appeal to everyone. The argument for mass marketing is that it should lead to the lowest costs and prices and create the largest potential market.

Product-differentiated marketing   Here the seller produces two or more products that have different features, styles, quality, sizes, and so on. Today Coca-Cola produces several soft drinks packaged in different sizes and containers. They are designed to offer variety to buyers rather than appeal to different market segments.

Target marketing   Here the seller identifies market segments, selects one or more of these segments, and develops products and marketing mixes tailored to each segment. For example, Coca-Cola developed Diet Coke to meet the needs of diet-conscious drinkers. Diet Coke met with remarkable success in Canada, becoming the leading diet soft drink brand one year after its introduction in 1982.[2] As well, Coca-Cola has targeted New Coke at the under 20s with slogans such as ''Catch the Wave'' and Coke Classic is aimed at the over 20s with themes like ''Red, White and You.''[3]

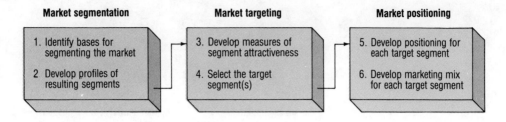

FIGURE 8-1
Steps in Market Segmentation, Targeting, and Positioning

Today's companies are moving away from mass marketing and product-differentiated marketing toward target marketing. Target marketing is more effective in helping sellers find marketing opportunities. The sellers can develop the right product for each target market. They can adjust their prices, distribution channels, and advertising to reach the target market efficiently. Instead of scattering their marketing effort ("shotgun" approach), they can focus it on the buyers who have the greater purchase interest ("rifle" approach).

Target marketing calls for three major steps (Figure 8-1). The first is *market segmentation*, dividing a market into distinct groups of buyers who might call for separate products or marketing mixes. The company identifies different ways to segment the market and develops profiles of the resulting market segments. The second step is *market targeting*, evaluating each segment's attractiveness and selecting one or more of the market segments to enter. The third step is *market positioning*, setting the competitive positioning for the product and a detailed marketing mix. This chapter will describe the principles of market segmentation, market targeting, and market positioning.

Market Segmentation

Markets consist of buyers, and buyers differ in one or more ways. They may differ in their wants, resources, locations, buying attitudes, and buying practices. Any of these variables can be used to segment a market.

The General Approach to Segmenting a Market

Figure 8-2A shows a market of six buyers. Each buyer is potentially a separate market because of unique needs and wants. Ideally, a seller might design a separate marketing program for each buyer. For example, a company like Budd Automotive of Kitchener, which produces car frames, faces only a few buyers

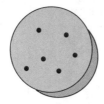

A. No market segmentation

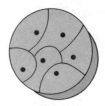

B. Complete market segmentation

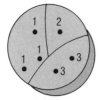

C. Market segmentation by income classes 1, 2, and 3

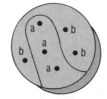

D. Market segmentation by age classes a and b

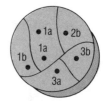

E. Market segmentation by income-age class

FIGURE 8-2
Different Segmentations of a Market

and treats them as separate markets. This complete market segmentation is shown in Figure 8-2B.

Most sellers will not find it worthwhile to "customize" their product to satisfy each specific buyer. Instead, the seller looks for broad classes of buyers who differ in their product needs or buying responses. For example, the seller may find that income groups differ in their wants. In Figure 8-2C, a number (1, 2, or 3) shows each buyer's income class. Lines are drawn around buyers in the same income class. Segmentation by income results in three segments.

On the other hand, the seller may find large differences between younger and older buyers. In Figure 8-2D, a letter (a or b) shows each buyer's age group. Segmentation by age results in two segments, each with three buyers.

Income and age may both count heavily in affecting the buyer's behavior toward the product. In this case, the market can be divided into five segments: 1a, 1b, 2b, 3a, and 3b. Figure 8-2E shows that segment 1a contains two buyers and the other segments contain one buyer.

Using more characteristics to segment the marker gives the seller finer precision, but this precision requires increasing the number of segments and reducing the population in each segment.

Bases for Segmenting Consumer Markets

There is no single way to segment a market. A marketer has to try different segmentation variables, alone and in combination, hoping to find the best way to view the market structure. Here we will look at the major geographic, demographic, psychographic, and behavior variables used in segmenting consumer markets (see Table 8-1).

TABLE 8-1
Major Segmentation Variables for Consumer Markets

Variable	Typical breakdowns
Geographic:	
Region	Maritimes, Ontario, Quebec, (Windsor-Quebec corridor), Prairies, British Columbia
City	Under 1000, 1000-2999, 3000-4999, 5000-9999, 10 000-14 999, 15 000-24 999, 25 000-49 999, 50 000-99 999, 100 000-199 999, 200 000-299 999, 300 000-399 999, 400 000-499 999, over 500 000
Density	Urban, suburban, rural
Climate	Pacific, Prairie, Central, Atlantic
Psychographic:	
Social class	Lower lowers, upper lowers, lower middles, upper middles, lower uppers, upper uppers
Life style	Use of one's time, values, beliefs
Personality	Compulsive, gregarious, authoritarian, ambitious
Behavioristic:	
Purchase occasion	Regular occasion, special occasion
Benefits sought	Quality, service, economy
User status	Nonuser, ex-user, potential user, first-time user, regular user
Usage rate	Light user, medium user, heavy user
Loyalty status	None, medium, strong, absolute
Readiness stage	Unaware, aware, informed, interested, desirous, intending to buy
Attitude toward product	Enthusiastic, positive, indifferent, negative, hostile
Demographic:	
Age	Under 6, 6-11, 12-19, 20-34, 35-49, 50-64, 65+
Sex	Male, female
Family size	1-2, 3-4, 5+
Family life cycle	Young, single; young, married, no children; young, married, youngest child under 6; young, married, youngest child 6 or over; older, married, with children; older, married, no children under 18; older, single; other
Income	Under $1000, 1000-9999, 10 000-14 999, 15 000-24 999, 25 000-34 999, 35 000-49 999, 50 000 and over
Occupation	Professional and technical; managers, officials, and proprietors; clerical, sales; craftspersons; operatives; farmers; retired; students; homemakers; unemployed
Education	Grade school or less; some high school; graduated high school; some university; graduated university
Religion	Catholic, Protestant, Jewish, Lutheran, other
Race	White, black, oriental, brown
Nationality	Canadian, American, British, French, German, Eastern European, Scandinavian, Italian, Latin American, Middle Eastern, Japanese, Chinese

Geographic Segmentation

Geographic segmentation divides the market into different geographical units such as nations, provinces, regions, counties, cities, or neighborhoods. The company decides to operate in one or a few geographical areas, or to operate in all areas but pay attention to geographical differences in needs and wants. For example, gasoline is sold nationally by Petro-Canada or Shell but is modified by region to accommodate differences in climate. Many beers in Canada have been brewed and sold on a regional basis, such as Moosehead in the Maritimes and Uncle Ben's in British Columbia.

Demographic Segmentation

Demographic segmentation divides the market into groups based on demographic variables such as age, sex, family size, family life cycle, income, occupation, education, religion, race, and nationality. Demographic factors are the most popular bases for segmenting customer groups. One reason is that consumer needs, wants, and usage rates often vary closely with demographic variables. Another is that demographic variables are easier to measure than most other types of variables. Even when market segments are first defined using bases such as personality or behavior, their demographic characteristics must be known in order to assess the size of the target market and to reach it efficiently.

Here we will show how certain demographic factors have been used in market segmentation.

Age and Life-Cycle Stage

Consumer needs and wants change with age. Some companies offer different products or use different marketing approaches for various age and life-cycle segments. For example, Richardson-Vicks offers four versions of its Life Stage vitamins, each designed for the special needs of specific age segments—chewable Children's Formula for children from 4 to 12 years; Teen's Formula for teenagers; and two adult versions (Men's Formula and Women's Formula). Johnson & Johnson developed Affinity Shampoo for women over 40 to help overcome age-related hair changes. National Trust, of Toronto, has offered a special savings account for children under 14 that includes a discount on a subscription to *Owl* magazine. Many retailers also recognize the importance of age. Firms such as Eaton's hold Senior Citizen days. Others, including Canadian Airline International and Air Canada, provide special discounts for people over 65 in an attempt to attract consumers from this rapidly growing age segment.

Age and life cycle can be tricky variables. For example, the Ford Motor Company considered the age of the buyer in developing the target market for its initial Mustang automobile. The car was designed to appeal to young people who wanted an inexpensive, sporty automobile. However, Ford found that the car was being purchased by all age groups. The company then realized that its target market was not the physically young but the psychologically young.

Ford built on the age and life-cycle strategy in the introduction of its new two-seater car. The target market is described as young adults aged 25 to 34, working women, or single parents with one or two children who want a small

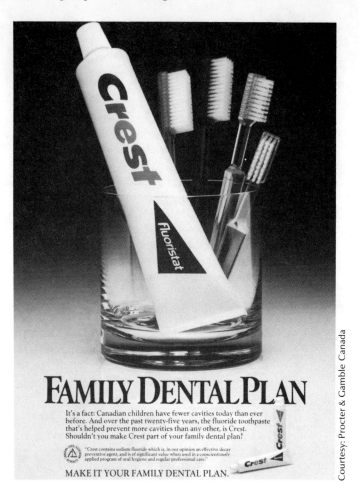

FAMILY DENTAL PLAN

It's a fact: Canadian children have fewer cavities today than ever before. And over the past twenty-five years, the fluoride toothpaste that's helped prevent more cavities than any other, is Crest. Shouldn't you make Crest part of your family dental plan?

"Crest contains sodium fluoride which is, in our opinion an effective decay preventive agent, and is of significant value when used in a conscientiously applied program of oral hygiene and regular professional care."

MAKE IT YOUR FAMILY DENTAL PLAN.

Courtesy: Procter & Gamble Canada

An example of family life-cycle segmentation.

practical car that has flair.[4] In this case, Ford used a combination of age, life-cycle, and psychographic segmentation.

Sex

Sex segmentation has long been used in clothing, hairdressing, cosmetics, and magazines. Occasionally other marketers will notice an opportunity for sex segmentation. The deodorant market provides a good example. Most deodorant brands are used by men and women alike. Procter and Gamble, however, developed Secret as the brand specially formulated for a woman's chemistry, and packaged and advertised the product to reinforce the female image. The automobile industry is also beginning to see the potential for sex segmentation. In the past, cars were designed to appeal to male and female family members. With more working women and women car owners, however, some manufacturers are designing cars especially for women drivers. Studies conducted by General Motors of Canada have identified the prime female market for Camaro as being between the ages of 27 and 35, with some buyers as young as 22. As well, 35% of the buyers of the sporty Mazda RX-7 in Canada are female.[5] Chrysler Canada has targeted the Le Baron for career and professional women under

40 and hopes to capture more of the younger working women car buyers with its Plymouth Turismo and Dodge Charger.[6]

Income

Income segmentation has long been used by the marketers of such products and services as automobiles, boats, clothing, cosmetics, and travel. Other industries sometimes see its possibilities. For example, Suntory, the Japanese liquor company, introduced a scotch selling for $75 to attract drinkers who want the very best.

At the same time, income does not always predict the customers for a given product. One would think that manual workers would buy Chevrolets and managers would buy Cadillacs. Yet many Chevrolets are bought by managers (often as a second car), and some Cadillacs are bought by manual workers (such as highly-paid plumbers and carpenters). Manual workers were among the first purchasers of color television sets; it was cheaper for them to buy these sets than to go out to movies and restaurants.

Psychographic Segmentation

In *psychographic segmentation*, buyers are divided into different groups based on social class, life style, or personality characteristics. People in the same demographic group can have very different psychographic profiles.

Social Class

We described the six social classes in Chapter 5 and showed that social class has a strong effect on preferences in cars, clothes, home furnishings, leisure activities, reading habits, and retailers. Many companies design products or services for specific social classes, building in features that appeal to the target social class.

Life Style

We saw in Chapter 5 that people's interest in various goods is affected by their life styles and that the goods they buy express their life styles. Marketers are increasingly segmenting their markets by consumer life styles. For example, a manufacturer of men's blue jeans will want to design jeans for a specific male life style group — the "active achiever," the "pleasure seeker," the " homebody," the "blue-collar outdoorsman," or the "business leader."[7] Each group would require different jeans designs, prices, advertising, and outlets. Unless the company states which specific life style group it is aiming at, its jeans may not appeal to any life style group at all.

Personality

Marketers have also used personality variables to segment markets. They give their products personalities that correspond to consumer personalities. Successful market segmentation strategies based on personality traits have been reported for such products as women's cosmetics, cigarettes, insurance, and liquor.[8] Burnett found that blood donors are low in self-esteem, low risk takers, and more concerned about their health; nondonors tend to be the opposite on all these dimensions.[9] This suggests that social agencies should use different marketing approaches for keeping current donors and attracting new ones.

Behavior Segmentation

In *behavior segmentation*, buyers are divided into groups based on their knowledge, attitude, use, or response to a product. Many marketers believe that behavior variables are the best starting point for building market segments.

Occasions

Buyers can be grouped according to occasions when they get an idea, make a purchase, or use a product. For example, air travel is triggered by occasions related to business, vacation, or family. Airlines such as Air Canada and Canadian can specialize in serving people who are flying for one of these occasions. Charter airlines such as Wardair serve people whose vacation includes flying somewhere.

Occasion segmentation can help firms build up product usage. For example, eggs are most often consumed at breakfast. The Canadian Egg Marketing

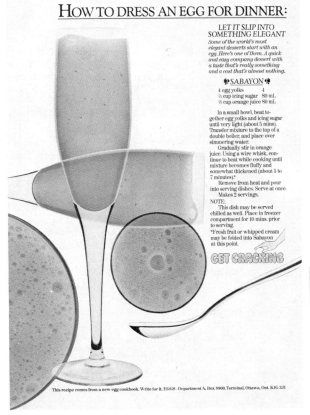

A well-known campaign promotes eggs for other occasions, not just for breakfast.

Courtesy: Canadian Egg Marketing Agency

Agency can promote eating eggs at lunch or dinner. Some holidays—Mother's Day and Father's Day, for example—were promoted partly to increase the sale of candy, flowers, cards, and other gifts.

Benefits Sought

A powerful form of segmentation is to group buyers according to the different benefits that they seek from the product. Yankelovich applied benefit segmentation to the purchase of watches. He found that "approximately 23% of the buyers bought for lowest price, another 46% bought for durability and general product quality, and 31% bought watches as symbols of some important occasion."[10] Most watch companies at the time focused strongly on the third segment by making expensive watches, stressing prestige, and selling through jewelry stores. The U.S. Time Company decided to focus on the first two segments. It created Timex watches and sold them through mass merchandisers. Using this segmentation strategy, U.S. Time became the world's largest watch company.

An interesting application of benefit segmentation was the study conducted by the Canadian Government Office of Tourism.[11] A survey of Americans who were potential vacation travelers to Canada identified six benefit segments as illustrated in Table 8-2. Through the use of advanced statistical techniques, a "perceptual map" can be constructed that links the benefits people are looking for, the kinds of people looking for each benefit, and the products or services that can deliver the benefits. A perceptual map of vacation travelers is illustrated in Figure 8-3.

TABLE 8-2

Benefit Segmentation of the Vacation Travel Market in Canada

Segment I. *Friends and relatives — nonactive visitor (29%)*. These vacationers seek familiar surroundings where they can visit friends and relatives. They are not very inclined to participate in any activity.

Segment II. *Friends and relatives — active city visitor (12%)*. These vacationers also seek familiar surroundings where they can visit friends and relatives, but they are more inclined to participate in activities — especially sightseeing, shopping, and cultural and other entertainment.

Segment III. *Family sightseers (6%)*. These vacationers are looking for a new vacation place that would be a treat for the children and an enriching experience.

Segment IV. *Outdoor vacationer (19%)*. These vacationers seek clean air, rest and quiet, and beautiful scenery. Many are campers and availability of recreation facilities is important. Children are also an important factor.

Segment V. *Resort vacationer (19%)*. These vacationers are most interested in water sports (e.g., swimming) and good weather. They prefer a popular place with a big city atmosphere.

Segment VI. *Foreign vacationer (26%)*. These vacationers look for vacations in a place they have never been before with a foreign atmosphere and beautiful scenery. Money is not of major concern but good accommodation and service are. They want an exciting, enriching experience.

Source: Shirley Young, Leland Ott, and Barbara Feigin, "Some Practical Considerations in Markets Segmentation," *Journal of Marketing Research*, August 1978, p. 408.

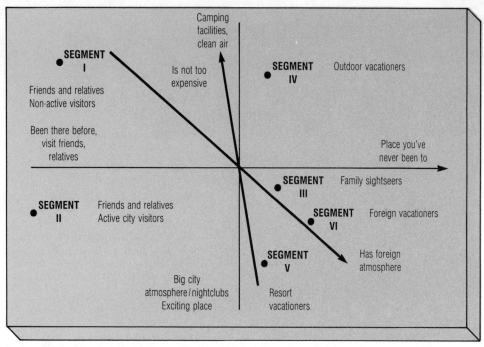

Source: Shirley Young, Leland Ott, and Barbara Feigin, "Some Practical Considerations in Markets Segmentation," *Journal of Marketing Research*, August 1978, p. 407.

FIGURE 8-3

A Perceptual Map of Vacation Benefits and Segments

Because of their relatively low vacation expenditures, segments I and II offered less attractive business potential than was offered by the other segments. Moreover, Canadian vacations could not provide an opportunity to visit with friends and relatives. The other segments had vacation needs and desires that could be delivered by various areas of Canada through different types of vacations. For each of these segments, data from the questionnaire were used to determine a profile in terms of behavior, psychographics, travel incentives, and image of a Canadian vacation.

Benefit segmentation requires finding out the major benefits people look for in the product class, the kinds of people who look for each benefit, and the major brands that deliver each benefit. One of the most successful benefit segmentations was reported by Haley, who studied the toothpaste market (see Table 8-3). Haley's research found four benefit segments: those seeking economy, protection, cosmetic, and taste benefits. Each benefit group had special demographic, behavior, and psychographic characteristics. For example, decay prevention seekers had large families, were heavy toothpaste users, and were conservative. Each segment also favored certain brands. A toothpaste company can use these results to clarify which benefit segment it is appealing to, its

TABLE 8-3
Benefit Segmentation of the Toothpaste Market

Benefit segments	Demographics	Behavior	Psychographics	Favored brands
Economy (low price)	Men	Heavy users	High autonomy, value oriented	Brands on sale
Medicinal (decay prevention)	Large families	Heavy users	Hypochondriac, conservative	Crest
Cosmetic (bright teeth)	Teens, young adults	Smokers	High sociability, active	Aqua-Fresh, Ultra Brite
Taste (good tasting)	Children	Spearmint lovers	High self-involvement, hedonistic	Colgate, Aim

Source: Adapted from Russell I. Haley, "Benefit Segmentation: A Decision Oriented Research Tool," Journal of Marketing, July 1963, pp. 30-35. See also Russell I. Haley, "Benefit Segmentation: Backwards and Forwards," Journal of Advertising Research, February-March 1984, pp. 19-25.

characteristics, and the major competitive brands. The company can also search for a new benefit and launch a brand that delivers this benefit.[12]

User Status

Many markets can be segmented into nonusers, ex-users, potential users, first-time users, and regular users of a product. High market share companies are particularly interested in attracting potential users, while smaller firms will try to attract regular users to their brand. Potential users and regular users require different kinds of marketing appeals.

Usage Rate

Markets can also be segmented into light-user, medium-user, and heavy-user groups. Heavy users are often a small percentage of the market but account for a high percentage of total buying. Using beer as an example, only 16% of the population accounts for 88% of total beer consumption. Heavy users drink over seven times as much beer as light users. Clearly a beer company would prefer to attract one heavy user to its brand over several light users. Most beer companies target the heavy beer drinker, using appeals such as Labatt's "me and the boys and our 50."

Loyalty Status

A market can also be segmented by consumer loyalty. Consumers can be loyal to brands (Old Vienna), stores (Eaton's), and companies (McCain Foods). Buyers can be divided into groups according to their degree of loyalty. Some consumers are completely loyal — they buy one brand all the time. Others are somewhat loyal — they are loyal to two or three brands of a given product, or favor one brand but buy others. Still other buyers show no loyalty to any brand. They want something different each time they buy, or always buy the brand on sale.

Each market is made up of different numbers of each type of buyer. A brand-loyal market has a high percentage of buyers with strong brand loyalty — the toothpaste market and the beer market seem to be fairly high brand-loyal markets. Companies selling in a brand-loyal market have a hard time gaining more market share, and companies trying to enter such a market have a hard time getting in.

A company can learn a lot by analyzing loyalty patterns in its market. It should study its own loyal customers. Colgate finds that its loyal buyers are more middle class, have larger families, and are more health conscious. This pinpoints the target market for Colgate. By studying its less loyal buyers, the company can pinpoint which brands are most competitive with its own. If many Colgate buyers also buy Crest, Colgate can attempt to improve its positioning against Crest, possibly by using direct comparison advertising. By looking at customers who are shifting away from its brand, the company can learn about its marketing weaknesses. As for nonloyals, the company can attract them by putting its brand on sale.

Buyer Readiness State

At any time, people are in different stages of readiness to buy a product. Some people are unaware of the product, some are aware, some are informed, some are interested, some want the product, and some intend to buy. The relative numbers make a big difference in designing the marketing program. Suppose a health agency wants women to take an annual Pap test to detect cervical cancer. At the beginning, most women may be unaware of the Pap test. The marketing effort should go into high-awareness building advertising, using a simple message. If successful, the advertising should then dramatize the benefits of the Pap test and the risks of not taking it, in order to move more women into the stage of desire. Facilities should be readied for handling the large number of women who may be moved to take the examination. In general, the marketing program must be adjusted to the changing distribution of buyer readiness.

Attitude

People in a market can be enthusiastic, positive, indifferent, negative, or hostile about a product. Door-to-door workers in a political campaign use the voter's attitude to determine how much time to spend with the voter. They thank enthusiastic voters and remind them to vote; they spend no time trying to change the attitudes of negative and hostile voters. They reinforce those who are positive and try to win the vote of the indifferent voters. In such marketing situations, attitudes can be effective segmentation variables.[13]

Bases for Segmenting Industrial Markets

Industrial markets can be segmented with many of the same variables used in consumer market segmentation. Industrial buyers can be segmented geographically and by several behavior variables: benefits sought, user status, usage rate, loyalty status, readiness stage, and attitudes.

A common way to segment industrial markets is by **end users**. Different end users often seek different benefits and can be approached with different marketing mixes. Consider the transistor market:

> The market for transistors consists of three submarkets: military, industrial, and commercial.
>
> The **military buyer** attaches great importance to product quality and availability. Firms selling transistors to the military market must make a large investment in R and D, use salespeople who know the military buying process, and specialize in limited-line products.
>
> **Industrial buyers**, such as computer manufacturers, look for high quality and good service. Price is not critical unless it becomes much too high. In this market, transistor manufacturers make a modest investment in R and D, use salespeople who have technical product knowledge, and offer a broad line.
>
> **Commercial buyers**, such as pocket-radio manufacturers, buy their components largely on price and delivery. Transistor manufacturers selling in this market need little or no R and D effort, use aggressive salespeople who are nontechnical, and offer common lines that can be mass-produced.

Customer size is another industrial segmentation variable. Many companies set up separate systems for dealing with major and minor customers. For example, Steelcase, a major manufacturer of office furniture, divides its customers into two groups:

> *Major accounts*   Accounts such as Petro-Canada and Dofasco are handled by national account managers working with field district managers.
>
> *Dealer accounts*   Smaller accounts are handled by field sales people working with dealers who sell Steelcase products.

Industrial companies typically define their target market opportunities by applying several segmentation variables at the same time.[14]

Requirements for Effective Segmentation

Clearly, there are many ways to segment a market, but not all segmentations are effective. For example, buyers of table salt could be divided into blond and brunette customers. However, hair color does not affect the purchase of salt. Furthermore, if all salt buyers buy the same amount of salt each month, believe all salt is the same, and want to pay the same price, the company would not benefit from segmenting this market.

To be useful, market segments must have the following characteristics:

Measurability   *The degree to which the size and purchasing power of the segments can be measured. Certain segmentation variables are difficult to measure. An illustration would be the size of the segment of teenage smokers who smoke primarily to rebel against their parents.*

Accessibility   *The degree to which the segments can be reached and served. Suppose a perfume company finds that heavy users of its brand are single women who are often out late at night and frequent bars. Unless this group lives or shops at certain places and is exposed to certain media, they will be difficult to reach.*

Substantiality   *The degree to which the segments are large or profitable. A segment should be the largest possible homogeneous group worth going after with a tailored marketing program. It would not pay, for example, for an automobile manufacturer to develop cars for persons whose height is less than four feet.*

Actionability   *The degree to which effective programs can be designed for attracting and serving the segments. A small airline, for example, identified seven market segments, but its staff was too small to develop separate marketing programs for each segment.*

Substantiality is a problem faced by Canadian marketers because of the relatively small size of the Canadian market. With a population of 26 million, many segments are not large and/or profitable enough for a company to pursue. The problem is also complicated by the geographic dispersion of the population, which increases the costs of distribution and advertising. To overcome these problems some Canadian companies have selected wider segments and developed strategies that appeal to a more general target market.[15]

Market Targeting

Marketing segmentation reveals the market segment opportunities facing the company. The company now has to decide on how many segments to cover and how to identify the best segments.

Three Market-Coverage Alternatives

The firm can adopt one of three market-coverage strategies, known as undifferentiated marketing, differentiated marketing, and concentrated marketing. These strategies are shown in Figure 8-4 and discussed below.

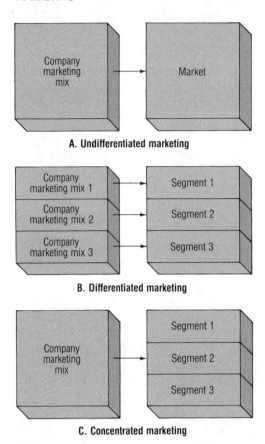

A. Undifferentiated marketing

B. Differentiated marketing

C. Concentrated marketing

FIGURE 8-4
Three Alternative Market Coverage Strategies

Undifferentiated Marketing

The company might decide to ignore market segment differences and go after the whole market with one market offer. By focusing on what is common in the needs of consumers, rather than on what is different, the company designs a product and marketing program that appeals to the most buyers. The company relies on mass distribution and mass advertising, and aims to give the product a superior image in people's minds.

Undifferentiated marketing provides cost economies. The narrow product line keeps down production, inventory, and transportation costs. The undifferentiated advertising program keeps down advertising costs. The absence of segment marketing research and planning lowers the costs of marketing research and product management. In Canada, some companies use this approach because of the small size of the total market.

However, most modern marketers have strong doubts about undifferentiated marketing. It is very difficult to develop a product or brand that will satisfy all consumers. The companies using undifferentiated marketing typically develop an offer aimed at the largest segments in the market. When several companies do this, there is heavy competition in the largest segments and less satisfaction in the smaller ones. The result is that the larger segments may be less profitable because they attract heavy competition. Recognition of this problem has resulted in a greater interest on the part of companies in smaller segments of the market.

Differentiated Marketing

Here the company decides to target several market segments and designs separate offers for each. General Motors tries to produce a car for every "purse, purpose, and personality." By offering product and marketing variations, it hopes for higher sales and a stronger position within each market segment. The company also hopes that a stronger position in several segments will strengthen consumers' overall identification of the company with the product category. In addition, General Motors hopes for greater repeat purchasing because the company's offer better matches the customer's desire.

A growing number of companies have adopted differentiated marketing. Here is an excellent example:[16]

> Dylex Limited operates a number of different retail chains, each appealing to a different market segment. Its clothing stores sell high-priced men's wear (Harry Rosen), medium-priced men's wear (Tip Top, Big Steel Man), moderate-priced men's wear (Thrifty's) and budget-priced men's wear (Family Fair). Often these stores will all be located in the same mall. Putting the stores near each other does not hurt them because they are aimed at different segments of the men's clothing market. Dylex also uses the strategy in women's wear (Fairweather, Town and Country, Suzy Shier, and Braemar). This strategy has helped Dylex more than double its sales every five years.

Chrysler Canada's Dodge Caravan and Chrysler Laser are aimed at market segments with quite different purses and personalities.

Differentiated marketing typically creates more total sales than undifferentiated marketing. Procter & Gamble Canada gets a higher total market share with five brands of hand soap than it could with only one. However, it also increases the costs of doing business. Modifying a product to meet different market segment requirements usually involves some R&D, engineering, or special tooling costs. It is usually more expensive to produce ten units of ten different products than 100 units of one product. Developing separate marketing plans for the separate segments requires extra marketing research, forecasting, sales analysis, promotion planning, and channel management. In addition, trying to reach different market segments with different advertising increases promotion costs. Therefore, the company must weigh increased sales against increased costs when deciding on a differentiated marketing strategy.

Concentrated Marketing

Many companies see a third possibility that is especially appealing when company resources are limited. Instead of going after a small share of a large market, the company goes after a large share of one or a few submarkets.

Many examples of concentrated marketing can be cited. Hewlett-Packard has concentrated on the high-priced calculator market and Richard D. Irwin on economics and business texts. Through concentrated marketing the company achieves a strong market position in the segments it serves, owing to its greater knowledge of the needs of the segment, and the special reputation it acquires. The company also enjoys many operating economies because of specialization in production, distribution, and promotion. If the segment is chosen well, the company can earn a high rate of return on its investment.

At the same time, concentrated marketing involves higher than normal risks. The particular market segment can turn sour or competitors may decide to enter the same segment. For these reasons, many companies prefer to diversify in several market segments.

Choosing a Market-Coverage Strategy

The following factors need to be considered in choosing a market-coverage strategy:[17]

Company resources   When the firm's resources are limited, concentrated marketing makes the most sense.

Product homogeneity   Undifferentiated marketing is more suited for homogeneous products such as grapefruit or steel. Products that can vary in design, such as cameras and automobiles, are more suited to differentiation or concentration.

Product stage in the life cycle   When a firm introduces a new product, it is practical to launch only one version, and undifferentiated marketing or concentrated marketing makes the most sense. In the mature stage of the product life cycle, differentiated marketing starts to make more sense.

> ***Market homogeneity***   *If buyers have the same tastes, buy the same amounts, and react the same way to marketing efforts, undifferentiated marketing is appropriate.*
>
> ***Competitive marketing strategies***   *When competitors segment the market, undifferentiated marketing can be disastrous. Conversely, when competitors use undifferentiated marketing, a firm can gain by using differentiated or concentrated marketing.*

Identifying Attractive Market Segments

Suppose the firm decides on concentrated marketing. It must now identify the most attractive segment to enter. Consider the following situation:

> A successful manufacturer of snow removal equipment is looking for a new product. Management reviews several opportunities and lands on the idea of producing snowmobiles. Management recognizes that it could make any of three product types: gasoline, diesel, or electric. It can design a snowmobile for any of three markets: consumer, industrial, or military. The nine product/market alternatives are shown in Figure 8-5. Assuming that the company wants to focus first on a single segment, management has to decide on which one.

The company needs to collect data on the nine market segments. The data would include current dollar sales, projected sales-growth rates, expected profit margins, strength of competition, marketing channel needs, and so on. The best segment would have large current sales, a high growth rate, a high profit

FIGURE 8-5
Product/Market Grid for Snowmobiles

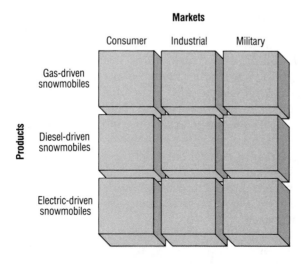

margin, weak competition, and simple marketing channel requirements. Usually no segment would be best in all these areas, and tradeoffs would have to be made.

After the company identifies the more objectively attractive segments, it must ask which segments fit its business strengths best. For example, the military market may be highly attractive, but the company may have had no experience in selling to the military. On the other hand, it may have lots of experience in selling to the consumer market. Thus the company seeks a segment that is attractive in itself and for which it has the necessary business strengths to succeed. It wants to target the segments in which it has the greatest strategic advantage.

Market Positioning

Once a company has decided which segments of the market it will enter, it must decide what "positions" it wants to occupy in those segments. A *product's position* is the way the product is **defined by consumers** on important attributes — the place the product occupies in consumers' minds relative to competing products. Thus Tide is positioned as an all-purpose, family detergent; Era is positioned as a concentrated liquid; Cheer is positioned as the detergent for all temperatures. Datsun and Toyota are positioned on economy; Mercedes and Cadillac are positioned on luxury.[18]

Consumers are overloaded with information about products and services. They cannot re-evaluate products every time they make a buying decision. To simplify buying decision making, consumers organize products into categories — they "position" products, services, and companies in their minds. A product's position is a complex set of consumer perceptions, impressions, and feelings that consumers hold for the product compared with competing products. Consumers position products with or without the help of marketers. However, marketers do not want to leave their products' positions to chance. They plan positions that will give their products the greatest advantage in selected target markets, and they design marketing mixes to create the planned positions.

The marketer can follow several positioning strategies.[19] It can position its product on specific **product attributes**: Hyundai advertises its low price; Saab promotes performance. Products can also be positioned on the needs they fill or the **benefits** they offer: Crest reduces cavities; Aim tastes good. Products can also be positioned according to **usage occasions**. In the summer, Gatorade can be positioned as a beverage for replacing athletes' body fluids; in the winter, it can be positioned as the drink to use when a doctor recommends drinking plenty of liquids. Another approach is to position the product for certain classes of **users**. Johnson & Johnson improved the market share for its baby shampoo from 3 to 14% by repositioning the product as one for adults who wash their hair often and need a gentle shampoo.

A product can be positioned directly **against a competitor**. In its famous "We're number two, so we try harder" campaign, Avis successfully positioned itself against larger Hertz. A product may also be positioned **away from com-**

In this advertisement, Kellogg's is positioning their breakfast cereals as nutritious to appeal to health-conscious consumers.

petitors — 7-Up became the number-three soft drink when it was positioned as the "un-cola," the fresh and thirst-quenching alternative to Coke and Pepsi.

Finally, the product can be positioned for different **product classes**. For example, some margarines are positioned against butter, others against cooking oils. Camay hand soap is positioned with bath oils rather than with soap. Marketers often use a combination of these positioning strategies. For example, Johnson & Johnson's Affinity shampoo is positioned as a hair conditioner for women over 40 (product class and user). Arm & Hammer baking soda has been positioned as a deodorizer for refrigerators or garbage disposals (product class and usage situation).

To plan a position for a current or new product, a company must first do a competitive analysis to identify the existing positions of its own and competing products. Suppose our snowmobile manufacturer learns that snowmobile buyers in its target segment are mostly interested in size and speed. Potential customers and dealers can be asked where they see competitors' snowmobiles along these dimensions. The findings are shown in the **product position map** in Figure 8-6. Competitor A is seen as producing small/fast snowmobiles; B, medium-size/medium-speed snowmobiles; C, small-to-medium-size/slow snowmobiles; and D, large/slow snowmobiles. The areas of the circles are proportional to the competitors' sales.[20]

Given these competitor positions, what position should the company seek? It has two choices. One is to establish a position next to one of the existing competitors and fight for market share. Management might do this if it feels that it can build a better snowmobile, the market is large enough for two competitors, the company has more resources than the competitor, or this position best fits the company's business strengths.

The other choice is to develop a snowmobile that is not now being offered to this market, such as a large/fast snowmobile. The company would win those customers seeking this type of snowmobile, since competitors are not offering it. Before making this decision, management has to be sure that enough buyers want a large/fast snowmobile and that it can build this snowmobile at the right

FIGURE 8-6
A Product Position Map Showing Perceived Offers of Four Competitors

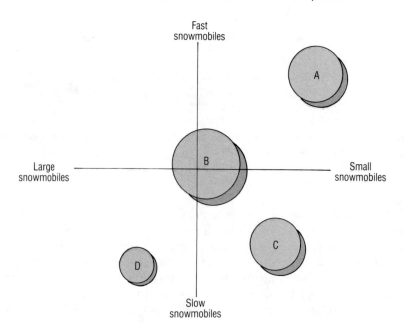

Courtesy: Bombardier Inc., Ski-doo

price level. If the answers are positive, the company has discovered a "hole" in the market and should move to fill it.

Suppose, however, that management decides there is more profit and less risk in building a small/fast snowmobile to compete with competitor A. In this case, it would study A's snowmobile and seek a way to differentiate its offer in the eyes of potential buyers. It can develop its competitive positioning on product features, style, quality, price, and other dimensions.

Once management decides on its positioning strategy, it can turn to the task of developing its detailed marketing mix. If the company decides to take the high-price/high-quality position in this market segment, it must develop superior product features and quality, find retailers who have a good reputation for service, develop advertising that appeals to affluent buyers, and so on.

The company's positioning decisions determine who its competitors will be. When setting its positioning strategy, the company should look at its competitive strengths and weaknesses compared to those of competitors, and select a position in which it can attain a strong competitive advantage.

Summary

Sellers can take three approaches to a market. **Mass marketing** is the decision to mass-produce and mass-distribute one product and attempt to attract all kinds of buyers. **Product differentiation** is the decision to produce two or more market offers differentiated in style, features, quality, or size, in order to offer variety to the market and set the seller's products apart from competitor's products. **Target marketing** is the decision to identify the different groups that make up a market and to develop products and marketing mixes for selected target markets. Sellers today are moving away from mass marketing and product differentiation toward target marketing because the latter is more helpful in spotting market opportunities and developing more effective products and marketing mixes.

The key steps in target marketing are market segmentation, market targeting, and market positioning. Market segmentation is the act of dividing a market into distinct groups of buyers who might merit separate products or marketing mixes. The marketer tries different variables to see which give the best segmentation opportunities. For consumer marketing, the major segmentation variables are geographic, demographic, psychographic, and behavioral. Industrial markets can be segmented by end use, customer size, geographic location, and product application. The effectiveness of the segmentation analysis depends upon finding segments that are measurable, accessible, substantial, and actionable.

Next, the seller has to target the best market segment(s). The first decision is how many segments to cover. The seller can ignore segment differences (undifferentiated marketing), develop different market offers for several segments (differentiated marketing), or go after one or a few market segments (concentrated marketing). Much depends on company resources, product and market homogeneity, product life-cycle stage, and competitive marketing strategies.

If the company decides to enter one segment, which one should it be? Market segments can be evaluated on their objective attractiveness and on company business strengths needed to succeed in that market segment.

Market selection, then, defines the company's competitors and positioning possibilities. The company researches the competitors' positions and decides whether to take a position similar to that of some competitor or to fill a hole in the market. If the company positions itself near another competitor, it must seek further differentiation through product features and price/quality differences. Its decision on positioning will then enable it to take the next step, planning the details of the marketing mix.

Questions for Discussion

1. When the Cadillac Cimarron was introduced, Cadillac officials said that even if they sold every car, they would consider the Cimarron a disaster if it had been sold only to traditional customers. The Cadillac merchandising director said: "Our salespeople will tell some buyers, 'This car isn't for you.'" Explain this sales rationale in terms of market segmentation.
2. After the market segmentation process has been completed, the organization should begin developing the marketing mix factors. Comment.
3. Discuss the three major steps in target marketing.

4. There is one single best way to segment a consumer market. Comment.

5. Give specific examples of marketers who have been successful in segmenting their markets on each of the following bases: low price; high quality; service.

6. Describe the requirements for effective segmentation and apply them to an example of your choice.

7. Differentiated marketing is always the best approach to target marketing. Comment.

Chapter 8 Key Terms

Behavior segmentation   Dividing a market into groups based on their knowledge, attitude, use, or response to a product.

Demographic segmentation   Dividing the market into groups based on demographic variables such as age, sex, family size, family life cycle, income, occupation, education, religion, race, and nationality.

Geographic segmentation   Dividing a market into different geographical units such as nations, provinces, regions, counties, cities, or neighborhoods.

Market   The set of all actual and potential buyers of a product.

Market positioning   Formulating a competitive positioning for a product and a detailed marketing mix.

Market segmentation   Dividing a market into distinct groups of buyers who might require separate products or marketing mixes.

Market targeting   Evaluating each market segment's attractiveness and selecting one or more segments to enter.

Product position   The way the product is defined by consumers on important attributes — the place the product occupies in consumers' minds relative to competing products.

Psychographic segmentation   Dividing a market into different groups based on social class, life style, or personality characteristics.

Cases for Chapter 8

Designing Products: Products, Brands, Packaging, and Services

Chapter Objectives

After reading this chapter, you should be able to:

1. Define product and the major classifications of consumer and industrial products.
2. Explain why companies use brands and identify the major branding decisions.
3. Describe the roles of product packaging.
4. Discuss the decisions that companies make when developing product lines and mixes.

When is ketchup more than just ketchup? When it's Heinz, of course! When is a headache tablet more than a headache tablet? When it's Aspirin. These are two classic examples of brands representing the product type almost as a generic term. In many cases these brand names become thoroughly entrenched in the consumer's mind and gain market dominance. Any competitor is at a severe disadvantage and must engage in a strategy that will make the brand stand out in the hope of capturing some portion of the remaining market. One way of accomplishing this is through distinctive packaging. The success of L'eggs pantyhose, Janitor in a Drum, and André's Cask Wines are, in part, due to unique packaging strategies.

The introduction of Miller beer in a long-neck bottle rather than the traditional brown stubby bottle helped it become one of the five top-selling brands in Canada. Labatt's countered with a long-neck bottle with a twist-top cap, and repackaging plans for other Labatt's brands. Molson responded by changing four of

their leading brands to new tall bottles. Clearly, the beer bottle packaging war was on.

When a company differentiates its product through packaging, that strategic element alone will not lead to success. While Heinz used packaging to revitalize interest by introducing the Keg O'Ketchup, this packaging strategy was employed in conjunction with the other parts of the marketing mix, which Heinz executed exceptionally well.

A small Toronto-based company, Grenadier Chocolate, had a product it felt could compete successfully with the chocolate-milk drink mixes marketed by the industry leaders: Cadbury's, Nestlé's (Quik), and Hershey's. Grenadier entered the market-place with a liquid milk mix, branded Milk Mate, in a plastic bottle. The product was physically differentiated from its major competition (bottle versus can, liquid versus solid). The shopper could easily relate to the bottled liquid form as many home products were packaged in this manner. Milk Mate's physical difference certainly made it eye-catching and somewhat appealing on the shelf; however, the shopper would be breaking long-established purchase and consumption habits by buying Milk Mate rather than an old familiar brand like Nestlé's Quik.

Along with a unique package and a differentiated product form, Milk Mate had to provide definite benefits or value to the consumer. Without some tangible benefits the incentive to switch brands might be too low. Milk Mate advertised the product extensively, focusing on a number of benefits including:

- Convenience—no awkward measuring as in the powdered form.
- No waste—doesn't solidify in chunks like the powder.
- No mess—no spoons on counters, in glasses.
- Dissolves easily.
- Kid proof—no mess, no waste, convenient.
- Same value—equal or lower cost per serving.

The advertising themes pointed out the advantages of the unique product form, as well as stressing the cost equivalency with the powdered-milk mixes on a per-serving basis. This promotional strategy attempted to reduce the risk in changing brands.

Milk Mate proved to be a successful new product entry into the market, a somewhat rare event in situations where there are well-established brands. Milk Mate was a differentiated, competitive product with a well-designed marketing strategy that included some excellent packaging ideas.

Milk Mate's success is based on developing an original and attractive product concept for its target market. Grenadier Chocolate is not just selling a milk modifier, but an augmented product that has achieved acceptance by the market. Marketers do not believe that "a product is a product is a product." Constructing the product concept is an important first step in marketing mix planning.[1]

The chapter begins with the question, what is a product? We will then look at ways to classify products in consumer and industrial markets, and look for links between types of products and marketing strategies. Next, we will see that each product involves several decisions beyond basic product design, such as branding, packaging, and the offering of various customer services. Finally, we will move from decisions about individual products to decisions about building product lines and product mixes.

What is a Product?

A Wilson tennis racquet, a Superclips haircut, a Bryan Adams concert, a Club Med vacation, a two-ton truck, Head skis, and a telephone answering service are all products. We define product as follows:

> *A product is anything that can be offered to a market for attention, acquisition, use, or consumption that might satisfy a want or need. It includes physical objects, services, persons, places, organizations, and ideas.*[2]

Product planners need to think about the product on three levels. The most basic level is the **core product**, which answers the question, what is the buyer really buying? Every product is really a package of problem-solving services.

A woman buying lipstick buys more than lip color. Charles Revson of Revlon saw this early: "In the factory, we make cosmetics; in the store, we sell hope." Theodore Levitt pointed out that buyers "do not buy quarter-inch drills; they buy quarter-inch holes." Super salesman Elmer Wheeler would say, "Don't sell the steak — sell the sizzle." Marketers must uncover the needs hiding under every product, and sell **benefits**, not **features**. The core product stands at the center of the total product, as illustrated in Figure 9-1.

The product planner has to turn the core product into an **actual product**. Perfume, computers, and political candidates are all actual products. Actual products may have as many as five characteristics: a **quality level**, **features**, **styling**, a **brand name**, and **packaging**.

Finally, the product planner may offer additional services and benefits that make up an **augmented product**. IBM's success is partly a result of its skillful augmentation of its actual product—the computer. While its competitors were busy selling computer features to buyers, IBM saw that customers wanted solutions, not hardware. Customers wanted instruction, canned software programs, programming services, quick repairs, and guarantees. IBM sold a system, not just a computer.

Product augmentation leads the marketer to look at the buyer's total consumption system. In this way, the marketer will find many ways to augment its offer and make it more competitive. According to Levitt:

> The *new* competition is not between what companies produce in their factories, but between what they add to their factory output in the form of packaging, services, advertising, customer advice, financing, delivery arrangements, warehousing, and other things that people value.[3]

FIGURE 9-1
Three Levels of Product

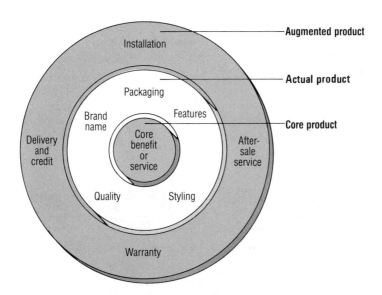

A product is more than a simple set of tangible features. In fact, some products (a haircut or a doctor's exam) have no tangible features. Consumers see products as complex bundles of benefits that satisfy their needs. When developing products, marketers must first identify the core consumer needs the product will satisfy. They must then design the actual product and find ways to augment the product to create the bundle of benefits that will best satisfy consumers.

Product Classifications

In seeking marketing strategies for individual products, marketers have developed several product classification schemes based on product characteristics.

Durable Goods, Nondurable Goods, and Services

Products can be classified into three groups according to their durability or tangibility:[4]

Nondurable goods *Tangible goods normally consumed in one or a few uses. Examples include beer, soap, and salt.*

Durable goods *Tangible goods that normally survive many uses. Examples include refrigerators, machine tools, and clothing.*

Services *Activities, benefits, or satisfactions that are offered for sale. Examples include haircuts and repairs.*

Because of the growing importance of services in our society, we will look at them more closely in Chapter 19.

Consumer Goods Classification

Consumer goods are those bought by final consumers for personal consumption. Marketers usually classify these goods based on **consumer shopping habits**. We can distinguish among convenience, shopping, specialty, and unsought goods (see Figure 9-2).[5]

FIGURE 9-2
Classification of Consumer Goods

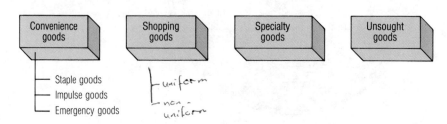

Convenience goods   *Consumer goods that the customer usually buys frequently, immediately, and with a minimum of comparison and buying effort. Examples include tobacco products, soap, and newspapers.*

Convenience goods can be further divided into staples, impulse goods, and emergency goods. **Staples** are goods that consumers buy on a regular basis, such as Heinz ketchup, Crest toothpaste, or Ritz crackers. **Impulse goods** are purchased without any planning or search effort. These goods are normally available in many places because consumers seldom look for them. Therefore, candy bars and magazines are often placed next to checkout counters because shoppers may not have thought of buying them. **Emergency goods** are purchased when a need is urgent—umbrellas during a rainstorm, boots and shovels during the first winter snowstorm. Manufacturers of emergency goods will place them in many outlets to avoid losing the sale when the customer needs these goods.

Shopping goods   *Consumer goods that the customer, in the process of selection and purchase, usually compares on such bases as suitability, quality, price, and style. Examples include furniture, clothing, used cars, and major appliances.*

In defining and providing examples of shopping goods, the marketer should remember that the description is for the typical customer. Many people do compare prices and brands, and shop around when purchasing furniture and appliances. For example, one study of Canadian furniture buyers found that the average buyer made about five store visits and sought information from two different sources before purchasing furniture.[6] However, some buyers went to only one store and did very little comparison shopping before buying. For these buyers, the process was more similar to routinized response behavior than limited or extensive problem solving. Marketing to these atypical buyers might emphasize convenience and ease of shopping.

Shopping goods can be divided into **uniform** and **nonuniform** goods. The buyer sees uniform shopping goods as being similar in quality but different enough in price to justify shopping comparisons. The seller has to "talk price" to the buyer. But in shopping for clothing, furniture, and more nonuniform goods, product features are often more important to the consumer than the price. If the buyer wants a new suit, the cut, fit, and look are likely to be more important than small price differences. The seller of nonuniform shopping goods must therefore carry a wide assortment to satisfy individual tastes and must have well-trained salespeople to give information and advice to customers.

Specialty goods   *Consumer goods with unique characteristics or brand identification for which a significant group of buyers is willing to make a special purchase effort. Examples include specific brands and types of fancy goods, cars, stereo components, photographic equipment, and men's suits.*

A Mercedes, for example, is a specialty good because buyers are willing to travel a great distance to buy one. Buyers do not compare specialty goods. They only invest time to reach the dealers carrying the wanted products. The dealers do not need convenient locations, but they must let buyers know their locations.

Unsought goods *Consumer goods that the consumer does not know about or knows about but does not normally think of buying. New products such as smoke detectors and compact disc players are unsought goods until the consumer is made aware of them through advertising. The classic examples of known but unsought goods are life insurance and encyclopedias.*

Industrial Goods Classification

Industrial goods are those bought by individuals and organizations for further processing or for use in conducting a business. The distinction between a consumer good and an industrial good is based on the purpose for which the product is purchased. If a consumer buys a lawnmower for use around the home, the lawnmower is a consumer good. If the same consumer buys the same lawnmower for use in a landscaping business, the lawnmower is an industrial good.

Industrial goods can be classified in terms of how they enter the production process and their cost. There are three groups: materials and parts, capital items, and supplies and services (see Figure 9-3).

Materials and parts *Industrial goods that enter the manufacturer's product completely. They fall into two classes: raw materials and manufactured materials and parts.*

Raw materials include farm products (wheat, livestock, fruits and vegetables) and natural products (fish, lumber, crude petroleum, iron ore). Each is marketed somewhat differently. Farm products are supplied by many small producers who turn them over to marketing intermediaries, who in turn process and sell them. In Canada, this intermediary function is frequently provided by a marketing board. Over 100 marketing boards have been established by producers to perform a variety of marketing functions. Some boards provide a means of buying and selling the products, such as the Pork Board in Ontario, which operates auction yards for its members. Other boards not only provide all the distribution functions but also control both production levels and prices for the products. For example, in the dairy industry and the egg industry, the marketing board governs how much a farmer can produce and at what prices the products will be sold. These two boards also actively promote their products. While there has been considerable controversy concerning the role of marketing boards in

FIGURE 9-3
Classification of Industrial Goods

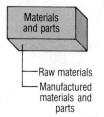

Materials and parts
— Raw materials
— Manufactured materials and parts

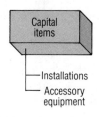

Capital items
— Installations
— Accessory equipment

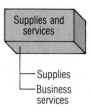

Supplies and services
— Supplies
— Business services

the Canadian economy, the boards have helped improve the distribution efficiency of farmers.[7]

Natural products are highly limited in supply. They usually have great bulk and low unit value and require lots of transportation from producer to user. There are fewer and larger producers, who tend to market them directly to industrial users. Because the users depend on these materials, long-term supply contracts are common. The uniformity of natural materials limits demand creation activity. Price and delivery are the major factors affecting the selection of suppliers.

Manufactured materials and parts include component materials (iron, yarn, cement, wires) and component parts (small motors, tires, castings). Component materials are usually processed further—for example, pig iron is made into steel and yarn is woven into cloth. The uniform nature of component materials usually means that price and supplier reliability are the most important purchase factors. Component parts enter the finished product completely with no further change in form, as when small motors are put into vacuum cleaners and tires are added to automobiles. Most manufactured materials and parts are sold directly to industrial users. Price and service are the major marketing factors, and branding and advertising tend to be less important.

Capital items   Industrial goods that enter the finished product partly. They include two groups: installations and accessory equipment.

Installations consist of buildings (factories, offices) and fixed equipment (generators, drill presses, computers, elevators). Installations are major purchases. They are usually bought directly from the producer after a long decision period. The producers use a top-notch salesforce, which often includes sales engineers. The producers have to be willing to design to specification and to supply postsale services. Advertising is used but is much less important than personal selling.

Accessory equipment includes portable factory equipment and tools (hand tools, lift trucks) and office equipment (typewriters, desks). These products do not become part of the finished product. They simply aid in the production process. They have a shorter life than installations, but a longer life than operating supplies. Most accessory equipment sellers use middlemen because the market is spread out geographically, the buyers are numerous, and the orders are small. Quality, features, price, and service are major factors in supplier selection. The salesforce tends to be more important than advertising, although advertising can be used effectively.

Supplies and services   Industrial goods that do not enter the finished product at all.

Supplies include operating supplies (lubricants, coal, typing paper, pencils) and maintenance and repair items (paint, nails, brooms). Supplies are the convenience goods of the industrial field because they are usually purchased with a minimum effort or comparison. They are normally marketed through resellers because of the low unit value of the goods and the great number of customers spread out across the country. Price and service are important factors because suppliers are quite similar and brand preference is not high.

Business services include maintenance and repair services (window cleaning, typewriter repair), and business advisory services (legal, management consulting, advertising). These services are usually supplied under contract. Maintenance services are often provided by small producers, and repair services are often available from the manufacturers of the original equipment. Business advisory services are normally new task-buying situations, and the industrial buyer will choose the supplier on the basis of the supplier's reputation and personnel.

We have seen that a product's characteristics will have a major effect on marketing strategy. At the same time, marketing strategy will also depend on such factors as the product's stage in the life cycle, the number of competitors, the degree of market segmentation, and the condition of the economy.

Brand Decisions

Consumers view a brand as an important part of the product, and branding can add value to the product. For example, most consumers would perceive a bottle of Chanel No. 5 as a high quality, expensive perfume. But the same perfume in an unmarked bottle would be viewed as lower in quality even though the fragrance is identical. Therefore, branding decisions are an important part of product strategy.

First, we should become familiar with the language of branding. Here are some key definitions:[8]

Brand   A name, term, sign, symbol, or design, or a combination of them intended to identify the goods or services of one seller or group of sellers and to differentiate them from those of competitors.

Brand name   That part of a brand that can be vocalized — the utterable. Examples are Avon, Chevrolet, and UBC (University of British Columbia).

Brand mark   That part of a brand that can be recognized but is not utterable, such as a symbol, design, or distinctive coloring or lettering. Examples are the Air Canada maple leaf and the Royal Bank lion.

Trademark   A brand or part of a brand that is given legal protection — it protects the seller's exclusive rights to use the brand name or brand mark.

Copyright   The exclusive legal right to reproduce, publish, and sell the matter and form of a literary, musical, or artistic work.

Branding creates difficult decisions for the marketer. The key decisions are shown in Figure 9-4 and discussed below.

Branding Decision

The company must first decide whether it should put a brand name on its product. Historically, most products went unbranded. Producers and middle-

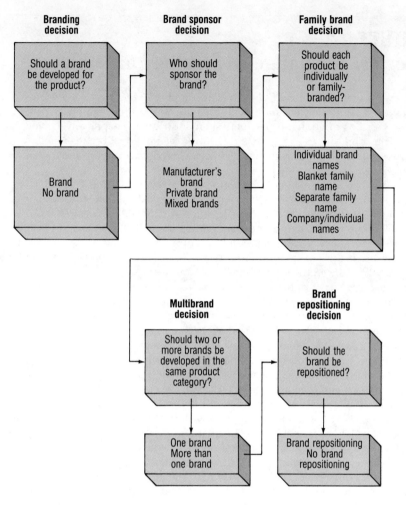

FIGURE 9-4
An Overview of Branding Decisions

men sold their goods directly out of barrels, bins, and cases without supplier identification. However, in Canada today hardly anything is sold unbranded. Salt is packaged in branded containers, oranges are stamped with growers' names, common nuts and bolts are packaged with a distributor's label, and automobile parts—spark plugs, tires, filters—bear brand names that differ from those of the automakers.

Recently there has been a return to "no branding" of certain consumer goods. These "generics" are plainly packaged with no manufacturer identification (see Exhibit 9-1). The intent of generics is to bring down the cost to the consumer by saving on packaging and advertising. As a result, the issue of branding versus no branding is very much alive today.

EXHIBIT 9-1
Generics: A Change in Strategy at Loblaws

Generics were first introduced in North America in 1977 by Jewel Food Stores, a large Chicago-based supermarket chain. Generics are unbranded, plainly packaged, less expensive versions of common products such as spaghetti, paper towels, and canned peaches. They offer prices as much as 30% lower than national brands. The lower price is made possible by lower-quality ingredients, lower-cost packaging, and lower advertising costs.

Two Canadian supermarkets, Dominion and Loblaws, followed Jewel Stores and introduced generics early in 1978. However, Loblaws quickly became the leader in generic sales. In the 15 months since 16 generic products first went on the shelf, Loblaws sold over 30 million no-name items and expanded the line to 120 products. By 1983 Loblaws carried over 500 generic products, which accounted for about 10% of their grocery volume. Of the total no-name products Loblaws introduced, about 60% ranked number one in the dollar sales in their categories.

The price savings of generics appeal strongly to consumers, but product quality remains an important factor in consumers' buying decisions. Generics have sold better in product areas where consumers care less about quality or see little quality difference between generics and national brands. Areas such as paper products, frozen foods, peanut butter, canned vegetables, plastic bags, disposable diapers, and dog food have been hardest hit by generics. Generics have had less success in such areas as health and beauty aids, where consumers are less willing to trade quality for price.

It appears that generics peaked in 1983. Since then, the market share for generics has dropped off a little. This decline has resulted partly from an improved economy—consumers now have more income than they did when generics exploded in the late 1970s and early 1980s. Furthermore, the inflation rate has declined. However, generics still hold about 15% share of supermarket sales in Canada.

Sales of generics at Loblaws, about 20% of total sales, are even higher than the national share, but with a difference. Loblaws offers two "generics": the "No-Name" label, which is a typical generic, and the "President's Choice" label, which is a house brand that is actively promoted by Loblaws. Loblaws is blurring the image of generics and gaining market share for its brands at the expense of brand-name manufacturers.

The overall decline in generics has also resulted from better marketing strategies by brand-name manufacturers. These marketers have responded by emphasizing brand image and quality. Another strategy is to cut costs and pass the savings along to consumers through lower prices and greater values. The brand-name manufacturer can also introduce lower-quality, lower-priced products that compete directly with generic products. Procter & Gamble, for example, introduced its line of Banner paper products.

This raises the questions: Why have branding in the first place? Who benefits? How do they benefit? At what cost?

Branding helps buyers in many ways. Brand names tell the buyer something about product quality. Buyers who always buy the same brand know that they will get the same quality each time they buy. Brand names also increase the shopper's efficiency. Imagine a buyer going into a supermarket and finding

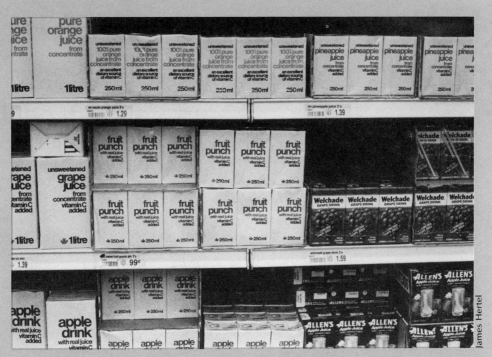

Consumers have the choice of generic or branded products.

Although this line offered less quality than other P&G brands, it offered greater quality than generics at a competitive price.

The brand-name marketers must convince consumers that their product's higher quality is worth the extra cost. Branded products that offer a large quality difference will not be hurt much by generics. Those most threatened are weak national brands and lower-price store brands that offer little additional quality. Why pay 20 to 40% more for a branded item, when its quality is not much different from that of its generic cousin?

Sources: Martha R. McEnally and Jon M. Hawes, "The Market for Generic Brand Grocery Products: A Review and Extension," *Journal of Marketing*, Winter 1984, pp. 75-83; Bernard Portis, Terry Deutscher, and Jorgen Rasmussen, "Trial and Satisfaction with Generic Grocery Products in Canada," *ASAC Conference, Marketing Division Proceedings* (Montreal: 1980), pp. 280-288; and Ben Fiber, "Loblaws Focuses on Own Products," *The Globe and Mail*, June 9 1986, p. B1.

thousands of unlabelled products. Finally, brand names help call consumers' attention to new products that might benefit them. Brands become the basis upon which a whole story can be built about the new product's special qualities.

Branding also gives the seller several advantages. The brand name makes it easier for the seller to process orders and track down problems. The seller's brand name and trademark provide legal protection of unique product features,

You make us better.

Here are some well-known brand marks.

Royal Bank of Canada brand mark used with permission of the Royal Bank of Canada
Esso brand mark used with permission of Imperial Oil Ltd.
Petro-Canada brand mark used with permission of Petro-Canada

which would otherwise be copied by competitors. Branding lets the seller attract a loyal and profitable set of customers. Branding also helps the seller to segment markets — P&G can offer five soap brands, not just one general product for all consumers.

Brand Sponsor Decision

In deciding to brand a product, the manufacturer has three sponsorship options. The product may be launched as a **manufacturer's brand** (also called a national brand). Alternatively, the manufacturer may sell the product to middlemen who put on a **private brand** (also called middlemen brand, distributor brand, or dealer brand). The manufacturer may also sell some output under its own brand names and some under private labels. Kellogg's and IBM sell almost all their output under their own brand names. The Canadian Appliance Manufacturing Company sells all its output under various distributors' names. Laura Secord makes puddings both under its own name and under a no-name or generic product. By doing this it holds the leading share among branded puddings as well as the generic field.[9]

Manufacturers' brands have dominated the Canadian scene. Consider such well-known brands as Campbell's soup and Heinz ketchup. Recently, however, large retailers and wholesalers have developed their own brands. Canadian Tire, Eaton's, Simpsons, The Bay, Woodwards, Loblaws, and other store chains are promoting their own brands.

Family Brand Decision

Manufacturers who brand their products face several further choices. There are at least four brand-name strategies:

1. **Individual brand names**   This policy is followed by Canada Packers (Maple Leaf, York, Domestic, Dial, and Devon).

2. **A blanket family name for all products**   This policy is followed by Heinz and Philips.

3. **Separate family names for all products**   This policy is followed by Greb

(Hush Puppies for leisure shoes, Kodiak for work boots, and Bauer for hockey equipment).

4. **Company trade name combined with individual product names**   This policy is followed by Kellogg's (Kellogg's Rice Krispies and Kellogg's Raisin Bran).

What are the advantages of an individual brand-names strategy? A major advantage is that the company does not tie its reputation to the product's acceptance. If the product fails, it does not hurt the company's name.

Using a blanket family name for all products also has some advantages. The cost of introducing the product will be less, because there is no need for heavy advertising to create brand recognition and preference. Furthermore, sales will be strong if the manufacturer's name is good. For example, new soups introduced under the Campbell brand name get instant recognition.

When a company produces very different products, it may not be best to use one blanket family name. Swift Canada uses separate family names for its turkeys (Butterball) and fertilizers (Vigoro). Companies will often invent different family brand names for different quality lines within the same product

Procter & Gamble uses an individual brand names strategy that allows the brands to compete in various market segments.

Courtesy: Procter & Gamble Canada

class. Thus A&P sells a first-grade, second-grade, and third-grade set of brands — Ann Page, Sultana, and Iona.

Finally, some manufacturers want to use their company name along with an individual brand name for each product. The company name adds familiarity to the new product, while the individual name sets it apart from other company products. Thus *Quaker Oats* in Quaker Oats Cap'n Crunch taps the company's reputation for breakfast cereal, while *Cap'n Crunch* sets apart and dramatizes the new product.

Multibrand Decision

A seller uses a multibrand strategy when it develops two or more brands in the same product category. This marketing practice was pioneered by P&G when it introduced Cheer as a competitor for its already successful Tide. Although Tide's sales dropped slightly, the combined sales of Cheer and Tide were higher. P&G now produces five detergent brands.

Manufacturers use multibrand strategies for several reasons. First, they can gain more shelf space, thus increasing the retailer's dependence on their brands. Second, few consumers are so loyal to a brand that they will not try another. The only way to capture the "brand switchers" is to offer several brands. Third, creating new brands develops healthy competition within the manufacturer's organization. Managers of different General Motors brands compete to outperform each other. Fourth, a multibrand strategy positions brands on different benefits and appeals, and each brand can attract a separate following.

Brand Repositioning Decision

However well a brand is initially positioned in a market, the company may have to reposition it later. A competitor may launch a brand next to the company's brand and cut into its market share, or customer wants may shift, leaving the company's brand with less demand. Marketers should consider repositioning existing brands before introducing new ones. In this way they can build on existing brand recognition and consumer loyalty.

Repositioning may require changing both the product and its image. P&G repositioned Bold detergent by adding a fabric softening ingredient. A brand can also be repositioned by changing only the product's image. Ivory Soap was repositioned without change from a "baby soap" to an "all natural soap" for adults who want healthy-looking skin.

Selecting a Brand Name

The brand name should be carefully chosen. Stern noted that a good brand name:

> . . . can save millions of dollars over the product's life because it carries its own meaning, describes the product's advantages, is instantly recognized and serves to differentiate the product ... often millions of dollars are spent to develop a

product and to see it just through its first year of public life. That is a lot of cash to bet on haphazard brand name development and vest-pocket testing.[10]

Most large marketing companies have developed a formal brand-name selection process. Finding the best brand name is a difficult task. It begins with a careful review of the product and its benefits, the target market, and proposed marketing strategies. Among the desirable qualities for a brand name are the following: (1) It should suggest something about the product's benefits and qualities. Examples: Beautyrest, Craftsman, Sunkist, Spic and Span, Zest. (2) It should be easy to pronounce, recognize, and remember (short names help). Examples: Tide, Crest. (3) It should be distinctive. Examples: Mustang, Kodak.

Once chosen, the brand name must be protected. Many firms try to build a brand name that will eventually become identified with the product category. Such brand names as Frigidaire, Kleenex, Levi's, Jello, Scotch Tape, and Fiberglas have succeeded in this way. However, their very success may threaten the the company's rights to the name. Cellophane, nylon, and shredded wheat are now names that any seller can use.

Packaging Decisions

Many products offered to the market have to be packaged. Some marketers have called packaging a fifth P, along with price, product, place, and promotion. Most marketers, however, treat packaging as an element of product strategy.

Packaging is the activities of designing and producing the container or wrapper for a product.

The container or wrapper is called the package. The package may include up to three levels of material. The **primary package** is the product's immediate container. The bottle holding Old Spice After-Shave Lotion is the primary package. The **secondary package** is the material that protects the primary package and that is thrown away when the product is about to be used. The cardboard box containing the bottle of after-shave lotion is a secondary package that allows for additional protection and promotion. The **shipping package** is packaging necessary to store, identify, and ship the product. A corrugated box carrying six dozen Old Spice After-Shave Lotions is a shipping package. Finally, **labelling** is part of packaging and consists of printed information appearing on or with the package.

Traditionally, packaging decisions were based mostly on cost and production factors; the primary function of the package was to contain and protect the product. In recent times, however, numerous factors have made packaging an important marketing tool. An increase in self-service means that packages must now perform many sales tasks, from attracting attention, to describing the product, to making the sale.[11] Rising consumer affluence means that consumers are willing to pay a little more for the convenience, appearance, dependability, and prestige of better packages.

James Hertel

Simple, classic, and attractive packaging helps create an image for a line of cosmetics.

Companies are realizing the power of good packaging to create instant consumer recognition of the company or brand. Every film buyer immediately recognizes the familiar yellow packaging of Kodak film. Innovative packaging can also give the company an advantage over competitors. When Imperial Oil switched from packaging motor oil in cans to plastic, the change was enthusiastically received by both service station operators and consumers. Chateau-Gai Wines packaged San Gabriel wine in a box made of polyethylene, foil, and cardboard, and it became a Canadian best-seller.[12]

Developing a good package for a new product requires many decisions. The first task is to establish the packaging concept. The packaging concept states what the package should *be* or *do* for the product. Should the main functions of the package be to offer product protection, introduce a new dispensing method, suggest certain qualities about the product or the company, or something else?

Decisions must be made on specific elements of the package—size, shape, materials, color, text, and brand mark. These various elements must work together to support the product's position and marketing strategy. The package must be consistent with the product's advertising, pricing, distribution, and other marketing strategies.

Companies usually consider several different package designs for a new product. To select the best package, the company must test the various designs to find the one that stands up best under normal use, that dealers find easiest to handle, and that consumers respond to most favorably.

After selecting and introducing the package, the company must check it regularly in the face of changing consumer preferences and advances in technology. In the past, a package design might last for 15 years before changes were needed. In today's rapidly changing environment, most companies must recheck their packaging every two or three years.[13] Keeping a package up to date usually requires only minor, but regular, changes—changes so subtle that they go unnoticed by most consumers.

Cost remains an important packaging consideration. Developing the packaging for a new product may cost a few hundred thousand dollars and take from a few months to a year. Converting to a new package may cost millions, as the major Canadian breweries learned when they entered the "packaging" wars that resulted in reduced profits for two years.[14] Marketers must weigh packaging costs against consumer perceptions of value added by the packaging, and against the role of packaging in helping to attain marketing objectives. In making packaging decisions, the company must also heed growing societal concerns about packaging and make decisions that serve society's interests as well as customer and company objectives (see Exhibit 9-2).

Packaging is an important part of L'eggs marketing mix.

James Hertel

EXHIBIT 9-2
Packaging and Public Policy

Packaging is attracting more and more public attention. Marketers should heed the following issues in making their packaging decisions.

1. *Fair packaging and labelling* The public has traditionally been concerned with packaging and labelling that might be false and misleading. Both the federal and provincial governments have responded to this concern by providing a considerable amount of legislation in regard to packaging. It is estimated that there are over 100 regulations in place affecting packages of all shapes and sizes. The four main pieces of legislation are:

- *The Consumer Packaging and Labelling Act* requires the net weight to be in metric units and the identity of the product to be on the main display surface in English and French.
- *The Food and Drug Act* requires ingredient listings in descending order of product importance, and, for perishable products, a "best before" date stamp must be included. All information must be in English and French.
- *The Hazardous Products Act* applies to products, listed on a schedule, that are considered to be a hazard to public health or safety. For those consumer products, the degree of hazard is identified with a series of symbols that warns of any potential danger, in English and French.
- *Bill 101* (Province of Quebec) requires French to be on the package or product, and any other language cannot occupy more space than the French listings.

Other legislation that directly affects the package and/or label includes the National Trademark and True Labelling Act and the Textile Labelling Act.

2. *Excessive cost* Critics have called packaging excessive in many cases, charging that it raises prices. They point to secondary "throwaway" packaging and question its

Customer Service Decisions

Customer service is another element of product strategy. A company's offer to the marketplace usually includes some services. Service can be a minor or a major part of the total offer. In fact, the offer can range from a pure good on the one hand to a pure service on the other. In Chapter 19 we discuss services as products themselves. Here we will discuss services that augment actual products. The marketer faces three decisions about customer services: (1) What customer service mix should be offered? (2) What level of service should be offered? (3) In what forms should the services be provided?

value to the consumer. It is estimated that packaging is a $6 billion-a-year business in Canada, and many would argue that packaging costs of approximately 22% of net sales in the food-processing business are too high. However, it appears that, in many cases, changing packaging types would not have a great effect on retail prices. Marketers also feel that critics do not understand all the functions performed by the package, such as convenience and the reduction of pilferage, and also that marketers, as much as anyone, want to keep packaging costs down.

3. *Scarce resource*   The growing concern over shortages of paper, aluminum, and other materials raises the question of whether industry should try harder to reduce its packaging. For example, the growth of non-returnable glass containers has resulted in using up to 17 times as much glass as with returnable containers. The throwaway bottle is also an energy waster, which can be ill afforded in this time of energy management. All provinces have passed laws prohibiting or taxing non-returnable containers.

4. *Pollution*   As much as 40% of the total solid waste in this country is made up of package material. Many packages end up in the form of broken bottles and bent cans littering the streets and countryside. All this packaging creates a major problem in solid waste disposal that is a huge consumer of labor and energy.

These questionable aspects of packaging have mobilized public action and interest in new laws that might further affect marketing decision making in the packaging area. Marketers must be equally concerned and must attempt to create ecological packaging when they develop packaging concepts for their products.

Sources: Martin Mehr, "Marketers Want Rules Applying to All," *Financial Post,* March 7 1981, p. 19; "An Energy Analysis of Consumer Products Packaging," unpublished report (Ottawa: Consumer and Corporate Affairs Canada, 1980); M. Dale Beckman, "An Analysis of Food Packaging Costs: Does Packaging Cost Too Much?" *ASAC Proceedings, Marketing Division* (London, 1978), pp. 25-42; Robert English, "Packaging Shows a Mixed Recovery," *Financial Post,* December 11 1983, p. 11.

Service Mix Decision

The marketer needs to survey customers to find out the main services that might be offered and their importance. For example, Canadian buyers of industrial equipment ranked 13 service elements in the following order of importance: (1) delivery reliability, (2) prompt price quotation, (3) technical advice, (4) discounts, (5) after-sales service, (6) sales representation, (7) ease of contact, (8) replacement guarantee, (9) wide range of manufacturer, (10) pattern design, (11) credit, (12) test facilities, (13) machining facilities.[15] These importance rankings suggest that in this market the seller should at least match competition on delivery reliability, prompt price quotation, technical advice, and other services deemed most important by customers.

However, the issue of which services to offer is often very subtle. A service can be very important to customers and yet not affect supplier selection if all the suppliers offer the service at the same level.

Service Level Decision

Customers not only want certain services, but also want them in the right amount and quality. If bank customers have to stand in long lines or face frowning bank tellers, they might switch to another bank.

Companies need to check on their own and competitors' service levels in relation to customers' expectations. The company can spot service problems in several ways: comparison shopping, customer surveys, suggestion boxes, and complaint systems. This lets the company know how it is doing and helps disappointed customers get satisfaction.

Service Form Decision

Marketers must also decide on the forms in which to offer various services. The first question is: how should each service be priced? For example, consider what Electrohome should offer in repair services on its television sets. Electrohome has three options. It could offer free repair service for a year with the sale of a set, or sell a service contract, or decide not to offer repair services at any price, but leave them to television repair specialists.

Another question is: how should the service be delivered? Electrohome could provide repair services in several ways. It could hire and train its own service people and locate them across the country, or arrange with distributors and dealers to provide repair services, or leave independent companies to provide repair services.

For each service, various options exist. The company's decision depends on customer needs and competitors' strategies.

Product Line Decisions

We have looked at product strategy decisions—branding, packaging, and services—for individual products. However, product strategy also calls for building a product line. We define **product line** as follows:

> A product line is a group of products that are closely related, either because they function in a similar manner, are sold to the same customer groups, are marketed through the same types of outlets, or fall within given price ranges.

Thus General Motors produces a line of cars, and Revlon produces a line of cosmetics. Each product line needs a marketing strategy. Most companies assign a specific person to manage each product line. This person faces a number of tough decisions on product line length and product line featuring.

Product Line Length Decision

Product line managers have to decide on product line length. The line is too short if the manager can increase profits by adding items; the line is too long if the manager can increase profits by dropping items.

Product line length is influenced by company objectives. Companies that want to be positioned as full-line companies or are seeking high market share and market growth will carry longer lines. They are less concerned when some items fail to add to profits. Companies that are keen on high profitability will carry shorter lines consisting of selected items.

Product lines tend to lengthen over time.[16] The company must plan this growth carefully. It can systematically increase the length of its product line in two ways: by stretching its line and by filling its line.

Product Line Stretching Decision

Every company's product line covers a certain range of the products offered by the industry as a whole. For example, BMW automobiles are located in the medium-high price range of the automobile market. Product line stretching occurs when a company lengthens its product line beyond its current range. As shown in Figure 9-5, the company can stretch its line downward, upward, or both ways.

FIGURE 9-5
Product Line Stretching Decision

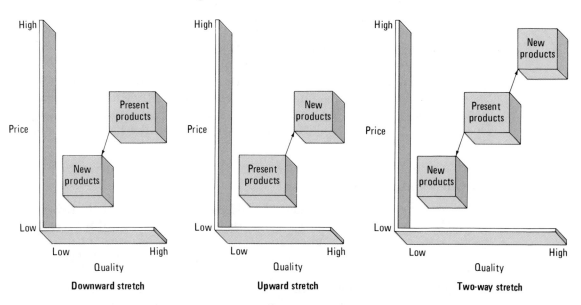

| Downward stretch | Upward stretch | Two-way stretch |

Downward Stretch

Many companies initially locate at the high end of the market and later stretch their lines downward. A company may stretch downward for any number of reasons. It may find faster growth taking place at the low end. The company may have first entered the high end to establish a quality image and intended to roll downward. The company may add a low-end product to plug a market hole that would otherwise attract a new competitor. The company may be attacked at the high end and respond by invading the low end.

One of the great miscalculations of several companies has been their unwillingness to plug holes in the lower end of their markets. General Motors resisted building smaller cars; Xerox, smaller copying machines; and Harley Davidson, smaller motorcycles. In each of these cases, Japanese companies found a major opening and moved in quickly and successfully.

Upward Stretch

Companies at the lower end of the market may want to enter the higher end. They may be attracted by a faster growth rate or higher margins at the higher end, or they may simply want to position themselves as full-line manufacturers.

An upward stretch decision can be risky. The higher-end competitors not only are well entrenched, but may also strike back by entering the lower end of the market. Prospective customers may not believe that the newcomer can produce quality products. Finally, the company's salespeople and distributors may lack the talent and training to serve the higher end of the market.

Two-way Stretch

Companies in the middle range of the market may decide to stretch their lines in both directions. Texas Instruments (TI) did this in the hand-calculator market. Before TI entered this market, the market was dominated by Bowmar at the low end and Hewlett-Packard at the high end. TI introduced its first calculators in the middle of the market. Gradually it added more machines at each end. It offered better calculators at the same or lower prices than Bowmar, ultimately destroying it. TI also designed high-quality calculators selling at lower prices than Hewlett-Packard, taking away a good share of HP's sales at the high end. This two-way stretch won TI the market leadership in the hand-calculator market.

Product Line Filling Decision

A product line can also be lengthened by adding more items within the present range of the line. Companies have several reasons for product line filling: reaching for extra profits, trying to satisfy dealers, trying to use excess capacity, trying to be the leading full-line company, and trying to plug holes to keep out competitors.

Line filling is overdone if it results in cannibalization and customer confusion. The company should make sure that new product items are noticeably different from present items.

Product Mix Decisions

An organization with several product lines has a product mix. We define **product mix** as follows.[17]

*A product mix (also called **product assortment**) is the set of all product lines and items that a particular seller offers for sale to buyers.*

Avon's product mix consists of four major product lines: cosmetics, jewelry, fashions, and household items. Each product line consists of several sublines. For example, cosmetics break down into lipstick, rouge, powder, and so on. Each line and subline has many individual items. Altogether, Avon's product mix includes 1300 items. A large supermarket handles as many as 14 000 items; a typical K mart stocks 15 000 items; Canadian Tire holds over 25 000 different automobile items, in each of its four supply depots, which can be shipped to any of their more than 300 stores within two days; and Canadian General Electric manufactures over 200 000 items ranging from hydraulic turbines to heavy machinery.

A company's product mix can be described as having a certain width, length, depth, and consistency. These concepts are illustrated in Table 9-1 in connection with selected Procter & Gamble Canada consumer products.

The **width** of P&G's product mix refers to how many different product lines the company carries. Table 9-1 shows a product mix width of six lines. (In fact, P&G produces many more lines, including mouthwash, shortening, soft drinks, and others.)

TABLE 9-1

Product Mix Width and Product Line Length Shown for Procter & Gamble Products

Product mix width

	Detergents	Toothpaste	Bar Soap	Deodorants	Disposable diapers	Shampoo
Product line length	Ivory Snow 1932 Dreft 1946 Tide 1948 Joy 2 1950 Cheer 1951 Oxydol 1958 Cascade 1962 Ivory Liquid 1958 Bold 3 1981 Cascade Liquid 1987	Crest 1961	Ivory 1916 Camay 1927 Zest 1958 Safeguard 1965 Coast 1979 Liquid Ivory 1984	Secret 1965	Pampers 1972 Luvs 1983	Head & Shoulders 1964 Pert 1981 Ivory Shampoo 1986

Source: Courtesy of Procter & Gamble Canada. Does not include all products of P&G.

The **length** of P&G's product mix refers to the total number of items the company carries. In Table 9-1, it is 23. We can also compute the average length of a line at P&G by dividing the total length (here 23) by the number of lines (here 6), or 3.8. The average P&G product line as represented in Table 9-1 consists of 3.8 brands.

The **depth** of P&G's product mix refers to how many versions are offered of each product in the line. Thus if Crest comes in three sizes and two formulations (regular and mint), Crest has a depth of six. By counting the number of versions within each brand, the average depth of P&G's product mix can be calculated.

The **consistency** of the product mix refers to how closely related the various product lines are in end use, production requirements, distribution channels, or in some other way. P&G's product lines are consistent in so far as they are consumer goods that go through the same distribution channels. The lines are less consistent insofar as they perform different functions for the buyers.

These four dimensions of the product mix provide a method for defining the company's product strategy. The company can increase its business in four ways. The company can add new product lines, thus widening its product mix. In this way, its new lines build on the company's reputation in its other lines. The company can lengthen its existing product lines to become a more full-line company. The company can add more product versions to each product and thus deepen its product mix. Finally, the company can pursue more product line consistency or less, depending upon whether it wants to have a strong reputation in a single field or in several fields.

Thus we see that product strategy is a complex subject calling for decisions on product mix, product line, branding, packaging, and service strategy. These decisions must be made with a full understanding of consumer wants and competitors' strategies.

Summary

A product is a complex concept that must be carefully defined. Product strategy calls for making coordinated decisions on product items, product lines, and the product mix.

Each product item offered to customers can be looked at on three levels. The **core product** is the essential service the buyer is really buying. The **actual product** is the features, styling, quality, brand name, and packaging of the product offered for sale. The **augmented product** is the actual product plus the various services offered with it, such as warranty, installation, maintenance, and free delivery.

There are several ways to classify products. For example, all products can be classified according to their durability (nondurable goods, durable goods, and services). Consumer goods are usually classified according to consumer shopping habits (convenience, shopping, specialty, and unsought goods). Industrial goods are classified according to their cost and how they enter the production process (materials and parts, capital items, and supplies and services).

Companies have to develop brand policies for the product items in their lines. They must decide whether to brand at all, whether to do manufacturing or private branding, whether to use family brand names or individual brand names, whether to put out several competing brands, and whether to reposition any of the brands.

Products require packaging decisions to create such benefits as protection, economy, convenience, and promotion. Marketers have to develop a packaging concept and test it to make sure it achieves the desired objectives and is compatible with public policy.

Companies have to develop customer services that are desired by customers and effective against competitors. The company has to decide on the most important services to offer, the level at which each service should be provided, and the form of each service.

Most companies produce not a single product but a product line. A product line is a group of products related in function, customer purchase needs, or distribution channels. Each product line requires a product strategy. Line stretching raises the question of whether a line should be extended downward, upward, or both ways. Line filling raises the question of whether additional items should be added within the present range of the line.

Product mix describes the set of product lines and items offered to customers by a particular seller. The product mix can be described by its width, length, depth, and consistency. The four dimensions of the product mix are the tools for developing the company's product strategy.

Questions for Discussion

1. How does the classification system for consumer goods differ from that for industrial goods? Explain.
2. How would you classify a Sony video cassette recorder? Explain.
3. Discuss the core, actual, and augmented product for the college degree you are pursuing.
4. A package can add significant value to a product. Comment.
5. In how many retail outlets in a particular geographic area must each type of consumer good (convenience, shopping, specialty, and unsought) be distributed?
6. Explain how customers and marketers benefit from the use of brand names.
7. Offer several examples of how firms have engaged in product-line stretch.

Chapter 9 Key Terms

Brand A name, term, sign, symbol, or design, or a combination of them intended to identify the goods or services of one seller or group of sellers and to differentiate them from those of competitors.

Brand mark That part of a brand that can be recognized but is not utterable, such as a symbol, design, or distinctive coloring or lettering.

Brand name That part of a brand that can be vocalized.

Capital items Industrial goods that enter the finished product partly, including installations and accessory equipment.

Consumer goods Those bought by final consumers for personal consumption.

Convenience goods Consumer goods that the customer usually buys frequently, immediately, and with the minimum of comparison and buying effort.

Copyright The exclusive legal right to reproduce, publish, and sell the matter and form of a literary, musical, or artistic work.

Durable goods Tangible goods that normally survive many uses.

Industrial goods Goods bought by individuals and organizations for further processing or for use in conducting a business.

Materials and parts Industrial goods that enter the manufacturer's product completely, including raw materials and manufactured materials and parts.

Nondurable goods Tangible goods normally consumed in one or a few uses.

Packaging The activities of designing and producing the container or wrapper for a product.

Product line A group of products that are closely related, either because they function in a similar manner, are sold to the same customer groups, are marketed through the same types of outlets, or fall within given price ranges.

Product mix The set of all product lines and items that a particular seller offers for sale to buyers.

Product Anything that can be offered to a market for attention, acquisition, use, or consumption that might satisfy a want or need. It includes physical objects, services, persons, places, organizations, and ideas.

Services Activities, benefits, or satisfactions that are offered for sale.

Shopping goods Consumer goods that the customer, in the process of selection and purchase, characteristically compares on such bases as suitability, quality, price, and style.

Specialty goods Consumer goods with unique characteristics or brand identification for which a significant group of buyers is willing to make a special purchase effort.

Supplies and services Industrial goods that do not enter the finished product at all.

Trademark A brand or part of a brand that is given legal protection — it protects the seller's exclusive rights to use the brand name or brand mark.

Unsought goods Consumer goods that the consumer does not know about or knows about but does not normally think of buying.

Cases for Chapter 9 ━━━━━━━━━━

Designing Products: New Product Development and Product Life-Cycle Strategies

Chapter Objectives

After reading this chapter, you should be able to:
1. List and define the steps in new product development.
2. Explain how companies find and develop new product ideas.
3. Describe the stages of the product life cycle.
4. Discuss how marketing strategy changes during a product's life cycle.

When a new product hits the market and "takes off", the rewards can be tremendous. Unfortunately, when the market cools, the results are often disastrous. Just ask the managers of Bombardier Inc. of Montreal, a company that experienced a number of ups and downs riding the snowmobile life cycle. The good years were the early 1970s. Bombardier was the market leader in snowmobile sales and in 1971-72 had an excellent year when the total market was 400 000 units. Then the oil crisis hit in 1973-74 and the market took a nose dive. In the 1980s, sales in North America were between 100 000 and 125 000 units. While Bombardier still operates in this market, it began a product diversification program in 1974 to reduce its dependence on one product. This program, described by some as helter-skelter, went first into other leisure products — motorcycles and sailboats. These new product ventures were not particularly successful and Bombardier lost $12-million in the two years ending in 1974.

The next diversification move, in late 1974, involved retooling some snowmobile capacity to make subway cars for the city of Montreal. Next, Bombardier purchased a manufacturer of diesel locomotives. Thus, in 1976 Bombardier was in two chancy businesses, snowmobiles and mass transit. By early 1981, it was engaged in the development, manufacture, and sale of a number of different recreational vehicles, trucks, railway cars, heat transfer products, all-terrain vehicles, aerospace components, marine and stationary engines, medium-speed diesel engines, and surface condensers for use in nuclear and fossil-fuel electrical stations.

In the past few years, Bombardier's marketing strategy has become more refined. Its goal is to manufacture and sell high technology products acquired through licensing agreements. It now has four major product lines: (1) mass transit (subway cars) and railway products (railcars, diesel engines), (2) recreation/utility vehicles (snowmobiles), (3) military vehicles (the Iltis, a four-wheel vehicle designed by Volkswagen), and (4) aerospace products. The last product line was obtained in late 1986 when Bombardier purchased Canadair, a Crown corporation that makes the Challenger Jet and other aerospace products.

For two reasons, experts regard the Canadian purchase as an excellent fit with Bombardier's existing business. First, putting a plane together is similar to putting a railcar together. It's basically installing electronics into a metal shell. Second, the marketing is similar, as the end users in both cases are governments and business.

Bombardier's strategy seems to be paying off. After suffering an $18.5 million loss in 1982, it has turned a profit every subsequent year, and sales in 1987 were over $1 billion. But for companies like Bombardier who market high technology products, the pressure is always there to pick the right products for the future.[1]

A company like Bombardier has to be good at identifying and developing new products. It also has to be good at managing them in the face of changing tastes, technologies, and competition. Every product seems to go through a life cycle —it is born, goes through several phases, and eventually dies as younger products come along that better serve consumer needs.

This product life cycle presents two major challenges. First, because all products eventually decline, the firm must find *new products* to replace aging ones (the problem of new product development). Second, the firm must understand how its products age, and adapt its marketing strategies as products pass through life-cycle stages (the problem of product life-cycle strategies). We will first look at the problem of finding and developing new products, and then at the problem of managing them successfully over their life cycle.

New Product Development Strategy

Given rapid changes in tastes, technology, and competition, a company cannot rely only on its existing products. Customers want and expect new and improved products. Competition will do its best to provide them. Every company needs a new product development program.

A company can obtain new products in two ways. One is through **acquisition**, by buying a whole company (for example, Bombardier's purchase of Canadair), a patent, or a license to produce someone else's product (Bombardier's licensing of the Iltis from Volkswagen). As the cost of developing and introducing a major new product climbed rapidly in the 1980s, many large companies decided to acquire existing brands rather than to create new ones. Following this direction, Procter & Gamble acquired Richardson-Vicks, R.J. Reynolds bought Nabisco, and Pepsico took over Seven-Up.[2]

The company can also obtain new products through *new product development*, by setting up its own research and development department. By "new

Courtesy: Ford Motor Company

The famous Edsel — launched 1957, buried 1959 — at a cost to Ford of $350 million.

products'' we mean original products, product improvements, product modifications, and new brands that the firm develops through its own R&D efforts. In this chapter, we will concentrate on new product development.

Innovation can be very risky. Ford lost $350 million on its Edsel automobile; RCA lost a staggering $580 million on its SelectaVision video-disc player; Xerox's venture into computers was a disaster; and the French Concorde aircraft will never pay back its investment. One study found that the new product failure rate was 40% for consumer products, 20% for industrial products, and 18% for services.[3] A recent study of 700 consumer and industrial firms found an overall success rate for new products of only 65%.[4]

Why do many new products fail? There are several reasons. A high-level executive might push a favorite idea in spite of poor marketing research findings. An idea may be good, but the market size may have been overestimated. The actual product may not be designed as well as it should have been. A product might be incorrectly positioned in the market, priced too high, or advertised poorly. Sometimes the costs of product development are higher than expected, or the competitors fight back harder than expected.

A major reason for failure of new industrial products in Canada is a poor marketing effort.[5] The marketing problems include inadequate attention to customer requirements, inadequate assessment of competitors' strengths, a lack of market research to identify product deficiencies, and pricing the new product too high.

Companies face a problem—they must develop new products, but the odds weigh heavily against success. The solution lies in strong new product planning, and in setting up a systematic **new product development process** for finding and nurturing new products. The major steps in this process are shown in Figure 10-1 and described below.

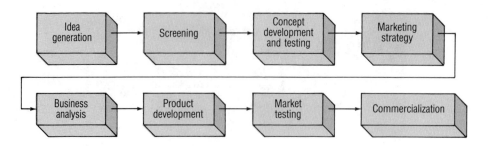

FIGURE 10-1
Major Stages in New Product Development

Idea Generation

New product development starts with *idea generation*, a systematic search for new ideas. A company typically has to generate many ideas in order to find a few good ones. The search for new product ideas should be systematic rather than haphazard, otherwise the company will expend energy in generating ideas that are not necessarily suited to its business.In one study of industrial manufacturing firms in Canada, the source or "trigger" for new product ideas came mainly from an assessment of market needs (27%); a general product policy decision such as extending the product line (22%); an application of a new technology (21%); customers seeking out the company (18%), and a reaction to competition (10%).[6] Most of the triggers for the new product ideas surprisingly came not from an active company policy of seeking new products but from other sources. For example, many new products were developed on the basis of customer requests, a haphazard way of generating new product ideas.

Top management can avoid this haphazard approach by carefully defining its new product development strategy. It should state what products and markets to emphasize. Management should also state what the company wants from the new products, whether it is high cash flow, market share, or some other objective. In addition, management should state the effort to be devoted to developing original producers, changing existing products, and imitating competitors' products.

To obtain flow of new product ideas, the company must tap many sources. Major sources of new product ideas include:

Internal sources   One study found that over 55% of all new product ideas come from within the company.[7] The company can find new ideas through formal research and development. It can seek advice and input from its scientists, engineers, and manufacturing people. Company executives can brainstorm for new product ideas. The company's salespeople are another good source because they are in daily contact with customers.

Customers   Almost 28% of all new product ideas come from watching and listening to customers. Consumer needs and wants can be looked at through consumer surveys. The company can analyze customer questions and complaints to find new products that can better solve consumer problems. Company engineers or salespeople can meet with customers to get suggestions. Finally, consumers often create new products on their own, and companies can benefit by finding these products and putting them on the market.[8]

Competitors About 27% of new product ideas come from analyzing competitors' products. Companies buy competing new products, take them apart to see how they work, analyze their sales, and decide whether the company should bring out a new product of its own. The company can also watch competitors' ads and other communications to get clues about their new products.

Distributors and suppliers Resellers are close to the market and can pass along information about consumer problems and new product possibilities. Suppliers can tell the company about new concepts, techniques, and materials that can be used to develop new products.

Other sources Other idea sources include trade magazines, shows, and seminars; government agencies; new product consultants; advertising agencies; marketing research firms; university and commercial laboratories; and inventors.

Idea Screening

The purpose of idea generation is to create a large number of ideas. The purpose of the succeeding stages is to **reduce** the number of ideas. The first idea-reducing stage is screening.

The purpose of *screening* is to spot good ideas and drop poor ones as soon as possible. Product development costs rise greatly in later stages. The company will want to proceed only with the product ideas that will turn into profitable products.

Most companies require their executives to write up new product ideas on a standard form that can be reviewed by a new product committee. They describe the product, the target market, and the competition, and make some rough estimates of market size, product price, development time and costs, manufacturing costs, and rate of return. They answer the questions: Is this idea good for our particular company? Does it mesh well with the company's objectives and strategies? Do we have the people, skills, and resources to make it succeed? Many companies have well designed systems for rating and screening new product ideas.

Concept Development and Testing

Surviving ideas must now be developed into product concepts. It is important to distinguish between a product idea, a product concept, and a product image. A *product idea* is an idea for a possible product that the company can see itself offering to the market. A *product concept* is a detailed version of the idea stated in meaningful consumer terms. A *product image* is the way consumers picture an actual or potential product.

Concept Development

As part of its effort to forecast the future demand for electrical power, British Columbia Hydro was interested in forecasting usage of electrically-powered vehicles by commercial fleets.[9] The utility decided to study fleet owners' reactions to electric trucks that had certain operating characteristics including speed, range, operation costs, price, and pollution standards.

This is a product idea. Customers, however, do not buy a product idea, they buy a product concept. The marketer's task is to develop this idea into some alternative product concepts, find out how attractive each concept is to customers, and choose the best one.

Among the product concepts tested for the electric truck were:

1. Speed of 64 km/h and a range of 64 km.
2. Operating costs of 5¢ per 1.6 km.
3. Price $8000.
4. Pollution level zero.
5. Electric propulsion system.

Concept Testing

Concept testing calls for testing these concepts with a group of target consumers. The concepts may be presented through word or picture descriptions. In this case, the consumers were the fleet personnel directly responsible for the vehicle purchase decisions. To increase the realism of the study, the consumers attended a seminar where they were shown an electrically powered van and given instructions on its operation. They were asked to evaluate the electric-truck concept against a conventional truck. The relative importance of various vehicle characteristics were determined by asking the consumers to rank a set of alternatives from most to least desirable. This required the consumer to "trade off" various characteristics—a situation faced by all buyers in real life. For example, consumers may be asked to decide whether they prefer an increased range (e.g., 100 km) or an increased payload (e.g., 1100 kg).[10]

The reaction of consumers in this situation was that electric vehicles would only be more desirable than conventional vehicles if they were sold at the same price as the conventional vehicle and were not constrained by limited speed or range. At the time of the study, it was not possible to build these characteristics into an electric vehicle.

Marketing Strategy Development

Let us assume that a similar study was conducted on a personal electric car, and that consumers reacted favorably to the following product concept:

> An efficient, fun-to-drive, electric-powered car in the subcompact class that seats four. Great for shopping trips and visits to friends. Costs half as much to operate as similar gasoline-driven cars. Goes up to 80 km/h and does not need to be recharged for 160 km. Priced at $6000.

The next step is *marketing strategy development*, designing an initial marketing strategy for introducing this car into the market.

Courtesy: Copper Development Association Inc.

The prototype of an electric car. This vehicle has a top speed of 100 km/h and an in-city driving range of 135 km.

The marketing strategy statement consists of three parts. The first part describes the target market, the planned product positioning, and the sales, market share, and profit goals for the first few years. Thus:

> The target market is households that need a second car for shopping trips and visits to friends. The car will be positioned as more economical to buy and operate, and more fun to drive, than cars now available to this market. The company will aim to sell 20 000 cars in the first year, are a loss of not more than $3 million. The second year will aim for sales of 30 000 cars and a profit of $5 million.

The second part of the marketing strategy statement outlines the product's planned price, distribution, and marketing budget for the first year:

> The electric car will be offered in three colors and will have optional air-conditioning and power-drive features. It will sell at a retail price of $8000, with 15% off the list price to dealers. Dealers who sell over ten cars per month will get an additional discount of 5% on each car sold that month. An advertising budget of $2 million will be split 50:50 between national and local advertising. Advertising will emphasize the car's economy and fun. During the first year, $100 000 will be spent on marketing research to find out who is buying the car and their satisfaction levels.

The third part of the marketing strategy statement describes the planned long-run sales and profit goals, and marketing mix strategy over time:

> The company intends to capture a 6% long-run share of the total auto market and realize an after-tax return on investment of 15%. To achieve this, product quality will start high and be improved over time. Price will be raised in the second and third years if competition permits. The total advertising budget will be raised each year by about 10%. Marketing research will be reduced to $60 000 per year after the first year.

Business Analysis

Once management has decided on the product concept and marketing strategy, it can evaluate the business attractiveness of the proposal. *Business analysis* involves a review of sales, costs, and profit projections to find out whether they satisfy the company's objectives. If they do, the product can move to the product development stage.

To estimate sales, the company should look at the sales history of similar products and survey market opinion. It should estimate minimum and maximum sales to learn the range of risk. After preparing the sales forecast, management can estimate the expected costs and profits for the product. The costs are estimated by the R&D, manufacturing, accounting, and finance departments. The planned marketing costs are included in the analysis. The company then uses the sales and costs figures to analyze the new product's financial attractiveness.

Product Development

If the product concept passes the business test, it moves into product development. Here R&D or engineering develop the product concept into a physical product. Until this point, the product concept existed only as a word description, a drawing, or a crude mockup. This step calls for a large jump in investment. It will show whether the product idea can be turned into a workable product.

The R&D department will develop one or more physical versions of the product concept. It hopes to find a prototype that meets the following criteria: (1) Consumers see it as having the key features described in the product concept statement; (2) it performs safely under normal use; (3) it can be produced for the budgeted costs.

Developing a successful prototype can take days, weeks, months, or even years. The prototype must have the required functional features and also convey the intended psychological characteristics. The electric car, for example, should strike consumers as being well built and safe. Management must learn how consumers decide how well a car is built. Some consumers slam the door to hear its "sound." If the car does not have "solid-sounding" doors, consumers will think it is poorly built.

When the prototypes are ready, they must be tested. Functional tests are conducted under laboratory and field conditions to make sure that the product performs safely and effectively. The new car must start well; it must be comfortable; it must be able to go around corners without overturning. Consumer tests are conducted, asking consumers to test-drive the car and rate the car and its attributes.

Market Testing

If the product passes functional and consumer tests, the next step is market testing. *Market testing* is the stage where the product and marketing program are introduced into more realistic market settings.

Market testing lets the marketer get experience with marketing the product, find potential problems, and learn where more information is needed before going to the great expense of full introduction. The basic purpose of market testing is to test the product itself in real market situations. However, market testing also allows the company to test the entire marketing program for the product—the positioning strategy, advertising, distribution, pricing, branding and packaging, and budget levels. The company uses market testing to learn how consumers and dealers will react to handling, using, and repurchasing the product. Market testing results can be used to make better sales and profit forecasts.[11]

The amount of market testing needed varies with each new product. Market testing costs can be enormous, and market testing takes time that competitors may use to gain an advantage. When the costs of developing and introducing the product are low or when management is already confident that the new product will succeed, the company may do little or no product testing. Minor modifications of current products or copies of successful competitor products, for example, might not need testing. When introducing the new product requires a large investment, or when management is not sure of the product or marketing program, the company may do a lot of market testing.

Commercialization

Market testing gives management the information needed to make a final decision about whether to launch the new product. If the company goes ahead with commercialization, it will face high costs. The company will have to build or rent a manufacturing facility. It may have to spend, in the case of a new consumer packaged good, between $1 million and $5 million for advertising and sales promotion alone in the first year. When Diet Coke was launched in Canada, total promotion expenditures were close to $4 million, including about $1 million spent on sampling.[12] Gillette Canada spent over $1.1 million on promotion to introduce its Mink shampoo and $750 000 to launch Tame, a new hair care line.[13]

In launching a new product, the company must make the following four decisions.

When

The first decision is whether it is the right time to introduce the new product. If sales of the electric car sales will cannibalize the sales of the company's other cars, its introduction may be delayed.[14] Or, if the electric car can be improved further, the company may wait to launch it next year. The company may also want to wait if the economy is down.

Where

The company must decide whether to launch the new product in a single location, one region, several regions, the national market, or the international market. Few companies have the confidence, capital, and capacity to launch new products into full national distribution. They will develop a planned market rollout over time. Small companies, in particular, will select an attractive city and put on a blitz campaign to enter the market. They will enter other cities one at a time. Large companies will introduce their product into a whole region and then move to the next region. Companies with national distribution networks, such as auto companies, will often launch their new models in the national market.

To Whom

Within the rollout markets, the company must target its distribution and promotion to the best prospect groups. The company has already profiled the prime prospects in earlier market testing. It must now fine-tune its market identification, looking especially for early adopters, heavy users, and opinion leaders.

How

The company must develop an action plan for introducing the new product into the selected markets. It must spend the marketing budget on the marketing mix and various other activities. Thus the electric car's launch may be supported by a publicity campaign, and then by offers of gifts to draw more people to the showrooms. The company must prepare a separate marketing plan for each new market.

In making these decisions, management should be guided by the findings in the field known as innovation diffusion and adoption theory (see Table 10-1).

TABLE 10-1

Major Findings of Innovation Diffusion and Adoption

In launching a new product, a firm should be guided by the major findings in the field of innovation diffusion and adoption theory. These findings are:

Stages of adoption   Individual consumers go through a series of stages of acceptance in the process of adopting a new product. The stages are awareness, interest, evaluation, trial, and adoption. Thus the manufacturer of a new electric car must think about what can be done to efficiently move people through each stage. For example, if people have awareness and interest but are not coming into a dealer's showrooms, the manufacturer must develop promotional incentives to attract people into the showrooms.

Consumer adopter types   People differ greatly in their readiness to try new products. There are innovators (the first 2.5% of the individuals to adopt a new product), early adopters (the next 13.5%), early majority (the next 34%), late majority (the next 34%), and laggards (the last 16%). The electric car manufacturer should try to identify the characteristics of people who are likely to be early adopters, such as having a high income and being active in the community, and should then focus its promotion on this group.

Role of personal influence   Personal influence plays a major role in the adoption of new products. The statements of other people about a new product carry heavy weight with a prospect, especially if the product is risky or costly. The electric car manufacturer will want to research what opinion leaders and early buyers say to others about the new electric car and to correct as soon as possible any product features that will give rise to complaints. The manufacturer may also want to use a ''testimonial advertising'' approach in which some attractive sources assure other people that the electric car is reliable and fun to drive.

Innovation characteristics   Certain characteristics of the innovation strongly affect the rate of adoption. The main ones are the innovation's relative advantage over other products, its compatibility with the person's life style, its complexity, its divisibility into small trial units, and its communicability. Thus an electric car will be more appealing to the extent that it saves buyers a lot of money, fits their life style, is simple to operate, can be test driven, and is easy to understand.

Source: These and other ideas are elaborated in Everett M. Rogers and F. Floyd Shoemaker, *Communication of Innovations* (New York: Free Press, 1971).

These findings clearly point out the high risks involved in new-product development and the careful planning that is needed to successfully launch a new product.

Product Life-Cycle Strategies

After launching the new product, management wants the product to enjoy a long and prosperous life. Although they do not expect the product to sell forever, management wants to earn a decent profit to cover all the effort and risk that went into it. Management is aware that each product will have a life cycle, although the exact shape and length is not known in advance.

The typical *product life cycle (PLC)* is a curve, as shown in Figure 10-2. It is marked by five distinct stages:

1. **Product development** begins when the company finds and develops a new product idea. During product development, sales are zero and the company's investment costs add up.

2. **Introduction** is a period of slow sales growth as the product is being introduced in the market. Profits are nonexistent in this stage because of the heavy expenses of product introduction.

3. **Growth** is a period of rapid market acceptance and increasing profits.

4. **Maturity** is a period of slowdown in sales growth because the product has achieved acceptance by most of the potential buyers. Profits level off or decline because of increased marketing outlays to defend the product against competition.

5. **Decline** is the period when sales fall off quickly and profits drop.

FIGURE 10-2
Sales and Profits over the Product's Life from Inception to Demise

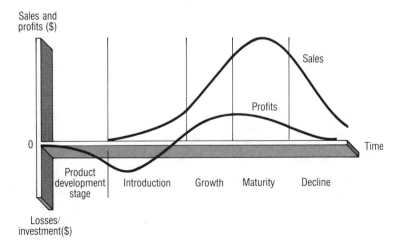

Not all products follow this S-shaped product life cycle. Some products are introduced and die quickly. Others stay in the mature stage for a long time. Some enter the decline stage, and then are cycled back into the growth stage through strong promotion or repositioning.

The PLC concept can describe a product class (gasoline-powered automobiles), a product form (station wagons), or a brand (Mustang). The PLC concept applies differently in each case. Product classes have the longest life cycles. The sales of many product classes stay in the mature stage for long time. Product forms, on the other hand, tend to have the standard PLC shape. Product forms such as the "dial telephone" and "cream deodorants" pass through a regular history of introduction, rapid growth, maturity, and decline. A specific brand's life cycle can change quickly because of changing competitive attacks and responses. The life cycles of several toothpaste brands are shown in Figure 10-3.

The PLC concept can also be applied to what are known as styles, fashions, and fads. Their special life-cycle features are described in Exhibit 10-1.

The PLC concept can be used by marketers as a useful framework for describing how products and markets work. However, using the PLC concept for forecasting product performance or for developing marketing strategies presents some practical problems.[15] For example, managers may have trouble identifying a product's current life-cycle stage, when it will move into the next stage, and the factors that affect how the product will move through the stages. In practice, it is very hard to forecast the sales level at each PLC stage, the length of each stage, and the shape of the PLC curve.

FIGURE 10-3
Product Life Cycles for Selected Toothpaste Brands from 1936 to 1982

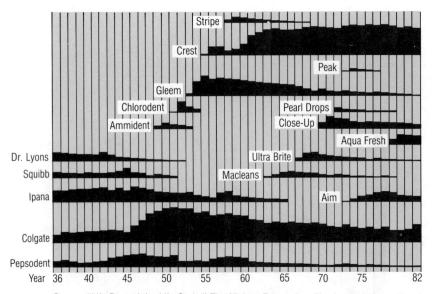

Source: "Life Beyond the Life Cycle," The Nielsen Researcher, Number 1, 1984, p. 3.

EXHIBIT 10-1
Style, Fashion, and Fad Cycles

In markets where style and fashion are influential, sales cycles occur. Marketers need to understand and predict these cycles.

A **style** is a basic and distinctive mode of expression appearing in a field of human activity. For example, styles appear in homes (colonial, ranch, Cape Cod), clothing (formal, casual), and art (realistic, surrealistic, abstract). Once a style is invented, it may last for generations, coming in and out of vogue. A style exhibits a cycle showing several periods of renewed interest.

A **fashion** is a currently accepted or popular style in a given field. For example, jeans are a fashion in today's clothing. Fashions pass through four stages. In the **distinctiveness stage**, some consumers take an interest in something new to set themselves apart from other consumers. The product may be custom-made or produced in small quantities by some manufacturers. In the **copying stage**, other consumers take an interest out of a desire to copy the fashion leaders, and additional manufacturers begin to produce larger quantities of the product. In the **mass fashion stage**, the fashion has become very popular and manufacturers have geared up for mass production. Finally, in the **decline stage**, consumers start moving toward other fashions that are beginning to catch their eye. Thus fashions tend to grow slowly, remain popular for a while, and decline slowly.

Fads are fashions that come quickly into the public eye, are adopted with great zeal, peak early, and decline very fast. Their acceptance cycle is short, and they tend to attract only a limited following. They often have a novel or quirky aspect, as when people started buying Rubik's cube. Fads appeal to people who are searching for excitement or who want to set themselves apart from others or have something to talk about to others. Fads do not survive because they normally do not satisfy a strong need or satisfy it well. It is difficult to predict whether something will only be a fad, and if so, how long it will last— a few days, weeks, or months. The amount of media attention it receives, along with other factors, will influence its duration.

Sources: Chester R. Wasson, "How Predictable Are Fashion and Other Product Life Cycles?" *Journal of Marketing*, July 1968, pp. 36-43; William H. Reynolds, "Cars and Clothing: Understanding Fashion Trends," *Journal of Marketing*, July 1968, pp. 44-49; and Dwight E. Robinson, "Style Changes: Cyclical, Inexorable and Foreseeable," *Harvard Business Review*, November-December 1975, pp. 121-31. See also George B. Sproles, "Analyzing Fashion Life Cycles—Principles and Perspectives," *Journal of Marketing*, Fall 1981, pp. 116-24.

Using the PLC concept to develop marketing strategy can be difficult because strategy is both a cause and result of the product's life cycle. The product's current PLC position suggests the best marketing strategies, and the resulting marketing strategies affect product performance in later life-cycle stages. Yet when used carefully the PLC concept can help in developing good marketing strategies for different stages of the product life cycle.

We looked at the product development stage of the product life cycle in the first part of the chapter. We now look at strategies for each of the other life-cycle stages.

Introduction Stage

The introduction stage starts when the new product is first distributed and made available for purchase. Introduction takes time, and sales growth is apt to be slow. Such well-known products as instant coffee, frozen orange juice, and powdered coffee creamers lingered for many years before they entered a stage of rapid growth.

In this stage, profits are negative or low because of low sales and high distribution and promotion expenses. Much money is needed to attract distributors and "fill the pipelines." Promotion spending is high to inform consumers of the new product and encourage them to try it.

There are only a few competitors, and they produce basic versions of the product, since the market is not ready for product refinements. The firms focus their selling on those buyers who are ready to buy, usually the higher-income groups.

Growth Stage

If the new product satisfies the market, it will enter the growth stage, and sales will start climbing quickly. The early adopters will continue to buy, and later buyers will start following their lead, especially if they hear favorable word of mouth. New competitors will enter the market attracted by the opportunities for profit. They will introduce new product features, and expand the market. The increase in competitors leads to an increase in the number of distribution outlets, and sales will jump in order to fill the pipelines.

Prices remain where they are or fall only slightly. Companies keep their promotion spending at the same or a slightly higher level to meet competition and continue educating the market.

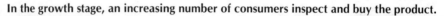

In the growth stage, an increasing number of consumers inspect and buy the product.

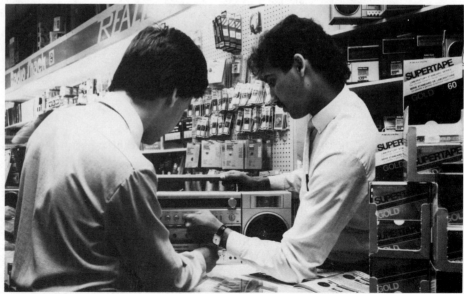

James Hertel

Profits increase during this growth stage as promotion costs are spread over a large volume and unit manufacturing costs fall due to the "experience curve" effect.[16] The firm uses several strategies to sustain rapid market growth as long as possible:

- Improves product quality and adds new product features and models.
- Enters new market segments.
- Enters new distribution channels.
- Shifts some advertising from building product awareness to building product conviction and purchase.
- Lowers prices at the right time to attract more buyers.

The firm in the growth stage faces a tradeoff between high market share and high current profit. By spending a lot of money on product improvement, promotion, and distribution, it can capture a dominant position. The firm gives up maximum current profit at this stage, but it hopes to make up the profit in the next stage.

Maturity Stage

At some point a product's sales growth will slow down, and the product will enter a maturity stage. This maturity stage normally lasts longer than the previous stages, and it poses strong challenges to marketing management. Most products are in the maturity stage of the life cycle, and therefore most of marketing management deals with the mature product.

The slowdown in sales growth results in many producers with many products to sell. This overcapacity leads to greater competition. Competitors begin marking down prices, and they increase their advertising and sales promotions. They also increase their R&D budgets to find better versions of the product. These steps mean a drop in profit, and some of the weaker competitors start dropping out. The industry eventually contains only well-established competitors.

The product manager should not simply defend the product. A good offense is the best defense. He or she should consider modifying the market, product, and marketing mix.

During the maturity stage, companies modify the features and styles of their products.

Courtesy: Sony of Canada Limited. Walkman is a registered TM of Sony Corporation.

Market Modification

Here the manager tries to increase the consumption of the current product. The manager looks for new users and market segments, as well as for ways to increase usage among present customers. The manager may want to reposition the brand to appeal to a larger or faster-growing segment.

Product Modification

The product manager can also change product characteristics—such as product quality, features, or style—to attract new users and more usage.

A strategy of **quality improvement** aims at increasing the performance of the product — its durability, reliability, speed, taste. This strategy is effective when the quality can be improved, buyers believe the claim of improved quality, and enough buyers want higher quality.

A strategy of **feature improvement** adds new features that expand the product's usefulness, safety, or convenience. Feature improvement has been successfully used by Japanese makers of watches, calculators, and copying machines. For example, Sony keeps adding new playing features to its Walkman line of miniature stereo players.

A strategy of **style improvement** aims to increase the attractiveness of the product. Thus car manufacturers restyle their cars to attract buyers who want a new look.

Marketing Mix Modification

The product manager can also try to improve sales by changing one or more marketing mix elements. Prices can be cut to attract new users and competitors' customers. A better advertising campaign can be sought. Aggressive sales promotions, such as trade deals, cents-off, gifts, and contests, can be used. The company can move into larger market channels, if these channels are growing, by using mass merchandisers. The company can offer new or improved services to the buyers.

Decline Stage

The sales of most product forms and brands eventually dip. The sales decline may be slow, as in the case of oatmeal cereal; or rapid, as for the Edsel automobile. Sales may plunge to zero or they may drop to a low level, in the decline stage, where they continue for many years.

Sales decline for many reasons, including technological advances, shifts in consumer tastes, and increased competition. As sales and profits decline, some firms withdraw from the market. Those that remain may reduce the number of their product offerings. They may drop smaller market segments and marginal trade channels, cut the promotion budget, and reduce their prices further.

Carrying a weak product can be very costly to the firm, and not only in profit terms. There are many hidden costs—the weak product may take up too much of management's time. Frequent price and inventory adjustments are often necessary for a weak product. It requires advertising and salesforce attention that might better be used to make the "healthy" products more profitable.

Its failing reputation can cause customer concerns about the company and its other products. The biggest cost may well lie in the future. Keeping weak products delays the search for replacement products, creates a lopsided product mix, and hurts current profits, weakening the company's foothold on the future.

For these reasons, companies need to pay more attention to their aging products. The first task is to identify those products in the declining stage by regularly reviewing the sales, market shares, cost, and profit trends on each of its products. For each declining product, management has to decide whether to maintain, harvest, or drop the product. Management may decide to maintain its brand without change in the hope that competitors will leave the industry. For example, Procter & Gamble remained in the declining liquid-soap business as others withdrew, and it made good profits. Alternatively, management may decide to reposition the brand in hopes of moving it back into the growth stage of the product life cycle, as Clairol did with Ban deodorant in the 1980s. It relaunched Ban with a $2.5 million promotion campaign targeted at "stylish" women in the hopes of gaining a greater share of the $100 million deodorant market in Canada.[17]

Management may decide to harvest the product, which means reducing various costs (plant and equipment, maintenance, R&D, advertising, sales force), and hoping that sales hold up fairly well for a while. If successful, harvesting will increase the company's profits in the short run. If management decides to drop the product from the line, it can sell the product to another firm or simply liquidate it at salvage value. If the company plans to find a buyer, it will not want to run down the product through harvesting.

The key characteristics of each stage of the product life cycle are summarized in Table 10-2. The table also lists the marketing responses made by companies in each stage.[18]

TABLE 10-2
Product Life Cycle: Characteristics and Responses

	Introduction	Growth	Maturity	Decline
Characteristics				
Sales	Low	Fast growth	Slow growth	Decline
Profits	Negligible	Peak levels	Declining	Low or zero
Cash flow	Negative	Moderate	High	Low
Customers	Innovative	Mass market	Mass market	Laggards
Competitors	Few	Growing	Many rivals	Declining number
Responses				
Strategic focus	Expand market	Market penetration	Defend share	Productivity
Mktg. expenditures	High	High (declining %)	Falling	Low
Mktg. emphasis	Product awareness	Brand preference	Brand loyalty	Selective
Distribution	Patchy	Intensive	Intensive	Selective
Price	High	Lower	Lowest	Rising
Product	Basic	Improved	Differentiated	Rationalized

Source: Peter Doyle, "The Realities of the Product Life Cycle," *Quarterly Review of Marketing* (UK), Summer 1976, p. 5.

Summary

Organizations need to develop new products and services. Their current products face limited life spans and must be replaced by newer products. However, new products can fail—the risks of innovation are as great as the rewards. The key to successful innovation lies in strong planning and a systematic new product development process.

The new product development process consists of eight stages: idea generation, idea screening, concept development and testing, marketing strategy development, business analysis, product development, market testing, and commercialization. The purpose of each stage is to decide whether the idea should be further developed or dropped. The company wants to minimize the chances of poor ideas moving forward and good ideas being rejected.

Each product has a life cycle marked by a changing set of problems and opportunities. The sales of the typical product follows an S-shaped curve made up of five stages. The cycle begins with the product development stage when the company finds and develops a new product idea. The introduction stage is marked by slow growth and low profits as the product is being pushed into distribution. If successful, the product enters a growth stage marked by rapid sales growth and increasing profits. During this stage the company tries to improve the product, enter new market segments and distribution channels, and reduce its prices slightly. Then comes a maturity stage in which sales growth slows down and profits stabilize. The company seeks strategies to renew sales growth, including market, product, and marketing mix modification. Finally, the product enters a decline stage where sales and profits fall off. The company's task during this stage is to identify the declining product and decide whether to maintain, harvest, or drop it. In the latter case, the product can be sold to another firm or liquidated for salvage value.

Questions for Discussion

1. It has been estimated that an average of 100 new products are introduced to the market each week, yet most do not meet the expectations of their marketer. Why do many new products fail?

2. What is the purpose of the idea-screening stage of the new-product development process?

3. Explain the importance of concept testing in the new-product development process.

4. Describe the level of sales and profits (losses) during each stage of the product life cycle.

5. Discuss the role and importance of promotional expenditures in each stage of the product life cycle.

6. Which one of the strategies discussed in the maturity stage did the following companies utilize? (a) Arm & Hammer baking soda, (b) State Farm insurance, and (c) Coca-Cola.

7. There is nothing the manager can do once a product reaches the decline stage. Comment.

Chapter 10 Key Terms

Business analysis   A review of the sales, costs, and profit projections for a new product to find out whether they satisfy the company's objectives.

Concept testing   Testing new product concept with a group of target consumers to find out if the concept has strong consumer appeal.

Decline stage   The product life cycle stage in which a product's sales decline.

Growth stage   The product life cycle stage in which the product's sales start climbing quickly.

Idea generation   The systematic search for new product ideas.

Idea screening   Screening new product ideas in order to spot good ideas and drop poor ones as soon as possible.

Introduction stage   The product life cycle stage in which the new product is first distributed and made available for purchase.

Marketing strategy development   Designing an initial marketing strategy for a new product based on the product concept.

Market testing   The stage of new product development in which the product and marketing program are tested in more realistic market settings.

Maturity stage   The stage in the product life cycle in which sales growth slows or levels off.

New product   A good, service, or idea that is perceived by some potential customers as new.

New product development   The development of original products, product improvements, product modifications, and new brands through the firm's own R&D efforts.

Product concept   A detailed version of the new product idea stated in meaningful consumer terms.

Product development   Developing the product concept into a physical product in order to ensure that the product idea can be turned into a workable product.

Product idea   An idea for a possible product that the company can see itself offering to the market.

Product image   The way consumers picture an actual or potential product.

Product life cycle (PLC)   The course of a product's sales and profits over its lifetime. It involves five distinct stages: product development, introduction, growth, maturity, and decline.

Cases for Chapter 10

Pricing Products: Pricing Considerations and Approaches

Chapter Objectives

After reading this chapter, you should be able to:

1. Discuss how marketing objectives and mix strategy, costs, and other internal company factors affect pricing decisions.
2. List and discuss factors outside the company that affect pricing decisions.
3. Explain how price setting depends on consumer perceptions of price and on the price-demand relationship.
4. Compare the three general pricing approaches.

A consumer buying a compact disc player faces a bewildering array of models and prices. Over 20 brands and 60 models are sold in Canada, ranging from a stripped-down player selling for less than $200 to a player that fits into the trunk of a car, changes up to 10 compact discs through remote control, and sells for over $1500. The consumer must decide whether the extra features such as shuffle play and linear remote tracking on the more expensive models are worth the extra price.

Consumers may have trouble choosing among the different prices, but manufacturers probably have more trouble **setting** the prices. Consider the case of Gendis Inc., the company selling Sony products in Canada. Through a joint venture, Gendis owns 51% of Sony Canada, and Toyko-based Sony Corp. holds the remaining 49%. Managers at Gendis must consider many factors in their complex price-setting process. They first consider the company's overall marketing objectives and the role of price in the marketing mix. Should Gendis price to maximize current profits on compact disc

players, or to maximize long-run market share? Should it use a high-price/low-volume strategy or a low-price/high-volume strategy?

When setting compact disc player prices, Gendis must also consider costs. These include the manufacturing costs, shipping and import duties, and the costs of storing, stocking, selling, and customer services. Gendis must price its compact disc players to cover these costs, plus a target profit. However, if Gendis considers only costs when setting prices, it ignores important demand and competitive factors.

The total demand for compact disc players has increased dramatically in Canada. In 1985, 60 000 units were sold; in 1986, 120 000 were sold; and the number doubled again in 1987. The increased demand is due in part to rapidly falling prices for the players. Gendis must determine how to price its players so that consumers will consider and buy their units. Consumer-oriented pricing starts with knowing consumer perceptions of each model's value. If Gendis charges more than buyers' perceived value, its compact disc players will sell poorly. If it charges less, its players will sell very well but will provide less revenue.

Gendis must also consider the quality and prices of competitors' compact disc players. If Sony players are similar to those of its major competitors, but it charges more, it risks losing sales. If it sets prices much lower than those of comparable products, it will win sales from competitors but lose profit opportunities.

Thus Gendis sets the prices of its basic compact disc players on the basis of costs, demand, and competitors' prices. For each player in its product line, Gendis must determine how consumers value different features and what features consumers prefer. Gendis has decided to use a premium price strategy for its line of compact disc players. Gendis sees the target market for Sony products, including compact disc players, as consumers who want "reliability, reputation, after-sale service and support" and are willing to pay for that "comfort." This strategy has paid off as Gendis sales of Sony products exceed $250 million in Canada each year.[1]

All profit organizations and many nonprofit organizations must set prices on their products or services. Price goes by many names. You pay **rent** for your apartment, **tuition** for your education, and a **fee** to your physician or dentist. A transportation company charges you a **fare**, the local bank charges you **interest** on a credit card, and the company that insures your car charges you a **premium**. Your regular lawyer may ask for a **retainer** to cover her services. The "price" of an executive is a **salary**, the price of a salesperson may be a **commission**, and the price of a worker is a **wage**.[2] Simply defined, price is the amount of money charged for a product or service. More broadly, *price* is the sum of the values consumers exchange for the benefits of having or using the product or service.

Price is the only element in the marketing mix that produces revenue; the other elements represent costs. However, many companies do not handle pricing well. The most common mistakes are pricing that is too cost-oriented, is not revised often enough to reflect market changes, does not take the rest of the marketing mix into account, and is not varied enough for different product items and market segments.

In this and the next chapter, we will look at the problem of setting prices. This chapter will look at the factors marketers must consider when setting prices, and at general pricing approaches. In the next chapter, we will examine pricing strategies for new product pricing, product-mix pricing, initiating and responding to price changes, and adjusting prices for buyer and situational factors.

Factors to Consider When Setting Prices

The company's pricing decisions are affected by many internal company factors and external environmental factors. These factors are shown in Figure 11-1. **Internal factors** include the company's marketing objectives, marketing mix strategy, costs, and organization. **External factors** include the nature of the market and demand, competition, and other environmental factors.

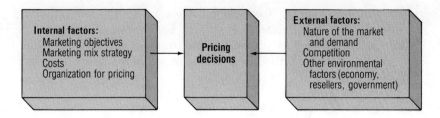

FIGURE 11-1
Factors Affecting Price Decisions

Internal Factors Affecting Pricing Decisions

Marketing Objectives

Before setting price, the company must decide on its strategy for the product. If the company has selected its target market and positioning carefully, then its marketing mix strategy (including price) will be fairly straightforward. For example, if Sony wants to produce high quality stereo and video components for the higher-income segments, this suggests charging higher prices. Thus pricing strategy is largely determined by past decisions on market positioning.

At the same time, the company may seek additional objectives. The clearer a firm is about its objectives, the easier it is to set price. Examples of common objectives are survival, current profit maximization, market-share maximization, and product quality leadership.

Survival

Companies set survival as their major objective if troubled by too much manufacturing capacity, heavy competition, or changing consumer wants. To keep the plant going, companies must set a low price in the hope that it will increase demand. Profits are less important than survival. In recent years, troubled companies such as Chrysler resorted to large price rebate programs in order to survive. As long as their prices cover variable costs and some fixed costs, they can stay in business for a while.

Current Profit Maximization

Many companies want to set a price that will maximize current profits. They estimate what the demand and costs will be at different prices, and choose the price that will produce the maximum current profit, cash flow, or return on investment. In all cases, the company wants to maximize current financial outcomes rather than long-run performance.

Market-Share Leadership

Many companies want to obtain the dominant market share. They believe that the company with the largest market share will enjoy the lowest costs and highest long-run profit. To become the market-share leader, they set prices as low as possible. A variation of this objective is to pursue a specific market-share gain. For example, if a company wants to increase its market share from 10% to 15% in one year, it will search for the price and marketing program to achieve this objective.

Product Quality Leadership

A company might decide it wants to have the highest quality product on the market. This normally calls for charging a high price to cover the high product quality and high cost of R&D. Michelin, the tire manufacturer, is a good example of a firm seeking product quality leadership. It continually introduces new tire features and longer-lasting tires, and prices its tires at a premium.

Other Objectives

A company might use price to attain other more specific objectives. It can set prices low to prevent competition from entering the market, or set prices at competitors' levels to stabilize the market. Prices can be set to keep the loyalty and support of resellers, or to avoid government intervention. Prices can be temporarily reduced to create excitement about a product or to draw more customers into a retail store. One product may be priced to help the sales of other products in the company's line. Thus pricing may play an important role in helping to accomplish the company's objectives at many levels.

Marketing Mix Strategy

Price is only one of the marketing mix tools that the company uses to achieve its marketing objectives. Price decisions must be coordinated with product design, distribution, and promotion decisions to form a consistent and effective marketing program. Decisions made for other marketing mix variables may affect pricing decisions. For example, producers who use many resellers and expect these resellers to support and promote their products may have to build larger reseller margins into their prices. The decision to develop a high-quality position will mean that the seller must charge a higher price to cover higher costs.

The company often makes its pricing decision first and then bases other marketing mix decisions on the price it wants to charge. For example, Ford discovered through research that a market segment existed for an affordable sporty car and designed the Mustang to sell within the price range that this segment was willing to pay. Here price was a key product positioning factor that defined the product's market, competition, and design. The intended price determined what product features could be offered and what production costs could be incurred.

Costs

Costs set the floor for the price that the company can set for its product. The company wants to charge a price that covers all its costs for producing, distributing, and selling the product, plus a fair rate of return for its effort and risk.

A company's costs take two forms, fixed and variable. *Fixed costs* (also known as overhead) are costs that do not vary with production or sales level. A company must pay bills each month for rent, heat, interest, and executive salaries, whatever the company's output. Fixed costs are incurred no matter what the production level.

Variable costs vary directly with the level of production. The production of each *Maclean's* magazine involves a cost of paper, ink, and other inputs. These costs tend to be the same for each unit produced. They are called variable because their total varies with the number of units produced.

Total costs are the sum of the fixed and variable costs for any given level of production. Management wants to charge a price that will at least cover the total production costs at a given level of production.

The company must watch its costs carefully. If it costs the company more than competitors to produce and sell its product, the company will have to charge a higher price or make less profit, putting it at a competitive disadvantage.

Organizational Considerations

Management must decide who, within the organization, should set prices. Companies handle pricing in a variety of ways. In small companies, prices are often set by top management rather than by the marketing or sales department. In large companies, pricing is typically handled by divisional or product line managers. In industrial markets, salespeople may be allowed to negotiate with customers within certain price ranges. Even here, top management sets the pricing objectives and policies and often approves the prices proposed by lower-level management or salespeople.[3] In industries where pricing is a key factor (steel, railroads, oil companies), companies will often have a pricing department to set prices or help others in setting the best prices. This department reports to the marketing department or top management.

External Factors Affecting Pricing Decisions

The Market and Demand

Costs set the floor for prices, and the market and demand set the ceiling. Both consumer and industrial buyers balance the price of a product or service against the benefits of owning it. Thus, before setting prices, the marketer must understand the relationship between price and demand for its product.

In this section, we will look at how the price-demand relationship varies for different types of markets, and at how buyer perceptions of price affect the pricing decision. Then we will discuss methods for measuring the price-demand relationship.

Pricing in Different Types of Markets

The seller's pricing freedom varies with different types of markets. Economists recognize four types of markets, each presenting a different pricing challenge.

Under *pure competition*, the market consists of many buyers and sellers trading in a uniform commodity such as wheat, copper, or financial securities. No single buyer or seller has much effect on the going market price. A seller cannot charge more than the going price, because buyers can obtain as much as they need at this price. Sellers would not charge less than the market price, because they can sell all they want at the market price. If the price and profits rise, new sellers can easily enter the market. Sellers in these markets do not spend much time on marketing strategy, since the role of marketing research, product development, pricing, advertising, and sales promotion is small as long as the market stays purely competitive.

Under *monopolistic competition*, the market consists of many buyers and sellers who trade over a range of prices rather than a single market price. The reason for the price range is that sellers are able to differentiate their offers to the buyers. Either the physical product can be varied in quality, features, or style, or the accompanying services can be varied. Buyers see differences in sellers' products and will pay different prices. Sellers try to develop differentiated offers for different customer segments and freely use branding, advertising, and personal selling, in addition to price, to set their offers apart. Because there are many competitors, each firm is less affected by competitors' marketing strategies than in oligopolistic markets.

In monopolistic competition, as in the small electronic product field, many sellers compete over a wide range of products.

James Hertel

Under *oligopolistic competition*, the market consists of a few sellers who are highly sensitive to each other's pricing and marketing strategies. The product can be uniform (steel, aluminum) or nonuniform (cars, computers). The reason for the few sellers is that it is difficult for new sellers to enter the market. Each seller is alert to competitors' strategies and moves. If a steel company like Algoma slashes its price by 10%, buyers will quickly switch to this supplier. The other steelmakers like Stelco and Dofasco will have to respond by lowering their prices or increasing their services. An oligopolist is never sure that it will gain anything permanent through a price cut. On the other hand, if the oligopolist raised the price, the competitors might not follow this lead. The oligopolist would have to retract its price increase or risk losing customers to competitors.

A *pure monopoly* consists of one seller. The seller may be a government monopoly (Canada Post), a private regulated monopoly (Hydro Quebec), or a private nonregulated monopoly (as Du Pont became when it introduced nylon). Pricing is handled differently in each case. A government monopoly can pursue a variety of pricing objectives. It might set a price below cost because the product is important to buyers and they cannot afford to pay full cost. Alternatively, the price might be set to cover costs or to produce fair revenues, or it might be set quite high to slow down consumption. In a regulated monopoly, the government permits a company, such as Bell Canada, to set rates that will yield a "fair return," one that will let the company maintain and expand its plant as needed.

Consumer Perceptions of Price and Value

In the end, the consumer will decide whether a product's price is right. When setting prices, the company must consider consumer perceptions of price and how these perceptions affect consumers' buying decisions. Nagle states that pricing decisions, like other marketing mix decisions, must be buyer oriented:

> . . . pricing requires more than mere technical expertise. It requires creative judgment and a keen awareness of buyers' motivations . . . the key to effective pricing is the same one that opens doors . . . in other marketing functions: a creative awareness of who buyers are, why they buy, and how they make their buying decisions. The recognition that buyers differ in these dimensions is as important for effective pricing as it is for effective promotion, distribution, or product development.[4]

When consumers buy a product, they exchange something of value (the price) to get something of value (the benefits of having or using the product). Effective buyer-oriented pricing involves understanding what value consumers place on the benefits they receive from the product, and setting a price that fits this value. The benefits include both actual and perceived benefits. When a consumer buys a meal at a fancy restaurant, it is easy to figure out the value of the meal's ingredients. But it is very difficult, even for the consumer, to measure the value of other satisfactions such as taste, a plush environment, relaxation, conversation, and status. These values will vary for different consumers and for different situations. As an example, when Domino's Pizza began operations in Canada, they conducted market surveys to determine what value Canadian consumers would attach to quality and service, the key "ingredients" of Domino's marketing strategy. The surveys revealed that consumers were willing to pay for these factors. Domino's charges a premium price for their pizzas and has captured 40% of the market in some areas of Ontario.[5]

Marketers must try to look at the consumer's reason for buying the product, and set price according to consumer perceptions of the product's value. Because consumers vary in the values they assign to different product features, marketers often vary their pricing strategies for different price segments. They offer different sets of product features at different prices. For example, jeans makers may offer lower-priced, rugged jeans for consumers who value utility and durability, and higher-priced designer jeans for customers who value fashion and status.

Buyer-oriented pricing means that the marketer cannot design a product and marketing program, and only then set the price. Good pricing begins with analyzing consumer needs and price perceptions. Price must be considered along with the other marketing mix variables before the marketing program is set.

Analyzing the Price-Demand Relationship

Each price the company might charge will lead to a different level of demand. The relation between the price charged and the resulting demand level is shown in the familiar demand curve in Figure 11-2A. The *demand curve* shows the number of units the market will buy in a given time period at different prices that might be charged. In the normal case, demand and price are inversely related. That is, the higher the price, the lower the demand. Therefore, the company would sell less if it raised its price from P_1 to P_2. Consumers with limited budgets will probably buy less of the item if its price is too high.

Most demand curves slope downward in either a straight or a curved line

FIGURE 11-2
Two Hypothetical Demand Schedules

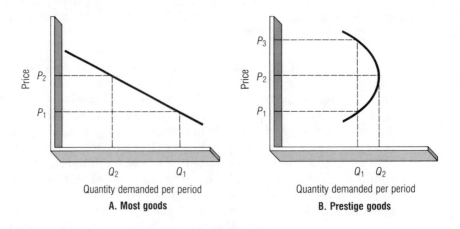

Price P_2 P_1

Q_2 Q_1
Quantity demanded per period
A. Most goods

Price P_3 P_2 P_1

Q_1 Q_2
Quantity demanded per period
B. Prestige goods

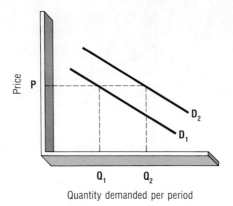

FIGURE 11-3
Effects of Promotion and Other Nonprice Variables on Demand, Shown through Shifts
of the Demand Curve

as in Figure 11-2A. But for prestige goods, the demand curve sometimes slopes
upward, as in Figure 11-2B. A perfume company found that by raising its price
from P_1 to P_2, it sold more perfume rather than less. Consumers thought the
higher price meant a better or more desirable perfume. However, if too high a
price is charged (P_3), the level of demand will be lower than at P_2.

Most companies try to measure their demand curves. The type of market
makes a difference. In a monopoly, the demand curve shows the total market
demand resulting from different prices. If the company faces competition, its
demand at different prices will depend on whether competitor's prices stay
constant or change with the company's prices. Here, we will assume that competitor's prices remain constant. Later in this chapter, we will discuss what
happens when competitor's prices change.

To measure a demand curve requires estimating demand at different prices.
In measuring the price-demand relationship, the market researcher must not
allow other factors affecting demand to vary. If a company raised its advertising
budget when it lowered its price, we would not know how much of the increased
demand was due to the lower price and how much to the increased advertising.

Economists show the impact of nonprice factors on demand through shifts
of the demand curve, rather than movements along the demand curve. Suppose
the initial demand curve in Figure 11-3 is D_1. The seller is charging P and selling
Q_1 units. Now suppose the economy suddenly improves, or the seller doubles
its advertising budget. The higher demand is reflected through an upward shift
of the demand curve from D_1 to D_2. Without changing the price P, the seller's
demand is now Q_2.

Price Elasticity of Demand

Marketers need to know *price elasticity*, or how responsive demand will be to
a change in price. Consider the two demand curves in Figure 11-4. In Figure

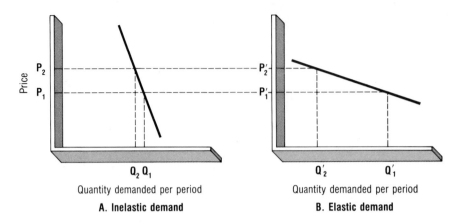

FIGURE 11-4
Inelastic and Elastic Demand

11-4A a price increase from P1 to P_2 leads to a relatively small drop in demand from Q_1 to Q_2. In Figure 11-4B the same price increase leads to a large drop in demand from Q'_1 to Q'_2. If demand hardly changes with a small change in price, we say the demand is inelastic. If demand changes a lot, we say the demand is elastic.

What determines the price elasticity of demand? Demand is likely to be less elastic under the following conditions: (1) there are few or no substitutes or competitors; (2) buyers do not readily notice the higher price; (3) buyers are slow to change their buying habits and search for lower prices; (4) buyers think the higher prices are justified by quality improvements or normal inflation.

If demand is elastic rather than inelastic, sellers will consider lowering their price. A lower price will produce more total revenue. This makes sense as long as the extra costs of producing and selling more do not exceed the extra revenue.

Competitors' Prices and Offers

Another external factor affecting the company's pricing decisions is competitors' prices and their possible reactions to the company's pricing moves. Consumers evaluate a product's price and value against the prices and values of comparable products. In addition, the company's pricing strategy may affect the nature of the competition it faces—a high-price, high-margin strategy may attract competition, whereas a low-price, low-margin strategy may stop competitors or drive them out of the market.

The company needs to learn the price and quality of each competitor's offer. This can be done in several ways. The firm can send out comparison shoppers to price and compare competitors' offers. The firm can get competitors' price lists and buy competitors' equipment and take it apart. The firm can also ask buyers how they view the price and quality of each competitor's offer.

Once the company is aware of competitors' prices and offers, it can use them as a starting point for its own pricing. If the firm's offer is similar to a major competitor's offer, the firm will have to price close to the competitor or lose sales. If the firm's offer is not as good, the firm will not be able to charge as much as the competitor. If the firm's offer is better, the firm can charge more than the competitor. Basically, the firm will use price to position its offer relative to competitors.

Other External Factors

When setting prices, the company must also consider other factors in its external environment. For example, **economic conditions** can have a strong impact on the results of the firm's pricing strategies. Economic factors such as inflation, boom, or recession, and interest rates affect pricing decisions because they affect both the costs of producing a product and consumer perceptions of the product's price and value.

The company must consider what impact its prices will have on other parties in its environment. How will **resellers** react to various prices? The company should set prices that give resellers a fair profit, encourage their support, and help them to sell the product effectively. The **government** is another important external influence on pricing decisions. Marketers need to know the laws affecting price and make sure their pricing policies are legal. The major laws affecting price are summarized in Exhibit 11-1 (p. 266).

General Pricing Approaches

The price the company charges will be somewhere between one that is too low to produce a profit and one that is too high to produce any demand. Figure 11-5 summarizes the major considerations in setting price. Product costs set a floor to the price; consumer perceptions of the product's value set the ceiling. The company must consider competitors' prices and other external and internal factors to find the best price between these two extremes.

FIGURE 11-5
Major Considerations in Setting Price

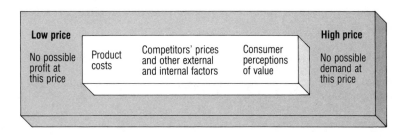

Companies set prices by selecting a general pricing approach that includes one or more of these three sets of factors. We will look at the following approaches: the cost-based approach (cost-plus pricing, breakeven analysis, and target profit pricing), the buyer-based approach (perceived-value pricing), and the competition-based approach (going-rate and sealed-bid pricing).

EXHIBIT 11-1
Price Decisions and Public Policy

Prior to 1986, the major federal laws dealing with pricing were contained in the Combines Investigation Act.[1] In 1986, the new Competition Act was enacted and the existing pricing laws were incorporated into this act. The laws cover price discrimination, predatory pricing, discriminatory promotional allowances, misleading price advertising, and resale price maintenance.

Price discrimination   Under Section 34a of the Act, it is illegal for a supplier to charge different prices to competitors purchasing similar quantities of goods. No supplier has been charged or prosecuted under this section of the Act, possibly because of ambiguities in the legislation.

Predatory pricing   Sections 34b and 34c of the Act prohibit pricing practices that can substantially lessen competition. The sections do not preclude price-cutting at the retail level. Few Canadian firms have been brought to court under these sections.

Discriminatory promotional allowances   Section 35 of the Act makes it illegal for sellers or their customers to receive or seek any type of promotional allowance, such as discounts or rebates, not offered on a proportional basis. No Canadian firms have been convicted under this section.

Misleading price advertising   Under Section 36 of the Act it is illegal to misrepresent the regular price at which a product is usually sold. The federal government has actively enforced this section and hundreds of convictions have occurred since the addition of this legislation in 1960. Companies convicted of misleading price advertising are fined and the cases are published for public knowledge.

Resale price maintenance   Section 38 of the Act prohibits manufacturers from requiring resellers to sell their products at a stipulated price. A number of court cases have been brought under this section of the Act.

[1]A summary of the court cases under the Combines Investigation Act until 1973 is contained in *Proposals for a New Competition Policy for Canada* (Ottawa: Department of Corporate Affairs, 1978); see also *Misleading Advertising Bulletin*, Department of Consumer and Corporate Affairs, Ottawa, various issues, and Competition Act, Catalog YX75-C-23-1986.

Cost-Based Pricing

Cost-Plus Pricing

The simplest pricing method is *cost-plus pricing*, which means adding a standard markup to the cost of the product. An appliance retailer might pay a manufacturer $20 for a toaster and mark it up to sell at $30, which is a 50% markup on cost. The retailer's gross margin is $10. If the store's operating costs amount to $8 per toaster sold, the retailer's profit margin will be $2.[6]

The manufacturer who made the toaster could also have used cost-plus pricing. If the manufacturer's standard cost of producing the toaster was $16, it might have added a 25% markup, setting the price to the retailer at $20. Construction companies calculate job bids by estimating the total project cost and adding a standard markup for profit. Lawyers and other professionals typically price by adding a standard markup to their costs. Some sellers tell their customers they will charge them cost plus a specified markup; for example, aerospace companies price this way to the government.

Markups vary a lot among different goods. Some common markups (on price, not cost) are 59% for bakeries, 48% for jewelry stores, and 19% for supermarkets.[7] In the retail grocery industry, coffee, canned milk, and sugar tend to have low markups, while frozen foods, jellies, and some canned products have high markups. The varying markups reflect differences in unit costs, sales, turnover, and manufacturers' brands versus private brands.

Does the use of standard markups to set prices seem logical? Generally, any pricing method that ignores current demand and competition is not likely to lead to the best price. The retail graveyard is full of merchants who insisted on using standard markups after their competitors had gone into discount pricing.

Still, markup pricing remains popular for many reasons. First, sellers are more certain about costs than about demand. By tying the price to cost, sellers simplify pricing — they do not have to make frequent adjustments as demand changes. Second, where all firms in the industry use this pricing method, prices tend to be similar, and price competition is minimized. Third, many people feel that cost-plus pricing is fairer to both buyers and sellers. Sellers do not take advantage of buyers when buyers' demand becomes great, yet the sellers earn a fair return on their investment.

Breakeven Analysis and Target Profit Pricing

Another cost-oriented pricing approach is *breakeven pricing* or **target profit pricing**. The firm tries to determine the price at which it will break even or make the profit it is seeking. Target pricing is used by General Motors, which prices its automobiles to achieve a 15 to 20% profit on its investment. This pricing method is also used by public utilities, which are constrained to make a fair return on their investment.

Target pricing uses the concept of a **breakeven chart**. A breakeven chart shows the total cost and total revenue expected at different levels of sales. Figure 11-6 shows a hypothetical breakeven chart and analysis. Fixed costs are $6-million regardless of sales volume. Variable costs of $5 per unit are added to

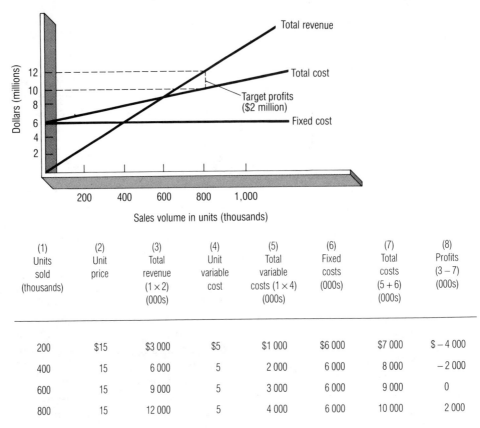

(1) Units sold (thousands)	(2) Unit price	(3) Total revenue (1 × 2) (000s)	(4) Unit variable cost	(5) Total variable costs (1 × 4) (000s)	(6) Fixed costs (000s)	(7) Total costs (5 + 6) (000s)	(8) Profits (3 − 7) (000s)
200	$15	$3 000	$5	$1 000	$6 000	$7 000	$ − 4 000
400	15	6 000	5	2 000	6 000	8 000	− 2 000
600	15	9 000	5	3 000	6 000	9 000	0
800	15	12 000	5	4 000	6 000	10 000	2 000

Break-even = the point where total revenue and total costs are equal
= fixed costs/(unit price − unit variable cost)

FIGURE 11-6
Breakeven Chart and Analysis Chart

fixed costs to form total costs, which rise with volume. The total revenue curve starts at zero and rises with each unit sold. The slope of the total revenue curve also reflects the price. Here the price is $15 (for example, the company's revenue is $12 million on 800 000 units, or $15 per unit).

At $15, the company must sell at least 600 000 units to break even; that is, for total revenue to cover total cost. If the company wants a target profit of $2-million, it must sell at least 800 000 units at a price of $15 each. If the company is willing to charge a higher price, say $20, it will not need to sell as many units to achieve its target profit. However, the market may not buy even this lower volume at the higher price, as much depends on the price elasticity of demand. This is not shown in the breakeven chart. This pricing method requires the company to consider the impact of different prices on the sales volume needed to pass the breakeven point and realize target profits, and the likelihood that this will happen with each possible price.

Buyer-Based Pricing

An increasing number of companies are basing their prices on the product's perceived value. *Perceived value pricing* uses the buyers' perception of value, not the seller's cost, as the key to pricing. The company uses the nonprice variables in the marketing mix to build up perceived value in the buyers' minds. Price is set to match the perceived value.

Consider the various prices that different restaurants charge for the same item. A consumer who wants a cup of coffee and a slice of apple pie may pay $1.25 in a fast-food outlet, $2.00 at a family restaurant, $3.50 at a hotel coffee shop, $5.00 for hotel room service, and $7.00 at an elegant restaurant. Each succeeding restaurant can charge more because of the value added by the atmosphere.

The company using perceived-value pricing must find out the value in the buyers' minds for different competitive offers. In the last example, consumers could be asked how much they would pay for the same coffee and pie in the

An example of perceived-value pricing.

different surroundings. Sometimes consumers could be asked how much they would pay for each benefit added to the offer.

If the seller charges more than the buyers' perceived value, the company's sales will suffer. Many companies overprice their products, and their products sell poorly. Other companies underprice. Although their products sell very well, they produce less revenue than if price was raised to the perceived value level.[8]

Competition-Based Pricing

Going-Rate Pricing

In *going-rate pricing*, the firm bases its price largely on competitors' prices, with less attention paid to its own costs or demand. The firm might charge the same, more, or less than its major competitors. In oligopolistic industries that sell a commodity such as steel, paper, or fertilizer, firms normally charge the same price. The smaller firms "follow the leader." They change their prices when the market leader's prices change, rather than when their own demand or cost changes. Some firms may charge more or less, but they hold the amount of difference constant. Thus minor gasoline retailers usually charge a cent less than the major oil companies, without letting the difference increase or decrease.

Going-rate pricing is quite popular. Where demand elasticity is difficult to measure, firms feel that the going price represents the collective wisdom of the industry concerning the price that will yield a fair return. They also feel that holding to the going price will avoid harmful price wars.

Sealed-Bid Pricing

Competition-based pricing is also used when firms bid for jobs. Using *sealed-bid pricing*, the firm bases its price on how it thinks competitors will price rather than on its own costs or demand. The firm wants to win the contract, and this requires pricing lower than the other firms.

Yet the firm cannot set its price below a certain level. It cannot price below cost without harming its position. On the other hand, the higher it sets its price above its costs, the lower its chance of getting the contract.

Summary

In spite of the increased role of nonprice factors in the modern marketing process, price remains an important element in the marketing mix. Many internal and external factors influence the company's pricing decisions. Internal factors include the firm's marketing objectives, marketing mix strategy, cost, and organization for pricing.

The pricing strategy is largely determined by the company's target market and positioning objectives. Common pricing objectives include survival, current profit maximization, market-share leadership, and product quality leadership.

Price is only one of the marketing mix tools the company uses to accomplish its objective, and pricing decisions affect and are affected by product design, distribution, and promotion decisions. Price decisions must be carefully coordinated with the other marketing mix decisions when designing the marketing program.

Cost sets the floor for the company's price — the price must cover all the costs of making and selling the product, plus a fair rate of return.

Management must decide who within the organization is responsible for setting price. In large companies, some pricing authority may be delegated to lower-level managers and salespeople, but top management usually sets pricing policies and approves proposed prices. Production, finance, and accounting managers also influence pricing.

External factors that influence pricing decisions include the nature of the market and demand, competitors' prices and offers, and other external factors such as the economy, reseller needs, and government actions. The seller's pricing freedom varies with different types of market. Pricing is specially challenging in markets characterized by monopolistic competition or oligopoly.

In the end, the consumer decides whether the company has set the right price. The consumer weighs the price against the perceived values of using the product — if the price exceeds the sum of the value, consumers will not buy the product. Consumers differ in the values they assign to different product features, and marketers often vary their pricing strategies for different price segments. When assessing the market and demand, the company estimates the demand schedule, which shows the probable quantity purchased per period at alternative price levels. The more inelastic the demand, the higher the company can set its price. Demand and consumer value perceptions set the ceiling for prices.

Consumers compare a product's price to the price of competitors' products. The company must learn the price and quality of competitors' offers and use them as an starting point for its own pricing.

The company can select one or a combination of three general pricing approaches: the cost-based approach (cost-plus or breakeven analysis and target profit pricing), the buyer-based (perceived-value) approach, and the competition-based (going-rate or sealed-bid pricing) approach.

Questions for Discussion

1. What are the most influential factors affecting the setting of price in each of the four market types discussed in this chapter?
2. What is the importance of the price elasticity of demand?
3. If a firm has selected its target market and positioning carefully, then its marketing-mix strategy, including price, will be straightforward. Comment.

4. Offer examples of firms whose marketing strategy might be survival, current profit maximization, market share maximization, or product-quality leadership.

5. Explain how an increase in production will cause the average fixed cost per unit to fall, thereby allowing a firm to lower its selling price without necessarily reducing its profit margin per unit.

6. If you had a chance to open a car wash where annual fixed costs were $100 000, variable costs were $0.50 per car washed, and you determined that a ''competitive'' price would be $1.50 per car, would you invest in this business?

7. Explain the major pricing issues with which public policymakers are most concerned.

8. If a company is to respond accurately to price changes, it must thoroughly understand its competitors. Comment.

Chapter 11 Key Terms

Breakeven pricing   Setting price to break even on the costs of making and marketing a product, or to make the desired profit.

Cost-plus pricing   Adding a standard markup to the cost of the product.

Demand curve   A curve that shows the number of units the market will buy in a given time period at different prices that might be charged.

Fixed costs   Costs that do not vary with production or sales level.

Going-rate pricing   Setting price based largely on following competitor's prices rather than on company cost or demand.

Monopolistic competition   A market in which many buyers and sellers trade over a range of prices rather than at a single market price.

Oligopolistic competition   A market in which there are a few sellers who are highly sensitive to each other's pricing and marketing strategies.

Perceived-value pricing   Setting price based on buyers' perception of value rather than on the seller's cost.

Price   The amount of money charged for a product or service, or the sum of the values consumers exchange for the benefits of having or using the product or service.

Price elasticity   A measure of the sensitivity of demand to changes in price.

Pure competition   A market in which many buyers and sellers trade in a uniform commodity — no single buyer or seller has much effect on the going market price.

Pure monopoly   A market in which there is a single seller — it may be a government monopoly, a private regulated monopoly, or a private nonregulated monopoly.

Sealed-bid pricing   Setting price based on how the firm thinks competitors will price rather than on its own costs or demand — used when a company bids for jobs.

Total costs   The sum of the fixed and variable costs for any given level of production.

Variable costs   Costs that vary directly with the level of production.

Cases for Chapter 11

Pricing Products: Pricing Strategies

Chapter Objectives

After reading this chapter, you should be able to:
1. Describe the major strategies for pricing new products.
2. Discuss how companies find a set of prices that maximizes the profits for the total product mix.
3. Explain how companies adjust their prices to take into account different types of customers and situations.
4. Tell why companies decide to change their prices.

Marketers of spirits in Canada — the earthly kind (gin, scotch, whisky) as opposed to the heavenly kind — are facing a difficult future. From 1982 to 1987, sales of spirits have experienced an average decline of 5% each year. One of the main reasons for the decline is rising prices due to provincial and federal taxes (up 44% in three years), which now account for 80% of the retail price of a bottle of spirits. For the distillers, pricing strategies must consider the impact of taxes along with consumer reaction.

One brand that was particularly hard hit by the taxation policy was Seagram's Crown Royal. This world famous brand with its distinctive royal purple cloth bag and drawstring enclosed in the classic box was costing more with every tax increase. The problem was that the bag and box were being taxed along with the liquid contents. The result was that sales went flat and then fell.

Seagram's marketing executives were on the horns of a dilemma. On the one hand the bag and box offered a distinct position for the brand. The Crown Royal bag was a tradition — its uses, for storing everything from children's marbles to jewelry, were legendary. On the other hand, because of taxes, the bag and box added about $6.00 to the retail price for a large bottle of Crown Royal, making it considerably more expensive than its main rival, Hiram Walker's Canada Club. Before making a final decision, a test market was conducted in Alberta. Crown Royal was sold at a lower price without the bag and box and consumers reacted positively to the change. That evidence convinced Seagram's to trade-off the bag and box for a lower price in Canada. Before the change was made in 1984, annual sales of Crown Royal were around 50 000 cases each year. After the change, sales increased dramatically. In 1986 200 000 cases were sold and sales are now exceeding 250 000 cases annually. In the case of Crown Royal, consumers are apparently willing to forgo attractive and unique packaging for a lower price.[1]

James Hertel

Crown Royal bottles without the famous bag and box.

In this chapter, we will look at pricing strategies. A company does not set a single price, but develops a pricing structure that covers different items in its line. This pricing structure changes over time as products move through their life cycles. The company adjusts product prices to reflect changing costs and demand, and to account for variations in buyers and situations. As the competitive environment changes, at times the company considers initiating price changes, and at times responds to price changes by other companies. This chapter will examine the major pricing strategies available to management.[2] We will look at **new product pricing strategies** for products in the introductory stage of the product life cycle; **product-mix pricing strategies** for related products in the product mix; **price-adjustment strategies** that account for customer differences and changing situations; and **strategies for initiating and responding to price changes**.

New Product Pricing Strategies ━━━━━━━━━

Pricing strategies usually change as the product passes through the product life cycle. The introductory stage is especially challenging. We can distinguish between pricing a real product innovation that is patent-protected and pricing a product that imitates existing products.

Pricing an Innovative Product

Companies introducing a new patent-protected innovative product can choose between market-skimming pricing and market penetration pricing.

Market-Skimming Pricing

Many companies that invent new products set high prices initially to "skim" the market. Du Pont is a prime user of *market skimming*. On its new discoveries —cellophane, nylon—it finds the highest price it can charge given the benefits of its new product over other products customers might buy. Du Pont sets a price that makes it just worthwhile for some segments of the market to adopt the new material. After the initial sales slow down, it lowers the price to draw in the next price-sensitive layer of customers. In this way, Du Pont skims a maximum amount of revenue from the various segments of the market. Market skimming was also used when Trivial Pursuit was introduced in Canada. After production levels increased to match demand, both the price of the game and the new card sets were lowered.

Market skimming makes sense only under certain conditions. Enough buyers must want the product at the higher price. The costs of producing a small volume cannot be so high that they cancel the advantage of charging the higher price. The product's quality and image should support the higher price and competitors should not be able to easily enter the market and undercut the high price.

Market Penetration Pricing

Other companies set a low price on their innovative product, hoping to attract a large number of buyers and win a large market share. Texas Instruments (TI) is a prime user of this *market penetration pricing*. TI will build a large plant, sets its price as low as possible, win a large market share, realize falling costs through experience curve effects, and cut its price further as costs fall.[3]

Several conditions favor setting a low price. The market must be highly price-sensitive so that a low price produces more market growth. Production and distribution costs must fall as production volume increases, and the low price must help to keep out the competition.

Pricing an Imitative New Product

A company that plans to develop an imitative new product faces a product-positioning problem. It must decide where to position the product on quality

FIGURE 12-1
Nine Marketing Mix Strategies on Price/Quality

and price. Figure 12-1 shows nine possible price-quality strategies. If the existing market leader has taken box 1 by producing the premium product and charging the highest price, the newcomer might prefer to use one of the other strategies. The newcomer could design a high-quality product and charge a medium price (box 2), design an average-quality product and charge an average price (box 5), and so on. The newcomer must consider the size and growth rate of the market in each box and the competitors it would face.

Product-Mix Pricing Strategies

The strategy for setting a price on a product has to be changed when the product is part of a product mix. In this case, the firm looks for a set of prices that maximizes the profits on the total product mix. Pricing is difficult because the various products have related demand and costs, and face different degrees of competition. We will look at four situations.

Product-Line Pricing

Companies usually develop product lines rather than single products. For example, Panasonic offers five different color video sound cameras, ranging from a simple one weighing 2.1 kilograms to a complex one weighing 2.9 kilograms that includes automatic focusing, fade control, and two-speed zoom lens. Each successive camera in the line offers more features. Management must decide on the price steps to set between the various cameras.

The price steps should take into account cost differences between the cameras, customer evaluations of the different features, and competitors' prices. If the price difference between two successive cameras is small, buyers will buy the more advanced camera, and this will increase company profits if the cost

Product line pricing: the different cameras in Panasonic's product line have prices to match costs, features, and consumers' perceptions of quality.

Courtesy: Matsushita Electric of Canada Limited

difference is smaller than the price difference. If the price difference is large, customers will buy the less advanced cameras.

In many industries, sellers use well-established price points for the products in their line. Thus men's clothing stores might carry men's suits at three price levels: $150, $220, and $310. The customers will associate low-, average-, and high-quality suits with the three price "points." Even if the three prices are raised a little, men will normally buy suits at their preferred price point. The seller's task is to establish perceived quality differences that support the price differences.

Optional Product Pricing

Many companies offer to sell optional or accessory products along with their main product. A car buyer can order electric windows, defoggers, and cruise control. Pricing these options is a sticky problem. Automobile companies have to decide which items to build into the base price and which items to offer as options. General Motors' normal pricing strategy is to advertise a stripped-down model for $8000 to pull people into showrooms, but to devote most of the showroom space to showing loaded cars at $10 000 or $12 000.

The economy model is stripped of so many comforts and conveniences that most buyers reject it. When GM launched its new front-wheel drive J-cars in the early 1980s, it took a clue from the Japanese automakers and included in the sticker price many useful items previously sold only as options. Now the advertised price represented a well-equipped car. Unfortunately, however, the price was high and many car shoppers balked.

Captive Product Pricing

Companies in some industries make products that must be used with the main product. Examples of captive products are razor blades and camera film. Producers of the main products (razors and cameras) often price them low and set high markups on the supplies. Thus Kodak prices its cameras low because it

Courtesy: Kodak Canada Inc.

Kodak uses a captive product strategy for its film.

makes its money on selling film. Those camera makers who do not sell film have to price their cameras higher in order to make the same overall profit.

By-Product Pricing

In producing processed meats, petroleum products, chemicals, and other products, there are often by-products. If the by-products have no value and getting rid of them is costly, this will affect the pricing of the main product. The manufacturer will seek a market for these by-products and should accept any price that covers more than the cost of storing and delivering them. This will let the seller reduce the main product's price to make it more competitive.

Price-Adjustment Strategies

Companies adjust their basic price to account for various customer differences and changing situations. We will look at the following adjustment strategies: discount pricing and allowances, discriminatory pricing, psychological pricing, promotional pricing, and geographical pricing.

Discount Pricing and Allowances

Most companies will adjust their basic price to reward customers for certain acts, such as early payment of bills, volume purchases, and off-season buying. These price adjustments — called discounts and allowances — are described below.

Cash Discounts

A *cash discount* is a price reduction to buyers who pay their bills promptly. A typical example is "2/10, net 30," which means that payment is due within 30 days, but the buyer can deduct 2% if the bill is paid within ten days. The discount must be granted to all buyers meeting these terms. Such discounts are customary in many industries and help to improve the sellers' cash situation and reduce credit collection costs and bad debts.

Quantity Discounts

A *quantity discount* is a price reduction to buyers who buy large volumes. A typical example is "$10 per unit for less than 100 units; $9 per unit for 100 or more units." Quantity discounts must be offered to all customers and must not exceed the seller's cost savings associated with selling large quantities. These savings include lower selling, inventory, and transportation expenses. Discounts provide an incentive to the customer to buy more from a given seller rather than buying from many sources.

Functional Discounts

A *functional discount* (also called a trade discount) is offered by the seller to trade channel members who perform certain functions such as selling, storing, and record keeping. Manufacturers may offer different functional discounts to different trade channels because of the varying services they perform, but manufacturers must offer the same functional discounts within each trade channel. Functional discounts, while a common practice in the U.S., are illegal in Canada under the price discrimination provisions of The Competition Act (see Exhibit 11-1, Chapter 11).

Seasonal Discounts

A *seasonal discount* is a price reduction to buyers who buy merchandise or services out of season. Seasonal discounts allow the seller to keep production

While ski manufacturers and resorts charge top prices in winter, they often offer discounts in other seasons.

Courtesy: Whistler Resort Association

steady during the year. Ski manufacturers will offer seasonal discounts to retailers in the spring and summer to encourage early ordering. Hotels, motels, and airlines will offer seasonal discounts in their slower selling periods.

Allowances

Allowances are other types of reductions from the list price. For example, *trade-in allowances* are price reductions given for turning in an old item when buying a new one. Trade-in allowances are most common in the automobile industry and are also given for some other durable goods. *Promotional allowances* are payments or price reductions to reward dealers for participating in advertising and sales-support programs.

Discriminatory Pricing

Companies will often adjust their basic prices to allow for differences in customers, products, and locations. In *discriminatory pricing*, the company sells a product or service at two or more prices, where the difference in prices is not based on differences in costs. Discriminatory pricing takes several forms:

Customer basis *Different customers pay different prices for the same product or service. For example, museums will charge a lower admission for students and senior citizens.*

Product-form basis *Different versions of the product are priced differently, but not according to differences in their costs. A dishwasher with a formica top might be priced at $460 and the same dishwasher with a wooden top might be priced at $480. Yet the wooden top only cost $5 more to make than the formica top.*

Place basis *Different locations are priced differently even though the cost of offering each location is the same. A theater varies its seat prices because of audience preferences for certain locations.*

Time basis *Prices are varied seasonally, by the day, and even by the hour. Public utilities vary their prices to commercial users by time of day and weekend versus weekday.*

If price discrimination is to work, certain conditions must exist. First, the market must be segmentable, and the segments must show different degrees of demand. Second, members of the segment paying the lower price should not be able to turn around and resell the product to the segment paying the higher price. Third, competitors should not be able to undersell the firm in the segment being charged the higher price. Fourth, the cost of segmenting and watching the market should not exceed the extra revenue obtained from price discrimination. Fifth, the practice should not lead to customer resentment and ill will. Sixth, the form of price discrimination used must be legal. With the current deregulation taking place in certain industries (such as airlines), companies in these industries have used more discriminatory pricing. Consider the price discrimination used by airlines:

> At one point, the passengers on a plane bound from Toronto to Vancouver were paying as many as eight different fares for the same flight due to the heated-up competition between Air Canada and Canadian Pacific/Pacific Western. Many of the fares were aimed at segments of the market. The eight possible fares were: (1) $641 one-way for first class; (2) $485 one-way for executive class; (3) $458 one-way for economy class; (4) $435 one-way special economy class; (5) $504 for a return fare if the ticket was purchased 14 days in advance; (6) $299 for a return fare if the ticket was purchased 21 days in advance; (7) $229 for a one-way youth standby; and (8) $366 for a return fare for senior citizens if the ticket was purchased 14 days in advance.

Psychological Pricing

Price says something about the product. For example, many consumers use price to judge quality. A $50 bottle of perfume may contain only $3 worth of scent, but people are willing to pay $50 because the price seems to indicate

Consumers often judge the quality of products by the prices charged.

James Hertel

something special. Buyers often take price to be a sign of product quality, especially for products that they cannot easily evaluate, like perfume. Bayer aspirin, although the highest-priced aspirin, continues to outsell lower-priced brands, indicating that people take its price and well-known brand name to be a sign of higher quality. Consumers often consider a higher-priced product to be of a better quality.[4] However, their judgment of product quality is also influenced by the brand name and the store selling the product.[5] Thus, using *psychological pricing*, sellers should consider the psychology of prices and not simply the economics.

Even small differences in price can suggest product differences to consumers. Consider a stereo priced at $300 compared to one priced at $299.95. The actual price difference is only five cents, but the psychological difference can be much greater. For example, some consumers will see the $299.95 as a price in the $200 range rather than the $300 range. The $299.95 will more likely be seen as a bargain price, and the $300 price will suggest more quality.

Promotional Pricing

With *promotional pricing*, companies will temporarily price their products below the list price, and sometimes even below cost. Promotional pricing takes several forms:

Loss leaders   Supermarkets and department stores will price a few product as loss leaders to attract customers to the store in the hope that they will buy other items at normal markups.

Special-event pricing   Sellers will also use special-event pricing in certain seasons to draw in more customers. Thus white sales are promotionally priced every January to attract shopping-weary customers into the stores.

Cash rebates   Manufacturers will sometimes offer cash rebates to consumers who buy the product from dealers within a specified time. The manufacturer sends the rebate directly to the customer. They have recently been popular with automakers, and with durable goods and small appliance producers.

Discounts   The seller may simply offer discounts from normal prices to increase sales and reduce inventories. One study of Canadian consumers' reactions to retail "price-offs" found that consumers thought the "best deal in town" was more likely when substantial savings were announced (for example, 50% off), and depended on the particular store doing the advertising (for example, a discount store).[6]

Geographical Pricing

The company must decide how to price its products to customers located in different parts of the country. Should the company charge higher prices to distant customers to cover the higher shipping costs, but thereby risk losing

A clearance sale is a form of promotional pricing.

their business? Or should the company charge the same to all customers regardless of location? We will look at five geographical pricing strategies for the following hypothetical situation:

> The Peerless Paper Company is located in Vancouver, British Columbia, and sells paper products to customers all over Canada and the United States. The cost of freight is high and affects the companies from whom customers buy their paper. Peerless wants to establish a geographical pricing policy. It is trying to determine how to price a $100 order to three specific customers: customer A (Edmonton); customer B (San Francisco, California); and customer C (Toronto).

FOB Origin Pricing

Peerless can ask each customer to pay the shipping cost from the Vancouver factory to the customer's location. All three customers would pay the same factory price of $100, with customer A paying, say, $10 for shipping, customer

B paying $15, and customer C paying $25. With *FOB origin pricing*, the goods are then placed free on board a carrier, at which point the title and responsibility pass to the customer, who pays the freight from the factory to the destination.

Supporters of FOB pricing feel that it is the fairest way to assess freight charges, because each customer picks up its own cost. The disadvantage, however, is that Peerless will be a high-cost firm to distant customers. If Peerless's main competitor is in Ontario, this competitor would outsell Peerless in Ontario. In fact, the competitor would outsell Peerless in most of the East, while Peerless would dominate the West. A vertical line could be drawn on a map connecting the cities where the two companies' price plus freight would just be equal. Peerless would have the price advantage west of this line, and its competitor would have the price advantage east of this line.

Uniform Delivered Pricing

Uniform delivered pricing is the exact opposite of FOB pricing. Here the company charges the same price plus freight to all customers regardless of their location. The freight charge is set at the average freight cost. Suppose the average freight cost is $15. Uniform delivered pricing therefore results in a high charge to the Edmonton customer (who pays $15 freight instead of $10) and a lower charge to the Toronto customer (who pay $15 instead of $25). The Edmonton customer would prefer to buy paper from another local paper company that uses FOB origin pricing. On the other hand, Peerless has a better chance to win the Toronto customer. Other advantages are that uniform delivered pricing is fairly easy to administer and lets the firm advertise its price nationally.

Zone Pricing

Zone pricing falls between FOB origin pricing and uniform delivered pricing. The company sets up two or more zones. All customers within a zone pay the same total price, and this price is higher in the more distant zones. Peerless might set up a West zone and charge $10 freight to all customers in this zone; a South zone and charge $15; and an East zone and charge $25. In this way, the customers within a given price zone receive no price advantage from the company. Customers in Edmonton and Regina pay the same total price to Peerless. The complaint, however, is that the Edmonton customer is paying part of the Regina customer's freight cost. In addition, a customer just on the east side of the line dividing the West and East pays much more than one just on the west side of the line, although they may be within a few miles of each other.

Basing-Point Pricing

Basing-point pricing allows the seller to select a particular city as a basing point and charge all customers the freight cost from that city to the customer location, regardless of the city from which the goods are actually shipped. For example, Peerless might set Winnipeg as the basing point and charge all customers $100 plus the freight from Winnipeg to their location. This means that an Edmonton customer pays the freight cost from Winnipeg to Edmonton even though the goods may be shipped from Vancouver. Using a basing-point location other than the factory raises the total price to customers near the factory and lowers the total price to customers far from the factory.

If all the sellers used the same basing-point city, delivered prices would be the same for all customers, and price competition would be eliminated. Such industries as sugar, cement, steel, and automobiles used basing-point pricing for years, but this method is less popular today. Some companies set up multiple basing points to create more flexibility. They would quote freight charges from the basing-point city nearest to the customer.

Freight Absorption Pricing

The seller who is anxious to do business with a certain customer or geographical area might use *freight absorption pricing*. This involves absorbing all or part of the actual freight charges in order to get the business. The seller might reason that if it can get more business, its average costs will fall and more than compensate for the extra freight cost. Freight absorption pricing is used for market penetration and also to hold on to increasingly competitive markets.

Price Changes

Initiating Price Changes

After developing their price structures and strategies, companies will face occasions when they will want to cut or raise prices.

Initiating Price Cuts

Several situations may lead a firm to consider cutting its price, even though this might cause a price war (see Exhibit 12-1). One situation is excess capacity. Here the firm needs more business and cannot get it through increased sales effort, product improvement, or other measures. In the late 1970s many companies dropped "follow-the-leader pricing" and turned to "flexible pricing" to boost their sales.[7]

Another situation is falling market share in the face of strong price competition. Several industries — automobiles and consumer electronics — have been losing market share to Japanese competitors whose high quality products carry lower prices than Canadian products. This may lead Canadian firms to more aggressive pricing action.

Companies will also cut prices in a drive to dominate the market through lower costs. Either the company starts with lower costs than its competitors, or it cuts prices in the hope of gaining market share that will lead to falling costs through larger volume.

EXHIBIT 12-1
Price Wars in the Cigarette Market: The Fight for Market Share

Canadian cigarette manufacturers operate in a declining market where any profit or sales growth comes from cost-cutting actions or taking share from the competition. Imperial Tobacco, a division of Imasco, has constantly gained share through effective marketing strategies and holds over 50% of the Canadian cigarette market. In late 1985, managers at Rothmans of Pall Mall of Canada decided that drastic action was necessary in order to regain lost share. In spite of the fact that for every $1.00 in cigarette sales provincial and federal taxes are $.67, Rothmans offered 30 Number 7 cigarettes for the price of 25. Imperial Tobacco quickly responded to protect their share. They cut $4.00 off the price of a carton of Peter Jackson. Benson and Hedges, another firm, created a new king size brand that they discounted, and RJR MacDonald entered the fray with a discounted 30-cigarette pack.

What was meant to be a temporary price cut by Rothmans to gain share has turned into a long-term price war. It is not certain who has gained or lost the most share, but clearly the costs are high. Estimates are that all the companies are losing money on the discounted brands and that it will cost Imperial $66 million a year to discount Peter Jackson.

Imperial's strategy is to maintain or gain share in the market. Because Imperial's domination and resources are so great, Rothmans and the two other manufacturers cannot attack it through price. Rothmans is likely, at some point, to raise its prices and attempt to gain share or increase profits through product innovation and other non-price marketing strategies.

Sources: Cathryn Motherwell, "Cigaret Price War Creates Rift in Industry," *The Globe and Mail*, November 6 1985, p. B9; Cathryn Motherwell, "Tobacco Firms Offer Bargain to Consumers," *The Globe and Mail*, September 17 1985, p. B6; and Cathryn Motherwell, "Cigaret Firms May Get Burned by Hoopla," *The Globe and Mail*, May 26 1986, p. B1.

Initiating Price Increases

Many companies have had to raise prices in recent years. They do this knowing that the price increases will be resented by customers, dealers, and the company's own salesforce. Yet a successful price increase can greatly increase profits. For example, if the company's profit margin is 3% of sales, a 1% price increase will increase profits by 33% if sales volume is unaffected.

A major situation leading to price increases is cost inflation.[8] Rising costs squeeze profit margins and lead companies to regular rounds of price increases. In anticipation of further inflation companies often raise their prices by more than the cost increase. Companies do not want to make long-run price agreements with customers — they fear that cost inflation will eat up their profit margins. Companies can increase their prices in a number of ways to fight inflation.[9]

Another factor leading to price increases is overdemand. When a company cannot supply all its customers' needs, it can raise its prices, ration products to customers, or both. Prices can be raised almost invisibly by dropping discounts and adding higher-priced units to the line, or prices can be pushed up openly.

Buyer Reactions to Price Changes

Whether the price is raised or lowered, the action will affect buyers, competitors, distributors, and suppliers, and may interest government as well.

Customers do not always put a straightforward interpretation on price changes. Customers may view a price cut in several ways.[10] They may think the item is about to be replaced by a later model, or that it has some fault and is not selling well. They may think that the firm is in financial trouble and may not stay in business to supply future parts. Alternatively, they may believe that the price will come down even further and it will pay to wait. They may believe that quality has been reduced.

A price increase, which would normally lower sales, may carry some positive meanings to the buyers. They may think that the item is very "hot" and may be unobtainable unless it is bought soon, or that the item is an unusually good value, or that the seller is greedy and is charging what the traffic will bear.

Competitor Reactions to Price Changes

A firm considering a price change has to worry about competitors' as well as customers' reactions. Competitors are very likely to react where the number of firms is small, the product is uniform, and the buyers are well informed.

How can the firm figure out the likely reactions of its competitors? Assume that the firm faces one large competitor. If the competitor reacts in a set way to price changes, the reaction can be anticipated. However, if the competitor treats each price change as a fresh challenge, and reacts according to its self-interest, the company will have to figure out what makes up the competitor's self-interest at the time.

The problem is complex because the competitor can interpret a company price cut in many ways. It might think that the company is trying to steal the market, or that the company is doing poorly and is trying to boost its sales, or that the company wants the whole industry to cut prices to increase total demand.

When there are several competitors, the company must guess each competitor's likely reaction. If all competitors behave alike, the company needs to analyze only a typical competitor. If the competitors do not behave alike because of differences in size, market shares, or policies, then separate analyses are necessary. If some competitors will match the price change, there is good reason to expect that the rest will also match it.

Responding to Price Changes

Here we reverse the question and ask how a firm should respond to a price change by a competitor, the situation faced by Imperial Tobacco when Rothmans cut the price of cigarettes (Exhibit 12-1). The firm needs to consider several issues. Why did the competitor change the price? Did it want to steal the market, to use excess capacity, to meet changing cost conditions, or to lead an industry-wide price change? Does the competitor plan to make the price change temporary or permanent? What will happen to the company's market share and profits if it doesn't respond? Are other companies going to respond? If so, what are the competitor's and other firms' responses likely to be to each possible reaction?

Besides these issues, the company must make a broader analysis. The company has to consider the product's stage in the life cycle, its importance in the company's product mix, the intentions and resources of the competitor, the price and value sensitivity of the market, the behavior of costs with volume, and the company's other opportunities.

The company cannot always make an extended analysis of its alternatives at the time of a price change. The competitor may have spent much time preparing this decision, but the company may have to react within hours or days. About the only way to cut down reaction time is to plan ahead for possible competitor's price changes and possible responses. Reaction programs for meeting price changes are most often used in industries where price changes occur often and where it is important to react quickly. Examples can be found in the meatpacking, lumber, and oil industries.[11]

Summary

Pricing is a dynamic process. Companies design a pricing structure that covers all their products. They change the structure over time, and adjust it to account for different customers and situations.

Pricing strategies usually change as a product passes through its life cycle. In pricing innovative new products, the company can follow a skimming policy by setting prices high initially to "skim" the maximum amount of revenue from various segments of the market. Alternatively, the company can use penetration pricing by setting a low initial price to win a large market share. When introducing an imitative product, the company can decide on one of nine price-quality strategies.

When the product is part of a product mix, the firm searches for a set of prices that will maximize the profits from the total mix. The company decides on the price zones for items in its product line and on the pricing of optional products, captive products, and by-products.

Companies apply a variety of price-adjustment strategies to account for differences in consumer segments and situations. One is geographical pricing, where the company decides how to price for distant customers, choosing from such alternatives as FOB pricing, uniform delivered pricing, zone pricing, basing-point pricing, and freight absorption pricing. A second is discount pricing and allowances, where the company establishes cash discounts, quantity discounts, functional discounts, seasonal discounts, and allowances. A third is discriminatory pricing, where the company sets different prices for different customers, product forms, places, or times. A fourth is psychological pricing, where the company adjusts the price to better communicate a product's intended position. A fifth is promotional pricing, where the company decides on loss-leader pricing, special-event pricing, and psychological discounting.

When a firm considers initiating a price change, it must consider customers' and competitors' reactions. Customers' reactions are influenced by the meaning customers perceive in the price change. Competitors' reactions flow from a set reaction policy or a fresh analysis of each situation. The firm initiating the price change must also anticipate the probable reactions of suppliers, middlemen, and government.

The firm that faces a price change initiated by a competitor must try to understand the competitor's intent and the likely duration of the change. If swiftness of reaction is desirable, the firm should preplan its reactions to different possible price actions by competitors.

Questions for Discussion

1. Discuss examples of firms that have engaged in market skimming or market-penetration pricing.

2. Explain the concept of optional product pricing and offer an example of this pricing strategy.

3. Garden Way, of Winnipeg, a popular manufacturer of gardening equipment, uses FOB origin pricing. What are the advantages and disadvantages of this pricing strategy?

4. In 1985 and 1986, auto manufacturers resorted to aggressive low-interest consumer financing programs in an attempt to sell more cars. What dangers exist with this pricing strategy?

5. Do the following companies practice market penetration or market skimming in pricing their products? (a) McDonald's, (b) Curtis Mathes television sets, and (c) Bic Corporation. If so, why?

6. How might customers interpret a price reduction just announced by the manufacturer of a popular personal computer?

7. Discuss the two major discount pricing tactics Head Skis might employ in dealing with the retail outlets that carry its products.

8. GE has invented a revolutionary new household bulb that will last five times longer than the typical 1000-hour life of ordinary incandescent bulbs and use only one-third as much electricity. It is thinking of pricing the bulb at $10 (this will save $20 over the bulb's rated life in lower electric bills). What

problems might GE have with this pricing policy? What suggestions would you make?

Chapter 12 Key Terms

Basing-point pricing   A geographic pricing strategy in which the seller designates some city as a basing point and charges all customers the freight cost from that city to the customer location, regardless of the city from which the goods are actually shipped.

Cash discount   A price reduction to buyers who pay their bills promptly.

Discriminatory pricing   Selling a product or service at two or more prices, where the difference in prices is not based on differences in costs.

FOB origin pricing   A geographic pricing strategy in which goods are placed free on board a carrier, and the customer pays the freight from the factory to the destination.

Freight absorption pricing   A geographic pricing strategy in which the company absorbs all or part of the actual freight charges in order to get the business.

Functional discount   A price reduction offered by the seller to trade channel members who perform certain functions such as selling, storing, and record keeping.

Market penetration pricing   Setting a low price for a new product in order to attract a large number of buyers and a large market share.

Market-skimming pricing   Setting a high price for a new product to skim maximum revenue from the segments willing to pay the high price; the company makes fewer but more profitable sales.

Promotional allowance   A payment or price reduction to reward dealers for participating in advertising and sales-support programs.

Promotional pricing   Temporarily pricing products below the list price, and sometimes even below cost, to increase short-run sales.

Psychological pricing   A pricing approach that considers the psychology of prices and not simply the economics — the price is used to say something about the product.

Quantity discount   A price reduction to buyers who buy large volumes.

Seasonal discount   A price reduction to buyers who buy merchandise or services out of season.

Trade-in allowance   A price reduction given for turning in an old item when buying a new one.

Uniform delivered pricing   A geographic pricing strategy in which the company charges the same price plus freight to all customers regardless of their location.

Zone pricing   A geographic pricing strategy in which the company sets up two or more zones — all customers within a zone pay the same total price, and this price is higher in the more distant zones.

Cases for Chapter 12 ▬▬▬▬▬▬▬▬

CHAPTER 13

Placing Products: Distribution Channels and Physical Distribution

Chapter Objectives

After reading this chapter, you should be able to:

1. Explain why companies use distribution channels and the functions these channels perform.
2. Discuss how channel members interact, and how they organize to do the work of the channel.
3. Identify the major distribution channel alternatives open to a company.
4. Tell how companies select, motivate, and evaluate channel members.
5. Discuss the issues firms face when setting up physical distribution systems.

Getting your product to market in Canada is easy—if your manufacturing plant is in Toronto and your market is Southern Ontario. National distribution, however, is more difficult and more expensive. Here are several elements that make distribution in Canada somewhat unique:

- The distance from coast to coast is 6400 km, and most of our population is in a narrow 300-km belt across the country. In fact, five population clusters contain most Canadians.

- Because of the geography, on a per capita basis Canada has twice the mileage of railway mainline as the United States and 40% more surfaced highway.

- Most of Canada's manufacturing is located in Quebec and Ontario (71%), while many large Western markets are thousands of kilometers away.

- About three-quarters of Canada's population resides in urban areas, the remaining 25% in areas that often have few transportation facilities.

- Transportation alternatives for many Canadian firms are limited: there are only two major railways, two major airlines, one cross-country highway, and only regional and seasonal connecting waterways.

Some of the managerial implications resulting from these unique aspects of Canadian distribution are:

- Firms deciding to operate on a national basis will face not only relatively high transportation costs but also additional costs such as: greater working capital requirements because goods are in transit longer; greater communication costs for personnel visiting markets and costs of transmitting information to and from distant markets; and extra packaging costs.

- For some firms it may be more profitable to limit their market coverage. This can be done in two ways; distribution to just the urban areas of Canada, or limited distribution to a specific geographic area such as Ontario and Quebec.

- Firms located outside Ontario and Quebec have a difficult time competing in these markets because of their higher distribution costs, yet most of Canada's buying power is contained in these two provinces.

- Because of the distances involved in reaching many Canadian markets, firms may lose some control over their ability to supply and service their customers at the level they consider appropriate.[1]

Marketing channel decisions are among the most important facing management. The company's channel decision directly affects every other marketing decision. The company's pricing depends on whether it uses large, high-quality dealers or medium size, medium-quality dealers. The firm's salesforce decisions depend on how much selling and training the dealers will need. In addition, the company's channel decisions often involve long-term commitment to other firms. When a truck manufacturer signs up independent dealers, it cannot easily replace them with company-owned branches if conditions change. Therefore management must choose channels with an eye on tomorrow's likely selling environment as well as today's.

In this chapter we will examine four major issues: (1) What is the nature of distribution channels? (2) How do channel firms interact and organize to do the work of the channel? (3) What problems do companies face in designing and managing their channels? (4) What role does physical distribution play in attracting and satisfying customers? In the next chapter we will look at distribution channel issues from the viewpoint of retailers and wholesalers.

The Nature of Distribution Channels

Most producers use middlemen to bring their products to market. They try to forge a distribution channel.

> A distribution channel is the set of firms and individuals that take title, or assist in transferring title, to a good or service as it moves from the producer to the consumer.

Why Are Middlemen Used?

Why do producers give some of the selling job to middlemen? Although they must give up some control over how and to whom the products are sold, producers gain certain advantages from using middlemen. These advantages are described below.

Many producers lack the financial resource to carry out direct marketing. For example, Ford of Canada sells its automobiles through over 750 independent dealers. Even Ford would be hard pressed to raise the cash to buy out its dealers. Similarly, Beaver Lumber Company, which had only company-owned stores until 1977, decided that it could obtain greater market penetration without stretching its financial resources by introducing franchise stores. Now Beaver

Lumber has over 100 franchise stores that account for most of the company's sales.[2]

Direct marketing would require many producers to become middlemen for the products of other producers in order to achieve mass-distribution economies. For example, the Adams Division of Warner-Lambert Canada would not find it practical to set up small retail gum shops around the country or to sell gum door to door or by mail order. It would have to sell gum along with many other small products, and would end up in the drugstore and foodstore business. Adams finds it easier to work through a network of privately owned distributors.

Even producers who can afford to set up their own channels can often earn a greater return by increasing their investment in their main business. If a company earns a 20% rate of return on manufacturing and foresees only a 10% return on retailing, it will not want to do its own retailing.

The use of middlemen largely boils down to their greater efficiency in making goods available to target markets. Through their contacts, experience, specialization, and scale of operation, middlemen usually offer the firm more than it can achieve on its own.

Figure 13-1 shows one way that using middlemen can be economical. Part A shows three producers each using direct marketing to reach three customers. This requires nine different contacts. Part B shows the three producers working through one distributor, who contacts the three customers. This system requires only six contacts. In this way, middlemen reduce the amount of work that must be done.

FIGURE 13-1
How a Distributor Reduces the Number of Channel Transactions

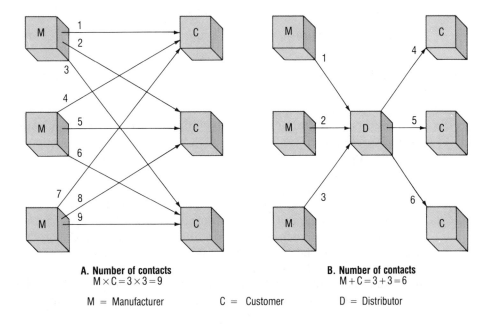

A. Number of contacts
$M \times C = 3 \times 3 = 9$

B. Number of contacts
$M + C = 3 + 3 = 6$

M = Manufacturer   C = Customer   D = Distributor

From the economic system's point of view, the role of middlemen is to transform the assortment of products made by producers into the assortments wanted by consumers. Producers make narrow assortments of products in large quantities, but consumers want broad assortments of products in small quantities. In the distribution channels, middlemen buy the large quantities of many producers and break them down into the smaller quantities and broader assortments wanted by consumers. Thus, middlemen play an important role in matching supply and demand.

Distribution Channel Functions

A distribution channel moves goods from producers to consumer. It overcomes the major time, place, and possession gaps that separate goods and services from those who would use them. Members of the marketing channel perform many key functions:

Research   Gathering of information needed for planning and aiding exchange.

Promotion   Developing and spreading persuasive communications about the offer.

Contact   Finding and communicating with prospective buyers.

Matching   Shaping and fitting the offer to the buyer's needs. This includes such activities as manufacturing, grading, assembling, and packaging.

Negotiation   Reaching an agreement on price and other terms of the offer so that ownership or possession can be transferred.

Physical distribution   Transporting and storing of the goods.

Financing   Acquiring and using funds to cover the costs of the channel work.

Risk taking   Assuming the risks in connection with carrying out the channel work.[3]

The first five functions help to complete transactions; the last three help fulfill the completed transactions.

The question is not *whether* these functions need to be performed (they must be), but rather *who* is to perform them. All the functions have three things in common: they use up scarce resources, they can often be performed better through specialization, and they can be shifted among channel members. To the extent that the manufacturer performs them, costs go up and prices have to be higher. When some functions are shifted to middlemen, the producer's costs and prices are lower, but the middlemen must add a charge to cover their work. In dividing up the work of the channel, the various functions should be assigned to the channel members who can perform them most efficiently and effectively to provide satisfactory assortments of goods to target consumers.

Number of Channel Levels

Distribution channels can be described by the number of channel levels. Each middleman that performs some work in bringing the product and its ownership closer to the final buyer is a **channel level**. Since the producer and the final consumer both perform some work, they are part of every channel. We will use the number of **intermediary levels** to indicate the **length** of a channel. Figure 13-2 shows several marketing channels of different length.

- A *zero-level channel* (also called a ***direct marketing channel***) consists of a manufacturer selling directly to consumers. The three major ways of direct selling are door-to-door, mail order, and manufacturer-owned stores. Avon's sales representatives sell cosmetics to homemakers on a door-to-door basis; Statistics Canada sells various reports through mail order; and Bata Shoes sells through its own stores.

- A *one-level channel* contains one middleman. In consumer markets this middleman is typically a retailer; in industrial markets it is often a sales agent or a broker.

- A *two-level channel* contains two middlemen. In consumer markets they are typically a wholesaler and a retailer; in industrial markets they may be an industrial distributor and dealers.

- A *three-level channel* contains three middlemen. For example, in the meatpacking industry jobbers usually come between wholesalers and retailers. The jobber buys from wholesalers and sells to the smaller retailers, who generally are not served by the large wholesalers.

FIGURE 13-2
Examples of Different-Level Channels

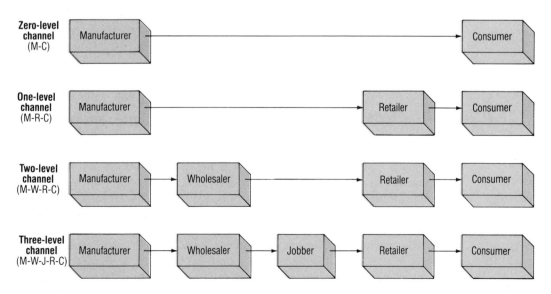

Distribution channels with more levels exist, but they are less common. From the producer's point of view, the greater the number of levels, the less control they have.

Channels in the Service Sector

The concept of distribution channels is not limited to the distribution of physical goods. Producers of services and ideas also face the problem of making their output *available* to target populations. They develop "educational distribution systems" and "health delivery systems." They must discover agencies and locations for reaching their targets:

> A University of Toronto study indicated that 50% of Canadians were not visiting a dentist regularly. The reasons included inconvenience, having to make an appointment up to two months in advance, and inaccessibility, as the locations were often far away from home or work. Two Toronto dentists decided to change that situation. Their company, Tri Dont Dental Centres, now has over 100 dental offices in large shopping malls in Canada. The offices are open seven days a week, emergency appointments can be made in 20 minutes and check-ups can be arranged for the same day a patient calls. Sales of Tri Dont now exceed $40 million each year.[4]

Channels normally describe a forward movement of products. We can also talk about **backward channels**. According to Zikmund and Stanton:

> The recycling of solid wastes is a major ecological goal. Although recycling is technologically feasible, reversing the flow of materials in the channel of distribution — marketing trash through a "backward" channel — presents a challenge. Existing backward channels are primitive, and financial incentives are inadequate. The consumer must be motivated to undergo a role change and become a producer — the initiating force in the reverse distribution process.[5]

The authors identify several middlemen that can play a role in "backward channels," including manufacturers' redemption centers, community groups, traditional middlemen such as soft drink middlemen, recycling centers, modernized "rag and junk men," and trash-recycling brokers.

Channel Behavior and Organization

Distribution channels are more than simple collections of firms tied together by various flows. They are complex behavioral systems in which people and companies interact to accomplish individual, company, and channel goals. Some channel systems consist of only informal interactions among loosely organized firms; others consist of formal interactions guided by strong organizational structures.

Channel systems do not stand still — new types of middlemen surface and whole new channel systems evolve. Here we will look at channel behavior and at how members organize to do the work of the channel.

Channel Behavior

A distribution channel is made up of unlike firms that have banded together for their common good. Each channel member is dependent on the other channel members. A Ford dealer depends on the Ford Motor Company to design cars that meet consumer needs. In turn, Ford depends on the dealer to attract consumers, persuade them to buy Ford cars, and service the cars after the sale. The Ford dealer also depends on other dealers to provide good sales and service that will uphold the reputation of Ford and its dealer network. In fact, the success of individual Ford dealers will depend on how well the entire Ford distribution channel competes with the channels of other auto manufacturers.

Each channel member plays a role in the channel and specializes in performing one or more function. IBM's role is to produce personal computers that consumers will like and to create demand through national advertising. Computerland's role is to display these computers in a convenient location, answer the buyers' questions, close sales, and provide service. The channel will be most effective when each member is assigned the tasks it can do best.

Ideally, because the success of individual channel members depends on overall channel success, all channel firms should work smoothly together. They should understand and accept their roles, coordinate their goals and activities with those of other channel members, and cooperate to attain overall channel goals. Manufacturers, wholesalers, and retailers should work together to produce greater profit than they could obtain individually. By cooperating, they can more effectively sense, serve, and satisfy the target market.

But individual channel members rarely take such a broad view. They are usually more concerned with their own short-run goals and their dealings with firms next to them in the channel. Cooperating to achieve overall channel goals sometimes means giving up individual company goals. Though channel members are dependent on one another, they often act alone in their own short-run best interests. They often disagree on the roles each should play — on who should do what and for what rewards. Such disagreements over goals and roles generate **channel conflict**.

Horizontal conflict is conflict between firms at the same level of the channel. Some Ford dealers in Montreal may complain about other dealers in the city stealing sales from them by being too aggressive in their pricing and advertising, or by selling outside their assigned territories. Some Harvey's franchises might complain about other Harvey's franchises cheating on ingredients, giving poor service, and hurting the overall Harvey's image.

Vertical conflict is even more common and refers to conflicts between different levels of the same channel. For example, General Motors came into conflict with its dealers some years ago when trying to enforce policies on service, pricing, and advertising. For the channel as a whole to perform well, each channel member's role must be specified, and channel conflict must be managed. Cooperation, assigning roles, and conflict management in the channel are attained through strong channel leadership. The channel will perform better if it contains a firm, agency, or mechanism that has the power to assign roles and manage conflict.

In a large, single company, the formal organization structure assigns roles and provides needed leadership. But in a distribution channel made up of independent firms, leadership and power are not formally set. Traditionally, distribution channels have lacked the leadership needed to assign roles and manage conflict. In recent years, however, new types of channel organizations have appeared that provide stronger leadership and improved performance. We will look now at these organizations.[6]

Channel Organization

Historically, distribution channels have been loose collections of independently owned and managed companies, each showing little concern for overall channel performance. These **conventional distribution channels** have lacked strong leadership and have been troubled by damaging conflict and poor performance.

Growth of Vertical Marketing Systems

One of the biggest recent developments has been the **vertical marketing systems** that have emerged to challenge conventional marketing channels. Figure 13-3 contrasts the two types of channel arrangement.

A *conventional distribution channel* consists of an independent producer(s), wholesaler(s), and retailer(s). Each is a separate business seeking to maximize its own profits, even at the expense of profits for the system as a whole. No channel member has much control over the other members, and there are no formal means for assigning roles and resolving channel conflict.

By contrast, a *vertical marketing system (VMS)* consists of the producer(s), wholesaler(s), and retailer(s) acting as a unified system. Either one channel member owns the others, or has contracts with them, or has so much power that they all cooperate.[7] The vertical marketing system can be dominated by the producer, wholesaler, or retailer. The VMSs came into being to control channel behavior and manage the channel conflict. They achieve economies through size, bargaining power, and elimination of duplicated services.

FIGURE 13-3

Comparison of Conventional Distribution Channel with Vertical Marketing System

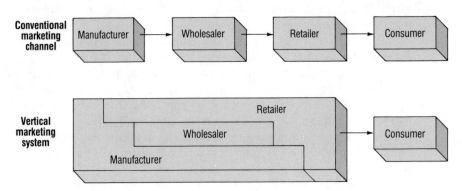

We will now look at the three major types of VMS shown in Figure 13-4. Each type uses a different means for setting up leadership and power in the channel. In a corporate VMS, coordination and conflict management are attained through common ownership at different levels of the channel. In a contractual VMS, they are attained through contractual agreements among channel members. In an administered VMS, leadership is assumed by one or a few dominant channel members.

FIGURE 13-4
Conventional Distribution Channels and Vertical Marketing Systems

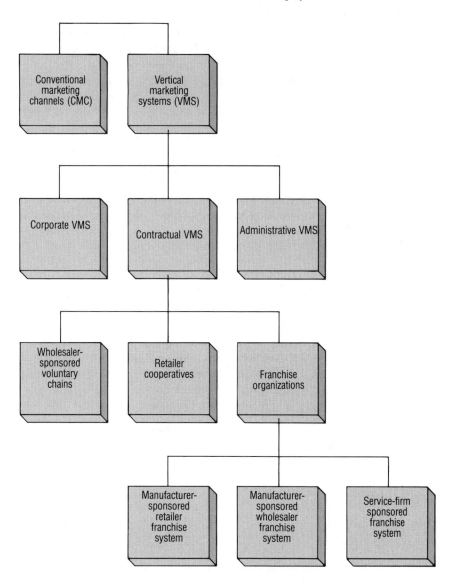

Corporate VMS

A *corporate VMS* combines successive stages of production and distribution under single ownership. For example, Bata Shoes, the largest shoe company in the world, has over 5000 company-owned retail stores. In addition, Bata sells shoes through independent retailers in a conventional distribution channel.

Contractual VMS

A *contractual VMS* consists of independent firms at different levels of production and distribution who join together through contracts to obtain more economies or sales impact than they could achieve alone. Contractual VMSs have expanded rapidly in recent years. There are three types of contractual VMSs.

1. ***Wholesaler-sponsored voluntary chains*** *Wholesalers organize voluntary chains of independent retailers to help them compete with large chain organizations. The wholesaler develops a program in which independent retailers standardize their selling practices and achieve buying economies that let the group compete effectively with chain organizations. Examples include the United Farmers of Alberta Co-op and Co-op Atlantic.*

2. ***Retailer cooperatives*** *Retailers organize a new, jointly owned business to carry on wholesaling and possibly production. Members buy most of their goods through the retailer co-op and plan their advertising jointly. Profits are passed back to members in proportion to their purchases. Nonmember retailers may also buy through the co-op but do not share in the profits. Examples include The Red River Co-op and The Scotsburn Co-operative.*

3. ***Franchise organizations*** *A channel member called a franchiser might link several stages in the production distribution process. Franchising has been the fastest growing retailing form in recent years. Although the basic idea is an old one, some forms of franchising are quite new. There are three forms of franchises.*

   *The first is the **manufacturer-sponsored retailer franchise system**, as found in the automobile industry. Ford, for example, licenses dealers to sell its cars — the dealers are independent business people who agree to meet various conditions of sales and service.*

   *The second is the **manufacturer-sponsored wholesaler franchise system**, as found in the soft-drink industry. Coca-Cola, for example, licenses bottlers (wholesalers) in various markets who buy its syrup concentrate and then carbonate, bottle, and sell it to retailers in local markets.*

   *The third is the **service-firm-sponsored retailer franchise system**. Here a service firm organizes a whole system for bringing its service to consumers. Examples are found in the auto rental business (Hertz, Tilden), fast-food service business (McDonald's, Harvey's, Burger*

Courtesy: Procter & Gamble Canada

Administered VMS: Because Procter & Gamble markets many popular brands, they can command extra cooperation from retailers.

King), and the personal care business (Colours, First Choice hair-cutting).

The various contractual VMSs are discussed in more detail in Chapter 14.

Administered VMS

An *administered VMS* coordinates successive stages of production and distribution, not through common ownership or contractual ties, but through the size and power of one of the parties. Manufacturers of a top brand can obtain strong trade cooperation and support from resellers. Thus Procter & Gamble, Arrow, and Campbell Soup can command unusual cooperation from resellers regarding displays, shelf space, promotions, and price policies.

Channel Design Decision

We will now look at several channel decision problems facing manufacturers. In designing marketing channels, manufacturers have to struggle between what is ideal and what is available. A new firm usually starts by selling in a limited market area. Since it has limited capital, it usually uses only a few existing middlemen in each market. For example, the majority of manufacturing firms start out in Ontario or Quebec, which have both 62% of the retail buying power and 62% of Canada's population.[8] In these provinces the number of middlemen are fairly extensive and the major problem may be to convince one or more of the middlemen to handle the line.

If the new firm is successful, it might branch out to new markets. Again, the manufacturer will tend to work through the existing middlemen, although this might mean using different types of marketing channels in different areas. In the smaller markets the firm might sell directly to retailers; in the larger markets it might sell through distributors. In one part of the country it might grant exclusive franchises because the merchants normally work this way; in another, it might sell through all outlets willing to handle the merchandise. The manufacturer's channel system thus evolves to meet local opportunities and conditions.

Designing a channel system calls for setting the channel objectives and constraints, identifying the major channel alternatives, and evaluating them.

Setting the Channel Objectives and Constraints

Good channel planning begins with deciding which markets are to be reached with what objectives. The objectives include the desired level of customer service and the functions middlemen should perform. The producer's objectives are influenced by the nature of its customers, product, middlemen, competitors, company policies, and the environment.

Customer characteristics   Channel design is greatly influenced by customer characteristics. When trying to reach a large or widely spread customer population, long channels are needed. If customers often buy small amounts, long channels are needed because of the high cost of filling small and frequent orders.

Product characteristics   Perishable products require more direct marketing because of the dangers caused by delays and too much handling. *Bulky products*, such as building materials or soft drinks, require channels that minimize the shipping distance and the amount of handling between producer and consumers. *Nonstandardized products*, such as custom-built machinery and special business forms, are sold directly by company salespeople because middlemen lack the needed knowledge. Products needing installation or service are usually sold and maintained by the company or its franchised dealers.

Middlemen characteristics   Channel design reflects the ability of different types of middlemen to handle various tasks. For example, manufacturers' representatives can contact customers at a low cost per customer because the total cost is shared by several clients. But the selling effort per customer is less intense than if the company's sales representatives did the selling. In general, middlemen differ in their abilities to handle promotion, customer contact, storage, contact, and credit.

Competitive characteristics   Channel design is influenced by competitors' channels. Producers may want to compete in or near the same outlets carrying the competitors' products. Thus food companies want their brands to be displayed next to competing brands. In other industries, producers may want to avoid the channels used by competitors. Avon decided not to compete with other cosmetics makers for scarce positions in retail stores and instead set up a profitable door-to-door selling operation.

Company characteristics   Company characteristics play an important role in channel selection. The company's *size* determines the size of its markets and its ability to get desired dealers. Its *financial resources* affect which marketing functions it can handle and which to give to middlemen. The company's *product mix* affects its channel pattern. The wider its product mix, the better the company can deal with customers directly. The greater the depth of the company's product mix, the more it might favor exclusive or selective dealers. The company's *marketing strategy* will affect channel design. Thus a policy of speedy customer delivery affects the functions the producer wants middlemen to perform, the number of outlets, and the choice of transportation methods.

Environmental characteristics   When *economic conditions* are depressed, producers want to move their goods to market in the most economical way. This means using shorter channels and dropping unneeded services that add to the final price of the goods.

Identifying the Major Alternatives

Suppose a company has defined its target market and desired positioning. It should next identify its major channel alternatives in terms of types of middlemen, number of middlemen, and the responsibilities of each channel member.

Types of Middlemen

The firm should identify the types of middlemen available to carry on its channel work. Consider the following example:

A manufacturer of test equipment developed an audio device that detects poor mechanical connections in any machine with moving parts.

The company executives felt that this product would have a market in all industries where electric, combustion, or steam engines were made or used. This meant such industries as aviation, automobile, railroad, food canning, construction, and oil. The company's salesforce was small, and the problem was how best to reach these different industries. The following channel alternatives came out of management discussion:

Company salesforce   Expand the company's direct salesforce. Assign salespeople to territories and have them contact all prospects in the area. Alternatively, develop separate company salesforces for the different industries.

Manufacturer's agency   Hire manufacturer's agencies in different regions or industries to sell the new test equipment.

Industrial distributors   Find distributors in the different regions or industries who will buy and carry the new line. Give them exclusive distribution, good margins, product training, and promotional support.[9]

Companies should also search for more innovative distribution channels. This happened when IBM (Canada) Limited decided to merchandise its typewriter products and related supplies by catalog in addition to using its regular salesforce. IBM sent the catalog to every Canadian customer who had bought an IBM typewriter. Within five months, 20% of IBM's total typewriter orders were being generated through catalog sales, five times more than the company anticipated.[10] In another example of a daring new channel, a group decided to merchandise books through the mails in the now famous Book-of-the-Month Club.

Sometimes a company has to develop a channel other than the one it prefers because of the difficulty or cost of using the preferred channel. The decision sometimes turns out extremely well. For example, the U.S. Time Company first tried to sell its inexpensive Timex watches through regular jewelry stores. But most jewelry stores refused to carry them. The company then managed to get its watches into mass-merchandise outlets. This turned out to be a wise decision because of the rapid growth of mass merchandising.

Number of Middlemen

Companies have to decide on the number of middlemen to use at each level. Three strategies are available.

Tobacco products, soft drinks, and candy are usually sold through intensive distribution.

James Hertel

Intensive distribution

Producers of convenience goods and common raw material typically seek *intensive distribution*—that is, stocking their product in as many outlets as possible. These goods must be available where and when consumers want them. Cigarettes, for example, sell in over 100 000 outlets to create maximum brand exposure and convenience.

Exclusive distribution

Some producers purposely limit the number of middlemen handling their products. The extreme form of this limiting is *exclusive distribution*, where a limited number of dealers are given the exclusive right to distribute the company's products in their territories. It often goes with **exclusive dealing**, where the manufacturer requires these dealers not to carry competing lines. Exclusive distribution is often found in the distribution of new automobiles, major appliances, and women's apparel brands. By granting exclusive distribution, the manufacturer hopes for stronger selling support from distributors and more control over middlemen's prices, promotion, credit, and services. Exclusive distribution often enhances the product's image and allows higher markups.

Selective distribution

Between intensive and exclusive distribution is *selective distribution*—the use of more than one but less than all the middlemen who are willing to carry the company's products. The company does not have to spread its efforts over many outlets, including many marginal ones. It can develop a good working relationship with the selected middlemen and expect a better than average selling effort. Selective distribution lets the producer gain good market coverage with more control and less cost than intensive distribution.

Evaluating the Major Channel Alternatives

Suppose a producer has identified several possible channels and wants to select the one that will best satisfy the firm's long-run objectives. Each alternative should be evaluated against economic, control, and adaptive criteria.

Using **economic** criteria, the company compares the likely profitability of the different channel alternatives. It estimates the sales that each channel would produce, and the costs of selling different volumes through each channel. The company must also consider **control** issues. Using middlemen usually means giving them some control over the marketing of the product, and some middlemen take more control than others. Other things being equal, the company prefers to keep as much control as possible. Finally, channels often involve long-term commitments to other firms, making it hard to **adapt** the channel to the changing marketing environment. The company wants to keep the channel as flexible as possible. To be considered, a channel involving a long commitment should be greatly superior on economic or control grounds.

Channel Management Decisions

Once the company has reviewed its channel alternatives and decided on the best channel design, it must implement and manage the chosen channel. Channel management calls for selecting and motivating individual middlemen and evaluating their performance over time.

Selecting Channel Members

Producers vary in their ability to attract qualified middlemen. Some producers have no trouble signing up middlemen. In some cases, the promise of exclusive or selective distribution for desirable product will draw enough applicants.

At the other extreme are producers who have to work hard to line up enough qualified middlemen. When Polaroid started, it could not convince photography stores to carry its new cameras and had to go to mass-merchandising outlets. Small food producers often find it difficult to persuade grocery stores to carry their products.

Motivating Channel Members

Once selected, middlemen must be continually motivated to do their best. The producer must sell not only through the middlemen, but to them. Most producers see the problem as finding ways to gain middlemen's cooperation.[11] They will use the carrot-and-stick approach. As positive motivators, producers may offer higher margins, special deals, premiums, cooperative advertising allowances, display allowances, and sales contests. At times they will use negative motivators such as threatening to reduce margins, slow down delivery, or end the relationship. The weakness of this approach is that the producer has not really studied the needs, problems, strengths, and weaknesses of the distributors.

More advanced companies try to forge a long-term partnership with their distributors. The manufacturer develops a clear sense of what it wants from its distributors and what its distributors can expect. The manufacturer seeks an agreement from its distributors on their roles and responsibilities, and rewards them accordingly.

Evaluating Channel Members

The producer must regularly check middlemen's performance against such standards as reaching sales quotas, average inventory levels, customer delivery time, treatment of damaged and lost goods, cooperation in company promotion and training programs, and services to the customer.

The producer typically sets sales quotas for the middlemen. After each period, the producer might circulate a list showing the sales performance of each middleman. This list should motivate middlemen at the bottom to do better and middlemen at the top to keep up their performance. Each middleman's sales performance can be compared with performance in the last period. The average percentage improvement for the group can be used as a norm.

Manufacturers need to be sensitive to their dealer. Those who treat their dealer lightly risk not only losing their support, but also provoking some legal actions. Exhibit 13-1 describes various legal aspects pertaining to manufacturers and their channel member.

EXHIBIT 13-1
Distribution Decisions and Public Policy

For the most part, manufacturers are free under the law to develop whatever channel arrangements suit them. In fact, the law affecting channels seeks to make sure that manufacturers are not prevented from using channels as the result of the exclusionary tactics of others. Most of the law is concerned with mutual rights and duties of the manufacturer and channel members once they have formed a relationship.

Exclusive dealing   Many manufacturers and wholesalers like to develop exclusive channels for their products. The policy is called **exclusive dealing** when the seller requires these outlets not to handle competitors' products. Both parties draw benefits from exclusive dealing, the seller achieving more dependable outlets without having to invest capital in them, and the distributors gaining a steady source of supply and seller support. However, the result is that other manufacturers are excluded from selling to these dealers. Under the Competition Act, exclusive dealing contracts are legal as long as they do not substantially lessen competition.

Tying agreements   Manufacturers of a strongly demanded brand occasionally sell it to dealers on condition that the dealers take some or all of the rest of the line. This practice is called **full-line forcing**. Such tying arrangements are not illegal per se, but they do run afoul of the Competition Act if they tend to lessen competition substantially.

As well, under the Competition Act a vertically integrated supplier cannot squeeze the margins of independent wholesalers or retailers for the purpose of impeding their entry or expansion in a market. Other anti-competitive actions, including restricting wholesalers or retailers to sell only to certain customers, are outlined in the Act.

Physical Distribution Decisions

We are now ready to look at physical distribution—how companies store, handle, and move goods so that they will be available to customers at the right time and place. Customers are greatly affected by the seller's physical distribution system. Here we will consider the nature, objectives, systems, and organizational aspects of physical distribution.

Nature of Physical Distribution

The main elements of the physical distribution mix are shown in Figure 13-5. We define physical distribution as follows:

> *Physical distribution is made up of the tasks involved in planning, implementing, and controlling the physical flow of materials and final goods from points of origin to points of use to meet the needs of customers at a profit.*

Management has become concerned about the total cost of physical distribution, and experts believe that large savings can be gained in the physical distribution area. Poor physical distribution decisions result in high costs. In a recent study of Canadian firms, most of them did not have the necessary cost data available to make coordinated physical-distribution decisions.[12] Not

FIGURE 13-5
Cost of Physical Distribution Elements as a Percent of Total Physical Distribution Cost

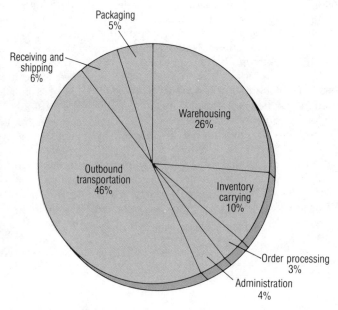

Source: Based on B. J. LaLonde and P. H. Zinszer, *Customer Service: Meaning and Measurement* (Chicago: National Council of Logistics Management, 1976).

enough use is being made of modern decision tools for coordinating inventory levels, transportation modes, and plant, warehouse, and store locations.

Physical distribution is not only a cost, it is a potent tool in demand creation. Companies can attract more customers by giving better service or lower prices through better physical distribution. Companies lose customers when they fail to supply goods on time. When John Labatt Limited introduced Budweiser beer in Canada, it did not have enough inventory on hand to supply the unexpected demand. Many customers had to settle for other brands when Budweiser was out of stock, resulting in lost sales for Labatt.

The Physical Distribution Objective

Many companies state their objective as getting the right goods to the right places at the right time for the least cost. Unfortunately, no physical distribution system can both maximize customer service and minimize distribution costs. Maximum customer service implies large inventories, the best transportation, and many warehouses, all of which raise distribution cost. Minimum distribution cost implies cheap transportation, low inventories, and few warehouses.

The company cannot simply let each physical distribution manager keep down his or her costs. Physical distribution costs interact, often in an inverse way:

- The traffic manager favors rail shipment over air shipment whenever possible. This reduces the company's freight bill. But because the railroads are slower, this ties up working capital longer, delays customer payment, and may cause the customer to buy from competitors offering faster service.

- The shipping department uses cheap containers to minimize shipping costs. This leads to a high rate of damaged goods in transit and customer ill will.

- The inventory manager favors low inventories to reduce inventory cost. However, this increases stockouts, back orders, paperwork, special production runs, and high-cost fast-freight shipments.

Because physical distribution activities involve strong tradeoffs, decisions must be made on a total system basis. The starting point for designing the system is to study what customers want and what competitors are offering. Customers want several things from suppliers: on-time delivery, large enough inventories, ability to meet emergency needs, careful handling of merchandise, good after-sale service, and willingness to take back or quickly replace defective goods. The company has to research the importance of these services to customers. For example, selection and availability are very important services in the auto parts business. Canadian Tire has acknowledged this by building four large depots in Edmonton, Toronto, Montreal, and Moncton. Twenty-five thousand auto parts are available through these depots for shipment to over 390 Canadian Tire Stores, and delivery is made anywhere in the country within two days of receiving an order.[13]

The company must look at competitors' service standards when setting its own, as it will normally want to offer at least the same level of service. But the objective is to maximize profits, not sales. The company has to look at the costs of providing higher levels of service. Some companies offer less service and charge a lower price. Other companies offer more service than competitors and charge a high price to cover their higher cost.

The company ultimately must set physical distribution objectives to guide its planning. For example, Coca-Cola wants "to put Coke within an arm's length of desire." Some companies go further and define standards for each service factor. One appliance manufacturer has set the following service standards: to deliver at least 95% of the dealer's order within seven days of order receipt, to fill the dealer's order with 99% accuracy, to answer dealer questions on order status within three hours, and to ensure that damage to merchandise in transit does not exceed 1%.

Given a set of objectives, the company is ready to design a physical distribution system that will minimize the cost of attaining these objectives. The major decision issues are: (1) How should orders be handled? (**order processing**) (2) Where should stocks be located? (**warehousing**) (3) How much stock should be kept on hand? (**inventory**), and (4) How should goods be shipped? (**transportation**). We will now look at these four issues.

Order Processing

Physical distribution begins with a customer order. The order department prepares invoices and sends them to various departments. Items out of stock are back-ordered. Shipped items are accompanied by shipping and billing documents with copies going to various departments.

The company and customers benefit when these steps are carried out quickly and accurately. Ideally, salespeople send in their orders every evening, in some cases phoning them in. The order department processes these quickly. The warehouse sends the goods out as soon as possible. Bills go out as soon as possible. The computer is often used to speed up the order-shipping-billing cycle.

Warehousing

Every company has to store its goods while they wait to be sold. A storage function is needed because production and consumption cycles rarely match. For example, many agricultural commodities are produced seasonally, but demand is continuous. The storage function overcomes differences in needed quantities and timing.

The company must decide on the best number of stocking locations. More stocking locations mean that goods can be delivered to customers more quickly. However, warehousing costs increase. In making the decision about the number of stocking locations, the company must balance the level of customer service against distribution costs.

Some company stock is kept at or near the plant, and the rest is located in warehouses around the country. The company might own private warehouses and rent space in public warehouses. Companies have more control in owned warehouses, but they tie up their capital and are less flexible if desired locations change. Public warehouses, on the other hand, charge for the rented space and provide additional services (at a cost) for inspecting goods, packaging them, shipping them, and invoicing them. In using public warehouses, companies have a wide choice of locations and warehouse types.

Companies use storage warehouses and distribution warehouses. Storage warehouses store goods for moderate to long periods of time. Distribution warehouses receive goods from various plants and suppliers and move them out as soon as possible.

The older, multi-storied warehouses with slow elevators and outdated materials-handling methods are facing competition from newer, single-storied **automated warehouses** with advanced materials-handling systems under the control of a central computer. In these automated warehouses, only a few employees are necessary. The computer reads orders and directs lift trucks, electric hoists, or robots to gather goods, move them to loading docks, and issue invoices. These warehouses have reduced worker injuries, labor costs, theft, and breakage and have improved inventory control. Canadian Tire and Home Hardware are two firms that have advanced this technology in Canada.

Inventory

Inventory levels also affect customer satisfaction. Marketers would like their companies to carry enough stock to fill all customer orders right away. However, it costs too much for a company to carry this much inventory. Inventory costs increase at an increasing rate as the customer service level approaches 100%. Management would need to know whether sales and profits would increase enough to justify larger inventories.

Inventory decisions involve knowing when to order, and how much to order. In deciding when to order, the company balances the risks of running out of stock against the costs of carrying too much stock. In deciding how much to order, the company needs to balance order-processing costs against inventory-carrying costs. Larger average order size means fewer orders and lower order-processing costs, but it also means larger inventory-carrying costs.

Transportation   Mode of Transportation

Marketers need to take an interest in their company's transportation decisions. The choice of transportation carriers affects the pricing of the products, delivery performance, and the condition of the goods when they arrive, all of which will affect customer satisfaction.

In shipping goods to its warehouses, dealers, and customers, the company can choose among four transportation modes: rail, water, truck, and air. Each transportation mode's characteristics are summarized in Table 13-1 and discussed in the following paragraphs.

Rail

Because most of Canada's population is contained in a belt that is less than 300 km wide but 6400 km long, railway remains the nation's largest transportation carrier, accounting for 39% of the nation's tonnage. Railways are one of the most cost-effective modes of transportation for shipping carload quantities of

TABLE 13-1

Characteristics of Major Transportation Modes

Transportation mode	1983 Tonne-kilometers (billions)	Percentage of total (weight)	1983 Percentage of total (weight)	Typical shipped products
Rail	226.0	38.5	40.5	Farm products, minerals, coal, chemicals, autos
Water	N/A	38.3	9.9	Oil, grain, sand, gravel, metallic ores, coal
Truck	41.8	23.1	46.6	Clothing, books, computers, paper goods
Air	1.0	1	3.0	Technical instruments, perishable food

Source: Canadian Transport Commission, *Transport Review*, II 12-5, 1985.

bulk products — coal, wheat, minerals, and forest products — over long land distances. In Canada, the rate costs for shipping merchandise by rail are quite complex, and require a historical perspective to be understood. The shipper's lowest rate comes from shipping carload rather than less-than-carload quantities. Manufacturers will often get together and combine shipments to common destinations to take advantage of lower rates. The Canadian railways have a number of customer-oriented services, including new kinds of equipment to handle categories of merchandise more efficiently, and flatcars that permit the carrying of truck trailers by rail (piggyback).

Water

A large amount of goods moves by ships and barges on coastal and inland waterways. The cost of water transportation is very low for shipping bulky, low-value, nonperishable products such as sand, coal, grain, oil, and metallic ores. On the other hand, water transportation is the slowest transportation mode and is sometimes affected by the weather. The St. Lawrence Seaway, for example, is closed for most of the winter season.

Truck

Trucks have steadily increased their share of transportation and now account for 23% of total tonnage carried. They account for the largest portion of transportation within cities as opposed to between cities. Trucks are highly flexible in their routing and time schedules. They can move goods door to door, saving shippers the need to transfer goods from truck to rail and back again at a loss of time and risk of theft or damage. Trucks are efficient for short hauls of high-value merchandise. Their rates are competitive with railway rates in many cases, and trucks can usually offer faster services.

Air

Air carriers transport less than 1% of the nation's goods but are becoming more important as a transportation mode. Although air freight rates are much higher than rail or truck rates, air freight is ideal where speed is needed or distant markets have to be reached. Among the most frequently airfreighted products are perishables (fresh fish, cut flowers) and high-value, low-bulk items (technical instruments, jewelry). Companies find that air freight reduces inventory levels, number of warehouses, and costs of packaging.

* pipelines

* wire

Choosing Transportation Modes

In choosing a transportation mode for a product, shippers consider as many as six criteria. Table 13-2 ranks the various modes on these criteria. If a shipper needs speed, air and truck are the prime choices. If the goal is low cost, then water might be best. Trucks appear to offer the most advantages, which explains their growing share.

Shippers are increasingly combining two or more modes of transportation, thanks to containerization. Containerization consists of putting the goods in boxes or trailers that are easy to transfer between two transportation modes. **Piggyback** describes the use of rail and trucks; **fishyback**, water and trucks; **trainship**, water and rail; and **airtruck**, air and truck. Each combination offers advantages to the shipper. For example, piggyback is cheaper than trucking alone, and yet provides flexibility and convenience. Canadian Pacific, with extensive investments in most of these modes of transportation, can offer a manufacturer many of these combinations for shipping products.

Organizational Responsibility for Physical Distribution

We can see that decisions on warehousing, inventory, and transportation require much coordination. A growing number of companies have set up a permanent

TABLE 13-2
Transportation Modes Ranked According to Major Shipper Criteria (1 = Highest Rank)

	Speed (door-to-door delivery time)	Frequency (scheduled shipments per day)	Dependability (meeting schedules on time)	Capability (ability to handle various products)	Availability (no. of geographic points served)	Cost (per ton-kil.)
Rail	3	3	2	2	2	2
Water	4	4	3	1	4	1
Truck	2	1	1	3	1	3
Air	1	2	4	4	3	4

Note: 1 = Most favorable rank

Source: Adapted from James L. Heskett, Robert J. Ivie, and Nicholas A. Glaskowsky, *Business Logistics* (New York: Ronald Press, 1964), pp. 71 ff. Copyright by John Wiley & Sons, Inc. Reprinted by permission.

committee made up of managers responsible for different physical distribution activities. This committee meets often to set policies for improving overall distribution efficiency. The goal is to coordinate the company's physical distribution and marketing activities in order to create high market satisfaction at a reasonable cost. One study of Canadian manufacturing firms concluded that only about one in five companies had made serious attempts to centralize or coordinate their physical distribution activities.[14] Among the reasons cited for these findings was the lack of internal pressure for adopting more centralization.

Summary

Distribution channel decisions are among the most complex and challenging decisions facing the firm. Each channel system creates a different level of sales and cost. Once a distribution channel has been chosen, the firm must usually stick with it for a long time. The chosen channel will strongly affect and be affected by the other elements in the marketing mix.

Each firm needs to identify alternative ways to reach the market. They vary from direct selling to using one, two, three, or more intermediary channel levels. Marketing channels face continual and sometimes dramatic change. An important trend is the growth of vertical marketing systems. This trend affects channel cooperation, conflict, and competition.

Channel design calls for identifying the major channel alternatives in terms of the types of intermediaries, the number of intermediaries, and the channel responsibilities. Each channel alternative has to be evaluated according to economic, control, and adaptive criteria.

Channel management calls for selecting qualified middlemen and motivating them. Individual channel members must be evaluated regularly against their own past sales and other channel members' sales.

Just as the marketing concept is receiving increased recognition, more business firms are paying attention to the physical distribution concept. Physical distribution is an area of potentially high cost savings and improved customer satisfaction. When order processors, warehouse planners, inventory managers, and transportation managers make decisions, they affect each other's cost and ability to handle demand. The physical distribution concept calls for treating all these decisions within a unified framework. The task is to design physical distribution systems that minimize the total cost of providing a desired level of customer services.

Questions for Discussion

1. Why do most producers use middlemen to distribute and sell their products to consumers?
2. How many channel levels are commonly used by the following companies? (a) Ford Motor Company, (b) Molsons Brewing Company, and (c) Loblaws.
3. Distinguish among the three major types of vertical marketing systems. Give an example of each.

4. Which of the following products would receive intensive, exclusive, and selective distribution, and why? (a) Rolex watches, (b) General Motors automobiles, (c) Bic Disposable Razors, and (d) Estee Lauder perfume.

5. There is no way to reduce channel conflict. Comment.

6. How do physical distribution decisions differ from channel decisions? What is the overriding objective of physical distribution?

7. In what ways has the computer facilitated physical distribution?

8. Which mode of transportation would probably be used to distribute the following products? (a) beer, (b) expensive jewelry, (c) natural gas, and (d) farm machinery.

Chapter 13 Key Terms

Administered VMS   A vertical marketing system that coordinates successive stages of production and distribution, not through common ownership or contractual ties, but through the size and power of one of the parties.

Contractual VMS   A vertical marketing system in which independent firms at different levels of production and distribution join together through contracts to obtain more economies or sales impact than they could achieve alone.

Conventional distribution channel   A channel consisting of an independent producer(s), wholesaler(s), and retailer(s), each a separate business seeking to maximize its own profits, even at the expense of profits for the system as a whole.

Corporate VMS   A vertical marketing system that combines successive stages of production and distribution under single ownership—channel leadership is established through common ownership.

Distribution channel   The set of firms and individuals that take title, or assist in transferring title, to a good or service as it moves from the producer to the consumer.

Exclusive distribution   Giving a limited number of dealers the exclusive right to distribute the company's products in their territories.

Intensive distribution   Stocking the product in as many outlets as possible.

Physical distribution   The tasks involved in planning, implementing, and controlling the physical flow of materials and final goods from points of origin to points of use to meet the needs of customers at a profit.

Selective distribution   The use of more than one but less than all the middlemen who are willing to carry the company's products.

Vertical marketing system (VMS)   A distribution channel structure in which the producer(s), wholesaler(s), and retailer(s) act as a unified system—either one channel member owns the others, or has contracts with them, or has so much power that they all cooperate.

Cases for Chapter 13

Placing Products:
Retailing and Wholesaling

Chapter Objectives

After reading this chapter, you should be able to:
1. Discuss the roles of retailers and wholesalers in the distribution channel.
2. Describe the major types of retailers and give examples of each.
3. Identify the major types of wholesalers and give examples of each.
4. Discuss the marketing decisions facing retailers and wholesalers.

Metropolitan Toronto is the largest single retail market in Canada, with sales of over $19 billion each year. Torontonians have the widest selection of products and stores in the nation. Every large retail chain operates in Toronto, aggressively pursuing consumers for an increased share of this massive market. The department stores have tried to blanket the market by moving out to where the consumer lives and locating in the large suburban malls. Eaton's, Simpsons, K mart, and Towers have been at the leading edge of the suburban shift. In more recent times, the department store chains have also aided in the revitalization and redevelopment of the downtown core. The Bay and Eaton's have led the "back-to-the-city" movement, with the Eaton Centre being the flagship of retailing in downtown Toronto.

In the midst of all the clamor and glamor of the "Store Wars" sits the unusual retail concept espoused by Ed Mirvish and institutionalized as Honest Ed's. Ed Mirvish has very few basic beliefs when it comes to business and retailing. One of his principal beliefs, and perhaps the main strategy of Honest Ed's, is to "go against the trends."

Honest Ed's central tactic is to give the customer good bargains without frills. When you think of modern department stores,

located downtown or in the suburbs, you think of their extensive services. Honest Ed's has none. The modern department store is spacious, with wide aisles, expansive display areas, and neatly organized goods. Honest Ed's is packed with goods in functional stacks arranged along narrow aisles in one 150 000 square foot location.

The modern department store believes in service and forward courtesy. Sales personnel approach the customer and ask if they can be of service. They prowl their area, searching for customers in need of help, and convincing customers who are close to the point of purchase. The staff at Honest Ed's, by contrast, don't speak until spoken to. They believe there is no need for aggressive selling techniques or "extended" courtesies. The goods can sell themselves and information will be provided when it is sought.

The modern department store has its own credit card system and may also accept Master Card and Visa. The credit system is convenient for the customer and helps increase potential sales. Honest Ed's accepts only cash.

Modern department stores are aware they are operating in a very competitive environment. Their advertising is high-powered, multimedia, and slick. They issue catalogs and flyers, and their TV and radio spots highlight seasonal specials and nationwide sales extravaganzas. Honest Ed laughs at himself in newspaper ads and clogs them with a multitude of products, accentuating the low price.

When he opened Honest Ed's in 1948, Ed Mirvish introduced the discount house to Canada. One might assume that Honest Ed's customers probably are from the lower income groups. However, shopping at Honest Ed's is an event, an experience, and all income groups are attracted to this landmark at Bathurst and Bloor. While it is a method of retailing that is certainly more appropriate for particular segments of the population, a customer's age, affluence, customs, habits, and tastes are meaningless at Honest Ed's. The distinctive concept — good prices and no frills — defines a target

market that cuts across age and income groups. Honest Ed's customers love a good bargain and that is all he promises and delivers. The strategy is simplistic, but it works. On busy days up to 20 000 customers will visit the store, helping to ring up sales of more than $50 million each year. Ed Mirvish has used the profits from this store to purchase the Royal Alexandra Theatre in Toronto, open restaurants, and engage in a wide variety of other activities.

Honest Ed's remains a unique retail concept in a world that has seen many rapid and dramatic changes in retailing. It is a simple and honest concept that has worked for over 30 years.

"Ed never spanked his kid. (But his prices hit bottom.)"

This chapter looks at retailing and wholesaling. In the first section we look at retailing's nature and importance, major types of retailers, decisions retailers make, and the future of retailing. In the second section, we discuss the same topics for wholesalers.

Retailing

What is retailing? We all know that Eaton's and The Bay are retailers, but so are the Avon lady, the local Holiday Inn, and a doctor seeing patients. We define retailing as follows:

Retailing is all activities involved in selling goods or services directly to (final)consumers for their personal, non-business use.

Many institutions — manufacturers, wholesalers, retailers — do retailing. But most retailing is done by retailers, businesses whose sales come primarily from retailing. Retailing can be done by person, mail, telephone, or vending machines; in stores, on the street, or in the consumer's home.

Retailing is a major industry in Canada. Total retail sales exceed $150 billion and over 700 000 people are employed in retailing. Sears Canada alone has over 52 000 personnel, making it one of Canada's largest employers.

Much of Canada's retailing is concentrated in a few large retail chains. Sixteen retail chains including Sears Canada, The Bay, Safeway Stores, Loblaws, Steinberg, Eaton's, Woolworth, Canadian Tire, Provigo, and Dylex have sales of over $1 billion annually.[1] These and other retail chains have a tremendous amount of buying power available and can frequently dictate terms and conditions to many of their suppliers. The Bay in particular, with its controlling interest in Fields, Zellers, Simpsons, and Marshall Wells, and its large minority interest in Robinsons and Sears Canada, can have a significant influence on manufacturers in Canada.

At the other end of the spectrum are the independent stores, usually owner-operated, and often described as "mom and pop" stores. Their importance and market share have been declining since the 1950s, although in recent years they have increased their share of total retail sales.[2] One reason for the turnaround of the independents is that many have banded together in voluntary retail groups.[3] These groups can provide increased buying power and expertise that would not be available to an independent operating alone.

Types of Retailers

Retailers come in all shapes and sizes, and new retailing forms keep emerging. Retailers can be classified by one or more of several characteristics: amount of service, product line sold, relative prices, nature of business premises, control of outlets, and type of store cluster. These classification elements and the corresponding retailer types, are shown in Table 14-1 and discussed below.

TABLE 14-1
Different Ways to Classify Retail Outlets

Amount of service	Product line sold	Relative price emphasis	Nature of business premises	Control of outlets	Type of store cluster
Self-service	Specialty store	Discount	Mail and	Corporate chain	Central business
Limited	Department store	store	telephone-	Voluntary chain	district
service	Supermarket	Warehouse	order retailing	and retailer	Regional shopping
Full service	Convenience store	Catalog	Automatic	cooperative	center
	Combination store	showroom	vending	Franchise	Community
	and superstore		Door-to-door	organization	shopping center
			retailing		Neighborhood
					shopping center

Amount of Service

Different products need different amounts of service, and customers' service preferences vary. Some customers will pay retailers for more service; others would rather have fewer services and pay a lower price. Thus several types of retailers have evolved offering different levels of service. Table 14-2 shows three levels of service and the retailers that use them.

TABLE 14-2
Classification of Retailers Based on the Amount of Customer Service

Decreasing services		Increasing services
Self-service	**Limited service**	**Full service**
Very few services	Small variety of services	Wide variety of services
Price appeal	Shopping goods	Fashion merchandise
Staple goods		Specialty merchandise
Convenience goods		
Warehouse retailing	Door-to-door sales	Specialty stores
Grocery stores	Department stores	Department stores
Discount retailing	Telephone sales	
Variety stores	Variety stores	
Mail-order retailing		
Automatic vending		

Source: Adapted from Larry D. Redinbaugh, *Retailing Management: A Planning Approach* (New York: McGraw-Hill, 1976), p. 12.

Self-service retailing grew rapidly in the 1930s. Customers were willing to carry out their own "locate-compare-select" process to save money. Today self-service is the basis of all discount operations and is typically used by sellers of convenience goods and nationally branded, fast-moving shopping goods.

Limited-service retailers such as Zellers provide more sales assistance because they carry more shopping goods for which customers need more information. They also offer additional services, such as credit and merchandise return, that are not usually offered by low-service stores. Their increased operating costs result in higher prices.

In **full-service retailing**, found in specialty stores and first-class department stores, salespeople assist customers in every phase of the locate-compare-select process. Full-service stores usually carry more specialty goods and slower-moving items such as cameras, jewelry, and fashions, for which customers like to be "waited on." They provide more liberal return policies, various credit plans, free delivery, home servicing, and extras such as lounges and restaurants. More services result in higher operating costs, which are passed along to customers as higher prices.

Product Line Sold

Retailers can be classified by the length and breadth of their product assortments. Among the most important types of stores are the specialty store, department store, supermarket, convenience store, and superstore.

Specialty Store

A *specialty store* carries a narrow product line with a deep assortment within that line. Examples include clothing stores, sporting goods stores, furniture stores, florists, and bookstores. Specialty stores can be further classified by the narrowness of their product lines. A clothing store is a **single-line store**, a men's clothing store is a **limited-line store**, and a men's custom shirt store is a **super-**

Specialty stores, such as Suzy Shier, can focus on the needs and tastes of a specific market segment.

specialty store. The increasing use of market segmentation, market targeting, and product specialization have resulted in the rapid growth of superspecialty stores such as Athlete's Foot (sport shoes), Pennington's (clothes for large women), and Computerland (personal computers).

The shopping center boom has also contributed to the recent growth of specialty stores. Specialty stores often occupy 60 to 70% of the total shopping center space. Although most specialty stores are independently owned, chain specialty stores show the strongest growth. The most successful chain specialty stores zero in on specific target market needs.

Suzy Shier is a young women's fashion clothing store chain operated by Dylex Limited. Suzy Shier specializes in clothes for the single working woman in the 18 to 35 age group. Merchandise selection and pricing decisions are based on market research conducted to identify Suzy Shier customers and their needs. Having defined its target market carefully, Suzy Shier is able to achieve a number of advantages. It can continually study the fashion interests of 18- to 35-year-old women; it can pretest new fashion ideas; it can build a unique image; it can aim its advertising carefully; and it can locate in shopping centers that are in areas with the right demographics.

Department Store

A *department store* carries a wide variety of product lines, typically clothing, home furnishings, and household goods. Each line is operated as a separate department managed by specialist buyers or merchandisers.

Department stores in Canada have been a dominant force in retailing and are well-known by most Canadians. However, since 1979 department stores have lost ground to other types of retailers. Several factors led to this decline, including greater competition from specialty stores, lack of clearly defined target markets, and reduced customer service. Some of the department stores are trying to arrest this trend by redesigning their stores (Sears) or repositioning them (Woodwards, Simpsons).[4]

Supermarket

Supermarkets are large, low-cost, low-margin, high-volume, self-service stores that carry a wide variety of food, laundry, and household maintenance products.

Seven supermarket chains control over one-half of the retail food industry in Canada, and each of the chains tends to be concentrated in a particular geographic area. For example, Safeway is the dominant chain in Western Canada with sales of around $3.5 billion annually, followed by Overwaitea and Loblaws. In Ontario, A&P is the dominant chain, followed by Loblaws, which also controls Zehr's, and a substantial minority of Sobey's, the leading Maritime chain. The other chains with strong market positions in Ontario are the Oshawa Group (with IGA and Food City), and Steinberg. In Quebec, Metro-Richelieu, Steinberg, and Provigo are the market leaders. Sobey's and Loblaws are dominant in the Maritimes. Sobey's also has a substantial interest in Provigo.

Supermarkets have faced a number of challenges in recent years, including the growth of fast-food outlets (McDonald's, Kentucky Fried Chicken, Pizza

A supermarket.

James Hertel

A convenience store.

Pizza). Canadians are now spending over 35% of their total food budgets outside of food stores.[5] In response, supermarkets have increased the number of their private brands (including generics), added more high-margin nonfood items, and added "takeout" delicatessens and bakery departments. As well, they are building larger stores and using "scrambled merchandising" strategies. Today many supermarkets are selling prescriptions, appliances, records, sporting goods, hardware, garden supplies, and even cameras, hoping to find high-margin lines to improve profit.

Convenience Store

Convenience stores are small stores that carry a limited line of high-turnover convenience goods. Examples include 7-Elevens, Mac's, and Beckers. These stores locate near residential areas and remain open long hours and seven days a week. Convenience stores must charge high prices to make up for higher operating costs and lower sales volume, but they satisfy an important consumer need. Consumers use convenience stores for "fill-in" purchases at off hours or when time is short, and they are willing to pay for the convenience. The "big three" convenience stores in Canada (Mac's, Beckers, and 7-Eleven) have over 1900 outlets and total sales in excess of $1 billion annually.[6]

Superstore and Combination Store

These two types of stores are larger than the conventional supermarket.

    Superstores (average size of 80 000 square feet) are about twice the size of regular supermarkets and carry a large assortment of routinely purchased food and nonfood items. They offer such services as laundry, dry cleaning, shoe

A superstore.

repair, video rentals, gasoline bars, and bargain lunch counters. An example is the Calgary Co-op, which has 12 superstores in Calgary each about twice the size of the average supermarket. Total annual sales exceed $370 million and the Co-op holds more than a 35% share of the Calgary retail food market.[7]

Combination stores are combined food and drug stores. Their average size is over 100 000 square feet and they are the latest weapon in the supermarket wars in Canada. Companies like Loblaws, Ferme Carnaval, and Safeway are opening "super-combos" from Halifax to Vancouver. They offer the consumer a wide selection of food, nonfood, and drug products at discount prices. Total sales from one super-combo store can exceed $75 million annually, up to seven times more than a conventional supermarket.[8]

Service Business

For some businesses, the "product line" is actually a service. Service retailers include hotels and motels, banks, airlines, colleges, hospitals, movie theaters, bowling alleys, restaurants, repair services, barber and beauty shops, and funeral homes. Service retailers in Canada are growing faster than product retailers, and each service industry has its own retailing drama. Banks look for new ways to distribute their services, including automatic tellers, direct deposit, and telephone banking. The amusement industry has spawned Disney World, Canada's Wonderland, and other theme parks. H&R Block has built a franchise network to help consumers pay as little as possible to the government.

Relative Prices

Retailers can also be classified by their prices. Most retailers charge regular prices and offer normal-quality goods and customer service. Some offer higher-quality goods and service at higher prices. Discount stores run lower-cost, lower-service operations and sell goods for lower prices. Here we will look at discount stores and two offshoots, warehouse stores and catalog showrooms.

Discount Store

A *discount store* sells standard merchandise at lower prices by accepting lower margins and selling higher volumes. The use of occasional discounts or specials does not make a discount store. Nor does selling inferior goods at low prices. A true discount store has five characteristics: (1) it regularly sells its merchandise at lower prices; (2) it sells mostly national brands, not inferior goods; (3) it operates on a self-service, minimum facilities basis; (4) it locates in a low-rent area and draws customers from fairly long distances; and (5) it has simple and functional fixtures.[9]

Competition in recent years, particularly from specialty stores and combination stores, has created problems for many discount retailers. For example, K mart, a general merchandise discount chain in Canada, has shown slow profit growth in the last five years. As well, two discount department stores, Horizon and Sayvette's, closed in the late 1970s.

Discount retailing has moved beyond general merchandise into special merchandise forms, such as discount sporting goods and discount stereo equipment stores. Discount food retailing is one of the more interesting developments, with the innovation of the "box" food store. Loblaws, with their "no frills" stores, Steinberg with the Valdi stores, and Kwik Save have pioneered this development in Canada. They are almost warehouse operations. Services are slashed to the barest minimum, with customers bagging their own groceries. These stores usually carry high-turnover items; none is perishable, thus eliminating the need for costly refrigeration. Prices are posted on signs rather than on merchandise, thus saving marking costs. In one year these no-frills stores captured 25% of the supermarket business in Ottawa and made substantial sales gains in many other areas.[10]

Warehouse Store

A *warehouse store* is a no-frills, reduced-service store that seeks high volume through low prices. One of its most interesting forms is the **furniture showroom warehouse**. Conventional furniture stores have run warehouse sales for years to clear out old stock. But this new concept has been most clearly developed in Canada by Leon's Furniture. Shoppers enter a large warehouse usually located in a low-rent suburban area. They enter the showroom section containing room settings of attractively displayed furniture and appliances. Customers select goods and place orders with salespeople. By the time the customer pays, leaves, and drives to the loading dock, the merchandise is ready. Leon's 23 outlets sell over $160 million each year with aggressive advertising, numerous sales, and a good product assortment.[11]

Catalog Showroom

A *catalog showroom* sells a wide selection of high-markup, fast-moving, brand-name goods at discount prices. These include jewelry, power tools, cameras, luggage, small appliances, toys, and sporting goods. Emerging in the late 1960s, these stores have become popular with consumers. They even threaten traditional discounters who have traded up to more service, higher markups, and higher prices. The catalog showroom industry is dominated in Canada by Consumers Distributing, with annual sales of over $1 billion.

Catalog showrooms make their money by cutting costs and margins to provide low prices that will attract a higher volume of sales. They carry presold, branded goods, lease stores in low-rent areas, and hire fewer salespeople.

Nature of Business Premises

Most goods and services are sold through stores, but **nonstore retailing** has been growing rapidly in Canada. Here we examine three forms of nonstore retailing: mail and telephone order retailing, vending machines, and door-to-door selling and in-house parties.

Mail and Telephone Order Retailing

Mail and telephone order retailing uses the mail or telephone to obtain orders or to aid delivery. These businesses take several forms.

Mail-order catalog sellers mail catalogs to a select group of customers. Some large mail-order houses carry a full line of goods. Sears Canada, the industry leader, sends out 4 million of its Christmas catalogs each year and generates between 30 and 40% of its total sales through catalog sales. Other Canadian retailers, notably Canadian Tire and Consumers Distributing, use catalogs as part of their marketing mix although the customer visits the store to purchase items shown in the catalog.

Direct response marketers run newspaper, magazine, radio, or television ads describing a product. The customer can write or phone for the product. The direct marketer selects the media vehicles that maximize the number of orders for a given advertising expenditure. This strategy works well with such products as records and tapes, books, and small appliances.

Direct mail marketers send mailing pieces — letters, fliers, and foldouts — to prospects who are on special mailing lists, or simply to "The Householder." Organizations ranging from IBM Canada to Eaton's, from the National Ballet of Canada to the United Way, all use direct mail as a means of marketing their products and services. Direct mail has proved very successful in promoting magazines, books, records, and insurance. Major charities use direct mail to raise over $350 million in Canada each year.[12] It is estimated that 1.7 billion pieces of direct mail are sent in Canada each year, 73 for each man, woman, and child. Direct mail is popular with marketers because it can be a very cost-effective form of advertising, and it is much easier to analyze the sales results of direct mail than those of broadcast media.

In **telemarketing**, direct marketers use the telephone to sell everything from

James Hertel

Catalogs are an important promotion tool for many retailers.

home repair services to newspaper subscriptions to zoo memberships. Some telephone marketers use computerized phoning systems where households are dialed automatically and computerized messages presented.

Several factors have caused the increase in mail and telephone order retailing. Working women have less shopping time. In-store shopping has become less appealing because of higher driving costs, traffic and parking headaches, less in-store service, and longer checkout lines. The development of toll-free lines and the longer operating hours of telephone retailers have also boosted this form of retailing.

Automatic Vending

Automatic vending through coin-operated machines generates annual sales of over $360 million in Canada.[13] Today's machines use space-age and computer technology to sell a wide variety of impulse goods — cigarettes, beverages, candy, newspapers, foods and snacks, hosiery, cosmetics, paperbacks, T-shirts, and insurance policies.

Vending machines are found in factories, offices, lobbies, retail stores, and gasoline stations. They increasingly supply entertainment services — pinball machines, jukeboxes, and electronic computer games. Automatic teller machines provide bank customers with checking, savings, withdrawals, and funds-transfer services.

Vending machines offer 24-hour selling, self-service, and less damaged goods. But automatic vending is costly, and prices of vended goods are often 15 to 20% higher than in other retail methods. Customers must put up with machine breakdowns, out-of-stocks, and the fact that merchandise cannot be returned.

Door-to-Door Retailing

Door-to-door retailing, which started centuries ago with roving peddlers, has grown into a substantial industry. In Canada, over 200 000 people are involved in selling door-to-door, office-to-office, or at home sales parties. The leading direct sales companies in Canada are Avon, Mary Kay Cosmetics, and Shaklee.

Door-to-door selling companies have sometimes been accused of pyramid selling, which is illegal under the Competition Act. The main feature of a pyramid sales company is that money is made through recruiting "representatives" and having them purchase the product. In such cases the product is sold through a number of recruiters rather than to the "final consumer."[14] Instances of pyramid selling have created a certain amount of distrust for direct sales firms.

The advantages of door-to-door selling are consumer convenience and personal attention, but the high costs of hiring, training, paying, and motivating the salesforce result in higher prices. Door-to-door selling has a somewhat uncertain future. The increase in the number of single-person and working-couple households decreases the chances of finding anyone at home. Recent advances in interactive telecommunication make it likely that the door-to-door salesperson may be replaced in the future by the household television or home computer.

Control of Outlets

Retailing institutions can be classified by form of ownership. Independent retail stores account for about 57% of all retail sales. Here we will look at several other forms of ownership — the corporate chain, voluntary chain and retailer cooperative, and franchise organization.

Corporate Chain

The chain store is one of the most important retail developments of this century. In the general merchandise field and in food retailing, corporate chain stores control a substantial share of the market. A chain store has been defined by Statistics Canada as an organization operating four or more retail outlets in the same kind of business, under the same legal ownership.[15] Beginning in 1869 with Timothy Eaton, generally acknowledged as the "father of the department store" in Canada, department stores have been a dominant force in retailing in Canada. By 1929, three chains accounted for 80% of all department store sales.[16] Since then the level of concentration declined as more competitors entered the market.

Today, the six largest department store chains — The Bay, Sears Canada, Woolworth, K mart, Woodwards, and Eaton's—have total sales exceeding $14.5 billion annually. These chains control the lion's share of sales, store locations, buying power, and financial resources in this market. Their dominance has been created by aggressive marketing, merchandising practices, central buying, and efficient distribution.

A similar picture exists in food retailing in Canada but with an interesting twist. The giant supermarket chains—A&P, Safeway, Loblaws, Provigo, Steinberg, The Oshawa Group—have frequently achieved growth through vertical integration. For example, George Weston controls Loblaws and also controls, either directly or through subsidiaries like Loblaws, bakeries, flour mills, cookie and biscuit factories, chocolate bar firms, dairies, sugar companies, fish canneries, oyster farms, grocery wholesalers, tea manufacturers, and grocery outlets in the United States, to name a few of their activities. This extensive vertical integration in the food industry allows Weston to achieve both economies of scale and control over the channel of distribution. George Weston is now the fifth largest company in Canada, with sales over $8.9 billion annually.

A number of specialty retail chains have also grown rapidly in recent years —Canadian Tire in the automotive and hardware business; Dylex, the Grafton Group, Reitman's, and Dalmys in the clothing field; and Beaver Lumber in the home improvement area. These corporate chains have many advantages over independents. Their size allows them to buy in large quantities at lower prices. They can afford to hire corporate-level specialists to deal with such areas as pricing, promotion, merchandising, inventory control, and sales forecasting. In addition, chains gain promotional economies because their advertising costs are spread over many stores and a large sales volume.

Voluntary Chain and Retailer Cooperative

The great success of corporate chains caused many independents to band together in one of two forms of contractual associations. One is the **voluntary chain**—a wholesaler sponsored group of independent retailers that engage in group buying and common merchandising. Examples include the United Farmers of Alberta Ltd. and Co-op Atlantic. The other is the **retailer cooperative**—a group of independent retailers that band together and set up a jointly owned central wholesale operation and conduct joint merchandising and promotion efforts. Examples include the Red River Co-op and The Scotsburn Co-operative. These organizations give independents the buying and promotion economies they need to meet the prices of corporate chains.

Franchise Organization

A *franchise* is a contractual association between a manufacturer, wholesaler, or service organization (the franchiser) and independent business people who buy the right to own and operate one or more units in the franchise system (franchisees). The main difference between a franchise and other contractual systems (voluntary chains and retail cooperatives) is that franchise systems are normally based on some unique product or service, or on a method of doing business, or on a trade name, goodwill, or patent that the franchiser has developed. In 1986 there were about 1.1 million people working in the franchise industry and total sales were $60 billion.[17]

Virtually anything and everything is now being franchised in Canada — from records to rent-a-wreck, from real estate to repair shops. Leading the way are firms such as Canadian Tire, McDonald's, Shoppers Drug Mart, Scott's

Franchises are a major form of retailing in Canada.

(Kentucky Fried Chicken), Coca-Cola, and Pepsi-Cola, all with sales of over $250 million annually. About one-half of the total retail sales through the more than 20 000 franchise outlets are accounted for by automobile and truck dealers and soft drink bottlers.

Type of Store Cluster

Most stores today cluster together to increase their customer pulling power and to give consumers the convenience of one-stop shopping. The main types of store clusters are the central business district and the shopping center.

Central Business District

Central business districts were the main form of retail cluster until the 1950s. Every large city and town had a central business district with department stores, specialty stores, banks, and movie theaters. When people began to move to the suburbs in the 1950s, these central business districts, with their traffic and parking problems, began to lose business. Downtown merchants opened branches in suburban shopping centers, and the decline of the central business districts continued. Only recently have the cities joined with merchants to try to revive downtown shopping areas by building malls and underground parking. Some central business districts have made a comeback; others remain in a slow and possibly irreversible decline.

Shopping Center

A *shopping center* is a group of retail businesses planned, developed, owned, and managed as a unit, and related in location, size, and type of store to the trade area that it serves.[18]

The **regional shopping center** is the largest and most dramatic of the shopping centers. A regional shopping center is like a mini-downtown. It contains from 40 to 100 stores and pulls customers from a wide area. In its early form, the regional shopping center had two strong department stores "anchoring" the ends, with specialty stores in between. With this design, consumers could easily compare products at various specialty and department stores. Regional centers have added new types of retailers over the years—dentists, health clubs, and even branch libraries. Larger regional malls now have several department stores and several shopping levels. Probably the most famous regional mall in

The West Edmonton Mall, the largest shopping center in Canada, draws visitors from as far away as Japan.

Courtesy: Triple-Five Corporation Limited

Canada is the West Edmonton Mall, which has a children's zoo, circus rides, and a variety of other activities to attract and entertain shoppers in Alberta.

A **community shopping center** contains 15 to 50 retail stores. The center normally contains a primary store (usually a branch of a department or variety store), a supermarket, specialty stores, convenience goods stores, professional offices, and sometimes a bank. The primary store usually locates at the middle of the center.

Most shopping centers are **neighborhood shopping centers** that contain five to 15 stores. They are close and convenient for consumers. They usually contain a supermarket as the anchor store and several service stores — a dry cleaner, self-service laundry, drugstore, a hair stylist shop, a hardware, or other stores located in an unplanned strip.

Retailer Marketing Decisions

We will now look at the major marketing decisions retailers must make about their target markets, product assortment and services, price, promotion, and place.

Target Market Decision

Retailers must first define the target market, and decide how they will be positioned in the target market. The retailer's positioning guides all other retailer marketing decisions. Product assortment, services, pricing, advertising, store decor, and other decisions must all support the retailer's position in its market segment.

Some stores define their target market and position quite well. A women's apparel store in Montreal positions itself as "fashions for the discriminating woman" and targets upper-income women between the ages of 30 and 35 living within 30 minutes' driving time from the store. But many retailers fail to clearly define their target markets and positions. They try to have "something for everyone" and end up not satisfying any market well. Even large department stores like Eaton's must define their major target markets so that they can design effective strategies for serving these markets.

Product Assortment and Services Decision

Retailers have to decide on three major product variables: product assortment, services mix, and store atmosphere.

The retailer's **product assortment** must match what target shoppers expect. In fact, assortment becomes a key element in the competitive battle with other retailers. The retailer has to decide on product assortment **width** and **depth**. Thus a restaurant can offer a narrow and shallow assortment (small lunch counter), a narrow and deep assortment (delicatessen), a wide and shallow assortment (cafeteria), or a wide and deep assortment (large restaurant). Another

TABLE 14-3
Typical Retail Services

Prepurchase services	Postpurchase services	Ancillary services
1. Accepting telephone orders	1. Delivery	1. Cheque cashing
2. Accepting mail orders (or purchases)	2. Regular wrapping (or bagging)	2. General information
		3. Free parking
3. Advertising	3. Gift wrapping	4. Restaurants
4. Window display	4. Adjustments	5. Repairs
5. Interior display	5. Returns	6. Interior decorating
6. Fitting rooms	6. Alterations	7. Credit
7. Shopping hours	7. Tailoring	8. Restrooms
8. Fashion shows	8. Installations	9. Baby attendant service
9. Trade-ins	9. Engraving	
	10. COD delivery	

Source: Carl M. Larson, Robert E. Weigand, and John S. Wright, *Basic Retailing* ©1982, p. 384. Reprinted by permission of Prentice-Hall, Inc.

product assortment element is the quality of the goods. The customer is interested not only in the range of choice, but also in the quality of the products.

Retailers also must decide on the **services mix** to offer customers. The old "mom and pop" grocery stores offered home delivery, credit, and conversation, services that today's supermarkets have dropped. Table 14-3 lists some of the major services full-service retailers can offer. The services mix is one of the key tools of nonprice competition for setting one store apart from another.

The store's **atmospherics** is a third element in its product arsenal. Every store has a physical layout that makes moving around difficult or easy. Every store has a "feel"; one store is dirty, another is charming, a third is plush, a fourth is somber. The store must have a planned atmosphere that suits the target market and moves them to buy. A bank should be quiet, solid, and peaceful, and a nightclub should be bright, loud, and vibrating.[19]

Price Decision

The retailer's prices are a key competitive factor and reflect the quality of goods carried and services offered. Retail prices are based on the cost of merchandise, and intelligent buying is a key factor in successful retailing. Beyond this, retailers must price carefully in many other ways. They can set low markups on some items that can work as traffic builders or loss leaders, and hope that customers will buy more items with higher markups once they are in the store. Retail management can also use markdowns on slower-moving merchandise. Shoe retailers, for example, expect to sell 50% of their shoes at a 60% markup, 25% at a 40% markup, and the remaining 25% at cost. They set their initial prices with these expected markdowns in mind.

Promotion Decision

Retailers use the normal promotion tools—advertising, personal selling, sales promotion, and publicity — to reach consumers. Retailers advertise in newspapers, magazines, radio, and television. The advertising may be supported by circulars and direct mail pieces. Personal selling requires careful training of salespeople in how to greet customers, meet their needs, and handle their complaints. Sales promotion may include in-store demonstrations, contests, and visiting celebrities. Publicity is always available to retailers who have something interesting to say.

Place Decision

The retailer's location is key to its ability to attract customers. The costs of building or leasing facilities also have a major impact on the retailer's profits. Thus site location decisions are among the most important the retailer makes. Small retailers may have to settle for whatever locations they can find or afford. Large retailers usually employ specialists who select locations using advanced site-location methods.[20]

The Future of Retailing

Several trends will affect the future of retailing. The slowdown in population and economic growth means that retailers will no longer have sales and profit growth through natural expansion in current and new markets. Growth will have to come from increasing their shares of current markets. But greater competition and new types of retailers will make it more difficult for retailers to improve their market shares. Consumer demographics, life styles, and shopping patterns are changing rapidly. To be successful, retailers will have to choose target segments carefully and position themselves strongly.

Rising costs will make more efficient operation and smarter buying essential to successful retailing. New methods such as computerized checkout and inventory control will help cut costs and provide new ways to serve consumers better.

Many retailing innovations are partially explained by the **wheel of retailing** concept.[21] According to this concept, many new types of retailing forms begin as low-margin, low-price, low-status operations. They challenge established retailers that have become "fat" over the years by letting their costs and margins increase. The new retailers' success leads them to upgrade their facilities and offer more services. This raises their cost and forces them to increase their prices. Eventually, the new retailers become like the conventional retailers they replaced. The cycle begins again when still newer types of retailers evolve with lower costs and prices.

New retail forms will continue to emerge to meet new consumer needs and new situations. But the life cycle of new retail forms is getting shorter. Department stores took about 100 years to reach the mature stage of the life cycle; more recent forms reach maturity in about ten years. Retailers can no longer sit back with a successful formula. To remain successful, they must keep adapting.

Wholesaling

Wholesaling includes all activities involved in selling goods and services to those buying for resale or business use. A retail bakery does wholesaling when it sells pastry to the local hotel. However, we will define *wholesalers* as those firms engaged *primarily* in wholesaling activity.

Wholesalers differ from retailers in several ways. First, because they deal mostly with business customers rather than final consumers, wholesalers pay less attention to promoting, to atmosphere, and to location. Second, wholesalers usually cover larger trade areas and have larger transactions than retailers.

Wholesalers buy mostly from producer and sell mostly to retailers, industrial consumers, and other wholesalers. But why are wholesalers used at all? For example, why would a producer use wholesalers rather than sell directly to retailers or consumers? The answer is that wholesalers are often better at performing one or more of the following channel functions:

Selling and promoting   *Wholesalers' salesforces help manufacturers reach many small customers at a low cost. The wholesaler has more contacts and is often better trusted by the buyer than the distant manufacturer.*

Buying and assortment building   *Wholesalers can select items and build assortments needed by their customers, thus saving the customers much work.*

Bulk breaking   *Wholesalers save their customers money by buying in carload lots and breaking bulk.*

Warehousing   *Wholesalers hold inventories, thereby reducing the inventory costs and risks of suppliers and customers.*

Transportation   *Wholesalers provide quicker delivery to buyers because they are closer.*

Financing   *Wholesalers finance their customers by giving credit, and they finance their suppliers by ordering early and paying bills on time.*

Risk bearing   *Wholesalers absorb some risk by taking title and bearing the cost of theft, damage, spoilage, and obsolescence.*

Market information   *Wholesalers give information to suppliers and customers about competitors, new products, and price developments.*

Management services and advice   *Wholesalers often help retailers to train their salesclerks, improve store layouts and displays, and set up accounting and inventory control systems.*

TABLE 14-4
Classification of Wholesalers

Merchant wholesalers	Brokers and agents	Manufacturers' and retailers' branches and offices
Full-service wholesalers	Brokers	Sales branches and offices
Wholesale merchants	Agents	Purchasing offices
Industrial distributors		
Limited-service wholesalers		
Cash-and-carry wholesalers		
Truck wholesalers		
Drop shippers		
Rack jobbers		
Producers' cooperatives		
Mail-order wholesalers		

Types of Wholesalers

Wholesalers fall into three major groups (see Table 14-4): merchant wholesalers, brokers and agents, and manufacturers' sales branches and offices. We will now look at each of these groups of wholesalers.

Merchant wholesalers are independently owned businesses that take title to the merchandise they handle. Merchant wholesalers are of two broad types: full-service and limited-service wholesalers.

Full-Service Wholesalers

Full-service wholesalers provide a full set of services such as carrying stock, using a salesforce, offering credit, making deliveries, and providing management assistance. They are either wholesale merchants or industrial distributors.

Wholesale merchants sell mostly to retailers and provide a full range of services. They vary in the width of their product line. Some carry several lines of goods to meet the needs of both general merchandise retailers and single-line retailers. Others carry one or two lines of goods in a greater depth of assortment. Examples are hardware wholesalers, drug wholesalers, and clothing wholesalers. Some specialty wholesalers carry only part of a line in great depth. Examples are health food, seafood, and automotive parts wholesalers. They offer customers deeper choice and greater product knowledge.

Industrial distributors are merchant wholesalers who sell to producers rather than to retailers. They provide inventory, credit, delivery, and other services. They may carry a broad range of merchandise, a general line, or a specialty line. Industrial distributors may focus on such lines as MRO items (maintenance, repair, and operating supplies), OEM items (original equipment supplies such as ball bearings, motors), or equipment (such as hand and power tools, and forklift trucks).

Limited-Service Wholesalers

Limited-service wholesalers offer fewer services to their suppliers and customers. There are several types of limited service wholesalers.

Cash-and-carry wholesalers have a limited line of fast-moving goods, sell to small retailers for cash, and normally do not deliver. A small fish store retailer, for example, normally drives at dawn to a cash-and-carry fish wholesaler and buys several crates of fish, pays on the spot, drives the merchandise back to the store and unloads it.

Truck wholesalers (also called truck jobbers) perform a selling and delivery function. They carry a limited line of goods (such as milk, bread, snack foods), which they sell for cash as they make their rounds of supermarkets, small groceries, hospitals, restaurants, factory cafeterias, and hotels.

Drop shippers operate in bulk industries such as coal, lumber, and heavy equipment. They do not carry inventory or handle the product. Once an order is received, they find a producer who ships the goods directly to the customer. The drop shipper takes title and risk from the time the order is accepted to the time it is delivered to the customer. Because drop shippers do not carry inventory, their costs are lower and they can pass on some savings to customers.

Rack jobbers serve grocery and drug retailers, mostly in the area of nonfood items. These retailers do not want to order and maintain displays of hundreds of nonfood items. The rack jobbers send delivery trucks to stores, and the delivery person sets up racks of toys, paperbacks, hardware items, health and beauty aids, or other items. They price the goods, keep them fresh, set up and keep inventory records. Rack jobbers sell on consignment, which means that they retain title to the goods and bill the retailers only for the goods sold to consumers. Thus they provide such services as delivery, shelving, inventory, and financing. They do little promotion because they carry many branded items that are highly advertised.

Mail-order wholesalers send catalogs to retail, industrial, and institutional customers offering jewelry, cosmetics, special foods, and other small items. Their main customers are businesses in small outlying areas. They have no salesforce to call on customers.

Brokers and Agents ⟶ *good question for test!*

Brokers and agents differ from merchant wholesalers in two ways: they do not take title to goods, and they perform only a few functions. Their main function is to aid in buying and selling, and for this they earn a commission ranging from 2 to 6% of the selling price. Like merchant wholesalers, they generally specialize by product line or customer types.

James Hertel

A country auction. The auctioneers are acting as wholesalers, linking producer and consumer.

Brokers

A *broker* brings buyers and sellers together and assists in negotiation. Brokers are paid by the party that hired them. They do not carry inventory, get involved in financing, or assume risk. The most familiar examples are food brokers, real estate brokers, insurance brokers, and security brokers.

Agents

Agents represent buyers or sellers on a more permanent basis. There are several types.

Manufacturers' agents (also called **manufacturers' representatives**) are the most numerous type of agent wholesaler. They represent two or more manufacturers of related lines. They have a formal agreement with each manufacturer covering prices, territories, order-handling procedures, delivery and warranties, and commission rates. They know each manufacturer's product line and use their wide contacts to sell the products. Manufacturers' agents are used in such lines as apparel, furniture, and electrical goods. Most manufacturers' agents are small businesses, with only a few employees who are skilled salespeople. They are hired by small producers who cannot afford to maintain their own field salesforces, and by large producers who want to open new territories or sell in areas that cannot support a full-time salesperson.

Selling agents contract to sell a producer's entire output when the manufacturer is either not interested in doing the selling or feels unqualified. The selling agent serves as a sales department and has considerable influence over prices, terms, and conditions of sale. The selling agent normally has no territory limits. Selling agents are found in such product areas as textiles, industrial machinery and equipment, coal and coke, chemicals, and metals.

Purchasing agents generally have a long-term relationship with buyers. They make purchases for buyers, and often receive, inspect, warehouse, and ship goods to the buyers. One type consists of **resident buyers** in major apparel markets, who look for apparel lines that can be carried by small retailers located in small cities. They know a lot and provide helpful market information to clients as well as obtaining the best goods and prices available.

Commission merchants (or houses) are agents that take physical possession of products and negotiate sales. They are not normally used on a long-term basis. They are used most often in agricultural marketing by farmers who do not want to sell their own output and do not belong to cooperatives. The commission merchant would take a truckload of farm products to a central market, sell it for the best price, deduct a commission and expenses, and pay the balance to the farmer.

Manufacturers' Sales Branches and Offices

The third major type of wholesaling is done in *manufacturers' sales branches and offices* by sellers or buyers themselves, rather than through independent wholesalers. There are two types.

Manufacturers often set up their own sales branches and offices to improve inventory control, selling, and promotion. **Sales branches** carry inventory and are found in such industries as lumber and automotive equipment and parts. **Sales offices** do not carry inventory and are most often found in dry goods and notion industries. Many retailers set up **purchasing offices** in major market centers such as Toronto and Vancouver. These purchasing offices perform a role similar to that of brokers or agents, but are part of the buyer's organization.

Wholesaler Marketing Decisions ━━━━━

Wholesalers also make decisions about target markets, product assortments and services, pricing, promotion, and place.

Target Market Decision

Wholesalers, like retailers, need to define their target market and not try to serve everyone. They can choose a target group by size of customer (only large retailers), type of customer (convenience food stores only), need for service (customers who need credit), or other factors. Within the target group, they can identify the more profitable customers in order to design stronger offers and build better relationships with these customers. They can propose automatic reordering systems, set up management training and advising systems, or even sponsor a voluntary chain. They can discourage less profitable customers by requiring larger orders or adding charges to smaller ones.

Product Assortment and Services Decision

The wholesaler's "product" is its assortment. Wholesalers are under great pressure to carry a full line and stock enough for immediate delivery, but this can damage profits. Wholesalers today are cutting down on the number of lines they carry, choosing to carry only the more profitable ones. Wholesalers are also rethinking which services count most in building strong customer relationships and which should be dropped or charged for. The key is to find the mix of services most valued by their target customers.

Pricing Decision

Wholesalers usually mark up the cost of goods by a standard percentage, say 20%. Expenses may run 17% of the gross margin, leaving a profit margin of 3%. In grocery wholesaling the average profit margin is often less than 2%. Wholesalers are now trying new pricing approaches. They may cut their margin on some lines in order to win important new customers. They will ask suppliers for a special price break when they can turn it into an increase in the supplier's sales.

Promotion Decision

Most wholesalers are not promotion-minded. Their use of trade advertising, sales promotion, publicity, and personal selling is largely scattered and unplanned. Many are behind the times in personal selling—they still see selling as a single salesperson talking to a single customer instead of a team effort to sell, build, and service major accounts. Wholesalers also need to adopt some of the nonpersonal promotion techniques used by retailers. They need to develop an overall promotion strategy and to make greater use of supplier promotion materials and programs.

Place Decision

Wholesalers typically locate in low-rent, low-tax areas and put little money into their physical setting and offices. Their materials-handling and order-processing systems are often out of date. To meet rising costs, large and progressive wholesalers are turning to the automated warehouse. Orders are fed into a computer, and the items are picked up by mechanical devices and automatically taken to the shipping platform where they are assembled. Many wholesalers are turning to computers and wordprocessing machines to carry out accounting, billing, inventory control, and forecasting. Progressive wholesalers are adapting their services to the needs of target customers and finding cost-reducing methods of doing business.

Summary

Retailing and wholesaling consist of many organizations bringing goods and services from the point of production to the point of use.

Retailing, one of the major industries in Canada, includes all the activities involved in selling goods or services directly to final consumers for their personal, non-business use. Retailers can be classified in several ways: by the amount of service they provide (self-service, self-selection, limited service, or full service); product line sold (specialty stores, department stores, supermarkets, convenience stores, combination stores, and superstores); relative prices (discount stores, warehouse stores, and catalog showrooms); nature of the business premises (mail and telephone order retailing, automatic vending, and door-to-door retailing); control of outlets (corporate chains, voluntary chains, retailer cooperatives, and franchise organizations); and type of store cluster (central business districts and shopping centers). Retailers make decisions on their target market, product assortment and services, pricing, promotion, and place. They need to find ways to improve their management and increase their productivity.

Wholesaling includes all the activities involved in selling goods or services to those who are buying for the purpose of resale or for business use. Wholesalers help manufacturers deliver their products to the many retailers and industrial users across the nation. Some of the many functions of wholesalers include selling and promoting, buying and assortment building, bulk-breaking, warehousing, transporting, financing, risk bearing, supplying market information, and providing management service and advice. Wholesalers fall into three groups. Merchant wholesalers take possession of the goods. They can be subclassified as full-service wholesalers (wholesale merchant, industrial distributors) and limited-service wholesalers (cash-and-carry wholesalers, truck wholesalers, drop shippers, rack jobbers, and mail order wholesalers). Agents and brokers do not take possession of the goods but are paid a commission for aiding buying and selling. Manufacturers' branches and offices are wholesaling operations conducted by nonwholesalers to bypass the wholesalers. Progressive wholesalers adapt their services to the needs of target customers and seek cost-reducing methods of doing business.

Questions for Discussion

1. Explain the major difference between retailing and wholesaling.
2. Retailers can be classified by one or more of several characteristics. Identify these characteristics and offer an example of each type of retailer.
3. What are the characteristics of a true discount store?
4. Many retail innovations can be explained by the wheel-of-retailing concept. Comment.

5. Explain the major differences between merchant wholesalers and agents and brokers.
6. If friends of yours were planning to open a greeting card shop, which type of store cluster would you recommend that they select? Why?
7. Would a small manufacturer of lawn and garden tools seek a manufacturer's agent or a selling agent to handle the merchandise? Why?
8. Most wholesalers are not promotion-minded. Comment.

Chapter 14 Key Terms

Agent   A wholesaler who represents buyers or sellers on a more permanent basis, performs only a few functions, and does not take title to goods.

Automatic vending   Selling through coin-operated machines.

Broker   A wholesaler who does not take title to goods and whose function is to bring buyers and sellers together and assist in negotiation.

Catalog showroom   A retail operation that sells a wide selection of high-markup, fast-moving, brand-name goods at discount prices.

Chain stores   An organization operating four or more retail outlets in the same kind of business, under the same legal ownership.

Convenience store   A small store, located near a residential area, open long hours seven days a week, and carrying a limited line of high-turnover convenience goods.

Department store   A retail organization that carries a wide variety of product lines—typically clothing, home furnishings, and household goods; each line is operated as a separate department managed by specialist buyers or merchandisers.

Discount store   A retail institution that sells standard merchandise at lower prices by accepting lower margins and selling higher volume.

Door-to-door retailing   Selling door-to-door, office-to-office, or at home sales parties.

Franchise   A contractual association between a manufacturer, wholesaler, or service organization (a franchiser) and independent business people who buy the right to own and operate one or more units in the franchise system (franchisees).

Mail and telephone order retailing   Selling that uses the mail or telephone to get orders or to aid in delivery.

Manufacturers' sales branches and offices   Wholesaling done by sellers or buyers themselves, rather than through independent wholesalers.

Merchant wholesaler   An independently owned business that takes title to the merchandise it handles.

Retailers   Businesses whose sales come primarily from retailing.

Retailing   All activities involved in selling goods or services directly to final consumers for their personal, non-business use.

Shopping center   A group of retail businesses planned, developed, owned, and managed as a unit, and related in location, size, and type of store to the trade area that it serves.

Specialty store   A retail outlet that carries a narrow product line with a deep assortment within that line.

Supermarkets   Large, low-cost, low-margin, high-volume, self-service stores that carry a wide variety of food, laundry, and household maintenance products.

Superstore   A store almost twice the size of a regular supermarket that carries a large assortment of routinely purchased food and nonfood items, and offers such services as laundry, dry cleaning, shoe repair, check cashing, bill paying, and bargain lunch counters.

Warehouse store   A no-frills, reduced-service store that seeks high volume through low prices.

Wholesalers   Firms engaged *primarily* in wholesaling activity.

Wholesaling   All activities involved in selling goods and services to those buying for resale or business use.

Cases for Chapter 14

Promoting Products: Communication and Promotion Strategy

Chapter Objectives

After reading this chapter, you should be able to:
1. Name and define the four tools of the promotion mix.
2. Discuss the elements of the marketing communication process.
3. Explain the methods for setting the promotion budget.
4. Discuss the factors that affect the design of the promotion mix.

Mother's Pizza Parlour & Spaghetti House is a Canadian theme restaurant with over 55 outlets in Canada and the U.S. grossing over $58 million annually. Mother's theme of old fashioned warmth and nostalgia is based on its 1925-1935 decor. The management of Mother's would like to project this theme on a consistent basis throughout their chain. If one of their stores does not deliver the desired message to its clientele, the entire operation is affected negatively. Mother's is in an active expansion stage and the consistency of quality and image is particularly crucial. Therefore the management, owners, and corporate officers stress this need for consistency in communicating Mother's concept through a number of marketing elements:

Interior store appearance Each store is decorated with $100 000 worth of antiques. Staff are dressed in attire of the 1920s and 1930s. Charlie Chaplin silent movies, with old-time music, are played to create an entertaining dining experience.

Exterior store appearance In the restaurant industry customers judge a book by its cover. For this reason, every store exterior is neat and

clean, just the way Mother likes it. The store readagraph is an effective marketing tool. It usually carries the message of a store special such as Noodle Night or a community service announcement.

Advertising Television, radio, outdoor, and newspaper advertisements provide important impressions of Mother's Restaurants. Generic television and radio commercials are designed to encourage the consumer to slip away to a simpler day and come home to Mother's. The stores are presented as a neighborhood restaurant where people enjoy good food while being treated like family.

Radio and newspaper support promotions These promotions create for consumers the impression that they can expect extra value from Mother's, whether it is a Monday Father's Night Special or a free glass for customers.

Community involvement Sponsoring teams in sport leagues, assisting community organizations, and helping disabled children is Mother's way of saying they are really are a neighborhood restaurant. It is important to be a good corporate citizen, making a positive contribution in the community.

Operations   This is the final impression and the most important. You must provide good food and service to deliver on the promise of performance. In the restaurant industry you are only as good as the last meal you have served.

If customers have a bad experience they will never come back. If they have a good experience, they will not only come back, but also bring their friends. Because Mother's ensures an enjoyable dining experience, its customer base is loyal and constantly growing, in large part because of a strong, consistent promotion and communication program.[1]

Modern marketing calls for more than developing a good product, pricing it attractively, and making it available to target customers. Companies must also communicate with their customers. What is communicated, however, should not be left to chance.

To communicate well, companies hire advertising agencies to develop effective ads, sales promotion specialists to design sales incentive programs, and public relations firms to develop the corporate image. They train their salespeople to be friendly, helpful, and persuasive. For most companies the question is not whether to communicate, but how much to spend and in what ways.

A modern company manages a complex marketing communications system (see Figure 15-1). The company communicates with its middlemen, consumers, and various publics. Its middlemen communicate with their consumers and publics. Consumers have word-of-mouth communication with each other and with other publics. Meanwhile each group provides feedback to every other group.

FIGURE 15-1
The Marketing Communications Systems

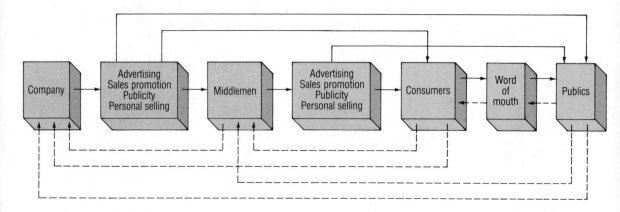

The marketing communications mix (also called the promotion mix) consists of four major tools:

Advertising   *Any paid form of nonpersonal presentation and promotion of ideas, goods, or services by an identified sponsor.*

Sales promotion   *Short-term incentives to encourage purchase or sales of a product or service.*

Publicity   *Nonpersonal stimulation of demand for a product, service, or business unit by planting commercially significant news about it in a published medium or obtaining favorable presentation of it on radio, television, or stage that is not paid for by the sponsor.*

Personal selling   *Oral presentation in a conversation with one or more prospective purchasers for the purpose of making sales.*[2]

Within the categories are specific tools such as sales presentations, point-of-purchase displays, specialty advertising, trade shows, fairs, demonstrations, catalogs, literature, press kits, posters, contests, premiums, and coupons. At the same time, communication goes beyond these specific tools. The product's design, its price, the package shape and color, and the salesperson's manner all communicate something to buyers. The whole marketing mix, not just the promotion mix, must be coordinated for greatest communication impact.

This chapter looks at two questions: What are the major steps in developing effective marketing communication? How should the promotion budget and mix be determined? Chapter 16 will look at mass communication tools—advertising, sales promotion, and publicity. Chapter 17 will look at the salesforce as a communication and promotion tool.

Steps in Developing Effective Communication

Marketers need to understand how communication works. Communication involves the nine elements shown in Figure 15-2. Two elements are the major parties in a communication — *sender* and *receiver*. Another two are the major communication tools — *message* and *media*. Four are major communication functions — *encoding, decoding, response,* and *feedback*. The last element is *noise* in the system. These elements are defined as follows:

Sender   *The party sending the message to another party.*

Encoding   *The process of putting thought into symbolic form.*

Message   *The set of symbols that the sender transmits.*

Media   *The communication channels through which the message moves from sender to receiver.*

Decoding   *The process by which the receiver assigns meaning to the symbols encoded by the sender.*

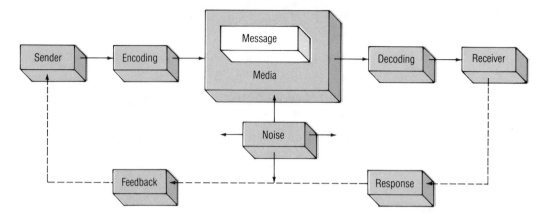

FIGURE 15-2
Elements in the Communication Process

Receiver The party receiving the message sent by another party.

Response The reactions of the receiver after being exposed to the message.

Feedback The part of the receiver's response communicated back to the sender.

Noise The unplanned static or distortion during the communication process that results in the receiver's getting a different message than the sender sent.

The model points out the key factors in good communication. Senders must know what audiences they want to reach and what responses they want. They must be good at encoding messages that take into account how the target audience decodes messages, and they must send the message through media that reach the target audience. Senders must develop feedback channels so that they can know the audience's response to the message.

Thus the marketing communicator must make the following decisions: (1) identify the target audience, (2) determine the response sought, (3) choose a message, (4) choose the media, (5) select the message source, and (6) collect feedback.

Identifying the Target Audience

A marketing communicator must start with a clear target audience in mind. The audience may be potential buyers, current users, deciders, or influencers. The audience may be individuals, groups, special publics, or the general public. The target audience will affect the communicator's decisions on *what* will be said, *how* it will be said, *when* it will be said, *where* it will be said, and *who* is to say it.

Determining the Response Sought

Once the target audience has been defined, the marketing communicator must decide what response is sought. Of course, the desired final response is purchase. But purchase is the result of a long process of consumer decision making. The marketing communicator needs to know where the target audience now stands and to which state it needs to be moved.

The target audience may be in any of the six buyer readiness states — awareness, knowledge, liking, preference, conviction, or purchase. These states are shown in Figure 15-3 and discussed below.

Awareness

The communicator must first know how aware the target audience is of the product or organization. The audience may be unaware of it, know only its name, or know one or a few things about it. If most of the target audience is unaware, the communicator tries to build awareness, perhaps just name recognition. This can be done with simple messages repeating the name. Even then, building awareness takes time.

> Suppose a small college in New Brunswick called Maritime College seeks applicants from Nova Scotia but has no name recognition in that province. Suppose in addition that there are 30 000 high school graduates in Nova Scotia who may potentially be interested in Maritime College. The college might set the objective of making 70% of these students aware of Maritime's name within one year.

Knowledge

The target audience might have company or product awareness, but not know much more. Maritime may want its target audience to know that it is a three-year college in the Saint John Valley with excellent programs in English and the language arts. Maritime College needs to learn how many people in the target audience have little, some, and much knowledge about Maritime. The college may decide to build up product knowledge as its first communication objective.

FIGURE 15-3
Buyer Readiness States

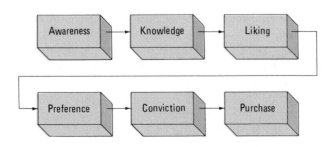

Liking

If the target audience knows the product, how do they feel about it? We can develop a scale covering degrees of liking — dislike very much, dislike somewhat, indifferent, like somewhat, like very much. If the audience looks unfavorably on Maritime College, the communicator has to find out why and then develop a communications campaign to build up favorable feelings. If the unfavorable view is based on real problems of the college, then communications will not do the job. Maritime would have to fix its problems and then communicate its quality. Good public relations call for "good deeds followed by good words."

Preference

The target audience might like the product, but prefer others more. In this case, the communicator will try to build consumer preference. The communicator will promote the product's quality, value, performance, and other features. The campaign's success can be checked by the communicator by measuring the audience's preferences again after the campaign.

Conviction

A target audience might prefer the product but not develop a conviction about buying it. Thus some high school graduates may prefer Maritime, but may not be sure that they want to go to college. The communicator's job is to build conviction that going to college is the right thing to do.

Purchase

Some members of the target audience might have conviction, but not quite get around to making the purchase. They may wait for more information or plan to act later. The communicator must lead these consumers to take the final step. This might include offering the product at a low price, offering a premium, or letting consumers try it on a limited basis.

The buyer readiness states are important to the marketing communicator. Buyers normally pass through these stages on their way to purchase. The communicator's task is to identify the stage most consumers are in and develop a communication campaign that will move them to the next stage.

Choosing a Message

Having defined the desired audience response, the communicator moves to developing an effective message. Ideally, the message should get **attention**, hold **interest**, arouse **desire**, and obtain **action** (known as the AIDA model). In practice, few messages take the consumer all the way from awareness to purchase, but the AIDA framework suggests the desirable qualities.

In putting together the message, the marketing communicator must solve three problems: what to say (message content), how to say it logically (message structure), and how to say it symbolically (message format).

Message Content

The communicator has to figure out an appeal or theme that will produce the desired response. There are three types of appeals. *Rational appeals* relate to the audience's self-interest. They show that the product will produce the claimed benefits. Examples would be messages showing a product's quality, economy, value, or performance.

Emotional appeals attempt to stir up negative or positive emotions that will motivate purchase. These include fear, guilt, and shame appeals that get people to do things they should (brush their teeth, have an annual health checkup) or stop doing things they should not (smoke, drink too much, overeat). Communicators also use positive emotional appeals such as love, humor, pride, and joy.

Moral appeals are directed to the audience's sense of what is right and proper. They are often used to urge people to support social causes such as a cleaner environment, equal rights for women, and aid to the needy. Moral appeals are less often used for everyday products.

Message Structure

The communicator has to decide on three message structure issues. The first is whether to draw a conclusion or leave it to the audience. Drawing a conclusion is usually more effective. The second is whether to present a one-sided or two-sided argument. Usually a one-sided argument is more effective in sales presentations, except where the audiences are highly educated and negatively disposed. The third is whether to present the strongest arguments first or last. Presenting them first gets strong attention, but may lead to an anticlimactic ending.[3]

Message Format

The communicator must use a strong format for the message. In a print ad, the communicator has to decide on the headline, copy, illustration, and color. To attract attention, advertisers can use novelty and contrast, eye-catching pictures and headlines, distinctive formats, message size and position, and color, shape, and movement.[4] If the message is to be carried over the radio, the communicator has to choose words, sounds, and voices. The "sound" of an announcer promoting a used car has to be different from one promoting quality furniture.

If the message is to be carried on television or in person, then all these elements, plus body language, have to be planned. Presenters must be aware of facial expressions, gestures, dress, posture, and hair style. If the message is carried on the product or its package, the communicator has to watch texture, scent, color, size, and shape.

> Color plays a major communication role in food preferences. When housewives sampled four cups of coffee that had been placed next to brown, blue, red, and yellow containers (all the coffee was identical, but this was unknown to the housewives), 75% felt that the coffee next to the brown container tasted too strong; nearly 85% judged the coffee next to the red container to be the richest; nearly

everyone felt that the coffee next to the blue container was mild and the coffee next to the yellow container was weak.

Choosing Media

The communicator must now select channels of communication. There are two broad types of communication channels—personal and nonpersonal.

Personal Communication Channels

In *personal communication channels*, two or more people communicate directly with each other. They might communicate face to face, person to audience, over the telephone, or even through the mail. Personal communication channels are effective because they allow for personal addressing and feedback.

Most marketers use personal communication channels. For example, company salespeople contact buyers in the target market. However, other communicators may also reach buyers about the product. These might include independent experts making statements to target buyers—consumer advocates, consumer buying guides, and others. Neighbors, friends, family members, and associates may also talk to target buyers about the product. This last channel, known as **word-of-mouth influence**, has considerable effect in many product areas.

Personal influence carries great weight for products that are expensive or risky, or for products that are highly visible. Buyers of automobiles and major appliances go beyond mass-media sources to seek the opinions of knowledgeable people.

Companies can take several steps to put personal influence channels to work for them. They can identify influential people and companies and devote extra effort to them. Companies can create opinion leaders by supplying certain people with the product on attractive terms. Companies can work through community members such as disc jockeys, class presidents, and presidents of local organizations. They can also use influential people in testimonial advertising, or develop advertising that has high "conversation value."[5]

Nonpersonal Communication Channels

Nonpersonal communication channels are media that carry messages without personal contact or feedback. They include mass and selective media, atmospheres, and events. *Mass and selective media* consist of print media (newspapers, magazines, direct mail), electronic media (radio, television), and display media (billboards, signs, posters). Mass media are aimed at large, often unsegmented audiences; selective media are aimed at smaller, selected audiences. *Atmospheres* are designed environments that create or reinforce the buyer's leanings toward consumption of the product. Thus lawyers' offices and banks are designed to communicate confidence and other qualities that might be valued by the clients.[6] *Events* are designed occurrences that communicate messages to target audiences. Public relations departments arrange news conferences or grand openings to communicate with an audience.

Nonpersonal communication affects buyers directly. In addition, mass media often helps to initiate more personal communication. Mass communication affects attitudes and behavior through a two-step, flow-of-communication process. "Ideas often flow from radio and print to opinion leaders and from these to the less active sections of the population."[7] This two-step flow means the effect of mass media is not as direct, powerful, and automatic as one might think. Rather, **opinion leaders**, people whose product opinions are sought by others, step between the mass media and their audiences. The opinion leaders are more exposed to mass media, and they carry messages to people who are less exposed to media.

The two-step flow concept challenges the notion that people's buying decisions are affected by a "trickle-down" of opinions and information from higher social classes. Since people mostly interact with others in their own social class, they pick up their fashion opinions and other ideas from people like themselves who are opinion leaders. The two-step flow concept also suggests that mass communicators should direct their messages directly to opinion leaders, letting them carry the message to others. Thus pharmaceutical firms first try to promote their new drugs to the most influential doctors.

Selecting the Message Source

The message's impact on the audience is affected by how the audience views the sender. Messages delivered by highly credible sources are more persuasive. Pharmaceutical companies want doctors to tell consumers about their products' benefits because doctors are very credible. Marketers hire well-known actors and athletes to deliver their messages.

What factors make a source credible? The three factors most often found are expertise, trustworthiness, and likability.[8] **Expertise** is the degree to which the communicator appears to have the authority needed to back the claim. Doctors, scientists, and professors rank high on expertise in their fields. **Trustworthiness** is related to how objective and honest the source appears to be. Friends are trusted more than salespople. **Likability** is how attractive the source is to the audience. People like sources who are open, humorous, and natural. Thus the most highly credible source would be a person who scored high on all three factors.[9]

Collecting Feedback

After sending the message, the communicator must research its effect on the target audience. This involves asking the target audience whether they remember the message, how many times they saw it, what points they recall, how they felt about the message, and their past and present attitudes toward the product and company. The communicator would also like to measure behavior resulting from the message, such as how many people bought the product and talked to others about it.

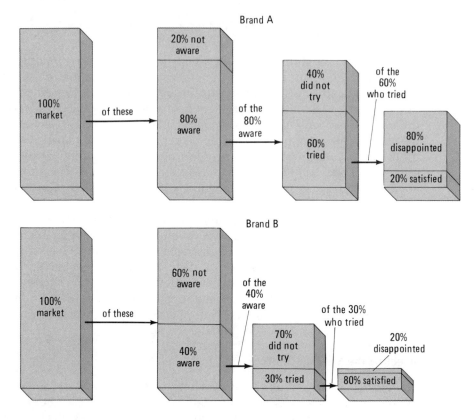

FIGURE 15-4
Current Consumer States for Two Brands

Figure 15-4 shows an example of feedback measurement. Looking at brand A, we find that 80% of the total market are aware of brand A, 60% of those who are aware have tried it, and only 20% of those who have tried it are satisfied. This suggests that the communication program is creating awareness, but that the product fails to give consumers what they expect. On the other hand, only 40% of the total market are aware of brand B, only 30% of those aware have tried it, but 80% of those who have tried it are satisfied. In this case, the communication program needs to be stronger to take advantage of the brand's power to obtain satisfaction.

Setting the Total Promotion Budget and Mix

We have looked at the steps in planning and sending communications to a target audience. But how does the company decide on (1) the total promotion budget, and (2) its division among the major promotional tools to create the promotion mix? We will now look at these questions.

Setting the Total Promotion Budget

One of the hardest marketing decisions facing companies is how much to spend on promotion. John Wanamaker, the department store magnate, said: "I know that half of my advertising is wasted, but l don't know which half. I spent $2 million for advertising, and I don't know if that is half enough or twice too much."

Thus it is not surprising that industries and companies vary greatly in how much they spend on promotion. Promotion spending may be 20 to 30% of sales in the cosmetics industry and only 5 to 10% in the industrial machinery industry.

Within a given industry, low- and high-spending companies can be found. Ford Canada, with sales over $13 billion, spends about $24 million on advertising. Chrysler Canada, with sales of $7 billion, spends about $21 million on advertising. Chrysler's larger expenditures as a percentage of sales are part of the companies' efforts to gain market share.

How do companies decide on their promotion budget? We will look at four common methods used to set the total budget for advertising.

Affordable Method

Many companies use the *affordable method*. They set the promotion budget at what they think the company can afford. One executive explained this method as follows: "Why, it's simple. First, I go upstairs to the controller and ask how much they can afford to give this year. He says a million and a half. Later, the boss comes to me and asks how much we should spend and I say 'Oh, about a million and a half.' "[10]

This method of setting budgets completely ignores the effect of promotion on sales volume. It leads to an uncertain annual promotion budget, which makes long-range market planning difficult.

Percentage-of-Sales Method

Many companies use the *percentage-of-sales method*, setting their promotion budget at a certain percentage of current or forecasted sales. Alternatively, they can budget a percentage of the sales price. Automobile companies usually budget a fixed percentage for promotion based on the planned car price. Oil companies set the budget at some fraction of a cent for each gallon of gasoline sold under their label.

A number of advantages are claimed for this method. First, the percentage-of-sales method means that promotion spending is likely to vary with what the company can "afford." Second, this method helps management to think about the relationship between promotion spending, selling price, and profit per unit. Third, this method creates competitive stability because competing firms tend to spend about the same percent of their sales on promotion.

In spite of these advantages, the percentage-of-sales method has little to justify it. It uses poor logic in viewing sales as the cause of promotion rather than as the result. As budget is based on availability of funds rather than on opportunities, it prevents the increased spending sometimes needed to turn around falling sales. Because the budget varies with year-to-year sales, long-range planning is difficult. Finally, the method does not provide any basis for choosing the specific percentage, except what has been done in the past or what competitors are doing.

Competitive-Parity Method

Some companies use the *competitive-parity method*, setting their promotion budgets to match competitors' outlays. They watch competitors' advertising, or get industry promotion spending estimates from publications or trade associations, and set their budgets based on the industry average.

Two arguments support this method. One is that competitors' budgets represent the collective wisdom of the industry. The other is that spending the same amount as competitors do helps prevent promotion wars.

Neither argument is valid. There are no grounds for believing that the competition has a better idea of what a company should be spending on promotion. Companies differ greatly, and each has its own special promotion needs. In addition, there is no evidence that budgets based on competitive parity prevent promotion wars.

Objective-and-Task Method

Using the *objective-and-task method*, marketers develop their promotion budget by (1) defining specific objectives, (2) determining the tasks that must be performed to achieve these objectives, and (3) estimating the costs of performing these tasks. The sum of these costs is the proposed promotion budget.

This is the most logical budget-setting method.[11] It makes management spell out its assumptions about the relationship between dollars spent and promotion results. However, it is also the most difficult method. It is often hard to figure out which specific task will achieve specific objectives. For example, suppose a company wants 95% awareness for its new product in the target market during a six-month introductory period. What specific advertising messages and media schedule would be needed to attain this objective? Management should think about such questions even though they are difficult to answer. With the objective-and-task method, the company sets its promotion budget based on what it wants to accomplish with promotion. The overall answer to how large the promotion budget should be depends on where the company's products are in their life cycles, how much they differ from competing products, whether they are routinely needed or have to be "sold," and other factors.

Setting the Promotion Mix

The *promotion mix* is the specific mix of advertising, personal selling, sales promotion, and publicity a company uses to pursue its advertising and marketing objectives. Companies within the same industry may differ widely in how they design their promotion mixes. Avon spends most of its promotion funds on personal selling while Revlon spends heavily on advertising. In selling vacuum cleaners, Electrolux spends heavily on a door-to-door salesforce, while Hoover relies more on advertising. Thus it is possible to achieve a given sales level with various mixes of advertising, personal selling, sales promotion, and publicity.

Companies are always looking for ways to improve promotion by replacing one promotion tool with a more economical one. Many companies have replaced some field sales activity with telephone sales and direct mail. Other companies have increased their sales promotion spending in relation to advertising to gain quicker sales.

Designing the promotion mix is even more complex when one tool must be used to promote another. Thus when McDonald's decides to run Million Dollar Sweepstakes in its fast-food outlets (a sales promotion), it has to run ads to inform the public. When General Mills uses a consumer advertising/sales promotion campaign to back a new cake mix, it has to set aside money to promote this campaign to the resellers to win their support.

Many factors influence the marketer's choice of promotion tools. We will now look at these factors.

Nature of Each Promotion Tool

Each promotion tool—advertising, personal selling, sales promotion, and publicity — has unique characteristics and costs. Marketers have to understand these characteristics in selecting the tools.

Advertising

Because of the many forms and uses of advertising, it is hard to generalize about its unique qualities as a part of the promotion mix. Yet the following qualities can be noted:[12]

It is public.   *Advertising's public nature suggests that the product is standard and legitimate. Because many people see ads for the product, buyers know that their motives for purchasing the product will be publicly understood.*

It is pervasive.   *Advertising enables the seller to repeat a message many times. It lets the buyer receive and compare the messages of various competitors. Large-scale advertising by a seller says something positive about the seller's size, popularity, and success.*

It is expressive.   *Advertising lets the company dramatize its products through the artful use of print, sound, and color.*

It is impersonal.   *Advertising cannot be as persuasive as a company salesperson. The audience does not feel that it has to pay attention or respond. Advertising is only able to carry on a one-way communication with the audience.*

On the one hand, advertising can be used to build up a long-term image for a product (such as Coca-Cola ads), and on the other, to trigger quick sales (as when Eaton's advertises a weekend sale). Advertising can reach masses of geographically spread out buyers at a low cost per exposure. Certain forms of advertising, such as TV advertising, require a large budget; other forms, such as newspaper advertising, can be done on a small budget.

Personal selling

Personal selling is the most effective tool at certain stages of the buying process, particularly in building up a buyer's preference, conviction, and action. The reason is that personal selling, as compared with advertising, has three unique qualities:[13]

It is personal.   *Personal selling involves personal interaction between two or more people. Each person can observe the other's needs and characteristics up close and make quick adjustments.*

It creates a relationship.   *Personal selling lets all kinds of relationships spring up, ranging from a matter-of-fact selling relationship to a deep personal friendship. The effective salesperson keeps the customer's interests at heart in order to build a long-term relationship.*

Personal selling draws a response from a consumer and may make a consumer more ready to try a new product, such as a computer.

James Hertel

It leads to a response. With personal selling, the buyer feels a greater need to listen and respond, even if the response is a polite "thank you."

These unique qualities come at a cost. Personal selling is the company's most expensive promotion tool, costing Canadian companies an average of over $150 a sales call.[14]

Sales promotion

Although sales promotion includes a wide assortment of tools—coupons, contests, premiums, and others—these tools have three unique characteristics:

They get attention. They attract consumers and provide information that may lead the consumer to the product.

They provide an incentive to buy. They provide some inducement or contribution that gives value to the consumer.

They invite quick response. They include a reward for quick consumer response.

Companies use sales promotion tools to create a stronger and quicker response. Sales promotion can be used to dramatize product offers and to boost sagging sales. Sales promotion effects are usually short-lived, however, and are not effective in building long-run brand preference.

Publicity

Publicity's appeal is based on its three unique qualities:

It is believable. News stories and features seem more real and believable to readers than ads.

It catches buyers. Publicity can reach many prospects who may avoid salespeople and advertisement. The message gets to the buyers as news rather than as a sales-directed communication.

It is dramatic. Like advertising, publicity can dramatize a company or product.

Marketers tend to underuse publicity or use it as an afterthought. Yet a well-thought-out publicity campaign used along with the other promotion mix elements can be very effective and much less costly.

Factors in Setting the Promotion Mix

Companies consider many factors when developing their promotion mixes. We will now look at these factors.

Type of Product/Market

The importance of the different promotion tools varies between consumer and industrial markets. The differences are shown in Figure 15-5. Consumer goods

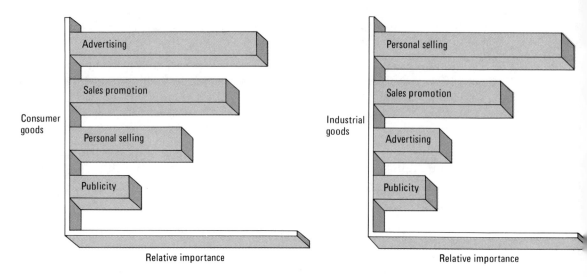

FIGURE 15-5
Relative Importance of Promotion Tools in Consumer Versus Industrial Markets

companies usually put more of their funds in advertising, followed by sales promotion, personal selling, and then publicity. Industrial goods companies put most of their funds in personal selling, followed by sales promotion, advertising, and publicity. In general, personal selling is more heavily used with expensive and risky goods and in markets with fewer and larger sellers.

Although advertising is less important than sales calls in industrial marketing, it still plays an important role. Advertising can build product awareness and knowledge, develop sales leads, and reassure buyers. Advertising's role in industrial marketing is shown dramatically in a McGraw-Hill ad (see Figure 15-6). With advertising, most of the statements the buyer makes in the ad can be prevented.

Similarly, personal selling can strongly reinforce a consumer goods marketing effort. It is not simply the case that "salesmen put products on shelves and advertising takes them off." Well-trained consumer goods salespeople can sign up more dealers to carry the brand, convince them to give the brand more shelf space, and urge them to use special displays and promotions.

Push Versus Pull Strategy

The promotion mix is heavily affected by whether the company chooses a push or a pull strategy. The two strategies are contrasted in Figure 15-7. A *push strategy* calls for using the salesforce and trade promotion to push the product through the channels. The producer promotes the product to wholesalers, the wholesalers promote the product to retailers, and the retailers promote the product to consumers.[15] A *pull strategy* calls for spending a lot of money on advertising and consumer promotion to build up consumer demand. If effective,

FIGURE 15-6
Advertising has a Role to Play in Industrial Selling

FIGURE 15-7
Push versus Pull Strategy

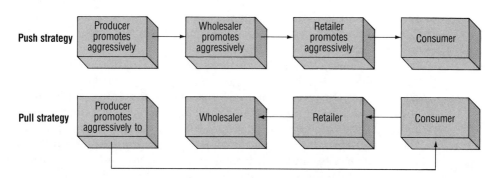

consumers will ask their retailers for the product, the retailers will ask the wholesalers for the product, and the wholesalers will ask the producers for the product.

Some small industrial goods companies use only push strategies; some direct marketing companies use only pull. Most large companies use some combination of push and pull. For example, Procter & Gamble uses mass-media advertising to pull its products, and a large salesforce and trade promotions to push its products through the channels.

Buyer Readiness Stage

Promotional tools vary in their effects at different stages of *buyer readiness*. In the awareness and knowledge stages, advertising, along with publicity, plays a more important role than "cold calls" from salespeople. Customer liking, preference, and conviction are more affected by personal selling, followed closely by advertising. Finally, closing the sale is mostly done with sales calls and sales promotion. Given its high costs, personal selling should clearly focus on the later stages of the customer buying process.

Product Life-Cycle Stage

The effects of different promotion tools also vary with stages of the product life cycle. In the introduction stage, advertising and publicity are good for producing high awareness, and sales promotion is useful in promoting early trial. Personal selling must be used to convince the trade to carry the product.

In the growth stage, advertising and publicity continue to be powerful, while sales promotion can be reduced because fewer incentives are needed.

In the mature stage, sales promotion again becomes important relative to advertising. Buyers know the brands and advertising is needed only to remind them.

In the decline stage, advertising is kept at a reminder level, publicity is dropped, and salespeople give the product only a little attention. Sales promotion, however, might continue to be strong.[16]

Responsibility for Marketing Communications Planning

Members of the marketing department often have different views on how to split the promotion budget. For example, a sales manager might prefer to hire two more salespeople than spend $100 000 on a single television commercial. The public relations manager may feel that he or she can do wonders with some money shifted from advertising to publicity.

In the past, companies left these decisions to different people. No one was responsible for thinking through the roles of the various promotion tools and coordinating the promotion mix. Today, companies are moving toward appointing a marketing communications director who is responsible for all of the company's marketing communications. This director develops policies for using the different promotion tools, keeps track of all promotion spending by product, tool, and results, and coordinates the promotion mix activities when major campaigns take place.

Summary

Promotion is one of the four major elements of the company's marketing mix. The main promotion tools — advertising, sales promotion, publicity, and personal selling — work together to achieve the company's communication objectives.

In preparing marketing communications, the communicator has to understand the nine elements of any communication process: sender, receiver, encoding, decoding, message, media, response, feedback, and noise. The communicator's first task is to identify the target audience and its characteristics. Next, the communicator has to define the response sought, whether it be awareness, knowledge, liking, preference, conviction, or purchase. Then a message should be constructed containing an effective content, structure, and format. Media must be selected, both for personal communication and nonpersonal communication. The message must be delivered by a credible source — someone who is an expert, trustworthy, and likable. Finally, the communicator must watch how much of the market becomes aware of the product, tries it and is satisfied in the process.

The company has to decide how much to spend for promotion. The most popular approaches are to spend what the company can afford, use a percentage of sales, base promotion on competitors' spending, or base promotion on an analysis and costing of the communication objectives and tasks.

The company has to split the promotion budget among the major tools to create the promotion mix. Companies are guided by the characteristics of each promotion tool, the type of product/market, whether the company needs a push or a pull strategy, the buyer's readiness stage, and the product life-cycle stage. The different promotion activities require strong coordination for maximum impact.

Questions for Discussion

1. Apply the four major tools in the marketing communication mix to your college or university.
2. How would the six buyer readiness states relate to your last purchase of a soft drink?
3. What type of message content is used by the following marketers? (a) Bell Canada, (b) Bic Disposable Razors, (c) L'Oreal Hair Coloring, (d) The United Way, and (e) Black & Decker.
4. What major types of communication channels can an organization utilize? When should each be used?
5. Discuss the three factors that make a source credible and offer an example of each.
6. How might a company set its promotion budget? Discuss the advantages of each approach.

7. The type of product being marketed has no relationship to the communication mix employed by the marketer. Explain.

8. Distinguish between a push and a pull strategy, offering an example of each.

Chapter 15 Key Terms

Advertising   Any paid form of nonpersonal presentation and promotion of ideas, goods, or services by an identified sponsor.

Affordable method   Setting the promotion budget at what management thinks the company can afford.

Atmospheres   Designed environments that create or reinforce the buyer's leanings toward consumption of a product.

Buyer readiness states   The stages consumers normally pass through on their way to purchase, including awareness, knowledge, liking, preference, conviction, or purchase.

Competitive-parity method   Setting the promotion budget to match competitors' outlays.

Emotional appeals   Message appeals that attempt to stir up negative or positive emotions that will motivate purchase; examples include fear, guilt, shame, love, humor, pride, and joy appeals.

Events   Designed occurrences that communicate messages to target audiences, such as news conferences, grand openings, or others.

Mass and selective media   Print media (newspapers, magazines, direct mail), electronic media (radio, television), and display media (billboards, signs, posters) aimed at large, unsegmented audiences (mass media) or at selected audiences (selective media).

Moral appeals   Message appeals that are directed to the audience's sense of what is right and proper.

Nonpersonal communication channels   Media that carry messages without personal contact or feedback, including mass and selective media, atmospheres, and events.

Objective-and-task method   Setting the promotion budget at a certain percentage of current or forecasted sales, or a percentage of the sales price.

Percentage-of-sales method   Setting the promotion budget at a certain percentage of current or forecasted sales, or as a percentage of the sales price.

Personal communication channels   Channels through which two or more people communicate directly with each other, including face to face, person to audience, over the telephone, or through the mail.

Personal selling   Oral presentation in a conversation with one or more prospective purchasers for the purpose of making sales.

Promotion mix   The specific mix of advertising, personal selling, sales promotion, and publicity that a company uses to pursue its advertising and marketing objectives.

Publicity   Nonpersonal stimulation of demand for a product, service, or business unit by planting commercially significant news about it in a published medium, or obtaining favorable presentation of it, on radio, television, or stage that is not paid for by the sponsor.

Pull strategy   A promotion strategy that calls for spending a lot on advertising and consumer promotion to build up consumer demand; if successful, consumers will ask their retailers for the product, the retailers will ask the wholesalers, and the wholesalers will ask the producers.

Push strategy   A promotion strategy that calls for using the salesforce and trade promotion to push the product through the channels; the producer promotes the product to wholesalers, the wholesalers promote to retailers, and the retailers promote to consumers.

Rational appeals   Message appeals that relate to the audience's self-interest and show that the product will produce the claimed benefits; examples include appeals of product quality, economy, value, or performance.

Sales promotion   Short-term incentives to encourage purchase or sales of a product or service.

Cases for Chapter 15

Promoting Products: Advertising, Sales Promotion, and Publicity

Chapter Objectives

After reading this chapter, you should be able to:
1. Define the roles of advertising, sales promotion, and publicity in the promotion mix.
2. Describe the major decisions in developing an advertising program.
3. Discuss how sales promotion campaigns are developed and implemented.
4. Explain how companies use publicity to communicate with their publics.

Three of the leading advertisers in Canada are breweries—Carling O'Keefe, Labatt's, and Molson. There are some obvious reasons why they spend about $88 million on advertising each year — most of the other marketing mix variables are fixed or controlled by government, and market share is a major objective of the game in this $4 billion industry—but what is interesting is the message.

Faced with mature markets and products that are usually sold for the same price on the basis of limited distribution (in most provinces through government outlets), managers in the beer business rely extensively on advertising to obtain and hold market share. Even here they are threatened by various provincial governments who restrict the kind of advertising allowed (e.g., Quebec) or limit the advertising (e.g., British Columbia). In spite of this, however, advertising remains the major weapon on the brewery battleground.

In their overriding objective of maintaining, or preferably, gaining market share, all three companies have launched competitive brands in the three main segments, light, regular, and premium—and, in some cases, offer more than one brand in a particular segment. The most frequent appeals used are designed to attract consumers with a life style or image portrayal that is consistent with their own. Perhaps the appeals are more appropriately described as a presentation to market segments of idealized life styles or self-images. Here are some examples:

- MOLSON EXPORT—"Like an old friend." The boys get together for some type of activity and then enjoy an Export or two.

- MOLSON GOLDEN — "The with-it crowd." The trendy young set are at the disco or around the pool making quips and enjoying a Golden.

- LABATT'S 50 — "Cutting out and going fishing." In this case it's just me and the boys and our 50.

- LABATT'S BLUE — "It's time to call for the Blue." People across Canada enjoying life with a Blue.

- CARLING O'KEEFE'S CARLSBERG—"Me and my friends." After helping friends move, everyone has a Carlsberg.

The list could go on but most of the themes have a common thread — an enjoyable social setting with people and scenes the potential customer may relate to. Who will win the battle for market share is dependent on a number of variables, but obviously life style advertising is the primary competitive weapon. To sell a beer in the Canadian market good taste just isn't enough; the appeal must touch some respon-sive chord. This means positioning the product in the consumer's mind. To carve out market share, the brewers need a creative mass-pro-motion technique. All three firms engage in the sponsoring of sports and other recreational events. Their total promotion spending, includ-ing advertising, is estimated at $400 million annually.[1]

Companies must do more than make good products — they must inform consumers of product benefits, and carefully position products in consumers' minds. To do this they must skillfully use the mass-promotion tools of adver-tising, sales promotion, and publicity. These tools are examined in this chapter.

Advertising

We define advertising as follows:

> *Advertising is any paid form of nonpersonal presentation and promotion of ideas, goods, or services by an identified sponsor.*

In 1987, advertising ran up a bill of over $7 billion.[2] The spenders included not only business firms, but museums, professionals, and social organizations that advertise their causes to various target publics. In fact, the largest adver-tising spender is a nonprofit organization — the Canadian federal government and two provincial governments, Ontario and Quebec, are among the top 25 advertisers in Canada.

Table 16-1 lists the top ten advertisers in 1986. Procter & Gamble is the leading business spender with $51 million, or 4.8% of its total sales. The other major spenders are found in the auto, food, beer, and tobacco industries. Gen-erally, advertising as a percentage of sales is low in the auto industry and high in food, drugs, toiletries, and cosmetics, followed by gum, candy, and soaps.

However, what Table 16-1 does not show is the tremendous spillover of advertising from the United States. Companies like Procter & Gamble, Kraft, and General Motors are entirely owned by U.S. parent companies. These, and other heavy advertisers, benefit from U.S. advertising that "spills over" into the Canadian market. Seventy percent of the top 50 commercial advertisers in Canada are foreign-owned and sell similar products in both Canada and the U.S.[3] The reason for the spillover is that most Canadians have access to U.S. television stations because they live close to the border and/or receive U.S.

TABLE 16-1
Top Ten National Advertisers in 1986

Rank	Company	Total advertising (millions)	Total sales (millions)	Advertising as a percent of sales
1	Government of Canada	$64	—	—
2	Procter & Gamble	51	$1 060	4.8
3	John Labatt	38	3 581	1.1
4	The Molson Companies	32	2 006	1.6
5	General Motors	27	18 532	.2
6	Unilever	27	890	3.0
7	Government of Ontario	26	—	—
8	The Thompson Group	24	1 030	2.3
9	RJ Reynolds	22	567	3.9
10	McDonald's Restaurants	21	1 087	1.9

Source: "Top National Advertisers 1986," *Marketing*, March 20 1987, p. 14. All advertising figures represent advertising expenditures in media measured in Canada by Media Measurement Services. The figures do not include media overflow from the United States, nor do they include retail or direct buys in broadcast. Sales figures from *Corporate Canada 500*, Canadian Business, June 1987.

stations on cable (about 64% of Canadian households have cable TV; about 43% have converters allowing them to receive up to 30 channels).[4] Many Canadian cable systems are now using a technique called simulcast, which reduces spillover by broadcasting only Canadian commercials when a television show is broadcast at the same time on both a Canadian and a U.S. station. However, a substantial number of Canadians watch U.S. television and view U.S. ads for many products that are sold in Canada. The same pattern holds true for radio. Probably the best example of the benefits of spillover was the introduction of Budweiser, a well-known American beer. It achieved a 6% national market share within a few months of being launched, and Labatt's could not keep up with demand.[5] Both Budweiser and Miller are among the top ten selling brands in Canada.

In regard to magazines, Canada is the largest foreign market for U.S. magazine publishers, accounting for 72% of the sales (worth over $390 million annually) of periodicals exported by the U.S.[6] For example, *National Geographic* is the third best-selling periodical in Canada, and *Penthouse, Woman's Day*, and *Family Circle* all have circulations of more than 250 000 in Canada.[7] Again, U.S. advertisers whose products are sold in both countries would benefit from ads in these magazines. Canadian magazine publishers have the advantages of Bill C-58, which prohibits the deduction for tax purposes of advertising expenditures made in media unless the media are at least 75% Canadian-owned and have at least 80% Canadian content.[8] While this bill has clearly helped Canadian consumer magazines, it has not stopped the sizeable U.S. magazine spillover in Canada.[9]

Media decisions for companies operating in Canada are complicated because of the spillover from the U.S. and the fragmented audiences for particular media. Some markets are also difficult to reach because of lack of media alternatives, differences in language, and local market conditions. All told, advertising in Canada requires special consideration from those involved in the decision.

Advertising takes a wide variety of forms and may be used to achieve many

EXHIBIT 16-1
How Does an Advertising Agency Work?

An advertising agency is an organization of marketing, creative, and media people involved in the creation and placement of advertising. In Canada, many of the large advertising agencies are subsidiaries of U.S. parent firms. Companies like J. Walter Thompson, Ogilvy and Mather, McCann-Erickson, Young and Rubicam, and Leo Burnett have Canadian operations entirely owned by the U.S. parent. In many cases, the Canadian subsidiary will handle the Canadian advertising while the U.S. parent agency will handle the U.S. advertising to allow for consistency of advertising messages between the two countries. It has been estimated that close to 40% of the accounts handled by U.S.-owned agencies in Canada are also handled by the parent company.

Even companies with a strong advertising department will use advertising agencies. The specialists at agencies can often perform advertising tasks better than the company's staff. Agencies also bring an outside point of view to solving the company's problems, along with considerable experience from working with different clients and situations. Agencies are paid from media discounts and cost the firm very little. Since the firm can cancel its agency contract at any time, an agency works hard to do a good job.

Advertising agencies usually have four departments: **creative**, which develops and produces ads; **media**, which selects media and places ads; **research**, which studies audience characteristics and wants; and **business**, which handles the agency's business activities. Each account is supervised by an account executive, and people in each department are assigned to work on one or more accounts.

Agencies often attract new business through their reputation or size. Generally, however, a client invites a few agencies to make a presentation for its business and then selects one of them.

Ad agencies are paid in the form of commissions and fees. Typically, the agency receives 15% of the media cost as a rebate. Suppose the agency buys $60 000 of magazine space for a client. The magazine bills the advertising agency for $51 000 ($60 000 less different goals. Advertising dollars go into many media: magazines and news-papers, radio and television, outdoor, direct mail, and others. In addition, advertising has many uses: to build an an organization's image, build a brand, announce a sale, or support an idea or cause.

Organizations handle advertising in different ways. In small companies, advertising might be handled by someone in the sales department. Large com-panies set up advertising departments, whose job is to set the advertising budget, work with the ad agency, and handle direct mail advertising, dealer displays, and other advertising not done by the agency. Most large companies use an outside advertising agency because it offers several advantages (see Exhibit 16-1).

15%), and the agency bills the client for $60 000, keeping the $9000 commission. If the client bought space directly from the magazine, it would have paid $60 000 because these commissions are only paid to recognized advertising agencies.

Both advertisers and agencies are becoming unhappy with the commission system. Larger advertisers complain that they pay more than smaller ones for the same services simply because they place more advertising. Advertisers also believe that the commission system drives agencies away from low-cost media and short advertising campaigns. Agen-cies are unhappy because they perform extra services for an account without getting any more pay. The trend today in Canada is toward paying either a straight fee or a combi-nation commission and fee.

Other trends are also hitting the advertising agency business. Full-service agencies are facing more competition from limited-service agencies specializing in media buying, advertising copy writing, or advertising production. Business managers in agencies are getting more power and demanding more profit-mindedness from the creative staff. Some advertisers have opened in-house agencies, thus quitting a longstanding relation-ship with their agency.

The introduction of fines or imprisonment for false or misleading advertising has resulted in some changes for advertising agencies. Many large agencies now have at least one person on staff whose job is to be familiar with all the laws and regulations governing advertising and to advise the agency accordingly. Most advertising in Canada is scruti-nized, monitored, or regulated by some organization other than the advertiser and the agency. Canada has some extremely strict requirements for advertising that must be considered before any commercials are aired.

Sources: Peter T. Zarry, "Advertising and Marketing Communication in Canada," in Donald N. Thompson and David S.R. Leighton, eds., *Canadian Marketing: Problems and Perspectives* (Toronto: Wiley, 1973), p. 241; Randy Scotland, "Commission System is Now on the Skids," *Marketing*, March 10 1986, p. 1, 7; "Canada's Top 100 Ad Agencies," *Marketing*, December 15 1986, p. 21-25; and Jennifer Wells, "Agencies Move From Commissions to Fees Gaining Momen-tum," *Financial Post*, March 9 1987, p.39.

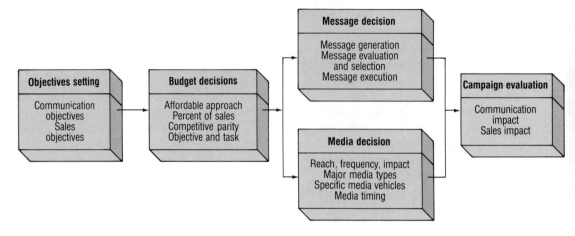

FIGURE 16-1
Major Decisions in Advertising

Major Decisions in Advertising

Marketing management must make five important decisions in developing an advertising program. These decisions are listed in Figure 16-1 and discussed below.

Setting Objectives

The first step in developing an advertising program is to set the advertising objectives. These objectives are based on past decisions about the target market, positioning, and marketing mix. The marketing positioning and mix strategy defines the job that advertising must do in the total marketing program.

Many communication and sales objectives can be set for advertising. Advertising objectives can be classified as to whether their aim is to inform, persuade, or remind. Table 16-2 lists examples of these objectives.

Informative advertising is used heavily when introducing a new product category, where the objective is to build primary demand. Thus the yogurt industry first had to inform consumers of yogurt's nutritional benefits and many uses. When Black & Decker took over the houseware products of Canadian General Electric, the company had to inform Canadian consumers that Black and Decker would maintain the reputation and quality of the brands. The first phase of the $15 million marketing campaign resulted in 80% of Canadians recognizing Black & Decker as a leader in small appliances.[10]

Persuasive advertising becomes more important as competition increases, and when a company's objective is to build selective demand. For example, the Fisher-Price ad in Figure 16-2 (p. 378) attempts to persuade an audience of parents of babies that the new product line, the Activity Center, enhances a baby's learning skills.

TABLE 16-2
Possible Advertising Objectives

Informative advertising	
Telling the market about a new product	Describing available services
Suggesting new uses for a product	Correcting false impressions
Informing the market of a price change	Reducing consumers' fears
Explaining how the product works	Building a company image
Persuasive advertising	
Building brand preference	Persuading customers to purchase now
Encouraging switching to your brand	Persuading customers to receive a sales call
Changing customer's perception of product attributes	
Reminder advertising	
Reminding consumers that the product may be needed in the near future	Keeping it in their minds during off seasons
Reminding them where to buy it	Maintaining its top-of-mind awareness

Some persuasive advertising has become *comparison advertising*, which compares one brand directly or indirectly to one or more other brands. In its classic comparison campaign, Avis positioned itself against Hertz, the market leader by claiming, ''We're number two, but we try harder.'' Comparison advertising is used in Canada for such products as deodorants, toothpastes, detergents, automobiles, and tires.[11]

Reminder advertising is important for mature products, to keep the consumer thinking about the product. The purpose of expensive Coca-Cola ads in magazines is to remind people about Coca-Cola, not to inform or persuade them.

Budget Decision

After setting advertising objectives, the company can next set its advertising budget for each product. The role of advertising is to affect demand for a product. The company wants to spend the amount needed to achieve the sales goal. Four common methods for setting the advertising budget were discussed in Chapter 15.

Message Decision

Given the advertising objectives and budget, management has to build a creative strategy. Advertisers go through three steps: message generation, message evaluation and selection, and message execution.

Message Generation

Creative people use different methods to find ideas for advertising messages. Many creative people start by talking to consumers, dealers, experts, and com-

Fisher-Price introduces data processing for the beginner.

What's up? What's down? What's in or out? What's hard, soft, loud or round?

Your baby is likely to process more information about the world in this first year than in any year after. Because a baby is the supreme beginner: curious,

Activity Center

open-minded, ambitious and ready to enjoy every new experience.

That's why Fisher-Price activity toys are so much fun. They satisfy that natural urge to know.

Our Activity Center gives babies a vivid display of buttons to press, knobs to

Turn & Learn Activity Center

turn and more. Everything they touch makes something else happen. At first it's just trial and error. But soon baby figures out that to make the bell ring, you push the red button. He doesn't know it, but he's applying the scientific method.

Babies also learn new ways to use their hands. On our Turn & Learn Activity Center there's a rabbit that

Floating Family

springs into motion, a phone dial, beads to slide. Each action requires a different

Bath Activity Center

move. A push of the palm, fitting one finger into a circle, grasping with thumb and forefinger.

Both these toys have

unbreakable mirrors, too, where a baby can discover the most marvelous thing of all—her own smile.

Baby's First Blocks

At bathtime, there's a surprising world of water to learn about, and our Bath Activity Center shows them how water pours or squirts or makes a wheel revolve. More delightful data for a growing baby.

Other Fisher-Price activity toys teach them colors and sizes and sounds and shapes. And when you watch your baby at play, you can almost hear the wheels go round in that little head. The eyes light up, the smile appears and the laugh happens.

Data processing has never been so much fun.

Crib & Playpen Toys by Fisher-Price.

Courtesy Fisher-Price Canada

Fisher-Price identified a market segment of parents who were concerned about their babies' development. The result was the Activity Center.

Your friends in the right places.

When you land in Calgary, stay right where you are.

The Chateau Airport is the only hotel connected to the airport terminal. You'll enjoy this modern sophisticated hotel with its complete fitness centre including a pool, sauna and whirlpool. And you'll sleep tight in the sound-proofed rooms.

At the Chateau Airport, our staff including Albin Stroniarz, maintenance dept., take care of all the details and surround you with warmth and friendliness.

Stay with friends at CP Hotels in Banff, Calgary, Edmonton, Halifax, Lake Louise, Mirabel, Montebello, Montréal, Peterborough, Québec, St. Andrews, Thunder Bay, Toronto, Trois-Rivières, Victoria, Frankfurt, Hamburg, Bremen (Spring 1985), Jerusalem and Tiberias.

CP Hotels [◀
Chateau Airport

2001 Airport Road N.E., Calgary International Airport, Calgary, Alberta

Reservations: 1-800-268-9411 Ontario and Québec 1-800-268-9420 Toronto 361-1400 Or your Travel Agent

CP and [◀ are registered trade marks of Canadian Pacific Limited

Courtesy CP Hotels

CP Hotels uses persuasive advertising very effectively in its campaign showing its welcoming atmosphere for business clients.

FIGURE 16-2
Advertising Creating a Position for a New Product

petitors. Other people try to imagine consumers using the product, and determine the benefits consumers seek when buying and using it. Generally, advertisers create many possible messages, only a few of which will be used.

Message Evaluation and Selection

The advertiser must evaluate the possible messages. Twedt suggests that messages should have three characteristics.[12] First, the message must make the product more desirable or interesting to consumers. Second, it must tell how the product is better than competing brands. Finally, the message must be believable. It may be hard to make the message believable as many consumers doubt the truth of advertising in general. One recent study found that, on average, consumers rate advertising messages as "somewhat unbelievable."[13]

In Canada, the advertiser must also consider whether the message is suitable for both English and French audiences. Literal translations of messages from one language to the other may not be suitable. For example, when the English message for Budweiser — "This Bud's for you" — was tested in Quebec, the response was very negative. As a result, the English slogan was replaced with "toute une bière," which roughly translates as "one hell of a beer."[14]

Message Execution

The message's impact depends not only on what is said, but also on how it is said. The advertiser has to put the message across in a way that wins the target market's attention and interest.

The advertiser usually prepares a copy strategy statement describing the objective, content, support, and tone of the desired ad. Creative people then must find a style, tone, words, and format for executing the message. Any message can be presented in different execution styles, such as:

Slice-of-life   This shows one or more people using the product in a normal setting. A family seated at the dinner table might express satisfaction with Heinz Ketchup.

Life style   This shows how a product fits in with a life style. A Dairy Bureau of Canada ad shows women exercising and talks about how milk adds to a healthy, active life style.

Fantasy   This creates a fantasy around the product or its use. Revlon's first ad for Jontue showed a barefoot woman wearing a chiffon dress and coming out of an old French barn, crossing a meadow, and meeting a handsome young man on a white horse, who carries her away.

Mood or image   This builds a mood or image around the product, such as beauty, love, or serenity. No claim is made about the product except through suggestion. Many coffee ads create mood.

Musical   This shows one or more people or cartoon characters singing a song about the product. Many cola ads have used this format.

Personality symbol   *This creates a character that represents the product. The character might be animated (Green Giant, Cap'n Crunch, Mr. Clean) or real (Robin Hood, Morris the Cat).*

Technical expertise   *This shows the company's expertise in making the product. Thus, Nabob shows that their coffee has been carefully prepared and packaged in a unique vacuum pack that preserves freshness for a year.*

Scientific evidence   *This presents survey or scientific evidence that the brand is better or better liked than one or more other brands. For years, Crest toothpaste has used scientific evidence to convince buyers that Crest is better at fighting cavities.*

Testimonial evidence   *This features a highly believable or likable source endorsing the product. It could be a celebrity like Wayne Gretzky (GWG Jeans) or Carling Bassett (C-Plus) or ordinary people saying how much they like the product.*

The advertiser must also choose a *tone* for the ad. Procter & Gamble always uses a positive tone: its ads say something very positive about the product. P&G avoids humor that might take attention away from the message. On the other hand, Volkswagen's classic ads for its famous Beetle used humor and poked fun at the car ("the Ugly Bug").

Memorable and attention-getting *words* must be found. The theme listed below on the left would have had much less impact without the creative phrasing on the right:[15]

Theme

- 7-Up is not a cola.

- Let us drive you in our bus instead of driving your car.

- Shop by turning the pages of the telephone directory.

- We don't rent as many cars, so we have to do more for our customers.

Creative Copy

- "The Uncola."

- "Take the bus, and leave the driving to us."

- "Let your fingers do the walking."

- "We're number 2, so we try harder."

Format elements such as headlines, ad size, color, and illustration will make a difference in the impact as well as the cost of an ad. A small change in the way an ad is designed can make a big difference in its effect. Larger-size ads gain more attention, although the attention may not necessarily cover their difference in cost. Full-color ads, instead of black and white, increase both ad effectiveness and ad cost.[16]

Media Decision

The advertiser must next choose advertising media to carry the advertising message. The steps are (1) deciding on reach, frequency, and impact; (2) choosing among major media types; (3) selecting specific media vehicles; and (4) deciding on media timing.

Deciding on Reach, Frequency, and Impact

To select media, the advertiser must decide which reach, frequency, and impact are needed to achieve the advertising objective:

1. *Reach*   *The advertiser must decide on reach, or how many people in the target market should be exposed to the ad campaign during the given period of time. For example, the advertiser might try to reach 70% of the target market during the first year.*

2. *Frequency*   *The advertiser must also decide on frequency, or how many times the average person in the target market should be exposed to the message. For example, the advertiser might want an average exposure frequency of three.*

3. *Impact*   *The advertiser must also decide what impact the exposure should have. Messages on television may have more impact than messages on radio because television uses sight and sound, not just sound. The same message in one magazine (say, Maclean's) may be more believable than in another (say, TV Times). For example, the advertiser may seek an impact of 1.5 where 1.0 is the impact of an ad in an average medium.*

Now suppose the advertiser's product might appeal to a market of 1 000 000 consumers. The goal is to reach 700 000 consumers (1 000 000 × 70%). Since the average consumer will receive three exposures, 2 100 000 exposures (700 000 × 3) must be bought. Since exposures of 1.5 impact are desired, a rated number of exposures of 3 150 000 (2 100 000 × 1.5) must be bought. If 1000 exposures with this impact cost $10, the advertising budget will have to be $31 500 (3150 × $10). In general, the more reach, frequency, and impact the advertiser seeks, the higher the advertising budget will have to be.

Choosing Among Major Media Types

The media planner has to know the reach, frequency, and impact of each of the major media types. The major advertising media are summarized in Table 16-3. In order of their advertising volume, the major media types are direct mail, newspapers, television, radio, outdoor, and magazines. Each medium has its advantages and limitations. Media planners consider many factors when making their media choices. The most important factors are:

1. *Target audience media habits*   *For example, radio and television are the best media for reaching teenagers.*

TABLE 16-3

Profiles of Major Media Types

Medium	Volumes in millions (1986)	Example of cost (1987)	Advantages	Limitations
Newspapers	$1500	$8700 one page, weekday *Vancouver Sun*	Flexibility; timeliness; good local market coverage; broad acceptance; high believability	Short life; poor reproduction quality; small "pass-along" audience
Television	1100	$20 500 for 30 seconds of prime time on 41 CBC stations	Combines sight, sound, and motion; appealing to the senses; high attention; high reach	High absolute cost; high clutter; fleeting exposure; less audience selectivity
Direct mail/catalogs	1600	Varies considerably	Audience selectivity; flexibility; no ad competition within the same medium; personalization	Relatively high cost; "junk mail" image
Radio	610	$7000 for 60-second slots of prime time on four Toronto stations	Mass use; high geographic and demographic selectivity; low cost	Audio presentation only; lower attention than television; non-standardized rate structures; fleeting exposure
Magazines	287	$23 400 one page, four-color, in the English edition of *Chatelaine*	High geographic and demographic selectivity; credibility and prestige; high-quality reproduction; long life; good pass-along readership	Long ad purchase lead time; some waste circulation; no guarantee of position
Outdoor	484	$72 400 for 135 billboards covering Toronto/Hamilton, Montreal, and Vancouver for one month	Flexibility; high repeat exposure; low cost; low competition	No audience selectivity; creative limitations

Note: The data in column 2 is from Ben Fiber, "Mass Media Growth Off, Further Fall Seen," *The Globe and Mail*, January 13 1987, p. B14, and does not include miscellaneous media. The data in column 3 is from Canadian Media Directors' Council Media Digest, 1986/7.

2. ***Product*** Women's dresses are best shown in color magazines, and Polaroid cameras are best demonstrated on television.

3. ***Messages*** A message announcing a major sale tomorrow will require radio or newspapers. A message with a lot of technical data might require magazines or mailings.

4. ***Cost*** Television is very expensive, while newspaper advertising costs much less. What counts is the cost per thousand exposures rather than the total cost.

Given these and other media characteristics, the media planner must decide how much of each media type to buy. For example, a firm launching a new shampoo might decide to spend $300 000 on daytime network television, $200 000 on women's magazines, and $100 000 on daily newspapers in 12 major markets.

If the company doing the advertising sold the product in both Canada and the U.S., the media planner might note how much the U.S. company was spending on advertising in the magazines that had high circulation in Canada. The planner might then consider this "spill-over" effect before making a final decision on where to spend the money in Canadian media.

Selecting Specific Media Vehicles

The media planner now chooses the best specific media vehicles. For example, if advertising is to be placed in magazines, the media planner looks up the circulation and costs of different ad sizes, color options, ad positions, and frequencies. The planner then evaluates the magazines on such factors as credibility, status, reproduction quality, editorial focus, and lead time. The media planner decides which vehicles give the best reach, frequency, and impact for the money.

Media planners compute the cost per thousand persons reached by a vehicle. If a full-page, four-color advertisement in *Maclean's* costs $19 000 and *Maclean's* readership is 650 000 people, the cost of reaching each one thousand

Specific media vehicles let potential advertisers know about their editorial climate and readership.

2.6 million Canadian consumers read Maclean's every week.

Think about it.
    Over the course of a year Maclean's offers its advertisers more than 100 million exposures.
    No other weekly newsmagazine can match us when it comes to exposing your products and services to the Canadian consumer market. And that's a fact. According to PMB '83 — the latest

We call that very decent exposure.

Canadian magazine readership survey — more Canadians read Maclean's than *any* other newsmagazine. PMB also confirms that the Canadians who read Maclean's are the people most likely to respond to your advertising message — affluent people, well-educated and aware. Have your media buyers check us out.

The medium that makes your message news.

CANADA'S WEEKLY NEWSMAGAZINE

Courtesy: Maclean's

persons is $29.20. The same advertisement in *Saturday Night* may cost $6600 but reach only 129 000 persons at a cost per thousand of $51.20. The media planner would rank each magazine by cost per thousand and initially favor those magazines with the lower cost per thousand.

The media planner must also consider the costs of producing ads for each medium. Newspaper ads may cost very little to produce, but the costs of television ads may run as high as $150 000. The media planner must add in production costs when computing the cost of using each medium.

The media planner must adjust these initial cost measures in several ways. First, the measures should be adjusted for audience quality. For a baby lotion advertisement, a magazine read by 100 000 young mothers would have a high exposure value; a magazine read by 100 000 older men would have a low exposure value. Second, the exposure value should be adjusted for audience attention. Readers of *Chatelaine*, for example, pay more attention to ads than readers of *Maclean's*. Third, the exposure value should be adjusted for the medium's editorial quality.

Deciding on Media Timing

The advertiser has to decide how to schedule the advertising over the year. Suppose sales of a product peak in December and drop off in March. The firm

EXHIBIT 16-2
The New Electronic Media

In recent years, advances in communication technology have led to some exciting new electronic media that marketers can use to reach selected target markets. Some of these new media are described here.

Telemarketing Telemarketing (telephone marketing) has become the major direct marketing tool. Telemarketing blossomed in the late 1960s with the introduction of Wide Area Telephone Service (WATS) and now generates around $7 billion sales each year in Canada. With WATS, marketers can use toll-free 800 numbers to handle customer service, or to receive orders from television ads, direct mail, or catalogs.

Cable television Today more than 64% of the Canadian population live in cable-equipped households. Cable systems allow narrow program formats such as all sports, all news, ethnic programs, arts programs, and others targeted at select segments. Advertisers can better target special market segments with cable advertising, rather than use the shotgun approach offered by network television.

Advertisers can buy space during cable programming in the same way they would using regular television. Recently, however, many new cable formats have been tried in Canada, including shopping channels—programs or channels dedicated to selling can vary its advertising to follow the seasonal pattern, to oppose the seasonal pattern, or to be the same all year. Most firms do seasonal advertising. Even with this choice, the firm still has to decide whether its advertising should come before or during a seasonal sale.

The advertiser also has to choose the pattern of the ads. *Continuity* means scheduling ads evenly within a given period. *Pulsing* means scheduling ads unevenly over the time period. Thus 52 ads could be scheduled at one per week during the year, or pulsed in several bursts. Those who favor pulsing feel that the audience will learn the message more completely and that money can be saved. Anheuser-Busch conducted research and found that Budweiser could drop advertising in a given market with no harm to sales for at least a year and a half.[17] Then the company could use a six-month burst of advertising and regain the past sales growth rate. This led Budweiser to adopt a pulsing strategy.

New Advertising Media

New communications technologies have brought about many new electronic media. The use of these new media has grown quickly, especially by direct marketers and others trying to reach special target segments. Several of these media are described in Exhibit 16-2.

goods and services. For example, the Shopping Network, The Canadian Home Shopping Club, and the Canadian Value Network are three programs that have been available to Canadians through cable television. To date, the success of these shopping programs in Canada has been mixed.

Videotext   Videotext is a two-way system that links consumers with computer data banks by cable or telephone lines. A videotext service makes up a computerized catalog of products offered by producers, retailers, banks, travel organizations, and others. Consumers use an ordinary television set that has a special keyboard device and is connected to the system by two-way cable. They sort through the catalog, compare products and prices, and place orders. Alternatively, the consumer might hook into the system by telephone using a home computer. A consumer wanting to buy a new stereo could request a list of all stereo brands in the computerized catalog, compare the brands, and order one using a charge card—all without leaving home.

These and other new electronic media are gaining an ever-greater share of advertising spending. Their importance will grow as more and more consumers discover the wonders of electronic shopping.

Sources: G. Scott Osborne, *Electronic Direct Marketing* (Englewood Cliffs, NJ: Prentice-Hall, 1984); Lawrence Strauss, *Electronic Marketing* (White Plains, NY: Knowledge Industry Publications, 1983); and Kenneth Kidd, "Getting Set to Sell Itself to Canadians," *The Toronto Star*, March 15 1987, pp. F1, F5.

Advertising Evaluation

The advertising program should regularly evaluate the communication and sales effects of advertising.

Measuring the Communication Effect

Measurement of the communication effect reveals whether an ad is communicating well. Called *copy testing*, it can be done before or after an ad is printed or broadcast. Before the ad is placed, the advertiser can show it to consumers, ask how they like it, and measure recall or attitude changes resulting from the ad. After the ad has run, the advertiser can measure how the ad affected consumer advertising recall, or product awareness, knowledge, and preference.

Measuring the Sales Effect

What sales are caused by an ad that increases brand awareness by 20% and brand preference by 10%? This sales effect of advertising is often harder to

EXHIBIT 16-3
Advertising Decisions and Public Policy

The Canadian advertiser faces regulation from five sources: federal law, provincial law, municipal law, industry codes, and media acceptance or clearing policies. The advertiser faces over 100 federal and provincial statutes regulating advertising, as well as city codes and industry codes. We will consider each in turn.

Federal laws The Competition Act covers such categories as misleading price advertising and misleading statements of fact. The Food and Drugs Act defines which drugs can and cannot be advertised and what can be said in drug advertising. The advertiser must be concerned with at least 15 federal statutes.

Provincial laws Each province has enacted its own laws dealing with advertising. Quebec probably has the most stringent laws, including a ban on all advertising intended for children under 13 years, and language (French and English) specifications for ads. The provinces have a variety of laws concerning liquor advertising. Prince Edward Island bans liquor advertising in all media; Ontario has banned "life style" beer and wine advertising.

City/municipal laws Various cities and municipalities have banned tobacco and liquor advertising in bus shelters and transit vehicles.

Industry codes The advertising industry has developed the Canadian Code of Advertising Standards, which defines acceptable advertising practices. The purpose of this self-regulation is to set and maintain standards of honesty in advertising.

measure than the communication effect. Sales are affected by many factors besides advertising, such as product features, price, and availability.

One way to measure the sales effect of advertising is to compare past sales with past advertising expenditures. Another way is through experiments. Du Pont was one of the first companies to use advertising experiments.[18] Du Pont's paint department divided 56 sales territories into high, average, and low market share territories. In one-third of the group, Du Pont spent the normal amount for advertising; in another third, two and one-half times the normal amount; and in the remaining third, four times the normal amount. At the end of the experiment, Du Pont estimated how many extra sales had been created by higher levels of advertising expenditure. Du Pont found that higher advertising spending increased sales at a diminishing rate, and that the sales increase was weaker in Du Pont's high market share territories.

To spend a large advertising budget wisely, advertisers must define their advertising objectives; make careful budget, message, and media decisions; and evaluate advertising's results. Advertising also draws much public attention, because of its power to affect life styles and opinions. Advertising has faced increased regulation to ensure that it performs responsibly (see Exhibit 16-3).

Broadcaster/media codes Most advertising media in Canada and particular broadcasters have established their own codes. For example, CBC has a commercial acceptance policy guideline, and the Telecaster Committee, made up of independent TV stations, has developed a code specifying acceptable commercials.

The result of this regulation is that a new television commercial for a product like breakfast cereal is likely to take the following path before it is put on the air. First, it goes to the agency's legal department, then the client's legal department. Then it is sent to the CRTC for clearance as to "good taste." The commercial is then sent to the health standards branch of the Department of Consumer and Corporate Affairs to ensure it complies with the Food and Drugs Act and the Competition Act. Then the commercial goes to the CRTC's Children's Advertising Committee and also to the children's section of the Advertising Standards Council. The commercial must then go to Quebec to see if it is classified as an ad aimed at children. If it is, it can't be shown. Assuming the commercial leaps these hurdles, it still must be approved by the CBC's Commercial Acceptance Department and the Telecaster Committee.

The legal environment for advertisers in Canada is fairly stringent. Expectations are that the future will continue to bring still more regulations into effect, thereby making companies more sensitive to the legalities of advertising.

Sources: Robert W. Sweitzer, et al., "Political Dimensions of Canadian Advertising Regulation," *The Canadian Marketer*, Fall 1979, pp. 3-8; "Quebec Led Provinces in Ad Legislation," *Marketing*, February 16 1981, p. 35; Marq De Villiers, "The Great Toilet Paper Cover Up," *Canadian Business*, May 1978, pp. 46-49, 70-74; Frances Phillips, "Self-Regulation May Save Children's Advertising," *Financial Post*, March 12 1983, p. 15; "Marketing Guide to Liquor Advertising Regulations," *Marketing*, August 4 1986, pp. 14-16.

Sales Promotion

Advertising is supplemented by two other mass-promotion tools, sales promotion and publicity.

Sales promotion consists of short-term incentives to encourage purchase or sales of a product or service.

Sales promotion includes a wide variety of promotion tools designed to stimulate earlier or stronger market response. It includes consumer promotion (samples, coupons, rebates, prices-off, premiums, contests, demonstrations), trade promotion (buying allowances, free goods, merchandise allowances, cooperative advertising, push money, dealer sales contests), and salesforce promotion (bonuses, contests, sales rallies).

Sales promotion tools are used by most organizations, including manufacturers, distributors, retailers, trade associations, and nonprofit institutions. For example, churches sponsor bingo games, theater parties, and raffles. Estimates of annual sales promotion spending run as high as $5 billion, and this spending has increased rapidly in recent years.[19]

Some sales promotion tools are "consumer franchise building" — they include a selling message along with the deal to build long-run consumer demand rather than temporary brand switching. These include samples; coupons, when they include a selling message; and premiums, when they are related to the product.[20] Sales promotion tools that are not consumer franchise building include price-off packs, consumer premiums not related to a product, contests and sweepstakes, refund offers, and trade allowances. Sellers frequently use franchise-building promotions because they have longer lasting effects.

Sales promotions seem most effective when used together with advertising. In one study, point-of-purchase displays related to current TV commercials were found to produce 15% more sales than similar displays not related to such advertising. In another, a heavy sampling approach along with TV advertising proved more successful than either TV alone or TV with coupons in introducing a product.[21]

In using sales promotion, a company must set objectives; select the tools; develop the program; pretest, implement, and control the program; and evaluate the results.[22]

Setting Sales Promotion Objectives

Sales promotion objectives are based on marketing objectives for the product. The objectives set for sales promotion will vary with the type of target market. For the consumer market, objectives include getting users to buy more of the product, building trial among nonusers, and attracting competitors' brand users. For the retail market, objectives include getting the retailer to carry new items and more inventory, getting them to advertise the product and give it more shelf space, and getting them to buy ahead. Concerning the salesforce, objectives include getting more salesforce support for current or new products, or getting salespeople to sign up new accounts.

Selecting Sales Promotion Tools

Many tools can be used to accomplish the sales promotion objectives. The promotion planner should consider the type of market, sales promotion objectives, the competition, and the costs and effectiveness of each tool. The main tools are described below.

Samples, Coupons, Price Packs, and Premiums

These tools make up the bulk of *consumer promotions*. **Samples** are offers of a small amount or trial of a product to consumers.[23] Some samples are free; for others the company charges a small amount to offset sampling costs. Samples might be delivered door-to-door, sent in the mail, picked up in the store, attached to another product, or offered in an ad. Sampling is the most effective but most expensive way to introduce a new product. Esprit shampoo was introduced to the Canadian market through sampling.

Coupons are certificates that give consumers a saving on the purchase of a product. Over 7 billion coupons are given out in Canada each year, and about 4% are redeemed.[24] Coupons can be mailed, included in other products, or placed in ads. They can stimulate sales of a mature brand and promote early trial of a new brand.

Price Packs (also called cents-off deals) offer consumers savings off the regular price of a product. The reduced prices are marked by the producer directly on the product's label or package. These can include single packages sold at a reduced price (such as two for the price of one). Or they might include

Companies send out over 7 billion coupons each year in Canada.

James Hertel

two related products banded together (such as a toothbrush and toothpaste). Price packs are very effective—even more than coupons—for stimulating short-term sales.

Premiums are goods offered free or at low cost as an incentive to buy a product. A with-pack premium comes with the product, inside (in-pack) or outside (on-pack) the package. The package itself, if reusable, may serve as a premium. Premiums are sometimes mailed to consumers who send in a proof of purchase, such as a boxtop. Manufacturers now offer consumers all kinds of premiums bearing the company's names.

Point-of-Purchase Displays and Demonstrations

POP displays and demonstrations take place at the point of sale. An example is a five-foot-high cardboard display of Cap'n Crunch next to Cap'n Crunch cereal boxes. Unfortunately, many retailers do not like to handle the hundreds of displays, signs, and posters they receive from manufacturers each year. Manufacturers are responding by offering better POP materials, tying them in with television or print messages, and offering to set them up. The L'eggs panty hose display is one of the most creative in the history of POP materials and a major factor in the success of this brand.

Trade Promotion

Manufacturers use many techniques to get the cooperation of wholesalers and retailers. They may offer a buying allowance, which is an offer of money off on each case purchased during a stated period. The offer encourages dealers to buy in quantity or carry a new item they might not usually buy.

Manufacturers may offer a merchandising allowance to reward dealers for featuring the manufacturer's products. An advertising allowance rewards dealers for advertising the product. A display allowance rewards them for using product displays.

Manufacturers may offer free goods such as extra cases of merchandise to middlemen who buy a larger quantity. They may offer push money, cash, or gifts to dealers or their salesforces to push the manufacturer's goods. Manufacturers may offer free specialty advertising items that carry the company's name, such as pens, pencils, calendars, paperweights, matchbooks, memo pads, and yardsticks.[25]

Business Conventions and Trade Shows

Industry associations organize annual conventions and may sponsor a trade show at the same time. Firms selling to the industry show their products at the trade show. The vendors who participate in Canadian industrial trade shows expect several benefits, including new products, meeting new buyers, maintaining company visibility, and contacting decision makers who might otherwise not be reached.[26]

Contests, Sweepstakes, and Games

These promotions give consumers, dealers, or salesforces the chance to win something—such as cash, trips, or goods—as a result of luck or extra effort. A

The Canadian/Premium/Incentive/Travel Show Convention provides an opportunity for marketers of sales promotions to display their products.

contest calls for consumers to submit an entry, such as a jingle, guess, or suggestion, to be judged by a panel that will select the best entries. A sweepstakes calls for consumers to submit their names for a draw. A game gives consumers something every time they buy—bingo numbers, missing letters—which may help them win a prize. A sales contest urges dealers or the salesforce to increase their efforts, with prizes going to the top performers.

Developing the Sales Promotion Program

The marketer must make some other decisions to define the full sales promotion program—how much incentive to offer, who can participate, how to advertise the sales promotion, how long it should last, when it should start, and how much to budget.

Size of Incentive

The marketer has to decide how much to offer. A certain minimum incentive is necessary if the promotion is to succeed. Up to a point, a larger incentive will produce more sales response. Some of the large consumer packaged-goods firms have a sales promotion manager who studies past promotions and recommends incentive levels to brand managers.

Conditions for Participation

Incentives might be offered to everyone or to select groups. A premium might be offered only to those who turn in boxtops. Sweepstakes might not be offered in certain provinces, or to families of company personnel, or to persons under a certain age.

Distribution of the Promotion

The marketer must decide how to promote and distribute the promotion program. A 15-cents-off coupon could be given out in a package, store, mail, or advertisement. Each distribution method involves a different level of reach and cost.

Length and Timing of the Promotion

If the sales promotion period is too short, many prospects will not be able to take advantage of the promotion since they may not be buying during that time. If the promotion runs too long, the deal will lose some of its "act now" force. According to one researcher, the best frequency is about three weeks per quarter, and the best length is the time of the average purchase cycle.[27]

Brand managers need to set calendar dates for the promotions. The dates will be used by production, sales, and distribution. Some unplanned promotions will also be needed, requiring cooperation on short notice.

Total Sales Promotion Budget

The sales promotion budget can be developed in two ways. The marketer can choose the promotions and estimate their total cost. The more common way, however, is to take a percentage of the total budget to use for sales promotion.

Strang found three major problems in how companies budget for sales promotion: (1) they do not consider cost effectiveness; (2) instead of spending to achieve objectives, they simply extend last year's spending, take a percentage of expected sales, or use the "affordable approach"; and (3) advertising and sales promotion budgets are prepared separately.[28]

Pretesting

Sales promotion tools should be pretested when possible to find out if they are appropriate and of the right incentive size. Yet fewer than 42% of premium offers are ever pretested.[29]

Implementing

For each promotion, companies should have implementation plans that cover lead time and sell-off time. Lead time is the time necessary to prepare the program before launching it. Sell-off time begins with the launch and ends when the promotion ends.

Evaluating the Results

Evaluation is very important, and yet, according to Strang, "evaluation of promotion programs receives . . . little attention. Even where an attempt is made to evaluate a promotion, it is likely to be superficial . . . Evaluation in terms of profitability is even less common."[30]

Manufacturers can use one of many methods to evaluate sales promotions. The most common method is to compare sales before, during, and after a promotion. Suppose a company has a 6% market share before the promotion, which jumps to 10% during the promotion, falls to 5% right after, and rises to 7% later on. The promotion seems to have attracted new triers and more buying from current customers. After the promotion, sales fell as consumers used up their inventories. The long-run rise to 7% means that the company gained some new users. If the brand's share returned to the old level, then the promotion only changed the timing of demand rather than the total demand.

Consumer panel data would reveals the kinds of people who responded to the promotion and what they did after the promotion. Consumer surveys can provide more information on how many consumers recall the promotion, what they thought of it, how many took advantage of it, and how it affected their buying. Sales promotions can also be evaluated through experiments that vary such factors as incentive value, length, and distribution method.

Clearly, sales promotion plays an important role in the total promotion mix. To use it well, the marketer must define the sales promotion objectives, select the best tools, design the sales promotion program, pretest it, implement it, and evaluate the results.

Publicity

In addition to sales promotion, another major mass promotion tool is publicity.

Publicity is nonpersonal stimulation of demand for a product, service, or business unit by planting commercially significant news about it in a published medium or obtaining favorable presentation of it on radio, television, or stage that is not paid for by the sponsor.

Publicity is used to promote products, people, places, ideas, activities, organizations, and even nations. Trade associations and marketing boards have used publicity to rebuild interest in declining commodities such as eggs, milk, and potatoes. Organizations have used publicity to attract attention or change a poor image. Nations have used publicity to attract more tourists, foreign investment, and international support.

Publicity is part of a larger concept, that of *public relations*. Company public relations has several objectives. It aims to obtain favorable publicity for the company, build up a good "corporate image," and handle unfavorable rumors and stories that break out. Public relations departments use many tools to carry out these objectives:[31]

Press relations   Placing newsworthy information into the news media to attract attention to a person, product, or service.

Product publicity   Publicizing specific products.

Corporate communications   Creating internal and external communications to promote understanding of the institution.

Lobbying   Dealing with legislators and government officials to promote or defeat legislation and regulation.

Counseling Advising management about public issues and company positions and image.

People skilled in publicity are usually found in the company's public relations department. The public relations department is usually located at corporate headquarters. Its staff is so busy dealing with various publics — stockholders, employees, legislators, city officials — that publicity to support product marketing objectives may be ignored. One solution is to add a publicity person to the marketing department.

Publicity is often described as a marketing stepchild because of its limited and scattered use. Yet publicity can have a strong impact on public awareness at a much lower cost than advertising. The company does not pay for the space or time in the media. It pays for a staff to develop and circulate the stories. If the company develops an interesting story, it could be picked by all the media, having the same effect as advertising that would cost millions of dollars. In addition, it would have more credibility than advertising.

In considering when and how to use product publicity, management should set the publicity objectives, choose the publicity messages and vehicles, implement the publicity plan, and evaluate the results.

Setting Publicity Objectives

The first task is to set objectives for the publicity. The objectives are then turned into specific goals so that final results can be evaluated.

Choosing Publicity Messages and Vehicles

The organization next finds interesting stories to tell about the product. Suppose a little known college wants more public recognition. It will search for possible stories. Do any faculty members have unusual backgrounds or are any working on unusual projects? Are any interesting new courses being taught, or any interesting events taking place on campus? Usually this search will uncover hundreds of stories, some of which can be fed to the press. The stories chosen should reflect the image this college wants.

If there are not enough stories, the college could sponsor newsworthy events. Here the organization creates rather than finds news. Ideas include hosting major academic conventions, inviting well-known speakers, and holding news conferences. Each event creates many stories for many different audiences.

Event creation is very important in publicizing fundraising drives for nonprofit organizations. Fundraisers have developed a large set of special events such as art exhibits, auctions, benefit evenings, bingo games, book sales, cake sales, contests, dances, dinners, fairs, fashion shows, phoneathons, rummage sales, tours, and walkathons. No sooner is one type of event created, such as a walkathon, than competitors create new versions such as readathons, bikeathons, and jogathons.

Implementing the Publicity Plan

Implementing publicity requires care. Take the matter of placing stories in the media. A great story is easy to place. However, most stories are not great, and they may not get past busy editors. One of the main assets of publicists is their personal relationships with media editors. Publicists are often ex-journalists who know many media editors and know what they want. Publicists look at media editors as a market to satisfy so that these editors will continue to use their stories.

Evaluating the Publicity Results

Publicity's contribution is difficult to measure because it is used with other promotion tools and its impact is indirect. If it is used before the other tools come into action, its contribution is easier to evaluate.

The easiest measure of publicity effectiveness is the number of exposures in the media. Publicists give the client a "clippings book" showing all the media that carried news about the product and a summary such as the following:

> Media coverage included 350 column inches of news and photographs in 35 publications with a combined circulation of 8 million; 250 minutes of air time on 29 radio stations and an estimated audience of 7 million; and 66 minutes of air time on 16 television stations with an estimated audience of 9 million. If this time and space had been purchased at advertising rates, it would have amounted to $1,047,000.[32]

This exposure measure is not very satisfying. It does not tell how many people actually read or heard the message, and what they thought afterward. It does not give information on the net audience reached, since the media overlap in readership or audience.

A better measure calls for finding out what change in product **awareness/ comprehension/attitude** occurred as a result of the publicity campaign (after allowing for the impact of other promotional tools). This requires the use of survey methodology to measure the before-after levels of these variables.

Sales and profit impacts are the most satisfactory measures, if obtainable. This is often difficult because all elements of the marketing mix contribute to sales. To estimate publicity's net contribution may not be possible.

Summary

Three major tools of mass promotion are advertising, sales promotion, and publicity. They are mass marketing tools as opposed to personal selling, which targets specific buyers.

Advertising — the use of paid media by a seller to inform, persuade, and remind about its products or organization — is a strong promotion tool. Canadian marketers spend over $7 billion each year on advertising, which takes many forms (national, regional, local; consumer, industrial, retail; product, brand, institutional). Advertising decision making is a five-step process consisting of setting objectives, budget decision, message decision, media decision, and evaluation. Advertisers should set clear goals as to whether the advertising is supposed to inform, persuade, or remind buyers. The advertising budget can be based on what is affordable, a percentage of sales, competitors' spending, or objectives and tasks. The message decision calls for designing messages, evaluating them, and executing them effectively. The media decision calls for defining reach, frequency, and impact goals; choosing major media types; selecting media vehicles; and scheduling the media. Finally, the communication and sales effects of advertising are evaluated before, while, and after the advertising is placed.

Sales promotion covers a wide variety of short-term incentive tools — coupons, premiums, contests, buying allowances — designed to stimulate consumers, the trade, and the company's own salesforce. Sales promotion spending has been growing faster than advertising spending in recent years. Sales promotion calls for setting sales promotion objectives; selecting tools; developing, pretesting, and implementing the sales promotion program; and evaluating results.

Publicity, which involves securing free editorial space or time, is the least used of the major promotion tools, although it has great potential for building awareness and preference. Publicity involves setting publicity objectives; choosing publicity messages and vehicles; implementing the publicity plan; and evaluating publicity results.

Questions for Discussion

1. Discuss the three possible objectives of advertising.
2. List the advantages and disadvantages of each of the "new media" and discuss when each could be best used. What other new media might appear in the next 15 years?
3. How might McDonald's evaluate whether its most recent national advertising campaign was successful?
4. Public policy makers need not be concerned with advertising decisions. Comment.
5. Distinguish between consumer promotion and trade promotion.
6. Many firms have faced negative rumors about their products in recent years — K mart coats from Taiwan with poisonous snakes nesting in them, McDonald's using worms in its hamburger meat, Pop Rocks candy making your stomach explode, Bubble Gum containing spider eggs. How can the company best deal with these rumors when using public relations and advertising?
7. Publicity is part of the larger concept of public relations. Comment.
8. Discuss how you would develop a publicity campaign for the Canadian Cancer Society.

■■■■ Award-Winning Advertisements

Advertising aims to inform, persuade, and remind consumers about products and services. To accomplish these objectives, the advertiser first makes decisions about budget, message, and media, then evaluates the campaign. A detailed discussion of the preparation and execution of advertising campaigns is provided in Chapter 16. The following pages present a number of advertisements that have won awards, given annually by *Marketing* Magazine (Maclean Hunter Limited) to honor Canadian advertising. As you examine these ads, you might ask:

- What appears to be the objective, that is, what do you think the advertiser is trying to accomplish?

- What target markets are the ads trying to reach?

- What messages are the ads trying to communicate to the target markets?

- What creative strategies are used in the ads to communicate the messages effectively to the target markets?

Advertisements are important components of the marketing strategies used by organizations. These advertisements were selected to illustrate a range of products and services.

■■■■ 1987 *Marketing* Gold Award   Category: Transit, Single
The marketers of Scrabble, Chieftain Products, use a humorous juxtaposition of image and copy to promote their game.
Courtesy of DDB Needham Worldwide Advertising Ltd., agency, and Chieftain Products Inc., client

1987 *Marketing* Silver Award   Category: Transit, Single

A variation on a familiar product from Christie Brown is announced with a strong visual image and a simple rhyme.

Courtesy of Christie Brown & Co., client, and McCann-Erickson Advertising of Canada Ltd., agency

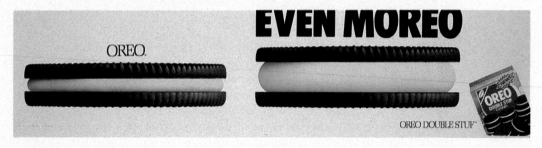

1987 *Marketing* Certificate   Category: Outdoor, Horizontal

A billboard ad presents Aspirin as an ongoing answer to consumer needs.

Courtesy of SMW Advertising Ltd., agency, and Sterling Drugs Ltd., client

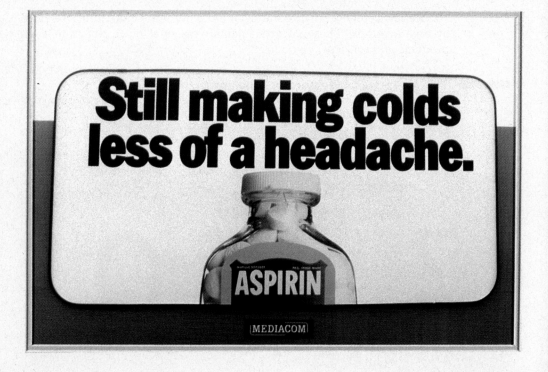

It says Dole on the outside.   It says Dole on the inside.

It says Dole on the outside.   It says Dole on the inside.

It says Dole on the outside.   It says Dole on the inside.

1987 *Marketing* **Certificate   Category: Transit Campaign**
An association theme emphasizes the natural flavors of the Dole products in these
three ads.
Courtesy of William Neilson Ltd., client, and Miller Myers Bruce DallaCosta, agency

1987 *Marketing* Certificate   Category: Business Press, Single
Heinz, the best-selling ketchup in Canada, connects the concept of achievement in
other fields to its own success, and announces its support of achievement in the arts.
Courtesy of Carder Gray Advertising Inc., agency, and H.J. Heinz Co. of Canada Ltd., client

To all of you who have succeeded in becoming a famous name, congratulations.

We know what you went through.

Heinz Ketchup, sponsor of the 1986 Casby Music Awards.

1987 *Marketing* Certificate   Category: Multi-Media Campaign

In this campaign, Tourism Canada presents the various landscapes and cultural experiences to be found in Canada.

Courtesy of Camp Associates Advertising Ltd., agency, and Tourism Canada, client

Gros Morne, western Newfoundland.

Set sail for foreign shores

Canada's Atlantic provinces–New Brunswick, Newfoundland, Nova Scotia and Prince Edward Island–bring together four different worlds, all close at hand but far away in feeling.

From the towering fjords of Newfoundland or the rugged grandeur of Nova Scotia's Cape Breton Island, to the warm saltwater beaches of Prince Edward Island or New Brunswick's Acadian coast, this is a compact region of contrasts, with some easygoing seaside cities, and a host of cozy coastal inns. Best of all, there's nothing in the world quite like a Maritime welcome–including the substantial premium on your U.S. dollars. And that welcome awaits you just over the border, in the world next door.

For information call: New Brunswick: 1-800-561-0123; Newfoundland: 1-800-563-6353; Nova Scotia: 1-800-341-6096 – from mainland U.S., or from Maine: 1-800-492-0643; Prince Edward Island: 1-800-565-9060, or, west of the Mississippi, (toll call) 1-902-368-4444.

On the beach
*Orby Head,
Prince Edward Island.*

Dancing to a different drummer
*Les Danseurs d'la Vallée Saint-Jean,
from New Brunswick's French-
speaking Madawaska Region.*

Sail the legend!
*Halifax harbour,
and the schooner
Bluenose II.*

**Scallops and
fiddleheads**
*A seasonal green
locally grown.*

Canada [*]
The World Next Door

Dalvay-By-the-Sea, Prince Edward Island.

The lure of Island hideaways

Campobello, Deer or Grand Manan, among New Brunswick's Fundy Isles. Nova Scotia's 'Highland' Island, Cape Breton. Prince Edward Island, our lush and lovely garden in the Gulf of St. Lawrence; or, for a world of difference, the rugged grandeur of Newfoundland.

Canada's Atlantic coast harbours a host of offshore discoveries, each unique in culture and customs, all sharing in the easygoing hospitality of island life. And all accessible by car via causeway or oceangoing ferry.

This summer, take advantage of the hefty premium on your U.S. dollars. Slip away for a while, and unwind to the ebb and flow of an island holiday.

For information, call New Brunswick: 1-800-561-0123; Newfoundland: 1-800-563-6353; Nova Scotia: 1-800-341-6096 – from mainland U.S., or from Maine: 1-800-492-0643; Prince Edward Island: 1-800-565-9060 or, west of the Mississippi, (toll call) 1-902-368-4444.

**Prelude to the 1987 International
Gathering of the Clans**
*A wee bit of Scottish tradition along
the Cabot Trail, Nova Scotia.*

**Seafood fresh
from the sea**
*And raised by
anyone.*

Seal Cove
*Grand Manan Island,
New Brunswick.*

**How to carve
a pheasant!**
*Whimsically Folk-art
Birds in Nova Scotia.*

Canada [*]
The World Next Door

FEED YOUR MIND ABOUT IT
a special exhibition at the
ONTARIO SCIENCE CENTRE
MARCH 6 - NOVEMBER 2, 1986.

In co-operation with AULT DAIRIES/CATELLI/OGILVIE: Companies of ☉ JOHN LABATT
Ontario Ministry of Agriculture and Food • Ontario Ministry of Citizenship and Culture

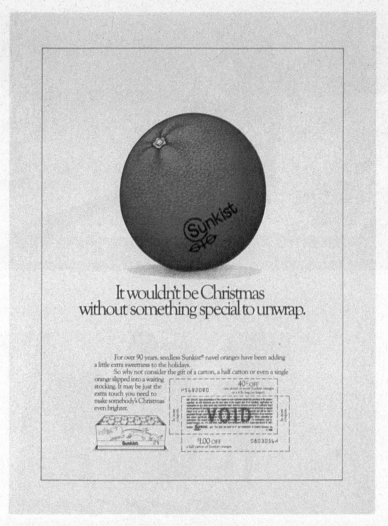

It wouldn't be Christmas
without something special to unwrap.

1987 *Marketing* Certificate   Category: Newspaper, Single

A seasonal tradition is linked to a branded product in this
Sunkist ad. A coupon encourages consumers to purchase
the product.

Courtesy of Foote, Cone & Belding Advertising Ltd., agency, and Sunkist
Growers Inc., client

1987 *Marketing* Certificate   Category: Outdoor, Vertical

A government-funded organization, the Ontario Science
Centre, advertises an exhibition with a provocative image
that will catch the attention of consumers.

Courtesy of Kuleba & Shyllit, agency, and the Ontario Science Centre,
client

■ 1987 *Marketing* Silver Award   Category: Outdoor, Horizontal
The contrast effect in these billboard ads for Club Med reminds Canadians of warmer
tourist destinations during winter.
Courtesy of The Nathan Fraser Agency and Club Med Sales Inc., client

Chapter 16 Key Terms

Advertising Any paid form of nonpersonal presentation and promotion of ideas, goods, or services by an identified sponsor.

Comparison advertising Advertising that compares one brand directly or indirectly to one or more other brands.

Consumer promotion Sales promotion designed to stimulate consumer purchasing, including samples, coupons, rebates, prices-off, premiums, contests, trading stamps, and demonstrations.

Continuity Scheduling ads evenly within a given period.

Copy testing Measuring the communication effect of an advertisement before or after it is printed or broadcast.

Frequency The number of times the average person in the target market is exposed to the advertising message during a given period.

Public relations Company activities that aim to obtain favorable publicity for the company, build up a good "corporate image," and handle unfavorable rumors and stories that break out.

Publicity Nonpersonal stimulation of demand for a product, service, or business unit by planting commercially significant news about it in a published medium or by obtaining favorable presentation of it on radio, television, or stage that is not paid for by the sponsor.

Pulsing Scheduling ads unevenly in bursts over a time period.

Reach The number of people in the target market exposed to the ad campaign during the given period.

Sales promotion Short-term incentives to encourage purchase or sales of a product or service.

Salesforce promotion Sales promotion designed to motivate the salesforce and make their selling efforts more effective, including bonuses, contests, and sales rallies.

Trade promotion Sales promotion designed to gain reseller support and to improve reseller selling efforts, including buying allowances, free goods, merchandise allowances, cooperative advertising, push money, and dealer sales contests.

Cases for Chapter 16

Promoting Products: Personal Selling and Sales Management

Chapter Objectives

After reading this chapter, you should be able to:
1. Discuss the role of a company's salesrepresentatives.
2. Identify the major salesforce management decisions.
3. Explain how companies set salesforce objectives and strategy.
4. Tell how companies recruit, select, and train salespeople.
5. Describe how companies supervise salespeople and evaluate their effectiveness.

Many people would not consider a career in sales because of the negative images associated with this occupation. Salespeople are often viewed as fast-talking, pushy individuals who are only interested in making a quick dollar by peddling their products to a gullible public. A few of these types may still be around but most successful salespeople today are a far cry from the old stereotype. Consider the following examples:

- Telecommunication Terminal Systems (TTS) of Toronto sells complex corporate telephone systems ranging in price from $6000 to millions of dollars. The competition includes Bell Information Systems and AT&T Canada. One of their top salespeople, who earns over $150 000 a year, puts her clients' needs first. As she says, "If you just forget about the commission and care about the client, I think that comes across." Or, as one buyer of a $3-million communication system from TTS commented, "she was able to coordinate her resources to meet our needs exceptionally well."

- ICL Computers Ltd. of Montreal sells "point-of-sale" computer systems to large retail chains. One of ICL's top salespeople describes the process she goes through in making a sale that may take up to two years to complete. She never approaches a company without first researching its ownership, finances, and likely readiness to buy. Next, she meets with managers of the company and learns what they would like in a computer system. Then she meets with ICL's technical experts to determine exactly how much ICL can deliver. Next, she works nights and weekends writing a proposal that is given to the client during a formal presentation. If ICL makes the short list, she conducts further negotiations until the contract is signed. She adds: "I don't neglect my client after the contract is signed. In fact, I work even harder to see that they come back to ICL."

- Xerox Canada sells photocopy machines in the highly competitive office copier market. The company is well known and regarded for its sales training program and professional sales force. The top sales performers at Xerox are experts on their products and competitive offerings. They have a very high business ethics level and are extremely motivated. They build long-term relationships based on trust and a knowledge of the customer's needs. As one Xerox salesperson said: "I get to know my customers well and if I think a competitor's machine will meet their needs better, I tell them."

Today's professional salespeople are sincere, hard working individuals who identify and meet customer needs by listening carefully and delivering what they promise. As good salespeople know, satisfied customers are the key to their success.[1]

Robert Louis Stevenson noted that "everyone lives by selling something." Salesforces are found in nonprofit as well as profit organizations. University recruiters are the university's salesforce for attracting students. Churches use membership committees to attract new members. Agriculture Canada sends agricultural specialists to sell farmers on using new farming methods. Hospitals and museums use fundraisers to contact and raise money from donors.

There are many stereotypes of salespeople. "Salesmen" may bring to mind the image of Arthur Miller's pitiable Willy Loman in *Death of a Salesman* or Meredith Willson's cigar-smoking, back-slapping, joke-telling Harold Hill in *The Music Man.* Salespeople are typically pictured as loving to be sociable — although many salespeople actually dislike it. They are blamed for forcing goods on people — although buyers often search out salespeople.

Actually the term *salesperson* covers a wide range of positions, where the differences are often greater than the similarities. McMurry offered the following classification of sales positions:[2]

- Positions where the salesperson's job is largely to deliver the product—milk, bread, fuel, oil.

- Positions where the salesperson is largely an inside order taker, such as the department store salesperson standing behind the counter.

- Positions where the salesperson is also largely an order taker but also works in the field, as the packing house, soap, or spice salesperson does.

- Positions where the salesperson is not expected or permitted to take an order but only builds goodwill or educates buyers — the distiller's "missionary person" or the "detailer" for a pharmaceutical company.

- Positions where the major emphasis is placed on technical knowledge —the engineering salesperson who is mostly a consultant to the client companies.

- Positions that demand the creative sale of tangible products like vacuum cleaners, refrigerators, siding, and encyclopedias.

- Positions requiring the creative sale of intangibles, such as insurance, advertising services, or education.

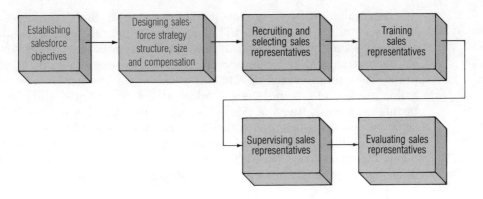

FIGURE 17-1
Major Steps in Salesforce Management

This list ranges from the least to the most creative types of selling. The jobs at the top of the list call for servicing accounts and taking orders, while the last ones call for locating buyers and persuading them to buy. We will focus on the more creative types of selling, and on the process of building and managing an effective salesforce. We define salesforce management as follows:

Salesforce management is the analysis, planning, implementation, and control of salesforce activities. It includes setting salesforce objectives; designing salesforce strategy; and recruiting, selecting, training, supervising, and evaluating the firm's salespeople.

The major salesforce management decisions are shown in Figure 17-1 and discussed in the following sections.[3]

Setting Salesforce Objectives

Companies set different objectives for their salesforces. IBM's salespeople are to "sell, install, and upgrade" customer computer equipment; Bell Canada salespeople should "develop, sell, and protect" accounts. Salespeople usually perform one or more of a variety of tasks for their companies. They find and develop new customers and communicate information about the company's products and services. They sell products by approaching, presenting, answering objections, and closing sales with customers. Salespeople provide services to customers, carry out market research and intelligence work, and fill in call reports.

Some companies are very specific about their salesforce objectives and activities. One company advises its salespeople to spend 80% of their time with current customers and 20% with prospects, and 85% of their time on current products and 15% on new products.[4] If norms are not set, salespeople tend to spend most of their time selling current products to current accounts, while neglecting new products and new prospects.[5]

As companies increase their market orientation, their salesforces need to become more market-oriented. The old view is that salespeople should worry about sales and the company should worry about profit. The newer view is that salespeople should know how to produce customer satisfaction and company profit. They should know how to look at sales data, measure market potential, gather market intelligence, and develop marketing strategies and plans. Salespeople need marketing analysis skills, especially at higher levels of sales management. A market-oriented rather than a sales-oriented salesforce will be more effective in the long run. This is particularly important for Canadian consumer goods manufacturers. The shift in channel power to retailers has meant that sales managers must consider the changing needs of Canada's large retailers.[6]

Designing Salesforce Strategy

Once the company has set its salesforce objectives, it is ready to face questions of salesforce strategy, structure, size, and compensation.

Salesforce Strategy

The company will be competing with others to get orders from customers. It must base its strategy on an understanding of the customer buying process. The company can use one or more of several sales approaches to contact customers. A salesperson talks to a prospect or customer in person or over the phone. Or the salesperson makes a sales presentation to a buying group. A sales team (such as a company executive, a salesperson, and a sales engineer) can make a sales presentation to a buying group.

In **conference selling**, a salesperson brings resource people from the company to meet with one or more buyers to discuss problems and opportunities. In **seminar selling**, company teams conduct an educational seminar for technical people in a customer company about state-of-the-art developments.

Thus the salesperson often acts as an "account manager" who arranges contacts between people in the buying and selling companies. Selling calls for teamwork. Salespeople need help from others in the company including top management, especially when major sales are at stake; technical people who provide customer services; and office staff such as sales analysts, order processors, and secretaries.

Salesforce Structure

The company must also decide on how to structure its salesforce. This is simple if the company sells one product line to one industry with customers in many locations—here the company would use a territorial salesforce function. If the company sells many products to many types of customers, it might need a product salesforce structure or customer salesforce structure. These three structures are discussed below.

Territorial Salesforce Structure

In the simplest sales organization, each salesperson is given an exclusive territory in which to sell the company's full line. This salesforce structure has many advantages. First, it clearly defines the salesperson's job. Because only one salesperson works the territory, she or he gets all the credit or blame for territory sales. Second, the territorial structure increases the salesperson's desire to build local business and personal ties. These ties improve the salesperson's selling effectiveness and personal life. Third, travel expenses are lower, since each salesperson travels within a smaller area.

Territorial sales organization is often supported by many levels of sales management positions. Several territories will be headed up by a district sales manager, several districts by a regional sales manager, and several regions by a national sales manager or sales vice-president.

Product Salesforce Structure

Salespeople must know their products, especially when the products are numerous, unrelated, and complex. This, together with the trend toward product management, has led many companies to structure their salesforces along product lines.

The product structure, however, can lead to problems if many of the company's products are bought by the same customers. For example, many companies have several product divisions, each with its own salesforce. It is possible that several salespeople from the same company could call on the same customer on the same day. This means that they travel over the same routes, and each waits to see the customer's purchasing agents. These extra costs must be compared to the benefits of better product knowledge and attention to individual products.

Customer Salesforce Structure

Companies often structure their salesforces along customer lines. Separate salesforces may be set up for different industries, for major industries, for major versus regular accounts, and for serving current customers versus finding new ones. The biggest advantage of customer specialization is that each salesforce can know more about specific customer needs. It can also reduce total salesforce costs. At one time a pump manufacturer used highly trained sales engineers to sell to all its customers—to manufacturers who needed highly technical assistance and to wholesalers who did not. Later the company split its salesforce and used lower-paid, less technical salespeople to deal with the wholesalers.

In Canada, sales managers of multiple-product firms face a dilemma. On the one hand, the wide geographic distribution of Canadian markets suggests that territorial-structured sales forces should be used to lower selling costs. On the other hand, the ready availability of new products, particularly for the Canadian subsidiaries of U.S. manufacturers, can result in product lines that are so broad as to spread the salesperson's efforts too thinly to be effective.[7] The decision as to what structure to use can be assisted by an analytic approach based on a sales response function.[8]

Salesforce Size

Once the company has set its strategy and structure, it is ready to consider salesforce size. Salespeople are one of the company's most productive and expensive assets. Increasing their number will increase both sales and costs.

Many companies use the **workload approach** to establish salesforce size.[9] The company might think as follows:

> Suppose we have 1000 Type A accounts and 2000 Type B accounts in Canada. Type A accounts require 36 calls a year and Type B accounts 12 calls a year. This means the company needs a salesforce that can make 60 000 calls a year. Suppose the average salesperson can make 1000 calls a year. The company would need 60 salespeople.

Salesforce Compensation

To attract the needed salespeople, the company has to have an attractive compensation plan. These plans vary considerably by industry and by company within the same industry. The level of compensation must be close to the "going rate" for the type of sales job and skills needed.

Compensation is made up of several elements—a fixed amount, a variable amount, expenses, and fringe benefits. The fixed amount, which might be salary or a drawing account, gives the salesperson some stable income. The variable amount, which might be commissions, a bonus, or profit sharing, rewards the salesperson for greater effort. Expense allowances let the salespeople undertake needed and desirable selling efforts. Fringe benefits, such as paid vacations, sickness or accident benefits, pensions, and life insurance, provide job security and satisfaction. Management must decide what mix of these compensation elements makes the most sense for each sales job.

Recruiting and Selecting Salespeople

Having set the strategy, structure, size, and compensation for the salesforce, the company now must set up systems for recruiting and selecting, training, supervising, and evaluating salespeople.

Importance of Careful Selection

At the heart of successful salesforce operation is the selection of good salespeople. The performance levels of an average and a top salesperson can be quite different. A survey of over 500 companies showed that, in a typical salesforce, 27% of the salespeople bring in over 52% of the sales.[10] Careful selection of salespeople can greatly increase overall salesforce performance.

Beyond the differences in sales performance, poor selection results in costly turnover. One study found an average annual salesforce turnover rate for all industries of almost 20%.[11] The costs of high turnover can be great. The company must spend more to hire and train replacements, and a salesforce with many new people is less productive.

What Makes a Good Salesperson?

Selecting salespeople would not be a problem if the company knew what traits to look for. If good salespeople are outgoing, aggressive, and energetic, these characteristics could be checked in applicants. However, many successful salespeople are also bashful, mild-mannered, and far from energetic.

Still, the search continues for the magic list of traits that spells sure-fire sales ability. Many lists have been drawn up. McMurry wrote that "the possessor of an effective sales personality is a habitual 'wooer,' an individual who has a compulsive need to win and hold the affection of others."[12] McMurry listed five additional traits of the super salesperson: "A high level of energy, abounding self-confidence, a chronic hunger for money, a well-established habit of industry, and a state of mind that regards each objection, resistance, or obstacle as a challenge."[13] Mayer and Greenberg have offered one of the shortest lists.[14] They concluded that the effective salesperson has at least two basic qualities: (1) empathy, the ability to feel as the customer does; and (2) ego drive, a strong personal need to make the sale. These two traits led in predicting good subsequent performance of applicants for sales positions in three different industries. Charles Garfield found that good salespeople are goal-directed risk takers who identify strongly with their customers (see Exhibit 17-1).

How can a company find out what traits salespeople in its industry should have? The job duties suggest some of the traits to look for. Is there a lot of paper work? Does the job call for much travel? Will the salesperson face a lot of rejections? The company should also look at the traits of its most successful salespeople for clues on needed traits.

Recruiting Procedures

After management has decided on the needed traits, it must recruit. The personnel department looks for applicants by getting names from current salespeople, using employment agencies, placing job ads, and contacting college students.

If successful, recruiting will attract many applicants, and the company must select the best ones. The selection procedure can vary from a single informal interview to lengthy testing and interviewing. Many companies give formal tests to sales applicants. Test scores provide only one piece of information in a set that includes personal characteristics, references, past employment history, and interviewer reactions. However, test results are weighted heavily by such companies as IBM, Prudential, Procter & Gamble, and Gillette.

Training Salespeople ━━━━━━━━━━━━━━━━━━

Many companies used to send their new salespeople into the field almost right away after hiring them. They would be given samples, order books, and instructions to sell west of Regina. Training programs were luxuries. A training program meant spending a lot for instructors, materials, and space; paying a person who was not yet selling; and losing opportunities because he or she was not in the field.

EXHIBIT 17-1
What Makes a Good Salesperson?

Charles Garfield, clinical professor of psychology at the University of California, San Francisco School of Medicine, claims his 20-year analysis of more than 1500 superachievers in every field of endeavor is the longest running to date. *Peak Performance—Mental Training Techniques of the World's Greatest Athletes*, the first book Garfield wrote about his findings, was published June 1. Although he says it will be followed shortly by a book on business that will cover supersalespeople, many companies (such as IBM, which took 3000) have ordered the current book for their sales forces. Garfield says that the complexity and speed of change in today's business world means that to be a peak performer in sales requires greater mastery of different fields than to be one in science, sports, or the arts. The following are the most common characteristics he has found in peak sales performance:

- Supersalespeople are always taking risks and making innovations. Unlike most people, they stay out of the "comfort zone" and try to surpass their previous levels of performance.
- Supersalespeople have a powerful sense of mission and set the short-, intermediate-, and long-term goals necessary to fulfill that mission. Their personal goals are always higher than the sales quotas set by their managers. Supersalespeople also work well with managers, especially if the managers also are interested in peak performance.
- Supersalespeople are more interested in solving problems than in placing blame or bluffing their way out of situations. Because they view themselves as professionals in training, they are always upgrading their skills.
- Supersalespeople see themselves as partners with their customers, and as team players rather than adversaries. Peak performers believe their task is to communicate with people, while mediocre salespeople psychologically change their customers into objects and talk about the number of calls and closes they made as if it had nothing to do with human beings.
- Supersalespeople take each rejection as information they can learn form, whereas mediocre salespeople personalize rejection.
- The most surprising finding is that, like peak performers in sports and the arts, supersalespeople use mental rehearsal. Before every sale they review it in their mind's eye, from shaking the customer's hand when they walk in to discussing his problems and asking for the order.

Source: "What Makes a Supersalesperson?" *Sales and Marketing Management*, August 13 1984, p. 86.

Today's new salespeople may spend a few weeks to many months in training. The median training period is 17 weeks in industrial products companies, and 20 in consumer products companies.[15] At IBM, new salespeople are not on their own for two years! IBM also expects its salespeople to spend 15% of their time each year in additional training.

The training programs have several goals:

1. ***Salespeople need to know and identify with the company***   *Most companies spend the first part of the training program describing the com-*

Courtesy: Procter & Gamble Canada

Most companies today have formal training programs for sale representatives and sales managers.

pany's history and objectives, its organization, its financial structure and facilities, and its chief products and markets.

2. ***Salespeople need to know the company's products*** Sales trainees are shown how products are produced and how they work in various uses.

3. ***Salespeople need to know customers' and competitors' characteristics*** They learn about the different types of customers and their needs, buying motives, and buying habits. They learn about the company's and competitors' strategies.

4. ***Salespeople need to know how to make effective presentations*** They get training in the principles of salesmanship. The company outlines the major sales arguments for each product, and some provide a sales script.

5. ***Salespeople need to understand field procedures and responsibilities*** They learn how to divide time between active and potential accounts, and how to use the expense account, prepare reports, and route effectively.

Principles of Salesmanship

One of the major objectives of training programs is to teach salespeople the art of selling. Companies spend millions of dollars on seminars, books, cassettes, and other materials. Almost a million copies of books on selling are purchased every year, with such tantalizing titles as *How to Outsell the Born Salesman*, *How to Sell Anything to Anybody*, *The Power of Enthusiastic Selling*, *How Power Selling Brought Me Success in 6 Hours*, *Where Do You Go from No.1*, and *1000 Ways a Salesman Can Increase His Sales*. One of the most lasting books is Dale Carnegie's *How to Win Friends and Influence People*.

All of the training approaches try to convert a salesperson from being a passive **order taker** to being an active **order getter**. Order takers assume that customers know their own needs, would resent any attempt at influence, and prefer salespeople who are polite and reserved. An example of an order taker would be a salesperson who calls on a dozen customers each day, simply asking if the customer needs anything.

There are two approaches to training salespeople to be order getters — a sales-oriented approach and a customer-oriented approach. The first one trains the salesperson in high-pressure selling techniques, such as those used in selling encyclopedias or automobiles. The techniques include overstating the product's merits, criticizing competing products, using a slick canned presentation, selling yourself, and offering some concession to get the order on the spot. This form of selling assumes the customers will not buy except under pressure; that they are influenced by a slick presentation; and that they will not be sorry after signing the order, or if they are, it does not matter.

The other approach trains salespeople in customer problem solving. The salesperson learns how to identify customer needs and find good solutions. This approach assumes that customer needs provide sales opportunities, that customers appreciate good suggestions, and that customers will be loyal to salespeople who have their long-term interests at heart. The problem solver salesperson fits better with the marketing concept than the hard seller or order taker.

Most training programs view the *selling process* as consisting of several steps that the salesperson must master. These steps are shown in Figure 17-2 and discussed below.[16]

Prospecting and Qualifying

The first step in the selling process is to identify prospects. The salesperson must approach many prospects to get a few sales. In one segment of the insurance industry, only one out of nine prospects becomes a customer. In the computer business, 125 phone calls result in 25 interviews leading to five demonstrations and one sale.[17] Although the company supplies leads, salespeople need skill in finding their own leads. Salespeople can obtain leads in many ways. They can ask current customers for the names of prospects. They can build referral sources, such as suppliers, dealers, noncompeting salespeople, and bankers. They can join organizations to which prospects belong, or engage in speaking and writing activities that will draw attention. Using news-

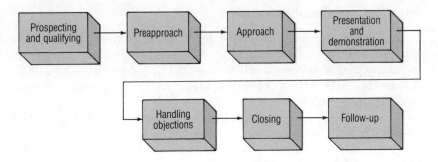

FIGURE 17-2
Major Steps in Effective Selling

papers or directories, they can search for names and use the telephone and mail to track down leads. Or they can drop in unannounced on various offices (cold calling).

Sales representatives need to know how to qualify leads, or screen out the poor ones. Prospects can be qualified by looking at their financial ability, volume of business, special needs, location, and possibilities for growth.

Preapproach

Before calling on a prospect, the salesperson should learn as much as possible about it (what it needs, who is involved in the buying) and its buyers (their characteristics and buying styles). The salesperson can consult standard sources (*Financial Post Survey of Industrials, Dun and Bradstreet*), acquaintances, and others to learn about the company. The salesperson should set **call objectives**, which might be to qualify the prospect, gather information, or make an immediate sale. Another task is to decide on the best approach, which might be a personal visit, a phonecall, or a letter. The best timing should be thought out because many prospects are busy at certain times. Finally, the salesperson should give thought to an overall sales strategy for the account.

Approach

The salesperson should know how to meet and greet the buyer to get the relationship off to a good start. This involves the salesperson's appearance, the opening lines, and the follow-up remarks. The salesperson should wear clothes similar to what the buyer wears; show courtesy and attention to the buyer; and avoid distracting mannerisms, such as pacing the floor or staring at the customer. The opening lines should be positive, such as "Mr. Smith, I am Yolanda Jones from the ABC Company. My company and I appreciate your willingness to see me. I will do my best to make this visit profitable and worthwhile for you and your company." This might be followed by some key questions or the showing of a display or sample to attract the buyer's attention and curiosity.

Presentation and Demonstration

The salesperson now tells the product "story" to the buyer, showing how the product will make or save money. The salesperson describes the product features but concentrates on selling the customer benefits. The salesperson will follow the AIDA formula of getting *attention*, holding *interest*, arousing *desire*, and obtaining *action*.

Companies use three styles of sales presentation. The oldest is the **canned approach**, which is a memorized sales talk covering the main points. An encyclopedia salesperson might describe the encyclopedia as "a once-in-a-lifetime buying opportunity" and focus on some beautiful four-color pages of sports pictures, hoping to trigger desire for the encyclopedia. Canned presentations are used mostly in door-to-door and telephone selling.

The **formula approach** first identifies the buyer's needs and buying style. The salesperson draws the buyer into a discussion that reveals the buyer's needs and attitudes. Then the salesperson moves into a formula presentation that shows how the product will satisfy that buyer's needs. It is not canned but follows a general plan.

The **need-satisfaction approach** starts with a search for the customer's real needs by getting the customer to do most of the talking. This approach calls for good listening and problem-solving skills. It is well described by an IBM salesperson: "I get inside the business of my key accounts. I uncover their key problems. I prescribe solutions for them, using my company's systems and even, at times, components from other suppliers. I prove beforehand that my systems will save money or make money for my accounts. Then I work with the account to install the system and make it prove out."[18]

Sales presentations can be improved with demonstration aids such as booklets, flip charts, slides, movies, and product samples. If buyers can see or handle the product, they will better remember its features and benefits.

A Procter & Gamble sales representative can describe how his or her company's products will increase profits for a retailer.

Courtesy: Procter & Gamble Canada

Handling Objections

Customers almost always have objections during the presentation or when asked to place an order. The problem can be logical or psychological. To handle these objections, the salesperson uses a positive approach, asks the buyer to clarify the objection, takes the objection as an opportunity to provide more information to the buyer, and turns the objection into a reason for buying. The salesperson needs training in the skills of handling objections.

Closing

The salesperson now tries to close the sale. Some salespeople do not get to this stage or do not handle it well. They lack confidence, or feel guilty about asking for the order, or do not recognize the right moment to close the sale. Salespeople need to know how to recognize closing signals from the buyer, including physical actions, comments, and questions. Salespeople can use one of several closing techniques. They can ask for the order, review the points of agreement, offer to help write up the order, ask whether the buyer wants A or B, get the buyer to make minor choices such as the color or size, or indicate that the buyer will lose out if the order is not placed now. The salesperson may offer the buyer special reasons to close, such as a lower price or an extra quantity at no charge.

Follow-Up

This last step is necessary if the salesperson wants to ensure customer satisfaction and repeat business. Right after closing, the salesperson should complete any details on delivery time, purchase terms, and other matters. The salesperson should schedule a follow-up call when the initial order is received to make sure there is proper installation, instruction, and servicing. This visit would show any problems, assure the buyer of the salesperson's interest, and reduce any buyer concerns that might have arisen.

Supervising Salespeople

New salespeople need more than a territory, compensation, and training—they need supervision. Through supervision, the company directs and motivates the salesforce to do a better job.

Directing Salespeople

Companies vary in how closely they supervise their salespeople. Salespeople who are paid mostly on commission and who are expected to hunt down their own prospects are generally left on their own. Those who are salaried and must cover assigned accounts are usually more closely supervised.

Developing Customer Targets and Call Norms

Most companies classify customers into A, B, and C accounts, based on the account's sales volume, profit potential, and growth potential. They set the desired number of calls per period on each account class. Thus A accounts may receive nine calls a year; B, six calls; and C, three calls. The call norms depend upon competitive call norms and profits expected from the account.

Developing Prospect Targets and Call Norms

Companies often specify how much time their salesforce should spend prospecting for new accounts. For example, a company may want its salespeople to spend 25% of their time prospecting, and to stop calling on a prospect after three unsuccessful calls.

Companies set up prospecting standards for several reasons. If left alone, many salespeople will spend most of their time with current customers. Current customers are better-known quantities. Salespeople can depend upon them for some business, whereas a prospect may never deliver any business. Unless salespeople are rewarded for opening new accounts, they may avoid new account development. Some companies rely on a special salesforce to open new accounts.

Using Sales Time Efficiently

Salespeople need to know how to use their time efficiently. One tool is the annual call schedule showing which customers and prospects to call on in which months, and which activities to carry out. The activities include taking part in trade shows, attending sales meetings, and carrying out marketing research.

The other tool is time-and-duty analysis. In addition to time spent selling, the salesperson spends time travelling, waiting, eating and taking breaks, and doing administrative chores. Actual selling time may amount to as little as 15% of total working time! If selling time could be raised from 15 to 20%, this would be a 33% increase in the time spent selling. Companies are always looking for ways to save time — using "phone power," simplifying recordkeeping forms, finding better call and routing plans, and supplying more and better customer information. Many companies are computerizing their call report and sales information systems to make salespeople more efficient.[19]

Motivating Salespeople

Some salespeople will do their best without any special urging from management. To them, selling is the most fascinating job in the world. They are ambitious and self-starters. Nevertheless, the selling job often involves frustration. Salespeople usually work alone, and they are sometimes away from home. They may face aggressive, competing salespeople and difficult customers. They sometimes do not have the authority to do what is needed to win a sale, and they may lose large orders they have worked hard to obtain. Thus salespeople often need special encouragement to work at their best level.

Management can boost salesforce morale and performance through its organizational climate, sales quotas, and positive incentives.

Organizational Climate

Organizational climate describes the feeling that the salespeople have about their opportunities, value, and rewards for a good performance. Some companies treat salespeople as if they are not very important. Other companies treat their salespeople as the prime movers and allow unlimited opportunity for income and promotion. The company's attitude toward its salespeople affects their behavior. If they are held in low esteem, there is much turnover and poor performance. If they are held in high esteem, there is little turnover and high performance.

Treatment from the salesperson's immediate superior is important. A good sales manager keeps in touch with the salesforce through letters and phone calls, visits in the field, and evaluation sessions in the home office. At different times the sales manager acts as the salesperson's boss, companion, coach, and confessor.

Sales Quotas

Many companies set quotas for their salespeople stating what they should sell during the year and by product. Their compensation is often related to how well they meet their quota.

Sales quotas are set when developing the annual marketing plan. The company first decides on a sales forecast that is reasonably achievable. Based on this forecast, management plans production, workforce size, and financial needs. It then sets sales quotas for its regions and territories. Sales quotas are set higher than the sales forecast to stretch sales managers and salespeople to their best effort. If they fail to make their quotas, the company may still make its sales forecast.

Positive Incentives

Companies use several incentives to increase salesforce effort. Sales meetings provide a social occasion, a break from routine, a chance to meet and talk with "company brass," and a chance to air feelings and to identify with a larger group. Companies also sponsor sales contests to spur the salesforce to make a selling effort above what would normally be expected. Other incentives include honors, awards, and profit-sharing plans.

Evaluating Salespeople

We have described how management communicates what the salespeople should be doing and motivates them to do it. However, this communication requires good feedback. Good feedback also means getting regular information from salespeople to evaluate their performance.

Sources of Information

Management gets information about its salespeople in several ways. The most important source is sales reports. Additional information comes from personal observation, customers' letters and complaints, customer surveys, and talks with other salespeople.

Sales reports are divided into plans for future activities and write-ups of completed activities. The best example of the first is the work plan, which salespeople submit a week or month in advance. The plan describes intended calls and routing. This report leads the salesforce to plan and schedule activities, informs management of their whereabouts, and provides a basis for comparing plans and performance. Salespeople can be evaluated on their ability to "plan their work and work their plan." Sometimes, management contacts individual salespeople after receiving their plans to suggest improvements.

Companies are beginning to require their salespeople to draft an annual territory marketing plan in which they outline their plans for building new accounts and increasing sales from existing accounts. The formats vary a lot— some ask for general ideas on territory development and others ask for detailed sales and profit estimates. This type of report casts salespeople into the role of marketing managers and profit centers. Their managers study these plans, make suggestions, and use them to develop sales quotas.

Salespeople write up their completed activities on call reports. Call reports keep sales management informed of the salesperson's activities, show what is happening with each customer's account, and provide information that might be useful in later calls. Salespeople also turn in expense reports for which they are partly or wholly repaid. Some companies also ask for reports on new business, reports on lost business, and reports on local business and economic conditions.

These reports supply the raw data from which sales management can evaluate salesforce performance. Are salespeople making too few calls per day? Are they spending too much time per call? Are they spending too much on entertainment? Are they closing enough orders per hundred calls? Are they finding enough new customers and holding on to the old customers?

Formal Evaluation of Performance

Using the salesforce reports and other information, sales management evaluates members of the salesforce. Formal evaluation produces three benefits. First, management must establish and communicate clear standards for judging performance. Second, management must gather well-rounded information about each salesperson. Third, salespeople know they will have to sit down one morning with the sales manager and explain their performance.

Comparing Salespeople's Performance

One type of evaluation is to compare and rank the sales performance of the different salespeople. Such comparisons, however, can be misleading. Salespeople may perform differently because of differences in factors such as territory potential, workload, level of competition, and company promotion effort. Furthermore, sales are not usually the best indicator of achievement. Management should be more interested in how much each salesperson contributes to net profits. This requires looking at each salesperson's sales mix and sales expenses.

Comparing Current Sales With Past Sales

A second type of evaluation is to compare a salesperson's current performance with past performance. This should directly indicate the person's progress. The comparison can show trends in sales and profits over the years for the salesperson. It can also show the salesperson's record on making calls and building new accounts. It cannot, however, tell why the salesperson's performance is moving in one direction or another.

Qualitative Evaluation of Salespeople

The evaluation usually looks at the salesperson's knowledge of the company, products, customers, competitors, territory, and tasks. Personal traits can be rated, such as general manner, appearance, speech, and temperament. The sales manager can also review any problems in motivation or compliance. Each company must decide what would be most useful to know. It should communicate these criteria to the salespeople so that they understand how their performance is evaluated and can make an effort to improve it.

Summary

Most companies use salespeople, and many companies assign them the key role in the marketing mix. The high cost of the salesforce calls for an effective sales management process consisting of six steps: setting salesforce objectives; designing salesforce strategy, structure, size, and compensation; recruiting and selecting; training; supervising; and evaluating.

As an element of the marketing mix, the salesforce is very effective in achieving certain marketing objectives and carrying on certain activities such as prospecting, communicating, selling and servicing, and information gathering. Under the marketing concept, the salesforce needs skills in marketing analysis and planning in addition to the traditional selling skills.

Once the salesforce objectives have been set, strategy answers the questions of what type of selling would be most effective (solo selling, team selling), what type of salesforce structure would work best (territorial, product, or customer structured), how large the salesforce should be, and how the salesforce should be compensated in terms of salary, commission, bonus, expenses, and fringe benefits.

Salespeople must be recruited and selected carefully to hold down the high costs of hiring the wrong people. Training programs familiarize new salespeople with the company's history, its products and policies, the characteristics of the market and competitors, and the art of selling. The art of selling involves a seven-step sales process: prospecting and qualifying, preapproach, approach, presentation and demonstration, handling objections, closing, and follow-up. Salespeople need supervision and continual encouragement because they must make many decisions and face many frustrations. Periodically, the company must evaluate their performance to help them do a better job.

Questions for Discussion

1. What are the advantages of personal selling over the other forms of promotion?
2. What personal qualities do you think are most important to a successful sales person? Why?
3. What are the relative advantages and disadvantages of the three salesforce structures?
4. The customer-oriented, problem-solving approach to training salespeople is consistent with the marketing concept. Comment.
5. A combination of straight salary and commission is probably the best way to compensate a salesforce. Comment.
6. You have just been hired by the World Book Encyclopedia Company to be a salesperson for the summer. Discuss how you would progress through the steps in effective selling.
7. How would your manager in question 6 go about evaluating your selling job for World Book at the end of the summer?
8. Salesperson to buyer is the only approach used to contact customers. Comment.

Chapter 17 Key Terms

Customer salesforce structure   A salesforce organization under which salespeople specialize in selling only to certain customers or industries.

Product salesforce structure   A salesforce organization under which salespeople specialize in selling only a portion of the company's products or lines.

Salesforce management   The analysis, planning, implementation and control of salesforce activities. It includes setting salesforce objectives; designing salesforce strategy; and recruiting, selecting, training, supervising, and evaluating the firm's salespeople.

Salesperson   An individual acting for a company who performs one or more of the following activities: prospecting, communicating, servicing, and information gathering.

Selling process   The steps that the salesperson follows when selling, which include prospecting and qualifying, preapproach, approach, presentation and demonstration, handling objections, closing, and follow-up.

Territorial salesforce structure   A salesforce organization that assigns each salesperson to an exclusive geographic territory in which the salesperson carries the company's full line.

Case for Chapter 17

Our processors squeezed by corn duty

By Renate Lerch

Ottawa Bureau Chief

A COUNTERVAILING duty designed to protect Canadian corn farmers from cheap

ronto, **St. Lawrence Starch Co.** of Mississauga, **Nacan Products Ltd.** of Brampton and **King Grain Ltd.** of Chatham. These companies buy about 24 mil-

tion from U.S. processors.

The CICU says the duty jeopardizes 700 production jobs in six Ontario communities where the four companies have invested

Grain prices have tumbled to about US$1.60-$1.70 a bushel this summer from US$3.60 in 1984. French corn growers joined the Canadians this week

solution should not come at the exp domestic industry. Processors h ready cut the price of glucose pro

The free trade gamble

By Deborah McGregor

Ottawa Bureau Chief

OTTAWA — The deal is done. But the battle is not won. In what is likely to be the most hotly contested fight for public opinion this country has ever witnessed, the opponents

virtually each passing hour, Canadian companies and workers in every sector and every region of the country were also part of the war.

But for most, the struggle was a more basic one of trying to decipher just exactly what the agreement contained and what it all meant.

To some, this spelled trouble. To others, it was a blessing

Alberta energy producers were pleased as th yoke of government restraint being lifted sales.

Ontario wine growers

REPORT ON BUSINESS

THE GLOBE AND MAIL, MONDAY, O

xport market helps keep Ya...cle maker m...

B.C. companies begin setting up shop in Washington

By DEBORAH JONES

Special to The Globe and Mail

YARMOUTH, N.S.

War is not only hell for the participants, but bad for business too, even if you're in the business of exporting ambulances — like Tri-Star Industries Ltd.

The seven-year conflict between Iran and Iraq has put an end to Tri-Star's sales to Iraq, its biggest customer. At one point, Yarmouth-based Tri-Star rented an airport runway to line up 376 of its ambulances destined for Baghdad.

Out of necessity, the manufacturer of specialized vehicles, which include hearses, custom vans and wreckers, turned its marketing attention elsewhere, winning customers in new export markets and winning several provincial government export awards in the process. On Sept. 1, it landed a $10.6-mil-

The Tri-Star division was formed in 1973 when the company's owners saw a need for a Canadian converter of stock vehicles to...

From its...show...

...Star con...up trucks and luxu... ...into emergency vehicles ...all terrains. It ships them, along with hearses produced by other converters, throughout Canada and to other countries.

The bulk of its sales effort goes toward winning small contracts in Canada, mainly in the Atlantic region, although Tri-Star has also won contracts from the Ontario Government to supply emergency vehicles, Mr. Condon said. But 60 per cent of its average $5-million in annual sales are in exports.

panies in the United States, are often too high pressure, he said.

In January, to cement tionship with Morocco a trade miss... companies... ment

INDUSTRY'S SURPR... NORTH OF THE BO...

Canada's boom is riding on m...

...hen Peter J. Nygard mo... Toronto after 20 years... nipeg, Man... he w... splash. So he celebrate... of his $150 million wo... ...ompany with a four-d... ...ded by 1,500 guests a... ...light of lasers beam... ...500-ft. observati... ...fanfare...

International Business

CANADA

British Gas buys bigger Bow Valley stake

BY BRIAN MILNER

The Globe and Mail

Expansion-minded British Gas PLC is extending its reach to Canada with an agreement to acquire control of Bow Valley Industries Ltd.

The Calgary-based oil and gas producer has reached a deal that could give British Gas up to 51 per cent of the company at a total cost of $1.37-billion.

...though, the huge British

would have to pay another $800-million for 33 million new common shares to move its stake to 51 per cent.

British Gas says it has no plans to make a tender offer for existing Bow Valley shares.

Completion of the deal, which is subject to approval by Bow Valley shareholders, the federal Government and other regulatory authorities, is expected by the end of September.

ious to expand into production elsewhere. The Bow Valley move is its first such step in this direction.

The board of British Gas thinks the proposed investment "will contribute to the development of an international base for our exploration and development activities," Sir Dennis said.

Mr. Seaman called the deal "a major vote of confidence" in Canadian oil and gas...

Without...

...from a recent

...inous signal to world markets'

..."competitive advantage in international commerce that would not exist but for government action." This ...would probably include Canada's regulated utility ...support of public inland waterways and other ...subsidies. Not only would such action ...Asian countries to retaliate ...in areas such as air- ...ed as a pre-

International Marketing

Chapter Objectives

After reading this chapter, you should be able to:
1. Discuss how foreign trade, economic, political-legal, and cultural environments affect a company's international marketing decisions.
2. Describe three approaches to entering foreign markets.
3. Explain how companies might adapt their marketing mixes for foreign markets.
4. Identify the three forms of international marketing organization.

Canada is one of the world's major trading nations with exports accounting for about 30% of the gross domestic product. Most of Canada's exports are raw materials or semi-finished products reflecting the country's rich natural resource base. Most imports to Canada are manufactured products. For decades, attempts have been made to break this pattern of Canadians as ''hewers of wood and drawers of water.'' While a number of suggestions and strategies have been considered and tried, the pattern continues. There are a variety of reasons for this:

• About 40% of Canada's manufacturing industry is controlled by foreign owners. This often constrains the Canadian subsidiary or ''branch plant'' from exporting because the parent firm is operating in most world markets. Further, productivity levels in many manufacturing industries in Canada are lower than comparable levels in the United States and other major manufacturing nations.

• Canada is a resource-based country and there is world demand for many of these resources (e.g., wheat, fish, metals and minerals, forest products).

• The relatively small Canadian market can mean establishing manufacturing plants on a scale unsuitable for world markets, or not competitive with them.

One recent strategy designed to increase the export of manufactured goods is a simple, yet appealing, concept — world product mandating. It recognizes that a large part of the manufacturing sector is made up of subsidiaries of foreign companies who depend on the parent firm for technology and often confine their sales to the Canadian market. The world-product mandating strategy seeks to use the power of the multinational parent company to sell a product or product line, manufactured by the Canadian-based subsidiary, on a world-wide basis. With the mandate, the subsidiary designs and manufactures a specific product and is responsible for marketing the product globally.

Like any strategy, world product mandating has pros and cons, but a number of success stories can be told:

• Litton Systems Canada, a subsidiary of the U.S. Litton Industries, developed a second-generation inertial navigation system for military and commercial aircraft. The system, introduced in 1971, accounted for sales of $100 million by 1980. The Canadian subsidiary now controls 65% of the world market for the product.

- Wabco Canada, a subsidiary of American Standard of New York, manufactured brakes for railway and transit cars. In 1984 Wabco Canada was operating at 20% capacity and the U.S. parent was considering closing the Ontario plant and manufacturing only in the U.S. The Canadian managers, with assistance from the Ontario Government, convinced the parent company to give them a world product mandate for brakes. Capacity at the plant has tripled and Wabco expects sales in 1990 to reach $150 million, about three times the 1985 total.

- Westinghouse Canada managers realized they needed a new strategic plan in the 1970s when profits were declining and tariffs around the world were coming down. The managers aggressively fought for mandates and now have 20 world product mandates, which account for 40% of production.

Other Canadian subsidiaries, including Black & Decker, CGE, NCR, Westinghouse, Garrett Manufacturing, Pratt and Whitney, and Xerox have successfully used world product mandating. These firms now regard the world as their market. A high level of skills is required — from technology to production expertise to marketing strategy — to operate in the international arena, and these Canadian companies have shown they have what it takes. While the risks are often great in international marketing, so are the rewards for successful firms.[1]

Because the Canadian market is relatively small, companies interested in growth will enter international marketing. The first step is usually the U.S. market, roughly ten times the size of the Canadian market, and with a similar social, political, economic, and technological environment. The U.S. is Canada's main trading partner; over 75% of Canada's exports and 70% of imports are with the United States. Other major markets where Canadian companies operate are the Asian Pacific market and the European Economic Community. Marketing in most of these countries requires managers to learn another language, deal with a different currency, face political and legal uncertainties, and often adapt the product to a different set of needs and expectations.

A major portion of Canada's exports are raw or semi-fabricated materials. Food, gas and oil, forest products, minerals, and chemicals account for 52% of exports; finished products account for 48%.[2] Most of the finished products are in transportation equipment such as cars and trucks, which are exported to the United States as part of the Auto Pact. This trade pattern reflects Canada's resource base and the control of much of the country's manufacturing sector by foreign owners.[3] The Canadian federal government has encouraged companies to expand their activities abroad in order to earn more foreign exchange and increase employment in Canada. In addition to establishing trade missions in most foreign markets, the Canadian government organized the Export Development Corporation, a Crown corporation that assists companies in financing foreign sales.

Many Canadian subsidiaries of U.S. firms operate in world markets through product mandating. In addition, a number of Canadian companies have gone into world marketing on such a large scale that they can be called multinational companies. Among Canadian companies selling more than 50% of their output abroad are Alcan, Seagram, Inco, MacMillan Bloedel, Noranda Mines, Moore, Abitibi, Bombardier, and Hiram Walker.[4] Well-known U.S. multinational firms such as General Motors, Ford, IBM, Xerox, and Coca-Cola operate in virtually all world markets. These North American multinationals compete with foreign multinational companies such as Royal Dutch/Shell, British Petroleum, Unilever, Philips, Volkswagenwerk, Nippon Steel, Siemens, Toyota Motor, and Nestlé.

In addition to U.S. multinational firms operating in Canada through subsidiaries, many other foreign companies have entered the Canadian market. Their names and brands have become household words, such as Sony, Honda, Datsun, Nestlé, Perrier, Norelco, Mercedes Benz, and Volkswagen, with many Canadians showing a preference for these brands over domestic brands.

In recent years Canadian firms have been investing in foreign markets at an accelerating rate. Most of this investment is in the United States, and Canada is now the third-largest investor in that country.[5] The major reasons why these firms are entering foreign markets are the greater rewards offered and, in some cases, a negative view of the Canadian economic and political environment.[6] Canadian real estate companies, such as Cadillac Fairview and Coscan, have been particularly active in the U.S., along with retailers like Loblaws, Shoppers Drug Mart, Dylex, and Consumer's Distributing, and manufacturers such as John Labatt. These firms have entered the international marketing arena to expand their operations and improve their growth and profitability, although some have not achieved these goals.[7] As one example, Canadian Tire's expansion into the United States was a disaster that cost the company over $55 million in losses in one year alone.

We might ask: Does international marketing, particularly for Canadian firms operating in the U.S., involve any new principles? In general the answer is no—the principles of marketing objectives, choosing target markets, developing marketing positions and mixes, and carrying out marketing control still apply. The principles are not new, but the differences between nations can be so great that the international marketer needs to understand foreign countries and how people in different countries respond to marketing efforts.

We will now look at the six decisions that a company faces in international marketing (see Figure 18-1).

FIGURE 18-1
Major Decisions in International Marketing

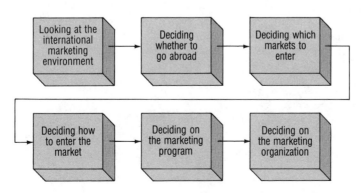

Looking at the International Marketing Environment

A company has to learn many things before deciding whether to sell abroad. The company must thoroughly understand the international marketing environment. That environment has changed very much since 1945, creating both new opportunities and new problems. World trade and investment have grown rapidly, and countries such as Japan have increased their economic power in world markets (see Exhibit 18-1). Canadian companies face increasing trade barriers put up to protect domestic markets against foreign competition. Nevertheless, attractive new markets are opening up in China, the USSR, and some Arab countries.

EXHIBIT 18-1
The World's Champion Marketers: The Japanese?

Few dispute that the Japanese have performed an economic miracle since World War II. In a very short time, they have achieved global market leadership in many industries: autos, motorcycles, watches, cameras, optical instruments, pianos, zippers, radios, television, and video recorders. Many theories have been offered to explain Japan's global success. Some point to their unique business and management practices. Others point to the help they get from Japan's government, powerful trading companies, and banks. Still others say Japan's success is based on low wage rates and unfair dumping policies.

One of the main keys to Japan's success is its skillful use of marketing. The Japanese know how to select a market, enter it in the right way, build market share, and protect their share against competitors.

Selecting Markets

The Japanese work hard to identify attractive global markets. They look for industries that require high skills, high labor intensity, and only small amounts of natural resources. These include consumer electronics, cameras, watches, motorcycles, and pharmaceuticals. The Japanese prefer product markets that are new and changing. They like markets where consumers around the world would be willing to buy the same product designs. Industries where the market leaders are complacent or underfinanced are also attractive to them.

Entering Markets

Japanese study teams spend several months in the target country evaluating the market. The teams search for market niches that are not currently being satisfied. Some-

The International Trade System

The Canadian company looking abroad must start by understanding the international trade system. When selling to another country, the Canadian firm will face various trade restrictions. The most common is the *tariff*, which is a tax levied by the foreign government against certain imported products. The tariff may be designed to raise revenue or to protect domestic firms. The exporter may also face a *quota*, which sets limits on the amount of goods that the importing country will accept in certain product categories. The purpose of the quota is to conserve on foreign exchange and protect local industry and employment. An embargo, under which some kinds of imports are totally banned, is the strongest form of quota. Canadian firms may face **exchange controls**, which limit the amount of foreign exchange and the exchange rate against other cur-

times they start with a low-price, stripped-down version of a product, sometimes with a product that is as good as those of the competitors but priced lower, sometimes with a product that has higher quality or new features. The Japanese line up good distribution in order to provide quick service to their customers, and use advertising to bring their products to the consumer's attention. Their entry strategy is to build market share rather than early profits. The Japanese are often willing to wait even a decade before realizing their profits.

Building Market Share

Once Japanese firms gain a market foothold, they begin to expand their market share. They pour money into product improvements and new models so that they can offer more and better features than the competition. They spot new opportunities through market segmentation, develop markets in new countries, and work to build a network of world markets and production locations.

Protecting Market Share

Once the Japanese achieve market leadership, they become defenders rather than attackers. Many multinational and domestic companies are fighting back. The Japanese defense strategy is a good offense through continuous product development and refined market segmentation. They aim to fill holes in the market before their competition can.

Source: Philip Kotler and Liam Fahey, "The World's Champion Marketers: The Japanese," *Journal of Business Strategy,* Summer 1982, pp. 3-13.

rencies. The company may also face **nontariff barriers**, such as bias against Canadian company bids, and product standards that go against Canadian product features. For example, the Dutch government bans tractors that run faster than 16 kilometers an hour, which means that most Canadian-made tractors are barred.

At the same time, certain forces help trade between nations, or at least between some nations. Certain countries have formed *economic communities*, the most important of which is the European Economic Community (EEC, also known as the Common Market). The EEC's members are the major Western European nations, and they are working together to reduce tariffs, reduce prices, and expand employment and investment. The EEC sets no tariffs on its members, but sets a uniform tariff for trade with nonmember nations. Since the EEC's formation, other economic communities have been formed, such as the Latin American Free Trade Association (LAFTA), the Central American Common Market (CACM), the Council for Mutual Economic Assistance (CMEA) (Eastern European countries), and the Association of South East Asian Nations (ASEAN).

Each nation has unique features that must be grasped. A nation's readiness for different products and services, and its attractiveness as a market to foreign firms, depend on its economic, political-legal, and cultural environments.

Economic Environment

In looking at foreign markets, the international marketer must study each country's economy. Two economic factors reflect the country's attractiveness as an export market.

The first is the country's **industrial structure**. The industrial structure of a country shapes its product and service needs, income levels, and employment levels. There are four types of industrial structures.

Subsistence economies *In a subsistence economy the vast majority of people engage in simple agriculture. They consume most of their output and barter the rest for simple goods and services. They offer few market opportunities.*

Raw-material exporting economies *These economies are rich in one or more natural resources but poor in other ways. Much of their revenue comes from exporting these resources. Examples are Chile (tin and copper), Congo (rubber), and Saudi Arabia (oil). These countries are good markets for large equipment, tools and supplies, and trucks. If there are many foreign residents and a wealthy upper class, they are also a market for luxury goods.*

Industrializing economies *In an industrializing economy, manufacturing accounts for between 10 and 20% of the country's economy. Examples include Egypt, the Philippines, India, and Brazil. As manufacturing increases, the country needs more imports of textile raw materials, steel, and heavy machinery, and fewer imports of finished textiles, paper products, and automobiles. The industrialization creates a new wealthy class* *and a small but growing middle class, both demanding new types of imported goods.*

Industrial economies   *Industrial economies are major exporters of manufactured goods and investment funds. They trade goods among themselves and also export them to other types of economies for raw materials and semifinished goods. The varied manufacturing activities of these industrial nations and their large middle class make them rich markets for all sorts of goods.*

The second economic factor is the country's **income distribution**. The international marketer might find countries with five different income-distribution patterns: (1) very low family incomes, (2) mostly low family incomes, (3) very low, very high family incomes, (4) low, medium, high family incomes, and (5) mostly medium family incomes. Consider the market for Lamborghinis, an automobile costing more than $50 000. The market would be very small in countries with type 1 or type 2 income patterns. The largest single market for Lamborghinis turns out to be Portugal (income pattern 3), the poorest country in Europe, but one with enough wealthy, status-conscious families to afford them.

Political-Legal Environment

Nations differ greatly in their political-legal environments. At least four such factors should be considered in deciding whether to do business in a given country.

Attitudes Toward International Buying

Some nations are very receptive to foreign firms, and others are very hostile. For example, Mexico for many years has been attracting foreign businesses by offering investment incentives and site-location services. On the other hand, India has created obstacles for foreign businesses with import quotas, currency restrictions, and limits on the number of non-nationals in the management team. IBM and Coca-Cola decided to leave India because of all the ''hassles.''

Political Stability

Stability is another issue. Governments change hands, sometimes violently. Even without a change, a government may decide to respond to new popular feelings. The foreign company's property may be taken over; or its currency holdings may be blocked; or import quotas or new duties may be set. International marketers may still find it profitable to do business in an unstable country, but the situation will affect how they handle business and financial matters.[8]

Monetary Regulations

Sellers want to take their profits in a currency of value to them. Ideally, the buyer can pay in the seller's currency or in other world currencies. Short of this, sellers might accept a blocked currency if they can buy other goods in that country that they need or can sell elsewhere for a needed currency. In the worst case they have to take their money out of the host country in the form of less marketable products that they can sell elsewhere only at a loss. Many Canadian firms are forced to engage in countertrade, buying goods of the foreign country in order to sell their products to that country.[9] Besides currency limits, a changing exchange rate also creates high risks for the seller.

Government Bureaucracy

A fourth factor is the extent to which the host government runs an efficient system for helping foreign companies; efficient customs handling, good market information, and other factors that aid in doing business.

Cultural Environment

Each country has its own folkways, norms, and taboos. The way foreign consumers think about and use certain products must be checked by the seller before planning the marketing program. Here are samples of some of the surprises in the consumer market:

- The average Frenchman uses almost twice as many cosmetics and beauty aids as does his wife.

- The Germans and the French eat more packaged, branded spaghetti than the Italians.

- Italian children like to eat a chocolate bar between two slices of bread as a snack.

- Women in Tanzania will not give their children eggs for fear of making them bald or impotent.

Business norms and behavior also vary from country to country. Here are some examples of different foreign business behavior:

- South Americans like to sit or stand very close to each other when they talk business — in fact, almost nose to nose. The Canadian business executive keeps backing away as the South American moves closer. Both end up being offended.

- In face-to-face communications, Japanese business executives rarely say no to a Canadian business executive. Canadians are frustrated and know where they stand. Canadians come to the point quickly. Japanese business executives find this offensive.

- In France, wholesalers do not want to promote a product. They ask their retailers what they want, and deliver it. If a Canadian company builds its strategy around the French wholesaler's cooperation in promotions, it is likely to fail.

- In Muslim countries it is not proper to give anyone anything with your left hand. If you hand a person a pen with your left hand to sign a contract, he might not do it.[10]

Each country and region has cultural traditions, preferences, and taboos that the marketer must study.

Deciding Whether To Go Abroad

Companies get involved in international marketing in one of two ways. Some-one—a domestic exporter, a foreign importer, a foreign government—asks the company to sell abroad. Or the company starts to think on its own about going abroad. It might face overcapacity or see better marketing opportunities in other countries than at home. For example, in one study of small and medium size Canadian manufacturers, 30% got into international marketing through unsolicited orders, while most of the rest entered because they saw good opportunities in other countries.[11]

Before going abroad, the company should try to define its international marketing objectives and policies. First, it should decide what volume of foreign sales it wants. Most companies start small when they go abroad. Some plan to stay small, seeing foreign sales as a small part of their business. Other companies have bigger plans, seeing foreign business as equal to or even more important than their domestic business.

Second, the company must choose between marketing in a few countries and marketing in many countries. Third, the company must decide on the types of countries to enter. Which countries are attractive will depend on the product, geographical factors, income and population, political climate, and other factors. The seller may prefer certain country groups or parts of the world.

Deciding Which Markets To Enter

After listing possible export markets, the company will have to screen and rank them. The countries should be ranked on several factors such as market size, market growth, cost of doing business, competitive advantage, and risk level. Information on these factors may be obtained from the Canadian federal government, which offers a wide range of services to exporters including information on foreign markets, assistance in visiting foreign markets, and identification of potential customers.[12] The goal is to figure out the market potential of each market, using indicators such as those shown in Table 18-1. Then the marketer must decide which markets will offer the greatest long-run return on investment.

TABLE 18-1
Indicators of Market Potential

1. Demographic characteristics	**4. Technological factors**
Size of population	Level of technological skill
Rate of population growth	Existing production technology
Degree of urbanization	Existing consumption technology
Population density	Education levels
Age structure and composition of the population	
	5. Sociocultural factors
2. Geographic characteristics	Dominant values
	Life-style patterns
Physical size of a country	Ethnic groups
Topographical characteristics	Linguistic fragmentation
Climate conditions	
	6. National goals and plans
3. Economic factors	
GNP per capita	Industry priorities
Income distribution	Infrastructure investment plans
Rate of growth of GNP	
Ratio of investment to GNP	

Source: Susan P. Douglas, C. Samuel Craig, and Warren Keegan, "Approaches to Assessing International Marketing Opportunities for Small and Medium-Sized Business," *Columbia Journal of World Business*, Fall 1982, pp. 26-32.

Deciding How To Enter the Market

Once a company has decided to sell to a country, it must determine the best mode of entry. Its choices are exporting, joint venturing, and direct investment abroad.[13] Each succeeding strategy involves more commitment, risk, and possible profits. The three market entry strategies are shown in Figure 18-2, along with the options under each.

Export

The simplest way to enter a foreign market is through *exporting*. The company may passively export its surpluses from time to time, or it may actively make a commitment to expand exports to a particular market. In either case the company produces all its goods in the home country. It may or may not modify them for the export market. Exporting involves the least change in the company's product lines, organization, investments, or mission. Because the U.S. market

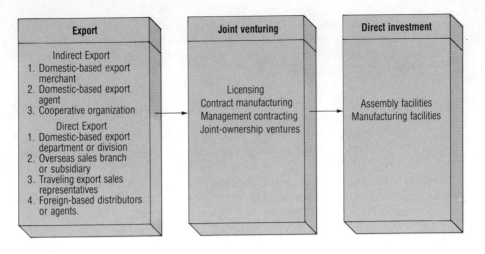

FIGURE 18-2
Market Entry Strategies

is so close and has a similar environment to the Canadian market, many Canadian firms engage in occasional or active exporting to the U.S.

A company can export its product in two ways. It can hire independent international marketing middlemen (indirect export) or handle its own exporting (direct export).

Indirect Export

Indirect export is more common in companies just beginning to export. First, it involves less investment. The firm does not need a foreign salesforce or a set of contacts. Second, it involves less risk. International marketing middlemen —domestic-based export merchants or agents, or cooperative organizations— bring knowhow and services to the relationship, and the seller normally makes fewer mistakes.

Direct Export

Sellers approached by foreign buyers are likely to use direct export. So will sellers whose exporters have grown large enough to do their own exporting. The investment and risk are somewhat greater, but so is the potential return.

The company can carry on direct exporting in several ways. First, it can set up a domestic export department that carries out export activities. Or it can set up an overseas sales branch that handles sales, distribution, and perhaps promotion. The sales branch gives the seller more presence and program control in the foreign market. It often serves as a display center and customer service center. Alternatively, the company can send home-based sales representatives abroad at certain times to find business. Finally, the company can do its exporting through foreign-based distributors who buy and own the goods, or through foreign-based agents who sell the goods on behalf of the company. In one study of Canadian exporters, most of the firms used the direct method. Smaller firms tended to use indirect methods, probably because of the high working capital costs of sales branches.[14]

Joint Venturing

A second method of entering a foreign market is through *joint venturing*, joining with foreign companies to set up production and marketing facilities. Joint venturing differs from exporting in that the company joins with a partner to set up some production facilities abroad. It differs from direct investment in that an association is formed with someone in the foreign country. There are four types of joint venture.

Licensing

Licensing is a simple way for a manufacturer to enter international marketing. The company enters an agreement with a licensee in the foreign market, offering the right to use a manufacturing process, trademark, patent, trade secret, or other items of value for a fee or royalty. The company gains entry into the market at little risk; the licensee gains production expertise, or a well-known product or name, without having to start from scratch. Coca-Cola carries out its international marketing by licensing bottlers around the world.

Licensing has potential disadvantages. The firm has less control over the licensee than if it had set up its own production facilities. Furthermore, if the licensee is very successful, the firm has given up these profits. If and when the contract ends, the firm may find that it has created a competitor. To avoid these dangers, the licensor must create a mutual advantage for the licensee. A key to doing this is to remain innovative so that the licensee continues to depend on the company.[15]

Contract Manufacturing

Another option is *contract manufacturing*, contracting with manufacturers in the foreign market to produce the product. Contract manufacturing has the drawback of less control over the manufacturing process, which may mean the loss of potential profits on manufacturing. On the other hand, it offers the company a chance to start faster with less risk, and with the opportunity to form a partnership with or buy out the local manufacturer later.

Management Contracting

Under *management contracting*, the domestic firm supplies the management knowhow to a foreign company that supplies the capital. The domestic firm is exporting management services rather than products. Hilton uses this arrangement in managing hotels around the world.

Management contracting is a low-risk method of getting into a foreign market, and it yields income from the beginning. The arrangement is very attractive if the contracting firm has an option to buy some share in the managed company later on. On the other hand, the arrangement is not sensible if the company can put its scarce management talent to better uses or if it can make greater profits by undertaking the whole venture. Management contracting prevents the company from setting up its own operations for a period of time.

Joint Ownership

Joint ownership ventures consist of the company joining with foreign investors to create a local business in which they share joint ownership and control. The company may buy an interest in a local firm, or the two parties may form a new business venture.

A jointly owned venture may be needed for economic or political reasons. The firm may lack the financial, physical, or managerial resources to undertake the venture alone. Or the foreign government may require joint ownership as a condition for entry. Many Canadian firms are entering the Japanese market on a joint venture basis. The advantages for the Canadian firms include: gaining an understanding of the complex Japanese business system, synergistic advantages, the availability of competent and reliable partners, and the diversification of risk and return. For the Japanese firms the main advantage is gaining access to technology or knowhow that the Japanese companies themselves do not possess.[16]

Joint ownership has certain drawbacks. The partners may disagree over investment, marketing, or other policies. Where many Canadian firms like to reinvest earnings for growth, local firms often like to take out these earnings. Where Canadian firms give a large role to marketing, local investors may rely on selling.[17]

Direct Investment

The biggest involvement in a foreign market comes through direct investment, developing foreign-based assembly or manufacturing facilities. As a company gains experience in exporting, and if the foreign market is large enough, foreign production facilities offer many advantages. First, the firm may have lower costs in the form of cheaper labor or raw materials, foreign government investment incentives, and freight savings. Second, the firm will gain a better image in the host country because it creates jobs. Third, the firm develops a deeper relationship with government, customers, local suppliers, and distributors, letting it adapt its products better to the local market. Fourth, the firm keeps full control over the investment and can therefore develop manufacturing and marketing policies that serve its long-term international objectives. Canadian firms are increasingly using the direct investment method of operating in foreign markets. Direct investment by Canadian firms in the U.S. alone is estimated at over $1 billion annually, and total direct investment by Canadian firms in the U.S. exceeds $20 billion.[18]

The main disadvantage is that the firm faces many risks in certain countries, such as restricted or devalued currencies, falling markets, or government takeover. In some cases, the firm has no choice but to accept these risks if it wants to operate in the host country.

Deciding on the Marketing Program ━━━━━

Companies that operate in one or more foreign markets must decide how much, if at all, to adapt their marketing mixes to local conditions. At one extreme are companies that use a *standardized marketing mix* worldwide. Standardization of the product, advertising, distribution channels, and other elements of the marketing mix promises the lowest costs because no major changes have been introduced.

EXHIBIT 18-2
Customization or Globalization?

Companies disagree on how much they should standardize their products and marketing programs across world markets. On the one hand are companies that customize their offerings to meet the varied needs of consumers in different markets. On the other hand are companies that sell their products about the same way worldwide. We will look at each side's position.

On the One Hand ...

Traditional international marketers hold that consumers in different countries vary a lot in their needs and wants, and that marketing programs will be more effective if they are tailored to specific market needs. Weir states:

> There is no "international" market ... from a marketing standpoint. Instead there are literally dozens of countries in which a country's products and services can be sold. All of these are different from one another in their economies, politics, traditions, cultures, and customer habits ... and ingrained consumer habits are hard to change.

Those who support customized marketing programs point out that countries differ in economic, political, legal, and cultural respects. Consumers in different countries have varied geographic, demographic, economic, and cultural characteristics, resulting in different needs and wants, spending power, product preferences, and shopping patterns. Most international marketers think that such differences across cultures call for customized products, prices, distribution channels, and promotion strategies.

One international marketer suggests that firms should "think globally but act locally to give the individual consumer more to say in what he or she wants." The corporate level gives strategic direction; local units focus on the individual consumer differences. This strategy is based on the belief that too much standardization places a company at a disadvantage against competitors who produce the goods that consumers want.

Thus most companies see differences in consumer needs and wants in different countries, assume that these differences are hard to change, and customize their products and marketing programs to serve unique consumer needs in each country.

At the other extreme is a *customized marketing mix*. The producer adjusts the marketing mix elements to each target market, bearing more costs but hoping for a larger market share and return. Between these two extremes, many possibilities exist (see Exhibit 18-2).

A recent survey of leading consumer packaged goods multinationals concluded: "To the successful multinational, it is not really important whether marketing programs are internationally standardized or differentiated; the important thing is that the *process* through which these programs are developed is standardized."[19]

On the Other Hand ...

Recently, many companies have moved toward **global marketing**. They have created "world brands" that are manufactured and marketed in much the same way worldwide. These global marketers believe that advances in communication, transportation, and travel are turning the world into a common marketplace. They claim that people around the world want the same products and lifestyles. All people want things that make life easier and increase their free time and buying power. Common needs and wants create global markets for standardized products.

Instead of focusing on differences between markets, and customizing products to meet these differences, the global corporation sells more or less the same product the same way to all consumers to take advantage of the lower costs resulting from standardization. It customizes products and marketing programs to meet local wants only when these wants cannot be changed or avoided. The global marketers realize lower costs through standardization of production, distribution, marketing, and management. Thus they can offer consumers high quality and more reliable products at lower prices.

Global marketers agree that there *are* differences in consumer wants and buying behavior in different markets, and that these differences cannot be entirely ignored. But they think the wants and behavior are changeable. According to Theodore Levitt, despite what consumers *say* they want, all consumers want good products at lower prices. He thinks that consumers will accept high-quality, lower-priced standardized products even if they are not entirely suitable.

If the price is low enough, they will take highly standardized world products, even if these aren't exactly what mother said was suitable, what immemorial custom decreed was right, or what market researchers ... asserted was preferred.

Which approach is best—customization or globalization? The answer is different for each company. It depends on the nature of each firm's products, markers, market position, financial resources, and other factors. But for most companies, the answer probably lies somewhere between the two extremes.

Sources: Based on Edward L. Weir, "Avoiding the Pitfalls of International Marketing," *Marketing and Media Decisions*, March 1983, pp. 80-82; "Modular Marketing Cracks International Markets," *Marketing News*, April 27 1984, p. 10; Mitchell Lynch, "Harvard's Levitt Called Global Marketing 'Guru,'" *Advertising Age*, June 25 1984, pp. 49-50; Theodore Levitt, "The Globalization of Markets," *Harvard Business Review*, May-June 1983, pp. 92-102. Excerpt reprinted by permission of the *Harvard Business Review*. Copyright 1983 by the President and Fellows of Harvard College, all rights reserved.

We will now look at possible changes in a company's product, promotion, price, and distribution as it goes abroad.

Product

Keegan lists five strategies for adapting product and promotion to a foreign market (see Figure 18-3).[20] Here we will look at the three product strategies, and later look at the two promotion strategies.

Straight extension means marketing the product in the foreign market without any change. Top management tells its marketing people: "Take the product as is and find customers for it." The first step, however, should be to find out whether the foreign consumers use that product. Deodorant usage among men ranges from 80% in Canada to 55% in Sweden, 28% in Italy, and 8% in the Philippines. Many Spaniards do not use such common products as butter and cheese.

Straight extension has been successful in some cases but a disaster in others. Massey-Ferguson designed a large-horsepower tractor with standard 74-inch treads and had little success selling it to corn farmers in the United States. The reason — the corn is planted in 30-inch rows there, and 74-inch treads would have trampled every third row.[21] Straight extension is tempting because it involves no additional product development costs, manufacturing changes, or new promotion.

Product adaptation involves changing the product to meet local conditions or wants. Heinz varies its baby-food products: in Australia it sells a baby food made from strained lamb brains and in the Netherlands, a baby food made from strained brown beans. General Foods blends different coffees for the British (who drink their coffee with milk), the French (who drink their coffee black), and Latin Americans (who want a chicory taste).

Product invention consists of creating something new. This can take two forms. Product invention might mean reintroducing earlier product forms that happen to be well adapted to the needs of that country. The National Cash Register Company reintroduced its crank-operated cash register, selling at half the price of a modern cash register, and sold large numbers in the Orient, Latin

FIGURE 18-3
Five International Product and Promotion Strategies

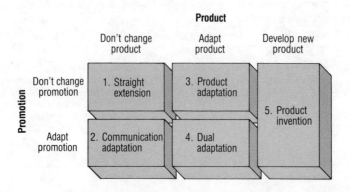

America, and Spain. Or the company might create a brand new product to meet a need in another country. There is an enormous need in less-developed countries for low-cost, high-protein foods.

Promotion

Companies can adopt the same promotion strategy they used in the home market or change it for each local market.

Consider the message. Many multinational companies use a standardized advertising theme around the world. Exxon used "Put a tiger in your tank" and gained international recognition. The copy is varied in a minor way, such as changing the colors to avoid taboos in other countries. Purple is associated with death in most of Latin America; white is a mourning color in Japan; and green is associated with jungle sickness in Malaysia. Even names have to be changed. In Germany, *scotch* (scotch tape) means "schmuck."

Other companies ask their international divisions to develop their own ads. For example, when Moosehead beer was launched in the U.S. market, both the package and promotion were changed. These changes along with a catchy slogan — "It stands head and antlers above the rest" — made it one of the top ten selling import beers in the U.S.[22]

Media also need to be adapted internationally because media availability varies from country to country. Commercial TV time is available for one hour each evening in Germany, and advertisers must buy time months in advance. In Sweden, there is no commercial TV time. There is no commercial radio in France and Scandinavia. Magazines are a major medium in Italy and a minor one in Austria. Newspapers are national in the United Kingdom and local in Spain.

Price

Manufacturers often price their products lower in foreign markets. Incomes may be low, and a low price is necessary to sell the goods. The manufacturer may set low prices to build a market share. Or the manufacturer may want to dump goods that have no market at home. If the manufacturer charges less in the foreign market than in the home market, this is called **dumping**. If the Canadian government finds dumping, it can levy a dumping tariff.

Manufacturers have little control over the retail prices charged by foreign middlemen who carry their products. Many foreign middlemen use high mark-ups, even though this means selling fewer units. They also like to buy on credit, and this increases the manufacturer's cost and risk.

Distribution Channels

The international company must take a **whole-channel** view of the problem of distributing products to final consumers.[23] Figure 18-4 shows the three major links between the seller and the final buyer. The first link, the seller's headquarters organization, supervises the channels between nations, and gets the products to the borders of the foreign nations. The third link, channels within nations, gets the products from their foreign entry point to the final consumers.

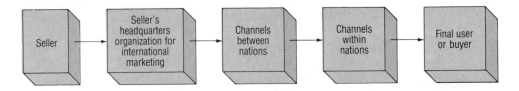

FIGURE 18-4
Whole-Channel Concept for International Marketing

Too many Canadian manufacturers think their job is done once the product leaves their hands. They should pay more attention to how it is handled within the foreign country.

Within-country channels of distribution vary a lot from country to country. There are large differences in the numbers and types of middlemen serving each foreign market. To get soap into Japan, a company has to work through what may be the most complex distribution system in the world. It must sell to a general wholesaler, who sells to a basic product specialty wholesaler, who sells to a specialty wholesaler, who sells to a regional wholesaler, who sells to a local wholesaler, who finally sells to retailers. All these distribution levels may double or triple the consumer's price over the importer's price.[24] If the company takes the same soap to tropical Africa, the company sells to an import wholesaler, who sells to a "mammy," who sells to a "petty mammy," who sells the soap door to door.

Another difference lies in the size and character of retail units abroad. Where large-scale retail chains dominate the Canadian scene, most foreign retailing is done by many small independent retailers. In India, millions of retailers operate tiny shops or sell in open markets. Their markups are high, but the real price is brought down through price haggling. Supermarkets could offer lower prices, but they are difficult to set up because of many economic and cultural barriers.[25] People's incomes are low, and they prefer to shop daily for small amounts rather than weekly for large amounts. They lack storage and refrigeration to keep food for several days. Packaging is not well developed because it would add too much to the cost. These factors have kept large-scale retailing from spreading rapidly in developing countries.

Deciding on the Marketing Organization

Companies manage their international marketing activities in at least three different ways. Most companies first organize an export department, then create an international division, and finally become a multinational organization.

Export Department

A firm normally gets into international marketing by simply shipping out the goods. If its international sales expand, the company organizes an export department with a sales manager and a few assistants. As sales increase, the export department expands to include various marketing services so that it can actively go after business. If the firm moves into joint ventures or direct investment, the export department will no longer be adequate.

International Division

Many companies get involved in several international markets and ventures. A company may export to one country, license to another, have a joint ownership venture in a third, and own a subsidiary in a fourth. Sooner or later it will create an international division or subsidiary to handle all its international activity.

Multinational Organization

Several firms have passed beyond the international division stage and become truly *multinational organizations*. They stop thinking of themselves as national marketers who sell abroad and start thinking of themselves as global marketers. The top corporate management and staff plan worldwide manufacturing facilities, marketing policies, financial flows, and logistical systems. The global operating units report directly to the chief executive or executive committee, not to the head of an international division. Executives are trained in worldwide operations, not just domestic *or* international. The company recruits from many countries; buys components and supplies where they cost the least; and invests where the expected returns are greatest.

Major companies must become more multinational in the 1980s and 1990s if they are going to grow. As foreign companies successfully invade the domestic market, Canadian companies must move more aggressively into foreign markets. They will have to change from companies that treat their foreign operations as secondary to companies viewing the entire world as a single market.[26]

Summary

Companies move into international marketing for many reasons. Some are pushed by poor opportunities in the home market, and some are pulled by better opportunities abroad. Given the risks of international marketing, companies need a systematic way to make their international marketing decisions.

First, the company must understand the international marketing environment, especially the international trade system. It must assess each foreign market's economic, political-legal, and cultural characteristics. Second, the company must consider what proportion of foreign to total sales it will seek, whether it will do business in a few or many countries, and what types of countries it wants to market in. Third, the company must decide which specific markets to enter. This calls for weighing the probable rate of return on investment against the level of risk. Fourth, the company has to decide how to enter each chosen market, whether through exporting, joint venturing, or direct investment. Many companies start as exporters, move to joint venturing, and finally make a direct investment. Companies must next decide how much their products, promotion, price, and channels should be adapted for each foreign market. Finally, the company must develop an effective organization for international marketing. Most firms start with an export department and graduate to an international division. A few pass to a multinational organization, which means that worldwide marketing is planned and managed by the top officers of the company.

Questions for Discussion

1. When appraising the international marketing environment, the economic environment of the country is the most important consideration for the firm. Comment.
2. International marketing does not involve any new principles of marketing. Comment.
3. Distinguish between a quota and an embargo.
4. Countries that are not classified as industrial economies should be avoided as an export markets. Comment.
5. Briefly discuss the three major strategies that a firm might use to enter a foreign market.
6. How does licensing differ from the other joint-venture possibilities?
7. What product strategy possibilities might a firm consider in expanding into international markets?
8. Which type of international marketing organization would you suggest for the following companies? (a) Huffy bicycles is planning to sell three models in the Far East; (b) a small manufacturer of toys is going to market its products in Europe; and (c) Dodge is contemplating selling its full line of cars and trucks in Kuwait.

Chapter 18 Key Terms

Contract manufacturing   Joint-venturing to enter a foreign market by contracting with manufacturers in the foreign market to produce the product.

Customized marketing mix   An international marketing strategy of adjusting the marketing mix elements to each international target market, bearing more costs but hoping for a larger market share and return.

Direct investment   Entering a foreign market by developing foreign-based assembly or manufacturing facilities.

Economic community   A group of nations organized to work toward common goals in the regulation of international trade; an example is the European Economic Community (EEC or Common Market).

Embargo   A ban on the import of a certain product.

Exporting   Entering a foreign market by exporting products and selling them through international marketing middlemen (indirect exporting) or through the company's own department, branch, or sales representatives or agents (direct exporting).

Joint venturing   Entering foreign markets by joining with companies in the foreign country to set up production and marketing facilities.

Joint ownership   Entering a foreign market by joining with foreign investors to create a local business in which the company shares joint ownership and control.

Licensing   A method of entering a foreign market in which the company enters an agreement with a licensee in the foreign market, offering the right to use a manufacturing process, trademark, patent, trade secret, or other item of value for a fee or royalty.

Management contracting   A joint venture in which the domestic firm supplies the management knowhow to a foreign company that supplies the capital; the domestic firm exports management services rather than products.

Multinational company   A company that operates in many countries and that has a major part of its operations outside its home country.

Quota   A limit on the amount of goods that an importing country will accept in certain product categories, designed to conserve on foreign exchange and protect local industry and employment.

Tariff   A tax levied by a government against certain imported products designed to raise revenue or protect domestic firms.

Standardized marketing mix   An international marketing strategy of using about the same product, advertising, distribution channels, and other elements of the marketing mix in all the company's international markets.

Case for Chapter 18 ▬▬▬▬▬▬▬▬▬▬▬▬▬

McLAUGHLIN PLANETARIUM

Services Marketing and Nonprofit Marketing

Chapter Objectives

After reading this chapter, you should be able to:

1. Define service and describe four characteristics that affect the marketing of a service.
2. Explain how organizations market themselves.
3. Discuss how persons and places are marketed.
4. Define social marketing and tell how social ideas are marketed.

Recently 11 hospitals in the Toronto area launched fund-raising campaigns with the objective of raising $154 million. They will be joined by another 11 Toronto hospitals who want an additional $140 million from the public. In entering the fund-raising sweepstakes these hospitals are in competition against each other, as well as against universities, orchestras, dance companies, and a host of charitable organizations.

Overall, the prospects are less than rosy for the cash-seeking hospitals. The federal government is cutting costs and handing out less money. Corporate donors are being squeezed from more and more sources: their alma mater universities are beginning or continuing fund-raising campaigns; the arts are linking corporate responsibility (and donations) to the development of cultural and artistic endeavors; and the charities are becoming increasingly sophisticated in their marketing, organization, and implementation strategies.

The hospitals face the problem of trying to market a voluntary donation fund in a very competitive market. The questions are: how do you differentiate yourself from the competition? What is your appeal? What philanthropic nerve are you trying to hit? What determines your approach to the target donors and specifically who are your donor groups? In light of

fund-raising needs and difficulties, the hospitals are forced to look at the vast complexity of their marketing challenges. A hospital has to understand exactly what the health needs of the community are; what image this community has of different hospitals; how their own patients feel about the hospital's service and care; what impression the physical facilities make; and so on.

To compete in the fund-raising market, hospitals are pursuing a variety of strategies including:

- hiring full-time fund-raising experts. More than 50 Canadian hospitals now have fund raisers on staff, who hold conferences on ways to raise money.

- employing advertising agencies to design professional promotion campaigns. The results include commercials on TV and radio, selling T-shirts and using slogans like "Help Us Care. Help Us Cure" and "Be A Saint. Give to St. Mike's."

Wherever the donations come from, a few things appear to be clear in the successful marketing of a fund-raising campaign: (1) recognition of the volunteers in the campaign and of the donors as a primary motivating force; (2) selection of key volunteers and donors; and (3) a comprehensive marketing strategy.[1]

Initially, marketing was developed for selling physical products such as toothpaste, cars, steel, and equipment. But this traditional focus on physical products may cause people to overlook the many other types of goods that are marketed. In this chapter we will look at the special marketing requirements for services, organizations, persons, places, and ideas.

Services Marketing

Service industries have grown very rapidly in Canada, and predictions are that the service sector will be the fastest-growing segment of the Canadian economy.[2] Seven out of every ten working Canadians are employed in service industries. This growth is the result of rising incomes, more leisure time, and the growing complexity of products that require servicing.

Service industries vary greatly. The government sector offers services with its courts, employment services, hospitals, loan agencies, military services, police and fire departments, postal service, regulatory agencies, and schools. The private nonprofit sector offers services with its museums, charities, churches, colleges, foundations, and hospitals. A good part of the business sector offers services with its airlines, banks, hotels, insurance companies, consulting firms, medical and law practices, entertainment companies, real estate firms, advertising and research agencies, and retailers.

Not only are there traditional service industries, but new types keep popping up all the time:

> For a fee, there are now companies that will balance your budget, baby-sit your plants, wake you up in the morning, drive you to work, or find you a new home, job, car, wife, clairvoyant, cat feeder, or gypsy violinist. Or perhaps you want to rent a garden tractor? A few cattle? Some original paintings? If it is business services you need, other companies will plan your conventions and sales meetings, design your products, handle your data processing, or supply temporary secretaries or even executives.[3]

Some service businesses are very large, with sales and assets in the billions. Table 19-1 shows the five largest service companies in each of five service categories. These, and thousands of other service companies compete in the over $200 billion service industry.

Nature and Characteristics of a Service

We define a service as follows:

> A service is any activity or benefit that one party can offer to another that is essentially intangible and does not result in the ownership of anything. Its production may or may not be tied to a physical product.

Renting a hotel room, depositing money in a bank, traveling on an airplane, visiting a psychiatrist, getting a haircut, having a car repaired, watching a professional sport, seeing a movie, having clothes cleaned at a dry-cleaners, getting advice from a lawyer—all involve buying a service.

TABLE 19-1

The Largest Canadian Service Companies

Commercial banking	Life insurance	Retailing	Utilities	Food and hospitality
Royal Bank of Canada	Sun Life	Canadian Tire	B.C. Telephone	McDonald's
Bank of Montreal	Manufacturers Life	Sears Canada	Canada Utilities	Scott's
Canadian Imperial Bank of Commerce	Great-West Life	Loblaw	Consumer's Gas	Four Seasons
Bank of Nova Scotia	Confederation Life	F.W. Woolworth	Noverco	V.S. Services
Toronto Dominion Bank	Mutual Life	Steinberg	Great Lakes Group	Cassidy's

Source: *Canadian Business 500*, 1987 Annual. Ranked by net income or assets.

The company must consider four service characteristics when designing marketing programs.

Intangibility

Services are intangible. They cannot be seen, tasted, felt, heard, or smelled before they are bought. The person getting a face lift cannot see the result before the purchase, and the patient in the psychiatrist's office cannot know the outcome in advance. The buyer has to have faith in the service provider.

Service providers can do certain things to improve the client's confidence. First, they can increase the service's tangibility. A plastic surgeon can make a drawing showing how the patient's face will look after the surgery. Second, service providers can emphasize the service's benefits rather than just describe its features. A college admissions officer can talk to prospective students about the great jobs its alumni have found instead of describing life on the campus. Third, service providers can develop brand names for their service to increase confidence, such as Magikist cleaning or Air Canada's Connoisseur service. Fourth, service providers can use a celebrity to create confidence in the service, as the Canadian Imperial Bank of Commerce has done with Anne Murray.

Inseparability

A service cannot exist separately from its providers, whether they are persons or machines. A service cannot be put on a shelf and bought by the consumer whenever needed. The service provider must be present. Surgery requires the presence of doctors and their equipment; checking the accuracy of a company's records requires the presence of an auditor.

Several strategies exist for getting around this limitation. The service provider can learn to work with larger groups. Some psychotherapists have moved from one-on-one therapy to small-group therapy to groups of over 300 people in a hotel ballroom getting "therapized." The service provider can learn to work faster—the psychotherapist can spend 30 minutes with each patient instead of 50 minutes and can see more patients. The service organization can train more service providers and build up client confidence, as H & R Block has done with its national network of trained tax consultants.

Variability

Services are highly variable—their quality depends on who provides them and when and where they are provided. A tennis lesson from Carling Bassett is likely to be of higher quality than one given by a local tennis pro. Bassett's lessons will vary, however, with her energy and frame of mind at the time of each lesson. Service buyers are often aware of this high variability and talk to others before choosing a provider.

Service firms can take two steps toward quality control. First, they can carefully select and train their personnel. Airlines, banks, and hotels spend large sums to train their employees to give good service. Consumers should find the same type of friendly and helpful personnel in every Canadian Pacific hotel. Second, the firm can regularly check customer satisfaction through suggestion and complaint systems, customer surveys, and comparison shopping. When poor service is found, it can be corrected.

Perishability

Services cannot be stored. The reason many doctors charge patients for missed appointments is that the service value only existed at that point when the patients did not show up. The perishability of services is not a problem when demand is steady, because it is easy to staff the services in advance. When demand fluctuates, service firms have difficult problems. For example, public transportation companies have to own much more equipment because of rush hour demand than they would need if demand were even throughout the day.

Sasser has described several strategies for producing a better match between demand and supply in a service business.[4]

On the demand side:

- Charging different prices at different times will shift some demand from peak to off-peak periods. Examples include low early-evening movie prices and weekend discount prices for car rentals.

- Nonpeak demand can be increased. McDonald's offered its Egg McMuffin breakfast and hotels developed their mini-vacation weekend.

- Complementary services can be offered during peak time to provide alternatives to waiting customers, such as cocktail lounges to sit in while waiting for a table and automatic tellers in banks.

- Reservation systems can help to manage the demand level. Airlines, hotels, and physicians employ them extensively.

Courtesy: Toronto Transit Commission

When demand for a service fluctuates, the service firm must be able to meet peak demand. Thus, a public transportation system must own enough buses and subway trains to handle rush-hour traffic.

On the supply side:

- Part-time employees can be hired to serve peak demand. Universities add part-time teachers when enrollment goes up, and restaurants call in part-time waiters and waitresses when needed.

- Peak-time demand can be handled more efficiently. Employees do only essential tasks during peak periods. Paramedics help doctors during busy times.

- Some tasks can be shifted to consumers, as when consumers fill out their own medical records or bag their own groceries.

- Providers can share services, as when several hospitals share an expensive piece of medical equipment.

- The firm can plan ahead for expansion, as when an amusement park buys surrounding land for later development.

Classification of Services

Services can be classified in a number of ways. First, is the service **people-based** or **equipment-based**? A psychiatrist needs almost no equipment, but a pilot needs an airplane. People-based services can involve professionals (accounting, management consulting), skilled labor (plumbing, car repair), and unskilled labor (janitorial service, lawn care). Equipment-based services can involve automated equipment (car washes, vending machines), equipment operated by unskilled labor (taxis, motion picture theaters), and equipment operated by skilled labor (airplanes, computers). Even within a given service industry, service providers vary in the amount of equipment they use. Sometimes the equipment adds value to the service (stereo amplification), and sometimes it reduces the amount of labor needed (automated car washes).

Second, is the **client's presence** necessary to the service? Brain surgery involves the client's presence, but a car repair does not. If the client must be present, the service provider has to be considerate of his or her needs. Thus beauty shop operators will decorate their shops, play background music, and talk pleasantly with customers.

Third, what about the **client's purchase motive**? Does the service meet a **personal need** (personal services) or a **business need** (business services)? Service providers typically develop different marketing programs for personal and business markets.

Fourth, what about the **service provider's motives** (profit or nonprofit) and **form** (private or public)? These two characteristics, when crossed, produce four quite different types of service organizations. Clearly the marketing programs of a private investor old-age home will differ from those of a private charity home or a veterans' home.[5]

The Importance of Marketing in the Service Sector

Service firms typically lag behind manufacturing firms in their use of marketing.[6] In many small service businesses (shoe repair, barbershops), the owners may think that marketing costs too much or is unneeded. In some service businesses (law and accounting firms), there is the belief that it is unprofessional to use marketing. Other services businesses (colleges, hospitals) had so much demand that they did not need marketing until recently.

Today, as competition increases, costs rise, productivity drops, and service quality falls off, more service firms are taking an interest in marketing. Airlines were one of the first service industries to study their consumers and competition and take positive steps to make trips easier and more pleasant for travelers. Banks and trust companies also moved quickly toward more active use of marketing. At first banks viewed marketing as consisting mainly of promotion and friendliness, but they have now set up marketing organization, information, planning, and control systems.[7] Now, banks and trust companies run mortgage burning contests and daily double sweepstakes, and offer a variety of accounts to attract specific segments of the market.[8] In stock brokerage, insurance, and hotels, the marketing concept has entered unevenly, with some leaders taking major marketing steps (Dominion Securities Pitfield, Holiday Inn), but many firms lagging behind.[9]

Organization Marketing

Organizations often carry out activities to "sell" the organization itself.

Organization marketing consists of activities undertaken to create, maintain, or change attitudes and behavior of target audiences toward an organization.

Look who's on Tony's team. Esso.

Tony's team is made up of a whole bunch of eager kids. They have one thing in common. Hockey.

Tony's team is important to Esso because it's a good healthy way for kids to grow and develop. That's why Esso got together with the Canadian Amateur Hockey Association, to sponsor Minor Hockey Week and the Esso Medals of Achievement awards for the Most Improved Player, Most Sportsmanlike Player, and Most Valuable Player on more than 20,000 amateur teams.

Tony has just been chosen his team's most valuable player. Not because he's the top scorer. In fact, his record is 0 goals, 1 assist. He was chosen because he demonstrated his importance to his team. Which just goes to show how valuable this kind of team training is to all our kids.

And that's why Esso agents and dealers in communities everywhere are so proud to be ...part of the team.

You make us better. (Esso)

Courtesy: Imperial Oil Limited

As part of public relations programs, companies support the arts, community groups, and sporting events.

Organization marketing has traditionally been handled by a public relations department. This is evident from the following definition of public relations:

> *Public relations is the management function that evaluates public attitudes, identifies an individual or an organization with the public interest, and plans and executes a program of action to earn public understanding and acceptance.*[10]

Public relations is marketing management shifted from a product or service to an organization.[11] The same skills are needed: knowledge of audience needs, wants, and behavior; communication skill; and ability to design and carry out programs that influence behavior. The similarities between marketing and public relations have led some companies to put both functions under single control. Organization marketing calls for assessing the organization's current image and developing a marketing plan to improve its image.

Image Assessment

The first step in image assessment is to research the organization's current image among key publics. The way an individual or a group sees an organization is called *organization image*. Different people can have different images of the same organization. The organization might be pleased with its public image or might find that it has serious image problems.

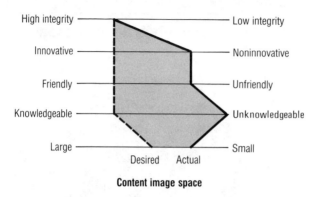

Content image space

FIGURE 19-1
Image Assessment

For example, suppose a bank does some marketing research to measure its image in the community. It finds its image to be that shown by the solid line in Figure 19-1. Thus current and potential customers view the bank as somewhat small, noninnovative, unfriendly, and unknowledgeable. The bank will want to change this image.

Image Planning and Control

Next the organization should figure out what image it would like to have and can achieve. For example, the bank might decide that it would like the image shown by the dashed line in Figure 19-1. It would like to be seen as giving more friendly and personal service, and as being more innovative, knowledgeable, and larger.

The firm now develops a marketing plan to shift its actual image toward the desired one. Suppose the bank first wants to improve its image so that it is perceived as giving friendly and personal service. The key step, of course, is to actually provide friendlier and more personal service. The bank can hire and train more personable and cooperative tellers and others who deal with customers. It can change its decor to make the bank seem warmer. When the bank is certain that it has improved performance on the important image measures, it can design a marketing program to communicate the new image to customers.[12]

The firm must resurvey its publics once in a while to see whether its activities are improving the firm's image. Images cannot be changed overnight because of limited funds and the "stickiness" of public images. If the firm is making no progress, either its marketing offer or its marketing program will have to be changed.

Person Marketing

Persons are also marketed. We define person marketing as follows:

Person marketing consists of activities undertaken to create, maintain, or change attitudes or behavior toward particular persons.

Two common forms of person marketing are celebrity marketing and political candidate marketing.

Celebrity Marketing

Although celebrity marketing has a long history going back to the Caesars, in recent times we more often associate it with the buildup of Hollywood stars and entertainers. Hollywood actors and actresses hire press agents to promote their stardom. The press agent places news about the star in the mass media and schedules highly visible public appearances. One of the great promoters was the late Brian Epstein, who managed the Beatles' rise to stardom and received more of the money than any Beatle.

Today celebrities are promoted by entire organizations. The release of Bryan Adams's record "Into The Fire" was just part of an extensive marketing effort that included a massive world tour, special promotions by A&M records, and a media blitz with stories in magazines like *Rolling Stone*. The objective was to vault Adams into the rock superstar category.[13]

Political Candidate Marketing

Political candidate marketing has become a major industry. Every few years the public is treated to numerous campaigns for municipal, provincial, and federal offices. In these political campaigns, the candidates go into the voter market and use marketing research and advertising to maximize voter "purchase." Interest in the marketing aspects of elections has been stimulated by the spectacular growth in political advertising, scientific opinion polling, computer analysis of voting patterns, and professional campaign management firms.[14]

Place Marketing

We define place marketing as follows:

> Place marketing *involves activities undertaken to create, maintain, or change attitudes or behavior toward particular places.*

There are four major types of place marketing: domicile marketing, business site marketing, land investment marketing, and vacation marketing.

Domicile Marketing

Domicile marketing involves the sale or rental of single-family dwellings, apartments, and other types of housing units. It has traditionally relied on classified want ads and real estate agents. More advanced marketing has been used for condominium selling and the development of total communities. Large builders research housing needs and develop housing products aimed at the price ranges and wants of specific market segments. Some high-rise apartments have been built for the jet set and some for the geriatric set, filled with the features, symbols, and services appropriate to each. Entire housing communities have been designed for certain life-cycle or life-style groups.

Business Site Marketing

Business site marketing involves developing, selling, or renting business sites such as factories, stores, offices, and warehouses. Large developers research companies' land needs and respond with real estate solutions, such as industrial parks, shopping centers, and new office buildings. Most provinces operate industrial development offices that try to sell companies on the advantages of locating new plants in their provinces. They spend large sums on advertising and offer to fly prospects to the site when necessary. Various cities, often through their Chamber of Commerce, attempt to do the same thing at the local level. Cities offer everything from lower housing prices to excellent transportation facilities to lower energy costs in trying to lure businesses to their area.[15]

Land Investment Marketing

Land investment marketing involves developing and selling for investment. The buyers — corporations, groups of professionals, small investors — hope to sell the land when it rises enough in value. Land investment marketing has played a major role in developing Whistler Mountain in British Columbia. Land developers have designed elaborate marketing programs involving mass-media advertising and publicity, direct mail, personal sales calls, free dinner meetings, and even free flights to the site.

Developers of new communities, such as the plan for this one in Florida, could market the climate, the pleasure of having palm trees on the lawn and water nearby, and the attractiveness of the homes.

Courtesy: Coscan Limited, Toronto, Canada

Vacation Marketing

Vacation marketing involves attracting vacationers to spas, resorts, cities, states, and even entire nations. The effort is carried on by travel agents, airlines, motor clubs, oil companies, hotels, motels, and governmental agencies. Tourism is a major industry in Canada worth over $18 billion a year. The federal and provincial governments spend millions trying to attract foreigners to Canada for a vacation. For example, the federal government developed a benefit segmentation of the tourist market in Canada, and designed marketing campaigns for selected segments.[16] Each year the federal government spends over $20 million in the United States to encourage Americans to visit "Canada—The World Next Door." The campaign focuses on three major benefits—a wild and open country, an old world rich in cultural heritage, and a new, exciting urban world — and attempts to market them separately. One successful vacations campaign was Expo '86, which drew over 22 million people to the world's fair in Vancouver. In total, the provincial and federal governments spend over $50 million each year trying to attract tourists to Canada or encourage Canadians to spend their vacations "at home."[17]

Idea Marketing

Ideas can also be marketed. In one sense, all marketing is the marketing of an idea, whether it be the idea of brushing your teeth or the idea that Crest is the most effective decay preventer. Here we will discuss only the marketing of social ideas, such as public health campaigns to reduce smoking, alcoholism, drug abuse, and overeating; environmental campaigns to promote wilderness protection, clean air, and conservation; and other campaigns such as family planning and human rights. This area has been called social marketing.[18]

> Social marketing is the design, implementation, and control of programs seeking to increase the acceptability of a social idea, cause, or practice in a target group.

Social marketers can pursue different objectives. They might want to produce understanding (knowing the nutritional value of different foods) or to trigger a one-time action (joining in a mass immunization campaign). They might want to change behavior (auto seat-belt campaign) or change a basic belief (convincing anti-abortionists to believe in a woman's right to abortion).

In designing social change strategies, social marketers go through a normal marketing planning process. First, they define the social change objective—for example, "to reduce the percentage of teenagers who smoke from 35% to 25% within five years." Next they analyze the attitudes, beliefs, values, and behavior of teenagers, and the forces that support teenage smoking. They consider communication and distribution approaches that might prevent teenagers from smoking (see Exhibit 19-1), develop a marketing plan, and build a marketing organization to carry out the plan. Finally, they evaluate and adjust the program to make it more effective.

Social marketing is new and its effectiveness relative to other social change strategies is hard to evaluate. It is difficult to produce social change with any

EXHIBIT 19-1
Can Social Marketing Reduce Cigarette Smoking?

Scientific evidence shows a link between cigarette smoking and lung cancer, heart disease, and emphysema. Most cigarette smokers know about the bad effects of cigarette smoking. The problem is to give them the means or the will to stop smoking. The four Ps suggest several possible approaches:

Product

- Require manufacturers to add a tart or bitter ingredient to the tobacco.
- Cut down further on the tar and nicotine in cigarettes.
- Find a new type of tobacco for cigarettes that tastes as good but is safe.
- Promote other products that will help people relieve their tensions, such as chewing gum.

Promotion

- Increase fear of early death among smokers.
- Create guilt or shame among cigarette users.
- Strengthen other goals of smokers and make them more important than smoking, such as the need for physical fitness.
- Urge smokers to cut down the number of cigarettes they smoke or to smoke only the first half of the cigarette.

Place

- Make cigarettes harder to obtain or unavailable.
- Make it easier for cigarette smokers to attend antismoking clinics.
- Make it harder to find public places that allow cigarette smoking.

Price

- Raise the price of cigarettes substantially.
- Raise the cost of life and health insurance to smokers.
- Offer a monetary or nonmonetary reward to smokers for each period they forgo smoking

strategy, let alone one that relies on voluntary response. Social marketing has mainly been applied to family planning,[19] environmental protection,[20] energy conservation,[21] improved nutrition, auto driver safety,[22] and public transportation — and there have been some encouraging successes. But more applications are needed before we can fully assess social marketing's potential for producing social change.

Courtesy: Canadian Cancer Society

One of the posters the Canadian Cancer Society uses in its campaign to reduce smoking.

Summary

Marketing has broadened in recent years to cover "marketable" entities other than products—namely, services, organizations, persons, places, and ideas.

Services are activities or benefits that one party can offer to another that are essentially intangible and do not result in the ownership of anything. They are intangible, inseparable, variable, and perishable. Services can be classified by whether they are people- or equipment-based, whether the client's presence is necessary, whether the client is a consumer or business, and whether the service provider is a profit or nonprofit firm in the private or public sector. Service industries lag behind manufacturing firms in adopting and using marketing concepts. Yet rising costs and increasing competition are forcing service industries to search for ways to increase their productivity. Marketing makes a contribution by calling for more systematic planning of service concepts and their pricing, distribution, and promotion.

Organizations can also be marketed. Organization marketing is undertaken to create, maintain, or change attitudes or behavior of target audiences toward an organization. It calls for assessing the organization's current image and developing a marketing plan for bringing about an improved image.

Person marketing consists of activities undertaken to create, maintain, or change attitudes or behavior toward particular persons. Two common forms are celebrity marketing and political candidate marketing.

Place marketing involves activities to create, maintain, or change attitudes or behavior toward particular places. The four most common types are domicile marketing, business site marketing, land investment marketing, and vacation marketing.

Idea marketing involves efforts to market ideas. In the case of social ideas it is called social marketing, and consists of the design, implementation, and control of programs seeking to increase the acceptability of a social idea, cause, or practice in a target group. The social marketer defines the social change objective, analyzes consumer attitudes and competitive forces, develops and tests alternative concepts, develops appropriate channels for the idea's communication and distribution, and finally, checks the results. Social marketing has been applied to family planning, environmental protection, energy conservation, antismoking campaigns, and other public issues.

Questions for Discussion

1. Relate the four characteristics of services to the purchase of a ticket to a concert.
2. Identify the ways in which a service may be classified.
3. How might image assessment be helpful to the local utility company?
4. Discuss an example of each of the two most common forms of person marketing.
5. Producers of services have historically been more marketing oriented than producers of products. Comment.
6. "Place marketing" refers exclusively to the sale and rental of single-family dwellings and apartments. Comment.

7. Explain how the distribution channel is important to the following service marketer: (a) Coopers and Lybrand (''Big 8'' accounting firm), (b) Paramount Pictures, (c) Joe's Repair Shop, and (d) the local repertory theater.

Chapter 19 Key Terms

Organization image   The way an individual or a group sees an organization.

Organization marketing   Activities undertaken to create, maintain, or change attitudes and behavior of target audiences toward an organization.

Person marketing   Activities undertaken to create, maintain, or change attitudes or behavior toward particular persons.

Place marketing   Activities undertaken to create, maintain, or change attitudes or behavior toward particular places.

Public relations   The management function that evaluates public attitudes, identifies an individual or an organization with the public interest, and plans and executes a program of action to earn public understanding and acceptance.

Service   Any activity or benefit that one party can offer to another that is essentially intangible and does not result in the ownership of anything.

Social marketing   The design, implementation, and control of programs seeking to increase the acceptability of a social idea, cause, or practice in a target group.

Cases for Chapter 19

Marketing and Society

Chapter Objectives

After reading this chapter you should be able to:
1. List and respond to the social criticisms of marketing.
2. Define consumerism and environmentalism and explain how they affect marketing strategies.
3. Describe the principles of socially responsible marketing.
4. Discuss the role of ethics in marketing.

In one study of shopping problems, Canadians were quick to voice their concerns. Asked about clothing and footwear, they noted problems with poor quality material and workmanship, sizes that were not standard and fabrics that did not live up to claims. Considering groceries, they felt prices were too high, and meat and produce were of poor quality. Automobile repair prices were a major problem area because of a felt lack of integrity by garage owners, the incompetence of mechanics, and the high cost of repair. They had similar complaints about home repair and renovation service. Poor quality workmanship and materials was one of the main complaints about furniture and appliances. When asked what could be done to rectify the situation, these Canadians had fairly simple answers — fair dealings, quality merchandise, after-sales service, and competent repair people.

In another study conducted by the Retail Council of Canada, the major complaint of consumers was the poor customer service provided by retailers. Consumers did not like the indifferent sales staff or the "vulture" -- the salesperson who constantly hovers around the customer. An interesting finding was that while trust companies were praised for having helpful staff, the banks were not. The survey also found that price was not a major factor in choosing where to shop. Most consumers were willing to pay a little more to get good service and a good returns policy or a warranty, particularly on big ticket items.

Some people, however, question whether Canadian business will respond. Consumer groups, like the Consumers' Association of Canada, advocate more control over business, and the federal and provincial governments are enacting more legislation to curtail unethical business practices. These activities seem to indicate that the problems in the marketplace have to be resolved by government as businesses will not respond voluntarily.

Yet, for every shoddy or questionable activity of a company, examples can be given of firms operating responsibly. These companies provide well-trained staff, reliable products, and quality customer service facilities. Such firms are responding positively to the new realities of consumerism and social responsibility. For these companies, future growth and profitability are tied to maintaining a strong and lasting relationship with their customers.[1]

Responsible marketers find out what consumers want and respond with the right products, priced to give good value to buyers and profit to the producer. The **marketing concept** is a philosophy of service and mutual gain. Its practice leads the economy by an invisible hand to satisfy the many and changing needs of millions of consumers.

Not all marketers follow the marketing concept. Some companies use questionable marketing practices. Some marketing actions that seem innocent in themselves strongly affect the larger society. Consider the sale of cigarettes. Ordinarily, companies should be free to sell cigarettes, and smokers should be free to buy them. However, this transaction affects the public interest. First, the smoker may be shortening his or her own life. Second, smoking places a burden on the smoker's family, and on society at large. Third, other people around the smoker may have to inhale the smoke and may suffer discomfort and harm. This is not to say that cigarettes should be banned. Rather, it shows that private transactions may involve larger questions of public policy.[2]

This chapter looks at the social effects of private marketing practices. It looks into the following questions: (1) What are the most frequent social criticisms of marketing? (2) What steps have private citizens taken to curb marketing ills? (3) What steps have legislators and government agencies taken to curb marketing ills? (4) What steps have enlightened companies taken to carry out socially responsible marketing?

Social Criticisms of Marketing

Some social critics claim that marketing hurts individual consumers, society as a whole, and other business firms.

Marketing's Impact on Individual Consumers

Consumer advocates, government agencies, and other critics have accused marketing of harming consumers through high prices, deceptive practices, high-pressure selling, shoddy or unsafe products, and planned obsolescence.

High Prices

Many critics charge that the Canadian marketing system causes prices to be higher than they would be under more "sensible" systems. They point to three factors.

High Costs of Distribution

A longstanding charge is that greedy middlemen mark up prices beyond the value of their services. Critics charge that there are too many middlemen or that middlemen are inefficient, provide unnecessary or duplicate services, and practice poor management and planning. As a result, distribution costs are too high, and consumers pay for these excessive costs in the form of higher prices.

How do retailers answer these charges? They argue as follows: First, middlemen do work that would otherwise have to be done by manufacturers or consumers. Second, the rising markup reflects improved services that consumers want — more convenience, larger stores and assortment, longer store hours, return privileges, and others. Third, the costs of operating stores keep rising and force retailers to raise their prices.

Fourth, retail competition is so intense that margins are actually quite low. For example, supermarket chains are left with barely 1% profit on their sales after taxes.

High Advertising and Promotion Costs

Modern marketing is also accused of pushing up prices because of heavy advertising and sales promotion. For example, a dozen tablets of a heavily-promoted brand of aspirin sell for the same price as 100 tablets of less-promoted brands. Critics feel that if many products were sold in bulk, their prices would be much lower. Differentiated products — cosmetics, detergents, toiletries — include costs of packaging and promotion that can amount to 40% or more of the manufacturer's price to the retailer.[3] Much of the packaging and promotion adds only psychological rather than functional value to the product. Retailers use additional promotion, such as advertising and games, which add several cents more to retail prices.

Marketers answer these charges in several ways. First, consumers want more than the functional qualities of products. They also want psychological benefits such as feeling wealthy, beautiful, or special. Consumers can usually buy functional versions of products at lower prices, but they are often willing to pay more for products that also provide these psychological benefits. Second, branding gives buyers confidence. A brand name means a certain quality, and consumers are willing to pay for well-known brands even if they cost a little more. Third, heavy advertising is needed to inform the millions of potential buyers of the merits of a brand. Fourth, heavy advertising and promotion are necessary for the firm when competitors are doing it. The business would lose ''share of mind'' if it did not match competitive spending. At the same time, companies are very cost conscious about promotion and try to spend their money wisely. Fifth, heavy sales promotion is needed from time to time because goods are produced ahead of demand in a mass-production economy. Special incentives have to be offered in order to sell inventories.

Excessive Markups

Critics charge that some companies mark up goods excessively. They point to the drug industry, where a pill costing five cents to make may cost the consumer 40 cents. They point to the pricing tactics of funeral homes that prey on the emotions of bereaved relatives. The high charges of television and auto repair people are also criticized.

Marketers respond that most businesses try to deal fairly with consumers because they want repeat business. Most consumer abuses are unintentional. When shady marketers do take advantage of consumers, they should be reported to Better Business Bureaus and other consumer protection groups. Marketers also respond that consumers often do not understand the reason for high markups. For example, pharmaceutical markups must cover the costs of purchasing, promoting, and distributing existing medicines, and the high research and development costs of searching for new medicines.

Deceptive Practices

Marketers are sometimes accused of deceptive practices that lead consumers to believe they will get more value than they actually do. Some industries draw more complaints than others. Among the worst offenders are insurance companies (claiming that policies are "guaranteed renewable" or underwritten by the government), publishing companies (selling subscriptions under false pretenses), mail order land sales organizations (misrepresenting land tracts or improvement costs), home improvement contractors (using bait-and-switch tactics), automotive repair shops (advertising low repair prices and then "discovering" a needed major repair), home freezer plans (overstating the savings), correspondence schools (overstating job opportunities), dance studios (signing up elderly people for lessons beyond their life expectancy), and companies selling medical devices (overstating therapeutic claims).

Marketers argue that most companies avoid deceptive practices because such practices harm their business in the long run. If consumers do not get what they expect, they will switch to more reliable products. In addition, consumers usually protect themselves from deception. Most consumers recognize the marketer's selling intent and are careful when they buy, sometimes to the point of not believing completely true product claims.

High-Pressure Selling

Salespeople are sometimes accused of high-pressure selling that gets people to buy goods they had no thought of buying. It is often said that encyclopedias, insurance, real estate, and jewelry are sold, not bought. The salespeople are trained to deliver smooth canned talks to entice purchase.[4] They sell hard because sales contests promise big prizes to those who sell the most.

Marketers know that buyers can often be talked into buying unwanted or unneeded things. Recent laws require door-to-door salespeople to announce that they are selling a product. Buyers in all provinces are allowed a "three-day cooling-off period" in which they can cancel a contract after rethinking it. In addition, consumers can complain to Better Business Bureaus or state consumer protection agencies when they feel that undue selling pressure was applied.

Shoddy or Unsafe Products

Another criticism is that products lack the quality they should have. One complaint is that products are not made well. Automobiles are the focus of many of the complaints — it seems that every new car has something wrong with it. Consumers grumble about rattles and pings, misalignments, dents, leaking and creaking. Consumers have also experienced considerable problems with car rust. For five years Ford Motor Company of Canada designed cars that were prematurely rusting. After a number of class action suits were launched in four provinces, Ford settled out of court with the car owners. Recently, the Honda Motor Car Company settled with consumers who had similar premature rusting problems.[5]

A second complaint is that some products deliver little benefit. Consumers got a shock on hearing that dry breakfast cereal may have little nutritional value. One nutrition expert stated: "In short, (the cereals) fatten but do little to prevent malnutrition. . . . The average cereal . . . fails as a complete meal even with milk added."[6] The expert added that consumers could often get more nutrition by eating the cereal package than the contents.

A third complaint concerns product safety. For years, *Consumer Reports* and *Canadian Consumer* have reported various hazards in tested products — electrical dangers in appliances, carbon monoxide poisoning from room heaters, finger risks in lawnmowers, and faulty steering in automobiles. Product quality has been a problem for several reasons, including occasional manufacturer indifference, increased production complexity, poorly trained labor, and poor quality control.

On the other hand, most manufacturers want to produce good quality. Consumers who are unhappy with one of the firm's products may avoid their other products and talk other consumers into doing the same. The way a company deals with product quality and safety problems can damage or help its reputation. Companies selling unsafe or poor-quality products risk damaging conflicts with consumer groups. For example, Ford Motor Company received a considerable amount of unfavorable publicity when Phil Edmunston formed the Rusty Ford Owners Association and began class action suits against the automaker. In addition to consumer groups, various laws require local, provincial, and federal government agencies to protect consumers against poor or unsafe products.

Planned Obsolescence

Critics have charged that some producers follow *planned obsolescence*, causing their products to become obsolete before they actually need replacement. In many cases, such as clothing fashions, producers have been accused of continually changing consumer-acceptable styles in order to encourage more and earlier buying. Producers have also been accused of holding back attractive functional features, then introducing them later to make older models obsolete. An example would be automobile manufacturers holding back safety and gasoline economy improvements. Finally, producers have been accused of using materials and components that will break, wear, rot, or rust sooner. For example, many drapery manufacturers are using a higher percentage of rayon in their drapes. They argue that rayon reduces the price of the drapes and has better holding power. Critics claim that rayon will cause the drapes to fall apart in two cleanings instead of four.

Marketers respond that consumers like style changes. They get tired of the old goods and want a new look in fashion or a new-styled car. No one has to buy the new look, and if not enough people like it, it will fail. Companies withhold new features when they are not fully tested, when they add more cost to the product than consumers are willing to pay, and for other good reasons. However, they do this at the risk of having a competitor introduce the new feature and steal the market. Furthermore, companies often put in new materials to lower their costs and prices. They do not design their products to break down earlier because they would lose their customers to other brands.

Marketing's Impact on Society as a Whole

The Canadian marketing system has been accused of adding to several "evils" in society. Here we will examine claims that marketing creates too much materialism, false wants, too few social goods, and cultural pollution.

Too Much Materialism

Critics have charged that the marketing system urges too much interest in material possessions. People are judged by what they own rather than by what they are. To be considered successful, people must own a suburban home, two cars, and the latest clothes and appliances.

Some of this may be changing. Some Canadians are losing their drive for possessions. They are relaxing more, playing more, and learning to get along with less. "Small is beautiful" and "less is more" describe this way of life. More emphasis is being placed on having close relationships and simple pleasures than on being "hooked on things."

False Wants

Interest in goods or services is seen by critics as not a natural state of mind but rather as false wants created by marketing. Business uses advertising to stimulate people's desires for goods. People work harder to earn the necessary money. Their purchases increase the output of Canadian industry, and industry in turn uses advertising to stimulate more desire for the industrial output. Thus marketing is seen as creating false wants that benefit industry more than they benefit consumers.

These criticisms overstate the power of business to create wants. People have strong defenses against advertising and other marketing tools. Marketers are most effective when they appeal to existing needs rather than attempt to create new ones. Furthermore, people seek information when making important purchases and do not rely on single sources of information. Even minor purchases, which may be affected by advertising messages, lead to repeat purchases only if the product performs as promised. Finally, the high failure rate of new products shows that companies are not able to control demand.

On a deeper level, our wants and values are influenced not only by marketers, but also by family, peer groups, religion, ethnic background, and education. If Canadians are highly materialistic, these values arose out of basic socialization processes that go much deeper than business and mass media could produce alone.

Too Few Social Goods

Business has been accused of overselling private goods (such as automobiles) at the expense of public goods (the roads that the automobiles are driven on). As private goods increase, they require more public services that are usually not forthcoming. For example, an increase in automobile ownership (private good) requires more highways, traffic control, parking spaces, and police services (public goods). The overselling of private goods results in "social costs." For cars, the social costs include excessive traffic congestion, air pollution, and deaths and injuries from car accidents.

A way must be found to restore a social balance between private and public goods. Producers could be made to bear the full social costs of their operations. In this way, they would build these costs into the price. If buyers found the price of the goods too high, the producers would disappear and resources would move to those users that could support the sum of the private and social costs.

Cultural Pollution

Critics charge the marketing system with creating **cultural pollution**. People's senses are constantly being assaulted by advertising. Serious programs are interrupted by commercials; printed matter is lost between pages of ads; beautiful scenery is marred by billboards. These interruptions continuously pollute people's minds with images of sex, power, or status. Though most people do not find advertising very annoying, and some even think it is the most interesting aspect of television, some critics call for sweeping changes.

Marketers answer the charges of commercial noise with these arguments: First, they hope that their ads primarily reach the target audience. Because of mass-communication channels, some ads are bound to reach people who have no interest in the product and are therefore bored or annoyed. People who buy magazines addressed to their interests — such as *Maclean's* or *Chatelaine* — rarely complain about the ads because they advertise products of interest. Second, the ads make radio and television free media and keep down the costs of magazines and newspapers. Most people think commercials are a small price to pay for this.

Marketing's Impact on Other Businesses

Critics also charge that a company's marketing practices can harm other companies and reduce competition. Three problems are involved: acquisitions of competitors, marketing practices that create barriers to entry, and unfair competitive marketing practices.

Critics claim firms are harmed and competition is reduced when companies expand by acquiring competitors rather than by developing their own new products. This is of particular concern in Canada because of the sizable number of takeovers and mergers that have recently occurred. While many of these mergers are of companies in unrelated industrials, for example, Hiram Walker (liquor) and Consumers Home (oil and gas), and would not be considered anti-competitive acquisitions, others such as the Bay-Simpsons-Zellers merger are considered a "travesty" of competition.[7] The concentration of newspapers by a few chains such as Thompson Newspapers Ltd., whose papers account for 26% of the total circulation of daily newspapers in Canada, was described as "monstrous" by the Royal Commission on Newspapers.[8] The effects of industry concentration are illustrated by the investigation of oil companies that concluded that four giants—Imperial, Shell, Gulf, and Texaco—had systematically overcharged consumers by $12.1 billion between 1953 and 1978.[9] Because of these types of business activity, there was considerable pressure, both from within and outside the federal government, to put some teeth into Canada's competition laws. The new Competition Act is designed to prohibit mergers and conspiracies that unduly lessen competition.[10]

Acquisition is a complex subject. Acquisitions can sometimes be good for a society. For example, the acquiring company may gain economies of scale leading to lower costs and lower prices. A well-managed company may take over a poorly managed company and improve its efficiency. An industry that was not very competitive might become more competitive after the acquisition. However, as acquisitions can sometimes be harmful, they are closely regulated by the government.

Critics have also charged that marketing practices add barriers to the entry of new companies into an industry. Large marketing companies can use heavy promotion spending, patents, and tie-ups of suppliers or dealers to keep out or drive out competitors. For example, as shopping center developers prefer dealing with chain stores, it is extremely difficult for an independent retailer to gain access to a shopping plaza.[11] This is a formidable entry barrier for many independent retailers who wish to grow by expanding the number of their stores.

Finally, some firms have used unfair competitive marketing practices with the intention of hurting or destroying other firms. They may set their prices below costs, threaten to cut off business with suppliers, or discourage the buying of the competitor's products. While the Competition Act has a section dealing with predatory competition, the difficulty has been to establish that the intent or action was really predatory. To date, no Canadian companies have been prosecuted for predatory competition.

Citizen Actions To Regulate Marketing

Because some people have viewed business as the cause of many economic and social ills, grassroots movements have arisen from time to time to keep business in line. The two major movements have been **consumerism** and **environmentalism**.

Consumerism

Up until 1945, Canada experienced little of the consumer activity that was taking place in the U.S.[12] In the U.S. the first consumer movement took place in the early 1900s. It was fueled by rising prices, Upton Sinclair's writings on conditions in the meat industry, and ethical drug scandals. The second consumer movement, in the mid-1930s, was sparked by both an upturn in consumer prices during the Depression and another drug scandal.

Since 1945, the Consumers' Association of Canada (CAC) has been the leading force in consumerism in Canada. Much of the CAC's early activity was focused on relatively specific purchase problems with food products, drugs, and clothing.[13] In the mid-1960s, the CAC became more involved in broader issues concerning product safety, labeling, and rising prices.[14] Government activity in this area grew rapidly with the inception of the Department of Consumer and Corporate Affairs in 1967. At that time, the federal government defined four goals to be achieved on behalf of consumers: protection against fraud and deception, protection against accident and health hazards, ensuring that the market system is competitive, and representation of the consumer in the councils of government.[15] At the provincial level, most governments created departments of consumer affairs and increased the level of resources devoted to consumer protection. During the 1970s a considerable amount of legislation was enacted to safeguard consumer rights in the areas of deceptive advertising, door-to-door selling, defective products and services, credit financing, and rental accommodation.[16]

The consumer movement has spread internationally and has become very strong in Scandinavia and the Low Countries. But what is the consumer movement?

Consumerism is an organized movement of citizens and government to improve the rights and power of buyers in relation to sellers.

The traditional sellers' rights include:

- The right to introduce any product in any size and style, provided it is not hazardous to personal health or safety; or, if it is, to include proper warnings and controls.

- The right to charge any price for a product, provided there is no discrimination among similar kinds of buyers.

- The right to spend any amount to promote a product, provided it is not defined as unfair competition.

- The right to use any product message, provided it is not misleading or dishonest in content or execution.

- The right to use any buying incentive schemes, provided they are not unfair or misleading.

The traditional buyers' rights include:

- The right not to buy a product that is offered for sale.

- The right to expect a product to be safe.

- The right to expect a product to perform as claimed.

Comparing these rights, many believe that the balance of power lies on the sellers' side. True, the buyer can refuse to buy. But critics feel that the buyer has too little information, education, and protection to make wise decisions when facing sophisticated sellers. Consumer advocates call for the following additional consumer rights:

- The right to be well informed about important aspects of a product.

- The right to be protected against questionable products and marketing practices.

- The right to influence products and marketing practices in ways that will improve the "quality of life."

Consumers have not only rights but responsibilities to protect themselves. Consumers who feel they got a bad deal can take action by writing to the company president or to the media; contacting federal, provincial, or local agencies; and going to small-claims courts.

Environmentalism

Where consumerists look at whether the marketing system is efficiently serving consumer wants, environmentalists look at how marketing affects the environment and at the costs of serving consumer needs and wants. In 1962, Rachel Carson's *Silent Spring* told about pesticide pollution of the environment.[17] It was no longer a matter of wasted resources, but of human survival. In 1970 the Ehrlichs coined the term "eco-catastrophe" to point out the harmful impact of certain Canadian business practices on the environment.[18] In 1972 the Meadowses published *The Limits to Growth*, which warned people that the quality of life would decline in the face of unchecked population growth, spreading pollution, and uncontrolled use of natural resources.[19] Pollution Probe, a Toronto-based environmental organization, has warned North Americans of the dangers of acid rain which could result in the "death" of 2500 lakes a year in Ontario, Quebec, and New England.[20]

These concerns are the basis for environmentalism.

Environmentalism is an organized movement of concerned citizens and government to protect and improve people's living environment.

Environmentalists are concerned with strip mining, forest depletion, factory smoke, billboards, and litter; with the loss of recreational areas; and with the increase in health problems caused by bad air and water, and chemically sprayed food.

Environmentalists are not against marketing and consumption; they simply want them to operate with more care for the environment. The marketing system's goal should not be to maximize consumption, consumer choice, or consumer satisfaction. The marketing system's goal should be to maximize life quality, which includes not only the quantity and quality of consumer goods and services, but also the quality of the environment. Environmentalists want environmental costs included in producer and consumer decision making.

Environmentalism has hit some industries hard. Steel companies and public utilities have had to invest millions of dollars in pollution-control equipment and costlier fuels. The auto industry has had to introduce expensive emission controls in cars. The packaging industry has had to find ways to reduce litter. The gasoline industry has had to create new low-lead and no-lead gasolines. These industries resent environmental regulations, especially when the regulations are imposed too rapidly to allow the companies to make the proper adjustments. These companies have absorbed large costs and have passed them on to buyers.

Public Actions To Regulate Marketing

Citizen concerns about marketing practices will usually lead to public attention and legislative proposals. New bills will be debated — many will be defeated, others will be modified, and a few will become workable laws.

We listed many of the laws affecting marketing in Chapter 5. The task is to translate these laws into the language that marketing executives will understand as they make decisions about competitive relations, products, price, promotion, and channels of distribution. Figure 20-1 shows the major issues facing marketing management when making decisions.

FIGURE 20-1
Major Marketing Decision Areas that May Be Called into Question under the Law

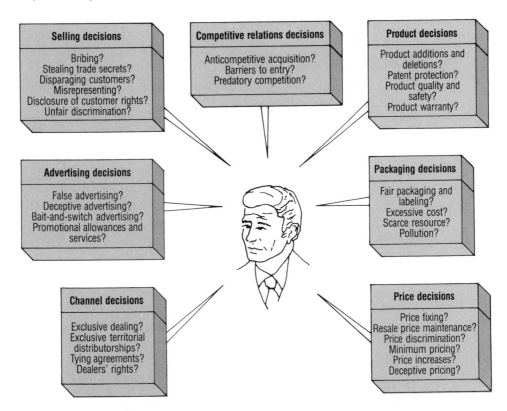

Selling decisions
Bribing?
Stealing trade secrets?
Disparaging customers?
Misrepresenting?
Disclosure of customer rights?
Unfair discrimination?

Competitive relations decisions
Anticompetitive acquisition?
Barriers to entry?
Predatory competition?

Product decisions
Product additions and deletions?
Patent protection?
Product quality and safety?
Product warranty?

Advertising decisions
False advertising?
Deceptive advertising?
Bait-and-switch advertising?
Promotional allowances and services?

Packaging decisions
Fair packaging and labeling?
Excessive cost?
Scarce resource?
Pollution?

Channel decisions
Exclusive dealing?
Exclusive territorial distributorships?
Tying agreements?
Dealers' rights?

Price decisions
Price fixing?
Resale price maintenance?
Price discrimination?
Minimum pricing?
Price increases?
Deceptive pricing?

Business Actions Toward Socially Responsible Marketing

At first, many companies opposed consumerism and environmentalism. They thought the criticisms were either unfair or unimportant. But by now, most companies have come around to accepting the new consumer rights in principle. They might oppose some pieces of legislation as not being the best way to solve certain consumer problems, but they recognize the consumer's right to information and protection. Many of these companies have responded positively to consumerism and environmentalism in order to better serve consumer needs. Here we will look at responsible business reactions to the changing marketing environment. We first outline a concept of enlightened marketing and then consider marketing ethics.

A Concept of Enlightened Marketing

The concept of *enlightened marketing* holds that the company's marketing should support the best long-run performance of the marketing system. Enlightened marketing consists of five principles.

Consumer-Oriented Marketing

The company should view and organize its marketing activities from the consumers' point of view. It should work hard to sense, serve, and satisfy the needs of a defined group of customers.

Innovative Marketing

The company should continually seek real product and marketing improvements. The company that overlooks new and better ways to develop and market products will eventually lose out to a company that has found a better way.

Value Marketing

The company should put most of its resources into value-building marketing investments. Many marketing strategies such as one-shot sales promotions, minor packaging changes, and advertising puffery may raise sales in the short run, but add less value than improvements in the product's quality, features, or convenience.

Sense-of-Mission Marketing

The company should define its mission in broad social terms rather than narrow product terms. When a company defines a social mission, company people feel better about their work and have a clearer sense of direction.

Societal Marketing

An enlightened company makes marketing decisions by considering consumers' wants, the company's requirements, consumers' long-run interests,

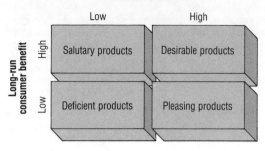

Immediate satisfaction

FIGURE 20-2
Classification of New Product Opportunities

and society's long-run interests. The company is aware that neglecting the last two factors is a disservice to consumers and society.

A societally oriented marketer wants to design not only pleasing but salutary products. The difference is shown in Figure 20-2. Products can be classified according to their degree of immediate consumer satisfaction and long-run consumer benefit. *Desirable products* give both high immediate satisfaction and high long-run benefits, such as tasty, nutritious breakfast foods. *Pleasing products* give high immediate satisfaction but may hurt consumers in the long run, such as cigarettes. *Salutary products* have low appeal but benefit consumers in the long run, such as seat belts. Finally, *deficient products* have neither immediate appeal nor long-run benefits, such as bad-tasting yet ineffective medicine.

The challenge posed by pleasing products is that they sell very well, but may end up hurting the consumer. The product opportunity, therefore, is to add long-run benefits without reducing the product's pleasing qualities. The challenge posed by salutary products is to add some pleasing qualities so that they will become more desirable in the consumers' minds.

Marketing Ethics

Even upright marketers face many moral dilemmas. The best course of action is often unclear. Not every manager has a fine moral sensitivity, so companies need to develop corporate marketing policies, broad guidelines that everyone in the organization must follow. These policies should cover distributor relations, advertising standards, customer service, pricing, product development, and general ethical standards.

The finest guidelines cannot resolve all the difficult ethical situations the marketer faces. Table 20-1 lists 14 difficult ethical situations marketers could face during their careers. If marketers choose immediate sales-producing actions in all 14 cases, their marketing behavior might be described as immoral or amoral. If they refuse to go along with *any* of the actions, they might be ineffective as marketing managers and unhappy because of the constant moral

TABLE 20-1

Some Morally Difficult Situations in Marketing

1. You work for a cigarette company and up to now have not been convinced that cigarettes cause cancer. A recent report has come across your desk that clearly establishes the connection between cigarette smoking and cancer. What would you do?

2. Your R&D department has modernized one of your products. It is not really "new and improved," but you know that putting this statement on the package and in the advertising will increase sales. What would you do?

3. You have been asked to add a stripped-down model to the low end of your line that could be advertised to attract customers. The product will not be very good, but the sales representatives could be depended upon to persuade buyers to buy the higher-priced units. You are asked to give the green light for developing this stripped-down version. What would you do?

4. You are interviewing a former product manager who just left a competitor's company. You are thinking of hiring him. He would be more than happy to tell you all the competitor's plans for the coming year. What would you do?

5. One of your dealers in an important territory has had family troubles recently and his sales have slipped. He was one of the company's top producers in the past. It is not clear how long it will take before his family trouble straightens out. In the meantime, many sales are being lost. There is a legal way to terminate the dealer's franchise and replace him. What would you do?

6. You have a chance to win a big account that will mean a lot to you and your company. The purchasing agent hinted that he would be influenced by a "gift". Your assistant recommends sending a fine color television set to his home. What would you do?

7. You have heard that a competitor has a new product feature that will make a big difference in sales. He will have a hospitality suite at the annual trade show and unveil this feature at a party thrown for his dealers. You can easily send a snooper to this meeting to learn what the new feature is. What would you do?

8. You are eager to win a big contract, and during sales negotiations you learn that the buyer is looking for a better job. You have no intention of hiring him, but if you hinted that you might, he would probably give you the order. What would you do?

9. You have to choose between three ad campaigns outlined by your agency for your new product. The first (A) is a soft-sell, honest information campaign. The second (B) uses sex-loaded emotional appeals and exaggerates the product's benefits. The third (C) involves a noisy, irritating commercial that is sure to gain audience attention. Preliminary tests show that the commercials are effective in the following order: C, B, and A. What would you do?

10. You are a marketing vice-president working for a beer company, and you have learned that a particularly lucrative province is planning to raise the minimum legal drinking age from 18 to 21. You have been asked to join other breweries in lobbying against this bill and make contributions. What would you do?

11. You want to interview a sample of customers about their reactions to a competitive product. It has been suggested that you invent an innocuous name like Marketing Research Institute and interview people. What would you do?

12. You produce an antidandruff shampoo that is effective with one application. Your assistant says that the product would turn over faster if the instructions on the label recommended two applications. What would you do?

13. You are interviewing a capable woman applicant for a job as sales representative. She is better qualified than the men just interviewed. At the same time, you suspect that some of your current salesmen will react negatively to her hiring, and you also know that some important customers may be ruffled. What would you do?

14. You are a sales manager in an encyclopedia company. A common way for encyclopedia representatives to get into homes is to pretend they are taking a survey. After they finish the survey, they switch to their sales pitch. This technique seems to be very effective and is used by most of your competitors. What would you do?

tension. Managers need a set of principles that will help them figure out the moral importance of each situation and how far they can go in good conscience.

Each company and marketing manager must work out a philosophy of socially responsible and ethical behavior. Under the societal marketing concept, each manager must look beyond what is legal and allowed, and develop standards based on personal integrity, corporate conscience, and long-run consumer welfare. A clear and responsible philosophy will help the marketing manager deal with the many knotty questions posed by marketing and other human activities.

Marketing executives of the 1980s and 1990s will face many challenges. They will have abundant marketing opportunities because of technological advances in solar energy, home computers and robots, cable television, modern medicine, and new forms of transportation, recreation, and communication. At the same time, forces in the socioeconomic environment will increase the limits under which marketing can be carried out. Those companies that are able to create new values and practice societally responsible marketing will have a world to conquer.

Summary

A marketing system should sense, serve, and satisfy consumer needs and improve the quality of consumers' lives. In working to meet consumer needs, marketers may take some actions that are not to everyone's liking or benefit. Marketing managers should be aware of the main criticisms.

Marketing's impact on consumer welfare has been criticized for high prices, deceptive practices, high-pressure selling, shoddy or unsafe products, and planned obsolescence. Marketing's impact on society has been criticized for creating too much materialism, false wants, too few social goods, and cultural pollution. Marketing has also been accused of harming competitors and reducing competition through acquisitions, practices that create barriers to entry, and unfair competitive marketing practices.

These concerns about the marketing system have led to citizen action movements — consumerism and environmentalism. Consumerism is an organized social movement that aims to strengthen the rights and power of consumers relative to sellers. Alert marketers view it as an opportunity to serve consumers better by providing more consumer information, education, and protection. Environmentalism is an organized social movement seeking to minimize the harm done to the environment and quality of life by marketing practices. It calls for curbing consumer wants when the satisfaction of these wants would create too much environmental cost.

Citizen action has led to the passage of many laws to protect consumers in the area of product safety, truth-in-packaging, truth-in-lending, and truth-in-advertising.

Many companies at first opposed these social movements and laws, but most of them now recognize a need for positive consumer information, education, and protection. Some companies have followed a policy of enlightened marketing based on the principles of consumer orientation, innovation, value creation, social mission, and societal orientation. These companies have provided company policies and guidelines to help their managers deal with moral questions.

Questions for Discussion

1. The cost of marketing is too high. Comment.
2. Critics of marketing's impact on society are really condemning our Canadian business system rather than just the area of marketing. Comment.
3. Planned obsolescence is not a valid criticism of marketing. Comment.
4. How does consumerism differ from environmentalism? Which poses the greater threat to marketing? Explain.
5. Discuss the five principles of enlightened marketing.
6. A societally oriented marketer wants to design only pleasing products. Comment.
7. What areas should be covered in a marketing code of ethics?

Chapter 20 Key Terms

Consumerism   An organized movement of citizens and government to improve the rights and power of buyers in relation to sellers.

Deficient products   Products that have neither immediate appeal nor long-run benefits, such as bad-tasting yet ineffective medicine.

Desirable products. Products that give both high immediate satisfaction and high long-run benefits, such as tasty, nutritious breakfast foods.

Enlightened marketing   A marketing philosophy that holds that the company's marketing should support the best long-run performance of the marketing system; its five principles include consumer-oriented marketing, innovative marketing, sense-of-mission marketing, value marketing, and societal marketing.

Environmentalism   An organized movement of concerned citizens and government to protect and improve people's living environment.

Planned obsolescence   A strategy of causing products to become obsolete before they actually need replacement; it includes style obsolescence, functional obsolescence, and material obsolescence.

Pleasing products   Products that give high immediate satisfaction but may hurt consumers in the long run, such as cigarettes.

Salutary products   Products that have low appeal but benefit consumers in the long run, such as seat belts.

Case for Chapter 20

Case 21   The Consumers' Association of Canada   520

Marketing Arithmetic

One aspect of marketing not discussed within the text is marketing arithmetic. The calculation of sales, costs, and certain ratios is important for many marketing decisions. The purpose of this appendix is to describe four major areas of marketing arithmetic: the operating statement, analytic ratios, markups and markdowns, and cost-volume-profit analysis.

Operating Statement

The operating statement and the balance sheet are the two main financial statements used by companies. The balance sheet shows the assets, liabilities, and net worth of a company at a given time. The operating statement (also called profit and loss statement or income statement) is the more important of the two for marketing information. It shows company sales, cost of goods sold, and expenses during the time period. By comparing the operating statement from one time period to the next, the firm can spot favorable or unfavorable trends and take the appropriate action.

Table A-1 shows the 1987 operating statement for Sandra Parsons, a ladieswear specialty store in New Brunswick. This statement is for a retailer; the operating statement for a manufacturer would be somewhat different. Specifically, the section "Cost of Goods Sold" would be replaced by "Cost of Goods Manufactured."

The outline of the operating statement follows a logical series of steps to arrive at the firm's $25 000 net profit figure:

Net sales	$300 000
Cost of goods sold	– 175 000
Gross margin	$125 000
Expenses	– 100 000
Net profit	$ 25 000

We will now look at major parts of the operating statement separately.

The first part details the amount that Parsons received for the goods she sold during the year. The sales figures consist of three items: gross sales, returns and allowances, and net sales. Gross sales is the total amount charged to cus-

TABLE A-1

Operating Statement for Sandra Parsons for the Year Ending December 31 1987

Gross Sales			$325 000
Less: sales returns and allowances			25 000
Net sales			$300 000
Cost of goods sold			
Beginning inventory, January 1, at cost		$ 60 000	
Gross purchases	$165 000		
Less: purchase discounts	15 000		
Net purchases	$150 000		
Plus: freight-in	10 000		
Net cost of delivered purchases		$160 000	
Cost of goods available for sale		$220 000	
Less: ending inventory, December 31, at cost		$ 45 000	
Cost of goods sold			$175 000
Gross margin			$125 000
Expenses			
Selling expenses			
Sales, salaries, and commissions	$ 40 000		
Advertising	5 000		
Delivery	5 000		
Total selling expenses		$ 50 000	
Administrative expenses			
Office salaries	$ 20 000		
Office supplies	5 000		
Miscellaneous (outside consultant)	5 000		
Total administrative expenses		$ 30 000	
General expenses			
Rent	$ 10 000		
Heat, light, telephone	5 000		
Miscellaneous (insurance, depreciation)	5 000		
Total general expenses		$ 20 000	
Total expenses			$100 000
Net profit			$ 25 000

tomers during the year for merchandise purchased in Parsons's store. As expected, some customers returned merchandise because of damage or a change of mind. If the customer gets a full refund or full credit on another purchase, this is called a "return." If the customer decides to keep the item provided Parsons reduces the price, this is called an "allowance." By subtracting returns and allowances from gross sales, we arrive at net sales — what Parsons earned in revenue from a year of selling merchandise:

Gross sales	$325 000
Returns and allowances	25 000
Net sales	$300 000

The second major part of the operating statement calculates the amount of sales revenue Sandra Parsons has left after paying the costs of the merchandise she sells. We start with the inventory in the store at the beginning of the year. During the year, Parsons bought $165 000 worth of dresses, slacks, blouses, handbags, jeans, and other goods. Suppliers gave the store discounts totaling $15 000, so that net purchases were $150 000. Because the store is located away from regular shipping routes, Parsons had to pay an additional $10 000 to get the products delivered, giving her a net cost of $160 000. Adding the beginning inventory, the cost of goods available for sale amounted to $220 000. The $45 000 ending inventory of clothes in the store on December 31 is then subtracted to come up with the figure $175 000 for cost of goods sold. Here again, we have followed a logical series of steps to figure out the cost of goods sold:

Amount Parsons started with (beginning inventory)	$ 60 000
Net amount purchased	+ 150 000
Any added costs to obtain these purchases	+ 10 000
Total cost of goods Parsons had available for sale during year	$220 000
Amount Parsons had left over (ending inventory)	− 45 000
Cost of goods actually sold	$175 000

The difference between what Parsons paid for the merchandise ($175 000) and what she sold it for ($300 000) is called the gross margin ($125 000).

In order to show the profit Parsons cleared at the end of the year, we must subtract from the gross margin the expenses incurred while doing business. The selling expenses included two sales employees, local newspaper and radio advertising, and the cost of delivering merchandise to customers after alterations. Selling expenses added up to $50 000 for the year. Administrative expenses included the salary for an office manager, office supplies such as stationery and business cards, and miscellaneous expenses, including an administrative audit conducted by an outside consultant. Administrative expenses totaled $30 000 in 1987. Finally, the general expenses of rent, utilities, insurance, and depreciation came to $20 000. Total expenses were therefore $100 000 for the year. By subtracting expenses ($100 000) from the gross margin ($125 000), we arrive at the net profit of $25 000 for Parsons during 1987.

Analytic Ratios

The operating statement provides the figures needed to compute some key ratios. These ratios are typically called operating ratios — the ratio of selected operating statement items to net sales. They let marketers compare the firm's performance in one year to that in previous years (or to industry standards and competitors in the same year). The most commonly used operating ratios are the gross margin percentage, the net profit percentage, the operating expense percentage, and the returns and allowances percentage.

Ratio	Formula	Computation from Table A-1
Gross margin percentage	$=\dfrac{\text{gross margin}}{\text{net sales}}$	$=\dfrac{\$125\ 000}{\$300\ 000}=42\%$
Net profit percentage	$=\dfrac{\text{net profit}}{\text{net sales}}$	$=\dfrac{\$25\ 000}{\$300\ 000}=8\%$
Operating expense percentage	$=\dfrac{\text{total expense}}{\text{net sales}}$	$=\dfrac{\$100\ 000}{\$300\ 000}=33\%$

Returns and allowances percentages

$$=\frac{\text{returns and allowances}}{\text{net sales}}=\frac{\$25\ 000}{\$300\ 000}=8\%$$

Another useful ratio is the stockturn rate. The stockturn rate is the number of times an inventory turns over or is sold during a specified time period (often one year). It may be computed on a cost, selling, or unit price basis. Thus the formula can be:

$$\text{Stockturn rate}=\frac{\text{cost of goods sold}}{\text{average inventory at cost}}$$

or

$$\text{Stockturn rate}=\frac{\text{selling price of goods sold}}{\text{average selling price of inventory}}$$

or

$$\text{Stockturn rate}=\frac{\text{sales in units}}{\text{average inventory units}}$$

We will use the first formula:

$$\frac{\$175\ 000}{\dfrac{\$60\ 000+\$45\ 000}{2}}=\frac{\$175\ 000}{\$52\ 500}=3.3$$

That is, Parsons's inventory turned over 3.3 times in 1987. Normally, the higher the stockturn rate, the higher management efficiency and company profitability.

Return on investment (ROI) is frequently used to measure managerial effectiveness. It uses figures from the firm's operating statement and balance sheet. A common formula for computing ROI is:

$$\text{ROI}=\frac{\text{net profit}}{\text{sales}}\times\frac{\text{sales}}{\text{investment}}$$

You may have two questions about this formula: Why use a two-step process when ROI could be computed simply as net profit divided by investment? What exactly is "investment"?

To answer these questions, let us look at how each component of the formula can affect the ROI. Suppose Sandra Parsons computed her ROI as follows:

$$ROI = \frac{\$25\ 000\ (\text{net profit})}{\$300\ 000\ (\text{sales})} \times \frac{\$300\ 000\ (\text{sales})}{\$150\ 000\ (\text{investment})}$$
$$8.3\% \quad \times \quad 2 \quad = 16.6\%$$

Suppose Parsons had worked to increase her share of market. She could have had the same ROI if her sales doubled while dollar profit and investment stayed the same. (She would accept a lower profit ratio to get a higher turnover and market share):

$$ROI = \frac{\$25\ 000\ (\text{net profit})}{\$600\ 000\ (\text{sales})} \times \frac{\$600\ 000\ (\text{sales})}{\$150\ 000\ (\text{investment})}$$
$$4.16\% \quad \times \quad 4 \quad = 16.6\%$$

Parsons might have increased her ROI by increasing net profit through more cost cutting and more efficient marketing:

$$ROI = \frac{\$50\ 000\ (\text{net profit})}{\$300\ 000\ (\text{sales})} \times \frac{\$300\ 000\ (\text{sales})}{\$150\ 000\ (\text{investment})}$$
$$16.6\% \quad \times \quad 2 \quad = 33.2\%$$

Another way to increase ROI is to find some way to get the same levels of sales and profits while decreasing investment (perhaps by cutting the size of Parsons's average inventory):

$$ROI = \frac{\$25\ 000\ (\text{net profit})}{\$300\ 000\ (\text{sales})} \times \frac{\$300\ 000\ (\text{sales})}{\$75\ 000\ (\text{investment})}$$
$$8.3\% \quad \times \quad 4 \quad = 33.2\%$$

What is "investment" in the ROI formula? Investment is often defined as the total assets of the firm. But many analysts now use other measures of return to assess performance. These measures include return on net assets (RONA), return on stockholders' equity (ROE), and return on assets managed (ROAM). Since investment is measured at a point in time, we usually compute ROI as the average investment between two time periods (say, January 1 and December 31 of the same year). We can also compute ROI as an "internal rate of return" by using discounted cash-flow analysis (see any financial textbook for more on this technique). The objective in using any of these measures is to figure out how well the company has been using its resources. As inflation, competitive pressures, and the cost of capital increase, the measures become increasingly important indicators of marketing and company performance.

Markups and Markdowns

Retailers and wholesalers must understand the concepts of markups and markdowns. They must make a profit to stay in business, and the markup percentage affects profits. Markups and markdowns are expressed as percentages.

There are two different ways to compute markups — on cost or on selling price:

$$\text{Markup percentage on cost} = \frac{\text{dollar markup}}{\text{cost}}$$

$$\text{Markup percentage on selling price} = \frac{\text{dollar markup}}{\text{selling price}}$$

Sandra Parsons must decide which formula to use. If Parsons bought blouses for $15 and wanted to mark them up $10, her markup percentage on cost would be $10/$15 = 67.7%. If she based markup on selling price, the percentage would be $10/$25 = 40%. In figuring markup percentage, most retailers use the selling price rather than the cost.

Suppose Parsons knew her cost ($12) and desired markup on price (25%) for a scarf, and wanted to compute the selling price. The formula is:

Selling price = cost ÷ (1 − margin)
Selling price = $12 ÷ .75 = $16

As a product moves through the channel of distribution, each channel member adds a markup before selling the product to the next member. This markup chain is shown for a dress purchased by a Parsons customer for $200:

		$ Amount	% of Selling Price
Manufacturer	Cost	$108	90%
	Markup	12	10
	Selling price	$120	100%
Wholesaler	Cost	$120	80%
	Markup	30	20
	Selling price	$150	100%
Retailer	Cost	$150	75%
	Markup	50	25
	Selling price	$200	100%

The retailer whose markup is 25% does not necessarily enjoy more profit than the manufacturer whose markup is 10%. Profit also depends on how many items with that profit margin can be sold (stockturn rate), as well as on operating efficiency (expenses).

Sometimes a retailer wants to convert markups based on selling price to markups based on cost, or vice versa. The formulas are:

$$\text{Markup percentage on selling price} = \frac{\text{markup percentage on cost}}{100\% + \text{markup percentage on cost}}$$

$$\text{Markup percentage on cost} = \frac{\text{markup percentage on selling price}}{100\% - \text{markup percentage on selling price}}$$

Suppose Parsons found that her competitor was using a markup of 30% based on cost, and she wanted to know what this would be as a percentage of selling price. The calculation would be:

$$\frac{30\%}{100\% + 30\%} = \frac{30\%}{130\%} = 23\%$$

Since Parsons was using a 25% markup on the selling price for dresses, she felt that her markup was suitable compared with that of the competitor.

Near the end of the summer Parsons found that she still had an inventory of summer slacks in stock. Thus she decided to use a markdown, a reduction from the original selling price. Before the summer, she had purchased 20 pairs of slacks at $10 each, and she had since sold ten pairs at $20 each. She marked down the other pairs to $15 and sold five pairs. We compute her markdown ratio as follows:

$$\text{Markdown percentage} = \frac{\text{dollar markdown}}{\text{total net sales in dollars}}$$

The dollar markdown is $25 (5 pairs @ $5 each) and total net sales are $275 (10 pairs @ $20 + 5 pairs @ $15). The ratio, then, is $25/$275 = 9%.

Larger retailers usually compute markdown ratios for each department rather than for individual items. The ratios provide a measure of relative marketing performance for each department and can be calculated and compared over time. Markdown ratios can also be used to compare the performance of different buyers and salespeople in a store's various departments.

Cost-Volume-Profit Analysis

The broad purpose of cost-volume-profit analysis is to examine the effects on profits of changes in costs, prices, and volumes. Sometimes referred to as sensitivity analysis, contribution analysis, or break-even analysis, it should be used whenever a decision is to be made that will alter existing costs or prices. The technique is useful in answering problems such as:

- How many additional units do we need to sell to break even, if we increase advertising expenditures by $5000?

- What contribution would we make if the selling price was increased by $1.00?

- Which product, A or B, provides a greater contribution to the firm?

To use this technique, a number of terms must be understood:

Variable costs   *Expenses that change with production or sales volume. Generally these costs vary directly with unit volume. For example, the costs of raw materials usually vary directly with production volume and sales commissions usually vary directly with sales volume.*

Fixed costs   *Expenses that remain constant regardless of production or sales volumes. For example, rent, depreciation, and advertising usually do not vary with production or sales volume.*

Contribution   *The difference between selling price and variable costs.*

Break-even point   *The point at which revenues equal expenses.*

The analysis may be based on either sales volume or units. It will depend on the information available and the question to be answered. Illustrations of how cost-volume-profit analysis is determined through the use of break-even analysis and sensitivity analysis are shown below, using a simple example: A firm selling electric hair dryers at $15 per unit has fixed costs of $42 000 (administrative expenses of $30 000 and advertising expenses of $12 000). Variable costs are $8 per unit.

Break-even Analysis

Objective: determine how many units or what volume of sales are required to break even. General equation: break-even = fixed costs/(selling price per unit – variable costs per unit)

- The number of units required to break-even = $42 000/($15 – $8) = 6000
- The sales volume required to break even = 6000 × $15 = $90 000

The sales volume required to break-even could also be calculated as follows:

- Break-even = fixed costs/contribution percentage per unit where the contribution percentage per unit = (selling price – variable costs)/selling price
- Break-even = $42 000/($15 – $8)/$15 = $90 000

Contribution Analysis

Objective: determine the unit or volume contribution at some specified sales level. General equation: contribution = selling price – variable costs. In the above example the contribution per unit is $7 (15 – $8). This is the amount that each unit sold will contribute toward covering fixed costs and profits. To illustrate, the question might be: What total contribution (expressed in units) is necessary to cover fixed costs and make a profit of $10 000?

- Total contribution necessary = $42 000 + $10 000 = $52 000
- Total contribution (in units) = $52 000/$7 = 7429 units

The advantage in using contribution analysis is that it is relatively easy to determine the financial impact of changes in costs or prices. For example, assume the firm currently sells 10 000 hair dryers a year:

1. The advertising manager proposed an increase in advertising expenditures of $2000 and expects sales to increase by 10%. What is the financial impact?

   Financial impact = additional contribution − additional expenses

   $$= \$7 \times 1000 - \$2000 = \$5000$$

2. The marketing manager proposed to increase the selling price from $15 to $17 and expects sales to decline by 5%. What is the financial impact?

   Financial impact = new contribution − previous contribution

   $$= \$9 \times 9500 - \$7 \times 10\ 000 = \$15\ 500$$

Sensitivity Analysis

Objective: to determine unit or volume contribution or profit under various cost, price, and volume assumptions. General equation: requires the application of break-even and/or contribution analysis.

Sensitivity analysis is often used to examine the financial impact of various alternatives at one time. For example, suppose the manufacturer of hair dryers was interested in the financial impact of a price change and a change in advertising expenditures at three different sales volumes. These alternatives can be handled in a contribution table as follows:

1. Assume that the two prices are low ($15) and high ($18).

2. Assume that the advertising expenditures are low ($12 000) and high ($20 000).

3. Assume that the three different sales volumes are low (8000 units), medium (10 000 units) and high (12 000 units).

Contribution Table (after advertising expenditures)

ADVERTISING

	Low			High		
Sales volume	8 000	10 000	12 000	8 000	10 000	12 000
Low price	$44 000	$58 000	$72 000	$36 000	$50 000	$64 000
High price	$68 000	$88 000	$108 000	$60 000	$80 000	$100 000

The contribution table is the first step in assessing various alternatives. The next step would be to assign various probabilities to each alternative (e.g., what is the probability that the firm will achieve 8000 unit sales with a low price and a low advertising budget?). Through the use of decision theory (which is not discussed here) the most suitable alternative can be determined. What is important here is to understand that sensitivity analysis is extremely useful in identifying the relationships between costs, volumes, and profits.

Case for Appendix A ━━━━━━━━━━━━━━━

Case 22   Financial Exercises for Marketing   522

Cases

1. SONY CORPORATION: WALKMAN/ WATCHMAN

Sony introduced the Walkman at the end of 1979. In 1980 they shipped 550 000 of these products worldwide, and by 1987 the product had become widely accepted and imitated. At least 20 companies entered the market with similar products. The Walkman and its competitors provide high-quality playback through lightweight earphones attached to a lightweight cassette player worn on the belt or around the neck. Sony management must now determine whether the Walkman-type product will continue to be popular and how it should compete in this market.

The Walkman was created by a young engineer who made it for fun. In time it was shown to Mr. Akio Morita, Sony's chairman, who adopted it for his personal use. He enthusiastically acted as the product development project leader, reducing the time between planning the product and its marketing to six months, from the usual one to two years. Product development and marketing ideas were obtained from high school and university students as they used and discussed the Walkman in a room especially equipped for observation.

Competition brought imitators and price cutting. Walkman stereo cassette players are being sold in mass retailing outlets for as low as $39. Competitors' products are sold for as much as 40% lower. Sony's response to this intense competition has been to maintain its premium prices, expand the line, and improve its products. Sony's innovative skills in trying to keep ahead of competition are evident in the new Walkman stereo cassette player. It incorporates a new earphone concept, and is as small as the plastic box that holds a standard cassette ($\frac{3}{4}$ inch by $2\frac{2}{3}$ inches by $4\frac{1}{4}$ inches) and uses one AA-cell battery. Each earphone fits into the ear sideways, with the speaker facing toward the front of the ear. The earphone does not slide around on the head, sounds better than most earphones, feels comfortable, and lets the user hear more environmental sounds.

In planning its Canadian marketing efforts for the Walkman, Sony is interested in knowing whether the product is more than a novelty. If Sony determines that the product serves one or more basic uses or functions, the market could be quite large and offer market segmentation opportunities. In any event, Sony will have to decide what, if any, competitive advantages it has and how best to use them in search of profit, while avoiding price competition as much as possible. It could concentrate on one or two models for all parts of the market or offer models designed especially for different segments.

Sony's newest related innovation is Watchman, a personal hand-held or vestpocket black-and-white TV. The Watchman was priced to sell for about $200, but has been advertised for as little as $149. Its two-inch screen gives clarity and picture definition that rival many larger conventional sets. Its brightness and luminance make the screen easy to watch at a football game, and words are easy to read. The Watchman uses a miniaturized cathode ray tube, just like most TVs. It is palm-sized — 9½ inches by 3 inches by 6 inches — and weighs 18 ounces. It is powered by four AA-cell batteries or an optional voltage adapter and is equipped with a telescoping antenna and a carrying strap.

In marketing the Watchman, Sony faces the same basic problems it does with the Walkman, but in a different phase of the product life cycle. The apparent similarity of the marketing characteristics of the two products suggests that they should be marketed to consumers in the same way. On the other hand, care must be taken to avoid the pitfall of reasoning by analogy.

Questions

1. What groups of potential buyers exist for the Walkman, and what can Sony do to increase the sale of the product to each of these groups?

2. Who are the potential buyers of the Watchman? Under what circumstances would they use it? How should the Watchman be marketed?

2. BICYCLE COURIERS LIMITED

Mr. Robert Jones, a successful entrepreneur, had been approached by Helen Smith with a proposal to invest in a bicycle courier business in Toronto. Ms. Smith had developed the idea after observing that the heavy traffic in Toronto made it difficult for courier vans to make deliveries within the city on a guaranteed two-hour delivery time. She felt she had a winning concept but needed an investor to provide funding for her venture. She had met Mr. Jones at a meeting of business entrepreneurs where Mr. Jones had discussed the criteria he used when deciding whether or not to invest in a new business. Ms. Smith thought her idea met these investment criteria and was hopeful that Mr. Jones would agree.

In large Canadian cities there are a substantial number of businesses that need to quickly send letters, documents, and small parcels to other firms within the city. For example, law firms need to send valuable legal documents to clients, frequently on a rush basis. They call a courier service that would guarantee a two-hour delivery at a price of $4.00 or $5.00. However, congested roads and traffic jams make the two-hour delivery difficult to achieve. Further, the high cost of parking tickets (courier vans would often park illegally during pickups and deliveries), vehicle maintenance, and insurance made it difficult for the traditional courier company to make money on intracity business.

Ms. Smith had observed this dilemma while working for one of Canada's leading couriers. She knew that some firms in the United States and Europe were using bicycle couriers and she thought the idea could work in Canada.

She felt that bicycles should be more efficient and economical than cars or trucks and that a bicycle service should be faster and cheaper. The total courier business in Canada which included both intra- and intercity sales, was worth about $625 million each year and was growing at a rate of 15% annually. No actual data was available on what proportion of the total courier business was intracity (e.g., within Toronto) versus intercity (e.g., between Toronto and Montreal) but Ms. Smith thought that the intracity courier business in Toronto could be as low as $2 million or as high as $5 million each year. Based on the limited information and her experience and interests, she estimated that the total number of deliveries within Toronto on an average day was approximately 3000. She felt that with the proper marketing plan she should be able to capture a large share of that business.

Ms. Smith then worked out some cost figures. The actual couriers would be paid on a commission basis, receiving 50% of the fees collected. However, they would be guaranteed the minimum wage of $3.50 per hour. If the business had a well organized delivery system, a courier should be able to deliver up to three items per hour. A dispatcher would be required to organize delivery routes, at a cost of $150 per week. As well, the couriers would require bicycles ($300 each), weatherproof saddlebags ($100 each), and two-way radios ($200 each) to communicate with the dispatchers. Telephone operators would be needed at $120 per week to handle the business calls. Office space located at the edge of the downtown core could be rented for $1000 per month and all other fixed costs (e.g., telephone, dispatch equipment, furnishings) were estimated at $20 000 per year.

Ms. Smith felt the key to the marketing plan was to offer cheaper, faster service than the traditional courier companies. She thought that she could guarantee a 1½ hour delivery time at a base rate of $2.50. If faster delivery was required (i.e., under one hour) the charge would be $4.00. She did have three concerns about her proposed business:

1. Would companies entrust valuable documents to people who delivered on bicycles? Customers might not view this service as reliable.

2. Would winter conditions put a halt to her business? She did some checking, and found that in Toronto there are only about 10 days a year when there is snow on the roads.

3. How should she begin marketing her idea and to whom?

Ms. Smith thought she would have to start with at least 20 couriers, two telephone operators, and one dispatcher. She approached Mr. Jones with an offer of 40% of the business for an investment of $50 000. She outlined the idea, left the information, and Mr. Jones agreed to call her with his decision in two days.

Questions

1. Would you recommend that Mr. Jones invest in the business?
2. Assume that Mr. Jones agrees to invest in the venture. Prepare a marketing plan for this service.

3. MARY SHOE COMPANY

The Mary Shoe Company is a major Canadian producer and marketer of foot-wear. The company has decided to review its marketing strategies and plans for three of its product lines. The first product line is sport shoes for the youth segment (under 20 years of age), which have been marketed under the "Blue Jay-Expo" brand. Over 30 different brands are offered in this highly competitive segment. The "Blue Jay-Expo" line is imported from the Far East, sold at a relatively low price, and has achieved a 15% share of the market. The line has been marginally profitable for the last few years. For the past five years the total segment has grown at 20% per year.

The second product line is "Eskimo" snow boots, produced in Canada for the youth market. The product is average in both price and quality among the six brands sold in this segment. It has a 20% market share and provides a reasonable profit for the company. Total segment sales have increased at 3% for the last few years.

The third product line is a high quality, high fashion footwear line for women marketed under the "Lascala" brand. This brand was targeted at the middle and upper middle income group of women who are fashion conscious. The "Lascala" brand is extremely profitable but has a very small share (3%) of this segment, in which 12 brands competed. The total segment had experienced increased growth of 30% per year for the past two years.

Questions
1. Outline an overall company strategy for these three product lines.
2. Recommend a marketing mix strategy for each brand.

4. THE CHANGING CANADIAN CONSUMER: THREATS AND OPPORTUNITIES

The dramatic changes that have occurred and will occur in the Canadian mar-ketplace create threats and opportunities for virtually all firms seeking to grow and remain profitable. The problem is to understand the impact these numerous trends will have on a particular business. Consider the following information:

1. Marketplace trends are caused by demographics, consumer resources (time, dollars, economics), technology, and attitudes.

2. By the year 2006, Canada will be in a steady state of population growth.

3. Household size is declining, down 50% over the last 20 years (from four persons per household to 2.8).

4. The baby boomers, born between 1946 and 1966, are now between 20 and 40 years of age. The largest individual age segments are between 20-29 and 30-39. In the next ten years, the big growth sector will be the 40-49 year olds — almost six times the growth rate of the overall population.

5. A number of new affluent segments are emerging:

- SKOTIES (Spoiled Kids Of The Eighties). With smaller families the norm, many children have lots of money and the time and freedom to spend it. One survey revealed that the average teenager (age 14 to 15) has $38 per week to spend, and ten year olds have $11 per week to spend.
- YUPPIES (Young Urban Professional People). Consumers who make over $50 000 per year constitute 4% of all households, or about 2 000 000 people.
- DINKS (Dual Income, No Kids). Dual income households are now the norm, and many of these consumers have decided not to have children.
- MUPPIES (Middle-Aged Urban Professionals). Of the 1.6 million families in the 50-64 age bracket, 300 000 of them make over $50 000 per year.
- WOOPIES (Well-Off Old People). On a per capita basis, people over 65 have the highest incomes.

Questions

1. Considering the above facts, what are the major threats and opportunities facing:
- A marketing manager for Campbell Soup Company.
- A marketing manager at Zellers.
- A marketing manager for the *Toronto Sun* newspaper.

5. TRIVIAL PURSUIT

Few products have matched the success of Trivial Pursuit. The game was introduced to the Canadian market in May 1982 and 100 000 games were sold in that year. In 1983 sales were 350 000 units in Canada and 1 million units in the United States. The biggest year for Trivial Pursuit was 1984 when over 20 million units were sold in the U.S. alone, adding up to more than $750 million at retail. By the end of 1986 over 41 million copies of Trivial Pursuit had been sold around the world, worth approximately $2 billion.

Trivial Pursuit is a simple board game in which winning is based on answering trivia questions. In 1980, Chris and John Haney and Scott Abbott invented the original game in about one hour, and then Chris and Scott spent six months on a beach in Spain thinking up the 6000 questions for the Genus edition. They test-marketed the game in 1981, selling all 1200 games they produced. Then they went to the banks to establish funds ($75 000) to get the game in full scale production. They were turned down by several banks before receiving the loan. After that, the rest is history. The initial game, with the Genus cards, was such a hot seller that the company, Horn Abbott, could not produce enough units to match demand even though the game sold for $30.

There were some interesting aspects to the initial marketing of the game. Where one might expect that the game would be distributed through department stores and game/toy stores, Trivial Pursuit was sold through virtually any type of store, ranging from supermarkets to drug stores to jewelry stores such as

Birks. The reason for this distribution pattern may have been that, as the product was such a hot seller, all kinds of stores wanted to carry the product and requested units. The $30 selling price was considered high for a board game (e.g., Scrabble could be purchased for under $15), but it clearly did not slow down sales. Finally, the game itself was attractively packaged and the board and cards were produced with good quality paper.

In the years following Trivial Pursuit's introduction, a number of predictable events occurred. First, the game's remarkable sales spawned a host of imitations, including Junior Trivia (two Vancouver boys developed this game for children aged 5 to 12 and sold 200 000 units in four months). Many other imitations, including Golden Trivia, Tour de Force, Trivia-Challenge, Superquiz, and I.Q. 2000, were developed in 1983. In 1984, Trivial Pursuit competed with over 50 other board games for a share of the now lucrative board game market, valued at $100 million each year in Canada. Since then, over 60 new board games have been introduced each year including Polarity, Scruples, Snap Judgement, Balderdash, and even a new game from the inventors of Trivial Pursuit called Ubi. Second, Trivial Pursuit has developed a number of editions that can be played with the game. These editions include Silver Screen, Sports, Baby Boomer, RPM, Genus II, and Young Players. Third, the price of the game and the editions is beginning to decline as retailers use them as "loss-leaders" or "price specials" to attract customers to their stores.

While the inventors and investors have made fortunes from Trivial Pursuit, it is not clear what the future holds for the game. Some people feel that the game can go on forever by adding new editions and extending the life of the product. However, others feel the game has reached the decline stage of its product life cycle and no further editions should be planned.

Questions

1. What factors have accounted for Trivial Pursuit's remarkable success?
2. What marketing strategy, on a worldwide basis, would you recommend for Trivial Pursuit for the next few years?
3. Do you think Trivial Pursuit is in the decline phase of its product life cycle? Why? Explain.

6. DISCOUNT MICROCOMPUTERS

In late 1986, Howard Cracower and David Matthews opened a discount computer store in Concord, a small town north of Toronto. The store, International Computer Clearance Warehouse Limited (ICCW), generated sales of $250 000 in the first three days of operation. Sales exceeded expectations and by the spring of 1987, they anticipated that sales in the first year of operations should reach $18 million — about three times greater than the original forecast. Now they are faced with a major decision: if and how they should expand.

Prior to starting the discount computer store, the partners operated a direct-marketing sales organization that sold microcomputers to the business sector.

Through this experience Mr. Cracower realized that there might be an opportunity for a computer retail store that focused on price and limited service. His primary objective was to have lower prices than everyone else in the business. He noted that most manufacturers and retailers concentrated on newer, faster, bigger, better, and more expensive products. He felt that many retailers regarded computers and their accessories as exotic products instead of viewing the entire computer market as one that was evolving from differentiated products into a true commodity market.

He and David Matthews invested $250 000 to get the business started. Both were well known in the computer business and they were able to negotiate credit lines with suppliers. They continually searched the "warehouses" of major world computer manufacturers and picked up "old" computers at large discounts. In the computer business, many models can be out of fashion in a few months and are then considered "old" by the manufacturer.

The partners designed a marketing mix that included discount prices, the "best" available product bargains around, and a full-time technical support staff of four people in the store. In addition, on the name brand merchandise that was sold, the manufacturer would provide warranties of up to two years. On the no-name clones and software not covered by manufacturers, ICCW offered a six-month warranty.

In spite of the initial success of ICCW, some people are skeptical about its future. One executive of a large retail computer chain wonders how long this concept will last. He points out that ongoing product development, service, and support are part of what customers are really paying for when they buy a new microcomputer. He suggests that ICCW's "no frills" approach will limit its ability to serve its customers. Furthermore, when these customers demand more service, ICCW's prices will have to go up.

Mr. Cracower is undaunted by these comments. He regards his major problem as how to decide on future expansion and sees the following options:

- Open up a number of franchise stores across Canada.

- Open up new stores on their own.

- Manufacture their own microcomputers in Singapore.

- Enter the U.S. market.

He would prefer to open his own stores because the profitability would be higher and the partners would have better control. However, this would limit the number of stores they could open because of the capital required. Entering the U.S. market would be challenging because many of the larger U.S. computer manufacturers might refuse to sell to ICCW to protect their own distribution systems and dealers. Manufacturing their own computers could offer a steady source of supply but limit their flexibility in terms of shopping for the best bargains around.

Questions

1. What are the major reasons for ICCW's success to date?
2. What future marketing strategy would you recommend for ICCW?

7. ATLANTIC JEANS

Ms. Jackson, the recently hired marketing manager for Atlantic Jeans, had just been given her first assignment. The president had met with her and made the following comments: "Our company is in trouble. We've been using a strategy of mass marketing for our jeans and I think we should consider a change. We've been losing sales and market share for the last three years. I want you to assess the market and prepare a report outlining how we should or could segment the market, and the implications for Atlantic Jeans of using a differentiated marketing strategy. As well, give me a proposal for a marketing mix that is based on the way you think the market should be segmented."

The first thing Ms. Jackson did was to look over her notes from the marketing course she had taken the year before. She remembered that the instructor had provided a diagram that illustrated how a firm might approach segmenting, targeting, and positioning. She studied the diagram (Figure 1) and then started collecting information.

Ms. Jackson then studied the marketing plan that had been used to support the company's mass marketing strategy. Atlantic currently produced a line of basic, durable blue jeans that appealed to a wide range of consumers. The jeans were priced within the typical retail price range for jeans—$25 to $40. The cost of goods for the line was approximately 60% of factory sales, and the promotion budget had fluctuated between $300 000 and $700 000 over the past five years.

Ms. Jackson then read any published articles she could obtain on the blue jean market. From various sources, including *Canadian Business*, *Financial Post*, *Business Week*, *Financial Times*, and *Report on Business*, she jotted down the following information:

- None of the major manufacturers, including Atlantic, Levi's, GWG, Lee, and Blue Bell, had done well in the last two years because of changing demographics and intense competition from smaller jean manufacturers.

- Blue Bell Canada had recently launched a campaign in major urban markets for its Wrangler 909 jeans. The budget for only one part of the campaign, a one-month outdoor poster program, was $300 000. The target was adults in the 18-49 age group, and the emphasis was placed on form-fitting style. This was a change from Blue Bell's previous approach with Wrangler Jeans, which had been known for their wide-leg, western style and fit.

- Pantorama, a Montreal based retailer, makes and sells Roberto jeans. They recently announced a major campaign to sell Roberto jeans across Canada, focusing on the youth market and emphasizing a young, trendy, and sexy image.

- Lee Canada did a market study and found that a Lee target market — women, aged 15 to 25 — liked Lee jeans for quality but found them unexciting. Lee responded by designing a new line that included white and pastel Lees in non-blue jean materials such as twill and chambray. To promote the line, $1-million was spent on advertising, including billboards, subway posters, and a TV campaign.

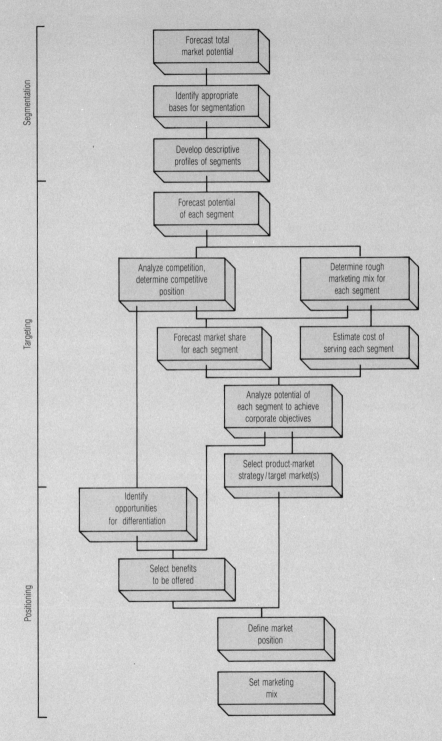

FIGURE 1
Framework for Segmentation, Targeting and Positioning

Ms. Jackson's next step was to collect demographic data from Statistics Canada and other sources. She then prepared a series of tables (1 to 4). With this information she started writing the report. She knew she would have to make some assumptions but it was important to get the job done.

Written by Arlene Bennett, Wilfrid Laurier University.

TABLE 1

Population by Province, 1986 (thousands of persons)

Total, Canada	25 622
Newfoundland	602 2,35 %
Prince Edward Island	127 0,50 %
Nova Scotia	884 3,45 %
New Brunswick	723 2,82 %
Quebec	6638 25,91 %
Ontario	9170 35,79 %
Manitoba	1080 4,22 %
Saskatchewan	1036 4,04 %
Alberta	2343 9,14 %
British Columbia	2946 11,50 %
Yukon	21 0,08 %
Northwest Territories	52 0,20 %

15,808 = 61,7 (handwritten, bracketing Quebec and Ontario)

Source: Statistics Canada.

TABLE 2

Population by Age Group and Sex, 1986 (thousands of persons)

Age	Male	Female
Total, Canada	12 676	12 946
Under 15 years	2792	2651 5443
15-19	994	945 1939
20-24	1196	1153 2349
25-29	1192	1193 2385
30-34	1094	1106 2200
35-39	1020	1021 2041
40-44	815	807 1622
45-49	664	661 1325
50-54	619	618 1237
55-59	599	617 1216
60-64	537	599 1136
65 and over	1154	1575 2729

(handwritten annotations: 28,8; 27,d; 15,47; 14,6; 10,66; 43,86 % off Ont/que 7382; 6934; 4988; 3589)

Source: Statistics Canada.

TABLE 3
Income Distribution, 1986

Income range	Number of people (thousands)
Under $10 000	4850
$10 000- 20 000	4500
$20 000- 30 000	3300
$30 000- 40 000	1700
$40 000- 50 000	750
$50 000-100 000	640
Over $100 000	110
Total	15 800

Source: Woods Gordon and Revenue Canada (based on all tax returns).

TABLE 4
Canadian Life styles

Life-style category	% all households
Urban	
Affluent	1
Upscale	7
Middle and upper middle class	16
Working (lower middle) class	15
Lower class	7
Young singles	4
Young couples	4
Empty nesters	9
Old and retired	4
Ethnic	3
Non-Urban	
Upscale and middle class	11
Working and lower class	16
Farming	3

Source: Compusearch Lifestyles Analysis.

Note: There are approximately 9.1 million households in Canada. The life-style categories are determined by dividing the population into groups with shared attitudes and similar buying patterns.

Questions

1. What further information would you want before preparing the report?
2. Using the existing information, assume you are Ms. Jackson and prepare the report.

8. PETITE SHOP (A)

Alice Wood had a decision to make. After working in a women's clothing store for several years she was now considering opening her own store for petite women in Prince George, British Columbia. In investigating the venture she had collected secondary information but was unsure how to go about estimating whether there was potential for another women's clothing store in that city.

Prince George was a city of 72 000 with a large trading area surrounding it. There were presently 22 clothing stores and five department stores that sold women's clothing in the city. During the past few years, Ms. Wood had saved $20 000 for this venture and had been learning all she could to ensure that her "Petite Shop" ladieswear store would be a success.

In anticipation of starting her own business, she enrolled in a small business management course at a local college. The instructor had stressed the importance of market research and mentioned several sources of secondary information that could assist in determining the market potential for a new business. As a result, Alice had obtained reports that she felt were relevant to her prospective business from Statistics Canada, *The Financial Post*, and the Prince George Chamber of Commerce. A summary of the information is contained in Tables 1, 2, and 3.

Now she had information, but was not sure how to proceed. She did not want to sell every type of women's clothing but planned a limited range of clothing that catered to the woman who was small—wearing dress sizes 3 to 9. Alice herself was small (5'1"), and felt that she understood the difficulties a woman of her size had in shopping for clothing. From her retailing experience, she estimated that about 18% of all clothing sales were in women's clothing of the type she planned to sell, and that 20% of all women fit in the size 3 to 9

TABLE 1

Prince George: Selected Data

Population	72 000
Number of households	25 000
Per capita disposable income	$13 000
Retail sales (annual)	$386 000 000

Source: Canadian Markets, *The Financial Post*.

TABLE 2

Prince George: Estimated Retail Space (selected establishments)

	sq. ft.
Food stores	200 000
Apparel stores	
Men's clothing stores	45 000
Women's clothing stores	80 000
Hardware stores	600 000
Department stores	650 000

Source: Prince George Chamber of Commerce.

TABLE 3

Canadian Family Expenditures on Clothing (percentage)

Family income	Percent
Under $7000	5.1
$ 7000- 9999	6.0
$10 000-14 999	6.1
$15 000-19 999	6.4
$20 000-24 999	5.8
$25 000-29 999	5.9
$30 000-34 999	6.2
$35 000-39 999	6.3
$40 000-49 999	6.4
$50 000 and over	5.9
All classes (average)	6.1

Source: *Market Research Handbook*, Statistics Canada.

Note: Families are equivalent to households.

category. Her decision to select a store directed at the small woman was arrived at after she visited all of the 22 clothing stores in Prince George and the women's clothing departments of the five department stores. She estimated that only about 10% of clothing stores' stock was sized 3 to 9 and that the five department stores had about 3500 square feet of selling space in total devoted to this size range. She felt that a small shop of about 1000 square feet could provide a much better selection to this market than these outlets presently provided.

Questions

1. Using the information provided, prepare an estimate of the market potential for the target market Alice Wood has focused on.

2. What portion of this market potential could Alice expect as Petite Shop's market share?

3. What non-quantitative considerations should be brought into this analysis?

Written by D. Wesley Balderson, University of Lethbridge.

9. PETITE SHOP (B)

Alice Wood had just finished estimating the market potential and market share for her proposed retail store in Prince George (see Petite Shop (A)). She now wanted to determine if the Petite Shop would provide an adequate return on her investment of $20 000. Ms. Wood had worked in a women's clothing store for several years and was planning to open her own store in Prince George, British Columbia.

Alice began by collecting information on the typical costs that would be incurred in operating the store. In investigating potential rental costs she found a 1000 square foot retail outlet for lease on a busy street in the central business district of Prince George. It looked like an ideal location for the Petite Shop. The site leased for $12 per square foot per year and there were no royalty payments except for a $550 per year payment to cover municipal taxes. The estimated utility expenses were $200 per month. The insurance cost for the retail shoe store that had previously leased the space was $1500 per year. Although Alice was excited with the potential of this site, she estimated that approximately $12 000 would have to be spent for leasehold improvements, of which only $8000 would be for depreciable items (depreciation rate of 20% per annum).

Ms. Wood felt that she could operate her new store with one other full-time person and some part-time help, at an estimated monthly cost of $1600. Other expenses would include a business license that would cost $100 each year. She estimated that all her miscellaneous expenses such as stationery, bad debt expense, credit expense, and telephone costs would total about $5000 per annum. These figures were based on her experience at the store where she presently worked.

Alice knew she would have to borrow some money to get started. She visited her local bank and discovered that the current interest rate for a business loan was 15%. She also learned that until she had a more concrete proposal her banker would not be very interested in considering a loan. Although she was a bit surprised at the bank's reaction, Alice was determined to prepare such a proposal. She knew she would have to do some advertising for her new store but did not know how much she should spend. The banker had suggested that the average for women's clothing stores was about 2% of sales and had given

TABLE 1

Key Business Ratios—Women's Clothing

Cost of goods sold	57.4%
Gross margin	42.6%
Current assets to current debt (ratio)	1.79
Profits on sales	3.6%
Profits on tangible net worth (ratio)	17.03
Sales to tangible net worth	4.75
Collection period (days)	13
Sales to inventory (ratio)	5.2
Fixed assets to tangible net worth	42.7%
Current debt to tangible net worth	94.2%
Number of firms reporting	2323

Source: Dun and Bradstreet Canada, Key Business Ratios Canada — Corporations

her a copy of a recent Dun and Bradstreet Financial Ratio sheet to assist her in calculating various expenses (Table 1).

Alice now found herself faced with the same dilemma as she was faced with when determining market potential and market share. She had a lot of information but was not sure how to proceed.

Written by D. Wesley Balderson, University of Lethbridge.

Questions

1. Using the information presented in Petite Shop (A) and this case, prepare an estimated income statement and return on investment calculation for the Petite Shop's first year of operation.
2. What areas has Alice overlooked in her investigation?
3. Given your analysis, what would you recommend to Alice Wood?

10. CANADIAN POPULATION AND HOUSEHOLD TRENDS

An important aspect of marketing is to determine the future implications of population and household trends. The three tables that follow provide past and future data on the Canadian population by age group, by geographic area, and by household.

TABLE 1

Population, Actual and Projected, By Age Group 1951-2006 (thousands)

Year	Population	Under 9	10-14	20-34	35-49	50-64	65 and over
Actual							
1951	14 010	3120	2190	3260	2610	1740	1090
1956	16 080	3790	2600	3540	3020	1890	1240
1961	18 240	4340	3290	3670	3400	2150	1390
1966	20 020	4500	3930	3950	3630	2470	1540
1971	21 570	4070	4420	4790	3760	2780	1750
1976	22 990	3620	4620	5760	3850	3140	2000
1981	24 340	3560	4240	6560	4220	3400	2360
1986	25 600	3630	3730	6940	4980	3590	2730
Projections							
1991	26 610	3570	3610	6750	5820	3690	3170
1996	27 350	3260	3680	6240	6560	4030	3580
2001	27 820	2880	3620	5770	6910	4760	3880
2006	28 090	2670	3310	5680	6740	5550	4410

Source: *Marketing Research Handbook*, Statistics Canada, ,Catalogue 63-224, various years. Projections based on moderate fertility rates, average net international migration, and a migration flow within Canada that partially reflects the late 1960s pattern.

TABLE 2

Population, Actual and Projected, By Geographic Area 1951-2006 (thousands)

Year	Total population	Maritime provinces	Quebec	Ontario	Prairie provinces	B.C. and Yukon/NWT
Actual						
1951	14 010	1620	4050	4600	2550	1190
1956	16 080	1760	4630	5410	2850	1430
1961	18 240	1900	5260	6230	3180	1670
1966	20 020	1980	5780	6960	3380	1920
1971	21 570	2060	6030	7700	3540	2240
1976	22 990	2180	6240	8260	3780	2530
1981	24 340	2230	6440	8630	4230	2810
1986	25 600	2320	6630	9110	4510	3030
Projections						
1991	26 610	2360	6750	9410	4800	3290
1996	27 350	2360	6780	9630	5040	3540
2001	27 820	2350	6740	9750	5240	3740
2006	28 090	2330	6660	9770	5400	3930

Source: *Marketing Research Handbook*, Statistics Canada, Catalogue 63-224, various years. Projections based on moderate fertility rates, average net international migration, and a migration flow within Canada that partially reflects the late 1960s pattern.

TABLE 3
Population, Actual and Projected, By Geographic Area 1966-2001 (thousands)

Year	Total households	Maritime provinces	Quebec	Ontario	Prairie provinces	B.C. and Yukon/NWT
Actual						
1966	5180	450	1390	1880	910	550
1971	6030	500	1600	2230	1020	680
1976	7170	600	1900	2640	1190	840
1981	8280	670	2170	2970	1450	1020
1986	9220	750	2340	3430	1590	1110
Projections						
1991	10 110	820	2510	3780	1760	1240
1996	10 680	860	2590	4020	1870	1340
2001	11 190	900	2650	4230	1980	1430

Source: *Marketing Research Handbook*, Statistics Canada, Catalogue 63-224, various years. Projections based on moderate fertility rates, average net international migration, and a migration flow within Canada that partially reflects the late 1960s pattern.

Note: Households include: single-detached, single-attached, apartments and flats, and mobile homes.

Questions

1. Analyze the tables and prepare a discussion of the marketing implications that are likely to occur in the decade from 1986 to 1996.
2. Contrast these changes with those that occurred in the decade from 1976 to 1986.

11. VULCAN PACKAGING LIMITED

Vulcan Packaging (VP), an Ontario-based company, manufactures and sells metal containers and operates a metal printing business. VP is one of the largest Canadian manufacturers of industrial pails and containers. It also has a lithography business through which it supplies multi-colored applications on a variety of consumer products. Company sales and profits have fluctuated in the past few years — in 1978 sales were $18.6 million (loss of $825 000), in 1983 sales were $64.3 million (profit of $243 000) and in 1985 sales were $68.5 million (profit of $1 900 000). However, company officials believe that a new product, Explosafe, will lead the firm to greater rewards in the future.

VP acquired the rights to Explosafe in the late 1970s, and since then has been developing, testing, and refining the product. Explosafe can be cut to fit any size and shape of container and, when installed, will prevent any materials in the container from exploding should the materials somehow be ignited. Explosafe is made of a thin aluminum alloy, which is expanded and slitted to form a mesh of hexagonal-shaped openings. Once installed, Explosafe acts to quench any explosive reaction by slowing down and stopping flames from spreading, and absorbing the heat released during the explosive reaction.

The product has been tested at the Rexdale, Ontario, plant and in a number of other situations. The most important tests, however, have been conducted by the U.S. Air Force. After four years of testing, the U.S.A.F., in a news release, stated that Explosafe "can effectively prevent explosions in the event of combat fire penetration or other ignition sources when fitted inside aircraft fuel tanks." The U.S.A.F. test report manual was released to military contractors at the same time. The manual allows Explosafe to be specified, by number, in applications requiring an explosion suppressant system. If all goes well, Explosafe sales to the military could be worth up to $150 million in the next five to seven years. VP has also received a contract (worth $500 000) to install engineered explosive support systems in the fuel tanks of 2768 2.5-ton military support vehicles for the Canadian Armed Forces.

Explosafe has also been tested by a U.S.-Canadian task force group of government agencies, chemical companies, and railway car representatives. The tests were conducted on scale-model containers (one-fifth real size). The containers were filled with 200 gallons of propane and subjected to fire-testing. The unprotected tanks exploded, while the tanks equipped with Explosafe boiled dry without rupture or explosion. Full-scale railway car tank testing is continuing.

Explosafe has also been successfully tested in five-gallon gasoline cans. When a mixture of propane and oxygen was detonated in a standard can, it blew up; a similar test with Explosafe left the can undamaged. Company officials were extremely optimistic about Explosafe and industry analysts feel that the company is at least five years ahead of any possible competitive product that might be developed. At issue is how the company could reach what is considered a large, untapped potential in both the consumer and industrial/military markets.

Assume that you have been requested to prepare a report recommending the major markets for the product and general approaches by which these markets could be reached at a profit. Your instructions from the company president include the following:

> I want your suggestions as to what markets look promising, and strategies we should adopt if we go into these markets. I do not expect you to provide any quantitative data in your report — especially with respect to the strategies you suggest we use in entering these markets. Thus, your reports will be essentially qualitative in nature. You are to present your reports at our next executive meeting with the understanding that once we, as a group, are agreed on what general strategies we have to adopt if we are to have any reasonable chance of being successful, you and your staff will be assigned the responsibility of detailing the precise strategies to be employed and the expenditures required. Following this we will meet and decide whether such an investment is feasible and desirable.

The market reports were to be rough in the sense that specific data were not required. Essentially, the reports would take the planners through the planning process in a quick and simplified way to get the "feel" of the problem and give corporate management ideas as a basis for further thought. Special attention was to be given to how the product would be used, why it would be selected over other products, who would buy it, where it would be bought, and how important price would be.

Questions

1. What four or five major questions would you pose to guide your preparation of a report on either the consumer or industrial market?
2. Diagram a market planning process you might use in drawing up a rough plan for Explosafe.
3. What opportunities for Explosafe exist in the consumer market?
4. List as many specific uses as possible for Explosafe in industry, government and other non-profit organizations. Use an outline, a series of lists, or some other basis for classifying your ideas.

12. LOCTITE CANADA

Loctite Canada is a wholly-owned subsidiary of the U.S. corporation Loctite, a manufacturer of adhesives and sealants, and related specialty chemicals. The U.S. parent has annual sales in the $200 million range while the Canadian subsidiary's sales are around $8 million. Both the parent and subsidiary have grown rapidly in recent years. The company's growth has been with the "wonder glues" (specifically the anaerobic type), which cure quickly in the absence of air, and the "crazy glues" (cyanoacrylates), which cure instantly upon exposure to moisture that is present in trace amounts on surfaces to be bonded. In the industrial market, this product sells for over $60 per pound; a pound contains roughly 30 000 drops and is generally applied a few drops at a time. Consumer packages are much smaller, containing about one-tenth of an ounce and selling for up to $2 per tube, or about $20 or more per ounce.

The company's phenomenal success in the industrial market has attracted competitors, including some large and aggressive ones, such as the 3M Company. Competitive anaerobic and cyanoacrylate products are being marketed in most countries where the company conducts business. The company has patent protection on its anaerobics in the United States and, to a lesser extent, in a number of foreign countries, including Canada. Nearly all competitive anaerobic sealants and adhesives are sold at prices lower than those of Loctite. Although the company has selectively reduced prices to meet competition from time to time, it believes that attention to technical service and customer needs has generally enabled it to maintain its market position without significant price reductions.

The company plans to intensify its "application engineering" approach, which helped it become the leader in the more competitive "crazy glue" or cyanoacrylates market. This approach casts well-trained technical service personnel as problem solvers for customers using Loctite's products, often especially formulated for the customer's application. The company has three principal user markets for its products: the industrial market, the consumer market, and the automotive after-market. In the Industrial Products Group, approximately 60% of sales are made through independent distributors, some of which sell adhesives and sealants made by others. The remainder of sales are made directly to end users. The company maintains close and continued contact with its distributors and major end users to provide technical assistance and support for the use of its products. In Canada and the United States, sales are made through approximately 120 technically trained district managers, sales engineers, and approximately 2800 independent industrial distributors.

Hoping to improve profitability, Loctite decided to try consumer goods marketing techniques in marketing RC 601, a puttylike adhesive for repairing worn machine parts. After going into the field to determine what potential customers wanted and studying the product from the customers' point of view, the company made certain changes in its marketing effort. The before-and-after contrast is shown in Table 1.

TABLE 1
Loctite's Market Survey — Summary

	Before	After
Market target	Design engineers[1]	Maintenance workers[2]
Product	Thin liquid	Gel
Package	Bottle (red)	Tube (silver)
Name	RC 601	Quick–Metal
Price	Cost based	Value based
Promotion	Technical description[3]	"Keeps machines running until parts arrive"
Sales effort	Routine	Special promotions and
Sales results		incentives at all levels
		700% increase after changes

1. Reluctant to try unproven products.
2. Able to buy anything anywhere needed to make machine operate.
3. Nonmigrating thoxotropic anaerobic gel.

The Industrial Products Division faces the problem of pricing three new products. The details are as follows:

Bond-a-matic   This is an instant glue applicator for assembly lines and is targeted at small and medium-sized manufacturers that put a lot of parts together. The product avoids "adhesive clog," a common and costly problem. The company is so confident of the product's performance that it will mail a demonstration kit for a 30-day free trial. The product should be priced low enough that it can be bought by production managers without the approval needed for a capital expenditure.

Quick Repair Kit   This includes an assortment of materials to make quick minor repairs requiring fast-curing adhesives and/or sealants to keep equipment running and minimize waste of materials in small shops and factories. The kit includes a pair of Vice-Grip pliers as a premium.

Quick-Metal   This is a puttylike adhesive for temporary repair of worn metal bearings and other machine parts. Equipment is ready to run in one hour, compared with 12 hours for "metalizers," the most commonly used alternative method. Loctite claims that the product can save the user over $4000 in time and labor. It is packaged in 50cc tubes.

All of these products are to be sold through the Industrial Products Division's distributors. In determining the suggested price to be charged by the distributors for each product, assume the following costs:

Loctite	Bond-a-matic	Quick Repair Kit	Quick-Metal
Cost to make	$27.00	$ 6.25	$1.50
All other costs	23.00	5.75	3.50
Total cost per unit	$50.00	$12.00	$5.00

Distributor:
Usual gross margin on this type of product is 33⅓ % of selling price.

Questions

1. What factors should be considered by Loctite in determining the suggested price its distributors should charge their customers?
2. What price would you recommend that Loctite suggest its distributors charge for each product?
3. How would you use the problem-solving marketing approach when selling through distributors and retailers?

13. BRAND LOYALTY

In late November Jim Ashman, the brand manager for a leading Canadian shampoo, met with his superior, Susan Keller, to discuss the advertising and sales promotion budget for next year. Susan began the conversation. "Jim, I think we should consider changing the amount we spend on advertising. This year, we've spent $1 100 000 on advertising and have just held on to our 14% share of the market. On the other hand, we've spent only $800 000 on sales promotions. One half went to trade allowances — we sold the shampoo to retail chains at reduced prices. The other $400 000 was spent on price specials to the consumer, including selling the large size (400 ml) for the price of the regular size (300ml). I think we should spend more of the budget on sales promotions and less on advertising. I don't think we get much brand loyalty with shampoo."

Jim responded, "No, I think we should spend the same amount next year on advertising and sales promotions as this year. Even though the competition is spending more on sales promotions and less on advertising than we are, we are holding our own. This is a product category where advertising can create brand loyalties." "I'm not sure," said Susan. "Look, there have been a number of articles written recently on brand loyalty in the wake of the Coca-Cola change. Why don't you review the articles and then we'll discuss it again." Susan was referring to the fact that, after the Coca-Cola Company changed the formulation of Coca-Cola and were forced to do an about-face and bring back the "Old Coke," a number of articles had been written about brand loyalty.

Jim then left Susan's office and spent a day compiling the articles that had discussed brand loyalty. He then summarized the main points from the articles.

- Consumer loyalty to big-name brands is on the wane in several product categories, eroded by wider selection and by price competition from aggressive name, generic, and store brands.

- Brand loyalty — that certain something that makes a consumer keep buying over and over again — is an elusive quality. It begins with the customer's preference for a product on the basis of objective reasons—the drink is sweeter, the paper towel more absorbent. The brand name is the customers' guarantee that they will get what they expect. But when a branded product has been around a long time and is heavily advertised, it can pick up emotional freight: it can become a part of a person's self-image or summon fond memories of days gone by.

- One study suggested that brand loyalties seem to be most intense with products that are ingested or close to the skin. As well, the more closely a brand is bound to people's self-image, the more likely they will be to resist any change in it.

- Brand loyalties seem to be greater, the more emotionally involved the customer is with a given purchase. The higher the level of involvement, the stronger the brand loyalty.

- Many marketers are beginning to worry that generic and other bargain products are making brand loyalty a thing of the past among increasingly savvy and recession-weary consumers.

- A research study has shown that few customers favor a single brand. They choose from two or three brands, making the decision in the store aisle, where display, price, and product availability are persuasive factors.

- The fact that many brands—Tide, Kleenex, and Kraft slices—have been the leading brands for many years suggests brand loyalty exists. However, some argue that people buy name brands out of habit, but do not necessarily feel loyal to them.

- One study of loyalty by an advertising agency provided some interesting results. The agency measured the degree of loyalty by asking people whether they would switch to another brand if it was sold at a 50% discount. The products where consumers most often said no were classed as high-loyalty products, those where consumers most often said yes were classed as low-loyalty products, and those in-between were classed as medium-loyalty products. The results are shown in Table 1.

After reviewing his notes, Jim was uncertain as to what proportion of the budget should be spent on advertising or sales promotion. He thought the best step he could take at this time would be to prepare a list of points for and against each method, in preparation for the meeting.

TABLE 1

High-loyalty products	Medium-loyalty products	Low-loyalty products
Cigarettes	Cola drinks	Paper towels
Laxatives	Margarine	Crackers
Cold remedies	Shampoo	Scouring powder
35-mm film	Hand lotion	Plastic trash bags
Toothpaste	Furniture polish	Facial tissues

Questions

1. Which is more effective in marketing shampoo, advertising or sales promotions?
2. Prepare pros and cons for both sides of the argument.

14. ALLIANCE COSMETICS

Alliance Cosmetics, a small cosmetics manufacturer in Manitoba, has a well-positioned set of mid-price-range facial cosmetic products. The quality of this product line, which retails in the $4 to $7 price range, is slightly above that of the major competitors such as Max Factor and Bonne Belle. The firm had sought and gained distribution through the major pharmacy stores in Ontario and Manitoba, and chains such as Shoppers Drug Mart had responded well to its product line.

The line's success was due to more than just the slightly higher quality-price relationship. The firm had initially contracted representation from an aggressive set of manufacturer's agents. This was necessary to get quick high-volume distribution, which appeared to be possible only through the drug mart chains. The majority of the agents had long-term relationships with the chain buyers and were able to open the doors for the firm's products. This rapid and fairly intensive distribution was a key factor.

Drug mart chains are interested in high turnover and good margins. Therefore, above-average retail mark-ups — in the neighborhood of 120% versus the more typical 100% on cost to retailer — were offered. Three years ago, the firm spent $200 000 on advertising in the introductory three-month launch of the initial product line, and has since spent about $600 000 per year on advertising.

With the success of the current mid-price-range product line, three drug chains had recently expressed an interest in the prospect of the firm producing top-of-the-line facial cosmetics. The firm had the following major facts to consider in pursuing this opportunity:

1. The plant had ample capacity. It could produce an extra 1 000 000 product units without overstraining the capacity of the equipment.

2. The fixed costs the company now faces per year are estimated at $650 000. This would likely increase by $175 000 with an additional product line.

3. The current average retail price of the company's product is $5.50. The company has an average selling price to retailers of $2.50 per unit.

4. The direct manufacturing costs per unit for the current line are $0.80. The direct overhead costs of the new line would be $1.00 per unit. Agent's commissions are 4% of the company's selling price.

5. Total advertising for all lines would be in the neighborhood of $1 million in the year the product is launched.

6. The average retail price of the line would have to be a minimum of $7.75 for it to be perceived as a high-quality good.

7. Some product samples had been produced and these were very well accepted by cosmeticians and models who had tried them.

This firm faces some interesting pricing problems. Price is often equated with quality in products like cosmetics. Here the consumer is purchasing in a very real sense "the total product concept." Cosmetics represent much more than the physical attributes of the product to the consumer. They represent glamor, beauty, and hope! Many buyers see price as a significant determinant of the quality of a product. To signify a premium-range product, a premium price has to be set. Unfortunately, as this premium price strategy is constrained by the firm's advertising budget, it cannot match the dollar volume of the large competitors in the industry. The higher the price, the greater the need for heavy and extensive advertising and promotional push. The company must have an advertising budget that will allow it to convince the public to pay the high price. The basic question is whether the planned $1 million in advertising expenditures is enough to support both product lines.

Questions

1. What pricing approach would you recommend for the new product line?
2. What price would you set for the new line? Why?

15. VIDEO MOVIES: PRICING DECISIONS

It is often difficult to set a price for a product or service. Balancing all the components—objectives, demand and cost analysis, competition, the effect on the company's other products or services, and legal considerations—to arrive at an optimum price requires considerable skill. Many of these components are relevant for the movie industry in its attempt to set prices for movies that are released on video cassettes for the home market.

A new market opened up for movie studios with the introduction of the video cassette recorder (VCR). Instead of having just one market for movies—the movie theater audience—multiple markets were now available. In fact, a movie studio can maximize the profits from films by reaching four markets: movie theaters, pay TV, network TV, and cassette sales for re-sale or rental. In particular, the rapid growth of VCRs in North America created a large market for the re-sale or rental of movies. In Canada, approximately 45 000 VCRs were sold in 1980. By the end of 1984, 23% of Canadian households had a VCR, by the end of 1985, 36%, and by the end of 1987 it was estimated that over 50% of the 9.1 million households in Canada had a VCR. A similar sales pattern and increase in household ownership was experienced in the United States.

Accompanying the growth in VCR sales was the establishment of video rental stores, which sprung up all over North America. Because it was one of the easiest businesses to get into (very low costs to enter), both new stores and existing retailers (e.g., convenience stores) entered the video rental business. Because of the proliferation of these businesses it is difficult to determine how large the total retail market is or how many stores are in existence at any given time. However, it was estimated that in 1984 there were approximately 35 000 video stores in North America (3500 in Canada and 31 500 in the U.S.). By 1987 approximately 80 000 video stores were in operation (8000 in Canada and 72 000 in the U.S.). Against this backdrop, the movie studios must make a pricing decision when releasing movies for the VCR market.

Your task is to analyze each of the following two decisions.

Decision A

In early 1984, two video cassettes were released in the same week, *Raiders of the Lost Ark* and *Tootsie*. *Raiders of the Lost Ark* was one of the most popular movies of all time, an action-adventure film that appealed to people of all ages. With this movie, the studio had an objective of getting a greater share of the retail revenue generated by the home video market, and it was decided to use a penetration pricing strategy with *Raiders*. The movie was sold to wholesalers for a price of $25.00, and retailed (both to consumers and video stores) for $39.95. Prior to this time, movies had been priced at $50 wholesale and $79.95 retail. *Tootsie* also had considerable success at the box office, although the comedic story of an unemployed actor (played by Dustin Hoffman) who gets a part in a daily soap opera as a female attracted a more adult, upscale audience than *Raiders*. This movie was released at the traditional wholesale price of $50 and retail price of $79.95.

Decision B

In early 1987, two video cassettes were released during the same week, *Top Gun* and *Stand By Me*. *Top Gun* was the top grossing movie of 1986. This adventure-action story of navy pilots at a flight competition appealed to a broad audience, although it was heavily aimed at the teenage market. *Top Gun* sold for a retail price of $27 and a wholesale price of $16. At this time, many movies were being sold at retail for $30. *Top Gun* reduced its price to $27 because Pepsi paid $3 per cassette to have a commercial for Pepsi included at the start of the film. *Stand By Me*, the poignant story of four young boys and their adventures over a few summer days, did reasonably well at the box office. It attracted a diverse audience, many of whom went because of the very favorable reviews received by the movie. *Stand By Me* sold for $90 retail and $55 wholesale, a higher price than usual in the market.

Questions

1. What factors should be considered in setting the price for a movie released on video cassette?
2. For each of the two examples, who do you think made the best pricing decision? Why?
3. For each decision, which of the two movies generated the largest total revenue for the studios?

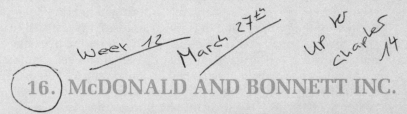

16. McDONALD AND BONNETT INC.

McDonald and Bonnett Inc. (M & B), a small Canadian import firm, was always on the look-out for new products to expand its line. Mr. McDonald, one of the two partners, met the owner of a Philippine manufacturing firm at a trade show. After some discussion, the manufacturer made Mr. McDonald an interesting offer — exclusive Canadian rights to import an innovative air freshening product. The active component of this product, tentatively branded "Odor Magnet," is a core of chemically treated, activated carbon that both absorbs odors and kills germs. The Odor Magnet does not cover smells, it eliminates them. It is effective for up to six months, although the instructions recommend that it be replaced every three months. The Philippine manufacturer of the Odor Magnet has already achieved some success with the product. Domestic sales have reached 24 000 units per year, and approximately 3 million units had been sold in Japan in a two year period. Canada has been chosen as a second international market. The Philippine manufacturer offered the product to M & B on the following basis: the offer was open for only 30 days, and it stipulated a minimum order of 1 million units.

The Philippine firm currently manufactures three air-freshener products. Mr. McDonald chose the Odor Magnet from this product line because it physically resembles several of the air-freshener products currently available in Canada. The case measures 3″ × 5″ × 1½″, and is made of white plastic. Slits are cut in the side faces of the rectangular case to allow airflow. The Odor Magnet is packaged in a cardboard box with a cutout window to show the product. The name is clearly marked in block letters on the front and sides of the package. On the back of the package are a complete list of product uses (i.e. refrigerator, bedroom, bathroom, and car), a detailed outline of the product benefits, and clear directions for use.

Upon returning from the trade show, Mr. McDonald met with his partner, and was adamant that they accept the offer immediately. "You must see it, Bonnett, this is the opportunity of a lifetime." Mr. Bonnett replied, "I don't know if we can take the risk, McDonald. We're a small operation with limited resources. This product doesn't fit with *any* of the lines we currently handle. We can't go head-to-head with the giants like S.C. Johnson. But . . . I have to agree with you—this product looks like a gold mine. There has to be some way for us to make some money from it. Let's get some data on the market and then decide.''

Over the next week, Mr. McDonald collected the following information on the Canadian market:

- Annual Canadian demand is approximately 15 million units.

- The success of air-freshening products stems from the fact that households have odors that their inhabitants find unpleasant. Currently there are a variety of solutions to this problem.
  - approximately 20 products (i.e. 20 brands, forms, or sizes) are currently on the market: Glade, Rolair, Flo Thru (S.C. Johnson); Wizard, Sahara, Stick-ons (Boyle-Midway); Airwick, Stick-ups (Airwick); Air Care (Bristol-Myers); Florient (Colgate-Palmolive); Twice-as-Fresh (Clorox); Lysol (Sterling Products); several "no name" store brands.
  - product forms include solids (three types: plastic case with a core of solid "perfume," which evaporates completely; plastic case with a core of heavy paper, soaked with "perfume," which evaporates from the paper; plastic bathroom tissue roll filled with "perfume" beads which release scent when the roll is turned), and aerosols.
  - most products are available in two to five scents (e.g. rose, lemon, baby powder, lilac, pine, etc.).

- S.C. Johnson is market leader, but no individual product has more than 10% market share.

- Solids are effective for one to two months. Aerosols last for two weeks to two months, depending on usage rate.

- Retail prices vary from $0.89 to $1.79 for solids, and from $1.09 to $2.69 for aerosols.

- Most small manufacturers of air-freshening products use manufacturer's agents to distribute their products to food, drug, and mass merchandise stores. These agents demand a 7% commission on sales. Other manufacturers use a company salesforce.

- Retail margin is approximately 15%.

- Although promotional activities are primarily limited to cooperative advertising, several brands have become widely recognized.

- A typical breakdown of the manufacturer's selling price for large companies, such as S.C. Johnson, is: cost of goods 60%, administrative expenses 10%, selling expenses (salesforce and advertising) 20%, profit margin 10%.

One unique competitor is Cow Brand Baking Soda. Cow Brand is marketed as an air-freshener, but only for specific applications—the refrigerator and the freezer. Even so, it cannot be ignored because it offers the same key advantage as the Odor Magnet; it eliminates odors. The only other competitor that claims this benefit is Lysol. The other aerosols overwhelm odors, and solids merely mask them.

Mr. McDonald as again confronted Mr. Bonnett in their office, this time armed with an analysis of the financial potential of the offer. "Bonnett, I've determined that the Odor Magnet can be brought to Toronto at a landed cost of $0.60 per unit. If we capture 10 percent of the Canadian market, with a selling price to retailers of $0.80, our gross margin will jump by $300 000. Of course, if we decide to use manufacturer's agents, that number will drop — but only by $84 000."

"I agree that your numbers *look* great, McDonald, but I don't know how you think we're going to do it! We can't get the share. You haven't included anything for advertising! I think that our only chance is to sell this to Loblaws or A & P as a store brand. Or we might work out a licensing agreement with S.C. Johnson. They know how to introduce a product like this — and they have the financial backing to handle it."

"I can't agree, Bonnett. The Odor Magnet is superior to any other product on the market and can be used everywhere from the bathroom to the baby's room to the refrigerator. Neither Lysol, nor Cow Brand, nor S.C. Johnson can claim all of those uses. The "Odor Magnet" brand name is too appealing to sell out as a store brand to a grocery chain. Why should we share the profit potential of this product?!"

Questions

1. Should M & B accept the offer?
2. If they accept the offer, what is the best strategy for introducing the new air-freshening product?

Written by Arlene Bennett, Wilfrid Laurier University.

17. WATTS FARM ENTERPRISES: PAMPERED BEEF®

Watts Farm Enterprises (WFE) is a small cattle farm near Drumbo, Ontario, which was started as a hobby by Dr. Ralph Watts over ten years ago. Dr. Watts, a dentist in Galt, Ontario, operates WFE to supply high quality beef to his family and acquaintances who are dissatisfied with the beef available from other sources. All cattle on the feedlot are carefully selected at local auction, then fattened on a diet of corn, hay and natural diet supplements. The result is Pampered Beef® — tender, flavorful beef, free of hormones and chemicals. In 1986, WFE operated with 24 head of cattle. For 1987, the herd was increased to 30 head. In fact, Dr. Watts felt that current market demand would have supported greater expansion. However, any further increase in the size of the herd would require the addition of a second barn at a cost of $25 000. Dr. Watts is considering this expansion for 1988, but only if sales can be increased significantly. He thinks this may be possible with improved distribution or promotion, but is not sure.

Pampered Beef commands a premium price both because of its tenderness and flavor, and because it is organically grown. Some customers simply prefer a more natural beef; others must avoid the hormones and chemicals because of severe allergies. The current price is $4.60/kg, approximately 10 to 15% higher than the average for volume beef purchases. It is sold in quarters, sides or whole carcasses, cut to customer specifications by a custom butchering service. Distribution is through only one outlet, the custom butcher's shop on Hwy. 53, east of Burford (Figure 1).

FIGURE 1
Watts Farm Enterprises Market Area

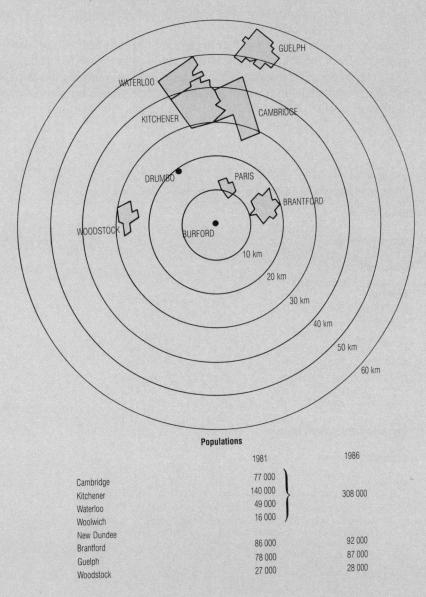

Populations

	1981	1986
Cambridge	77 000	
Kitchener	140 000	308 000
Waterloo	49 000	
Woolwich	16 000	
New Dundee		
Brantford	86 000	92 000
Guelph	78 000	87 000
Woodstock	27 000	28 000

In 1986, 49 customers purchased Pampered Beef. These sales were very geographically concentrated. Many customers live in Cambridge, largely due to contacts made by Dr. Watts at his dentistry office in that area. Overall, most WFE customers (past and present) live in Kitchener, Waterloo, or Cambridge (Galt/Hespeler). For logistical reasons, Dr. Watts is reluctant to expand this market base—particularly when he feels that the potential of the area has barely been tapped. The three primary types of competition for Pampered Beef in the K-W and Cambridge area are:

1. farms and wholesalers that offer volume beef purchases at low prices,

2. large supermarkets that offer standard cuts of beef at standard prices,

3. small butcher shops that offer standard and custom cuts at higher prices.

None of these competitors offers organically grown beef. Chemical-free beef is available from local Mennonite farms, but on a very limited scale.

Promotion of Pampered Beef, to date, has been largely by word-of-mouth. Dr. Watts has also implemented a friendly, personal, but professional direct-mail campaign. A letter and comment form are sent annually to present cus-

TABLE 1
Watts Farm Enterprises Income Statement for Year Ended December 31 1986

Sales[1]		27 962.55
Cost of goods sold		23 658.63
Gross profit		4303.92
Expenses		
General[2]	3507.47	
Insurance	843.65	
Interest	3311.72	
Marketing	238.99	
Total		7901.83
Loss before extraordinary income		3597.91
Extraordinary income[3]		3538.47
Net loss		59.44

[1]Twenty-two head of cattle were butchered and sold in 1986.
[2]Includes maintenance, automobile, office expenses.
[3]Includes custom work and rebates (tax, insurance, and fuel).

tomers, to thank them for their patronage, solicit an order and invite recommendations for changes to the product or service. Past customers receive a letter that inquires why their business has been lost, and a form for their comments and recommendations. Potential customers, identified through customer referrals, are sent a letter that outlines the development of WFE, describes the benefits of Pampered Beef and solicits future orders. Current customers receive a discount for successful referrals of new customers. The income statement and balance sheet for 1986 are provided in Tables 1 and 2.

TABLE 2
Watts Farm Enterprises Balance Sheet as of December 31 1986

Assets

Current assets

Bank	(89.84)	
Inventory (crops)	5640.29	
Prepaid expense	469.20	
Total current assets		6019.65

Fixed assets

Land		26 500.00
Building	26 530.42	
Less depreciation	2950.00	23 579.42
Equipment	39 517.53	
Less depreciation	2594.00	36 923.83
Automobile	11 740.00	
Less depreciation	1176.00	10 564.00
Total fixed assets		97 567.25
Total assets		103 586.90

Liabilities and owner's equity

Liabilities

Term bank loan		11 800.00
Contracts payable		2387.26
Tile loan		1205.32
Less prepaid finance charge		(117.99)
Total liabilities		15 274.59

Owner's equity

Capital (Dec. 31/85)	101 014.50	
Less drawings	12 642.75	88 371.75
Less Loss		59.44
Capital (Dec. 31/86)		88 312.31
Total liabilities and owner's equity		103 586.90

The comment forms returned through WFE's direct mail campaign have proved invaluable to Dr. Watts in making marketing decisions for Pampered Beef. He is confident, after ten years of operation with steadily increasing sales, that the product is appropriately priced. His experience also suggests that, given the scale of WFE, it is only financially feasible to sell Pampered Beef in bulk quantities. Dr. Watts has considered providing direct delivery—or at least establishing a pick-up depot in Kitchener. However, this would be a costly move, and his current customers seemed quite content to pick up their orders at the butcher's shop.

Having given fair consideration to changes in all areas of the market mix, Dr. Watts has reverted to his first instinct. His sense for the business tells him that the best way to increase sales of Pampered Beef is through improved distribution or increased promotion. But how can distribution or promotion be improved? Would improvement increase sales enough to justify the capital investment?

Questions

1. Recommend a promotion and distribution strategy for next year.

Written by Arlene Bennett, Wilfrid Laurier University.

18. HOME CLEANING SERVICES

Home Cleaning Services is a small Regina-based firm specializing in home cleaning services. The company's principal product is a weekly housecleaning service. For $75 per visit, two bonded cleaners clean and vacuum an entire house, wash the kitchen and bathroom floors, and, on an alternative visit schedule, clean the woodwork and wax and polish the hardwood floors. One team can clean two homes a day. These cleaning people are paid $6 per hour, with each home visit requiring three hours, and travel between homes averaged half an hour. Annual fixed costs, which include all clearning materials, travel expenses, etc., are $35 000.

The company, which originally consisted of owner-manager Tom Jones and two cleaners, had in less than four years grown to a staff of ten cleaners servicing 50 regular customers.

Initially, Jones had built his business by calling personally door-to-door in an attempt to solicit new customers. For the past year, however, most of his time was taken in supervising the cleaning teams and in general administration. Thus, most of the firm's recent growth had developed through personal referrals from existing customers.

Jones thought that there was a large untapped market for cleaning services, and was anxious to move rapidly to exploit the opportunities. Although the firm could not afford to invest a lot of money, Jones believed he could allocate $2000 to $3000 initially, and as much as $10 000 on selling and promotion during the current year, if he could be assured of at least 25 new regular customers.

While Jones was not sure of the best approach to increasing sales, he had considered a number of possibilities and wondered how he should appraise them.

Questions

Recommend a marketing plan for Mr. Jones for his next year of operations. The following questions can be used as guidelines in developing the marketing plan.

1. What alternatives can you think of for Jones to increase sales of his home cleaning service?
2. How would you suggest that these possible alternatives be evaluated?
3. Based on your analysis of the likely customers for a home cleaning service, how well do you think each of the approaches identified in question 2 would work?
4. What communications tasks does Jones wish to accomplish?

19. J.T. ELECTRONICS

Jack Booth, sales manager for J.T. Electronics, had just finished reviewing selected performance measures for 1987. He was concerned because market share had declined. There seemed to be a major problem in the Ontario region. He wondered if he should consider changing the compensation plan for the sales force, or at least talk to the salespeople in Ontario. "Something has to be done," he thought, "but I'm not sure what."

J.T. Electronics was a leading manufacturer and marketer of quality stereo equipment in Canada. The product line included stereos (receivers and amplifiers), compact disc players, and cassette decks. The company was jointly owned by a Canadian firm and Japanese firm. The Japanese partner manufactured most of the product line and the Canadian partner was responsible for distributing and marketing the products in Canada. One major task was to get distribution through the large department stores (e.g., Eaton's) and specialty stereo stores (e.g., Atlantic Sound). J.T. Electronics used a salesforce to accomplish this job.

For any stereo manufacturer, distribution is difficult because of the intense competition in the industry. At least eight large manufacturers and over 20 smaller companies competed in this market. Thus, retailers had a wide range of manufacturers they could choose to do business with, and consequently, they could often dictate terms to any manufacturer. Retailers could demand larger margins, request co-op advertising (where the manufacturer paid part of the retailer's advertising cost when that manufacturer's brands were advertised), and seek favorable credit terms.

The task for J.T. Electronics sales force was to work closely with retailers, particularly the large chains, and encourage them to carry, promote, and sell J.T. Electronics products. It was in this area that Jack Smith felt there could be a problem. He knew, based on market research studies, that J.T. Electronics products were well regarded by the stereo buying consumer, that the prices charged by J.T. were perceived as fair, and that the products were being carried by a reasonable number of stores. Even so, Jack Smith thought that possibly the salespeople were not establishing a strong working relationship with the retailers and that, as a result, the retailers were promoting competing brands rather than J.T. brands. "Maybe if the salespeople were put on commission or a combination of commission and salary, instead of straight salary, we'd do better," he thought. With that, he began reviewing the data again.

As Jack Booth looked through the tables (1 to 4) he thought about the three salespeople in the Ontario region. He felt that Phil Gowing had the most difficult

TABLE 1
J.T. Electronics—Market Share

Year	J.T. Electronics sales (millions)	Industry sales (millions)	J.T. Electronics (market share)
1987	$30.6	$180.0	17%
1986	31.5	175.0	18%
1985	26.6	140.0	19%
1984	25.7	135.0	19%
1983	25.1	132.0	19%

TABLE 2
J.T. Electronics—Sales Performance, By Region, 1987

Region	Buying power index (%)	Sales target	Actual sales	Percentage difference	Dollar difference
Maritimes	8.1	$ 2 575 000	$ 2 500 000	97	$ − 75 000
Quebec	24.8	7 880 000	8 100 000	103	+ 220 000
Ontario	38.5	12 240 000	10 710 000	88	− 1 530 000
Prairies	17.4	5 530 000	5 490 000	99	− 40 000
B.C.	11.2	3 575 000	3 800 000	106	+ 225 000
Total	100.0	$31 800 000	$30 600 000	96	$ − 1 200 000

Note: Sales target based on buying power index. The buying power index was based on personal disposable income by region.

TABLE 3

J.T. Electronics—Sales Performance, By Product Line, Ontario

Product	Sales target	Actual sales	Percentage difference	Dollar difference
Stereos	$ 7 640 000	$ 6 490 000	85	$ – 1 150 000
Compact disc players	1 300 000	1 120 000	86	– 180 000
Cassette decks	3 300 000	3 100 000	93	– 200 000
	$12 240 000	$10 710 000	88	$ – 1 530 000

TABLE 4

J.T. Electronics—Sales Performance, By Sales Representative, Ontario

Sales representative	Sales target	Actual sales	Percentage difference	Dollar difference
Phil Gowing				
Stereos	$2 570 000	$2 560 000	100	$ – 10 000
Compact disc players	400 000	410 000	103	+ 10 000
Cassette decks	1 200 000	1 180 000	98	– 20 000
	$4 170 000	$4 150 000	100	$ – 20 000
Martin Abell				
Stereos	$2 400 000	$1 770 000	74	$ – 630 000
Compact disc players	500 000	410 000	82	– 90 000
Cassette decks	1 100 000	960 000	87	– 140 000
	$4 000 000	$3 140 000	79	$ – 860 000
Lucy Johnson				
Stereos	$2 670 000	$2 160 000	81	$ – 510 000
Compact disc players	400 000	300 000	75	– 100 000
Cassette decks	1 000 000	960 000	96	– 40 000
	$4 070 000	$3 420 000	84	$ – 650 000

territory (primarily Western Ontario) where a lot of travel was involved. Jack knew that Phil was a very conscientious individual and a "self-starter" who was fairly motivated. Martin Abell was a different type of individual. Jack felt that Martin had a very good sales presentation and manner but was a rather easygoing individual who had the attitude of a "fair day's work for a fair day's pay." Martin had a territory in Central Ontario, and little overnight travelling was involved. The third salesperson, Lucy Johnson, had an engaging personality and seemed well suited to a career in sales. However, Jack felt she could be more forceful in some of her sales presentations. She was a diligent worker and covered her territory in Eastern Ontario in a very efficient manner.

Jack Booth knew that something had to be done. He debated whether he should collect more data or talk to the salespeople now.

Questions

1. What course of action would you recommend for Jack Booth?

20. WORLD PRODUCT MANDATING

One of the major problems that Canada faces in trying to increase its export trade is that approximately 60% of the manufacturing firms in the country are foreign-owned. As a result, Canadian subsidiaries of these foreign-controlled firms (usually U.S.) tend to be operated as branch plants that are designed to serve the Canadian market. For example, Colgate-Palmolive of Canada manufactures for the Canadian market; they do not engage in export activities. Those decisions are made by the U.S. parent. This pattern is quite prevalent in the Canadian manufacturing sector, leading some to refer to Canada's "branch plant economy."

In this branch plant form of operation, the Canadian subsidiary typically manufactures a wide range of products primarily for the Canadian market. The small size of this market often means the subsidiary does not achieve the economies of scale that are required to compete on an international basis. In many cases, the Canadian subsidiary is only profitable in Canada because of high Canadian tariffs.

Given this situation, one proposal that addresses both the foreign ownership issue and the pressure for more manufactured exports is world or global product mandating. A pure world-product-mandating strategy would assign a subsidiary total responsibility for particular products or operations. This implies responsibility for all aspects of research and development, including conceptual or basic research; responsibility for manufacturing; and direct responsibility for international marketing. However, variations from the "pure" strategy are likely to be the usual practice. For example, Black & Decker Canada Inc. obtained the world mandate for the Workmate, a portable work center for the home handyman, after it had been designed in the United Kingdom. The Canadian division produces and markets the Workmate on a world-wide basis, selling over 1 000 000 units annually.

The basic arguments in favor of world product mandating are:

- The branch plant system is no longer viable in today's world. Multinational corporations are rationalizing and consolidating operations, and weak branch plants are being phased out.

- When a subsidiary obtains a mandate, it can increase the scale of its production runs, lower unit costs, and become competitive on a world basis. A mandate can also lead to increased production, more research and development, greater profitability, and more jobs.

- Mandating changes the nature of the firm. The subsidiary achieves a greater degree of autonomy and the focus of management shifts from day-to-day operations and the domestic market toward a world view of opportunities in the long-term.

- Mandating requires the firm to be up-to-date on changing technologies that affect their products.

- Mandating uses the strengths of the multinational to market products on a world-wide basis.

Some argue that world product mandating is a naive idea because:

- Multinational firms have no real motivation to pursue mandating. In fact, mandating usually requires increased investment by the parent firm. In addition, the parent may become more dependent on the subsidiary. Many multinationals are opposed to this situation.

- Multinational firms are leery of "national" programs where governments get involved and dictate what companies shall or shall not do.

- Multinational firms prefer to conduct research and development at corporate headquarters to maintain control over this activity.

- Risk and uncertainty will be increased for the multinational firm if they grant a world product mandate to a subsidiary.

In summary, multinationals could be reluctant to adopt a world product-mandating strategy because they may lose some control over their subsidiaries.

While there are some examples of highly successful world product mandates in Canada — Black & Decker, Westinghouse, NCR, Litton, Xerox — less than 5% of most Canadian subsidiaries' activities are world product mandates. This strategy has a long way to go before it will have a sizable impact on Canada's exports in the manufacturing sector.

Questions

1. What actions could the federal or provincial governments of Canada take to encourage world product mandating?
2. For what kind of products is world product mandating in Canada likely to be most successful? Least successful? Why?

3. What are the main reasons a multinational would engage in world product mandating?

4. What other strategies are available to Canadian governments to increase exports in the manufacturing sector? How do they compare to world product mandating?

21. THE CONSUMERS' ASSOCIATION OF CANADA

The Consumers' Association of Canada (CAC) was established in 1947 as a voluntary, non-profit organization with four objectives:

1. To provide a channel for bringing the views of consumers to the attention of government, producers, and trade and industry.

2. To study consumer problems and make recommendations for their solution.

3. To circulate information on matters of consumer interest concerning goods, qualities, standards, services, and values.

4. To provide a strong voice for consumers.

Today, 40 years later, CAC is the only national consumer organization in Canada. It sees its main functions as representing, educating, and protecting consumers, and conducting independent research on consumer problems and comparative tests of consumer products. Over the years, CAC has been instrumental in the enactment of fair-packaging legislation, the creation of the Department of Consumer and Corporate Affairs, and the promotion of consumer interests on issues such as the competition laws, regulation of credit and interest, and food policy. CAC members have worked with groups like the Canadian Standards Association to achieve better product standards. They have also served on advisory committees to professional associations and marketing boards.

Most of CAC's approximately $4 million yearly income comes from the members who pay $25 a year. Members receive twelve issues of *Canadian Consumer* or *Le Consommateur Canadien*, plus the *Annual Buying Guide*. *Canadian Consumer* provides test results for various products and general consumer information. The *Buying Guide* issue contains ratings on all products tested by CAC and is usually over 100 pages long. Some revenue is received from newsstand sales of *Canadian Consumer* (priced at $2.50), and occasional grants from private organizations. While CAC wants to protect its independence and does not allow any advertising in its magazine, it has received considerable financial support through the years from the federal government.

In any voluntary group, members often disagree as to the purpose and priorities of the organization. This has certainly been true of CAC. There has been a struggle within the organization as to the extent of resources that should be allocated to consumer advocacy or to the testing and publishing function. The consumer advocacy function includes such activities as:

1. Meeting with government officials to put forth the consumers' view on a wide variety of issues. For example, CAC members might meet with Environment Canada to present proposals dealing with clean air.

2. Representing the consumer interest at rate hearings. For example, when Bell Canada applies for an increase in telephone rates, CAC could have members appear at the hearings to present a brief on the consumers' behalf.

Consumer advocacy is performed through the Regulated Industries Program, which employs lawyers to intervene before regulatory tribunals. The interventions attempt to minimize rate increases and foster responsiveness to the consumer interest in industries that operate under government regulatory legislation.

In essence, those who would like to see "consumer advocacy" as CAC's top priority would have the organization devote much of its time and resources to protecting consumer interests. They argue that CAC is the only organized voice for the consumer in Canada.

The testing and publishing function includes product testing and reporting of results in *Canadian Consumer* and the *Annual Buying Guide*. Those arguing for an increase in these activities feel that it is CAC's most important function and a critical service for its members.

In the early 1980s, this priority issue came to a head. CAC decided to expand the testing and publishing function and to restrict the consumer advocacy activities. The logic behind the decision was that CAC would have a sounder financial basis for the future by expanding an immediately tangible product — the product testing and publishing function. As the financial returns from this program increased, CAC would then be able to expand its other services including consumer advocacy.

While the executive of CAC hopes that it made the best decision, it will always face the question: How can CAC serve consumers most effectively with its limited resources?

Questions

1. From a marketing point of view, what strategy should CAC pursue in expanding its product testing and publications program? Briefly outline your ideas and reasons for each of the following categories:
   - Target markets
   - Product/service line
   - Pricing/fund raising
   - Distribution/place
   - Communication (advertising, publicity, promotion, personal selling).
2. What should be CAC's role in the consumer movement?
   (a) What services should be offered beyond product testing and publishing?
   (b) How should each service be financed?
3. Should CAC take an active role in sponsoring causes?

22. FINANCIAL EXERCISES FOR MARKETING

1. Mr. Johnson, owner of Johnson's Fine Furniture, is preparing for a year-end performance review of his two stores. The following financial data have been collected.

	Store 1	Store 2
Purchases at cost	$384 000	$519 000
Depreciation	3 000	5 000
Advertising	6 000	70 000
Returns and allowances	28 000	63 000
Rent and utilities	9 000	30 000
Beginning inventory	86 000	235 000
Administrative salaries	25 000	35 000
Telephone	500	500
Commissions	30 000	105 000
Salesforce salaries	—	89 000
Office expenses	7 000	10 000
Ending inventory	109 000	184 000
Sales	530 000	1 042 000
Investment	350 000	675 000

a) Prepare operating statements for each store.
b) Using ratio analysis, compare the performances of the two stores. What are the implications of this analysis?

2. Jennifer Smith makes hand-braided mats, at a cost of $25 per mat, to sell at local craft shows. She has 25 mats on hand for the next show, and expects to sell them all for a total of $1000. What is Jennifer's:
a) mark-up% on selling?
b) mark-up on cost?
c) margin?

3. A new multi-purpose clamp, the Vice-Master, has a retail selling price of $15. The retail margin is 50%, and the wholesale margin is 20%. The manufacturer's cost per unit is $2.
a) What dollar mark-up does each channel member receive?
b) Which channel member receives the greatest margin? Is this reasonable? Why?

4. John Thompson, owner of Thompson's Jewelery, purchased a large shipment of watches for $15. each. He expected to sell each watch for $40, but a major competitor is now advertising the same watch for $30. John feels he must match this price. What is his markdown percentage if he reduces the price on the entire shipment?

5. The Ontario Electronics Company (OEC) manufactures portable cassette players. The factory selling price of the cassette player is $115. Variable cost

per unit is $55 and total fixed costs are $200 000. How many units must OEC sell to:

a) break-even?

b) make $50 000 profit?

6. New Tech Corporation has completed development of a new electronic toy. The following financial and sales data have been assembled.

Projected market share	20%
Total market size	100 000 units
Retail selling price	$60
Retail margin	50%
Parts cost/unit	$5.00
Assembly cost/unit	$6.00
Packaging cost/unit	$1.00
Sales force salaries and expenses	$145 000
Manufacturing overhead	$ 76 000
Administrative expenses	$ 68 000
Sales promotion and advertising	$ 35 000

Prepare a financial summary for the new toy, including: variable cost per unit, contribution per unit, total contribution, total fixed costs, break-even volume, gross margin, and net profit.

7. Sweetless Candy Company is preparing to introduce a new low-calorie chocolate bar, Choco-lite. Two alternative marketing plans have been developed. The first plan positions the new product directly against all regular chocolate bars. The second plan positions Choco-lite as an exclusive alternative to high-calorie regular bars. Which plan should be adopted? Why?

	Plan 1	Plan 2
Retail selling price	$0.60	$1.00
Factory selling price	$0.34	$0.56
Materials/labor	$0.18/unit	$0.18/unit
Packaging	$0.06/unit	$0.10/unit
Total overhead	$200 000	$200 000
Advertising and Promotion	$600 000	$1 200 000
Total market	— 200 000 000	bars —
Projected market share	5%	3%

8. Jackson Knitwear (JK) manufactures the pantyhose brand "Leggy." Sales of "Leggy" will total 2 million pair in the current year. JK is considering adding a new line of run-proof pantyhose, "Tuff-Stuff," next year. First year sales of "Tuff-Stuff" are projected at 3 million pair. It is expected that these sales would be achieved by: selling to new customers (15%), taking sales from competing brands (45%), and taking sales from JK's brand "Leggy" (40%). If "Tuff-Stuff" was not introduced, sales of "Leggy" are forecast to remain the same as last year. Dan Jordeen, manager of the Pantyhose Division, is concerned about the cannibalization of "Leggy" sales by "Tuff-Stuff." How

would the introduction of "Tuff-Stuff" affect JK's net profit? Should "Tuff-Stuff" be introduced?

	Current	Year 1 with new line	
	"Leggy"	"Leggy"	"Tuff-Stuff"
Factory selling price	$1.90	$1.90	$2.35
Variable costs	$1.15	$1.15	$1.60
Fixed costs	$825 000	$645 000	$1 510 000

Prepared by Arlene Bennett, Wilfrid Laurier University.

References

Chapter 1

1. Peter F. Drucker, *Management: Tasks, Responsibilities, Practices* (New York: Harper & Row, 1973), pp. 64-65.

2. Here are some other definitions: "Marketing is the process of planning and executing the conception, pricing, promotion, and distribution of ideas, goods, and services to create exchanges that satisfy individual and organizational objectives." "Marketing is getting the right goods and services to the right people at the right place at the right time at the right price with the right communication and promotion." "Marketing is the creation and delivery of a standard of living." For further definitions, see Ernest F. Cooke, C.L. Abercrombie, and J. Michael Rayburn, "Problems with the AMA's New Definition of Marketing Offer Opportunity to Develop an Even Better Definition," *Marketing Educator*, Spring 1986, pp. 1, 5.

3. See Theodore Levitt's classic article, "Marketing Myopia," *Harvard Business Review*, July-August 1960, pp. 45-56.

4. For more discussion on marketing as an exchange process, see Philip Kotler, "A Generic Concept of Marketing," *Journal of Marketing*, April 1972, pp. 46-54; and Richard P. Bagozzi, "Toward a Formal Theory of Marketing Exchanges," in *Conceptual and Theoretical Development in Marketing*, eds. O.C. Ferrell, Stephen W. Brown, and Charles W. Lamb (Chicago: American Marketing Association, 1979), pp. 431-47.

5. For more discussion, see Wroe Alderson, "Factors Governing the Development of Marketing Channels," in *Marketing Channels for Manufactured Products*, ed. Richard M. Clewett (Homewood, IL.: Richard D. Irwin, 1957), pp. 211-14. The number of transactions in a decentralized exchange system is given by $N(N-1)/2$. With four persons, this means $4(4-1)/2 = 6$ transactions. In a centralized exchange system, the number of transactions is given by N, here 4. Thus a centralized exchange system reduces the number of transactions needed for exchange.

6. "Texas Instruments Shows U.S. Business How to Survive in the 1980s," *Business Week*, September 18 1978, pp. 66ff; and "The Long-Term Damage from TI's Bombshell," *Business Week*, June 15 1981, p. 36; and "Texas Instruments Cleans Up Its Act," *Business Week*, September 19 1983, pp. 56-64.

7. See Irving J. Rein, *Rudy's Red Wagon: Communication Strategies in Contemporary Society* (Glenview, IL: Scott, Foresman, 1972).

8. See John B. McKitterick, "What Is the Marketing Management Concept?" *The Frontiers of Marketing Thought and Action* (Chicago: American Marketing Association, 1957), pp. 71-82; Fred J. Borch, "The Marketing Philosophy as a Way of Business Life," *The Marketing Concept: Its Meaning to Management*, Marketing Series, No. 99 (New York: American Management Association, 1957), pp. 3-5; and Robert J. Keith, "The Marketing Revolution," *Journal of Marketing*, January 1960, pp. 35-38. For some current views on the marketing concept, see Franklin S. Houston, "The Marketing Concept: What It Is and What It Is Not," *Journal of Marketing*, April 1986, pp. 81-87.

9. Peter M. Banting and Randolph E. Ross, "The Marketing Masquerade," *Business Quarterly* (Canada), Spring 1974, pp. 19-27. Also see Philip Kotler, "From Sales

Obsession to Marketing Effectiveness," *Harvard Business Review*, November-December 1977, pp. 67-75.

10. Roger C. Bennett and Robert G. Cooper, "Beyond the Marketing Concept," *Business Horizons*, June 1979, p. 76.

11. Robert H. Hayes and William J. Abarnathy, "Managing Our Way to Economic Decline," *Harvard Business Review*, July-August 1980, pp. 67-77.

12. Bennett and Cooper, "Beyond the Marketing Concept," p. 81.

13. Laurence P. Feldman, "Societal Adaptation: A New Challenge for Marketing," *Journal of Marketing*, July 1971, pp. 54-60; Martin L. Bell and C. William Emery, "The Faltering Marketing Concept," *Journal of Marketing*, October 1971, pp. 37-42; and Donald P. Robin and R. Eric Reidenbach, "Social Responsibility, Ethics, and Marketing Strategy: Closing the Gap Between Concept and Application," *Journal of Marketing*, January 1987, pp. 44-48.

14. Quotation appearing in Richard W. Pollay, "The Distorted Mirror: Reflections on the Unintended Consequences of Advertising," *Journal of Marketing*, April 1986, pp. 18-36.

15. William J. Stanton, *Fundamentals of Marketing*, Seventh ed. (New York: McGraw-Hill, 1984), p. 9.

16. Bruce Gates, "Marketing Skills Key in Quest For CEO's," *The Financial Post*, February 26, 1986, p. 24.

17. Robert MacKay, "The Dentists' New Marketing Push," *Financial Times*, November 24, 1980, pp. 19, 24; Kirk Makin, "Got Legal Woes? Hire Crazy Joe's," *The Globe and Mail*, December 30 1986, p. B1; and Joan Breckenridge, "Chain Offers Walk-in Legal Centres," *The Globe and Mail*, November 12 1986, p. B1; and Marina Strauss, "While You're Shopping, Go in for a Medical Too," *The Globe and Mail*, March 2 1987, p. B1, 12.

18. Thomas V. Greer, *Marketing in the Soviet Union* (New York: Holt, Rinehart & Winston, 1973).

19. Jacob Naor, "Towards A Socialist Marketing Concept—The Case of Romania," *Journal of Marketing*, January 1986, pp. 28-39.

20. For a good review of nonprofit marketing, see Christopher H. Lovelock and Charles B. Weinberg, "Public and Nonprofit Marketing Comes of Age," in *Review of Marketing 1978*, eds. Gerald Zaltman and Thomas V. Bonoma (Chicago: American Marketing Association, 1978).

Chapter 2

1. Based on information found in Dylex Annual Reports.

2. Melville C. Branch, *The Corporate Planning Process* (New York: American Management Association, 1962), pp. 48-49.

3. See Peter Drucker, *Management: Tasks, Responsibilities, Practices* (New York: Harper & Row, 1973), Ch. 7.

4. Theodore Levitt, "Marketing Myopia," *Harvard Business Review*, July-August 1960, pp. 45-56.

5. For additional reading on this and other portfolio analysis approaches, see Philippe Haspeslagh, "Portfolio Planning: Limits and Uses," *Harvard Business Review*, January-February 1982, pp. 58-73; Yoram Wind and Vijay Mahajan, "Designing Product and Business Portfolios," *Harvard Business Review*, January-February 1981, pp. 155-65; and Yoram Wind, Vijay Mahajan, and Donald J. Swire, "An Empirical Comparison of Standardized Portfolio Models," *Journal of Marketing*, Spring 1985, pp. 89-99.

6. "The New Breed of Strategic Planner," *Business Week*, September 17 1984, p. 63.

7. Carolyn R. Farguhar and Stanley J. Shapiro, *Strategic Business Planning in Canada*, Conference Board of Canada, April 1983.

8. H. Igor Ansoff, "Strategies for Diversification," *Harvard Business Review*, September-October 1957, pp. 113-24.

9. For more reading on marketing's role, see Paul F. Anderson, "Marketing, Strategic Planning and the Theory of the Firm," *Journal of Marketing*, Spring 1982, pp. 15-26; and Yoram Wind and Thomas S. Robertson, "Marketing Strategy: New Directions for Theory and Research," *Journal of Marketing*, Spring 1983, pp. 12-25.

10. The four P classification was first suggested by E. Jerome McCarthy, *Basic Marketing: A Managerial Approach*, (Homewood, IL: Irwin, 1960).

Chapter 3

1. Written by the author and based on Martin Dewey, "How an Idea Revived the Hardware Business," *The Globe and Mail*, May 7 1979, p. 31,and Henry Koch, "Home Hardware is 20, Has 910 Stores," *Kitchener-Waterloo Record*, April 7 1984, p. B10.

2. For more on diagnosing implementation problems, see Thomas V. Bonoma, "Making Your Marketing Strategy Work," *Harvard Business Review*, March-April 1984, pp. 70-71; and "The New Breed of Strategic Planner: Number-Crunching Professionals Are Giving Way to Line Managers," *Business Week*, March-April 1984, pp. 70-71.

3. This figure is styled after several models of organizational design components. For examples, see Jay R. Galbraith, *Organizational Design* (Reading, MA: Addison-Wesley, 1977); (Englewood Cliffs, NJ: Prentice-Hall, 1982), p. 95; David L. Aaker, *Strategic Market Management* (New York: Wiley, 1984), Chap. 9; and Carl R. Anderson, *Management Skills, Functions, and Organization Performance* (Dubuque, IA: Wm. C. Brown, 1984), pp. 409-13.

4. See Thomas J. Peters and Robert H. Waterman, *In Search of Excellence: Lessons from America's Best-Run Companies* (New York: Harper & Row, 1982). For an excellent summary of the study's findings on structure, see Aaker, *Strategic Market Management*, pp. 154-57.

5. See "Who's Excellent Now?" *Business Week*, November 5 1984, pp. 76-78; and Daniel T. Carroll, "A Disappointing Search for Excellence," *Harvard Business Review*, November-December 1983, pp. 78-79ff.

6. This example is adapted from those found in Robert M. Tomasko, "Focusing Company Reward Systems to Help Achieve Business Objectives," *Management Review*, (New York: AMA Membership Publications Division, American Management Associations, October 1982), pp. 8-12.

7. Peters and Waterman, *In Search of Excellence*, pp. 75-76.

8. A.M. Ragab and A.W. Babcock, "An Investigation into the Practice of the Product Manager Concept by Selected Canadian Companies," in Bent Stidsen, ed., *Marketing in the 1970's and Beyond*. Proceedings, Marketing Division, Canadian Association of Administrative Sciences, Edmonton, 1975.

9. Jade Hemeon, "Inside Procter and Gamble," *Financial Times*, March 9 1981, pp. 1, 21.

10. For details, see Philip Kotler, William Gregor, and William Rodgers, "The Marketing Audit Comes of Age," *Sloan Management Review*, Winter 1977, pp. 25-43. A preliminary marketing audit tool is described in Philip Kotler, "From Sales Obsession to Marketing Effectiveness," *Harvard Business Review*, November-December 1977, pp. 67-75.

Chapter 4

1. Based on numerous sources including "Coke 'Family' Sales Fly as New Coke Stumbles," *Advertising Age*, January 17 1986, p. 1ff; Scott Scredon and Marc Frons, "Coke's Man on the Spot," *Business Week*, July 29 1985, pp. 56-61; Cathryn Matherwell, "Canada Getting Coke Classic," *The Globe and Mail*, July 24 1985, p. B5; and Andrew Cohen, "Escalating Cola Wars Leave Bitter After Taste," *Financial Post*, July 13 1985, p. 5. The quoted material is from Jack Honomichl, "Missing Ingredients in 'New' Coke's Research," *Advertising Age*, July 22 1985, p. 1ff, and Anne B. Fisher, "Coke's Brand Loyalty Lesson," *Fortune*, August 5 1985, pp. 44-46.

2. Marion Harper, Jr., "A New Profession to Aid Management," *Journal of Marketing*, January 1961, p. 1.

3. This definition is adapted from "Marketing Information Systems: An Introductory Overview," in *Readings in Marketing Information Systems*, Samuel V. Smith, Richard H. Brien, and James E. Stafford, eds. (Boston: Houghton Mifflin, 1968), p. 7.

4. Donald S. Tull and Del I. Hawkins, *Marketing Research: Measurement and Method*, (Third ed.) (New York: Macmillan, 1984), pp. 46-73.

5. James Walker, "At Pizza Pizza the Computer's the BOSS," *Financial Times*, September 12 1983, p. 6.

6. See Joyce Cheng, David Conway, and George Haines, Jr., "A Comparison of Business Use of Marketing Research in Canada and the United States," in *ASAC Marketing Proceedings*, Thomas E. Muller (ed.), Whistler, 1986, p. 297; and Jared Mitchell, "The Truth is Not for the Squeamish," *Report on Business Magazine*, March 1987 pp. 74-76.

7. See Bobby J. Calder, "Focus Groups and the Nature of Qualitative Marketing Research," *Journal of Marketing*, August 1977, pp. 353-64, and Edward F. Fern, "The Use of Focus Groups for Idea Generation: The Effect of Group Size, Acquaintanceship, and Moderator on Response Quantity and Quality," *Journal of Marketing Research*, February 1982, pp. 1-13.

8. For an overview of mechanical devices, see Roger D. Blackwell, James S. Hensel, Michael B. Phillips, and Brian Sternthal, *Laboratory Equipment for Marketing Research* (Dubuque, IA: Kendall/Hunt, 1970), pp. 7-8, and P.J. Watson and R.J. Gatchel, "Automatic Measures of Advertising," *Journal of Advertising Research*, June 1979, pp. 18-24.

9. The Pacific Western example is based on material obtained from Pacific Western Airlines.

10. For more on statistical analysis, consult a standard text such as Tull and Hawkins, 1984. For a review of marketing models, see Gary L. Lilian and Philip Kotler, *Marketing Decision Making: A Model Building Approach* (New York: Harper & Row, 1983); also see John D. C. Little, "Decision Support Systems for Marketing Managers," *Journal of Marketing*, Summer 1979, pp. 9-26.

11. See Feter Nulty, "How Personal Computers Change Managers' Lives," *Fortune*, September 3 1984, pp. 38-48.

Chapter 5

1. From various sources, including Campbell Soup Company Ltd., Annual Reports; "Marketing's New Look," *Business Week*, January 26 1987, pp. 64-69; Oliver Bertin, "New Lines, Marketing Add Spice to Campbell Soup," *The Globe and Mail*, June 3 1985, p. B3; and Tessa Eilmott, "Campbell Blends Corporate Vision Into Its Product Mix," *Financial Post*, November 23 1985, p. 26.

2. The statistical data in this chapter are drawn from; *Marketing Research Handbook 1985-86*, Statistics Canada, Revised Edition, 1986, Catalogue 63-224; *Canadian Markets 1986*, Financial Post, Sixty-first edition, 1986; and *Tomorrow's Customers*, Clarkson Gordon/Woods Gordon, 1986.

3. Ken Romain, "Ford's First 'Singles' Two-seaters Roll Off Talbotville Assembly Line," *The Globe and Mail*, February 16 1981, p. B9.

4. Philip Marchand, "Life Inside the Population Bulge," *Saturday Night*, October 1979, pp. 17-34.

5. First Annual Report of the Council on Environmental Quality (Washington, DC: Government Printing Office, 1970), p. 158.

6. See Charles Panat, *Breakthroughs* (Boston: Houghton Mifflin, 1980); and "Technologies for the '80s," *Business Week*, July 6 1981, pp. 48ff.

7. Robert Steklosa, "R&D Spending is up as Renovation of Economy Starts to Take Hold," *Financial Post*, December 10 1983, p. 24.

8. See Pierre Bourgault and Harold Crookell, "Commercial Innovation in a Secondary Industry," *The Business Quarterly*, Autumn 1979, pp. 56-64; and Alexander Bruce, "CMA Warns R&D Shortfall Threatens Future Exports," *The Globe and Mail*, March 17, 1987, p. B3.

9. R. Mansfield, *Research and Development in the Modern Corporation* (New York: Macmillan, 1971).

10. See Norman W. McGuinness and Blair Little, "The Influence of Product Characteristics on the Export Performance of New Industrial Products," *Journal of Marketing*, Spring 1981, pp. 110-122; and Peter Hanel and Kristian S. Palda, "The Export Connection to Innovativeness Among Canadian Manufacturers," in *Marketing: ASAC Proceedings*, ed. Michael Laroche, Ottawa, 1982, pp. 90-97.

11. *Report of the Royal Commission on Corporate Concentration*, Supplies and Services Canada, Ottawa, 1978, p. 158. For an excellent historical review of competition policy see Donald N. Thompson, "Competition Policy and Marketing Regulation," in *Canadian Marketing: Problems and Prospects*, eds. Donald N. Thompson and David S.R. Leighton (Toronto: Wiley Publishers of Canada, 1973), pp. 13-43.

12. W.T. Stanbury and Stephen Cook, "Competition Policy: The Retreat Begins," *Canadian Consumer*, Consumers Association of Canada, February 1978, p. 36.

13. Leo Greenland, "Advertisers Must Stop Conning Consumers," *Harvard Business Review*, July-August 1974, p. 18.

14. J.D. Forbes, "The Law and Canadian Consumers," in *Macromarketing: A Canadian Perspective*, ed. Donald N. Thompson, et al. (American Marketing Association, 1980), pp. 225-250.

15. For an interesting view of how Consumers Association of Canada members differ from the "average" consumer, see Jacques C. Bourgeois and James G. Barnes, "Viability and Profile of the Consumerist Segment," *Journal of Consumer Research*, March 1979, pp. 217-228.

16. Madeleine Saint-Jacques, "The French-Canadian Market," in *Advertising in Canada: Its Theory and Practice*, eds. Peter T. Zarry and Robert D. Wilson (Toronto: McGraw-Hill Ryerson, 1981), pp. 349-368.

Chapter 6

1. See Daniel Stoffman, "Hungry Competition," *Canadian Business*, December 1986, pp. 46-50, 149; and Terry Brodie, "Red Lobster Casts Its Net Over Canada," *Financial Times*, January 19 1987, pp. 4, 49.

2. Estimates based on *Market Research Handbook 1985-86*, Revised Edition, Statistics Canada, Catalogue 63-224 Annual.

3. Madeleine Saint-Jacques, "The French Canadian Market," in *Advertising in Canada: Its Theory and Practice*, eds. Peter T. Zarry and Robert T. Wilson (Toronto: McGraw-Hill Ryerson, 1981), pp. 349-368.

4. "Average University Student Profiled by Campus Plus," *Marketing*, August 19 1985, p. 5.

5. This classification was originally developed by W. Lloyd Warner and Paul S. Lundt in *The Social Life of a Modern Community* (New Haven, CT: Yale University Press. 1941). For a summary of more recent classifications, see Richard P. Coleman, "The Continuing Significance of Social Class to Marketers," *Journal of Consumer Research*, December 1983, pp. 265-80.

6. William O. Bearden and Michael J. Etzel, "Reference Group Influence on Product and Brand Purchase Decisions," *Journal of Consumer Research*, September 1982, p. 185.

7. Pierre Filiatrault and J.R. Brent Ritchie, "Joint Purchasing Decisions: A Comparison of Influence Structure in Family and Couple Decision-Making Units," *Journal of Consumer Research*, September 1980, pp. 131-140.

8. In some cases, income is more important than family life cycle. See Janet Wagner and Sherman Hanna, "The Effectiveness of Family Life Cycle Variables in Consumer Expenditure Research," *Journal of Consumer Research*, December 1983, pp. 281-291.

9. Patrick E. Murphy and William A. Staples, "A Modernized Family Life Cycle," *Journal of Consumer Research*, June 1979, pp. 12-22.

10. *Market Research Handbook 1985-86*, Revised Edition, Statistics Canada, Catologue 63-224 Annual.

11. John D. Claxton, Joseph N. Fry and Bernard Portis, "A Taxonomy of Prepurchase Information Gathering Patterns," *Journal of Consumer Research*, December 1974, pp. 35-42.

12. See William D. Wells, "Psychographics: A Critical Review," *Journal of Marketing Research*, May 1975, pp. 196-213; Stephen C. Cosmas, "Life Styles and Consumption Patterns," *Journal of Consumer Research*, March 1984, pp. 453-455; John L. Lastovicka, "On the Validation of Lifestyle Traits: A Review and Illustration," *Journal of Marketing Research*, February 1982, pp. 126-138.

13. Jan Pearson, "Social Studies," *Canadian Business*, December 1985, pp. 67-73.

14. For more reading on the pros and cons of using the life style concept, see Sonia Yuspeh, "Syndicated Values/Lifestyles Segmentation Schemes: Use Them as Descriptive Tools, Not to Select Targets," *Marketing News*, May 25 1984, p. 1; and "SRI's Response to Yuspeh: Demographics Aren't Enough," *Marketing News*, May 25 1984.

15. See Raymond L. Horton, "Some Relationships Between Personality and Consumer Decision-Making," *Journal of Marketing Research*, May 1979, pp. 244-45; and James F. Engel, Roger D. Blackwell and Paul W. Miniard, *Consumer Behavior*, Fifth ed. (New York: Dryden Press, 1986), Ch. 11.

16. See M. Joseph Sirgy, "Self-Concept in Consumer Behavior; A Critical Review," *Journal of Consumer Research*, December 1982, pp. 287-300.

17. Abraham H. Maslow, *Motivation and Personality* (New York: Harper & Row, 1954), pp. 80-106.

18. Bernard Berelson and Gary A. Steiner, *Human Behavior: An Inventory of Scientific Findings* (New York: Harcourt Brace Jovanovich, 1964), p. 88.

19. See David Krech, Richard S. Crutchfield, and Egerton L. Ballachey, *Individual in Society* New York: McGraw-Hill, 1962), Ch. 2.

20. Several models of the consumer buying process have been developed by marketing scholars. The most prominent models are those of John A. Howard and Jagdish N. Sheth, *The Theory of Buyer Behavior* (New York: Wiley, 1969); James F. Engel, Roger D. Blackwell, and Paul W. Miniard, *Consumer Behavior*, Fifth Ed. (New York: Dryden Press, 1986); James R. Bettman, *An Information Processing Theory of Con-*

sumer Choice (Reading, MA: Addison-Wesley, 1979); and Henry Assael , *Consumer Behavior and Marketing Action*, Second Ed. (Boston: Kent Publishing, 1984).

21. John A. Howard and Jagdish N. Sheth, *The Theory of Buyer Behavior* (New York: John Wiley, 1969), pp. 27-28.

22. See Raymond A. Bauer, "Consumer Behavior as Risk Taking" in *Risk Taking and Information Handling in Consumer Behavior*, ed. Donald F. Cox (Boston: Division of Research, Harvard Business School, 1967); James W. Taylor, "The Role of Risk in Consumer Behavior," *Journal of Marketing*, April 1974, pp 54-60; and Laurent, Gilles, and Jean-Noel Kapferer, "Measuring Consumer Involvement Profiles," *Journal of Marketing Research*, February 1985, pp. 41-53.

23. See Jagdish N. Sheth, "An Investigation of Relationships Among Evaluative Beliefs, Affect, Behavioral Intention, and Behavior," in *Consumer Behavior: Theory and Application*, John U. Farley, John A. Howard, and L. Winston Ring, eds. (Boston: Allyn & Bacon, 1974), pp. 89-114.

24. See John E. Swan and Linda Jones Combs, "Product Performance and Consumer Satisfaction: A New Concept," *Journal of Marketing*, April 1976, pp. 25-33.

Chapter 7 ━━━━━━━━━━━━━━━━━━━━━━━━━━━━━━━━━━━━━

1. Information obtained from V.S. Services Annual Reports, various years.

2. *Marketing Research Handbook*, 1985-86, Statistics Canada, Catalogue 63-224.

3. *Marketing Research Handbook*, 1985-86, Statistics Canada.

4. Some authors argue that there are more similarities than differences. See Edward F. Fern and James R. Brown, "The Industrial/Consumer Marketing Dichotomy: A Case of Insufficient Justification," *Journal of Marketing*, Spring 1984, pp. 68-77.

5. *Canadian Markets 1986*, Financial Post, Toronto, Maclean Hunter, 1986.

6. Thomas V. Bonoma, "Major Sales: Who Really Does The Buying?" *Harvard Business Review*, May-June 1982, pp. 111-119.

7. Frederick E. Webster, Jr., and Yoram Wind, *Organizational Buying Behavior* (Englewood Cliffs, NJ: Prentice-Hall, 1972), p. 2.

8. For a discussion of other organizational buyer behavior models, see Raymond L. Horton, *Buyer Behavior: A Decision-Making Approach* (Columbus, OH: Charles E. Merrill, 1984), Ch. 16.

9. Patrick J. Robinson, Charles W. Faris, and Yoram Wind, *Industrial Buying Behavior and Creative Marketing* (Boston: Allyn & Bacon, 1967).

10. Webster and Wind, *Organizational Buying Behavior*, 1972, p. 6. For more reading on buying centers, see Bonoma, 1982, "Major Sales: Who Really Does the Buying"; and Wesley J. Johnston and Thomas V. Bonoma, "Purchase Process for Capital Equipment and Services," *Industrial Marketing Management*, 10 (1981), pp. 253-64.

11. Webster and Wind, *Organizational Buying Behavior*, 1972, pp. 33-37.

12. Bonoma, 1982, "Major Sales," p. 114.

13. Robinson, Faris, and Wind, 1967, *Industrial Buying*.

14. Johnston and Bonoma, 1981, "Purchase Process," p. 261.

15. David L. Blenkhorn and Peter M. Banting, "Non-Food Retail Chain New Product Adoption Decision Criteria," in Robert Wyckham, ed., *Proceedings of the Marketing Division* (Halifax: ASAC, 1981), pp. 28-35.

16. For more reading on similarities and differences, see Jagdish N. Sheth, Robert F. Williams, and Richard M. Hill, "Government and Business Buying: How Similar Are They?" *Journal of Purchasing and Materials Management*, Winter 1983, pp. 7-13.

17. *How to Do Business with the Department of Supply and Services* (Ottawa: Information Canada, 1967).

18. *Weekly Bulletin of Business Opportunities*, Department of Supply and Services, Ottawa. For more details on various aspects of marketing to governments, see "Selling to Government," *Financial Post*, March 9 1987, pp. 20-25.

Chapter 8

1. Written by the author using material from Terry Poulton, "Plump Profits," *Canadian Business*, June 1978, pp. 54-57, 90-92; "Fashioning Large-Size Profits", *Financial Times*, March 2 1987, p. 42; and various annual reports of Pennington's Stores Limited.

2. James Walker, "Diet Coke's Success Formula," *Financial Times*, August 22 1983, pp. 2-6.

3. Jaimie Hubbard, "The Cola Wars," *Financial Post*, December 15 1986, p. 12.

4. Rob Wilson, "Ford's Double Bid to Re-coupe Youth Market," *Marketing*, March 9 1981, pp. 10-11.

5. Edward Clifford, "Sporty Cars Attracting More Women Buyers," *The Globe and Mail*, January 30 1984, p. B1.

6. Rob Wilson, "Chrysler's Come a Long Way, Baby," *Marketing*, January 27 1986, pp. 1, 3.

7. Joseph T. Plummer, "Life Style Patterns: New Constraint for Mass Communications Research," *Journal of Broadcasting*, Winter 1971-72, pp. 79-89.

8. Shirley Young, "The Dynamics of Measuring Unchange," in *Attitude Research in Transition*, Russell I. Haley, ed. (Chicago: American Marketing Association, 1972), pp. 61-82.

9. John J. Burnett, "Psychographic and Demographic Characteristics of Blood Donors," *Journal of Consumer Research*, June 1981, pp. 62-66.

10. See Daniel Yankelovich, "New Criteria for Market Segmentation," *Harvard Business Review*, March-April 1964, pp. 83-90, here p. 85.

11. Shirley Young, Leland Ott, and Barbara Feigen, "Some Practical Considerations in Market Segmentation," *Journal of Marketing Research*, August 1978, pp. 405-412.

12. For more reading on benefit segmentation, see Russell I. Haley, "Benefit Segmentation: Backwards and Forwards," *Journal of Advertising Research*, February-March 1984, pp. 19-25.

13. For more on consumer segmentation variables, see Yoram Wind, "Issues and Advances in Segmentation Research," *Journal of Marketing Research*, August 1978, pp. 317-37; Terry Elrod and Russell S. Winer, "An Empirical Evaluation of Aggregation Approaches for Developing Market Segments," *Journal of Marketing*, Fall 1982, pp. 56-63; and Lynn R. Kahle, "The Nine Nations of North America and the Value Basis of Geographic Segmentation," *Journal of Marketing*, April 1986, pp. 37-47.

14. For more on industrial segmentation variables, see Benson P. Shapiro and Thomas V. Bonoma, "How to Segment Industrial Markets," *Harvard Business Review*, May-June 1984, pp. 104-110; Peter Doyle and John Saunders, "Market Segmentation and Positioning in Specialized Industrial Markets," *Journal of Marketing*, Spring 1985, pp. 24-32; and Richard N. Cardozo, "Situational Segmentation of Industrial Markets," *European Journal of Marketing*, Fall 1980, pp. 264-276.

15. For a review of segmentation issues in Canada, see John Oldland, "The Closing Window of Market Segmentation," *Marketing*, May 5 1986, p. 14; "Emerging Trends in Market Segmentation," *Marketing*, May 12 1986; and "Segmentation: Where Does the Future Lie?," *Marketing*, May 19 1986, p. 30.

16. Information obtained from annual reports, Dylex Limited.

17. R. William Kotrba, "The Strategy Selection Chart," *Journal of Marketing*, July 1966, pp. 22-25.

18. For more reading on positioning, see Yoram Wind, "New Twists for Some Old Tricks," *The Wharton Magazine*, Spring 1980, pp. 34-39; David A. Aaker and J. Gary Shansby, "Positioning Your Product," *Business Horizon*, May-June 1982, pp. 56-62; and Al Ries and Jack Trout, *Positioning: The Battle for Your Mind* (New York, McGraw-Hill, 1981).

19. See Wind, "New Twists," p. 36; and Aaker and Shansby, "Positioning Your Product," pp. 67-58.

20. These maps must be interpreted with care. Not all customers share the same perceptions. The map shows the average perceptions. Attention should also be paid to the scatter of perceptions.

Chapter 9

1. For a detailed discussion of the introduction of Milk Mate, see "Grenadier Chocolate Company Limited" in Blair Little, et al., *Canadian Problems in Marketing*, Fourth ed. (Toronto: McGraw-Hill Ryerson, 1978), pp. 501-07. Other reference material includes Randy Scotland, "Beer Bottles are Shaping Up," *Marketing*, March 19 1984, p. 1, and "Labatt's Adds New Twist to its Beer Bottle Caps," *Toronto Star*, March 24 1984, p. D2.

2. See *Marketing Definitions: A Glossary of Marketing Terms*, compiled by the Committee on Definitions of the American Marketing Association (Chicago: American Marketing Association, 1960).

3. Theodore Levitt, *The Marketing Mode* (New York: McGraw-Hill, 1969), p. 2.

4. The three definitions can be found in *Marketing Definitions*.

5. The first three definitions can be found in *Marketing Definitions*. For further reading on this classification of goods, see Richard H. Holton, "The Distinction between Convenience Goods, Shopping Goods, and Specialty Goods," *Journal of Marketing*, July 1958, pp. 53-56; and Gordon E. Miracle, "Product Characteristics and Marketing Strategy," *Journal of Marketing*, January 1965, pp. 18-24. For a more recent classification of products, see Patrick E. Murphy and Ben M. Enis, "Classifying Products Strategically," *Journal of Marketing*, July 1986, pp. 24-42.

6. John D. Claxton, Joseph N. Fry, and Bernard Portis, "A Taxonomy of Prepurchase Information Gathering Patterns," *Journal of Consumer Research*, December 1974, pp. 35-42.

7. For those interested in the pros and cons of marketing boards in Canada, see J.D. Forbes, D.R. Hughes and T.K. Warley, *Economic Intervention and Regulation in Canadian Agriculture*, Economic Council of Canada (Ottawa: Supply and Services Canada, 1982); R.M.A. Lyons, "Marketing Boards: The Irrelevance and Irreverence of Economic Analysis," in Donald N. Thompson, et al. (eds.), *Macromarketing: A Canadian Perspective* (Chicago: American Marketing Association, 1980), pp. 196-224; John Spears, "Guardians of Farm Prices Face Critics," *Toronto Star*, November 9 1986, p. F1-2; and Oliver Bertin, "Group Wants Marketing Boards Curbed," *The Globe and Mail*, September 27 1986, p. B3.

8. The first four definitions can be found in *Marketing Definitions*.

9. Patricia Lush, "Packagers Told Power in Food Industry Shifting From Manufacturers to Retailers," *The Globe and Mail*, March 4 1981, p. B12.

10. Walter Stern, "A Good Name Could Mean a Brand of Fame," *Advertising Age*, January 17 1983, pp. M53-M54.

11. Charles A. Moldenhauer, "Packaging Designers Must Be Cognizant of Right Cues If the Consumer Base Is to Expand," *Marketing News*, March 30 1984, p. 14; and Elliot C. Young, "Judging a Package by Its Cover," *Madison Avenue*, August 1983, p. 17.

12. Jennifer Hunter, "Drug Tampering Cases Put Spotlight on Packaging," *The Globe and Mail*, December 12 1983, p. B3. See also: Janet Marchant, "Packager, Contain Thyself," in *Readings in Canadian Marketing*, U. De Brentane and M. Laroche (eds), (Dubuque, Iowa, Kendall/Hunt: 1983), pp. 106-109.

13. Moldenhauer, "Packaging Designers," p. 14.

14. Jaimie Hubbard, "The Soaring Cost of Selling Beer," *Financial Post*, June 28 1986, p. 11.

15. Peter G. Banting, "Customer Service in Industrial Marketing: A Comparative Study," *European Journal of Marketing* 10, no. 3 (1976), p. 140.

16. See Benson P. Shapiro, *Industrial Product Policy: Managing the Existing Product Line* (Cambridge, MA: Marketing Science Institute, September 1977), pp. 9-10.

17. This definition can be found in *Marketing Definitions*.

Chapter 10

1. Written by the author, based on material in Robert Gibens, "Dealers, Manufacturers of Snowmobiles Hope for March Cold Snap to Help Sales," *The Globe and Mail*, February 28 1981, p. B1; "Bombardier: Making a Second Leap from Snowmobile to Mass Transit," *Business Week*, February 23 1981, pp. 137, 140; Peter Menyasz, "Bombardier's Formula for Growth," *Financial Times*, November 28 1983, p. 5; Matthew Horsmeen, "Car Venture Revs Up," *Financial Post*, June 21 1986, p. 1, 2; Alan D. Gray, "Bombardier Step Into the Billion-Dollar Class," *Financial Times*, August 25 1986, p. 6; and David Stewart-Patterson, "Ottawa Selling Canadian to Bombardier," *The Globe and Mail*, August 19 1986, p. B1, B2.

2. Ranking Corporate Performance in Canada, *Report on Business Magazine*, July 1986, pp. 93-94.

3. David S. Hopkins and Earl L. Bailey, "New Product Pressures," *Conference Board Record*, June 1971, pp. 16-24.

4. *New Product Management for the 1980s* (New York: Booz, Allen & Hamilton, 1982). For a review of studies on new product failure rates, see C. Merle Crawford, "New Product Failure Rates," *Research Management*, September 1979, pp. 9-13.

5. See Robert G. Cooper, "The Dimensions of Industrial New Product Success and Failure," *Journal of Marketing*, Summer 1979, pp. 93-103; and Roger J. Calantone and Roger G. Cooper, "New Product Scenarios: Prospects for Success," *Journal of Marketing*, Spring 1981, pp. 48-60.

6. Blair Little, "New Focus on New Product Ideas," *The Right New Product*, ed. Blair Little (London: The University of Western Ontario, 1974).

7. See Leigh Lawton and A. Parasuraman, "So You Want Your New Product Planning to Be Productive," *Business Horizons*, December 1980, pp. 29-34.

8. See Eric vonHipple, "Get New Products from Consumers," *Harvard Business Review*, March-April 1982, pp. 117-22.

9. The following example is taken from George Hargreaves, John D. Claxton and Frederick H. Siller, "New Product Evaluation: Electric Vehicles for Commercial Applications," *Journal of Marketing*, January 1976, pp. 74-77.

10. For more on product concept testing, see William L. Moore, "Concept Testing," *Journal of Business Research*, 10 (1982), pp. 279-94; and David A. Schwartz, "Concept Testing Can Be Improved—and Here's How," *Marketing News*, January 6 1984, pp. 22-23.

11. For more on market testing, see Edward M. Tauber, "Forecasting Sales Prior to Test Market," *Journal of Marketing*, January 1977, pp. 80-84; Jay E. Klompmaker, G.

David Hughes, and Russell I. Haley, "Test Marketing in New Product Development," *Harvard Business Review*, May-June 1976, pp. 128-138; and "How to Improve Your Chances for Test Market Success," *Marketing News*, January 6 1984, pp. 12-13.

12. James Walker, "Diet Coke's Success Formula," *Financial Times*, August 22 1983, pp. 2, 6.

13. "Gillette Gives Shampoo Expensive Treatment," *Marketing*, January 16, 1984, p.1; and Gail Chaisson, "Gillette Introduces Hair-Care Items With $750,000 Campaign," *Marketing*, August 11, 1986, p. 2.

14. See Roger A. Kerin, Michael G. Harvey, and James T. Rothe, "Cannibalism and New Product Development," *Business Horizons*, October 1978, pp. 25-31.

15. See George S. Day, "The Product Life Cycle: Analysis and Applications Issues," *Journal of Marketing*, Fall 1981, pp. 60-67; and John E. Swan and David R. Rink, "Fitting Market Strategy to Varying Product Life Cycles," *Business Horizons*, January-February 1982, pp. 72-76.

16. The experience curve describes the rate at which costs fall as a function of accumulated production experience. See "Selling Business: a Theory of Economics," *Business Week*, September 8 1973, pp. 86-88; Walter Kiechell III, "The Decline of the Experience Curve," *Fortune*, October 5 1981, pp. 46-48; George S. Day and David B. Montgomery, "Diagnosing the Experience Curve," *Journal of Marketing*, Spring 1983, pp. 44-58; and Bruce D. Henderson, "The Application and Misapplication of the Experience Curve," *Journal of Business Strategy*, Winter 1984, pp. 3-9.

17. Ian Timberlake, "2.5 Million Backs Ban's Relaunch," *Marketing*, August 25 1986, p. 3.

18. For further reading on the product life-cycle concept, see Theodore Levitt, "Exploit the Product Life Cycle," *Harvard Business Review*, November-December 1965, pp. 81-94; Nariman K. Dhalla and Sonia Yuspeh, "Forget the Product Life Cycle Concept!" *Harvard Business Review*, January-February 1976, pp. 102-12; the special section of articles on the product life cycle in the Fall 1981 issue of the *Journal of Marketing*; D.R. Rink and J.E. Swan, "Product Life Cycle Research: A Literature Review," *Journal of Business Research*, September 1979, pp. 219-42; and Carl R. Anderson and Carl P. Zeithaml, "Stages of the Product Life Cycle, Business Strategy, and Business Performance," *Academy of Management Journal*, March 1984, pp. 5-24.

Chapter 11 ▬▬▬▬▬▬▬▬▬▬▬▬▬▬▬▬▬▬▬▬▬▬▬▬

1. From various sources, including Renate Lerch, "Sony Not Afraid of Competition," *The Financial Post*, April 26 1986, p. 45.

2. David J. Schwartz, *Marketing Today: A Basic Approach* (Third ed.) (New York: Harcourt Brace Jovanovich, 1981), p. 271.

3. See P. Ronald Stephenson, William L. Cron, and Gary L. Frazier, "Delegating Pricing Authority to the Sales Force: The Effects on Sales and Profit Performance," *Journal of Marketing*, Spring 1979, pp. 21-28.

4. Thomas Nagle, "Pricing as Creative Marketing," *Business Horizons*, July-August 1981, p. 19.

5. Shonee McKay, "Pricing Strategies: How to Choose the One That's Right For You," *Canadian Business*, July 1986, pp. 69-71.

6. The arithmetic of markups and margins is discussed in Appendix A, "Marketing Arithmetic."

7. *Marketing Research Handbook, 1985-86*, Statistics Canada, Catalogue 63-224.

8. See Daniel A. Nimer, "Pricing the Profitable Sale Has a Lot to Do with Perception," *Sales Management*, May 19 1975, pp. 13-14. For more on value-based pricing, see

Benson P. Shapiro and Barbara B. Jackson, "Industrial Pricing to Meet Customer Needs," *Harvard Business Review*, November-December 1978, pp. 119-27; and John L. Forbis and Nitin T. Mehta, "Value-Based Strategies for Industrial Products," *Business Horizons*, May-June 1981, pp. 32-42.

Chapter 12

1. From various sources, including: Alan D. Gray, "Liquor's Sobering Future," *Financial Times*, August 15 1983, pp. 1, 26-27; Farrell Crook, "Price Cut For Seagram Rye Out of the Bag," *The Toronto Star*, March 24 1984, p. D1; "Statistics Show Distillers Getting Stiffed by Taxes," *Marketing*, December 19 1983, p.8; Cathryn Motherwell, "Distillers Dreading Effect of Latest Tax Rise on Sales," *The Globe and Mail*, March 13 1986, p. B1; and Alan D. Gray, "Pitching The Montreal Expos," *Financial Times*, February 16 1987, p.7, 22.

2. For an excellent review of pricing strategies, see Gerard J. Telles, "Beyond The Many Faces of Price: An Integration of Pricing Strategies," *Journal of Marketing*, October 1986, pp. 146-160, and the Special Section of the *Journal of Business*, (1, 2, 1984), which examines various aspects of pricing decisions.

3. See Bruce D. Henderson, "The Application and Misapplication of the Experience Curve," *Journal of Business Strategy*, Winter 1984, pp.3-9.

4. For example see R.A. Peterson, "The Price-Perceived Quality Relationship: Experimental Evidence," *Journal of Marketing Research*, November 1970, pp. 525-28; and James E. Stafford and Ben M. Enis, "The Price-Quality Relationship: An Extension," *Journal of Marketing Research*, November 1969, pp. 456-58.

5. For reviews of consumers' perceptions of price, see Kent B. Monroe, "Buyers' Subjective Perceptions of Price," *Journal of Marketing Research*, February 1973, pp. 70-80; and Kent B. Monroe and S.M. Petroshius, "Buyers' Perceptions of Price: An Update of the Evidence," in *Perspectives in Consumer Behavior*, H.H. Kassarjian and T.S. Robertson, eds. Glenview, IL., Scott, Foresman and Company, 1981, 43-45.

6. J.N. Fry and G.H.G. McDougall, "Consumer Appraisal of Retail Price Advertisements," *Journal of Marketing*, July 1974, pp. 64-67.

7. See "Flexible Pricing," *Business Week*, December 12 1977, pp. 78-88.

8. See "Pricing Strategy in an Inflation Economy," *Business Week*, April 6 1974, pp. 43-49.

9. Norman H. Fuss, Jr., "How to Raise Prices — Judiciously to Meet Today's Conditions," *Harvard Business Review*, May-June 1975, pp. 10ff; and Mary Louise Hatten, "Don't Get Caught with Your Prices Down," *Business Horizons*, March-April 1982, pp. 23-28.

10. See Alfred R. Oxenfeldt, "A Decision-Making Structure for Price Decisions," *Journal of Marketing*, January 1973, pp. 48-53.

11. See, for example, William M. Morgenroth, "A Method for Understanding Price Determinants," *Journal of Marketing Research*, August 1964, pp. 17-26.

Chapter 13

1. Prepared from various sources, including: James D. Forbes, "Some Managerial Implications of Canada's Unique Distribution System," in Donald N. Thompson and Davis S.R. Leighton, eds., *Canadian Marketing: Problems and Prospects* (Toronto: Wiley Publishers of Canada Limited, 1973), pp. 145-59; Gerald Byers and Charles S. Mayer, "Physical Distribution in Canada," and Ronald E. Turner, "Canadian Freight Transportation Modes," both in Donald N. Thompson, ed., *Problems*

in Canadian Marketing (Chicago: American Marketing Association, 1975), pp. 85-110, and pp. 111-30.

2. "Beaver Goes Company-Owned Way," *Financial Post*, February 14 1981, p. 21; and Gary Lamphier, "Franchising: A Boom That Just Won't Quit," *Financial Times*, November 19 1984, p. 1, 10.

3. For other lists, see Edmund D. McGarry, "Some Functions of Marketing Reconsidered," in *Theory in Marketing*, Reavis Cox and Wroe Alderson, eds. (Homewood, IL: Irwin, 1950), pp. 269-73; and Louis P. Bucklin, *A Theory of Distribution Channel Structure* (Berkeley: Institute of Business and Economic Research, University of California, 1966), pp. 10-11.

4. Joan Breckenridge, "Storefront Dentistry Becomes $40 Million Business," *The Globe and Mail*, September 24 1984, p. B8.

5. William G. Zikmund and William J. Stanton, "Recycling Solid Wastes: A Channels-of-Distribution Problem," *Journal of Marketing*, July 1971, p. 34.

6. For an excellent summary of channel conflict and power, see Louis W. Stern and Adel I. El-Ansary, *Marketing Channels* (Second ed.) (Englewood Cliffs, NJ: Prentice-Hall, 1982), pp. 291-92, Chaps. 6 and 7.

7. See Bert C. McCammon, Jr., "Perspectives for Distribution Programming," in *Vertical Marketing Systems*, Louis P. Bucklin, ed. (Glenview, IL: Scott Foresman, 1970), pp. 32-51.

8. *Canadian Markets 1986*, *The Financial Post*, Toronto: Maclean Hunter, 1986.

9. For reading on industrial distributors, see Frederick E. Webster, Jr., "The Role of the Industrial Distributor," *Journal of Marketing*, July 1976, pp. 10-16; and James D. Hlavacek and Tommy J. McCuiston, "Industrial Distributors — When, Who, and How?" *Harvard Business Review*, March-April 1983, pp. 96-101.

10. Jade Hemeon, "More Firms Turn to Direct Mail," *Financial Times*, March 2 1981, p. 10.

11. See Bert Rosenbloom, *Marketing Channels: A Management View* (Hinsdale, IL: Dryden Press, 1978), pp. 192-203.

12. Douglas M. Lambert and Robert H. Quinn, "Increasing Profitability By Managing the Distribution Factor," *Business Quarterly*, Spring 1981, pp. 56-64.

13. Canadian Tire Corporation Limited, *Annual Report*, 1986.

14. Gerald Byers and Charles S. Mayer, "Physical Distribution Management in Canada", in Donald N. Thompson, ed., *Problems in Canadian Marketing* (American Marketing Association, 1977), pp. 85-110.

Chapter 14

1. *The Financial Post 500*, Toronto: Maclean Hunter, Summer 1986.

2. Mel S. Moyer and Hart E. Sernick, "The Decline of the Independent Store in Canada: Some Public Policy Questions," in Donald N. Thompson, et al., eds., *Macromarketing: A Canadian Perspective* (Chicago: American Marketing Association, Proceedings Series, 1980), pp. 124-46; Paul Goldstein, "Big Stores Fail to Meet Sales Demands," *The Globe and Mail*, June 30 1986, p. B1, 10; and Leonard Kubas, "Tougher Times for Retailers," *Marketing*, January 26 1987, pp. 34-35.

3. John Dart, "Voluntary Retail Groups: Performance and Promise," in Vernon J. Jones, ed., *Marketing ASAC Proceedings* (Montreal, 1980), pp. 117-25.

4. See Frances Phillips, "Big Stores Fight Back," *Financial Post*, February 8, 1986, pp. 1-2; and Daniel Stoffman, "That Elusive Simpsons Spirit," *Report on Business Magazine*, March 1987, pp. 34-40.

5. James Purdie, "A Major Shake-Up," *Financial Times*, February 9 1981, p. 30.

6. William Annett, "7-Eleven Pushes to be No. 1 in Canada," *Financial Times*, December 22 1986, pp. 6, 8.

7. Barry Nelson, "Co-op Takes on Giants in Calgary Food Fight," *Financial Times*, October 13 1986, pp. 27.

8. Paul Goldstein, "Super-combos a Bitter Pill for Drug Giants," *The Globe and Mail*, May 21 1985, pp. B1, 4.

9. Ronald R. Gist, *Retailing Concepts and Decisions* (New York: Wiley, 1968), pp. 45-46. This list of elements is slightly modified from Gist's.

10. Lawrence Moule, "Supermarkets Brace for Industry Shake-Out," *The Toronto Star*, January 9 1982, p. G1.

11. Terry Brodie, "Ambitious Leon's Refocuses on Canada," *Financial Times*, March 17 1986, pp. 4, 6.

12. Geoffrey Bailey, "Direct Hit," *Canadian Business*, February 1984, pp. 75-78.

13. *Vending Machine Operators*, Ottawa: Statistics Canada, Catalogue 63-213.

14. Ann Silversides, "Fine Line Separates Pyramids, Multi-Level Marketing," *The Globe and Mail*, May 30 1981, p. B1.

15. This definition is contained in the review of *Department Stores in Canada: 1923-1976* (Ottawa: Statistics Canada, 1979).

16. *Department Stores in Canada: 1923-1976*, 1979.

17. Jennifer Wells, "Other People's Experience," *Canadian Business*, October 1986, pp. 111-127.

18. This definition is based on one from the Urban Land Institute found in Roger A. Dickinson, *Retail Management: A Channels Approach* (Belmont, CA: Wadsworth, 1974), p. 9.

19. For more discussion, see Philip Kotler, "Atmospherics as a Marketing Tool," *Journal of Retailing*, Winter 1973-74, pp. 48-64.

20. For more on retail site location, see Lewis A. Spaulding, "Beating the Bushes for New Store Locations," *Stores*, October 1980, pp. 30-35; and "How to Use Foresight in Site Selection," *Discount Store News*, November 5 1979.

21. Malcolm P. McNair, "Significant Trends and Developments in the Postwar Period," in *Competitive Distribution in a Free, High-Level Economy and Its Implications for the University*, A.B. Smith, ed. (Pittsburgh: University of Pittsburgh Press, 1958), pp. 1-25. Also see the critical discussion by Stanley C. Hollander, "The Wheel of Retailing," *Journal of Marketing*, July 1960, pp. 37-42. For other theories of retail change, see Ronald R. Gist, *Retailing Concepts and Decisions* (New York: Wiley, 1968), Ch. 4.

Chapter 15

1. Prepared by M. McMullen, based on discussions with and material supplied by Chris Robinson of Mother's Restaurants Incorporated (Burlington, Ontario), and the reference source, Paul Goldstein, "Mother's Has Rise is Profit: Expects 15% in Sales," *The Globe and Mail*, March 30 1984, p. B4.

2. These definitions, except for *sales promotion*, are from *Marketing Definitions: A Glossary of Marketing Terms* (Chicago: American Marketing Association, 1960). The AMA definition of *sales promotion* covers, in addition to incentives, such marketing media as displays, shows and exhibitions, and demonstrations that can better be classified as forms of advertising, personal selling, or publicity. Some marketing scholars have also suggested adding *packaging* as a fifth element of the promotion mix, although others classify it as a product element.

3. For more on message content and structure, see Leon G. Schiffman and Leslie Lazar Kanuk, *Consumer Behavior* (Second ed.) (Englewood Cliffs, NJ: Prentice-Hall, 1983), pp. 270-77.

4. For a discussion of these devices, see James F. Engel, Roger D. Blackwell, and Paul W. Miniard, *Consumer Behavior* (Fifth ed.) (Hinsdale, IL.: Dryden Press, 1986), Ch. 9.

5. These and other points are discussed in Thomas S. Robertson, *Innovative Behavior and Communication* (New York: Holt, Rinehart & Winston, 1971), Ch. 9.

6. See Philip Kotler, "Atmospherics as a Marketing Tool," *Journal of Retailing*, Winter 1973-74, pp. 48-64.

7. P.F. Lazarsfeld, B. Berelson, and H. Gaudet, *The People's Choice* (Second ed.)(New York: Columbia University Press, 1948), p. 151.

8. Herbert C. Kelman and Carl I. Hovland, "Reinstatement of the Communication in Delayed Measurement of Opinion Change," *Journal of Abnormal and Social Psychology*, 48 (1953), pp. 327-35.

9. For more on source credibility, see Engel, Blackwell, and Miniard, *Consumer Behavior*, pp. 468-471.

10. Quoted in Daniel Seligman, "How Much for Advertising?" *Fortune*, December 1956, p. 123.

11. Charles H. Patti and Vincent Blanks, "Budgeting Practices of Big Advertisers," *Journal of Advertising Research*, December 1981, pp. 23-30.

12. See Sidney J. Levy, *Promotional Behavior* (Glenview, IL.: Scott, Foresman, 1971), Ch. 4.

13. Levy, 1971, Ch. 4.

14. "The High Cost of a Personal Sales Pitch," *Marketing*, November 25 1985, p. B11.

15. For more on push strategies, see Michael Levy, John Webster, and Roger Kerin, "Formulating Push Marketing Strategies: A Method and Application," *Journal of Marketing*, Winter 1983, pp. 25-34.

16. For more on advertising and the product life cycle, see John E. Swan and David R. Rink, "Fitting Market Strategy to Product Life Cycles," *Business Horizons*, January-February 1982, pp. 60-67.

Chapter 16 ▬▬▬▬▬▬▬▬▬▬▬▬▬▬▬▬▬▬▬▬▬▬▬▬

1. From various sources, including: Theresa Tedesco, "Beer, Tobacco Campaigns Back in the Hotseat," *Financial Post*, March 8 1986, p. 52, and "Molson Gearing Up For Bicentennial Marketing Push," *Financial Post*, March 8 1986, p. 56.

2. Ben Fiber, "Mass Media Growth Off, Further Fall Seen," *The Globe and Mail*, January 13 1987, p. B14.

3. Based on a review of the Top National Advertisers 1985, *Marketing*, June 16 1985, p. 1, and "Ranking Corporate Performance in Canada," *Report on Business Magazine*, July 1986.

4. The Canadian Media Directors' Council Media Digest, 1986/87, *Marketing*, January 1987.

5. Tracy Le May, "Can Bud Lead Labatt To the Top?" *Financial Times*, June 1 1981, pp. 2, 14.

6. "U.S. Magazines Find a Hungry Market in Canada," *Marketing*, June 22 1981, p. 34, and John Picton, "This Trivial Pursuit Designed Exclusively for Canadians," *The Toronto Star*, April 15, 1984, p. A10.

7. The Canadian Media Directors' Council Media Digest, 1986/87, *Marketing*, January 1987.

8. For two perspectives on Bill C-58, see Vernon Jones and Sherry Monahan, "An Investigation Into the Effects of Bill C-58 on Advertising Media Decisions," in

G.H.G. McDougall and R. Drolet, eds., *Marketing '77: The Canadian Perspective* (Fredericton: ASAC Proceedings, 1977), pp. 82-90; and I.A. Litvak and C.J. Maule, *The Impact of Bill C-58 on English Language Periodicals in Canada* (Ottawa: Secretary of State, 1978).

9. Leonard Kubas, "Local Advertisers Add Vitality to the 'Cinderella' Medium," *Marketing*.

10. Michael Ryval, "Target: 600 Million Impressions," *Financial Times*, March 3 1986, pp. 1, 6.

11. See William L. Wilke and Paul W. Farris, "Comparison Advertising: Problem and Potential," *Journal of Marketing*, October 1975, pp. 7-15, and Gordon H.G. McDougall, "Comparative Advertising in Canada: Practices and Consumer Reactions," *The Canadian Marketer*, Vol. 9, No. 2, 1978, pp. 14-20.

12. Dik Warren Twedt, "How to Plan New Products, Improve Old Ones, and Create Better Advertising," *Journal of Marketing*, January 1969, pp. 53-57.

13. See "Ad Quality Good, Believability Low," *Advertising Age*, May 31 1984, p. 3.

14. Dan Westall, "Quebec-Based Agencies Play Vital Function," *The Globe and Mail*, April 15 1981, p. B4.

15. L. Greenland, "Is This the Era of Positioning?" *Advertising Age*, May 19 1972.

16. For more on copy approaches, see David Ogilvy and Joel Raphaelson, "Research on Advertising Techniques That Work — and Don't Work," *Harvard Business Review*, July-August 1982, pp. 14-18.

17. Philip H. Dougherty, "Bud 'Pulses' the Market," *New York Times*, February 18 1975, p. 40.

18 See Robert D. Buzzell, "E.I. Du Pont de Nemours & Co.: Measurement of Effects of Advertising," in his *Mathematical Models and Marketing Management* (Boston: Division of Research, Graduate School of Business Administration, Harvard University, 1964), pp. 157-79.

19. Kenneth Kidd, "Marketing Battles Spawn Billions of Coupons A Year," *The Sunday Star*, April 20 1986, p. F2.

20. See Roger Strang, Robert M. Prentice, and Alden G. Clayton, *The Relationship Between Advertising and Promotion in Brand Strategy* (Cambridge, MA: Marketing Science Institute, 1975), Ch. 5.

21. Roger A. Strang, "Sales Promotion — Fast Growth, Faulty Management," Harvard Business Review, July-August, 1976, pp. 115-24.

22. For an interesting study of the effectiveness of various sales promotions in Canada, see Kenneth G. Hardy, "Key Success Factors for Manufacturers' Sales Promotions in Package Goods," *Journal of Marketing*, July 1986, pp. 13-23, and for some examples of point-of-purchase promotions, see Shelley Gillen, "How to Put More POP in your Sales," *Consumer Business*, February 1987, pp. 25-27.

23. Most of the definitions in this section have been adapted from John F. Luch and William Lee Siegler, *Sales Promotion and Modern Merchandising* (New York: McGraw-Hill, 1968).

24. Wayne Mowland, "Coupons, A Key to Value Marketing," *Marketing*, March 2 1987, p. 2.

25. For more on trade promotion, see John A. Quelch, "It's Time to Make Trade Promotion More Effective," *Harvard Business Review*, May-June 1983, pp. 130-36.

26. Peter M. Banting, "Industrial Trade Shows: A Comparative Perspective," in G.H.G. McDougall and R. Drolet, eds., *Marketing '77: The Canadian Perspective* (Fredericton: ASAC Proceedings, 1977), pp. 73-81.

27. Arthur Stern, "Measuring the Effectiveness of Package Goods Promotion Strategies" (paper presented to the Association of National Advertisers, Glen Cover, February 1978).

28. Strang, "Sales Promotion," 1976, p. 119.

29. Russell D. Bowman, "Merchandising and Promotion Grow Big in Marketing World," *Advertising Age*, December 1974, p. 21.

30. Strang, "Sales Promotion," 1976, p. 120.

31. Adapted from Scott M. Cutlip and Allen H. Center, *Effective Public Relations* (Third ed.) (Englewood Cliffs, NJ: Prentice-Hall, 1964), pp. 10-14.

32. Arthur M. Merims, "Marketing's Stepchild: Product Publicity," *Harvard Business Review*, November-December 1972, pp. 111-12.

Chapter 17

1. From various sources, including David Silburt, "Secrets of the Super Sellers," *Canadian Business*, January 1987, pp. 54-59 and Rona Maynard,"Depth of a Saleswoman," *Financial Post Magazine*, December 1 1985, pp. 26-32.

2. Robert N. McMurry, "The Mystique of Super-Salesmanship," *Harvard Business Review*, March-April 1961, p. 114.

3. For a review of the strategic, tactical, and operational decisions in sales management see Adrian B. Ryans and Charles B. Weinberg, "Sales Force Management: Integrating Research Advances," *California Management Review*, Fall 1981, pp. 75-89.

4. See William R. Dixon, "Redetermining the Size of the Sales Force: A Case Study," in *Changing Perspectives in Marketing Management*, Martin R. Warshaw (Ann Arbor: University of Michigan, Michigan Business Reports, 1962), No. 37, p. 58.

5. See Terry Deutscher, Judith Marshall, and David Burgoyne, "The Process of Obtaining New Accounts," *Industrial Marketing Management*, 11, 1982, pp. 173-181.

6. Gary Grundman, David Burgoyne and Terry Deutscher, "Market Realities Demand New Sales Management Approaches," *Business Quarterly*, Summer 1981, pp. 34-39.

7. Ronald E. Turner, "Sales Force Specialization," *Journal of the Academy of Marketing Science*, Winter 1975, pp. 99-108.

8. Turner, 1975, pp. 99-108.

9. For more on the workload and other approaches, see Walter J. Talley, "How to Design Sales Territories," *Journal of Marketing*, January 1961, pp. 7-13; and Gilbert A. Churchill, Jr., Neil M. Ford, and Orville C. Walker, Jr., *Sales Force Management* (Homewood, IL: Irwin, 1981), pp. 160-67.

10. The survey was conducted for the Sales Executives Club of New York and was reported in *Business Week*, February 1 1964, p. 52.

11. "1984 Survey of Selling Costs," *Sales and Marketing Management*, February 20 1984, p. 67.

12. McMurry, 1961, p. 117.

13. McMurry, 1961, p. 118

14. David Mayer and Herbert M. Greenberg, "What Makes a Good Salesman?" *Harvard Business Review*, July-August 1964, pp. 119-25.

15. "1984 Survey of Selling Costs," p. 68.

16. Some of the following discussion is based on W.J.E. Crissy, William H.Cunningham, and Isabella C.M. Cunningham, *Selling: The Personal Force in Marketing* (New York: Wiley, 1977), pp. 119-29.

17. Vincent L. Zirpoli, "You Can't 'Control' the Prospect, So Manage the Presale Activities to Increase Performance," *Marketing News*, March 16 1984, p. 1.

18. Mark Hanan, "Join the Systems Sell and You Can't Be Beat," *Sales and Marketing Management*, August 21 1972, p. 44. Also see Mark Hanan, James Cribbin, and

Herman Heiser, *Consultative Selling* (New York: American Management Association, 1970).

19. For examples, see "S&MM's Special Computers in Marketing Section," *Sales and Marketing Management*, December 5 1983.

Chapter 18

1. Sources include Tom Messer, "Council Seeks New Policies Encouraging Multinationals to Grant World Product Mandate to Subsidiaries," *Marketing*, October 27, 1980, pp. 24-25; Jennifer Grass, "Soft Talk Won't Increase Product Mandating," *Financial Post*, May 2 1981, p. 10; Mark Witten, "Branch Plants Bear New Fruit," *Canadian Business*, November 1980, pp. 54-56, 169-178; Mark Lukasiewicz, "'80s Expected to be Tough Times for Exporters," *The Globe and Mail*, February 5 1982, p. B1; Alan M. Rugman and Jocelyn Bennett, "Technology Transfer and World Product Mandatory in Canada," *Columbia Journal of World Business*, Winter 1982, pp. 58-62; Patrice Lush, "Going, Going, Gone," *Report on Business Magazine*, January 1987, pp. 36-40; and Ronald Anderson, "Product Mandate Could Have Flaws," *The Globe and Mail*, January 8, 1986, p. B2.

2. See *Outlook '87*, *The Financial Post*, Winter 1986-87 and "Effects of Stronger Dollar Unevenly Spread," *The Globe and Mail*, March 19 1987, p. B1.

3. For an overview of the international business issues facing Canada, see K.D. Dhawan, Hamid Etemad, and Richard W. Wright, eds., *International Business: A Canadian Perspective* (Don Mills: Addison-Wesley, 1981).

4. For more details, see I.A. Litvak and C.J. Maule, *The Canadian Multinationals* (Toronto: Butterworth, 1981) and "The Top Fifty Exporters," *Financial Post 500*, Summer 1986, p. 111.

5. Anthony Whittingham, "The New Imperialists," *Maclean's*, August 11 1980, pp. 32-36.

6. See I.A. Litvak and C.J. Maule, "The Emerging Challenge of Canadian Direct Investment Abroad," *The Business Quarterly*, Spring 1978, pp. 24-37 and Jaimie Hubbard, "Labatt's U.S. Assault," *Financial Post*, May 4 1987, pp. 1, 2.

7. Gary Lamphier, "Hard Lessons from the U.S., "*Financial Times*, March 25 1985, pp. 1, 24.

8. For a system of rating the political stability of different nations, see F.T. Haner, "Rating Investment Risks Abroad," *Business Horizons*, April 1979, pp. 18-23.

9. Thad McIlroy and Peter Raymont, "The Barter Barrier," *Canadian Business*, October 1984, pp. 151-156.

10. Len Butcher, "Passport to Profit," *Financial Post Magazine*, March 1 1984, pp. 66-68.

11. Paul W. Beamish and Hugh Munro, "The Export Performance of Small and Medium-Sized Canadian Manufacturers," *Canadian Journal of Administrative Sciences*, June 1986, pp. 29-40.

12. F.H. Rolf Seringhaus, "The Impact of Government Export Marketing Assistance," *International Marketing Review*, Summer 1986, pp. 55-66.

13. The discussion of entry strategies in this section is based on the discussion in Gordon E. Miracle and Gerald S. Albaum, *International Marketing Management* (Homewood, IL: Irwin, 1970), Ch. 14-16.

14. Harold Crookell and Ian Graham, "International Marketing and Canadian Industrial Strategy," *The Business Quarterly*, Spring 1979, pp. 28-34.

15. For more on licensing, see Allan C. Reddy, "International Licensing May Be Best for Companies Seeking Foreign Markets," *Marketing News*, November 12 1982, pp. 6-7.

16. Richard W. Wright, "Canadian Joint Ventures in Japan," *The Business Quarterly*, Spring 1979, pp. 28-34.

17. For more on joint ventures, see Paul W. Beamish, "The Characteristics of Joint Ventures in Development and Developing Countries," *Columbia Journal of World Business*, Fall 1985, pp. 13-19.

18. Whittingham, "The New Imperialists," 1980, and Alan D. Gray, "Making It in the U.S.A.," *Financial Times*, December 22 1986, pp. 1-31.

19. Ralph Z. Sorenson and Ulrich E. Wiechmann, "How Multinationals View Marketing Standardization," *Harvard Business Review*, May-June 1975, pp. 38-54.

20. Warren J. Keegan, "Multinational Product Planning: Strategic Alternatives," *Journal of Marketing*, January 1969, pp. 58-62.

21. Diane Francis, "Bailing Out the Titanic," *Canadian Business*, June 1981, pp. 47-50, 132, 137-142.

22. Tobie Sullivan, "Imported Beers Take Spotlight," *Advertising Age*, August 4 1980, pp. 5, 31-33, Christy Marshall, "Imports: Heineken Sails, Moosehead Charges," *Advertising Age*, November 2 1981, p. 36; and Kevin T. Higgins, "Beer Importers Upbeat About Future, Despite Warning Signs," *Marketing News*, October 25 1985, pp. 1, 10.

23. See Miracle and Albaum, *International Marketing Management*, pp. 317-19.

24. See William D. Hartley, "How Not to Do It: Cumbersome Japanese Distribution System Stumps U.S. Concerns," *Wall Street Journal*, March 2 1972, pp. 1, 8.

25. However, see Arieh Goldman, "Outreach of Consumers and the Modernization of Urban Food Retailing in Developing Countries," *Journal of Marketing*, October 1974, pp. 8-16.

26. See Yoram Wind, Susan P. Douglas, and Howard V. Perlmutter, "Guidelines for Developing International Marketing Strategies," *Journal of Marketing*, April 1973, pp. 14-23.

Chapter 19

1. Sources include: "Ailing Hospitals Turn to Fund Raisers," *The Toronto Star*, October 19 1981; "Strategic Planning in Non-Profit Organizations," *Business Quarterly*, Summer 1981; and Louise Brown, "Why Metro Hospitals Are Pleading for Money," *The Toronto Star*, January 18 1987, pp. H1, H4.

2. *Tomorrow's Customers* (Twentieth Ed.), Toronto, Clarkson Gordon/Woods Gordon, 1987.

3. "Services Grow While the Quality Shrinks," *Business Week*, October 1971, p. 50.

4. See W. Earl Sasser, "Match Supply and Demand in Service Industries," *Harvard Business Review*, November-December 1976, pp. 133-40.

5. For more on classifying services, see Christopher H. Lovelock, "Classifying Services to Gain Strategic Marketing Insights," *Journal of Marketing*, Summer 1983, pp. 9-20.

6. See A. Parasuraman, Leonard L. Berry, and Valerie A. Zeithaml, "Service Firms Need More Marketing," *Business Horizons*, November-December 1983, pp. 28-31.

7. See G. Lynn Shostack, "Banks Sell Services — Not Things," *Bankers Magazine*, Winter 1977, pp. 40-45; and Steven Mintz, "Banking on Marketing," *Sales and Marketing Management*, June 6 1983, pp. 43-48.

8. Allan Gould, "Carnival Tactics," *Canadian Business*, October 1984, pp. 44-51.

9. For more on marketing services, see Leonard L. Berry, "Services Marketing is Different," Christopher H. Lovelock, ed., *Services Marketing* (Englewood Cliffs, N.J.: Prentice-Hall, 1984) pp. 28-37; G. Lynn Shostock, "Service Positioning Through

Structural Change," *Journal of Marketing*, January 1987, pp. 34-43; and Valerie A. Zeithaml, A. Parasuraman, and Leonard L. Berry, "Problems and Strategies in Service Marketing," *Journal of Marketing*, Spring 1985, pp. 33-46.

10. *Public Relations News*, October 27 1947.

11. For this argument, see Philip Kotler and William Mindak, "Marketing and Public Relations," *Journal of Marketing*, October 1978, pp. 13-20.

12. For more on ways to market the services of a professional service firm, see Philip Kotler and Paul N. Bloom, *Marketing Professional Services* (Englewood Cliffs. NJ: Prentice-Hall, 1984).

13. Peter Goddard, "Into The Fire Forges A New Adams," *The Sunday Star*, March 15 1987, pp. C1, C8.

14. For an interesting example of how segmentation could be applied to a leadership campaign, see Philip J. Rosson, "Voter Decision Making: The 1976 Progressive Conservative Leadership Convention," in G.H.G. McDougall and R. Drolet, eds., *Marketing '77: The Canadian Perspective* (Fredericton: ASAC Proceedings, 1977), pp. 137-46.

15. See "Industrial Locations," Special Report, *Financial Times*, August 10 1981, pp. IL1-IL60.

16. Shirley Young, Leland Ott and Barbara Feigin, "Some Practical Considerations in Market Segmentation," *Journal of Marketing Research*, August 1978, pp. 405-12.

17. David Hayes, "Tomorrow Country," *Report on Business Magazine*, December 1985, pp. 58-65; and Sid Tafler, "Corporate Sponsors Give Expo 86 Big Boost," *Financial Times*, November 11 1985, pp. 28-29; and Mark Smyka, "Tourism Tries Three Routes," *Marketing*, February 17 1986, pp. 1-3.

18. See Philip Kotler and Gerald Zaltman, "Social Marketing: An Approach to Planned Social Change," *Journal of Marketing*, July 1971, pp. 3-12.

19. See Eduardo Roberto, *Strategic Decision-Making in a Social Program: The Case of Family-Planning Diffusion* (Lexington, MA: Lexington Books, 1975).

20. See Karl E. Henion II, *Ecological Marketing* (Columbus, OH: Grid, 1976).

21. See John D. Claxton, C. Dennis Anderson, J.R. Brent Ritchie, and Gordon H.G. McDougall, eds., *Consumer and Energy Conservation* (New York: Praeger Publishers, 1981).

22. S. Brown and J.D. Forbes, "Social Marketing in Canada — The Seat-Belt Experience," in Robert D. Tamilia, ed., *Developments in Canadian Marketing* (Saskatoon: ASAC Proceedings, 1979), pp. 176-85.

Chapter 20

1. The studies referred to are John D. Claxton and J.R. Brent Ritchie, "Consumer Prepurchase Shopping Problems: A Focus on the Retailing Component," *Journal of Retailing*, Fall 1979, pp. 24-43; and "Customers Not Impressed With Level of Retail Service", *Marketing*, April 21 1986, p. 6.

2. For an overview of some of the major public policy issues in marketing in Canada, see Stanley J. Shapiro and Louise Heslop, eds., *Marketplace Canada: Some Controversial Dimensions* (Toronto: McGraw-Hill Ryerson, 1982).

3. M. Dale Beckman, "An Analysis of Food Packaging Costs: Does Packaging Cost Too Much?" in J. M. Boisvert and R. Savitt, eds., *Marketing 1978* (London: ASAC Proceedings, 1978), pp. 25-42.

4. For examples of these practices, see Ellen Roseman and Phil Edmonston, *Canadian Consumers' Survival Book* (Don Mills, Ont.: General Publishing, 1977).

5. Roseman and Edmonston, 1977, p. 157.

6. "The Breakfast of Fatties?" *Chicago Today*, July 24 1970. For an example of some of the consequences of advertising to children, see Marvin E. Goldberg and Gerald J. Gorn, "Some Unintended Consequences of TV Advertising to Children," *Journal of Consumer Research*, June 1978, pp. 22-29.

7. Amy Booth, "Empires—Old Sultanates and New," *Financial Post Magazine*, June 1981, pp. 8-20.

8. Ross Laver, "Force Canada's Newspaper Chains to Sell Some Holdings, Inquiry Says," *The Globe and Mail*, August 19 1981, pp. 1-2.

9. Carol Goar, "Combating Corporate Cannibalism," *The Toronto Star*, May 31 1981, p. E2.

10. Avery Shenfeld and Stephen Tanny, "Competition Act Looks At Efficiency," *Financial Post*, March 9 1987, p. 19.

11. Albert Sigurdson, "Independent Booksellers Find Plaza Access Tough," *The Globe and Mail*, July 22 1981, p. B5.

12. Maryon Brechin, "Consumer Protection," *Encyclopedia Canadiana* (Toronto: Grolier, 1970), pp. 94-98.

13. David S.R. Leighton, ed, *Canadian Marketing: Problems and Prospects* (Toronto: Wiley Publishers, 1973), pp. 3-12.

14. For some examples of achievements of the Consumers' Association of Canada, see Maryon Brechin, "The Consumer Movement in Canada," in Vishnu H. Kirpalani and Ronald H. Rotenberg, eds., *Cases and Readings in Marketing* (Toronto: Holt Rinehart and Winston, 1974), pp. 141-46.

15. Herb Gray, "Functions and Objectives of the Department of Consumer and Corporate Affairs," in Vishnu H. Kirpalani and Ronald H. Rotenberg, eds., *Cases and Readings in Marketing* (Toronto: Holt Rinehart and Winston, 1974), pp. 147-57.

16. See Michael J. Trebilcock, *Help! Handbook of Consumer Rights in Canada* (Toronto: CBC Learning Systems, 1978).

17. Rachel Carson, *Silent Spring* (Boston: Houghton Mifflin, 1962).

18. Paul R. Ehrlich and Ann H. Ehrlich, *Population, Resources, Environment: Issues in Human Ecology* (San Francisco: W.H. Freeman, 1970).

19. Donnella H. Meadows. Dennis L. Meadows, Jorgen Randers, and William W. Benrens III, *The Limits to Growth* (New York: Universe Books, 1972).

20. Roy MacGregor, "Acid Rain," *Maclean's*, June 30 1980, pp. 40-44.

Glossary

Action Program A detailed program that shows what must be done, who will do it, and how decisions and actions will be coordinated to implement marketing plans and strategy.

Administered VMS A vertical marketing system that coordinates successive stages of production and distribution, not through common ownership or contractual ties, but through the size and power of one of the parties.

Advertising Any paid form of nonpersonal presentation and promotion of ideas, goods, or services by an identified sponsor.

Affordable Method Setting the promotion budget at what management thinks the company can afford.

Agent A wholesaler who represents buyers or sellers on a more permanent basis, performs only a few functions, and does not take title to goods.

Annual Plan Control Evaluation and corrective action to ensure that the company achieves the sales, profits, and other goals set out in its annual plan.

Atmospheres Designed environments that create or reinforce the buyer's leaning toward consumption of a product.

Attitude A person's enduring favorable or unfavorable cognitive evaluations, emotional feelings, and action tendencies toward some object or idea.

Automatic Vending Selling through coin-operated machines.

Baby Boom The major increase in the annual birthrate following World War II and lasting until the early 1960s. The "baby boomers," now moving into middle age, are a prime target for marketers.

Basing-Point Pricing A geographic pricing strategy in which the seller designates some city as a basing point and charges all customers the freight cost from that city to the customer location, regardless of the city from which the goods are actually shipped.

Behavior Segmentation Dividing a market into groups based on their knowledge, attitude, use, or response to a product.

Belief A descriptive thought that a person holds about something.

Brand A name, term, sign, symbol, or design, or a combination of them intended to identify the goods or services of one seller or group of sellers and to differentiate them from those of competitors.

Brand Mark That part of a brand that can be recognized but is not utterable, such as a symbol, design, or distinctive coloring or lettering.

Brand Name That part of a brand that can be vocalized.

Breakeven Pricing Setting price to break even on the costs of making and marketing a product, or to make the desired profit.

Broker A wholesaler who does not take title to goods and whose function is to bring buyers and sellers together and assist in negotiation.

Business Analysis A review of the sales, costs, and profit projections for a new product to find out whether they satisfy the company's objectives.

Business Portfolio The collection of businesses and products that make up the company.

Buyer Readiness States The stages consumers normally pass through on their way to purchase, including awareness, knowledge, liking, preference, conviction, or purchase.

547

Buying Center All the individuals and groups who participate in the buying decision process, who share some common goals and the risks arising from the decisions.

Cash Cows Low-growth, high-share businesses or products — established and successful units that generate cash that the company uses to pay its bills and support other business units that need investment.

Cash Discount A price reduction to buyers who pay their bills promptly.

Capital Items Industrial goods that enter the finished product partly, including installations and accessory equipment.

Catalog Showroom A retail operation that sells a wide selection of high-markup, fast-moving, brand-name goods at discount prices.

Causal Research Marketing research to test hypotheses about cause-and-effect relationships.

Chain Stores An organization operating four or more retail outlets in the same kind of business under the same legal ownership.

Company Culture A system of values and beliefs shared by people in an organization — the company's collective identity and meaning.

Company Marketing Opportunity An attractive arena for marketing action in which the company would enjoy a competitive advantage.

Company Marketing Environment The actors and forces outside of marketing that affect marketing management's ability to develop and maintain successful transactions with its target customers.

Comparison Advertising Advertising that compares one brand directly or indirectly to one or more other brands.

Competitive-Parity Method Setting the promotion budget to match competitors' outlays.

Concept Testing Testing new product concepts with a group of target consumers to find out if the concept has strong consumer appeal.

Consumer Goods Those bought by final consumers for personal consumption.

Consumer Market All the individuals and households who buy or acquire goods and services for personal consumption.

Consumer Promotion Sales promotion designed to stimulate consumer purchasing, including samples, coupons, rebates, prices-off, premiums, contests, trading stamps, and demonstrations.

Consumerism An organized movement of citizens and government to improve the rights and power of buyers in relation to sellers.

Continuity Scheduling ads evenly within a given period.

Contract Manufacturing Joint-venturing to enter a foreign market by contracting with manufacturers in the foreign market to produce the product.

Contractual VMS A vertical marketing system in which independent firms and different levels of production and distribution join together through contracts to obtain more economies or sales impact than they could achieve alone.

Convenience Goods Consumer goods that the customer usually buys frequently, immediately, and with the minimum of comparison and buying effort.

Convenience Store A small store, located near a residential area, open long hours seven days a week, and carrying a limited line of high-turnover convenience goods.

Conventional Distribution Channel A channel consisting of an independent producer(s), wholesaler(s), and retailer(s), each a separate business seeking to maximize its own profits, even at the expense of profits for the system as a whole.

Copy Testing Measuring the communication effect of an advertisement before or after it is printed or broadcast.

Copyright The exclusive legal right to reproduce, publish, and sell the matter and form of a literary, musical, or artistic work.

Corporate VMS A vertical marketing system that combines successive stages of production and distribution under single ownership — channel leadership is established through common ownership.

Cost-Plus Pricing Setting price by adding a standard markup to the cost of the product.

Cultural Environment Institutions and other forces that affect society's basic values, perceptions, preferences, and behaviors.

Culture The set of basic values, perceptions, wants, and behaviors learned by a member of society from family and other important institutions.

Customized Marketing Mix An international marketing strategy of adjusting the marketing mix elements to each international target market, bearing more costs but hoping for a larger market share and return.

Customer Salesforce Structure   A salesforce organization under which salespeople specialize in selling only to certain customers or industries.

Decline Stage   The product life cycle stage in which a product's sales decline.

Deficient Products   Products that have neither immediate appeal nor long-run benefits, such as bad-tasting yet ineffective medicine.

Demands   Human wants that are backed by buying power.

Demand Curve   A curve that shows the number of units the market will buy in a given time period at different prices that might be charged.

Demographic Segmentation   Dividing the market into groups based on demographic variables such as age, sex, family size, family life cycle, income, occupation, education, religion, race, and nationality.

Demography   The study of human populations in terms of size, density, location, age, sex, race, occupation, and other statistics.

Department Store   A retailing organization that carries a wide variety of product lines — typically clothing, home furnishings, and household goods; each line is operated as a separate department managed by specialist buyers or merchandisers.

Descriptive Research   Marketing research to better describe marketing problems, situations, or markets — such as the market potential for a product, or the demographics and attitudes of consumers.

Desirable Products   Products that give both high immediate satisfaction and high long-run benefits, such as tasty, nutritious breakfast foods.

Direct Investment   Entering a foreign market by developing foreign-based assembly or manufacturing facilities.

Discount Store   A retailing institution that sells standard merchandise at lower prices by accepting lower margins and selling higher volume.

Discriminatory Pricing   Selling a product or service at two or more prices, where the difference in prices is not based on differences in costs.

Distribution Channel   The set of firms and individuals that take title, or assist in transferring title, to a good or service as it moves from the producer to the consumer.

Diversification   A strategy for company growth by starting up or acquiring businesses outside the company's current products and markets.

Dogs   Low-growth, low-share businesses and products that may generate enough cash to maintain themselves, but do not promise to be a large source of cash.

Door-to-Door Retailing   Selling, door-to-door, office-to-office, or at home sales parties.

Durable Goods   Tangible goods that normally survive many uses.

Economic Community   A group of nations organized to work toward common goals in the regulation of international trade; an example is the European Economic Community (EEC or Common Market).

Economic Environment   Factors that affect consumer purchasing power and spending patterns.

Embargo   A ban on the import of a certain product.

Emotional Appeals   Message appeals that attempt to stir up negative or positive emotions that will motivate purchase: examples include fear, guilt, shame, love, humor, pride, and joy appeals.

Enlightened Marketing   A marketing philosophy that holds that the company's marketing should support the best long-run performance of the market system; its five principles include consumer-oriented marketing, innovative marketing, sense-of-mission marketing, value marketing, and societal marketing.

Environmentalism   An organized movement of concerned citizens and government to protect and improve people's living environment.

Events   Designed occurrences that communicate messages to target audiences, such as news conferences, grand openings, or others.

Exchange   The act of obtaining a desired object from someone by offering something in return.

Exclusive Distribution   Giving a limited number of dealers the exclusive right to distribute the company's products in their territories.

Experimental Research   The gathering of primary data by selecting matched groups of subjects, giving them different treatments, controlling related factors, and checking for differences in group responses.

Exploratory Research   Marketing research to gather preliminary information that will help to better define problems and suggest hypotheses.

Exporting   Entering a foreign market by exporting products and selling them through international marketing middlemen (indirect exporting) or through the company's own department, branch, or sales representatives or agents (direct exporting).

Fixed Costs   Costs that do not vary with production or sales level.

FOB Origin Pricing   A geographic pricing strategy in which goods are placed free on board a carrier, and the customer pays the freight from the factory to the destination.

Focus Group Interviewing   Personal interviewing that consists of inviting six to ten people to gather for a few hours with a trained interviewer to talk about a product, service, or organization. The interviewer "focuses" the group discussion on important issues.

Franchise   A contractual association between a manufacturer, wholesaler, or service organization (a franchiser) and independent business people who buy the right to own and operate one or more units in the franchise system (franchisees).

Freight Absorption Pricing   A geographic pricing strategy in which the company absorbs all or part of the actual freight charges in order to get the business.

Frequency   The number of times the average person in the target market is exposed to the advertising message during a given period.

Functional Discount   A price reduction offered by the seller to trade channel members who perform certain functions such as selling, storing, and record keeping.

Functional Organization   An organization structure in which marketing specialists are in charge of different marketing activities or functions such as advertising, marketing, research, sales management, and others.

Geographic Organization   An organization structure in which a company's national sales force (and perhaps other functions) specializes by geographic area.

Geographic Segmentation   Dividing the market into different geographical units such as nations, provinces, regions, counties, cities, or neighborhoods.

Going-Rate Pricing   Setting price based largely on following competitors' prices rather than on company costs or demand.

Government Market   Governmental units — federal, provincial and municipal — that purchase or rent goods and services for carrying out the main functions of government.

Growth Stage   The product life cycle stage when the product's sales start climbing quickly.

Human Need   A state of felt deprivation in a person.

Human Want   The form that a human need takes as shaped by culture and individual personality.

Industrial Market   All the individuals and organizations that acquire goods and services that enter into the production of other products and services, that are in turn sold, rented, or supplied to others.

Industrial Goods   Goods bought by individuals and organizations for further processing or for use in conducting a business.

Idea Generation   The systematic search for new product ideas.

Idea Screening   Screening new product ideas in order to spot good ideas and drop poor ones as soon as possible.

Introduction Stage   The product life cycle stage in which the new product is first distributed and made available for purchase.

Intensive Distribution   Stocking the product in as many outlets as possible.

Joint Ownership   Entering foreign markets by joining with foreign investors to create a local business in which the company shares joint ownership and control.

Joint Venturing   Entering foreign markets by joining with companies in the foreign country to set up production and marketing facilities.

Learning   Changes in an individual's behavior arising from experience.

Licensing   A method of entering a foreign market in which the company enters an agreement with a licensee in the foreign market, offering the right to use a manufacturing process, trademark, patent, trade secret, or other item of value for a fee or royalty.

Life Style A person's pattern of living as expressed in his or her activities, interests, and opinions.

Macroenvironment The larger societal forces that affect the whole microenvironment — demographic, economic, natural, technological, political, and cultural forces.

Mail and Telephone Order Retailing Selling that uses the mail or telephone to get orders or to aid in delivery.

Management Contracting A joint venture in which the domestic firm supplies the management knowhow to a foreign company that supplies the capital; the domestic firm exports management services rather than products.

Managerial Climate The company climate resulting from the way managers work with others in the company.

Manufacturers' Sales Branches and Offices Wholesaling done by sellers or buyers themselves, rather than through independent wholesalers.

Market The set of actual and potential buyers of a product.

Market Development A strategy for company growth by identifying and developing new market segments for current company products.

Market Management Organization An organization structure in which market managers are responsible for developing plans for sales and profits in their specific markets.

Market Penetration A strategy for company growth by increasing sales of current products to current market segments without changing the product in any way.

Market Penetration Pricing Setting a low price for a new product in order to attract a large number of buyers and a large market share.

Market Positioning Formulating a competitive positioning for a product and a detailed marketing mix.

Market Segment A group of consumers who respond in a similar way to a given set of marketing stimuli.

Market Segmentation The process of classifying customers into groups with different needs, characteristics, or behavior. Dividing a market into distinct groups of buyers who might require separate products or marketing mixes.

Market-Skimming Pricing Setting a high price for a new product to skim maximum revenue from the segments willing to pay the high price; the company makes fewer but more profitable sales.

Market Targeting Evaluating each market segment's attractiveness and selecting one or more segments to enter.

Market Testing The stage of new product development in which the product and marketing program are tested in more realistic market settings.

Marketing Human activity directed at satisfying needs and wants through exchange processes.

Marketing Audit A comprehensive, systematic, independent, and periodic examination of a company's environment, objectives, strategies, and activities to determine problem areas and opportunities and to recommend a plan of action to improve the company's marketing performance.

Marketing Concept The marketing management philosophy that holds that achieving organizational goals depends on determining the needs and wants of target markets and delivering the desired satisfactions more effectively and efficiently than competitors.

Marketing Control The process of measuring and evaluating the results of marketing strategies and plans, and taking corrective action to ensure that marketing objectives are attained.

Marketing Implementation The process that turns marketing strategies and plans into marketing actions in order to accomplish strategic marketing objectives.

Marketing Information Systems (MIS) A structure of people, equipment, and procedures to gather, sort, analyze, evaluate, and distribute needed, timely, and accurate information to marketing decision makers.

Marketing Intelligence Everyday information about developments in the marketing environment that helps managers prepare and adjust marketing plans.

Marketing Intermediaries Firms that help the company to promote, sell, and distribute its goods to final buyers; they include middlemen, physical distribution firms, marketing service agencies, and financial intermediaries.

Marketing Management The analysis, planning, implementation, and control of programs designed to create, build, and maintain beneficial exchanges with target buyers for the purpose of achieving organizational objectives.

Marketing Manager   A person who is involved in marketing analysis, planning, implementation, and control activities.

Marketing Mix   The set of controllable marketing variables that the firm blends to produce the response it wants in the target market.

Marketing Research   The systematic design, collection, analysis, and reporting of data and findings relevant to a specific marketing situation facing the company.

Marketing Strategy   The marketing logic by which the business unit hopes to achieve its marketing objectives. Marketing strategy consists of specific strategies for target markets, marketing mix, and marketing expenditure level.

Marketing Strategy Development   Designing an initial marketing strategy for a new product based on the product concept.

Mass and Selective Media   Print media (newspapers, magazines, direct mail), electronic media (radio, television), and display media (billboards, signs, posters) aimed at large, unsegmented audiences (mass media) or at selected audiences (selective media).

Materials and Parts   Industrial goods that enter the manufacturer's product completely, including raw materials and manufactured materials and parts.

Maturity Stage   The stage in the product life cycle in which sales growth slows or levels off.

Merchant Wholesaler   An independently owned business that takes title to the merchandise it handles.

Microenvironment   The forces close to the company that affect its ability to serve its customers — the company, market channel firms, customer markets, competitors, and publics.

Mission Statement   A statement of the organization's purpose, what it wants to accomplish in the larger environment.

Monopolistic Competition   A market in which many buyers and sellers trade over a range of prices rather than a single market price.

Moral Appeals   Message appeals that are directed to the audience's sense of what is right and proper.

Motive (or Drive)   A need that is sufficiently pressing to direct the person to seek satisfaction of the need.

Multinational Company   A company that operates in many countries and that has a major part of its operations outside its home country.

Natural Environment   Natural resources that are needed as inputs by marketers or that are affected by marketing activities.

New Product   A good, service, or idea that is perceived by some potential customers as new.

New Product Development   The development of original products, product improvements, product modifications, and new brands through the firm's own R&D efforts.

Nondurable Goods   Tangible goods normally consumed in one or a few uses.

Nonpersonal Communication Channels   Media that carry messages without personal contact or feedback, including mass and selective media, atmospheres, and events.

Objective-and-Task Method   Developing the promotion budget by (1) defining specific objectives, (2) determining the tasks that must be performed to achieve these objectives, and (3) estimating the costs of performing these tasks; the sum of these costs is the proposed promotion budget.

Observational Research   The gathering of primary data by observing relevant people, actions, and situations.

Oligopolistic Competition   A market in which there are few sellers who are highly sensitive to each other's pricing and marketing strategies.

Organization Image   The way an individual or a group sees an organization.

Organization Marketing   Activities undertaken to create, maintain, or change attitudes and behavior of target audiences toward an organization.

Organizational Buying   The decision-making process by which formal organizations establish the need for purchased products and services, and identify, evaluate, and choose among alternative brands and suppliers.

Packaging   The activities of designing and producing the container or wrapper for a product.

Perceived-Value Pricing   Setting price based on buyers' perception of value rather than on the seller's cost.

Percentage-of-Sales Method Setting the promotion budget at a certain percentage of current or forecasted sales, or as a percentage of the sales price.

Perception The process by which an individual selects, organizes, and interprets information inputs to create a meaningful picture of the world.

Person Marketing Activities undertaken to create, maintain, or change attitudes or behavior toward particular persons.

Personal Influence The effect of statements made by one person on another's attitude or probability of purchase.

Personal Communication Channels Channels through which two or more people communicate directly with each other, including face to face, person to audience, over the telephone, or through the mail.

Personal Selling Oral presentation in a conversation with one or more prospective purchasers for the purpose of making sales.

Personality A person's distinguishing psychological characteristics that lead to relatively consistent and lasting response to his or her own environment.

Physical Distribution The tasks involved in planning, implementing, and controlling the physical flow of materials and final goods from points of origin to points of use to meet the needs of customers at a profit.

Planned Obsolescence A strategy of causing products to become obsolete before they actually need replacement; it includes style obsolescence, functional obsolescence, and material obsolescence.

Place Marketing Activities undertaken to create, maintain, or change attitudes or behavior toward particular places.

Pleasing Products Products that give high immediate satisfaction but may hurt consumers in the long run, such as cigarettes.

Political Environment Laws, government agencies, and pressure groups that influence and limit various organizations and individuals in society.

Price The amount of money charged for a product or service, or the sum of the values consumers exchange for the benefits of having or using the product or service.

Price Elasticity A measure of the sensitivity of demand to changes in price.

Primary Data Information collected for the specific purpose at hand.

Product Anything that can be offered to a market for attention, acquisition, use, or consumption that might satisfy a want or need. It includes physical objects, services, persons, places, organizations, and ideas.

Product Concept A detailed version of the new product idea stated in meaningful consumer terms.

Product Development Developing the product concept into a physical product in order to ensure that the product idea can be turned into a workable product.

Product Idea An idea for a possible product that the company can see itself offering to the market.

Product Image The way consumers picture an actual or potential product.

Product Life Cycle (PLC) The course of a product's sales and profits over its lifetime. It involves five distinct stages: product development, introduction, growth, maturity, and decline.

Product Line A group of products that are closely related, either because they function in a similar manner, are sold to the same customer groups, are marketed through the same types of outlets, or fall within given price ranges.

Product Management Organization An organization structure in which product managers are responsible for developing and implementing marketing strategies and plans for a specific product or brand.

Product Mix The set of all product lines and items that a particular seller offers for sale to buyers.

Product Positioning The way the product is defined by consumers on important attributes — the place the product occupies in consumers' minds relative to competing products.

Product Salesforce Structure A salesforce organization under which salespeople specialize in selling only a portion of the company's products or lines.

Production Concept The philosophy that consumers will favor products that are available and highly affordable, and therefore management should focus on improving production and distribution efficiency.

Profitability Control Evaluation and corrective action to ensure the profitability of a company's various products, territories, customer groups, trade channels, and order sizes.

Promotion Mix The specific mix of advertising, personal selling, sales promotion, and publicity a company uses to pursue its advertising and marketing objectives.

Promotional Allowance   A payment or price reduction to reward dealers for participating in advertising and sales-support programs.

Promotional Pricing   Temporarily pricing products below the list price, and sometimes even below cost, to increase short-run sales.

Psychographic Segmentation   Dividing a market into different groups based on social class, life style, or personality characteristics.

Psychological Pricing   A pricing approach that considers the psychology of prices and not simply the economics — the price is used to say something about the product.

Public   Any group that has an actual or potential interest in or impact on an organization's ability to achieve its objectives.

Public Relations   The management function that evaluates public attitudes, identifies an individual or an organization with the public interest, and plans and executes a program of action to earn public understanding and acceptance.

Publicity   Nonpersonal stimulation of demand for a product, service, or business unit by planting commercially significant news about it in a published medium or obtaining favorable presentation of it on radio, television, or stage that is not paid for by the sponsor.

Pull Strategy   A promotion strategy that calls for spending a lot on advertising and consumer promotion to build up consumer demand; if successful, consumers will ask their retailers for the product, the retailers will ask the wholesalers, and the wholesalers will ask the producers.

Pulsing   Scheduling ads unevenly in bursts over time.

Pure Competition   A market in which many buyers and sellers trade in a uniform commodity — no single buyer or seller has much effect on the going market price.

Pure Monopoly   A market in which there is a single seller — it may be a government monopoly, a private regulated monopoly, or a private nonregulated monopoly.

Push Strategy   A promotion strategy that calls for using the salesforce and trade promotion to push the product through the channels; the producer promotes the

product to wholesalers, the wholesalers promote to retailers, and the retailers promote to consumers.

Quantity Discount   A price reduction to buyers who buy large volumes.

Question Marks   Low-share business units in high-growth markets that require a lot of cash to hold their share or build into stars.

Quota   A limit on the amount that an importing country will accept in certain product categories, designed to conserve on foreign exchange and protect local industry and employment.

Rational Appeals   Message appeals that relate to the audience's self-interest and show that the product will produce the claimed benefits; examples include appeals of product quality, economy, value, or performance.

Reach   The number of people in the target market exposed to the ad campaign during the given period.

Reference Groups   Groups that have a direct (face-to-face) or indirect influence on the person's attitude or behavior.

Reseller Market   All the individuals and organizations that acquire goods for the purpose of reselling or renting them to others at a profit.

Retailers   Businesses whose sales come primarily from retailing.

Retailing   All activities involved in selling goods or services directly to final consumers for their personal, nonbusiness use.

Role   The activities a person is expected to perform according to the persons around him or her.

Sales Promotion   Short-term incentives to encourage purchase or sales of a product or service.

Salesforce Management   The analysis, planning, implementation, and control of salesforce activities. It includes setting salesforce objectives; designing salesforce strategy; and recruiting, selecting, training, supervising, and evaluating the firm's salespeople.

Salesforce Promotion   Sales promotion designed to motivate the salesforce and make salesforce selling efforts more effective, including bonuses, contests, sales rallies, and others.

Salesperson   An individual acting for a

company who performs one or more of the following activities: prospecting, communicating, servicing, and information gathering.

Salutary Products Products that have low appeal but benefit consumers in the long run, such as seat belts.

Sample A segment of the population selected for marketing research to represent the population as a whole.

Seasonal Discount A price reduction to buyers who buy merchandise or services out of season.

Sealed-Bid Pricing Setting price based on how the firm thinks competitors will price rather than on its own costs or demand — used when a company bids for jobs.

Secondary Data Information that already exists somewhere, having been collected for another purpose.

Selective Distribution The use of more than one but less than all the middlemen who are willing to carry the company's products.

Selling Concept The idea that consumers will not buy enough of the organization's products unless the organization undertakes a large selling and promotion effort.

Selling Process The steps that the salesperson follows when selling, which include prospecting and qualifying, preapproach, approach, presentation, and demonstration, handling objections, closing, and follow-up.

Service Any activity or benefit that one party can offer to another that is essentially intangible and does not result in the ownership of anything. Its production may or may not be tied to a physical product.

Services Activities, benefits, or satisfactions that are offered for sale.

Shopping Center A group of retail businesses planned, developed, owned, and managed as a unit, and related in location, size, and type of store to the trade area that it serves.

Shopping Goods Consumer goods that the customer, in the process of selection and purchase, characteristically compares on such bases as suitability, quality, price, and style.

Social Classes Relatively permanent and ordered divisions in a society whose members share similar values, interests, and behaviors.

Social Marketing The design,

implementation, and control of programs seeking to increase the acceptability of a social idea, cause, or practice in a target group.

Societal Marketing Concept The idea that the organization should determine the needs, wants, and interests of target markets and deliver the desired satisfactions more effectively and efficiently than competitors in a way that maintains or improves the consumer's and society's well-being.

Specialty Goods Consumer goods with unique characteristics or brand identification for which a significant group of buyers is willing to make a special purchase effort.

Specialty Store A retail outlet that carries a narrow product line with a deep assortment within that line.

Standardized Marketing Mix An international marketing strategy of using the same product, advertising, distribution channels, and other elements of the marketing mix in all the company's international markets.

Stars High-growth, high-share businesses or products. They often require heavy investment to finance their rapid growth.

Status The general esteem given to a role by society.

Strategic Business Unit (SBU) A unit of the company that has a separate mission and objectives, which can be planned independently from other company businesses. An SBU can be a company division, a product line within a division, or sometimes a single product or brand.

Strategic Planning The process of developing and maintaining a strategic fit between the organization's goals and capabilities and its changing marketing opportunities. It relies on developing a clear company mission, supporting objectives, a sound business portfolio, and co-ordinated functional strategies.

Strategic Control A critical review of the company's overall marketing effectiveness.

Subculture A group of people with shared value systems based on common life experiences and situations.

Supermarkets Large, low-cost, low-margin, high-volume, self-service stores that carry a wide variety of food, laundry, and household maintenance products.

Superstore A store almost twice the size of a regular supermarket that carries a large assortment of routinely purchased food and nonfood items, and offers such services as laundry, dry cleaning, shoe repair, check cashing, bill paying, and bargain counters.

Supplies and Services   Industrial goods that do not enter the finished product at all.

Suppliers   Firms and individuals that provide the resources needed by the company and its competitors to produce goods and services.

Survey Research   The gathering of primary data by asking people questions about their knowledge, attitudes, preferences, and buying behavior.

Systems Buying   Buying a whole solution to a problem and not making all the separate decisions involved.

Tariff   A tax levied by a government against certain imported products designed to raise revenue or protect domestic firms.

Technological Environment   Forces that create new technologies, creating new product and market opportunities.

Territorial Salesforce Structure   A salesforce organization that assigns each salesperson to an exclusive geographic territory in which the salesperson carries the company's full line.

Trade-In Allowance   A price reduction given for turning in an old item when buying a new one.

Trade Promotion   Sales promotion designed to gain reseller support and to improve reseller selling efforts, including buying allowances, free goods, merchandise allowances, cooperative advertising, push money, and dealer sales contests.

Trademark   A brand or part of a brand that is given legal protection — it protects the seller's exclusive rights to use the brand name or brand mark.

Total Costs   The sum of the fixed and variable costs for any given level of production.

Transaction   A trade between two parties that involves at least two things of value, agreed-upon conditions, a time of agreement, and a place of agreement.

Uniform Delivered Pricing   A geographical pricing strategy in which the company charges the same price plus freight to all customers regardless of their location.

Unsought Goods   Consumer goods that the consumer does not know about or knows about but does not normally think of buying.

Value Analysis   An approach to cost reduction in which components are carefully studied to determine if they can be redesigned or standardized or made by cheaper methods of production.

Variable Costs   Costs that vary directly with the level of production.

Vertical Marketing System (VMS)   A distribution channel structure in which the producer(s), wholesaler(s), and retailer(s) act as a unified system — either one channel member owns the others, or has contracts with them, or has so much power that they all cooperate.

Warehouse Store   A no-frills, reduced-service store that seeks high volume through low prices.

Wholesalers   Firms engaged primarily in wholesaling activity.

Wholesaling   All activities involved in selling goods and services to those buying for resale or business use.

Zone Pricing   A geographic pricing strategy in which the company sets up two or more zones — all customers within a zone pay the same total price, and this price is higher in the more distant zones.

Name Index

Subject Index